CHINA:
A Political History, 1917–1980

Also of Interest

† *China in World Affairs: The Foreign Policy of the PRC Since 1970*, Golam W. Choudhury

† *China Briefing, 1981*, edited by Robert B. Oxnam and Richard C. Bush

† *China's Economic Development: Growth and Structural Change*, Chu-yuan Cheng

Technology, Politics, and Society in China, Rudi Volti

† *The Chinese Military System: An Organizational Study of the Chinese People's Liberation Army*, Second Edition, Revised and Updated, Harvey W. Nelsen

The Forgotten Ambassador: The Reports of John Leighton Stuart, 1946-1949, edited by Kenneth W. Rea and John C. Brewer

† *China, the Soviet Union, and the West: Strategic and Political Dimensions for the 1980s*, edited by Douglas T. Stuart and William T. Tow

China's Quest for Independence: Policy Evolution in the 1970s, edited by Thomas Fingar and the *Stanford Journal of International Studies*

† *Huadong: The Story of a Chinese People's Commune*, Gordon Bennett

† *Law Without Lawyers: A Comparative View of Law in the United States and China*, Victor H. Li

The People's Republic of China: A Handbook, edited by Harold C. Hinton

† *China's Four Modernizations: The New Technological Revolution*, edited by Richard Baum

China at the Crossroads: Nationalists and Communists, 1927-1949, edited by Gilbert F. Chan

Treaties of the People's Republic of China, 1949-1978: An Annotated Compilation, Grant F. Rhode and Reid E. Whitlock

Chinese Communist Power and Policy in Xinjiang, 1949-1977, Donald H. McMillen

Painting in the People's Republic of China: The Politics of Style, Arnold Chang

† *The Chinese Agricultural Economy*, edited by Randolph Barker and Radha P. Sinha

† *Food for One Billion: China's Agriculture Since 1949*, Robert C. Hsu

† *Economic Reform in the PRC: In Which China's Economists Make Known What Went Wrong, Why, and What Should Be Done About It*, edited and translated by George C. Wang

† Available in hardcover and paperback.

About the Book and Author

CHINA: A Political History, 1917–1980

Richard C. Thornton

The People's Republic of China is changing. It is modernizing, shifting ideological gears, becoming realistic about development needs and goals, and moving away from its isolationist past toward a much more open and pragmatic assessment of its present and future position in the world. In the post-Mao period, China also seems to be willing to engage, albeit reluctantly, in the painful internal reshuffling of priorities and functions necessary to speed development. But change has not been easy: there have been major problems, both domestic and international.

Richard Thornton puts the events of the past eight years in China into historical perspective in this updated and expanded version of his textbook on China's political history since 1917 (first published in 1973 as *China: The Struggle for Power, 1917-1972*). With the additional material, the book now stands as the most detailed account available. Professor Thornton deals with every significant issue that has confronted the leaders of revolutionary China and discusses the origins of the People's Republic. How did communism first take root in China? How did Mao first gain control of the Communist movement? What were the ingredients of Mao's victory and emergence as the undisputed master of the most populous country in the world? What was the origin of the Sino-Soviet alliance and what caused its collapse in the fifties? And in what sense were the tumultuous events of the Cultural Revolution of the sixties a prelude to the emergence of the new pragmatism and the Sino–U.S. rapprochement in the seventies? There has been very little stability in China's recent past, but Professor Thornton points out that there has been a historical logic in the sequence of China's history. An awareness of this logic is vital to understanding China's future.

Richard C. Thornton is now professor of history and international affairs at the Institute for Sino-Soviet Studies, George Washington University, and previously was a research associate at the Far Eastern and Russian Institute, University of Washington–Seattle. He is the author of numerous books and articles on Russian, Chinese, and U.S. affairs including *The Bear and the Dragon, Sino-Soviet Relations and the Political Evolution of the Chinese People's Republic,* and *The Comintern and the Chinese Communists.*

CHINA:
A Political History,
1917–1980———————————

Richard C. Thornton

Westview Press / Boulder, Colorado

First edition published in 1973, as *China: The Struggle for Power, 1917-1972,* by Indiana University Press.

Copyright © 1982 by Westview Press, Inc.

Published in 1982 in the United States of America by
  Westview Press, Inc.
  5500 Central Avenue
  Boulder, Colorado 80301
  Frederick A. Praeger, President and Publisher

Library of Congress Cataloging in Publication Data
Thornton, Richard C.
    China, a political history, 1917-1980.
    Rev. ed. of: China, the struggle for power, 1917-1972. 1973.
    Bibliography: p.
    Includes index.
    1. China—Politics and government—1912-1949. 2. China—Politics and government—
1949-   . 3. Communism—China—History. I. Title.
DS775.7.T48 1982   951.04   81-21885
ISBN 0-86531-197-8   AACR2
ISBN 0-86531-198-6 (pbk.)

Printed and bound in the United States of America

To
Joanne

History is the record of man's achievement and aspiration; the task of the historian is to measure the one in terms of the other.

R.C.T.

Contents

Preface xv

Part I
The Origin and Development of Chinese Communism, 1917–1941

  I   To Build a Communist Movement in China, 1917–1927 3

        The Bolshevik Experience 4
        The Soviet Union Aids the Kuomintang 6
        Chiang Kai-shek and the Communists 8
        The Communist Attempt to Seize Power 10
        Stalin, Trotsky, and the Chinese Revolution 16
        The Communists in Revolt 19

  II   The "Soviet" Experiment, 1927–1931 24

        Moscow's Policy in Practice 28
        Moscow's Misgivings 30
        The Chinese Eastern Railway Crisis 32
        The Formulation of the Li Li-san Line 34
        The Fateful Decision to Adopt the Li Li-san Line 39
        The Tide Turns Against Li Li-san 42
        The Comintern Reasserts Control 44

 III   Defeat in Kiangsi, 1931–1934 49

        The Internationalists "Bolshevize" the Party 50
        The Establishment of the Chinese Soviet Republic 54

Tokyo, Moscow, and Juichin. 56
The Fourth Encirclement Campaign–Stalemate 58
Mobilization for Armageddon 65
The Fukien Rebellion. 69
Defeat and Flight from the Central Soviet Area. 74

IV   From the Long March to the United Front, 1934–1937 76

Long March–The First Six Hundred Miles 76
The Tsunyi Conference. 78
Long March–Phase Two: The Conflict with Chang Kuo-t'ao 81
Organizational Reconstitution of the Communist System 87
International United Front 88
The CCP and the United Front. 90
Turning Point at Sian. 95
Continuation of the Internal Struggle 98

V   The Road to War, 1937–1941 100

United Front Policy in China. 102
Stalin, Wang Ming, and Mao Tse-tung 105
The Two-Front War Danger Mounts 110
From the Nazi-Soviet Pact to the Fall of France 114
Strategic Impact of the Fall of France 121

Part II
The American Experience in China, 1941–1949

VI   World War II, the United States and China, 1941–1944. 127

The Strategic Defensive 127
Chiang Kai-shek, Mao Tse-tung, and World War II 130
Mao Gains Command of the CCP .133
World War II, the Turning Point 137
Cairo-Tehran-Cairo 141
The Final Counteroffensive and America's "China Policy" 144
Nationalists and Communists Negotiate. 146
Shifts in American Policy Emphasis 149
China Crisis–Japanese and American. 151
Renewed American Efforts Toward Unification 156

VII The United States, the Soviet Union, and China, 1945 160

Yalta, Outline for the Postwar World. 160
The Immediate Repercussions of Yalta 163
Chiang Initiates and Mao Responds to "Constitutional
    Government" 165
The "Victory" of Mao Tse-tung 169
Gnawing Doubts Weaken the Prospects for
    Soviet-American Cooperation 171
The Effort to Stabilize Manchuria. 178
The Soviet Union, the United States, and China 180
The Appointment of General Marshall. 184

VIII Strategies in Conflict, 1946-1949. 188

Marshall Arranges a Settlement, December 22-March 11. 188
Chiang Kai-shek Takes the Initiative 193
America's Failure in China 196
The Soviet Achievement in China. 205
The Truman Doctrine and American China Policy 207
Victory of the Chinese Communists 212
The Chinese Revolution in Global Perspective. 216

Part III
The Sino-Soviet Relationship, 1949-1968

IX The Soviet Union and the Chinese People's Republic, 1949-1959. . 227

Strategy of Conflict. 227
The Establishment of the Chinese People's Republic 231
The Politics of Centralization. 233
Stalin's Death and the Succession Struggle 238
Twentieth Party Congress of the CPSU and Its Aftermath 242
Eighth Party Congress of the Chinese Communist Party 244
Great Leap Forward: The Choice for Independent Action. 249

X The Polarization of Communist Politics, 1959-1965 252

The Military Response to the Great Leap. 253
Breach in Sino-Soviet Relations 255
Economic Crisis and Organizational Conflict. 256

Mao Tse-tung and the PLA 259
Army Corps, Regional Forces, and Militia 261
Struggle for the Provincial Apparatus, Phase I. 264
Struggle for the Provincial Apparatus, Phase II 267
The Fall of Khrushchev and Vietnam 271

XI The Great Proletarian Cultural Revolution—
      I: The Mounting Crisis, 1965–1967. 278

The Decision to Initiate the "Cultural" Revolution 278
Mao Tse-tung Takes the Offensive. 282
The Great "Proletarian" Cultural Revolution—Initial Strategy 285
The Red Guards, Mao's Student Left. 289
The Attempt to "Seize Power" 294
Crisis in Peking over Greater PLA Involvement 298
Mao Alters the Theoretical Basis of the Cultural Revolution 302
The Mounting Crisis, February–March 1967 306

XII The Great Proletarian Cultural Revolution—
      II: Protracted Crisis, 1967–1968. 310

"Carry the Cultural Revolution Through to the Very End" 310
Failure of Mao's Policy and Increase in Violence 314
To Whom the Leading Role, Rebels or Soldiers? 318
The Attempt to Construct a Civil-Military "Balance" 324
Cultural Revolution on the Verge of Success. 328
The Decision to Terminate the Cultural Revolution 331
"Unity and Strength Under Chairman Mao and
     Vice-Chairman Lin". 335
The Soviet Legacy 338

Part IV
The Evolution of U.S.-China Relations, 1969–1980

XIII China in a Tri-Polar World, 1969–1973 341

The Soviet Union Probes China's Defenses 341
The Continuing Struggle in Peking: The Challenge of Lin Piao 345
The Second Plenum of the Chinese Communist Party. 347
The "Lin Piao Incident". 350
Peking, Washington, and Moscow 355

XIV The End of the Maoist Era, 1973–1976 361

The Return to Power of Teng Hsiao-p'ing and Moscow's Offer 361
From the Tenth Party Congress to the Fourth National
    People's Congress 367
Internal Change and Foreign Policy Stagnation 372
The Death of Chou En-lai and Designation of Mao's Heir 378
Dissolution of the Maoist Coalition. 383

XV The Struggle for Succession, 1976–1978 386

The Fall of the Gang of Four. 386
The "Selection" of Chairman Hua Kuo-feng. 389
Hua Kuo-feng, Yeh Chien-ying, Teng Hsiao-p'ing—
    Triumvirate Inchoate 391
Teng Hsiao-p'ing's Return to Power and Peking's
    Uneasy Coalition. 396
The Soviet Decision to Increase Military Pressure on China 400
Strategy, Counterstrategy, and Normalization 403
The Rise to Power of Teng Hsiao-p'ing 407

XVI Whither China? The Uncertain Future, 1978–1980 411

The Third Plenum of the Chinese Communist Party 411
The War with Vietnam: Lesson That Backfired
    or Signal to Moscow?. 417
The Abortive Opening to Moscow. 422
The Fifth Plenum and the Fate of Hua Kuo-feng. 427
Teng Hsiao-p'ing in Command of Chinese Politics 431
Implications for the Future 435

Notes 441
Suggested Readings 498
Index 500

Preface

It is the purpose of this work to provide an integrated analytical framework that will serve as a guide to further study of the vast and complex subject of Chinese Communist politics. The outpouring of materials from U.S., Soviet, Chinese Communist, and Chinese Nationalist sources in recent years has greatly enriched our fund of knowledge about China. For the historian of Chinese politics the new data have provided answers to hitherto unresolved problems and raised questions about seemingly settled issues. Although it is now possible to piece together the main outlines of the struggle for power in China, obviously no single volume can presume to encompass all aspects of the story.

Selection of topic and theme being unavoidable, I have chosen to emphasize two pervasive themes and four separate but related topics that seem to me to form an especially important underpinning for our understanding of Chinese political history. The two principal themes intertwine at virtually every critical point in the story. One is the tremendous impact that external forces have had on the course of events in China, particularly the impact of the Soviet Union as well as that of the United States and Japan on the decision-making process of the Chinese Communist Party. Soviet involvement in the political evolution of Chinese Communism has been continuous and has helped to create the very basis for the conflicts described in this book. An ideological and organizational heritage from the USSR conditioned the initial orientation of the People's Republic of China toward the Soviet Union. Chinese leaders, whether trained in Moscow (as many were) or not, operated within the political parameters of the international Communist movement— a factor that greatly shaped the policy alternatives they perceived to be open to them. They were obliged to determine policy in terms of China's relationship with the Soviet Union. Even when they subsequently made the decision to develop independently of the Soviets, the new alternatives were also shaped to a great extent by that relationship. The choice was never between Communism and Democracy; rather the issue was, should there be greater or less Soviet influence and control over Chinese affairs? The decision was in favor of the latter alternative, but the cost was high, particularly in terms of China's economic development.

A second theme is constant conflict within the Chinese Communist Party apparatus. The form and content of the struggle, of course, has varied over time depending on the political relationships existing within the Soviet and Chinese leaderships. I treat four general topics in this context. The first is the growth and development of the Chinese Communist Party and the rise to power of Mao Tse-tung; that story makes up Part I of the book. The second is the struggle between Nationalists and Communists for state power, a story that reaches its climax in Part II. The third is the establishment and decay of the Sino-Soviet alliance—the history of the post-1949 period extending up to 1968; this forms Part III of the book. Finally, the evolution of the Sino-American relationship from 1969 through 1980 and the political revolution following the death of Mao Tse-tung in 1976 form Part IV.

I would like to express my deepest appreciation to George Washington University's Institute for Sino-Soviet Studies and especially to Dr. Gaston J. Sigur, its director, whose support contributed greatly to preparation of the revised edition, and to the Institute's faculty and students, whose stimulating discussion and searching criticism helped me to clarify my own thoughts. Special thanks go to Dorothy Wedge, Sheila Murphy, and Suzanne Rudd for their unstinting secretarial support, to Susan McRory of Westview Press for her skillful copyediting, and to Edythe Porpa, who compiled the comprehensive index.

Richard C. Thornton
Washington, D.C.

PART I
The Origin and Development of Chinese Communism, 1917–1941

I

To Build a Communist Movement in China, 1917-1927

The final collapse of the Ch'ing dynasty in 1911 created a political vacuum in China, intensifying the struggle for hegemony over the mainland of Asia, which had begun in the nineteenth century. World War I further upset the balance of power in the Far East as European battlefields drew the attention and energies of the major powers away from Asia. The Russian revolution, too, forced a temporary withdrawal from Far Eastern affairs as the Bolsheviks battled in civil strife to secure their victorious *coup d'état.* Japan emerged from the cataclysmic events of war and revolution the most powerful and expansionistic state in Asia. Under these circumstances, Japan's drive to expand into China was as inevitable as were the efforts by the major powers to contain the Japanese.

The fledgling Soviet regime was most immediately and directly affected by the absence of a balance of power in Asia. Japanese dominance of China would place the Soviet Union at severe strategic disadvantage; therefore, after the revolution, Soviet leaders strove to repel the Japanese advance. The Bolshevik revolution dramatically altered the means and objectives of traditional Russian foreign relations. The concepts of class struggle, imperialism, and world revolution, as developed by Marx and Lenin, liberated Soviet leaders from the limiting effects of the nation-state concept. The Bolsheviks were not confined to traditional ways of conducting international relations. Their aims could be pursued on a worldwide front—by conventional diplomatic and unconventional revolutionary means—promoting and assisting what they termed the "class struggle" wherever it was deemed in their interest to do so.

The Soviet Union was, of course, still too weak to assist directly in the promotion of revolution. The Communist International, or Comintern, established in 1919, gave the young Communist regime greater operational flexibility. After initial expectation that revolution would erupt spontaneously had faded, Bolshevik leaders turned to the task of organizing the world revolution. Radical socialist groups all over the world had sprung up proclaiming allegiance to the Soviet state. To these groups the Soviet leaders, primarily through the organization of the Comintern, sought to give direction and cohesion, with the objective of creating organizations around the world responsive to the Soviet will.

To an extraordinary degree the Bolsheviks applied the experience and perspectives of their own revolutionary effort in Russia to the international scene. They did so in more than the commonly understood sense of extending on a world scale the Leninist party organization. A much deeper conception of the revolutionary process dominated Bolshevik attitudes and policies—a conception which actually had only a superficial relationship to the thoughts of Marx and Engels. That conception derived from the chain of events which unfolded in Russia from the dissolution of the monarchy through the Bolshevik coup to the consolidation of the regime during the civil war period. It was *dvoevlastie,* or dual power.[1]

The Bolshevik Experience

In Russia after the fall of the monarchy in March 1917, two organs of power quickly formed: the Provisional Government, composed of former Duma members, and the soviets of workers', peasants', and soldiers' deputies, controlled by the Menshevik faction of the Russian Social Democratic Labor Party. Over the course of the year, for various reasons, real power shifted from the Provisional Government to the soviets. Initially, the Bolsheviks participated in but did not control the soviets. By September, however, they managed to gain a majority in them and created their own military force, the Red Guard, which was the primary instrument employed in the coup of October 25 (November 7). Throughout, Lenin's strategy was to support the soviets versus the Provisional Government, even though his group did not initially control the soviets. He directed the Bolsheviks to work for control of the existing revolutionary alternative, the soviets, rather than create a third force.

The soviet of workers', peasants', and soldiers' deputies was the symbol of revolution in Russia in 1917.

When Soviet leaders undertook to formulate revolutionary policy for the "colonial and semi-colonial east" their discussions reflected the dual power conception of their own revolutionary experience. The decisive phase of the policy-making process occurred at the Second Congress of the Comintern, in August 1920. The policy alternatives which emerged from the discussions were contained in the positions expressed by Lenin and M. N. Roy, an Indian Communist. Although both agreed on the elemental premise of dual power, each proposed a different course of action in response to the question: What were the immediate steps necessary to foster the growth of a revolutionary movement in China?

Roy held that China's chaotic conditions permitted the immediate establishment of an independent, openly Communist-led and controlled revolutionary movement on the basis of soviets. Lenin disagreed, arguing that the prerequisites for an independently based Communist movement were yet to be established in China, a fertile but unplowed ground. Time was the necessary condition to permit the incubation of the movement. It would require some time to educate the masses in the concepts of Marxism-Leninism and to organize a revolutionary "vanguard." Therefore, Lenin postulated, in the beginning it would be necessary to support an existing revolutionary grouping ("national revolutionaries," it was agreed to call them) that already commanded a substantial following.[2] To do otherwise would be to risk the total destruction of the movement before it could be firmly established, because the warlords, "bourgeois revolutionaries," and imperialists all would combine to attack the nascent Communist organization. Lenin's proposals prevailed, but Roy's position was duly noted, being included in the congress's published resolutions because it reflected a policy which could be followed if conditions evolved that were capable of supporting an independent movement. The policy followed toward China, until 1928, when circumstances forced a change, was Lenin's.

Once it had been decided to build a revolutionary movement by working through an existing "bourgeois" revolutionary organization, rather than by establishing an independent Communist movement based on "soviets," the next question was: which revolutionary grouping should the Soviet Union support? The criteria for selection were obvious. The most desirable "national revolutionary" organization to support would be one that was popular but vulnerable to penetration. Warlords Wu P'ei-fu and Feng Yü-hsiang both controlled independent armed forces in the north and northwest, but were less susceptible to penetration than a revolutionary organization in south China led by Sun Yat-sen. Sun's Kuomintang, or Nationalist party, was a highly popular, quite disorganized revolutionary group in Kwangtung province subsisting largely at the mercy of local warlord troops because it had virtually no military force of its own. Moreover, the Nationalists espoused an ideology, the *San Min Chu Yi*, or Three People's Principles, which was not incompatible with Bolshevism's minimum program of the bourgeois-democratic revolution.

The Soviet Union Aids the Kuomintang

After protracted negotiations, the Soviet Union entered into an agreement to aid the Kuomintang. This was the Sun-Joffe agreement of January 27, 1923.[3] The decision to support the Kuomintang was fully in accordance with the larger objective of creating the conditions of dual power in China. The "revolutionary" Kuomintang would counterpose the "legal" government at Peking. The Soviet Union would assist the Kuomintang in its struggle for power while at the same time attempting to gain control of it from within. In this task the Chinese Communists played a crucial role.

Efforts toward the formation of a Chinese Communist Party were begun shortly after the establishment of the Communist International. It was part of the larger effort to give greater cohesion to the radical groupings around the globe clamoring for direction from the makers of the Russian revolution. Such basic organizational work would be undertaken in any case, regardless of the outcome of higher-level strategy discussions in the Soviet Union and Soviet negotiations with the various groupings inside China itself. When the Comintern's agent, Grigorii Voitinsky, arrived in China in the spring of 1920, the groundwork had already been laid and he quickly made contact with leaders of these groups, of whom Li Ta-chao and Ch'en Tu-hsiu were most notable. By the fall of that year, half a dozen small "Marxist study groups" were functioning in China, with a group in Japan and one in Paris composed of Chinese students abroad on work-study programs.

At the end of July 1921 (the exact date is unclear), the founding congress of the Chinese Communist Party (CCP) was held under the auspices of another Comintern agent, one Henry Sneevliet (alias Maring).[4] The Chinese Communists immediately became active in the labor and youth fields, in agitation and propaganda, translating the works of Marx and Lenin, publishing pamphlets and other literature. These endeavors met with but a modicum of success, but some organizational cohesion was realized. As it became apparent that the Kuomintang (KMT) would be the vehicle for Soviet influence in China, the Chinese Communists, not entirely willingly, began to join the Kuomintang as individuals.[5] When the Sun-Joffe agreement was signed in January 1923, the Chinese Communists were well on the road to forming a Bolshevik faction within the Nationalist party.

Soviet aid to the Kuomintang centered around two major interrelated programs, the political reorganization of the Nationalist party and the establishment of a national-revolutionary army. In October 1923 Michael Borodin arrived in Canton as the representative of the Soviet Government, and by the following January he had rewritten the party constitution, thoroughly restructuring the KMT along the lines of "democratic centralism." The First National Congress of the Kuomintang, held that month, officially concluded an alliance with the CCP. Soviet influence was especially strong at the Whampoa Military Academy, which had been established in April. Headed by General Galen, scores of Soviet military advisors and instructors drilled Chinese cadets in Soviet methods, using Soviet weapons, equipment, and supplies.[6] In addition to actual military training, weapons instruction, tactics of attack and deployment, and so forth, the curriculum included political economy, the theory of imperialism, the Three People's Principles of Sun Yat-sen, the history of China, and the history of the revolutionary movement in the West.

The striking feature of the Soviet military aid program was the organization of a political commissar system in the army which created twin political and military command systems from the top to the company level, with the political commissar having the power to countermand orders of the military commander. Although Chiang Kai-shek was military commander of the Whampoa Academy, the Chinese Communists built a strong position for themselves in the political section. Chou En-lai, who as a student in Paris had been one of the founders of the French branch of the CCP, held appointment as head of the political section at the academy. At this stage, however, Chiang's position as commandant cannot be interpreted as an attempt to balance the Communists and non-Communists. Chiang had returned in January 1924 from several months' study in the Soviet Union. Undoubtedly his assignment as commandant of the military academy was looked upon by Moscow with pleasure. It suggested that persons willing to cooperate with the Soviets were in command of both the military and political sections at Whampoa.

Within the short space of a year the massive Soviet aid effort began to show signs of success. The first Soviet arms shipment arrived at Whampoa on October 7, 1924 and was shortly followed by others.[7] By the end of the year the young Nationalist army disbanded the local militia and in the first eastern expedition early the next year routed regional forces which earlier had been troublesome,[8] providing a secure base on which in July to establish a "National Government." Under these conditions the CCP, too, expanded by leaps and bounds, increasing its power within the KMT. From a total of about fifty in 1921, CCP membership exceeded twelve thousand by 1926.[9] At the First Congress of the Kuomintang in January 1924, seven Communists were elected to the Central Committee and to several other key posts, including that of the Organization Department, which was headed by the Communist T'an P'ing-shan. The Second Congress of the Kuomintang, held in January 1926, saw the further extension of Communist power. Of thirty-six regular Central Committee members, seven were Communists, and seven other Communists were named as alternate members, including Mao Tse-tung, who also served briefly as head of the Propaganda Department. Most important, three of the nine members of the Central Executive Committee were Communists.[10]

Chiang Kai-shek and the Communists

Sun (and after his death on March 12, 1925, Chiang) was not oblivious to the growing Communist position in the Kuomintang, but was willing to take some risks because of the high returns accruing from Soviet aid. With Sun's death the principal candidates in the succession struggle were Chiang and Wang Ching-wei. Chiang's steps to secure his own position led him to oppose the Soviets because they had thrown their support to Wang. Chiang's first move was precipitated by an alleged Communist plot to kidnap him by taking him on board the gunboat *Chungshan*, anchored in the river near the Whampoa Military Academy. Instead, during the night of March 19-20, 1926, Chiang's men arrested the political commissars in the detachments under his command (about fifty Communists), detained all Soviet advisors in Canton, raided the headquarters of the Hong Kong Strike Committee, confiscating all arms found there, and disarmed the "Workers' Guard," a disguised CCP military formation. By the morning of the 20th, Chiang had stripped the Communists from power in military units under his command and had taken undisputed control over a significant part of the army, especially his own First Army Corps.

Borodin was out of the city when the coup took place. He had gone to the northwest to discuss with Feng Yü-hsiang the conditions under which the warlord would assist in the planned "Northern Campaign" against the Peking government. Upon his hasty return to Canton, Chiang confronted Borodin with a *fait accompli,* demanding that the northern campaign be initiated immediately. Borodin reluctantly agreed to continued Soviet aid for the campaign, in return for which Chiang released those whom he had arrested.[11] Borodin's reluctance to agree to the immediate beginning of the northern campaign is quite understandable, even apart from the events of March 20. The Communists had secured a strong position in the Kuomintang before March 20, but one not strong enough to be decisive in any showdown with Chiang. After the 20th, Borodin had even less reason to believe that the Communists could secure victory within the Kuomintang in an open contest with Chiang. Still, his choice was either to withdraw altogether, which would remove all possibility of having another opportunity to gain control, or to continue assistance in the hope that another opportunity would arise. So Borodin assented. Chiang, of course, preferred an early start for the campaign because a victory would give him access to alternate sources of funds and materiel from the businessmen and arsenals of the economically relatively advanced Yangtze River area. Such access would make him less dependent upon Soviet arms, money, and advisors.

Having gained acquiescence to begin the northern campaign immediately, Chiang discussed with Borodin the battle plan. Borodin urged a march on Wuhan, which would enable KMT forces to coordinate action with Feng Yü-hsiang; Chiang agreed. The mobilization order of July 1 reflected the Soviet proposal precisely. But while accepting this plan,

Chiang supplemented it by sending his own First Army Corps, commanded by Ho Ying-ch'in, through the coastal provinces of Fukien and Chekiang toward Nanking and Shanghai.[12] On July 9, the National Government at Canton appointed Chiang commander-in-chief of all forces in the northern campaign. Three days later Nationalist forces captured Ch'angsha and within a month they destroyed the forces of Wu P'ei-fu, marking a successful first phase of the campaign. During the initial phase Borodin and the KMT Central Executive Committee accompanied Nationalist forces on the march toward Wuhan, while Chiang remained in Canton. It was not until Nationalist armies stood at the gate of Wuhan in August that Chiang went into the field to assume on-the-spot direction of the campaign.[13]

The struggle against the tri-city complex was long and arduous, and when Wuhan finally capitulated on October 10, the Communists, who had led strikes within the city and gained control of it, delivered it to the KMT Left. This, combined with military developments in the field, placed Chiang in a dangerous position. During the siege the warlord Sun Chuan-fang had shifted his forces in an attempt to attack the Nationalists from behind. Chiang's supply of arms was now imperiled, for the Communists were unlikely to supply Chiang's forces from the Hanyang arsenal in Wuhan, and if Sun Chuan-fang's moves were successful, arms could no longer be obtained from Canton. Against the heated protests of the Soviet advisors, Chiang decided to move trusted forces eastward toward Nanchang, Nanking, and Shanghai to break the encircling movement by Sun, and, in the process, to capture the arsenals at Nanking and Shanghai.[14] After a difficult struggle Nanchang was captured in early November, making not only a figurative but a literal split in the KMT, with the Left at Wuhan and the Right at Nanchang. For the next few months each side maneuvered to win over the other, to no avail. Meanwhile, in Moscow the struggle between Stalin and Trotsky for Lenin's mantle was reaching its climax and China policy became a critical element in that struggle.

The Communist Attempt to Seize Power

The victorious surge of Nationalist armies northward provided both the Nationalists and the Chinese Communists with unparalleled opportunities for expansion of their power. Operating in the vanguard of the armed columns as propagandists and organizers of rural and urban populations along the line of march, the Communists reaped the political fruits of military victory. It was they who entered and took control of many of the cities and towns which the army conquered, while the military forces moved on to engage the enemy elsewhere in the field. In this way, Communist power increased tremendously during the northern expedition.

However, Chiang Kai-shek's strength, due to an unprecedented growth in the size of the army, increased even more rapidly than did Communist power. As Nationalist armies moved like an unstoppable juggernaut across the face of China, enemy commanders, one after the other, joined the revolutionary forces. Many of these men had been classmates of Chiang at the Paoting Military Academy, and this, coupled with the fact that Chiang was commander-in-chief, made it easy for him to enlist them in his ranks. In addition, since this growth, which increased Nationalist forces tenfold by the end of 1926, took place after Chiang had excluded the Communists from units under his command, Chiang, and not the Communists, was the principal beneficiary of this development.

Both of these trends were evident to the leaders in Moscow, but their significance was interpreted differently by Trotsky and by the Stalin-Bukharin coalition. Trotsky in late 1926 was losing, if he had not already lost, his struggle against Stalin for power in the Soviet Union. His interpretation of the situation in China and his policy prescription were part of a last-ditch effort to stem the political tide which was now running full against him. But Trotsky sought to oppose Stalin in a futile way, by opposing the position Lenin had espoused in 1920.

Recall that the issue at the Second Congress of the Comintern was how best to generate a revolutionary movement in the colonial and semi-colonial east. Roy had urged the immediate buildup of an independent Communist movement on the basis of soviets. Lenin had opposed this proposal on the grounds that the conditions that would support an openly Communist movement had not yet matured and prescribed instead that Communists support an existing revolutionary movement. This was the course adopted in China and was the policy which Stalin strenuously sought to uphold against Trotsky. In their struggle, Stalin stood on the solid ground of Leninist orthodoxy and Trotsky in the position of opposing Lenin, just as he had in 1905.

Thus, both Trotsky and Stalin perceived the polarization of the Kuomintang, but each responded differently. In Trotsky's view, the masses were moving left and the bourgeoisie were moving right; the Kuomintang was bourgeois. No worker, he said, would join the Chinese Communist Party if it supported a government which suppressed their demands. From these two propositions followed Trotsky's proposal. To him the polarization of the Kuomintang meant that "all the pre-conditions of a successful proletarian movement in the Soviet manner were present." [15] The suppressive character of the KMT required the Chinese Communist Party to withdraw from the Kuomintang and form an independent movement. Trotsky's position, of course, was quite simplistic and designed primarily to sway opinion in the party. He failed to add to his analysis the central fact that the Chinese Communists had been unsuccessful in efforts to gain control of the army, the major portion of which was now firmly under Chiang Kai-shek's control.

Stalin and Bukharin, at this time allied against Trotsky, faced the task of making policy at this critical juncture. They groped toward a policy which would enable the Chinese Communists to build an armed force to counter Chiang's and to accomplish the main objective of capturing the Kuomintang from within. The Kuomintang had not yet formally split and was in the process of organizing an administrative apparatus to govern the vast new territories it had acquired. On paper, therefore, the Communist position appeared to be quite strong. Combined with the Left-KMT, the Chinese Communist Party had controlled the majority of votes at the Second Kuomintang Congress the previous January (168 of a total of 278),[16] and there was every reason to expect that the party had strengthened its position as a result of the northern expedition.

As an immediate step to exploit the opportunities created by the northern expedition, the Stalin-Bukharin coalition directed the Chinese Communists to capture the new administrative apparatus. The target was the peasantry; the slogan, the "agrarian revolution"; the technique, organizational manipulation. These instructions were contained in the resolutions of the Seventh Plenum of the Executive Committee of the Comintern (ECCI), which convened from November 22 through December 16, 1926. First and foremost, the Communist revolution had to be identified with the agrarian revolution. The "basic demand" of a proletarian agrarian program must eventually be nationalization, but for the present, agrarian tactics could be set according to differing conditions. "In territory under the KMT National Government," the instructions stipulated, the CCP should strive to draw the peasantry over to the side of the revolution by supporting their demands, such as rent reduction, abolition of taxes, arming of the poor and middle peasantry, and so forth. These measures were merely:

> steps towards a more developed phase of the agrarian revolution . . . [to be] carried out by creating peasant committees under communist leadership. As the revolution develops, the peasant committees will acquire the authority and strength [to advance] . . . more radical demands.[17]

Second, as the Kuomintang pushed northward, conquering province after province, it had set up state organizations which Stalin now directed the CCP to capture. As stated in the resolution:

> The machinery of the National Revolutionary Government provides an extremely effective channel for approaching the peasantry and the communist party must make use of it. In the recently liberated provinces a state apparatus of the Canton type will be established. The task of the communists and their revolutionary allies is to permeate the new government apparatus in order to give practical expression to the agrarian programme of the national revolution. This can be achieved by using the State machine to confiscate lands, lower taxes, and give real powers to the peasant committees, thus gradually introducing reforms based on a revolutionary programme.[18]

In this manner, Stalin sought to capture the KMT from within, but events in China were overtaking this policy even as it was being formulated. At a Central Executive Committee meeting of the Kuomintang in December, Borodin persuaded the leaders of the left wing of the KMT to move the seat of government from Canton to Wuhan, in opposition to Chiang, who was demanding that the government be moved to Nanchang. Borodin won out and the government was moved to Wuhan, making the KMT split geographical as well as political—a situation which simultaneously made it easier and yet more difficult for the Chinese Communists to pursue the Comintern's plans. It made it easier in the sense that the Left-KMT at Wuhan was now free of the conservative elements which had opposed the Chinese Communists, yet more difficult because the actual balance of military power was concentrated in Chiang's hands and he was no longer dependent on the

Soviet Union for military supplies, now having access to alternate sources on China's east coast.

Having won the battle over the location of the government, the Chinese Communists, in alliance with the Left-Kuomintang, moved to gain control over the army. At its Third Plenum, on March 10, 1927, the Kuomintang Central Executive Committee not only refused Chiang's demand that the seat of the government be moved to Nanchang, but attempted to strip military power from him. Under the slogan "all power to the Party," the Left revoked emergency powers delegated to Chiang the year before to carry the revolutionary campaign northward, and reestablished the military council, to which Chiang was formally subordinated. The Third Plenum also passed a resolution on KMT-CCP cooperation, restoring the Communists to the status enjoyed before Chiang's March 1926 coup. As part of this latter development, the plenum appointed Communists to head the ministries of labor and agriculture, and to jurisdiction over the police and security apparatuses.

Chiang's reaction to the decision of the Third Plenum was publicly to acquiesce, but privately to act forcefully to strengthen his own position. On the 22nd of March, Chiang's forces took Shanghai, and on the 24th Nanking. Two days later, on the 26th, in a provisional emergency session of the KMT Central Supervisory Committee in Nanchang, Chiang's supporters passed a resolution stating that there was evidence of a planned Communist uprising and authorized him to take whatever measures he considered necessary to meet the threat.

At this point Wang Ching-wei returned from abroad after a self-imposed exile of approximately one year. Arriving on April 1 by way of Moscow, where he had had discussions with top Soviet leaders, Wang professed a desire to reunite the KMT. In response, Chiang announced on April 3 that he would henceforth act only on orders from the KMT Central Executive Committee in Wuhan. This led to a brief surge of propaganda from both the Comintern and the Chinese Communist Party to the effect that Chiang was "submitting to discipline" and that the Kuomintang right and left wings would soon be unified, but ensuing discussions foundered upon the issue of how to treat the Communists.[19] Five days after his arrival, on April 6, Wang secretly slipped off to Wuhan with Ch'en Tu-hsiu, secretary general of the Chinese Communist Party.

Wang's departure freed Chiang's hands. On the very next day he called a secret military conference in Shanghai which was attended by top military leaders Li Tsung-jen, Li Chi-shen, Pai Chung-hsi, and Huang Shao-hsiung, all of whom pledged to support Chiang against the Communists. On April 12, Chiang began to eliminate Communists in areas under his control in Shanghai, Canton, and Nanking. As Chiang's intention to purge the Communists became clear, the KMT Left at Wuhan, now led by Wang Ching-wei, formally expelled Chiang Kai-shek and his supporters from the party. On the following day, April 13, Chiang countered by formally establishing the government at Nanking in direct opposition to the one at Wuhan.

Under these new circumstances of formal cleavage in the Kuomintang, the Chinese Communist Party held its Fifth Party Congress (April 27–May 5) at which it pledged support to Wuhan and attacked Nanking as a counterrevolutionary regime. So as not to antagonize its Left-KMT allies, the Communists adopted a mild land policy, confiscating only land owned by landlords, but not that of army officers. Wang Ching-wei attended the main session of the congress as an honored guest. At the congress, Moscow's representatives, Borodin and M. N. Roy, disagreed on the policy to be pursued; the issue was resolved in Borodin's favor when Wang Ching-wei sided with Borodin. Wang and Borodin agreed on a plan, which, if successful, would not only unify China but bring Chiang Kai-shek to heel. The plan was to move the Left-KMT's forces northward, avoiding conflict with Chiang's troops, engaging instead the forces under the command of Chang Hsüeh-liang. Chang controlled north China and Peking, the symbol of political legitimacy and national unity. Feng Yü-hsiang, who had recently returned from Moscow and was receiving regular supplies of arms and money from the Soviet Union, was to be the linchpin in this plan. He was to join forces with those of the Left-KMT in the drive on Peking. Once the traditional capital was taken and China's northeast fell into Communist hands, Chiang would presumably be forced to capitulate. Roy opposed this plan, urging, instead, that the Communists gather their own forces together in the original base at Canton. He argued that the revolution was in its most advanced stage in south China and that the Communists would be best able to rebuild their own forces quickly there. Although Roy was overruled, his plan was adopted after Borodin's scheme to gain control of Peking failed and there was no other alternative.

In early May, Left-Kuomintang troops moved into Honan province and by mid-June they had delivered a stunning blow to the northern forces, but Feng Yü-hsiang never committed his troops to battle, moving in only after the fighting was over. The result was that the Left-Kuomintang's forces were badly mauled, gaining what could only be called a Pyrrhic victory. The real victor was Feng Yü-hsiang, who, as commander of the strategic force in the area, now attempted to play the role of broker in the reunification of the KMT. He demanded on June 12 that the Kuomintang reunite and expel the Communists!

Stalin, Trotsky, and the Chinese Revolution

Meanwhile, paralleling these events, the Eighth ECCI Plenum convened in Moscow from 18 to 30 May, at which time the Stalin-Trotsky feud over China policy reached a climax. Ironically, though Trotsky proved correct in his predictions about the course of the revolution in China, his predictions and arguments were based on incorrect data. In his theses of May 7, which were refused publication by the Stalin group, Trotsky reiterated his demands that the Chinese Communists withdraw from the Kuomintang and "appeal to the workers under its own name and banner, organize them, support every forward step of the Kuomintang, oppose every step backward. . . ." He loudly proclaimed that Chiang's April slaughter was the outcome of the Soviet Union's bureaucratic leadership, that is, of Stalin's "opportunist policy." [20]

Trotsky stated Stalin's policy correctly, saying that he proposed arming the workers but not forming soviets because soviets would conflict with the Left-KMT. But in attempting to refute Stalin's policies, Trotsky confused the issue. He queried: ". . . against whom were the workers to be armed if not against that [Left-Kuomintang] government?" The point was that arming the workers and establishing soviets were related but separate propositions, which Trotsky muddled together. Trotsky conveniently ignored the original motive for supporting the Kuomintang, which was to take it over from within. Stalin's policies were clearly focused on this objective. It mattered little whether or not the Communists obtained anything more than the Kuomintang's name. Revolutionary legitimacy was the prize, nothing more, nothing less. Once they secured the KMT "banner," they would have secured the shell of an organization which they could fill with their own policies. It mattered little whether any members of the Kuomintang came along with the name. In fact, Stalin was at that moment ordering the Communists to prepare to eliminate "vacillating groups" in the Left-KMT, that is, to purge the Left-KMT at the very time he was paying lip-service to CCP-KMT unity! Moreover, Trotsky's analysis of the Left-KMT left much to be desired from a purely factual standpoint. In his effort to discredit the Left-KMT and minimize its value, he asserted that it had no forces at its disposal. Yet, at that very moment, the Left-KMT forces were engaging in a critical battle with the forces of Chang Hsüeh-liang in which they lost over 14,000 men. Second, Trotsky argued that the Left-KMT government was "a fiction," missing the entire point of the Soviet Union's policy. A Left-KMT governmental apparatus existed capable of supporting an armed force of several thousand men.[21]

In his speech to the Eighth Plenum, Stalin clearly formulated the issue in terms of the concept of dual power.

> To form Soviets of workers' and peasants' deputies *at the present time* in the area of activity, say, of the Wuhan government, would mean establishing a dual power and issuing the slogan of a struggle for the overthrow of the Left-KMT and the establishment of a new Soviet power in China. . . . The appearance of Soviets of workers' and peasants' deputies cannot but create a dual power, and, given a dual power, the question whom all power should belong to cannot but become an acute issue.[22]

The questions of legitimacy and allegiance of the masses were implied in Stalin's words. The Left-KMT was formally the legitimate repository of power. Chiang had established his Nanking government in opposition to it. The juxtaposition of the Left- and Right-KMT made the question of allegiance clear. To add soviets to this conception as a third element would only divide and confuse the forces of the Left, which were not all-powerful, and weaken them still further.

The final resolutions of the plenum contained the signal for the Chinese Communists to attempt to take over the Left-KMT from within. All of the instructions in the resolutions, including creating a workers' guard, were intended to forward this objective. Stalin's policy was not to withdraw from the KMT as Trotsky demanded, but to organize a military force to capture it. The thrust of the policy can best be illustrated by the following excerpt from the plenum records. The prize—a Soviet controlled China—was worth the desperate effort.

Precisely because the KMT banner is the most weighty political factor in the country, the bourgeois leaders led by Chiang Kai-shek are trying to appear under its colors. CP tactics should not provide a screen for this political maneuver, which would be the case if the party left the KMT. . . .

The ECCI does not consider it appropriate at the present time to advance the slogan of Soviets of workers' and peasants' deputies (in the territory of Wuhan) which is equivalent to the slogan of proclaiming Soviet power. To advance the slogan of the immediate formation of Soviets . . . would inevitably mean to work for dual power, for the overthrow of the Wuhan Government, jumping over the KMT form of organizing the masses . . . the Left-KMT Wuhan Government is not a dictatorship of the proletariat and peasantry, but is on the road to such a dictatorship. . . . The ECCI believes that the CCP should take a most energetic part in the work of the Wuhan "Provisional revolutionary government". . . .

The ECCI believes . . . that the CCP must work to change the KMT into a really mass organization. . . . Only such a policy will make it possible to institute the strongest counter-measures against the eventual and inevitable desertion of the vacillating groups among the Left-KMT [!].

Agrarian revolution, including confiscation and nationalization of the land—that is the fundamental internal socio-economic content of the new stage of the Chinese revolution. . . . At the same time, within the Government, the communist party should pursue a policy which will further the development of the agrarian revolution. At the present stage this can be done only by transforming the present Government into the political center of the workers' and peasants' revolution and into an organ of the revolutionary democratic dictatorship of the proletariat and peasantry. Only with such a policy, moreover, pursued at the base and at the top, will it be possible to create really promising armed detachments and reorganize the entire army on a sound, revolutionary basis.

The ECCI also believes that at the present moment it is a matter of urgency to consider the question of reorganizing the army, of creating absolutely reliable revolutionary detachments, of the links between the army and workers' and peasants' organizations, of securing the cadres in the army, of turning the army from a mercenary into a regular army of the revolution, etc. Special attention should be paid to forming absolutely reliable detachments of revolutionary peasants and workers, to infiltrating communists and sound Left-KMT people into the army, purging it of counter-revolutionary elements, creating a workers' guard. . . .[23]

The essence of the plenum's decisions was telegraphed to the Comintern's representatives in China, among whom was Roy. Believing that Wang Ching-wei would support the new policy, Roy showed him the telegram. It had the opposite effect from that intended by Roy. The information that the Communists intended to purge recalcitrant elements in the Wuhan apparatus (which placed Wang himself in the position of follower rather than leader), combined with the defection of Feng Yü-hsiang to Chiang Kai-shek, left Wang Ching-wei little choice but to acquiesce to Chiang's ultimatum, delivered at the end of June, to expel the Communists. At the beginning of July the two Communist ministers in the Wuhan government resigned and on the 15th the reunified KMT political council expelled all Communists from the Nationalist party.

Again, events outpaced the Comintern. Even as the Wuhan leaders were expelling the Communists from their ranks, the ECCI was formulating another change in policy, calling upon the Chinese Communists "demonstratively" to leave the Wuhan government, but to remain within the KMT! No longer able to exert any influence at the top, the ECCI instructed the Chinese Communists to expend every effort toward a last gasp attempt from below. They were to establish closer ties with the KMT rank and file to prepare for the coming KMT National Congress, and, to give themselves greater influence, they were to push the agrarian revolution to a higher stage by arming the masses.

Yet even as the new instructions were being telegraphed to China they were obsolete. Having expelled the Communists, the Left-KMT leadership was emulating Chiang in conducting a systematic purge of Communists from their ranks. At the end of July, Borodin had been packed off to Moscow and the Communist rank and file were in flight, in hiding, or in revolt. Whether out of frustration or fear, and despite Comintern admonitions to be cautious, the Chinese Communists undertook several uprisings during the latter months of 1927, all of which were unsuccessful.

The Communists in Revolt

The Fourth Corps, the best of the Left-KMT's military units, staged the first uprising at Nanchang on August 1. Under Communist commanders Ho Lung and Yeh T'ing, the Fourth Corps had been marching southward from Honan province, where it had participated in the bloody conflict with Chang Hsüeh-liang's forces, toward the province of Kwangtung. At Nanchang, the Communists hoped to win over vacillating Nationalist military leaders and their troops to provide the nucleus for an all-Communist force to be formed in the Canton area. The revolt failed and the plan never materialized. A troop of 21,000 men when it left Nanchang, by the time the Corps reached Kwangtung its numbers had been whittled down by Nationalist forces to about 1,000 weary men.

The interpretation of Comintern instructions by the Central Committee of the CCP (and by Comintern representatives) over whether or not to carry out the Nanchang uprising suggests an increasingly widening gulf between Moscow and the Chinese Communists during this period of crisis. In a telegram to the CCP leadership, the Comintern expressed serious reservations about attempting a revolt at Nanchang. The telegram read: "If there is no chance at all of victory then it will be all right not to start the Nanchang revolt." The CCP Central Standing Committee interpreted the telegram differently. In a letter written shortly afterward, it wrote of the Comintern instruction: "This is as much as to say: 'Unless there is no chance at all of victory, the Nanchang revolt ought to be started.' " [24]

On August 7, a week after the Nanchang revolt, Besso Lominadze and Heinz Neumann, the Comintern's new representatives to the CCP, who replaced Borodin and Roy, called an emergency conference of the party. They cast out the Ch'en Tu-hsiu leadership, elected a new one headed by Ch'ü Ch'iu-pai, and determined upon plans for additional uprisings, still under the banner of the KMT. It is clear from the historical record that these new "reps," as they were called, were sent with instructions to convene an emergency meeting and install a new party leadership. It is much less clear whether they were instructed to instigate the uprisings that followed. While sent by Stalin to guide the CCP in its critical hour, both Lominadze and Neumann had ideas of their own about the proper policy to be followed in China. Believing that the Chinese revolution was in a state of continuous upsurge, they seemed to feel that uprising had to follow uprising until victory was achieved.[25] Thus they agreed to preparations for insurrections, the most extensive of which were at Ch'angsha (the Autumn Harvest Uprising) in September, Wuhan in October, and Canton in December. Although the Wuhan insurrection was canceled, the Ch'angsha and Canton revolts were carried out with bloody consequences.

Mao Tse-tung was assigned the task of organizing and carrying out the Autumn Harvest Uprising at Ch'angsha. The Communist leaders intended to establish a revolutionary regime based upon the peasant committees established earlier during the northern expedition—still under the Kuomintang cloak of legitimacy. But Mao acted otherwise, attempting to organize soviets and a "workers' and peasants' army," for which, after the uprising failed utterly, he was removed from his leadership posts in the party.[26] Long before he received the news of his demotion, however, Mao had already led the remnants of the force which had been involved in the Ch'angsha uprising to safety in the Ching Kang Mountains, thus laying the foundation for one of the first revolutionary bases.

One of the important consequences of the failure at Ch'angsha was the decision by Moscow to abandon further attempts to act within the KMT and to relinquish the quest for the Nationalist banner. By this time, the left and right wings of the KMT had reunited and it was pointless to continue attempts to gain control. Therefore, on September 30, *Pravda* announced that the Chinese revolution had moved into the "soviet" stage, a term that had specific meaning but which, for the time being, had an uncertain content. It meant that the twin poles of dual power would henceforth be the KMT and the Chinese soviets. Some Communists attributed the name *soviets* to their enclaves immediately after the new phase of the revolution was announced, but it would be several months before a specific policy would be formulated.

Meanwhile, the fusion of the left and right wings of the KMT had not been achieved without incident. General T'ang Sheng-chih, whose forces had been the mainstay of the Wuhan regime, refused to accept the reconciliation. The Nanking leaders (Chiang Kai-shek had resigned in August and a triumvirate consisting of Li Tsung-jen, Ho Ying-ch'in, and Pai Chung-hsi was in command) decided to send troops to Wuhan. The Chinese Communists recognized that General T'ang stood no chance of victory and in the wake of T'ang's defeat planned to carry out an uprising in Wuhan. Though the Comintern representative, Lominadze, approved of the plan, it was called off for lack of adequate preparation and sufficient forces.[27]

Early in November, the Chinese Communists held another plenary session. Led by the Comintern "reps," Lominadze and Neumann, and the Chinese Ch'ü Ch'iu-pai, these "left-extremists" decided to launch a series of uninterrupted "uprisings in cities and villages" under the slogan of the newly sanctioned soviets in the belief that only by "permanent revolution" could the Chinese revolution be victorious. The fruits of this decision were a series of scattered peasant uprisings and the disastrous Canton revolt of early December.

In Kwangtung province, two rival Nationalist generals, Li Chi-shen and Chang Fa-k'uei, shared power. Wang Ching-wei, seeking to reverse his waning political fortunes, plotted with Chang Fa-k'uei to oust Li Chi-shen from Canton, the provincial center of power. Their plans became known to the Chinese Communists, who sought to benefit from the struggle between the rival generals. When Chang Fa-k'uei carried out his coup, taking over the city on November 17, the Chinese Communist leadership quickly made plans of their own to instigate a revolt, setting December 11 as the date. The uprising was initially successful, enabling the Communists to hold the city for two days, but by the 13th, reinforcements had been sent to the city and the Communist forces, badly outnumbered, were savagely beaten.

In Moscow, Trotsky charged that the Canton revolt by the Communists was timed to coincide with the Fifteenth Party Congress of the Soviet Union, which convened from December 3 through 17, 1927. He claimed that Stalin used the "victory" at Canton to cover up the "purge" of the Trotskyite opposition. This charge, while plausible, seems unlikely. In the few available documents which emanated from Moscow, Stalin urged caution, not revolution. On the other hand, Comintern representatives on the spot clearly called for, and engineered, the uprisings. If the Canton revolt was timed at all, it was timed by a left-extremist faction in the Comintern whose China group included Lominadze, Neumann, and Ch'ü Ch'iu-pai, among others.[28]

Furthermore the idea of returning to the "base" of the revolution, Kwangtung, had been proposed several months before by Roy (another of the impatient revolutionaries) at the Fifth Chinese Communist Party Congress, and Communist troops, after the failure of Borodin's plan to take Peking, had since then begun a general southward movement. The Nanchang uprising and subsequent attacks on Swatow and Ch'aoch'ow in Kwangtung grew out of this general movement. The Canton revolt could be considered the culmination of attempts to reestablish the revolution's "base" in Kwangtung.

The Canton revolt marked the end of a chapter in the history of Chinese Communism, a chapter which witnessed the nearly total elimination of the Chinese Communist Party as it had been laboriously built up over the previous six years. Paradoxically, however, while the party itself had reached a low point, the Communist movement in China was, perhaps for the first time, becoming an independent force. In fact, Chinese politics from this point onward could not be carried on without careful consideration of the Communist position.

II
The "Soviet" Experiment,
1927–1931

The year 1927–1928 is one of the great watersheds in the history of Sino-Soviet relations. It marks a Soviet decision to support the establishment of a Communist state in China. Contrary to long held opinion, Stalin did not order the Chinese Communists to exhaust themselves in futile nationwide uprisings against the vastly superior Nationalists and their allies.[1] Instead, the Chinese Communists were instructed to begin the establishment of their own political regime—a state within a state—which in time would be capable of challenging the KMT for control of China. Of course, formulating a new policy, while not without its complications, was far simpler than executing it. Internal squabbling among the Chinese Communist leaders appointed to carry out the new policy brought the Communist movement to near destruction on several occasions.

The failure of the Chinese Communists to capture the KMT in 1927 triggered a lengthy debate in Moscow over the outlines of a new policy. The strategic concept of dual power remained the same, but the elements in that conception were altered. Where before the split the Communists sought to achieve power within the KMT, afterward they competed with the Nationalists as an independent political unit. With the downfall of the Peking government, the KMT now became the antagonist of the soviets, the Communists' own political instrument.

In the Moscow debate, which spanned a period of ten months and four major meetings,[2] three groups vigorously put forward three different policy proposals. The alignment of the groups was determined partly by the configuration of the power struggle which was just then reaching its climax in the Soviet Union. In that struggle, the "centrist" Stalin, in alliance with the "rightist" Bukharin, defeated the "leftist" Trotsky. With

Trotsky's defeat, the full force of that alliance was turned against a group of "left-extremists" who were proposing a policy of immediate, nation-wide uprisings.

The left-extremists, Lominadze and Neumann, the Comintern representatives responsible for the revolutionary rampage on which the Chinese Communists had embarked during the latter months of 1927, and a group in the CCP led by Ch'ü Ch'iu-pai, who headed the party during those months, proposed a policy of immediate uprisings in China. They buttressed their policy proposals with ideological arguments, but their basic assumption was that the chance for a revolutionary victory was best now, before the KMT was able to consolidate its power.

The Stalin-Bukharin alliance was sufficiently powerful to defeat the left-extremists, but each man based his policy position on different estimations of the possibilities for success of the Chinese revolution, making theirs an uneasy alliance. Bukharin saw no chance for the immediate victory of the Chinese revolution and proposed continued but limited cooperation between Communist and bourgeois elements in China.

Stalin took an intermediate position between Bukharin and the left-extremists. He compromised with Bukharin over the question of cooperation with bourgeois elements, differentiating between national and petty bourgeoisie and agreeing to Chinese Communist cooperation with the latter. At the same time, Stalin pushed for immediate action, but not nationwide uprisings, in the form of guerrilla warfare and subversion in support of the larger political objective of establishing Communist power in China. This was, in fact, the policy communicated to the Chinese Communists at their Sixth National Congress, which convened in Moscow in June–July 1928.[3]

In concept, the Comintern's new policy was the essence of simplicity. It called for the Chinese Communists to focus on the development of party, state, and military systems—the basic components of a Communist state—parts of which were already in rudimentary existence. The Chinese Communists were to use, as some were already using, their surviving forces and resources to establish revolutionary bases—"soviets"—in the Chinese hinterland. These soviets were to become the bases of Communist political power in China. The fledgling Red Army and guerrilla forces would provide a protective shield for the soviet areas, giving them time to develop and grow, and would eventually permit the establishment of a nationwide soviet regime as a genuine competitor to the KMT for popular support.

Although much has been written concerning the "originality" of Mao Tse-tung as the creator of a new set of guerrilla warfare techniques, this is not only erroneous but beside the point. Moscow made policy for the Chinese Communists in 1928, not Mao. All Chinese Communist guerrilla leaders were following the identical policy and by no stretch of the imagination or of fact could it be argued that Mao Tse-tung was in command of the movement in 1928. Guerrilla tactics were only part, although an important part, of a larger policy of building a Communist state in China.

The new Comintern policy bore the outlines of dual power. On the one side were the centers of state power, the large cities and industrial areas, under KMT control. On the other were the soviet areas, the Communist bases located in the Chinese hinterland out of easy reach of KMT forces. In between lay the vast, politically vulnerable countryside, which was the main theatre of operation for Communist forces. After selecting a target in the countryside, the Chinese Communists would first employ their guerrilla forces in an attempt to establish effective control over the area. Once successful in disrupting the ability of KMT forces to provide security for the inhabitants of the area, Communist "armed propaganda" teams would enter the target zone to organize the éléments déclassé into peasant unions, peasant committees, etc., and to agitate against the "establishment." Where these activities bore fruit a successful uprising would be carried out. Immediately afterward popular elections would be held, soviet power established, and the groundwork laid for the thorough restructuring of the social system, centering around the confiscation of landlord land and its redistribution to the landless and the land poor.

Once a soviet was established in one locality, the procedure would be repeated in an adjacent one, gradually expanding the territory under Communist control. In addition to restructuring the social order in the soviet areas, these areas were also used to create, arm, and train detachments for the Red Army, which also grew as soviet areas expanded. In terms of strategy as a whole, Communist activity in the larger cities, which were under firm KMT control, was designed to keep them in turmoil. While the party recruited students and workers from the cities, strikes, propaganda, terror, and subversion diverted the Nationalist efforts from the main forces of the Chinese Communists in the countryside.

This was the new policy, in theory, as it was set forth by the Comintern in resolutions of the Sixth Congress of the CCP.[4] In practice a leadership struggle within the CCP reduced the effectiveness of the new policy at the start. Conflict was built into the CCP leadership in two principal ways: first, the new Chinese Politburo itself reflected the Stalin-Bukharin alliance, since of the seven members chosen in Moscow three were selected by Stalin and three by Bukharin. One, Hsiang Chung-fa, was accepted by both for the formal leadership position of the party, the general secretaryship. The three men selected by Stalin were Li Li-san, Chou En-lai, and Ch'ü Ch'iu-pai; the three chosen by Bukharin were Chang Kuo-t'ao, Hsiang Ying, and Ts'ai Ho-shen. While the Politburo as selected was evenly balanced between the left and right wings of the CCP, Stalin manipulated the composition of the delegation that returned to China in Li Li-san's favor. He managed this by the simple expedient of detaining Chang Kuo-t'ao and Ch'ü Ch'iu-pai in Moscow on the ground that they disagreed sharply at the party congress and could not be expected to work together effectively in China.[5] Since Ch'ü was a member of the extreme-left faction, which was to the left of Stalin, the latter actually gained by preventing Ch'ü from returning to China, while Bukharin lost a great deal when Chang was kept back, for he was the strongest of the leaders of the "right" group. The Politburo leaders who returned to China in the fall of 1928 were thus Hsiang Chung-fa, Li Li-san, Chou En-lai, Hsiang Ying, and Ts'ai Ho-shen. Hsiang Chung-fa was secretary-general, but Li Li-san was *de facto* leader of the party.

The new policy greatly altered the locus of power within the party. Under the previous policy of cooperation with the KMT, the party's principal activities were agitation-propaganda and organizational penetration of the KMT. Power in the party lay with those who controlled these activities—the Party Politburo. Under the new policy of building state power in the hinterland, power began to gravitate to those who were actually engaged in carving out the soviet bases with military forces. While it was formally true that the leadership of the party controlled all of the party's resources, including its military forces, in fact real power increasingly was shifting from Central Headquarters in Shanghai to military commanders in the field.

In effect, the new policy decentralized the party's power structure by creating several power centers—the party, soviet areas, and Red Army forces—where previously there had been only the party. Stated another way, the Comintern called for the creation of state and military systems in addition to restrengthening the party system. Although the party leader was to be in overall command, real power tended to gravitate to those who commanded military forces.

Moscow's Policy in Practice

Between the time that Comintern policy was formulated and the new CCP leadership arrived in China—a period of several months—local Communist leaders were endeavoring to put the new policy into practice. Several enclaves had already been formed in the countryside, of which Mao's soviet in the Ching Kang Mountains, straddling the Hunan-Kiangsi border area, was but one. When Li Li-san arrived in Shanghai, where the party's central offices were located, he set about the task of rebuilding the shattered party apparatus while simultaneously attempting to direct the party on its new course. The task proved to be far more difficult than expected and led to the bizarre episode in Chinese Communist history known as the "Li Li-san line."

Soon after he arrived in China, Li Li-san began to reconstruct the party. Those groups which were in large urban areas, such as Shanghai, and those soviet areas which lay close to Shanghai, were relatively easy to control. The urban organizations had no military force and the close-in soviets were susceptible to greater pressure from the party center to submit to party discipline. Soviet areas located a great distance from the party center were another matter. In particular, the soviet led by Mao Tse-tung and military leader Chu Teh, which had been formed in April 1928, was in the Ching Kang Mountains, fully five hundred miles from Shanghai. Since what strength the party had lay in the nascent soviet areas, there could be no thought of unifying the party apparatus as long as the soviet areas remained outside central control and direction.

Li's general procedure in reasserting central control over the various party groupings was to establish inspection committees which would report on conditions in the unit in question. Li would then adopt the appropriate means to "bolshevize" the unit. To a great extent the establishment of central control was equivalent to building an organization personally loyal to Li Li-san and the "bolshevization" process was not always achieved harmoniously. In most cases, however, it was achieved. Mao Tse-tung presented Li Li-san with a special problem, having control of a local soviet, a military force, and the party organization, located a great distance from Shanghai.

Li Li-san's own power base lay in the urban organizations of the party; he had no military force directly under his command. Theoretically, of course, all the party's forces were at his command, but in actual fact none were. At any rate, Li did not control the forces of Mao Tse-tung. Under conditions of the KMT's strong control of the cities, which became more effective as the Nationalists consolidated their regime, no great insight was required to see that the possessors of independent military, government, and party systems in the countryside eventually would be in a position to direct the fortunes of the Chinese Communist movement. As long as Mao's forces lay outside Li's control, any increase in Mao's strength endangered Li's position of leadership. Yet the Comintern called on Li Li-san to support the buildup of the Red Army and the soviets as well as the party organizations. If Li carried out the policy of building a Red Army and the soviets before he could control them, he would be undercutting his own position. If he failed to carry out this policy, he would be opposing the Comintern and it would only be a matter of time before he was replaced.

Li's initial strategy *vis-à-vis* Mao Tse-tung (all the while attempting to equate his policies with those of the Comintern) was to delay the strengthening of Mao's position while endeavoring to gain control of his forces.[6] Translated into policy terms, instead of encouraging the consolidation of Mao's guerrilla units into a Red Army as called for by the Comintern, Li ordered Mao to disperse his forces over the countryside, at one point even ordering him to withdraw from command. Mao declined to follow these orders, at first respectfully, but with increasingly open hostility. The difficulty with this policy, of course, was that it flatly contradicted Comintern policy; Moscow had no vested interest in preserving the leadership of the party for Li Li-san. Its primary interest was in fostering the buildup of a political-military force in China which would function as an instrument serving Moscow's own immediate and long-range foreign policy ends.

Moscow's Misgivings

As early as February 1929, scarcely four months after Li Li-san had returned to China, the Comintern sent the first of several directives criticizing the new leadership's work in the urban areas and cautioning against "revolutionary impatience." [7] Later in June the Comintern sent a second directive, which called for a radical change in policy toward the rich peasant—from non-antagonism to complete opposition. The policy change was the result of two developments: the end of the Stalin-Bukharin alliance, and Li's application of the peasant policy in China.

The policy of non-antagonism toward the rich peasant was the result of the Stalin-Bukharin compromise made in 1928 over the larger issue of Communist policy toward the bourgeoisie. The compromise was the price each paid to uphold their alliance against the left-extremist group in the Comintern that was unsuccessfully challenging their policies at the Sixth Congress. By mid-1929, however, Stalin had defeated Bukharin, taking over effective command of the Comintern and the Soviet state apparatus. It was therefore no longer necessary to honor the agreement made with Bukharin.

The second factor lay in the ambiguity of the policy itself, which Li Li-san had turned to his advantage in his struggle with Mao Tse-tung. While the policy called for support to "progressive" elements among the rich peasantry (an attempt to split this stratum), Li Li-san, in letters to Mao, interpreted this to mean an alliance with all rich peasants. Li's interpretation was incorrect, but definitely advantageous to himself, for if Mao complied with these instructions he would find it impossible to ally with the rich peasantry and emphasize the main theme of peasant policy—full support to the poor peasantry. Attempts to gain the support of both the rich and the poor peasantry in any given locality could only result in confusion among the masses about CCP policy. Given his conflict with Mao, Li undoubtedly anticipated this result as part of his strategy of delaying the consolidation of Mao's strength. The Comintern was not pleased over the confusion and ordered a policy change to eliminate it.

There was yet another factor which prompted the Comintern to dispatch its June letter—a heated dispute within the CCP Politburo.[8] When Li first arrived in China, he sent Hsiang Ying, one of the seven originally selected in Moscow, out of Shanghai to work in a local party bureau. This reduced the original Politburo membership in Shanghai to four: Li Li-san, Hsiang Chung-fa, Chou En-lai, and Ts'ai Ho-shen. Hsiang Chung-fa, by his own admission, was thoroughly won over by Li; this gave the latter a commanding voice in any issue which came to a vote in the Politburo. Ts'ai Ho-shen found himself in a minority in the Politburo, and when he disagreed with Li Li-san over the interpretation of peasant policy, he returned to Moscow rather than be outvoted by Li. When Ts'ai left, only Li, Chou, and Hsiang—all Stalin's appointees—remained of the original group selected in Moscow at the Sixth CCP Congress. Ts'ai's departure now permitted Li to consolidate his position in the party leadership still further, and to this end Li convened the Second Plenum of the CCP in June 1929. At the plenum, every effort was made to equate the party's policies with those of the Comintern. Yet the resolutions of the plenum did not in the least reflect the change in policy toward the rich peasant called for by the Comintern in its June letter. On the contrary, the Second Plenum resolved to continue the policy of non-antagonism toward the rich peasant! No mention was made of the existence of a directive from the Comintern. In a party circular issued a month later describing the plenum's accomplishments, the same position was put forward. Paradoxically, five months later, the new policy change was made without fanfare by simple inclusion of the Comintern directive (dated June 1929) in a party pamphlet containing the resolutions of the Second Plenum, implying that the change had been made in June!

Li delayed acknowledgment of the letter because to acknowledge its receipt would have required a change of policy at the plenum. Such a change in turn would have indicated to the party membership that the Comintern had disagreed with Li's interpretation of the peasant policy and would damage his chance of securing his leadership position (the Comintern letter had actually named Li Li-san as one following an incorrect policy). Having made the decision not to admit having received a directive, Li was forced at the plenum to uphold his own previous interpretation of peasant policy. Later, after consolidating his position, he slipped the letter into the party's November pamphlet of the Second Plenum's resolutions. Li's scheme worked in the short run, but it had several important repercussions. Chou En-lai proved unwilling to go along with the scheme, which led to a falling out between them. The Comintern now became increasingly suspicious (from reports of those

who returned to Moscow, first Ts'ai and later Chou himself) that Li
Li-san was taking an independent line.

The Chinese Eastern Railway Crisis

Superimposed upon Comintern-CCP developments during these
months was a growing Sino-Soviet crisis of another order of magnitude,
a crisis which was to dominate the attention and energies of both
Moscow and the CCP—but in different ways—throughout the latter half
of 1929, and which was to play an important part in the development of
the "Li Li-san line." Beginning in January, Chinese Nationalist authorities began to raid Soviet consulates and commercial offices all along the
Chinese Eastern Railway. Finally, in July, they seized the entire railway,
closing Soviet commercial enterprises and deporting many Soviet
citizens. The result was a break-off in diplomatic relations between the
Soviet Union and the Republic of China and the beginning of military
conflict over the railway. In mid-August Soviet armed forces under
General Galen (who had been military advisor to the KMT during the
Borodin mission) initiated military probing actions all along the Man-
churian-Siberian border, describing these activities as defensive "replies"
to "White Guard forces" (i.e., Russian *émigrés*) equipped and incited by
Chinese authorities. For the next few months military action alternated
with diplomatic sortie, but no settlement was reached.

Until mid-November the conflict was purely a border affair. Nanking
relied on the armies of Chang Hsüeh-liang in Manchuria; the Soviets
used troops of the newly formed Far Eastern Army, reportedly a small
(3,000) but well-equipped force supported by a few aircraft. The Soviets,
however, had decided to retake the Chinese Eastern Railway and in
mid-November the Far Eastern Army changed its tactics, driving 125
miles into Chinese territory and securing key points along the railway.
From this position of strength the Soviet Union agreed to resume
negotiations, and a final settlement—the Khabarovsk protocol—was
reached on December 22 which restored the *status quo ante* regarding
Soviet rights along the railway, consulates, and commercial enterprises.

The Chinese Eastern Railway crisis formed the backdrop for the
development of Comintern-CCP relations during the second half of
1929. Throughout the crisis the CCP adopted the position of staunch
"proletarian internationalism" in defense of the Soviet Union. This

stance provided the opportunity for Ch'en Tu-hsiu, a deposed former leader who was still in the party although a relatively minor figure, to oppose the CCP Politburo. He attacked the party leadership for adopting an inappropriate slogan (perhaps without realizing that Moscow had commanded it), arguing that "defense of the Soviet Union" only strengthened the hand of the KMT against the CCP. In an increasingly heated exchange of letters with the Politburo, Ch'en moved from a simple attack on the party's slogan to a broader excoriation of Li Li-san's leadership, for which he was expelled from the party in mid-November 1929.

The Chinese Eastern Railway crisis, which evoked Ch'en Tu-hsiu's outcry, also greatly disturbed Moscow. As long as the conflict had been restricted to the immediate frontier area there was small cause for alarm. When the Soviet Union decided to widen the conflict, some thought had to be given to Chinese retaliatory capabilities. Moscow had to consider the possibility that a thrust into Chinese territory would provoke a counterattack, and that at some level of commitment the Russians would be hard pressed to match the Chinese, soldier for soldier, the logistical situation favoring the Chinese. Moscow needed, therefore, to prevent large numbers of reinforcements from being sent into Manchuria and to achieve this end ordered Chinese Communist forces to step up military activity. Such action would pin down Nationalist troops which could otherwise be sent to support Chang Hsüeh-liang in Manchuria.

The order to increase military activities was contained in the Comintern's directive to the CCP of October 26, 1929. In it Moscow commanded the Chinese Communists to

> strengthen and extend the guerrilla movement of Mao Tse-tung and Ho Lung, and especially in the area of Manchuria. . . . There must be more attention paid to work among the soldiers; try to arm as many worker and peasant detachments as possible at the expense of militarist units, disarming them and taking possession of their equipment. Capture the districts evacuated by the militarists [those sent to help Chang Hsüeh-liang?] and build up a strong position in them. . . .[8]

The directive achieved the desired effect. Chinese Communist military activity did prevent substantial KMT reinforcements from being sent to aid Chang Hsüeh-liang, and the Soviet Union obtained the restoration of its former position on the Chinese Eastern Railway. But the directive had long-range effects that were largely, if not totally, unforeseen by Moscow, for the October directive provided the critical impetus for the development of the "Li Li-san line."

The Formulation of the Li Li-san Line

The problem of Li Li-san, as of any Communist leader, was always that of maintaining his leadership in the party and at the same time carrying out Comintern policy and directives. As long as the directives remained sufficiently broad to permit him some degree of latitude in application, and as long as the Comintern did not press for policies which would be detrimental to his position of leadership, conflict could be resolved without difficulty. But when the Comintern in its October directive specifically instructed Li Li-san to develop the guerrilla movement of Mao Tse-tung, it was asking Li Li-san to support the increase in strength of his chief rival! Under these circumstances, Li was forced to alter his policy toward Mao, although his objectives remained the same—to hinder Mao's consolidation of power in the countryside, and to attempt to gain control of Mao's forces. Now, however, new means were required to achieve these ends; in December 1929 Li took the first, still veiled, step toward the formation of his own "line." Describing his orders as part of the general CCP effort to "defend the USSR" in the Chinese Eastern Railway crisis, Li reversed his previous policy toward Mao and the Red Army. Instead of urging dispersion, he urged concentration of forces so that the Red Army could carry out attacks on large cities in the near future when a nationwide revolutionary tide would have arrived. Li directed the party to

> expand the Red Army's organization and concentrate its fighting power. Propaganda must be employed to the greatest extent possible to draw the peasant masses into the Red Army. The armed peasant masses must be brought together and turned into a formal Red Army. . . . Second, each provincial committee must have a concentrated organization and a jointly developed plan for its own Red Army units. Each local Red Army unit must act in accordance with the general plan. Third, the development of the Red Army must be carried out on a large scale . . . the former strategy of avoiding to take important large cities must be changed . . . we must attack important cities and even occupy them. Taking possession of them in the

shortest possible time would have the greatest political significance. The Red Army's execution of this strategy must be coordinated with the nationwide workers', peasants', and soldiers' struggle to bring closer the great revolutionary tide.[9]

At this point, Li's position on the buildup of a Red Army appeared to coincide for the first time with Comintern policy, but the two policies coincided in appearance only. The policy of attacking and occupying important large cities "in the near future" was not the principal purpose envisaged by the Comintern for the Red Army, as Mao also shortly observed. Beyond that, Li's new policy of expanding the Red Army was designed to gain control of it. He sought to achieve this by lodging control in the hands of "concentrated" provincial committees, not military commanders, and by "packing" the Red Army with new organizations as well as with new troops. These measures would, he hoped, ensure party control over the military commanders from above, and mass pressure on them from below.

While Li Li-san was basically altering his strategy, Mao was greatly strengthening his own position. In December Mao convened the Ninth Conference of Red Army Delegates at Ku T'ien in western Fukien. The conference itself signified the consolidation of Mao's control over the growing Red Army in the Kiangsi-Fukien area. More importantly, it was Mao's initial attempt at independent policy formulation. In the conference resolution, Mao strongly opposed Li's policies—without mentioning either Central Circular Number 60 or Li Li-san by name. In the section "on the ideology of roving bandits," Mao acknowledged the "ideological struggle" then taking place in the Red Army and party organizations.

(1) Some people want to increase our political influence only by means of roving guerrilla actions, but are unwilling to increase it by undertaking the difficult tasks of building up base areas and establishing the people's political power. (2) In expanding the Red Army, some people follow the line of "hiring men and buying horses" and "recruiting deserters and accepting mutineers," rather than the line of expanding the local Red Guards and the local troops and thus developing the main forces of the Red Army. (3) Some people lack the patience to carry on arduous struggles together with the masses and only want to go to the big cities to feast. . . . The eradication of this ideology is an important objective in the ideological struggle within the Red Army and party organizations.[10]

"Some people," of course, referred to the Li Li-san leadership. "Hiring men and buying horses" and an impatience to "go to the big cities" referred to Li's policies of expanding the Red Army and launching attacks on large cities. Mao's espousal of the gradual establishment of soviet base areas, aside from being in complete agreement with Comintern policy, was undoubtedly viewed by him as the best means to increase his own power, both in an absolute sense and in relation to that of Li Li-san.

A few weeks later, on January 5, in his letter "A Single Spark Can Start a Prairie Fire," Mao referred to plans for "nationwide armed insurrection" as lacking "deep understanding." The policy he saw as "undoubtedly correct" was the one which he himself was pursuing:

> the policy of establishing base areas; of systematically setting up political power; of deepening the agrarian revolution; of expanding the people's armed forces by a comprehensive process. . . .[11]

From this strictly orthodox standpoint, Mao criticized Li Li-san's policy as "unrealistic." The Ku T'ien conference and the "Spark" letter mark the end of Mao's passive resistance to Li Li-san. From this point onward, Mao acts increasingly independently on the basis of his greatly strengthened political-military position.

The threatening buildup of Mao's power forced Li Li-san into a further elaboration of his own plans. In early February Li announced a conference of soviet area delegates to be held on May 1, a conference which would unite the soviet areas and the Red Army under firm central leadership. Recent developments certainly justified a conference of this sort. The soviet movement in general had grown rapidly in the year and a half since its adoption at the Sixth CCP Congress. Moreover, on the broader board of Chinese politics, warlords were jockeying for partners and positions for a renewed struggle against Chiang Kai-shek. Feng Yü-hsiang and Yen Hsi-shan, powerful warlords, had already allied themselves and they were soon joined by Chang Fa-k'uei and Li Tsung-jen. It appeared in early 1930 that a coalition of forces was forming which might be sufficiently powerful to topple the Nationalist regime. This external situation also impelled Li Li-san to mobilize the party's forces to ensure that the Chinese Communists would be in position to benefit from the coming struggle between Chiang Kai-shek and the insurgent coalition. Perhaps Li saw in the conference an opportunity to strengthen the party, gain control of the soviet force, defeat Mao, and satisfy Moscow all at the same time.

Meanwhile, Mao was holding another conference of his own, the "February 7 Conference." This marked the establishment of the Kiangsi provincial soviet, of which Mao was made chairman. It was

> attended by local representatives from the Party, the Army and the Government. . . . It was resolved to carry out land redistribution and [to] quicken the formation of Soviets.[12]

Now as chairman of a provincial soviet Mao could assume full command of Red Army forces in accordance with the restriction Li Li-san had placed on field commander powers in Central Circular Number 60. Mao had also taken the first step in a plan which he had proposed some weeks earlier to capture the entire province of Kiangsi and, to this end, had enacted his own land policy. These steps were further indications of a dramatic increase in Mao's strength.

Mao's preemptive action left Li Li-san with no feasible alternative but to disclose his own plans. In another Central Circular (Number 70, of February 26, 1930) Li set forth the first comprehensive and unveiled statement of what was later termed the "Li Li-san line." His "line" consisted of promoting great industrial strikes, which would lead to urban revolts, widespread peasant uprisings, troop rebellion in the armies of the warlords, and Red Army attacks on selected large cities, all of which, he hoped, would lead to the establishment of an urban-based Communist, or "soviet," regime in China.[13]

Central Circular Number 70 occasioned the final break between Li Li-san and Chou En-lai, who returned to Moscow at this time. If Stalin was not already aware of Li's deviation from established Comintern policy, Chou certainly informed him of it upon his arrival. In any case, Moscow's reaction to Li's policy was to send a carefully selected and loyal group of Chinese, then undergoing training at Moscow's Sun Yat-sen University, back to China in an effort to bring Li's policy into line. In the spring of 1930 this group, led by Ch'en Shao-yü (Wang Ming) and called the Russian Returned Students, or the Twenty-Eight Bolsheviks, returned to China.

Back in Shanghai, Chou's departure had made the dilemma implicit in

Li's position painfully explicit. Li had consistently chosen to achieve personal power at the expense of the Communist movement as a whole. Despite his efforts, however, real power had slipped inexorably from his grasp to that of the party leaders in the countryside, although it was not yet held by any one individual. Mao Tse-tung was apparently the first of the rural leaders to recognize that power had *in fact* passed from the Shanghai-based Central Politburo to the hands of the field commanders. Hence the intense struggle between them. Because of the risk of suffering an eclipse of his own position, Li would not fully support the soviet movement until he could fully control it. By so behaving, however, he contravened Comintern policy, which specifically called for the buildup of soviet political and military power in the countryside.

Chou's departure for Moscow, therefore, forced Li's hand, yet simultaneously made it easier for him to act. Over the next few months in *Hung Ch'i*, which became the party's theoretical journal at this time, Li attempted to construct a conceptual basis for his plans for revolution. Li's central proposition was that the arrival of a "nationwide revolutionary high tide in one or several provinces" was imminent. The Comintern had repeatedly cautioned Li against such grandiose formulations; nevertheless, he extended his proposition even further by arguing, as Lenin had argued for Russia in 1917, that a revolution in China would spark a worldwide conflagration.

While developing his concept of a "nationwide revolutionary high tide," Li was also striving to complete arrangements for the May conference of soviets' delegates. He had sent several communications to Mao in this regard, but Mao refused to answer. There could obviously be no satisfactory unification of the soviet movement without the participation of Mao Tse-tung, who was leader of a major soviet and who now controlled the single most powerful armed force in the movement. In the absence of a reply from Mao, Li grew panicky as the time drew near for the conference opening and he postponed it for one month. Mao simply refused to reply to Li's request for him to come to Shanghai; instead, he continued his independent operations in the Kiangsi-Fukien area.

Finally, at the end of May, Li Li-san decided that he could postpone the conference no longer lest he permit a golden opportunity to pass—the outbreak of war between Chiang Kai-shek and the "Yen-Feng" insurgent coalition. On April 3, Yen Hsi-shan had declared war on Chiang Kai-shek, simultaneously naming Feng Yü-hsiang and Li

Tsung-jen as his deputy commanders. Chang Fa-k'uei also joined this group. From April 5 on, the insurgent coalition converged on Chiang's forces from three directions. Yen himself moved forces southward from Hopeh into Shantung. Feng advanced eastward from Shensi into northern Honan, and Chang moved northward toward Ch'angsha from his base in Canton. Their plan was to crush Chiang in a gigantic pincer movement. By late May the insurgents were preparing to close in on Chiang along a front stretching from Tsinan in Shantung province to Ch'angsha in Hunan. Chang Fa-k'uei's troops had already reached Ch'angsha and Yen Hsi-shan's forces were nearing Tsinan. At this point, when Li Li-san felt compelled to open the conference of soviet area delegates without Mao, the actual balance of forces lay with the rebels, although Chiang's forces appeared, on paper, to be superior. The reason for this was that Chang Hsüeh-liang, who had been named commander of Chiang's forces, had not yet committed any of his own troops to battle. By late May, 1930, Chiang Kai-shek's position was precarious.

The Fateful Decision to Adopt the Li Li-san Line

The decisions of the Soviet Areas Conference and of the Central Politburo meeting which followed it mark the apogee in the history of the Li Li-san leadership. These decisions constituted the "Li Li-san line," the plan to carry out a nationwide uprising to overthrow the Nationalist regime of Chiang Kai-shek. The adoption of Li's resolution, however, did not carry without argument. The May conference provided an opportunity for prominent leaders in the party to level criticism of the Li Li-san leadership. Both Ho Meng-hsiung, a leader in the Shanghai party organization with a broad following among the party rank and file, and Ch'en Shao-yü used the conference to air grievances against Li and his policies. Ch'en, in particular, used the forum to intensify criticisms he had expressed since his return to China with the rest of the Twenty-Eight Bolsheviks. Li Li-san, Ch'en said, had ignored the most important function of the Communist movement in China, which was to establish soviet power at all levels from the local to the national. Ch'en's criticisms served to underscore the total divergence of Li's policies from those of the Comintern. The Comintern sought the establishment of a national soviet government for China as a part of the dual power conception and urged the party to hold a congress which would achieve the objective. Li

Li-san did hold a conference but used it to garner support for his policy of transforming the soviet movement into an instrument for imminent revolutionary action, not to proclaim the establishment of "Soviet China."

Li Li-san overcame the criticism leveled at him at the conference principally because his critics were divided among themselves. While both Ho and Ch'en opposed Li and therefore should have been natural allies, they were also in opposition to each other. Later, after Li's removal from power, Ch'en and Ho led groups which contended for control over the party apparatus.

A few days after the conference the Central Politburo sanctioned Li's plan—the well-known resolution of June 11, "A New Revolutionary High Tide and an Initial Victory in One or Several Provinces"—and a battle plan, which included reorganization of the Red Army and its command.[14] The four main Red Armies were reorganized into army corps. The Chu-Mao forces were formed into the First Red Army Corps, the forces of Ho Lung in western Hunan were renamed the Second Red Army Corps, P'eng Teh-huai's troops in northwestern Kiangsi became the Third Red Army Corps, and the guerrilla bands under the general direction of Hsü Hsiang-ch'ien in the mountains north of the Yangtze were renamed the Fourth Red Army Corps.

According to the battle plan the First Corps under Chu and Mao was to move from central Kiangsi to Nanchang. After taking Nanchang they were to move on to Kiukiang, then westward along the Yangtze to Wuhan. Ho Lung's Second Corps would move from the west and Hsü Hsiang-ch'ien's Fourth Corps from the north on to Wuhan. P'eng Teh-huai's Third Corps was to move from its base in northwest Kiangsi to attack Ch'angsha, after which it would link up with the rest of the forces in the attack on Wuhan. The Red Army attacks would be coordinated with workers' uprisings within target cities and local peasant uprisings in the countryside. Kuomintang and warlord armies would be immobilized by mutinies within their units.

The most surprising feature of Li's plans was the stipulation that all Red Army forces were to be placed under a single, centralized command with Chu Teh as commander-in-chief and Mao Tse-tung as supreme political commissar! Undoubtedly, Li Li-san assumed that Mao would be more tractable if directly subordinate to the Central Politburo in the chain of command. Li also assigned the First Corps the brunt of the fighting—to ensure that Mao's forces would see plenty of action, perhaps hoping that whatever the outcome of his plan, Mao would personally be weakened. But as events were to prove, Li made a fundamental error in judgment by assigning to Mao a role in which he could ensure the failure of Li's plans.

When Moscow learned of Li's plans through the Comintern representatives, who, of course, were present at the meetings, they immediately responded by bombarding the party's central headquarters with telegrams instructing Li to abandon his plans. Moscow's leaders undoubtedly expected that once news of their opposition was received by the Comintern "reps," as well as by Ch'en Shao-yü and the rest of the Twenty-Eight Bolsheviks, it would be sufficient pressure to restrain Li Li-san. But Li would brook no further opposition to his plans. He isolated the Comintern representatives (at this time two Germans who spoke no Chinese) from party members and placed the Twenty-Eight Bolsheviks on six months' probation, excluding them from participation in party affairs. While doing this, Li completed the organization, begun months before, of "action committees" at every level paralleling the party's organizations. The functions of the latter he either restricted severely or abolished altogether. This gave him, on paper, direct command over all party units from top to bottom.

According to plan, on July 16, 1930 nationwide demonstrations against the Warlord War erupted in major cities throughout China. These demonstrations were the signal for the arrival of a "revolutionary high tide" and a direct revolutionary situation. By July 22 demonstrations were in progress in several cities, although none had yet led to uprisings, and the Red Army had moved into position.

Fortunately for Li Li-san, the Warlord War had reached one of its critical junctures in June and July, providing favorable circumstances for Communist forces. On June 4 Chang Fa-k'uei had captured Ch'angsha and moved on to Wuhan, and in a major victory for the insurgent coalition Yen Hsi-shan captured Tsinan on the 25th. Although Hunanese forces recaptured Ch'angsha for Chiang Kai-shek on the 17th of June, their allegiance was uncertain. During the period, therefore, from early June until mid-August, when Chiang was finally able to wrest Tsinan from Yen's possession, Nationalist fortunes were at low ebb. The possibility of a Communist victory of some sort in the wake of the warlord conflict appeared promising.

The Tide Turns Against Li Li-san

At this crucial moment, on July 23, a letter from the Comintern arrived, the first such formal policy statement since the October letter of the previous year during the Chinese Eastern Railway crisis.[15] In its letter the Comintern opposed virtually every major policy measure that Li Li-san had advocated since the promulgation of Central Circular Number 70 the previous February. The Comintern disagreed with Li Li-san on the timing of the establishment of a national soviet government, on the function of the Red Army and guerrilla warfare, on policies in the soviet and non-soviet areas, and, most important, on the estimation of the current revolutionary situation. In an explicit rejection of Li Li-san's "line" the Comintern letter stated:

> In analyzing the present struggle, it should be noted that for the time being we still do not have an all-China objective revolutionary situation. The waves of the workers' and peasants' movements have not merged into one. Even combined these movements still do not guarantee the necessary forces to attack imperialist and Kuomintang control.[16]

Li Li-san responded to the damaging Comintern directive by temporarily suppressing it as he had earlier directives. He pressed forward with Red Army attacks on Wuhan and surrounding cities, although it is clear that he had radio contact with troop units in the field and could have called off the attacks had he so desired. On July 27 P'eng Teh-huai's Third Army Corps attacked and occupied Ch'angsha, holding it for ten days before being forced to retreat. On July 31 the First Army Corps under Mao and Chu attacked Nanchang, was repulsed, and moved westward toward Wuhan.

After the initial high point of the capture of Ch'angsha, Li's entire position began to crumble rapidly. No other military success followed the short-lived victory at Ch'angsha, where an all-China soviet regime was promulgated with Li named as chairman. Workers' demonstrations in the cities—particularly in Wuhan—failed to precipitate urban uprisings. Peasant revolts were expected to inflame the countryside, but sputtered futilely. Troop rebellions were supposed to immobilize Nationalist and warlord forces, but did not. To make matters worse, party leaders were beginning to press Li to account for Comintern telegrams, calling on him to stop the attacks. Li's reply was that "the Comintern does not understand Chinese conditions and cannot lead the Chinese revolution."[17]

His scheme failing rapidly and pressure mounting at home and abroad, Li Li-san nevertheless pressed for renewed Red Army attacks on Ch'angsha and Wuhan. A second attack on Ch'angsha began on September 7 and continued until the 13th, failing as had the first. The primary reason for his military failure was simply the overwhelming superiority of the Nationalist forces, even though some Nationalist units were still engaged in battle with vestiges of the insurgent warlord coalition. Contributing to his defeat was the fact that the workers' uprisings, peasant rebellions, and troop mutinies within KMT and warlord forces did not materialize.

Mao Tse-tung, moreover, made defeat certain. Before the second attack on Ch'angsha began, Mao questioned the wisdom of Li's order, but was outvoted by the assembled military commanders. After a week of fighting, Mao and Chu, on their own initiative, withdrew the First Army Corps, ending the assault on Ch'angsha and forcing the cancellation of the attack on Wuhan. Mao's move effectively brought to an end the "Li Li-san line." In his account to Edgar Snow, Mao admitted as much. Speaking of the second attack on Ch'angsha, Mao said: "This failure helped to destroy the Li Li-san line, and saved the Red Army from what would probably have been a catastrophic attack on Wuhan, which Li was demanding."[18] What Mao omitted in his account was that it was he himself who was in part responsible for the failure of the second attack.

By the time the second attack on Ch'angsha had ended, criticism of Li Li-san within the party had reached a crescendo. Ho Meng-hsiung led the attack, publicly denouncing Li Li-san as following an anti-Comintern line and calling for the removal of the entire central leadership. A powerful opponent of Li Li-san and ally of Chang Kuo-t'ao, Ho's criticisms were difficult to allay and the failure of Li's policies was a fact which gained Ho considerable support within the party rank and file for his own claim to leadership of the party. By this time, also, two more Comintern representatives had reached China. They were none other than Chou En-lai and Ch'ü Ch'iu-pai, who arrived with Comintern instructions to bring the "Li Li-san line" to an end. In the latter part of September they arranged to convene the party's third plenary session since the Sixth Congress of 1928.

The Comintern Reasserts Control

It required sustained effort from late September 1930 until early January 1931 for the Comintern to bring the CCP's policies back into line. There were two interrelated phases of this effort: the Third Plenum, held in late September, and the post-Third Plenum phase, which began with the Comintern's letter of November 16 and culminated in the Fourth Plenum in January 1931. First quietly and prudently, then with increasing openness and heavy-handedness, the Comintern applied the pressures and gathered the forces necessary to win the struggle with the CCP central leadership, which was itself in conflict with opposing factions in the party. In the end the Comintern had superior guns. It removed the Li Li-san leadership and inserted its own carefully selected and trained group as the new leaders of the CCP.

The Third Plenum convened at Lushan from September 24 through 28. The meeting was held secretly and attendance was limited. Although the Comintern clearly and consistently opposed Li Li-san's policies and sent Chou En-lai and Ch'ü Ch'iu-pai specifically to repudiate them, the Third Plenum came to what must have been to Moscow a startling conclusion. The final position adopted by the Third Plenum was that, "The Central's line was correct and identical to the Comintern's line [!] . . . but that the Central Politburo had made several individual, tactical mistakes," which had already been corrected. It was the "right opportunists" in the party, led by Ho Meng-hsiung, who, "by distorting the Comintern's line, were attempting to use these individual errors to attack the Central's political line."[19] The Third Plenum could not have reached this conclusion without the consent of Chou En-lai and Ch'ü Ch'iu-pai, who had been sent expressly to reestablish the Comintern's line. To do this would have necessitated a comprehensive denunciation of Li Li-san and his policies. What accounts for their shift?

When Chou and Ch'ü arrived in China, it quickly became apparent that their task would not be easy. The utter failure of Li's policies and his ruthless suppression of opposition had generated seething discontent among the party's leaders, of whom Ho Meng-hsiung was most virulent.

Under these circumstances, if Chou and Ch'ü condemned Li as the Comintern wished, they would in effect have supported Ho Meng-hsiung's bid for power and undercut their own positions. The issue was broader than it appeared. Both Chou and Ch'ü belonged with Li to the original left faction of the Politburo, which had been selected in 1928; Ho Meng-hsiung was a member of the party's right wing, a supporter of Chang Kuo-t'ao. Ho's attack on Li Li-san, therefore, was not simply an individual attack, but an attempt by the right wing in the CCP to oust the left. It is this which explains the reactions of Chou and Ch'ü, who sought to preserve and protect the leadership position of the left wing in the party against the attack from the right. To do so, however, they were constrained to disobey the Comintern's instructions.

The Comintern's objectives at the Third Plenum were apparently limited to the removal of Li Li-san from party leadership and the curtailment of his policies. These objectives were only partly achieved. Li's actual policy of attacking key cities in China in an attempt to bring down the Nationalist regime was quietly brought to a halt, but Li Li-san was not removed from the leadership and his policies were only mildly criticized. In the short run, Ch'ü Ch'iu-pai, whose idea it was to support Li, emerged from the plenum as *de facto* leader of the party, sharing power with Li Li-san, who remained in the Politburo. There was one serious flaw to the scheme. The Left had saved their own positions, but at the cost of disregarding the Comintern's instructions, and it was inevitable that they should reap the consequences of this decision.

As soon as the Comintern's resident representative (a non-Chinese) realized that the Third Plenum's final resolutions did not reflect the Comintern's position, he immediately wired Moscow of the outcome. Meanwhile, other party members—at the instigation of the Ho Meng-hsiung faction—showed increasing dissatisfaction with the party leadership and began to agitate against the embattled Central, which was still led by the left faction of Li Li-san, Ch'ü Ch'iu-pai, Chou En-lai, and Hsiang Chung-fa.

The Third Plenum failed to resolve the internal party conflict or to reconcile the differences between the CCP and the Comintern. Although the Comintern learned of the plenum's resolutions shortly after its close, it did not immediately respond.[20] It was not until mid-November that the Comintern made its next move. Meanwhile, the situation within the CCP was, if anything, worse than before. Ho Meng-hsiung, goaded by a frontal attack made on him at the plenum, now campaigned openly for the removal of the leadership and for his own candidacy. Both the Ho faction and the Central now sought to win over Ch'en Shao-yü and others of the Twenty-Eight Bolsheviks. During the following month and a half a curious three-cornered power struggle developed: the struggle continued between the Central and Ho factions, conflict erupted between the Ch'en and Ho factions, and a tacit but uneasy peace lay between the Central and Ch'en factions.

The Comintern entered the picture decisively with its letter of November 16, which represented a decided shift in its tactics toward the conflict with the CCP. Up to this point the Comintern had attempted to dispose of the Li Li-san problem discreetly, restricting the conflict—to the extent possible under the circumstances—to the top party leadership. The Third Plenum, however, demonstrated both the inadequacy of this method and the length to which the party's leaders would go to retain power. The November letter, therefore, brought the conflict into the open: it exhorted the entire party rank and file to oppose Li Li-san and made his dethronement a foregone conclusion.

The November letter flatly contradicted the Third Plenum's conclusion that the Li Li-san line was identical to the Comintern line. Li's policies, it stated, did not consist of

> mere occasional disagreements or differences of secondary importance in the evaluation of the situation and the understanding of tactical tasks. It is necessary to make completely clear that in the most critical moment of the Chinese revolution, two political lines differing in principle confronted each other. To conceal the differences in principle between these two opposed and mutually exclusive political lines would not only be harmful but would also involve the great danger that these mistakes might be repeated in the future.[21]

The essence of the Li Li-san line, it continued, was contained in the thesis "a victory in one or several provinces signified a nationwide direct revolutionary situation. . . ." This had been the principal theoretical deviation of Li Li-san, yet it had contained a kernel of orthodoxy. The Comintern had, after all, called for a victory in one or several provinces; Li's deviation lay in expanding this plan for limited conquest into a nationwide attempt to overthrow the Nationalist Government.

The November letter itself was sufficient to cause the removal of Li

Li-san from the Central Politburo; he was shortly called to Moscow to account for his policies. The Comintern was now bent on a much larger objective—removal of the entire left faction from the party leadership. To ensure that there would be no mistake this time, the Comintern sent its top man in CCP affairs, Pavel Mif, who arrived some time in late November after the Comintern's letter had already begun to have its impact. His arrival tipped the balance among the factions heavily in favor of the Twenty-Eight Bolsheviks, all of whom had been his proteges in Moscow.

Mif's conduct in China during this period is a classic example of coalition political gamesmanship. Three groups vied for the leadership of the party after Li's fall: the Ch'en group, supported by Mif; the Central faction—minus Li Li-san—which was striving to retain its position; and the Ho Meng-hsiung faction, which had strong support from the party rank and file. Shortly after his arrival, Mif formed a coalition with the Central against the Ho faction and in addition split the Central faction by obtaining the secret defection of Chou En-lai and Hsiang Chung-fa. Under these political circumstances the Fourth Plenum was held in early January 1931.

At the Fourth Plenum the Li Li-san line was formally repudiated and the Comintern line, first formulated in 1928, reestablished. The new party leadership reflected the coalition of the Central and Ch'en factions. Ch'en Shao-yü and several other members of the Twenty-Eight Bolsheviks were moved up into leadership positions. The right opposition suffered total defeat. Shortly after the plenum, its dissolution was completed when Ho Meng-hsiung was arrested and executed by the KMT. Mif kept his agreement with the Central faction. The new leadership elected at the Fourth Plenum saw Hsiang Chung-fa reelected as general secretary. Chou En-lai remained on the Central standing committee. Ch'ü Ch'iu-pai was retained in the Central leadership but demoted from his briefly held position of *de facto* leader and made head of the organizational bureau.

The Central faction appeared to retain its dominant position, but the appearance was deceptive and short-lived. As soon as the right opposition had been disposed of, Mif turned against the Central faction and against Ch'ü Ch'iu-pai in particular. In a general reshuffle of the leadership a few days after the plenum, Ch'ü Ch'iu-pai and all other members of the Central faction—except Chou En-lai and Hsiang

Chung-fa, who had defected to Mif—were dropped from the Politburo and replaced by members of the Twenty-Eight Bolsheviks. The composition of the reorganized Politburo was: Hsiang Chung-fa as general secretary and Chou En-lai as a member of the Politburo standing committee, their reward for defection from the Central faction and for proving themselves "good" Communists. All other posts were filled by Mif's Twenty-Eight Bolsheviks. Ch'en Shao-yü was raised to a position on the standing committee, Shen Tse-min was named to the Politburo, Chang Wen-t'ien, Ch'in Pang-hsien, Wang Yun-ch'eng, and three others were also given leading posts in the Central apparatus.

The right and left factions as they had existed since the Sixth Congress of 1928 were disestablished. Li Li-san stood "trial" in Moscow and was condemned to "study" there. He remained in Moscow for the next fifteen years, reappearing in China only when World War II ended. The removal of Li Li-san and the reestablishment of Comintern policy at the Fourth Plenum opened the way for unhindered expansion of armed Communist power in the Chinese countryside and set the stage for the rise of Mao Tse-tung.

III
Defeat in Kiangsi, 1931–1934

The period of the Kiangsi Soviet is perhaps the least clear of all periods of Chinese Communist history. Until recently, little documentation has been available outside of that which came from Maoist sources, written for the most part in the early forties after Mao had consolidated a commanding position in the party. Newly available documents from the early thirties now enable us to lift, partly, the veil of historical darkness surrounding these critical years and make it possible to trace the broad outlines of the period and its significance in the historical development of Soviet-Chinese Communist relations.[1]

From an overall perspective, these years witnessed an almost total defeat of the Communist movement and of Mao Tse-tung. Within the party, these were years of intense struggle between Mao and the Internationalists (the Moscow group), a struggle which unmistakably took shape in terms of Comintern strategy, policies, and directives. Initially, the Internationalists, led successively by Wang Ming (Ch'en Shao-yü) and later by Ch'in Pang-hsien (Po Ku), succeeded in stripping first military and then political power from Mao Tse-tung. Later, during the Long March, Mao was able to discredit their leadership and recoup his lost power, gaining an ascendant position within the party when the movement itself was in its apparent death throes.

Paradoxically, the KMT, which nearly destroyed the Communists, played an important role in Mao's rise to power by undermining the power of his party opponents. As Mao moved into a dominant position, but before the KMT could apply the *coup de grace,* successive waves of Japanese invaders forced the reallocation of KMT resources to meet the threat of foreign invasion and forestalled the destruction of the Communists. The delay was fortunate for Mao Tse-tung and the Communist movement; it proved fatal for the KMT.

The Internationalists "Bolshevize" the Party

Having achieved command of the party's central apparatus—with Moscow's direct assistance—at the Fourth Plenum, in January 1931, the Internationalists moved to extend their control to the rest of the party. Extending control was a two-step operation which involved purging opponents and inserting supporters into key posts. Under the rubrics of anti-rightist and anti-Li-Li-san campaigns, the Internationalists rebuilt or "bolshevized" the party. The purge was ruthless, but highly effective, resulting in the defection of thousands of party members to the KMT. Within a few months the Moscow trained leadership had a firm grip on the party's urban and rural apparatus.

While the party was being purged from within, the KMT was exerting pressure from without, with an extensive drive against the Communists. The most visible aspects of this drive were the bandit suppression campaigns undertaken against the soviet areas. Police pressure on the party's urban organizations was less visible but equally important, giving added incentive to those under fire in the party to leave its ranks.

The first of the bandit suppression campaigns began in December 1930 and lasted until January 1931. It failed. Local troops from Hunan, Hupeh, and Kiangsi, under local command, were ambushed and attacked, unit by unit, by the highly mobile Red Army forces under Mao Tse-tung's leadership. The second campaign got under way in February and continued through May, meeting the fate of the first. In June, Chiang Kai-shek himself took command of the third campaign and, employing five divisions of his own well-trained troops, drove directly toward Juichin in three strongly armed columns. Although Communist detachments managed to avoid heavy losses and constantly harassed the oncoming columns, there was little they could do to prevent the advance of Chiang's forces. By September 13, Juichin was in grave danger.

Meanwhile, intensive police activity, punctuated by periodic arrests of party leaders, made the cities under KMT control increasingly unsafe for the Communists. In April 1931, KMT police apprehended the head of the party's secret police apparatus, Ku Hsun-chang, who transferred his allegiance to the KMT and assisted them in uncovering other Communist organizations and personnel. (In reprisal, Chou En-lai ordered the extermination of Ku's entire family. Forty-eight persons, in all, were found slain later that year in Shanghai's foreign concession.) From Ku's information and from information supplied by British authorities, KMT police raided the Comintern's secluded Far Eastern Bureau in Shanghai, netting several important Comintern and Communist party personnel.

Earlier, British authorities in Singapore had arrested a Comintern agent, Ducroux (or Serge Lefranc). Ducroux had been on an important mission to inspect the newly reorganized Comintern apparatus in Southeast Asia (the old Nanyang or South Seas Party had been divided into two parts, the Indo Chinese and Malayan parties). Under interrogation, Ducroux revealed the names and addresses of important Comintern and Communist party personnel in several important cities. Armed with this information, British and KMT police conducted coordinated raids on the Communist apparatus in Hong Kong, Shanghai, and elsewhere, leading to the arrest of many important party leaders. Ho Chi-minh was arrested in Hong Kong; Hsiang Chung-fa, the General Secretary of the CCP, Hilaire and Gertrude Noulens, Comintern agents, and others were picked up in the Shanghai raid. The British deported Ho Chi-minh, who made his way back to Moscow, but the KMT police executed Hsiang Chung-fa within twenty-four hours after capture. The Noulens couple were held incommunicado for over a year and only after Moscow had mounted a worldwide propaganda campaign were they released. At any rate, such police pressure forced the party's leaders hurriedly to arrange for the transfer of the main Central apparatus from Shanghai to the soviet areas, a transfer which was completed over the course of the next several months.[2] A branch of the Central Bureau was left in Shanghai, but it functioned for only a few months before being discovered by KMT authorities.

The dislodgement of the Central apparatus from Shanghai coincided with the extension of Central control over the soviets' forces at a time when the KMT was also increasing pressure on the soviet areas. The first step had been taken on January 15, shortly after the conclusion of the Fourth Plenum, when a Central Bureau of Soviet Areas was established. Accompanying its establishment, a major reorganization of the soviet areas was announced. The soviet districts were reorganized into six general areas, with the Hunan-Hupeh-Kiangsi area designated as the Central Area and the future location of the capital of the national Soviet Republic, which was to be established later in the year. The Red Army composition was changed from four to seven armies, and the party front committees in the army were abolished and replaced by political commissars whose branch units were directly responsible to the Central Bureau.

In this fashion the Internationalist leadership under Wang Ming attempted to extend control over the Chinese Communists in the countryside and create a more centralized yet more complex movement, with separate governmental, military, and party systems. For Mao Tse-tung, the net effect of these new policies was to separate him from direct control over his power base. The reorganization of soviet districts split Mao's power base in Kiangsi. (In addition to the Central Soviet area, the Kiangsi base was further divided into two other areas, the Kiangsi-Fukien-Anhwei and Fukien-Kwangtung-Kiangsi areas.) The abolition of front committees stripped the power of direct command over troops from Mao and the increase in the number of armies also divided and separated the forces formerly under Mao's direct control.

At the same time that the Internationalists were dismantling the organizational basis of Mao's power in Kiangsi, they attempted to absorb him into the top leadership. Consequently, Mao was included as one of the nine-man committee which headed the Central Bureau of the Soviet Areas[3] and was appointed head of the General Political Department. This apparent paradox was virtually the only feasible alternative open to the Internationalists, for Mao was highly regarded by the Comintern. Comintern directives as early as June 1929 frequently mentioned Mao Tse-tung favorably, making it almost impossible to exclude him from the leadership. After all, Mao had built the single most powerful Communist force in the movement up to that time. The Comintern's favorable disposition toward him did not mean that Mao would be unopposed, it simply dictated the terms of the struggle against him; it meant that the struggle would be carried on indirectly.

In September Ch'in Pang-hsien (Po Ku) replaced Wang Ming (Ch'en Shao-yü) as Secretary General of the Politburo Standing Committee after the latter's reassignment to Moscow as CCP representative to the ECCI. At this time the party opened a veiled attack on Mao Tse-tung. In Central circulars the Internationalist leadership criticized "erroneous tendencies" within the party, the most serious of which were: guerrillaism, factionalism, narrow empiricism, peasant mentality, and party monopolization. Mao's later defense against these charges in the "Resolution on Some Historical Questions" confirms that he was in fact the target of this indirect criticism.⁴ Guerrillaism was scored not as a military tactic but as an organizational style. As a military tactic it was encouraged, but the reference was to Mao's fusing of party, state, and military systems into one while tenaciously retaining control over all through the party front committee. Party monopolization, factionalism, narrow empiricism, and peasant mentality were outgrowths of Mao's gradual and successful buildup of a strong power base.⁵ Mao was building an independent kingdom in the Communist movement and every act was deliberated from the perspective of whether it would further or hinder his personal fortunes. The fortunes of the movement were relegated to second place. He could hardly have done otherwise and yet retain a power position in the party.

A position of power was in itself grounds enough for the struggle against Mao, since he was not one of the Internationalist group. The Comintern's strategy required the formation of a state within a state. Its August 26, 1931 directive renewed the call of the July 23, 1930 directive for the formal establishment of a Central Soviet government on the basis of the soviet areas and strenuously urged that "all measures . . . be taken to strengthen the leadership of the center and party organizations in the soviet areas." ⁶ Moscow demanded the regularization and professionalization of the movement's forces.

It is beside the point to argue whether or not Mao's policies were compatible with these objectives. Neither Mao nor the Internationalists opposed the Comintern at this time. When the regime was founded it would have to be protected; this would require a change in military style. Pure guerrilla warfare could no longer suffice. Arguments over policy came later. Now the issue was: Who would control the new organs that were being created? Mao was at a disadvantage because the Central leadership initiated and controlled the reorganization procedure and only his earlier success saved him from being quietly shunted aside as so many other leaders were at this time. As it was, he was shackled with whatever mistakes the party had committed. His power was being reorganized out from under him and there was little that he could do to prevent it. Later when Mao gained control, he would turn the tables on the Internationalists with his "Resolution on Some Historical Questions." But for the time being he could only wait.

As the internal party reorganization and the KMT's third encirclement campaign were reaching their climaxes, an international crisis drastically altered the course of events. On September 18, 1931, Japanese military units began the occupation of Manchuria. The grave international crisis which resulted from this action forced an abrupt change in KMT policies. The third encirclement campaign was halted, KMT forces were withdrawn, and an attempt was made to negotiate a settlement with the Japanese. The fourth campaign, therefore, was not begun until the following June, 1932, giving the Communists a nine-month respite. The Chinese Communists used the relaxation of pressure to advantage. They expanded into areas left unprotected by withdrawing KMT troops and in November held their first congress formally establishing the Chinese Soviet Republic at Juichin, Kiangsi. The Internationalist leadership also used this brief period while the party was free from external attack to make another major organizational move against Mao Tse-tung, removing him from direct control over a military force.

The Establishment of the Chinese Soviet Republic

The first National Soviet Congress convened on November 7, 1931, formally establishing the Chinese Soviet Republic. The worldwide Communist press wildly trumpeted the congress as the culmination of a development which presented a national alternative to the "corrupt, decadent" Kuomintang. Dual power now existed in China. According to the congress's documents, over six hundred delegates from soviet areas, Red Army units, worker and peasant organizations, and so forth, attended.[7] Although termed a republic, the form of government designated in the constitution adopted at the congress was a revolutionary democratic dictatorship of the workers and peasants, a transitional step to a dictatorship of the proletariat, in which "exploiters" were to be deprived of political rights and freedoms. The congress also promulgated a land law, a labor law, resolutions on economic and minorities policies, and a resolution on the further centralization of the Red Army. The form and content of the Chinese Soviet regime derived directly from Comintern policies, in particular from its directive of July 23, 1930. To insure the enaction of Comintern policy, a new Comintern "advisor" had been sent out, Li Teh (aliases Otto Braun and Albert List).

The significant accomplishment of the congress was the creation of separate state and military structures at the national level. Separating civil from military commands was the means the Internationalists employed to wrest command over military forces from Mao's grasp, but, in return, Mao obtained the newly created post of chairman of the embryonic "state." In short, a compromise was reached between Mao and the Internationalists and the evidence suggests that chance played a critical role in determining this outcome. The chance factor was the absence of at least two important party leaders who might have been expected to carry the day against Mao Tse-tung—Chou En-lai and Chang Kuo-t'ao. Chang Kuo-t'ao had returned from Moscow in February and assumed the leadership of the Oyuwan soviet in the Hupeh-Honan-Anhwei border area, and Chou En-lai, secretary of the Central Soviet Bureau, was still in Shanghai. Neither man attended the First Congress; Chou En-lai arrived in Juichin only in mid-December. Thus, Mao was named chairman of the Soviet Republic of China and Chou En-lai did not receive a top state position. Chang Kuo-t'ao was named *in absentia* as co-vice-chairman of the Soviet government with Hsiang Ying, who had been sent as secretary of the Central Bureau to Kiangsi in January.

The reorganization of the top Red Army command, however, saw Mao's power hedged in several ways. Up to the third KMT extermination campaign, which ended in September 1931, Mao had served concurrently as Political Commissar in the General Headquarters of the First Front Army and the Red First Army. Chu Teh also served concurrently as commander-in-chief of the First Front Army and commander of the Red First Army.[8] From January 1931 Mao had also held the post of head of the General Political Department. The congress elevated Mao to the post of political commissar of the entire Red Army (a post which he held only until May 1933, when Chou En-lai replaced him) but removed him from direct contact with the armed forces. The Central Revolutionary Military Commission was created by the congress and assumed supreme command over the Red Army. The composition of this group was: Chairman, Hsiang Ying;[9] Vice-Chairman, Chou En-lai; Chief of Staff, Liu Po-ch'eng; Chief of the General Political Department, Wang Chia-hsiang. Mao was excluded from this military body, having been removed from the position of head of the General Political Department. Although Mao was elected political commissar of the Red Army, the congress stipulated that the General Political Department would control all political commissars in army units, and it further stipulated that the General Political Department would come under the direct command of the Central Revolutionary Commission. Furthermore, all non-military party units formerly in the army were abolished.

Finally, Mao was removed from both posts in the First Front and Red Armies. Chou En-lai assumed the post of political commissar of the First Front Army and Nieh Jung-chen became political commissar of the Red First Army. Chu Teh remained commander-in-chief of the First Front Army but Lin Piao advanced from command of the Red Fourth Corps to command of the Red First Army.[10]

The net effect of the redistribution of political power at the First Congress of Soviets was that Mao obtained a strong position in the newly created state apparatus, but was forced to relinquish his hold over the Red Army. He became political commissar of the entire Red Army, but was effectively removed from a position of direct command. Military command was lodged firmly in the hands of the Internationalists: Hsiang Ying, Wang Chia-hsiang, Chou En-lai, and Chu Teh.

Tokyo, Moscow, and Juichin

Between September 18, when the Japanese Kwantung Army began the invasion of Manchuria by occupying Mukden, and the end of the year, the Japanese had seized control of several key areas. They had immediately taken the cities of Mukden, Changchun, and Harbin, and within two months had occupied the entire province of Heilungchiang on the Soviet border. Japanese expansion into Manchuria posed a direct threat to the Soviet Union's eastern flank and Moscow sought to deflect further aggressive movement away from Soviet borders. While hastily shoring up its Far Eastern defenses, the Comintern generated a worldwide propaganda campaign for the defense of the Soviet Union, support of the Chinese revolution, and defeat of the Kuomintang. To divert the center of conflict to the south, Moscow readopted the strategy it had employed in the Chinese Eastern Railway crisis of 1929, commanding the Chinese Communists to step up their military activity. In a telegram to the CCP dated December 29, 1931, the Comintern called for a "national revolutionary war to oppose Japanese imperialists and all other imperialists," which first required, however, "a popular revolution to overthrow the Kuomintang." The directive, which deserves quotation at length, read as follows:

The central slogan shall aim at arming the people for a national revolutionary war to oppose Japanese imperialists and all other imperialists in order to win the liberation of the Chinese nation and to promote the independence and unification of China. It shall call for the overthrow of the Kuomintang government that has sold out and humiliated the Chinese nation. A popular revolution to overthrow the Kuomintang is the prerequisite of the triumph of the national revolutionary war against imperialism. It should be explained that only the China Soviet and the Chinese Red Army could guarantee the independence and liberation of the Chinese nation and the unification of China. The China Soviet and the Chinese Red Army are forces capable of overthrowing the imperialist enslavement, feudalistic bondage, and militarist oppression. The Soviet government should call on people throughout the country to defend China with armed force. Develop the strike movement. Through your pickets, seize control over the movement for boycotting Japanese goods. Call for enlistment in the Red Army and seizure of weapons to develop guerrilla warfare. Lead the student movement and have the students stir up the peasant masses in Kuomintang-ruled areas. Take advantage of every opportunity to engage in open propaganda agitation through written or oral messages. Set up mass anti-imperialist organizations. Set up your own armed self-defense corps, if necessary, under the cover of your military education organizations. Step up your work among troops of the militarists. Call on the soldiers and civilians to unite for the revolutionary war against the imperialists and the Kuomintang.[11]

The Chinese Communist Red Army in December 1931 was a far more formidable force than the one Moscow called into action in 1929. In the earlier instance, the Red Army was primarily a guerrilla force, but in the intervening two years it had grown into a large, mobile force estimated at close to 200,000 men.

Less than two days after receipt of the Comintern's telegram, the party Central issued a "statement on the current situation," in which it called upon the Chinese people to rally round the Chinese Soviet Republic and Red Army in an effort to overthrow the Kuomintang and the imperialists.[12] A week later the Chinese Communist leadership adopted a "resolution on the seizure of revolutionary victory first in one or more provinces," outlining the Red Army's coming offensive. The Japanese occupation of Manchuria, it said, posed a threat of military attack on the Soviet Union. "Hence, the task of the party is to organize, prepare, lead, and arm hundreds of millions of proletarian and peasant masses to wage a war of national liberation to defend China against the Japanese and all other imperialists, and to win China's liberation, independence, and unification." [13]

The major objective of the offensive, despite the avowal to overthrow the Kuomintang, was the consolidation of scattered soviets into two major areas, one south and one north of the Yangtze River. The forces north of the Yangtze, located to the north and west of Wuhan, doubled the area under their control between January and March. Under the commands of Chang Kuo-t'ao and Ho Lung, these forces built strong positions along the Yangtze River and the Peking-Hankow Railroad, threatening the major industrial complex of Wuhan and endangering the movement of forces along the railroad. Communist forces south of the Yangtze, although able to expand in the rural areas, taking several small towns, failed to capture any key cities. Planning to attack such Kiangsi urban centers as Nanchang, Fuchow, and Chian, the Red Army initially besieged the city of Kanchow in January, but was forced to withdraw in March.

The first Japanese invasion forced the redeployment of Nationalist forces northward to meet the Japanese along the Great Wall and prompted the Red Army offensive against the KMT. A second Japanese thrust, this time farther south at Shanghai on January 28, further staggered the KMT, forcing the removal of the government from Nanking inland to Loyang. Nationalist troops pressed into the defense of the beleaguered city left additional areas exposed to the Red Army. The response of the CCP to the Japanese occupation of Shanghai was the call, on February 2, for a general strike in the city. Faithfully echoing the slogans contained in the Comintern's December 29 telegram, the CCP exhorted the people to arm themselves to topple the Kuomintang, support the Chinese Soviet Republic, the Red Army, and the USSR.

The Fourth Encirclement Campaign—Stalemate

Although the Shanghai incident was not formally settled until May, the situation had become sufficiently stable by March 1 to permit the KMT to begin shifting troops to Wuhan for another push against the soviet areas. By this time the Chinese Communists had consolidated three major soviet areas, the Hupeh-Honan-Anhwei area, the Hunan-West Hupeh area north of the Yangtze, and the Central Soviet area in south Kiangsi. Observing the deployment of Nationalist troops, the CCP leaders formulated their own counter-strategy, which was outlined in the Central's "Letter to the Hupeh-Honan-Anhwei Soviet Area" of March 6. The two major soviets north of the Yangtze were not to attack Wuhan, but were to "surround Wuhan with soviet areas and peasant unrest . . . gain a genuine control of Yangtze River communications . . . [and] cut off military movement from Honan." [14] This was to be the general strategy. Red Army forces of the northern soviets positioned along the Peking-Hankow Railroad were to attack Nationalist troops moving along the railway, while the main force of the Red Army in Kiangsi would prepare for the coming Nationalist offensive.

The Nationalists thwarted this strategy by first striking at the northern soviets. In late May 1932 two Nationalist troop concentrations commanded by Chiang Kai-shek and General Ch'en Ch'eng struck simultaneously at the Hupeh-Honan-Anhwei soviet area north of Wuhan, and the Hunan-West Hupeh soviet area along the rail line south of Wuhan. During the first phase of the campaign, which lasted until the end of the year, KMT forces, 500,000 strong, were pitted against the two northern soviets, temporarily leaving the Kiangsi base free from major attack although local troops continued harassing activities.

One hundred thousand men under Chiang's command moved against the Hunan-West Hupeh soviet at Hung Hu (Lake Hung) a few miles west of the point where the railway crosses the Yangtze River. By September Chiang had forced the Red Army troops, commanded by Ho Lung and political commissar Hsia Hsi, from the Hung Hu base. By November, the original Communist force of 30,000 had been reduced to 5,000. Harried to the northwest, they carried on small-unit guerrilla activities in the mountainous border area where Szech'uan, Kweichow, Hupeh, and Hunan all join.

The larger Nationalist force under Ch'en Ch'eng invaded the Hupeh-Honan-Anhwei soviet area to the north of Wuhan. By September Ch'en's troops had also defeated the main Communist force led by Chang Kuo-t'ao and Hsü Hsiang-ch'ien, halving its original strength of 100,000 men. In early October Chang evacuated his forces to the northwest along the northern edge of the Ta Pieh Mountains, which form the natural border between Honan and Hupeh. By December 1932 Chang's Red Army remnants had passed through the southern part of Shensi into northern Szech'uan, where they occupied the small mountain town of

60

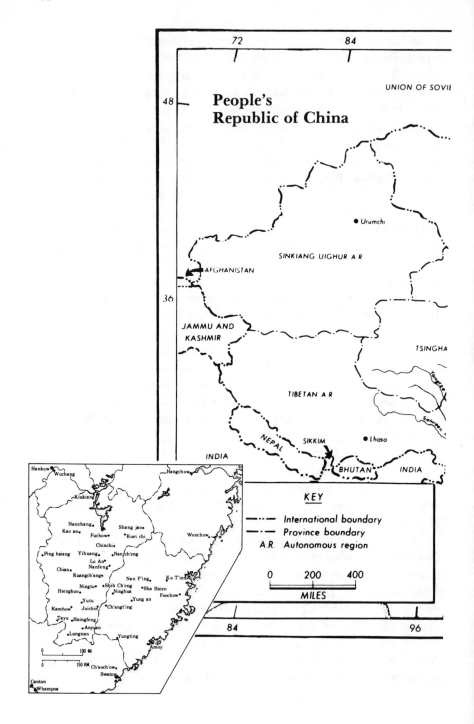

People's
Republic of China

UNION OF SOVIE

● Urumchi

SINKIANG UIGHUR A R

AFGHANISTAN

JAMMU AND
KASHMIR

TSINGHA

TIBETAN A R

● Lhasa

NEPAL   SIKKIM

INDIA

BHUTAN   INDIA

KEY

–··–··– International boundary
–··–··– Province boundary
A.R. Autonomous region

0   200   400

MILES

Hankow ● Wuchang

Kiukiang

Nanchang
Kao an   Shang jao
      Fuchow   Kuei chi
            Chinchi
Ping hsiang Yihuang   Nan ch'eng
      Lo An
      Nanfeng
   Chian
      Kuangch'ang
            Nan P'ing   Ku T'ien
   Ningtu   Shih Ch'eng   Sha Hsien
Hsingkuo   Ninghua   Foochow
   Yutu   Juichi   Yung an
Kanchow   Ch'angt'ing
   Tayu   Hsingfeng
      Anyuan
   Lungnan   Yungting
               Amoy

0   100 Mi.

0   150 KM   Ch'aoch'ow
            Swatow

Canton
Whampoa

Hangchow

Wenchow

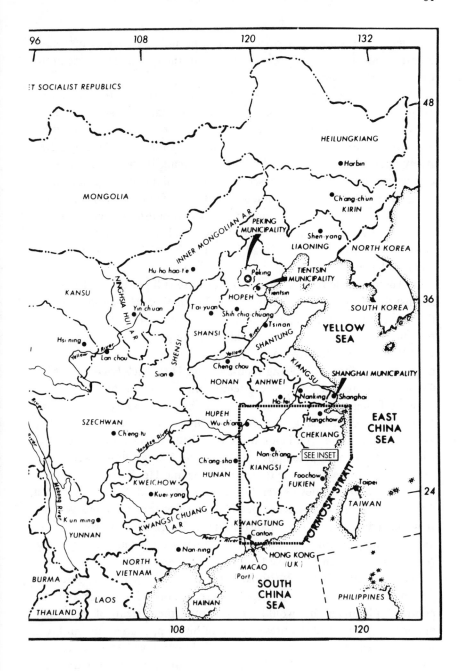

T'ungchiang, setting up a soviet there. The military defeats of Chang Kuo-t'ao and Ho Lung prepared the way for their political eclipse in the Central party apparatus.

Soon after the fourth campaign began it was evident that the soviet areas north of the Yangtze River stood little chance of survival unless aided by troops from the Central Soviet area in Kiangsi. Even then there was considerable doubt whether the combined forces of the entire Red Army could defeat the KMT buildup at Wuhan. It was not a matter of correct tactics, as Mao later asserted;[15] the positions of the soviets north of the Yangtze were simply untenable. Besides facing an overwhelming superiority in troops and firepower, the Communists' principal asset—mobility—was sharply discounted by the rapid movement afforded the government forces by the railroad system in the Wuhan area and by the Yangtze River.

In August, while the Nationalist forces were still poised for the assault against the Hupeh-Honan-Anhwei and Hunan-West Hupeh soviet areas, the Communist party high command had convened a conference at Ningtu, a few miles north of Juichin. At Ningtu, the immediate issue was: What should the Red Army in Kiangsi do in the face of imminent defeat for the forces of Chang Kuo-t'ao and Ho Lung? Except for Mao Tse-tung, all agreed that some attempt must be made to alleviate the pressure being placed upon them. Chou En-lai, supported by Hsiang Ying, Wang Chia-hsiang, Jen Pi-shih, Chu Teh, P'eng Teh-huai, Liu Po-ch'eng and Ch'en Yi, favored the so-called "forward offensive line," which centered on a preemptive strike by the Kiangsi-based Red Army to relieve the pressure on the forces of Chang and Ho. Properly executed, this policy would achieve several objectives. It would divide Nationalist troops, reducing the disadvantageous balance of forces around Wuhan. It would frustrate the Nationalist strategy of dividing the soviet areas and defeating them one at a time. Finally, it would surprise the Nationalists with an offensive for which they were unprepared.

Mao Tse-tung dissented. Probably because of an astute judgment of the military situation, and also because of the long range internal political advantage he would derive from the defeat of his party opponents' forces and the preservation of his own, Mao argued in favor of the strategy which had been successfully employed to date, that of "luring the enemy in deep." This, of course, meant meeting the Nationalists deep in Kiangsi, where no railroads and few auto roads penetrated and, in effect, leaving Chang Kuo-t'ao and Ho Lung to their own fates.

The secondary issue at Ningtu was the continuing struggle between Mao and the Internationalists for control of the Red Army. Elevated to the level of a debate over correct strategy, the Ningtu conference was the second round—the first occurring the previous November—in an organizational battle for political power. The issues were: (1) the regularization of the army, (2) civil-military command, and (3) the nature of party control within the army.

Mao could not accept regularization of the Red Army while he was still excluded from the policy-making group. If he acquiesced to regularization while still on the outside, the resultant command structure could see him placed in a position from which it would be extremely difficult, if not impossible, to gain control. Of course, once on the inside as a member of the formal policy-making group, Mao favored the regularization of the Red Army because he then was able to shape the reorganization process and ensure that opponents could not threaten his position. But as long as Mao did not command a strong position in the Red Army hierarchy, he would not agree to its regularization executed by an opponent.

Therefore, when the Internationalist leadership called for increasing military regularization, Mao countered with the necessity of raising guerrilla tactics to a higher degree of efficiency. He did not oppose regularization *per se,* but only at this point in time. In December 1936, after he had secured a strong position in the Red Army structure, Mao reversed his earlier position, noting that "guerrillaism" was characterized by

> irregularity, that is, decentralization, lack of uniformity, absence of strict discipline, simple methods of work. These features stemmed from the Red Army's infancy, and some of them were just what was needed at the time. As the Red Army reaches a higher stage, we must gradually and consciously eliminate them so as to make the Red Army more centralized, more unified, more disciplined and more thorough in its work—in short, more regular in character.[16]

The second issue was command of the Red Army. The Internationalists argued for the preservation of the command structure set up the previous November. This meant that the Revolutionary Military Commission would retain command over the Red Army. Mao naturally opposed this setup, since he was excluded from the Commission. From his posts as general political commissar of the Red Army and chairman of the Soviet Republic, however, Mao managed to place his followers in key military and political posts. For instance, Mao appointed both Lin Piao and Teng Hsiao-p'ing to army posts, much to the consternation of the Internationalists, who felt that the power of military appointment should lie with the Revolutionary Military Commission.

Finally, there were differences over the nature of party control at lower levels of the army. The Internationalists supported continuation of the political commissar system in the army, while Mao argued for the restoration of the party "front committees." The political commissars were organizationally subordinate to the Revolutionary Military Commission, so it was only natural that Mao opposed this political control system, over which he had no influence, in favor of the organization through which he had built his position earlier in Kiangsi. Mao's later accounts, written from the vantage point of the victor in the internal party struggle, do not reflect the controversy accurately, since the purpose of such writings as the 1945 resolution on "Some Historical Questions in the Party" was to discredit his fallen opposition and prepare the ground for his own legitimacy.

Mao Tse-tung failed in his bid to regain a position in the military at Ningtu, and his policy proposals were labeled "right opportunism." The policy adopted was the "forward and offensive line"—a preemptive attack to the north. To protect the Red Army's rear, guerrilla forces in Kiangsi were instructed to attack on all fronts in order to link up the soviet areas and create a strong, consolidated position which would prevent exposure of the Red Army's rear to local government forces in the provinces of Kwangtung and Fukien, which were then preparing to move against the Communist base area.

Mao fell ill after the conference. He was inactive for several months and Chou En-lai assumed the post of political commissar of the Red Army in Mao's stead, a post to which he was formally assigned in May 1933.

While the Nationalist government transported troops southward from Wuhan for the next phase of the campaign, the Chinese Communists, according to the preemptive strike plan, prepared for a large-scale engagement in the area of Lo An and Yihuang. Both of these towns were located on the northern edge of the mountainous region through which the Nationalist armies would have to pass to reach Juichin. After ambushing the government's troops there, the Red Army planned to follow up the hoped for advantage with a sharp offensive which would drive the Nationalists from Kiangsi.

Before the campaign began, however, the Japanese army entered the picture once more. Threatening north China, the Kwantung Army again forced an alteration in the balance of forces between the Nationalists and the Communists as it had the previous year at the same time. Between January and April 1933, before hostilities were brought to an end by the Tangku truce, Japanese military units occupied Chinchow, moved through the Shan Hai pass onto the north China plain, and attempted to pour through the mountain passes along the Great Wall. The Japanese thrusts endangered Peking and Tientsin and required a rapid redeployment of troops from Kiangsi to north China. The resultant weakening of the campaign force in Kiangsi gave the Communists a golden opportunity.

Beginning in January 1933, as Nationalist troops were being withdrawn from Kiangsi for transfer north to fight the Japanese, the Red Army opened a full-scale offensive which staggered the Nationalists but did not rout them. Although both sides sustained heavy losses in pitched battles during February and March, the Communist offensive failed to drive the Nationalists out of Kiangsi. By March, Kuomintang forces managed to stabilize a position in the Lo An–Yihuang region, where the Communist offensive originated, but the fourth campaign failed to oust the Communists from their main base.

Mobilization for Armageddon

Communist morale deteriorated as Nationalist forces pressed forward in campaign after seemingly endless campaign, despite some Red Army successes on the battlefield. Beset on all sides by enemy forces, a feeling of panic, pessimism, and imminent disaster grew among both party members and populace alike. The breakdown of morale during this period of crisis forced the leadership to take stringent measures to prevent the total collapse of the fledgling soviet republic. In frenzied mobilization campaigns, begun in early February while the fourth encirclement campaign was still in progress, Chinese Communist leaders strove to achieve three principal objectives: to consolidate the party, to insure allegiance to the regime, and to expand the army.

The front-line party cadres, whether commissar or commander, were not immune to the growing feeling of panic. Some refused to obey the command to conduct offensive operations and, describing their actions as guerrilla tactics, hid in the mountains from oncoming enemy troops. To steel its cadres, the party leaders initiated the "anti-Lo-Ming line," which, however, was not without its internal political ramifications. While helping to stiffen the resolve of front line party cadres, it was also a thinly veiled move to undercut further the position of Mao Tse-tung by eliminating his supporters among the cadre rank and file.

The campaign against Lo Ming began on February 15, 1933, with the promulgation of a Central Bureau resolution in which it was determined "to immediately unfold a struggle against the opportunistic line as represented by Comrade Lo Ming." [17] Lo was dismissed from his posts and replaced by an interim standing committee. Over the next several months any deviation from the "forward and offensive line" was interpreted as a manifestation of the Lo Ming line and its practitioner was removed from his post and given a reprimand. Among those attacked in this way were Mao Tse-tung's brother, Mao Tse-ching, Teng Hsiao-p'ing, T'an Chen-lin, and Ku Pai. In fact, the great majority of those branded as followers of Lo Ming were Mao's supporters and the internal political effect of the campaign saw the further consolidation of the International group at Mao's expense. As earlier, the struggle against Mao could not be conducted openly because of Mao's prominence; it had to be done indirectly.

The corollary to the anti-Lo-Ming line in the party was the drive, begun in June 1933, to secure the support of the general population, which, in increasing numbers, was leaving the Central Soviet area for the sanctuary of the mountains. To prevent the flight of the people the Chinese Communists carried out the so-called "land rectification" campaign, which, like the anti-Lo-Ming line, was not without its internal political consequences adversely affecting Mao Tse-tung. The basic thrust of the "rectification" campaign was a reclassification of the population into landlord, rich peasant, middle peasant, or poor peasant. Those found to be landlords or rich peasants (as the Communists defined them, landlords could be those owning one pig) would be fined, dispossessed of land, and, in selected cases, executed. Their land would then be redistributed among those classified as middle or poor peasants. As a result of the campaign, the Communists secured needed grain, funds, and recruits for the Red Army, as well as identifying and suppressing discontent among the population.

According to Mao Tse-tung's later report to the Second Congress of Soviets, over 13,000 families were classified as landlords or rich peasants and their belongings confiscated. Although the campaign was carried out by Mao through his governmental apparatus, he evidently opposed the policy from the beginning on the ground that it would hinder grain production. Therefore, Mao issued regulations during the campaign which encouraged peasants to seek to obtain lower classifications and thus be liable for smaller requisitions. (The Internationalist leadership repudiated this policy at the Fifth Plenum in January 1934 and Mao was excluded from yet another post, this time in his own governmental hierarchy.)[18]

The party experienced great difficulty in building up the strength of the Red Army. Recruitment campaigns were an endemic feature in the soviet areas, but during the fourth and fifth encirclement campaigns, the leadership made a major effort to expand the Red Army to one million men. Drive after drive failed to bring satisfactory results, forcing the party's leaders to reprimand, and in some cases dismiss for "opportunistic vacillation," party cadres who failed to reach enlistment quotas. The latter, in turn, increasingly resorted to brute force and terroristic methods to comply with instructions from higher levels. And still recruitment lagged. The Red Army failed to reach even the half-million mark. The peasantry fled into the mountains despite increasingly harsh methods to impress them into service in the Red Army.

While the Communists were sparing no effort to prepare for the coming battle, the Nationalists' new strategy, conceived the previous fall, was beginning to take shape. In part the new strategy constituted an attempt to turn against the Communists their own highly successful social mobilization techniques. Later to be dubbed the "new life" movement, when first employed fully during the fifth encirclement campaign it was termed simply the "seventy-percent political, thirty-percent military plan."

The 70-30 plan did not imply a decreased emphasis on military force. Rather, it signaled greater attention to accompanying political measures, particularly and primarily in the areas retaken from the Communists. The new plan centered around the creation of four organizations at the village level: the *chia, pao, teng,* and *niang. Chia* was the grouping of ten families in a given village. Each *chia* was administered by one of its number, a *chia chang,* appointed by the district police chief. *Pao* was the grouping of ten *chia,* headed by a similarly appointed *pao chang. Teng* and *niang* were organizations created within a *pao.* The *teng* was the grouping of non-combatants, who served as sentries, stretcher-bearers, and whatnot, performing general liaison duties. The *niang,* on the other hand, consisted of an armed, local military formation, called the *min t'uan.* The *min t'uan* of every five *niang* were unified into a single fighting unit commanded by a military officer appointed by the central government. The commanders of these five-unit districts were empowered to settle all local problems, thus giving the central government direct control over local affairs, and bypassing the provincial authorities. The power of the commanders included the settlement of the land problem in those districts in which the "red bandits" were or had been active, and the establishment of peasant co-ops and banks.

The 70-30 plan also provided for the strengthening of the economic blockade of the ever constricting soviet areas and the construction of an elaborate system of roads and blockhouses. Prohibition on trade between soviet and non-soviet areas was strictly enforced; violators were executed. Bans were placed on all vital commodities, particularly cooking oil and salt. Finally, an intricate blockhouse system with connecting roads was constructed to facilitate the blockade.

The social thread tying the system together was the concept of mutual responsibility. Each organizational unit was responsible and answerable for the conduct of the individuals in it. The effect of the *pao-chia* system in the war zone was to tighten the social organization under Nationalist control and make it difficult for the Communists to penetrate the villages and carry out agitational and organizational activities. The final step, in direct emulation of the Communists' social control system, was the assignment of what could only be called political commissars to the villages. Each political commissar, who was easily recognizable by the blue shirt he wore (giving the name to the organization), stood careful watch over the activities which took place in villages under his supervision.

By mid-1933 the 70-30 plan was operational in most of the projected combat areas and Nationalist military forces were positioning themselves for what proved to be the final, but not uninterrupted, assault on the Central Soviet area. The first phase of the campaign began in late August with Nationalist troops converging on the Central Soviet area from the north, south, east, and west. Their advance was deliberate and accompanied by the rapid construction of blockhouses in each newly-won area. At first, despite the relentless Nationalist advance, there was no decisive breakthrough, and it appeared as if the Communist strategy of "halting the enemy beyond the gate" might succeed. Furthermore, in November a dramatic event occurred which potentially increased the chances for a successful Communist defense. On November 20 the 19th Route Army, which formed the core of the eastern quadrant in the encircling forces, and a group of dissidents including the provincial leadership, rebelled against the Nationalists and established a People's Revolutionary Government at Foochow, Fukien.

The Fukien Rebellion

The People's Revolutionary Government, although surviving for less than two months, was a significant episode in the history of the Chinese Communist Movement in that its fate directly affected that of the Kiangsi Soviet and the career of Mao Tse-tung.

The 19th Route Army had been reassigned to Fukien after its sterling defense of Shanghai against the Japanese in 1932. Under the command of Ts'ai T'ing-k'ai it had clashed with the Red Army, being battered on several occasions. Stridently anti-Japanese, the 19th Route Army, along with the provincial leadership of Fukien, became increasingly disaffected with Chiang Kai-shek and his strategy of eliminating the Communists before fighting the Japanese. Taking seriously the Chinese Communist offer, made the previous January, to unite with any military group to resist Japan and the Kuomintang, the rebels made contact with Communist representatives sometime in the spring of 1933. After requesting instructions from Moscow, which favored military cooperation but no party commitment,[19] the Communist leadership concluded a secret preliminary agreement with the rebels, calling in essence for a truce and the preparation for military action against the forces of Chiang Kai-shek.

The rebellion itself compelled the Nationalists to shift troops from the encirclement in Kiangsi to Fukien in an effort to crush the rebels quickly lest others similarly inclined follow their example. Chiang's plan was straightforward and obvious to all; he intended, first, to preclude the possibility of joint operations between the Communists and the rebels. Therefore, he marshalled forces for a swift strike to capture Nan P'ing, a key railroad junction city a few miles to the northwest of Foochow and situated between the main forces of the Red Army and the 19th Route Army. Both Communists and rebels anticipated this strategy. On December 20 the Communists sent a telegram to the Foochow regime, signed by Chu Teh and Mao Tse-tung, noting the Nationalist troop deployment and urging the rebels to take positive steps to fight. They flatly stated their readiness to unite with the Foochow regime against Chiang and to conclude a fighting agreement for this purpose. In reply to this telegram, the rebels urgently requested that the Communists immediately send troops to Sha Hsien, a small town a few miles to the southwest of Nan P'ing, where the Communists could join forces with the 19th Route Army against the expected thrust of the Nationalists.

The Communists wired their acceptance of this request and appointed P'eng Teh-huai to lead a force consisting of the Third, Fifth, and Seventh Corps to aid the rebels. But before the force departed, a serious disagreement broke out between Mao Tse-tung and the Internationalists over the nature of support to be given the rebels. It seems that Mao, from the start wary of cooperation with the rebel regime, may have believed that the entire episode was a ruse to entrap the Red Army. Indeed, in his speech to the Second Congress of Soviets a few weeks later, he said that the Fukien People's Revolutionary Government was a "decoy," a "trick," and a "new device to deceive the people." [20] Rather than send troops to Sha Hsien, Mao wanted the rebels to send troops to northwest Fukien to join Communist forces there.[21]

At any rate, Mao's opposition delayed the departure of the rescue force, which permitted Chiang to reach Nan P'ing before the Red Army, successfully preventing the formation of a joint Red Army-rebel fighting front. Outmaneuvered, the Red Army force could only, as Mao advocated, "sit idly by and watch the tigers fight." [22] The result was that the Foochow regime collapsed within ten days after Chiang began operations against it on January 5. Nationalist naval units captured Amoy on the 10th and land forces occupied Foochow itself on the 15th, after which all organized resistance collapsed.

Extremely complex, the history of the Fukien rebellion has yet to be completely unravelled. The known facts, however, suggest the following interpretation regarding its significance both to the Communist movement and to Mao. The failure of the rebellion delivered a critical blow to the Chinese Communists. Had it succeeded, the Communists would have gained access to the coastal ports and would have been able to receive desperately needed supplies by sea from the Soviet Union. The importance of this possibility cannot be underestimated, for it would have altered the entire complexion of the revolutionary movement. Kung Ch'u, a onetime chief of staff in the Red Army who defected at the beginning of the Long March, noted that large quantities of military supplies were ready for shipment from Vladivostok whenever the Fukien ports would be opened to the Communists.[23] Mao Tse-tung was blamed for the failure to support the Fukien rebels as Moscow had instructed, and the Kremlin thereupon ordered his removal from all posts.[24]

Before, during, and after the Fukien rebellion, Moscow consistently advocated the policy of Chinese Communist military cooperation with anti-Chiang forces. Understanding of the Soviet position in regard to Fukien is clouded by a shift in strategy which took place during these years in the concept of the "main enemy," a shift which is often confused with the Soviet policy position on the Fukien events. Under the "United Front from below" strategy, the "main enemy" was the ruling groups of various countries; in China, Chiang Kai-shek and the Nationalists. Military agreements with anti-Chiang forces were entirely consistent with this strategy. As Germany and Japan became greater threats to Soviet security, Moscow raised the main enemy from the national to the international level, from individual governments to Fascism and imperialism. In China the main enemy became Japan, with the struggle against Chiang linked, but subordinate, to ·the struggle against Japanese imperialism. Although Soviet accounts later interpret the Fukien rebellion in terms of the strategy of the "United Front from above," the Soviet policy position remained consistent and was not a retrospective development. It was Mao who changed his position on the rebellion and understandably so. By swinging round to agreement with the Communist International's position, Mao admitted his error and removed an issue on which he could have been attacked by his opponents. Mao began to swing over to the Soviet position as early as the Tsunyi conference of

January 1935 and maintained it thereafter, in fact labeling the Internationalists with the policy of opposing support for the Fukien rebels.[25]

The Fifth Plenum of the CCP convened January 15 to 18, 1934, to carry out Moscow's order to remove Mao from his posts. In the third major round in his struggle with the Internationalist group, Mao was removed from all important posts, excluded from the Politburo and from chairmanship of the Council of People's Commissars, but he managed to retain the chairmanship of the Central Executive Committee of the Soviet Government. Even that position, however, was hedged by the Internationalists. Indeed, as Mao says, the Fifth Plenum was the "peak" of the development of the "third left line." [26]

At the plenum, Mao and his closest supporters, Ku Pai, Liu Shao-ch'i, and Teng Hsiao-p'ing, were sharply censured. Ku was denounced as an opportunist for exhibiting a negative attitude toward the Red Army expansion plan, Liu for opportunistic errors in the Shanghai trade union movement, and Teng for engaging in "anti-party factionalism." Apart from his role in the Fukien rebellion, Mao was charged on two other principal counts: his political and organizational support of Teng Hsiao-p'ing, and his publication of the "Decision on Certain Problems in the Land Struggle" during the land rectification campaign of the previous year. Severe reprimands were meted out to Mao's followers, but, in agreement with Chang Wen-t'ien's proposal, Mao's case was to be reviewed by the party group elected at the Second All-China Congress of Soviets to follow. Later it was decided that Mao's policy during the rectification campaign had an "erroneous influence" on party work, but that he had given only political and not organizational support to Teng. For this Mao was given a "serious final warning" which was withheld from public announcement.

As a result of the Fifth Plenum, Mao was dropped from the Politburo and excluded from the Central leadership of the party, although he remained a Central committee member and could attend all enlarged meetings. The newly elected Politburo standing committee consisted of five men: Ch'in Pang-hsien, Chang Wen-t'ien, Chou En-lai, Hsiang Ying, and Ch'en Yün.[27] Chou became chairman of the Revolutionary Military Council, assuming overall command of the Red Army and displacing Hsiang Ying. In general, the Fifth Plenum saw the further exclusion of Mao and his supporters from the Central leadership and the tightening of control by the Internationalists. As a result of the Fukien affair the course of the movement was altered considerably, as was Mao's own career, for he entered a period of virtual political exile which, except for a brief appearance at the May emergency conference after the Red Army's major defeat at the battle of Kuangchang, lasted until the Tsunyi conference of January 1935.

The Second All-China Congress of Soviets convened on January 22, four days after the close of the Fifth Plenum, and was reportedly attended by 700 delegates. Reports were given by: Mao Tse-tung, on the work of the Central Executive Committee; Chu Teh, on the buildup of the Red Army; Wu Liang-ping, on soviet construction; and Lin Pai-chu, on economic construction. Mao's report reflected the decisions of the party leadership. His denunciation of the Fukien rebels, placing blame for the failure entirely on them, was the public position taken by the party on this issue and only happened to coincide with his own view.

The elections to high office in the Soviet Government resulted in the further downgrading of Mao and his group. This is shown most clearly by a comparison of Mao's position in the governmental hierarchy after the First and Second Congresses. After the First Congress, Mao alone was chairman of the Central Executive Committee, which had 63 members; after the Second, he shared his power with a 17-man presidium, and the Central Executive Committee had 175 regular and 36 alternate members. Mao's supporters were excluded from the presidium.[28] After the First Congress, Mao headed both the Central Executive Committee and the Council of People's Commissars; after the Second, while Mao remained chairman of the Central Executive Committee, Chang Wen-t'ien became "premier" of the Council of People's Commissars.[29]

The political situation inside the party after the Second All-China Congress of Soviets represented the zenith of power for the Internationalist group and the nadir for Mao Tse-tung. All important positions in both military and state hierarchies were held by the Internationalists with one exception, the chairmanship of the Central Executive Committee of the Soviet Government. With the exclusion of Mao's supporters from positions of power, Mao was little more than a titular figure who contributed to none of the party decisions made during the remainder of 1934, including the decision to embark on the Long March.

Defeat and Flight from the Central Soviet Area

The Second All-China Congress of Soviets ended prematurely on February 1, six days earlier than originally scheduled, as Nationalist forces resumed the fifth campaign against the Communists after disposing of the Fukien problem. Encircled, the Communist leadership adopted a new tactic of "fast and close strike," devised by the Comintern representative assigned to the Red Army, Li Teh (Otto Braun, Albert List). While seeking to defend the core of soviet territory, Li Teh advocated swift, disruptive strikes against advancing Nationalist forces which would permit Red Army units to engage the enemy's troops before they could be reinforced from the pillboxes and rear areas. In early April the Red Army tested this new tactic at Kuangchang, gateway to the Central Soviet area about twenty miles north of Ningtu. In a battle which raged for over three weeks, from April 4 to 28, the Red Army suffered a stunning defeat, losing Kuangchang and opening the way for a final thrust into the heart of the soviet area.

At this juncture, in early May, the party held an emergency conference to determine its policy. Mao Tse-tung was permitted to attend this meeting, since it was the equivalent of an enlarged Politburo conference to which all Central Committee members were invited. Mao proposed dividing the Red Army into four major troop formations and engaging the Nationalist forces outside the Central Soviet area where there were no blockhouses. He urged that the Red Army strike outward, seeking battle in Fukien, Chekiang, Kiangsu, and Hunan, after which it should return to the Central Soviet area for its defense. In essence, Mao wanted to continue the battle against the Nationalists, but his plan was rejected by the party leadership. Instead, Chou En-lai's plan calling for withdrawal from the Central Soviet area was adopted.

The plan itself was designed to give the Communists maximum time to prepare for what they hoped would be a temporary evacuation, not a permanent withdrawal, from the Kiangsi Soviet. First, in an effort to draw away some of the encircling forces, designated units would attempt a breakthrough of Nationalist lines under the rubric of "advanced detachments of the anti-Japanese army." At the same time, the Communists would construct a heavily fortified defense line just to the north of Shih Ch'eng, the eastern point of a triangle bounded on the west by Ningtu and Kuangchang. Finally, secret arrangements were made to stockpile food and military supplies, while an intensive recruitment campaign was initiated to conscript the local populace in the Red Army to make up for the anticipated losses to be suffered in the last-ditch defense at Shih Ch'eng.[30]

May, June, and July saw frantic efforts to complete preparations before the final onslaught began. In early July a 9,000-man "anti-Japanese force" commanded by Fang Chih-min attempted to break through the Nationalist encirclement northeastward into Fukien, but by January 1935 the bulk of this force had been destroyed and Fang Chih-min had been captured and executed. Toward the end of July a second force under Hsiao K'o drove northward into Hunan and, although managing to link up with the forces of Ho Lung in the Hunan-Szech'uan-Kweichow border area, lost 85 percent of the original force of 7,000 men. Both of these attempts failed to divert the Nationalists' main thrust from the Central Soviet area. Throughout August and September Nationalist and Communist forces were locked in fierce battles in the Shih Ch'eng area. By the end of September, with the aid of artillery and aerial bombardment, Nationalist forces breached the fortified Shih Ch'eng-Yichien line, reducing Communist alternatives to flight or destruction.

After radio consultation with Moscow, which urged immediate abandonment of Kiangsi and a retreat to the northwest,[31] the Communists prepared to depart. Leaving a token force of some 28,000 men, including 20,000 wounded, under the command of Hsiang Ying and Ch'en Yi to carry out a rearguard action which included a frenzied campaign of terror against all those who could be labeled landlords, rich peasants or traitors, the main force of the Red Army departed on October 16, 1934. Accompanied, but not in any sense led, by Mao Tse-tung, who was still under a political cloud, the Communists, numbering approximately 100,000, fled westward, abandoning the Kiangsi stronghold they had held for over half a decade.

IV

From the Long March to the United Front, 1934–1937

The Long March, a frantic flight by the Chinese Communists from otherwise certain destruction by the Nationalists, brought about a reversal of power relationships within the Chinese Communist Party. The serious losses suffered by the party and the Red Army during the first two and a half months of the march created a situation in which Mao Tse-tung was able to lead a revolt against the Internationalist-dominated leadership. Mao assumed chairmanship of the Revolutionary Military Committee, which gave him a voice in the formulation of party policy. Henceforth, although his power was clearly limited, Mao would exert an ever more powerful influence on the direction and development of the Chinese Communist movement.

Long March—The First Six Hundred Miles

On October 14, 1934, the first contingents of the Central Soviet area force set out on what ultimately became known as the Long March, a trek which in meandering fashion covered some 6,000 miles and took just over one year to complete. The first leg of the journey, a succession of forced marches from Yütu, Kiangsi, to Tsunyi, Kweichow, was fateful to the further development of the Communist movement and to the career of Mao Tse-tung.

The Communists, organized into a large central column flanked by mobile fighting units, broke through the Nationalist encirclement of the Central Soviet area and marched southward through Hsinfeng and across the Kiangsi border into northern Kwangtung province. On the first leg they were led by Ch'in Pang-hsien, Chou En-lai, and Li Teh. Mao accompanied the Central leadership but did not contribute to its decisions. Their immediate objective was to consolidate the existing forces of the Red Army scattered by the encirclement campaigns. Before setting out from Yütu they radioed both Ho Lung and Chang Kuo-t'ao of their plan.[1] Ho was operating with a small force of 6,000 men in the mountains of northwestern Hunan, where he had been driven during the first phase of the fifth encirclement campaign; he was instructed to carry out a diversionary attack on Nationalist forces in the T'aoyuan area to prevent enemy forces there from taking up the pursuit of the fleeing central column. After this, Ho was to effect a link-up with the central column in the mountains of southwestern Hunan. Chang Kuo-t'ao, who had suffered a fate similar to that of Ho during the fifth campaign, had set up a soviet in T'ungchiang in northern Szech'uan. He was also alerted to the general plan and instructed to prepare to move his 30,000-man force (the Fourth Army) toward the central column.

The general objective of permanently unifying all the fighting forces of the Red Army was never accomplished on the Long March. It would not be until June 1935 that the Red Army forces would be joined and then only briefly and partially. Ho Lung's forces remained embattled in western Hunan until November 1935, and were not involved in the Long March, strictly speaking.

Nor was the objective of establishing a soviet in the mountainous region of western Hunan fulfilled, although that was evidently the reason most of the heavy equipment, printing presses, arsenal, mint machinery, supplies, and large radio transmitter were brought along. Burdened with heavy equipment, the central column was a cumbersome, lumbering force constantly worried by Nationalist troops from all sides. Under continuous fire, the Communists edged their way westward across northern Kwangtung, roughly following the Kwangtung-Hunan-Kiangsi border. On November 16 they slipped over into southern Hunan to take Linwu and on the 25th trudged over the Yun Gan pass into northeast Kwangsi. Their plan was to cross the Hsiang River, scale the Hsiyen Mountains, and then march northward to join the forces of Ho Lung that were moving south.

The Nationalists were alert to this maneuver and prevented the merger by setting up blocking movements all along the route of march. Striking the Communist forces as they attempted to cross the Hsiang River, Nationalist units wiped out, in Liu Po-ch'eng's words, "more than half our troops." [2] When the Communists had crossed the Hsiyen Mountains and taken T'ungkao, they found another huge concentration of Nationalist forces blocking the planned route north. For the time being, abandoning all thought of joining forces with Ho Lung, they swung westward into Kweichow, occupying Liping on December 14.

At Liping on the following day, the leadership convened an emergency meeting to decide what to do next. Counsel was divided: some urged renewed efforts to join Ho in western Hunan, advocating a march to the east; others wanted to join forces with the Fourth Army forces of Chang Kuo-t'ao and Hsü Hsiang-ch'ien, and therefore supported a march to the north; still others advocated the establishment of a new base in Yunnan and a march to the west. After lengthy discussion, elements of each one of these proposals were combined in a plan designed to permit the exhausted forces of the Red Army to avoid combat and recoup spent energies. It was decided to move into northern Kweichow, where, if possible, they would establish a base and from there attempt to join up with both Ho Lung and Chang Kuo-t'ao. Therefore, the central column set out from Liping in a northwesterly direction, taking, without a shot, the small town of Tsunyi on January 5, 1935.

Only 30,000 of the 100,000 who had started out on the Long March on October 14 were with the central column (the First Front Army) when it arrived at Tsunyi. In the short space of less than three months 70 percent of the fighting forces had been lost! Under constant attack from Nationalist and allied provincial forces, the slow-moving central column had fared badly. As losses mounted, thought turned increasingly to simple survival, resulting in the abandonment of the greater part of the heavy equipment carried along, including the large transmitter which had been used to send communications to the Comintern;[3] presumably the reception of signals *from* the Comintern remained possible. Tsunyi offered a brief respite from battle, there being no enemy troops close by, but also the opportunity for several strongly dissatisfied leaders, including Mao Tse-tung, to challenge the party leadership.

The Tsunyi Conference

The day after their arrival at Tsunyi the leadership convened a conference whose agenda was to be simply a discussion of the current situation and the next move for the Red Army. Under the strident criticisms of P'eng Teh-huai, Mao Tse-tung, and especially Liu Shao-ch'i, the conference agenda was broadened into an accusation session which covered the entire range of party policies since the Fourth Plenum of January 1931. Following Chou En-lai's military report, P'eng opened the criticism by deploring the plan to evacuate all the heavy equipment with the Red Army. He complained that this slowed down the Red Army's movement and made it easy prey for pursuing Nationalist forces. Mao then condemned what he called the purely static defensive tactics employed during the fifth encirclement campaign, arguing once again in favor of the principle of engaging the enemy in the open areas where there were no blockhouses and where the Red Army could maneuver. It was Liu Shao-ch'i, however, who broadened the criticism by impugning the correctness, not only of the party's military policies, but also of its political line since the Fourth Plenum.

In the heated criticism—self-criticism—which followed, Ch'in Pang-hsien, Chou En-lai, and Li Teh (Albert List) came under heavy verbal attack from party leaders. After prolonged discussion, Chou En-lai accepted criticism of his mistakes and Liu Po-ch'eng, who had opposed Mao's policies consistently since 1931, altered his position to support Mao, marking a significant shift of party leadership opinion in favor of the policies of Mao Tse-tung.

It would be an overstatement to say that Mao, Liu, and P'eng were acting in unison at this point. Mao did not yet command a faction in the Central Committee, but the Tsunyi conference provided the basis for just such a future development. At the conference Mao skillfully managed to exploit general dissatisfaction within the party for his own gain.

Helping him, possibly unintentionally, Chang Wen-t'ien suggested a compromise, which was reluctantly accepted by the leadership. In the interests of party unity Chang suggested that the conference, in its final resolution, state agreement with the party's political line since the Fourth Plenum, but register sharp disapproval of the military policies employed during the fifth encirclement campaign and the westward flight. Blame, he said, should be placed upon the principal party leaders, the chairman of the Revolutionary Military Committee, and the Comintern advisor. This meant Ch'in Pang-hsien, Chou En-lai, and Li Teh (Albert List), respectively.

The final resolution of the Tsunyi conference carried the subtitle "A Review of the Errors in the Military Line of Comrades Po Ku (Ch'in Pang-hsien), Chou En-lai, and List." Reflecting the compromise suggested by Chang Wen-t'ien, it approved the party's political line, but denounced the party leadership for the military policies carried out during the fifth encirclement campaign and the subsequent withdrawal maneuvers of the Red Army. Rejecting the tactic of "fast and close strike," the resolution adopted Mao's point of view, stating that the party "should have adopted the principle of offensive (positive) defense so as to change the overall defense into regional attacks and to turn the fighting from inner to outer circles to bring about a change for the better." [4]

The resolution condemning Ch'in, Chou, and Li Teh resulted in a major reorganization of the top party leadership and a setback for the Internationalist group. Ch'in was removed from the post of secretary general of the party and appointed director of the General Political Department of the Red Army, a powerless post into which Mao had once been shunted. Chang Wen-t'ien replaced Ch'in as secretary general, possibly because he was a member of the Internationalist group sympathetic to Mao. More importantly, the appointment of an Internationalist indicated that the relations between the Comintern and the Chinese Communist Party were not in question. Chou En-lai was dropped from chairman to vice-chairman of the Revolutionary Military Committee. Mao Tse-tung assumed the chairmanship of the Revolutionary Military Committee and was elected to the Politburo and also to the Politburo Standing Committee, replacing Hsiang Ying, who was still in Juichin commanding the rearguard action in the Central Soviet area.

Chance once again played a role in determining Mao Tse-tung's fortunes. On the westward flight one of the heavy items discarded was the long-range transmitter used to contact Moscow. Its loss meant that Moscow had no immediate knowledge of the Tsunyi meeting and therefore could not affect its outcome. However, one of the decisions of the conference was to send Ch'en Yün to Moscow to obtain Comintern approval of its proceedings.

A fine but important distinction must be made here concerning Mao's victory. The fact that Mao advanced in the party's hierarchy at the expense of the Internationalist or Moscow group did not mean that he opposed Moscow—nor vice versa. At Tsunyi, though the struggle was waged in policy terms, the issue was only incidentally policy. The real issue was party power. It was: who would lead the Communist party of China? It was not: should the Chinese party oppose Moscow? (In the fifties, this would become precisely the question, but such was not the case in 1935.) No leader—least of all Mao Tse-tung—could have survived in the Communist movement in flagrant opposition to the headquarters of the international revolution and still have claimed to be a part of that revolution. In the Chinese party alone, not to speak of the other Communist parties of the world, the list of those who had tried to take such a stand and failed included Ch'en Tu-hsiu, Ch'ü Ch'iu-pai, and Li Li-san. None survived Moscow's opposition. This speaks both of the difficulty of maintaining an international organization and of the *ultimate* power of the Comintern in deposing opponents in national parties. There is little reason to suppose that Mao could have survived, even if he had gained complete control of the party at Tsunyi, which he had not.

It would be over two decades before Mao could build a position strong enough to act independently of Moscow in broader policy matters. To speak of Mao's rise to power in opposition to Moscow at this time, in my view, is to project the present into the past; I speak here, of course, not of Mao's personal wishes, which probably were at variance with many of the directives and broad policy decisions emanating from Moscow. No doubt, Communist party members the world over had similar feelings. That is beside the point. To have openly sought to build a position in a Communist party on the basis of open opposition to Moscow would have been political suicide and Mao was anything but a fool. On the contrary, regardless of his personal feelings, he submitted to "party discipline" concerning policy matters.

Long March—Phase Two: The Conflict with Chang Kuo-t'ao

On January 15, after the close of the Tsunyi conference, the forces of the central column, now designated as the First Front Army, set out in a northwesterly direction, hoping to enter southern Szech'uan by way of northern Kweichow. Their objective was to join forces with Chang Kuo-t'ao's Fourth Front Army in northern Szech'uan. Engaged in continual combat along the way, the First Army discovered upon reaching Tucheng on the Ch'ih Sui River that the route into Szech'uan was blocked by a large concentration of Nationalist forces. The First Army was forced back by the KMT into an area bounded by the Ch'ih Sui and Wu rivers in northern Kweichow. Tsunyi was located in the center of this area and, by the end of February, the First Army again found itself at Tsunyi, but this time with Nationalist and allied provincial forces slowly closing in on its position.

Nationalist strategy was to prevent the scattered forces of the Communists from merging and to attack their groupings separately. Chiang Kai-shek also sought to involve as many as possible of the provincial warlords in the "Communist encirclement campaigns," for it gave him an excellent opportunity to secure the loyalty of these forces, many of which were as yet uncommitted, or loyal in name only, to the Nationalist Government. With Chiang in general command of operations, tactical headquarters were set up in northern Szech'uan at Kuangyuan under Hu Tsung-nan, who directed operations against the Fourth Front Army, and in southern Kweichow at Kweiyang under Hsüeh Yüeh, who directed operations against the First Front Army. By early April, the encirclement of the First Front Army in the Ch'ih Sui and Wu rivers area had begun; in the north the Fourth Front Army had managed to elude an attempt by Nationalist forces to destroy it at the Chia Ling River near Kuangyuan.

The First Front Army, using feinting maneuvers, quick marches, and other deceptive ploys, moved quickly to the southwest after perceiving the move to encircle it in northern Kweichow. Feigning an attack on Lungli to the southeast of Kweiyang, it sped across the P'ei P'an River through Hsingyi and, on April 24, crossed into the province of Yunnan. By this tactic the First Front Army evaded the Nationalist attempt to encircle and destroy it in Kweichow, but it was prevented from carrying out its plan to sweep through the relatively easy terrain of the western Szech'uan basin to north Szech'uan. Instead, it was forced to swing farther westward across northeast Yunnan, turning northward into the difficult mountainous terrain of western Szech'uan. Completing the crossing of the Chin Sha River by the first week in May, the dwindling forces of the First Front Army crossed the Tatu River and scaled the Chiaching Mountains, reaching the city of Maokung on the 16th of June. Fewer than 10,000 of the 100,000 who had begun the trip eight months before survived the march to Maokung.

The Fourth Front Army, meanwhile, was 80,000 strong in the T'ungkiang area of northern Szech'uan. Receiving telegraphic instructions from the party leadership at Tsunyi of the plan to join forces in Northern Szech'uan, the Fourth Army set out in a westward direction from T'ungkiang.[5] After fighting through an attempted encirclement by forces under the command of Hu Tsung-nan in the Kuangyuan area, it crossed the Chia Ling River on March 20, a month-long operation which required the building of boats and floating bridges. After crossing the river, the Fourth Front Army moved slowly westward, engaging in incessant battle and suffering 10,000 casualties. Still, when the Fourth Front Army reached Maokung in early June, it had a complement of some 70,000 men, compared to the 10,000 men of the "beggar army," which was the descriptive term applied to the First Front Army by Fourth Front Army personnel.

After joining forces in the Maokung area, the leaders of the First and Fourth Front Armies held a conference at nearby Lianghok'ou, a meeting which marked the beginning of a three-year struggle between Chang Kuo-t'ao and the leaders of the former Central Soviet area. Although taking varied forms, the struggle was one of contrasting political philosophies, a conflict between Communist right and left wings. At bottom, the issues resembled those which manifested themselves at the Sixth Congress of the party in 1928, the right wing believing that the victorious revolution was only a distant chimerical illusion, and the left wing asserting the possibility of immediate success of armed revolution based on the power of soviets. These elemental differences determined basic attitudes toward all political problems. At the Sixth Congress, it will be recalled that Chang and Bukharin, representatives of the right wing, had argued for extended cooperation with the Chinese bourgeoisie instead of immediate revolution, in opposition to Stalin, who had supported guerrilla action and establishment of soviets in China. The principal difference between 1928 and 1935, of course, was that armed revolution could no longer be disavowed. The question of soviets, however, was another matter and, although the situation had changed since 1928, at Lianghok'ou Chang continued to argue along lines similar to those of 1928.

The contending groups at Lianghok'ou were the leaders of the First and Fourth Front Armies.[6] Both groups vied for control over the Red Army, the basis of political power in the Chinese Communist movement. The effect of the struggle between First and Fourth Front Army groups was to smooth over the conflict between Mao and the Internationalists within the First Front Army, who united in the face of Chang's challenge. Chang Kuo-t'ao argued that no revolutionary situation existed, Mao argued that the revolution was on an upward swing. Chang condemned the party's political line as being in error since 1928, particularly in the decision to establish soviets in China! Mao and the Internationalists sharply disagreed. Chang found the soviet system "unsuitable" for China, asserting that the form of government which the Communists established should be acceptable to the local people of the area. Mao countered by saying that soviets were the only acceptable form of government. When the question of the Communists' next move arose, Chang proposed to establish a base (but not a soviet) on the Szech'uan-Sik'ang border. Mao urged that all forces continue northward to Liu Chih-tan's soviet base in Shensi, a proposal which was agreed upon by the majority of the leadership.

At this point, Chang called into question the Tsunyi conference, arguing that the party reorganization which had taken place there was invalid because it was not done by a party congress nor accepted by the Comintern. Mao's rejoinder was that it was valid under wartime conditions and that the Comintern's approval was forthcoming. In order to forestall further argument on the Tsunyi reorganization, about which Chang was technically correct, it was proposed to enlarge the Central Committee by co-opting eight members of the Fourth Front Army. This quieted Chang but pointed up the fact that, far from achieving the unification of Communist forces, the conference at Lianghok'ou resulted in only a temporizing compromise which soon broke down.

While the Communist leadership conferred and their troops rested, the Nationalists continued pursuit. Having failed to prevent the linkup of the First and Fourth Armies, although successfully blocking Ho Lung from joining them, the Nationalists now deployed to bottle them up in northern Szech'uan. The northern Nationalist force under Hu Tsung-nan had shifted to Sungp'an to the west of Kuangyuan, in order to block Communist movement northward into Shensi and Kansu. Nationalist forces in the southern sector under Hsüeh Yüeh had also redeployed, trailing along behind the First Front Army and retaking towns along its route of march. By the end of July these forces, which were made up primarily of Szech'uanese troops with Nationalist advisors, had reached Maokung and were on the heels of the Communists.

The mounting Nationalist pressure forced the Communists to stop on August 5 to decide upon an escape plan. The emergency conference was held at Maoerhkai in northern Szech'uan, where conflict again erupted between Chang Kuo-t'ao and Mao Tse-tung. Once more Chang proposed to construct a base in western Szech'uan from which the Communists would be able to expand into the Ch'engtu plain. Chang's proposal was rejected by both Chang Wen-t'ien and Mao Tse-tung, who, along with the majority of the Central Committee, decided to continue toward Shensi, where they could join forces with Liu Chih-tan and open up direct contact with the Soviet Union. To have accepted Chang's proposal would have meant marching directly into the face of Nationalist troops advancing from the south under Hsüeh Yüeh.

At Maoerhkai a further reorganization of the Revolutionary Military Committee took place, as well as changes in the command and composition of the armed forces. Mao remained chairman of the Revolutionary Military Committee, with Chou En-lai and Chang Kuo-t'ao vice-chairmen. The military command structure saw Chu Teh as commander-in-chief, Chang Kuo-t'ao as Red Army political commissar (a post recreated earlier at Maokung), P'eng Teh-huai as commander of the First Front Army, and Hsü Hsiang-ch'ien as commander of the Fourth Front Army. Finally, the Red Army's forces were realigned into two columns and some attempt to balance them politically was made. The "right column," under Mao and the Internationalists, consisted of the 1st and 3rd regiments of the First Front Army, and the 4th and 30th regiments of the Fourth Front Army. The "left column," under Chu Teh and Chang Kuo-t'ao, was composed of the 9th and 31st regiments of the Fourth Front Army and the 5th and 9th regiments of the First Front Army.[7]

It took eighteen days at Maoerhkai for the Communists to accomplish this reorganization and in the interim Nationalist forces drew ever nearer. The forces of Hsüeh Yüeh were closing in from the south, and those of Hu Tsung-nan stood squarely in the path of a move into Shensi. In this situation, while part of the "right column" (the 4th and 30th regiments of the Fourth Front Army under Ch'en Ch'ang-hao) was engaged in battle with the forces of Hu Tsung-nan (a battle in which several thousand troops were lost), the remainder (the 1st and 3rd regiments of the First Front Army), about 6,000 men, including Mao, Chou, the Internationalists, P'eng, and Lin Piao, surreptitiously slipped through the resulting gap in Nationalist lines leaving the rest of the Communist forces behind!

Those left behind were astounded and enraged at what they felt was

Mao's perfidy. Chang thereafter refused to run the gauntlet of Nationalist forces, despite repeated orders to do so from the central leadership, which had already safely broken through. Instead, he led the remainder of the Communist forces, about 60,000 troops, in the direction he had originally advocated—southward, avoiding the forces of Hsüeh Yüeh and setting up a parallel and separate central committee in western Szech'uan, where he had originally intended to establish himself. On Chang's central committee besides the eight Fourth Front Army members elected at Lianghok'ou were Chu Teh, Ch'en Ch'ang-hao, Liu Po-ch'eng, Li Cho-jan, Ho Chang-kung, and Shao Shih-ping, of those First Front Army units left behind. From early September 1935 until the summer of 1936, therefore, two central committees functioned in China.

Mao's small force, redesignated the "Worker-Peasant Red Army's Shensi-Kansu Guerrilla Contingent," continued on the Long March. Struggling through the Min Mountains, they reached Hatapu in southern Kansu in early September and, after several encounters with enemy troops, reached Wu Chi in northern Shensi on October 19, 1935. The Guerrilla Contingent arrived in northern Shensi with only 2,000 men and joined the 7,000 men of the Red 15th Corps commanded by Hsü Hai-tung, which itself had recently been formed by a merger of the 25th, 26th, and 27th regiments.

Arriving in northern Shensi, Mao's group found itself in the middle of a bloody factional struggle between a "central" faction, sent by the central leadership before it had started on the Long March, and a local faction. The central faction, led by Chu Li-chih and Kuo Hung-tao, had opposed and carried out a violent "counter-revolutionary" campaign against local Communist leaders and their supporters. When Mao's Guerrilla Contingent arrived, Liu Chih-tan and Kao Kang, the local leaders, had already been incarcerated and marked for execution. Attempting to bring about a semblance of unity, the party's central leadership, which had arrived with Mao, curtailed the counterrevolutionary campaign and quietly transferred Chu Li-chih and Kuo Hung-tao elsewhere. They criticized their subordinates for carrying out an erroneous policy, and released Kao Kang, Liu Chih-tan, and their supporters. Although providing a temporary solution, Kao Kang registered public dissatisfaction with the party solution, claiming that Chu and Kuo should have been punished for their misdeeds.[8]

Organizational Reconstitution of the Communist System

On the Long March, a natural tendency was for decision making increasingly to become concentrated in the military organization, rather than in the state or even party structure. State and party structures were largely irrelevant to the tasks facing the Communists while on the run and, as a consequence, fell into disuse. When the Guerrilla Contingent arrived in northern Shensi, it was decided to restore the central state and party organizations and begin to relegate the military organization to its former status. At Wayaopao the first important steps were taken toward the attainment of this objective.[9]

First, the Shensi-Kansu Guerrilla Contingent was abolished and redesignated the 1st and 3rd corps of the First Front Army. The command structure of the Red Army forces in northern Shensi, thus, was: Lin Piao, commander of the First Corps; Yang Shang-k'un, political commissar; Hsü Hai-tung, commander of the 15th Corps; Liu Chih-tan, political commissar. In the Revolutionary Military Committee, Mao retained the chairmanship he had gained at Tsunyi, Chou En-lai remained as vice-chairman, Yeh Chien-ying became chief of staff, and Li Fu-ch'un assumed the directorship of the General Political Department. Chang Kuo-t'ao, who was absent, was now excluded from the Revolutionary Military Committee entirely. The Internationalist group was also adversely affected by the Wayaopao reorganization. Mao and his supporters gained a firm grip on the military apparatus, excluding leaders of the Internationalist group from important positions in the Revolutionary Military Committee.

Reorganization of the party and state apparatuses was a different matter and the product of formal compromises among the Mao, Internationalist, and Chang groups, although many of those named to top party and state posts were not present to assume them, leaving real power to those who were on hand. The Executive Committee of the Central Soviet Government was composed of Mao as chairman and Hsiang Ying and Chang Kuo-t'ao as vice-chairmen. Neither Hsiang Ying nor Chang Kuo-t'ao was present to assume these posts, giving Mao sole effective control over this arm of the state apparatus. In the Council of People's Commissars, Ch'in Pang-hsien replaced Chang Wen-t'ien as chairman, Hsieh Chueh-tsai was secretary general and Wang Chia-hsiang was foreign minister. Although Wang was in the Soviet Union receiving treatment for battlefield injuries, the Internationalist group held firm control over this organ of state.

The party Central Committee was headed, as at Tsunyi, by Chang Wen-t'ien. Mao, as chairman of the Revolutionary Military Committee, was a member as were Lo Mai, director of the Organization Department; Liu Shao-ch'i, secretary of the Trade Union Movement Committee; Chou En-lai, secretary of the Committee for Work Among White Troops; Wu Liang-ping, director of the Propaganda Department; Ts'ai Ch'ang, director of the Women's Department; Tu Cheng-nung, chief secretary of the Central Committee, and Chang Hao (Lin Yu-ying), deputy secretary. The balance of formal power in the Central Committee lay with the Internationalist group, but if it can be asserted that Mao, Chou, and Liu constituted Mao's group at this time, together they comprised a powerful voice in the Central Committee.

By December 1935, Mao Tse-tung had effectively achieved control of the central organs of both the military apparatus and the Soviet government, while the Internationalist group held a commanding position in the Council of People's Commissars and the party Central Committee, on the surface a relatively even balance of power. Mao's command of the central military apparatus, however, proved decisive in the subsequent internal struggles.

International United Front

While the Chinese Communists were being pursued and decimated in the Chinese hinterland, Moscow made a major foreign policy *démarche*. As the threats of Germany and Japan grew, Moscow had reversed its isolationist policy of 1928 and from late 1933 onward sought to mobilize opposition to the expansionist powers. The effort to mobilize opposition included activities which led to recognition by the United States (November 1933), entrance into the League of Nations (September 1934), the conclusion of defense pacts with France and Czechoslovakia (May 1935), and, later, the extension of military aid to the republican side in the Spanish civil war (August 1936) and to the Chinese Nationalists (August 1937). As a key part of this broad effort, at the Seventh World Congress of the Comintern, held from July 25 through August 20, 1935, the world's Communist parties were called upon to unite with non-Communist parties against the forces of "fascism and militarism."

The new united front policy consisted primarily of three elements. First, the Communists called for the creation of anti-fascist "fronts" in Europe and anti-imperialist "fronts" in Asia. Second, Moscow proclaimed the willingness of the Communists to participate in all popular front *governments*. Dimitrov, general secretary of the Comintern, in his keynote speech to the congress, stated bluntly the role which Communists hoped to play:

> If we Communists are asked whether we advocate the united front only in the fight for partial demands, or whether we are prepared to share the responsibility even when it will be a question of forming a government on the basis of the united front, then we say with a full sense of our responsibility: Yes, we recognize that a situation may arise in which the formation of a government of the proletarian united front, or of an anti-fascist People's Front, will become not only possible but necessary in the interests of the proletariat.[10]

To justify such a marked doctrinal change, it was claimed that Communist participation in a bourgeois government would transform it into a "democracy of a new type," purging capitalism of its fascist contents. Third, in all such cases, Communists would amend their social and economic policies to make them compatible with "new democracy."

Wang Ming, the CCP's representative on the ECCI, delivered the major speech outlining the policy to be adopted in the colonial and semi-colonial areas. Amplifying the points made by Dimitrov, Wang stated that the united anti-imperialist front in Asia would also lead to a period of "new democracy" following the inclusion of Communists in governments. In the case of China, Wang urged that the central committee of the CCP and the Soviet government issue a joint appeal

> to all the peoples, to all parties, groups, troops, mass organizations, and to all prominent political and social leaders to organize together with us an All-China People's Government of National Defense.[11]

In a plain and obvious attempt to come to terms with the Kuomintang without saying so outright, Wang Ming further listed four concessions which the Chinese Communists would make in return for a united front against the Japanese. They would agree: first, to cease the struggle against the Nationalists; second, to rename and broaden the Soviet government to include non-Communist groups; third, to subordinate the Red Army to the Nationalist Government; and fourth, to amend their economic policies. Specifically he announced a relaxation of the hitherto stringent political and economic policies, including curtailment of the policy of confiscating the land of the small landowners.

The CCP and the United Front

The Comintern's policies eventually were carried out to the letter by the Chinese Communists, although in the beginning there was a delay in communication and a difference of opinion among the party leadership. It would take approximately two years and the outbreak of the Sino-Japanese war to bring about the Comintern's desired policy of a united front in China, but there can be no doubt about the origin of the policy—it was not devised by the Chinese Communists in Shensi, but by the Comintern in Moscow.

The Chinese Communists on the Long March were unaware of Moscow's policy turnabout. Only in October, after their arrival in northern Shensi, did they learn of the momentous change promulgated at the Comintern's Seventh World Congress. At that time, however, they were still ignorant of the specific role which they were to play in the new policy. It was not until December 1935, when Chang Hao (Lin Yu-ying) arrived at the northern Shensi base from Moscow, that the party central leadership received specific instructions.

On the 25th of December the central leadership convened a Politburo conference at Wayaopao to discuss the new policy. The "resolution on the current political situation and the party's tasks" marked the first formal CCP proclamation on the new united front policy, but it masked the sharp division within the party leadership over the advisability of adopting the new policy in the specific form called for by Moscow. At issue was not the united front; on this there was apparently full agreement, although Mao Tse-tung, in his report to the conference "On Tactics against Japanese Imperialism," suggested that there were differences over this question as well.[12] The sharp disagreement concerned the political forces to be included in the united front. Some advocated the Comintern line of a full united front including, and subordinate to,

Chiang Kai-shek. Wang Ming and Chang Kuo-t'ao, who were not present at the Wayaopao conference, later became the principal spokesmen for this view. Others, led by Mao Tse-tung, advocated a united front without Chiang Kai-shek. Mao's position was couched in terms of his evaluation of the national bourgeoisie as a camp of traitors led by their chieftain, Chiang Kai-shek. He asserted that the national bourgeoisie would vacillate under pressure and "when the national crisis reaches a crucial point, splits will occur in the Kuomintang camp." [13]

The final resolution of the Wayaopao conference reflected Mao's position; it called for a united front without Chiang Kai-shek. Undoubtedly, this was because Mao commanded the support of the majority of the party delegates who attended the conference. Those aspects of the Comintern's policy which were consistent with his position were included in the final resolution; those which were not were omitted. The major omission, however, constituted a fundamental revision of the entire policy. Consistent with Mao's position were the establishment of an anti-Japanese united front, a joint proposal for a government of national defense, the renaming of the Soviet Workers' and Peasants' Republic to the Soviet People's Republic, and the relaxation of social and economic policies to attract broader popular support. All of these were points made by Wang Ming at the Seventh Comintern Congress and in subsequent articles. [14]

Omitted from the resolution was the proposal to establish a united front with Chiang Kai-shek and the Kuomintang, a union Moscow intended. In fact, Chiang was specifically excluded from the united front, which the Communists themselves proposed to lead! The Wayaopao resolution, therefore, clearly contravened the main thrust of the Seventh Comintern Congress, which, although not explicitly, had implicitly called for just such an alliance. Based on Mao's belief that the Kuomintang would split under the impact of the Japanese invasion, the Wayaopao resolution read:

> The party's strategic line is to rally and organize all revolutionary forces of the whole Chinese nation to oppose the presently superior enemies—Japanese imperialists and traitor Chiang Kai-shek. All persons, all factions and all armed units, so long as they are opposed to Japanese imperialists and traitor Chiang Kai-shek, should unite. . . . The Communists should seek to obtain their right to leadership of the anti-Japanese front. [15]

In the resolution Mao attempted to strike a middle position among the policy options available. (His own position deviated from the Comintern's at this time, but later he swung round to the Comintern's view after the internal party conflict with Chang Kuo-t'ao was resolved.) Referring to divergent views within the party, the resolution stated that the party must struggle against "left exclusionism" (which meant no united front at all), as well as "right opportunism" (the subordination of everything for collaboration with Chiang Kai-shek). By this definition of terms Mao by implication labeled the Comintern's policy as "right opportunism" and assumed a centrist position himself.

How to explain Mao's position? Given the nearly total destruction of the Chinese Communist forces at this time, Mao was not merely delivering a gratuitous insult to Moscow. The party's and his own fortunes were low enough. Defiantly opposing Moscow, the only source of succor, was obviously not the reason for his position. Therefore, although Mao was in command of the leadership, the grouping of forces in the party as a whole must have been such as to force him to adopt the position he did. What were these forces? We must revert to the spectrum of opinion in the party, and, again, to the right and left wings.[16] The extreme left wing position is clear enough—no compromise. It was the right wing position that posed a danger for Mao. The fundamental predilection of the right wing was its willingness to cooperate with the bourgeoisie in the belief that the victory of the revolution was a distant possibility, not a short-run likelihood. As long as the Comintern pursued a policy of non-cooperation with the bourgeoisie and continued an armed struggle against it (a policy it had been following since 1928), there was no possibility that a right wing leader could ever ascend to the party leadership. A left wing policy ensured the future of the left wing leader. But now the Comintern was swinging from a left to a right wing policy! Therefore, party leaders who had advocated policies of cooperation with the bourgeoisie could expect to advance in the party hierarchy. Such a leader was Chang Kuo-t'ao.

The problem for Mao Tse-tung, therefore, was to preempt the policy field from Chang Kuo-t'ao and thereby prevent him from making a bid for the party leadership on the basis of the new policy line. Fortunately for Mao, Chang Kuo-t'ao was isolated from the party center, both physically and in terms of party support. Mao already had a substantial grip on the reins of power in the party, but the danger was no less because of this. Chang still commanded considerable support in the party, had his own central committee, and a sizable armed force. There was also an ever enlarging group which was willing to come to terms with non-Communist elements against Japan. If Mao had merely echoed the Comintern's new policy at Wayaopao, he would have found himself swinging over to a position which Chang had advocated all along and deserting some of his own relatively hard-line leftist supporters. For purely internal political reasons, Mao could not respond too quickly to the new line. As soon as Chang Kuo-t'ao's political fate had been sealed, however, Mao could and would shift quickly to the Comintern's line. Until that time (August 1936), Mao moved extremely cautiously toward acceptance of the Comintern line.

Mao's first step toward the full implementation of the Comintern's line was the issuance in May, after Red Army troops had suffered a severe defeat in western Shansi, of a declaration in which the Communists announced a troop withdrawal and expressed a willingness "to negotiate a ceasefire within a month with all forces that are currently attacking the anti-Japanese Red Army." [17] The withdrawal ostensibly was to demonstrate the Red Army's "sincerity to the Nanking government." But words were not enough to offset the fact that the Communists were in serious difficulty, their forces badly depleted. The following month Nationalist troops attacked Wayaopao, forcing evacuation of the central leadership to Paoan, where it remained until January 1937.

June 1936, however, was a critical month in the inner party struggle. At this time, Mao initiated a plan which ultimately led to Chang Kuo-t'ao's political defeat in the party. Sometime in June (the exact date is unknown) Chang Kuo-t'ao received a radio message from Chang Hao at central headquarters. Chang Hao, claiming Comintern authorization, proposed to mediate the dispute between Chang Kuo-t'ao and Mao Tse-tung. Essentially his proposal was that both the central leadership at Paoan and Chang's central committee should dissolve and reestablish as northwestern and southwestern "bureaus." Later, when their armed forces were joined, the bureau leaders would merge to establish a new central leadership. In the meantime, both bureaus should cooperate in making independent thrusts into Ninghsia and Kansu, striving eventually to open contact with the Soviet Union through Sinkiang.[18]

Chang Kuo-t'ao accepted this proposal, dissolved his central committee, established a southwest bureau, and began to discuss military operations with his comrades. Chang wanted to remain with all his forces in Sikang until a new joint policy could be worked out. Chu Teh and Jen Pi-shih, political commissar of Ho Lung's Second Army, disagreed, urging that Chang set out to join forces with the others in northern Shensi.[19] Finally, Chang gave in and his Fourth and Ho Lung's Second Armies set out to join Mao's First Army. By the end of October 1936, after numerous battles, Chang's troops made contact with advance units of the First Army at Huining, Ninghsia.

At this point Chang discovered to his astonishment and rage that Mao's committee had not dissolved at all, but had continued to function as the central leadership of the party! Outmaneuvered, he thereupon reorganized his forces into the Western Route Army and radioed the central leadership, informing them of his decision to move through the Kansu corridor to open up direct communication with the Soviet Union as originally proposed by Chang Hao the previous June.

When Chang Kuo-t'ao dissolved his central committee, Mao knew that his party opponent was sufficiently weakened for Mao to proceed to broaden his own policy position. The following month, on August 25, the central leadership at Paoan issued a "message to the Kuomintang." In it for the first time, the Chinese Communists referred to Chiang Kai-shek as "generalissimo" and recognized the "absolute necessity" of concentrating all forces under the direction of a central authority, as the Kuomintang had advocated in its own message a few days before, following its Fifth Congress.[20] Ignoring this message, Chiang Kai-shek proceeded to set up a National Defense Council without the Communists and began preparations to convene a National Assembly which would unify Chinese forces against Japan.[21] In effect, Chiang had beaten the Communists at their own game. Each side had sought to establish a united front excluding the other and the KMT had succeeded. It was they who formed and controlled the united front, not the Communists.

With no possibility of leading the anti-Japanese struggle and with the distinct probability that it would be excluded from the Nationalist-led united front altogether, the Communist central leadership moved quickly to make a place for itself in the Nationalist camp. On September 17, the party Politburo adopted the "Resolution on the New Situation of the Anti-Japanese National Salvation Movement and the Democratic Republic." The Communists asserted that the best means of achieving the anti-Japanese united front was to establish a "democratic republic," of which they, of course, would be a part. Though wishing to be a part of the democratic republic which they proposed, and to elect representatives to parliament, the Communists were determined to retain control over their own territory and armed forces.

> In the process of the struggle for establishing the anti-Japanese national united front and realizing the democratic republic, the strength of the Soviet and Red Army should never be weakened. The National Defense Government and allied anti-Japanese armed forces in the anti-Japanese national united front represent but a political and military agreement reached by the Soviet and Red Army with other regimes and armed forces on a certain program. This does not mean that they will merge with other regimes and armed forces. They may be placed under the unified command of the National Defense Government and allied anti-Japanese armed forces, but the independence of the Soviet and Red Army in their organization and leadership shall not be abolished.[22]

In effect, of the two remaining points of the policy announced by the Comintern at the Seventh Congress—Communist willingness to enter into united front governments (which would transform them into "new democratic" governments), and to subordinate their military forces to these governments—the Chinese Communists had now completely agreed to the first, but were not yet committed to the second, although they hinted at this possibility.

Turning Point at Sian

In early November after he had organized the Western Route Army, Chang Kuo-t'ao took his forces across the Yellow River and northwest along the Kansu corridor in an attempt to establish a link with the Soviet Union in Sinkiang. Attacked at Kulang, Kansu, by Moslem forces under General Ma Pu-fang, Chang's forces engaged in a series of firefights and were in danger of being wiped out. In an emergency meeting with Mao Tse-tung at T'unghsin, Ninghsia, in mid-November, Chang entreated Mao to send rescue forces to his beleaguered troops. He believed that a small force would tip the balance in favor of the Communists and, once the Nationalist forces were eliminated from the area, the corridor to Sinkiang could be opened up. Mao refused and Chang's forces suffered a serious defeat.[23] Chang returned to Paoan in early December 1936, a beaten man, the basis of his political power severely weakened. By his inaction, Mao had effectively eliminated the military power of a serious right wing rival.

Meanwhile, the Nationalists brought mounting pressure on the Paoan base and by late November the encirclement of the area was nearing completion. The Japanese increased pressure of their own by attacking Suiyuan, forcing another division of Nationalist armies to meet the threat of a Japanese thrust through Inner Mongolia. Ignoring a Communist plea for a ceasefire issued on December 1, Chiang flew to Sian on the 4th of December to make the final arrangements for the extermination of the Communists at Paoan and to assess the danger created by the Japanese move. Chiang's presence was necessary at Sian for Chang Hsüeh-liang, commander of the Nationalist forces assigned to the Paoan operation, had succumbed to Communist blandishments and would not attack them as Chiang had ordered. After persuasion failed to win Chang over, Chiang had no recourse but to relieve him of command. On the 10th of December, Chiang appointed Chiang Ting-wen in Chang Hsüeh-liang's place, but at dawn on the 12th Chang's men took Chiang Kai-shek captive, holding him for two weeks in what has subsequently been termed the "Sian incident."

News that Chiang had been placed under arrest at Sian and that the Chinese Communists were calling for his execution as a national traitor stunned Moscow. At one stroke, efforts to build a unified opposition to Japan around Chiang Kai-shek were threatened with complete failure. At that very moment secret talks were under way between the Soviet Union and the Nationalist Government concerning aid to the Nationalists, talks which had taken a favorable turn just before the Sian incident occurred. Chiang's death would have ended all hopes of an agreement between the Soviet Union and the Kuomintang and of building a unified resistance to Japan, which was Moscow's primary purpose. Therefore, from the 14th of December onward both *Pravda* and *Izvestia* carried articles condemning the seizure, demanding a peaceful settlement of the "incident" and proclaiming that there could be national unity only under Chiang Kai-shek. A telegram to this effect was also sent to the Chinese Communists.

Pandemonium reigned in the Chinese Communist camp when they learned the news of Chiang's arrest. Here was a golden opportunity to settle old scores with the man they had called the "butcher of China."

Moreover, it was decidedly in their interests to eliminate him, for they were threatened with exclusion from the united front which Chiang was slowly building. His death would disorganize the Nationalists, possibly even split them, and give the Communists new life and an opportunity to gain control over the resistance movement. A good *prima facie* case could certainly have been made that Chiang had refused to lead the people against the Japanese and that the CCP had always espoused resistance to civil war.

This was clearly the attitude of Mao Tse-tung, who had moved slowly toward the Comintern's position during the course of the previous year. Now that the opportunity to take the initiative had arisen, Mao reverted to the position he had espoused at Wayaopao—formation of a united front without Chiang Kai-shek. At a mass meeting in Paoan, Mao led cries for the public trial and execution of Chiang Kai-shek as a national traitor. All along Mao had argued that under sufficient pressure the Nationalists would split and, indeed, after Chiang's capture, they had split. One faction demanded that a punitive expedition be sent to rescue Chiang, the other that such a step would only ensure the Generalissimo's death. Mao therefore urged the Chinese Communist leadership to capitalize on this once-in-a-lifetime opportunity.

The telegram from Moscow threw a damper on Mao's plans. Although it was in the interests of the Chinese Communists to eliminate Chiang Kai-shek, his death would have ruined Moscow's attempt to build general Chinese resistance to Japan. A split in the Nationalist camp would only weaken the available forces; some would probably come to terms with the Japanese. Therefore, the telegram contained the order for the Chinese Communists to bring about a "peaceful settlement" of the incident and ensure that no harm befell Chiang Kai-shek.

The majority of the party leadership, in particular the Internationalist group, accepted the order without hesitation and, notwithstanding Mao Tse-tung's violent opposition to this decision—opposition which included vituperative denunciations and foot-stomping—the Communists did indeed play an important role in bringing about a peaceful settlement of the incident.[24] The settlement paved the way for the establishment of a united front of precisely the nature proposed by the Soviet Union in 1935 and led to the conclusion of a Soviet Union-Nationalist nonaggression treaty, which was signed the following August.

These developments were not immediately obvious after the settlement of the Sian incident. When released, Chiang publicly asserted that nothing had changed, but he quietly called off the projected offensive against the Communists and reassigned the assembled forces elsewhere. With the withdrawal of military pressure, the Communists, in January, moved their headquarters from Paoan to Yenan, where it remained until 1949. Immediately after their arrival, they published a statement containing the points which Chiang allegedly agreed to at Sian. Although the Nationalists made no formal reply, in February 1937 both parties issued separate statements containing the proposals for cessation of the civil war and joint efforts to make the concessions offered at Wayaopao and more. In addition to joining in a united front government, recognizing the Soviet government as a "special region" of the National government, and putting into effect more lenient economic and social policies, the Communists now proclaimed their willingness to redesignate their armed forces as units of the Nationalist army and accept "guidance" from the Central government on military matters! Every offer made by Wang Ming at the Seventh Comintern Congress in 1935, had now been made by the Communists at Yenan. This is how matters stood between the Chinese Communists and the KMT until the Japanese embarked on the full-scale attempt to subjugate China on July 7, 1937.

Continuation of the Internal Struggle

Within the Communist party the power struggle continued. In March the final defeat of the Western Route Army triggered an upsurge in the struggle between Mao and Chang Kuo-t'ao, and the May party conference saw the renewal of conflict between Mao and the Internationalists. When news of the defeat of the Western Route Army arrived at Yenan, Mao and his followers immediately initiated a party-wide propaganda campaign condemning "Chang Kuo-t'ao's erroneous right-opportunist line." The Maoists attempted to follow up the propaganda campaign with a move to oust Chang Kuo-t'ao at the enlarged Politburo conference of April, but failed. The conference turned into a fierce mutual recrimination session but with no result, indicating that Chang's influence within the leadership, if not his actual political-military power, was still quite high. The conference stalemate thus deferred the final act in the struggle between Mao and Chang Kuo-t'ao.[25]

In May (3 to 20), the party convened a conference to reaffirm the pledges made to the Kuomintang in February. Mao's report was one of two principal items on the agenda. The other item was a report by Liu Shao-ch'i which provoked a heated controversy. Mao, who this time had gathered around himself a substantial group of leaders, renewed the struggle against the Internationalist group. The attempt to discredit the Internationalists came in the form of Liu's report on the party's activity during the 1927–1937 decade and was an undisguised attempt to undermine the leadership position of the Internationalists by heaping the blame for past setbacks upon their shoulders.

At Tsunyi, Liu had denounced the Internationalists for their blunders since the Fourth Plenum. Backed by Mao Tse-tung, Liu resumed that attack. The response by the Internationalists, Chang Wen-t'ien, Ch'in Pang-hsien, Ho Kai-feng, Chen Keng, and others, was vitriolic. They countered that Liu's interpretation was a distortion not only of the party's correct leadership, but also of the Comintern's rule, and labeled Liu's views nothing more than Trotskyite-Ch'en Tu-hsiu "cliché." The shouting match which followed forced the Politburo to declare a recess and in a private extraordinary session Liu was severely reprimanded and his report stricken from the record. When the conference reconvened Chang Wen-t'ien delivered a substitute report containing a more positive view of the party's past leaders, which was passed without incident.

After the conference ended, Liu was demoted from secretary of the North China Party Bureau to a minor post in the central organization department. Since he was a member of Mao's group, however, he was shortly promoted director of the central cadres administration, after which his fortunes took a marked turn for the better. Chang Kuo-t'ao played only a minor role in the conference. After making a short comment at the opening of the conference, he walked out and refused to participate.[26]

The lesson which Mao Tse-tung learned from the conference was that the Internationalists could not be defeated by frontal attack. When the opportunity to strike against his internal party opponents again arose, Mao strove to divide his opposition before attempting to conquer. His next opportunity was not long in coming, occurring in the early days of all-out war against Japan.

V

The Road to War,
1937–1941

Soviet relations with the Communist Chinese during the years 1937 to 1941 must be interpreted primarily in the context of the events which led to World War II. Soviet actions and the role played by the Chinese Communists are comprehensible only if seen as the response to an increasingly threatening probability of a two-front war. In an effort to avoid involvement in a major European war, Soviet leaders followed three basic strategic principles.

First, they attempted to prevent the formation of anti-Soviet coalitions. This strategic principle was translated into attempts to prevent German coalitions with other European and Asian powers. The obverse of this policy was to attempt to create pro-Soviet alignments and to establish coalitions which would isolate Germany. The Franco-Soviet, Czech-Soviet, and Polish-Soviet pacts fell into this category. Collective security and popular front efforts were also part of this strategy.

Second, if conflict was unavoidable, it had to be contained or diverted as far from Soviet borders as possible. Unofficial Soviet involvement in the Spanish civil war had this as one of its many purposes. Another purpose was to prevent French capitulation to the forming Axis group. Third, the Soviets attempted to avoid war by direct negotiations and alliances with the aggressor states. From the mid-thirties on, Soviet leaders attempted to reach an understanding with Nazi Germany itself, but were unsuccessful until circumstances in 1939 made possible a temporary rapprochement.

Soviet leaders applied the same three strategic principles in the Far East, where an aggressively expansionistic Japan had already occupied Manchuria and north China and where border incidents between Soviet and Japanese troops were becoming increasingly frequent. The great Soviet fear was the evolution of a Japanese-Chinese coalition, or even truce. An agreement between Japan and China, or even a truce, would present great danger to the Soviet Union's eastern front, for it would free Japan from its entanglement with China to concentrate on its problems with, or designs on, the Soviet Union. It would also free the Nationalists to concentrate fully on their own internal Communist problem. The need for the Soviet Union to prevent a coalition of any sort between China and Japan was therefore absolute. In secret talks during 1936, the Soviets attempted to draw the Nationalists into an agreement, an attempt which showed little progress until the Sian incident of December 1936. Two reasons for the lack of success on the part of the Soviets were that during 1936, talks were in progress between Nanking and Tokyo concerning a settlement of differences. In addition, German advisers and technology were playing an important role in Nanking's armament program.

The Sian incident, however, was the catalyst that determined the structure of international politics in the Far East for the coming conflict. After Sian, the Chinese Nationalists turned away from even a tacit settlement at that time with Japan and moved toward a more favorable position *vis-à-vis* both the Chinese Communists and the Soviet Union. This momentous realignment undoubtedly spurred Japan to act sooner than she had planned. The resultant war hardened the respective positions of the involved powers, and diminished the possibility of a Japan-Soviet war, but did not eliminate it. The Soviet Union, by materially supporting the Nationalist war effort and concluding a mutual nonaggression pact with them, attempted to insure against the possibility of the Nationalists capitulating.

In the pact of August 21, 1937, the Soviets agreed to send monetary, technical, and advisory assistance to enable the Nationalists to prosecute the war against Japan. Most important to the Soviet Union in terms of its first strategic principle—that of preventing the formation of opposing coalitions—was article II of the pact, which stipulated that in the event of an attack on one of the parties by a third power, neither of the signatories would render assistance of any kind to the third power. By this measure, the Soviet Union attempted to insure against a settlement of the Sino-Japanese war on the basis of Chinese aid in an attack on the Soviets.

The pact was also the successful application of the second strategic principle—diverting an unavoidable conflict as far from Soviet borders as possible. Later, in 1941, the Soviets succeeded in applying the third principle as well by concluding a five-year neutrality pact with the Japanese—a pact which flagrantly violated article II of the Soviet-Chinese nonaggression pact of 1937. The Soviet-Japanese pact also served the larger purpose of inserting a wedge between the principal partners of the anti-Comintern pact, Germany and Japan; or, in other terms, it was the application of the corollary to strategic principle number one, the effective disestablishment of an opposing coalition.

United Front Policy in China

The Chinese Communists, despite vicious intraparty strife which sometimes delayed the adoption of the Soviet line, ultimately pursued policies which consistently complemented those of the Soviet Union. Strictly speaking, it was not in the interests of the Chinese Communists to support the Nationalists against Japan. Nationalist success would reduce the Communists' own chances for victory, as some Communists, including Mao Tse-tung, realized. Yet the policies the Communists adopted were those which supported the Soviet Union's international position.

The Nationalist-Communist United Front was formally initiated on the 22nd of August, one day after the signing by the Nationalist Government of the nonaggression treaty with the Soviet Union. On that day the Nationalist military council formally designated Communist party members Chu Teh and P'eng Teh-huai as commanders-in-chief of Communist troops, which were henceforth to be named the Eighth Route Army of the National Revolutionary Forces. This army was to be composed of three divisions totaling 20,000 men and was to operate in the second war zone in northern Shansi under the overall command of Yen Hsi-shan. At the same time, the government of the Communist area surrounding Yenan was renamed the Shen-Kan-Ning Border Area Government. Communist leader Lin Tsu-han (Lin Po-ch'u) was appointed chairman and Chang Kuo-t'ao vice-chairman of this government.

On the 25th of August the Chinese Communists held a conference at Lochuan, northern Shensi, to discuss their role in the united front.[1] While agreeing to the formation of the Eighth Route Army, they had heated differences of opinion over the extent of cooperation with the Nationalists. In every instance Mao Tse-tung took the negative position, arguing against truly unified action. None of Mao's extreme proposals was accepted by the leadership.

As to the organizational form of the Eighth Route Army, Chu Teh and Chou En-lai argued that it should conform to the Nationalist system of military organization, since the Communists had agreed to unity of command and had requested the Nationalists to integrate the forces. Mao and Jen Pi-shih, however, disagreed, calling for the continuance of the existing military organization of the Red Army. The upshot of this disagreement was the first of several compromises arranged within the party by Chang Wen-t'ien. Except for accepting the three division plan set up by the Nationalists, only minor, inconsequential changes in the Communists' own military system of organization would be made. For example, political commissars would be called deputy commanders or directors of political departments as in the Nationalist organization, but the basic system would remain unchanged. The three divisions which were to compose the Eighth Route Army were thus the 115th, commanded by Lin Piao, the 120th, commanded by Ho Lung, and the 129th, commanded by Liu Po-ch'eng.

Chou En-lai and Chu Teh again sided with each other on the question of whether or not Nationalist staff officers should be permitted to accompany Eighth Route Army troops into action. They stated that some Nationalist officers should be accepted, if only to show good faith. Mao and Jen opposed this view and again Chang Wen-t'ien brought forth an acceptable compromise. The Communists would accept a token number of Nationalist staff officers at Yenan for liaison purposes, but would permit none to accompany troops in the field.

On Eighth Route Army strategy in Shansi, Chu Teh urged coordinated operations with Yen Hsi-shan, but Mao argued that the small 20,000-man Communist force would make no appreciable difference in the conflict no matter how well they fought. He advocated, instead, that they disperse their troops behind enemy lines and fight independent, guerrilla battles. In still another compromise, it was decided that initially the Eighth Route Army's troops would act under Nationalist orders. This would make good propaganda. When the Japanese moved against them, they would then disperse and wage independent, guerrilla operations in the enemy's rear and establish bases there.

The final issue discussed at Lochuan was the evaluation of the war and the Communist role in it. On this issue, differences in the party were reflected in the positions of Mao and Chang Kuo-t'ao. Chang, expressing the right wing view, maintained that the war gave the Nationalists prestige, as a result of which they would be able to mobilize the entire country under the Nationalist banner. This, he reasoned, made the possibility of an internal split of the Kuomintang unlikely and, therefore, dictated for the Communists a policy of united action against Japan. Mao dissented from this view, continuing to argue, as he had for some time, that the Nationalists would split under the impact of full-scale war, with the pro-Japanese element surrendering and the anti-Japanese Left joining the Communists. Once the split occurred, the Chinese Communists would assume the leading role in the war, which would result in the defeat of both the Japanese and Chiang Kai-shek. Therefore, Mao argued, no concessions should be made to the Nationalists. Chang Wen-t'ien again negotiated an acceptable compromise. No whole-hearted, long-term cooperation with the Nationalists was envisaged, although the Communists would profess adherence to the policy of the united front.

The essence of the decisions taken at Lochuan was that the Communists would build "good will" during the early stages of the war, and build their own power bases afterward. Publicly, they proclaimed support of the policy of the united front, despite the deep disagreement within the party's leadership ranks. Opposition to the united front centered around Mao Tse-tung, who, although suffering a minor policy setback at Lochuan, succeeded in forcing a split in the Internationalist group, a split reflected in Chang Wen-t'ien's mediating efforts. In the long run, it was the split in the Internationalist group which enabled Mao to capture control of the party.

On September 22, the Communists made another public pledge for a "joint effort" against Japan. Voicing support for the Three Peoples' Principles of Sun Yat-sen, they declared their intention to: abandon armed struggle against the Nationalists, abolish the Soviet government, establish democratic rule, and reorganize and subordinate their armed forces under Nationalist command. The next day Chiang Kai-shek issued a statement proclaiming the triumph of "national consciousness" over "prejudice," and expressing the hope that, "like everybody else," the Communists would rally to the Nationalists in defense of the country. The united front was consummated.

Although Nationalist-Communist cooperation had been formally established, Mao's dissenting voice could still be heard. In an article published on September 29, Mao wrote that the Communists "shared" with their Nationalist "comrades" the responsibility for saving the nation, but that it was absolutely necessary to establish a new government which would carry out systematic and widespread reform of both governmental and military systems.[2] Here Mao publicly disagreed with the Comintern's position, which was that, reform or not, the Kuomintang must be supported. Mao's outspokenness on this critical policy question disturbed Moscow. To insure that an apparently vacillating Chinese Communist Party leadership would strictly adhere to the policy of the united front, Moscow sent back to China a group of tried and true revolutionary leaders.

Stalin, Wang Ming, and Mao Tse-tung

In late October the Soviet Union sent back to China several Chinese Communist Party leaders along with some equipment in order to show its good intentions in connection with the newly adopted policy of Communist-Nationalist cooperation and to facilitate improved communication between Moscow and Yenan.[3] The leaders flown in by Soviet aircraft were Wang Ming (Ch'en Shao-yü), Ch'en Yün, K'ang Sheng, and Tseng Shan. (This move was reminiscent of the critical situation during the summer of 1930, when Moscow sent the Twenty-Eight Bolsheviks to China to bring pressure on Li Li-san to conform to the policy line. Then, too, the principal figure involved was Wang Ming.) The equipment forwarded included a powerful transmitter and a few antiaircraft weapons.

The Chinese Communists were overjoyed by the arrival of Wang Ming and his companions. For most, his arrival aboard a Soviet aircraft meant that the Comintern had not abandoned its Chinese "section." Mao Tse-tung was less enthusiastic in his welcome, but Wang carried instructions from Stalin himself that were, indeed, for Mao Tse-tung a heartening surprise. Stalin, although he thought that Mao's ignorance of Marxism-Leninism and his narrow empiricist problem-solving attitude were "defects," supported his candidacy as a party leader because he had proven his mettle in the revolution. Perhaps with dual purpose, Stalin instructed the Russian-trained party members to "help" Mao ideologically and to build the leadership around him.

Wang Ming also delivered important instructions concerning two other party leaders, Chang Wen-t'ien and Chang Kuo-t'ao. Chang Wen-t'ien was considered by Moscow unsuitable to continue as general secretary of the party because Trotskyites had been discovered in a Moscow party cell of which he had been a leader. Although there was no question of Chang's personal loyalty, his leadership ability was now suspect. Wang's further instruction concerned the internal strife between Mao and Chang Kuo-t'ao. Stalin thought the struggle against Chang "overdone," and instructed the party to correct this errant policy.[4]

While Wang Ming's arrival offered positive benefits for Mao Tse-tung, namely personal recognition from Stalin, it also marked the beginning of a new stage in the struggle between the Mao and Internationalist groups. The instructions Wang carried from Moscow regarding Mao, Chang Kuo-t'ao, and Chang Wen-t'ien constituted the opening move in that contest. By upgrading Chang Kuo-t'ao, Mao's opponent, and downgrading Chang Wen-t'ien, Mao's ally, Stalin hoped to give greater weight in the Politburo to those who wholeheartedly supported his policy of the united front. Since the Tsunyi conference Chang Wen-t'ien, in effect, had shifted from the Internationalist to the Mao group. As general secretary his role was to mediate intraparty policy disputes. In each case, however, his mediation tended to favor Mao's position, as, for instance, at Lochuan. In fact, it had been Chang Wen-t'ien whose "compromise proposal" was the crucial act in Mao's ascension to control of the Revolutionary Military Committee at the Tsunyi conference. His removal from the post of general secretary opened up the possibility that Wang Ming could capture that post.

The reintroduction of Wang Ming into the Chinese political scene caused a polarization of party leadership around Wang and Mao. The lines of struggle were drawn at a Politburo conference which convened from December 9 through 13, 1937. The agenda of the conference included three major items: first, an evaluation of the war; next, the question of reestablishing the party organizations destroyed by the Kuomintang; finally, the problem of reorganizing the central leadership.[5] On each issue Wang Ming leveled a direct challenge to Mao Tse-tung.

In the major policy speech of the plenum regarding the present war situation, Wang struck a positive note. Contradicting Mao's views, stated publicly the previous month,[6] which was a primary reason for Wang's presence in Yenan, Wang stressed that beyond question the Kuomintang was the national government of China and should be supported by all patriotic Chinese. Waging a war of total resistance (not partial resistance as Mao charged), the Nationalist Government was to be strengthened, not reorganized or reformed. Finally, again directly contradicting Mao, he stated that it was not the Chinese Communist Party, but the Kuomintang which was leading the struggle against Japan. The current critical situation, he noted, was no time to engage in a power struggle with the Kuomintang.

Wang Ming's position was accepted by the party leaders in assemblage, even by Mao Tse-tung, for obvious reasons. The task of keeping the Nationalists in the war against Japan was paramount for Soviet leaders and for the survival of the Chinese Communists. Wang noted in his speech that the Japanese government had requested the German ambassador to China, O. P. Trautman, to mediate a peace settlement between Nanking and Tokyo. Even more serious, on December 2, 1937, Chiang had held discussions with his own military leaders, who unanimously advised him to settle the conflict, and on the same day Chiang informed Trautman of his acceptance of Japanese terms as a basis for discussion. (Chiang subsequently procrastinated and the Japanese broke off negotiations after the fall of Nanking on December 13.) But the issue of possible Nationalist capitulation was paramount in the minds of the Chinese Communist leaders at the conference. Nationalist surrender would create an extremely dangerous situation for the Soviet Union in the Far East, not to speak of the position of the Chinese Communists themselves, and had to be prevented at all costs. It was therefore not unusual that all of the Chinese Communist leaders, including Mao, agreed that everything had to be subordinated to resistance to the Japanese by working with the Kuomintang.

On the question of party reconstruction, Wang Ming struck a second blow at Mao, which the latter again had to accept. It was decided that the party should restore the organizations destroyed by the Nationalists during the extermination campaigns. Therefore, the North, Yangtze, and Southeast party bureaus were reestablished, in each case with men of Wang Ming's choosing. Yang Shang-k'un, one of the original Twenty-Eight Bolsheviks, was named head of the North China Bureau. Its location unknown, the North China Bureau coordinated guerrilla activities and base building behind Japanese lines. The number two man, Chu Jui, director of the Organization Department, was later succeeded by Li Hsueh-feng, who was one of Mao's supporters, but at this point the northern bureau was under Wang's control. Wang himself took charge of the Yangtze Bureau, which was located in Wuhan. Ch'in Pang-hsien was named director of the Organization Department. In addition to coordinating guerrilla and other activities in east central China, Wang, through the Yangtze Bureau, controlled the *New China Daily*, which began publication from Wuhan on January 11, 1938. Finally, Hsiang Ying was appointed secretary of the Southeast China Bureau and Tseng Shan director of the Organization Department. Located in Nanchang, the Southeast Bureau directed party activities in southeast China in addition to commanding the New Fourth Army. Yeh T'ing, who had defected from the party in 1927, returned from self-imposed exile in Germany to assume nominal command. Actual command responsibility lay with Hsiang Ying, whose formal post was deputy commander. Although granted permission by the Nationalists to form the New Fourth Army in October 1937, it was not until early 1938 that the Communists could make this force operational. Its main area of activity was in Anhwei province on both sides of the Yangtze River.

The third item on the agenda of the December 1937 Politburo conference was the reorganization of the central leadership, called for in the instructions brought back by Wang Ming the previous October. Following the letter of the instructions, but not the spirit, Mao agreed to the removal of Chang Wen-t'ien from the post of general secretary, but managed to gain party acceptance for the abolition of the post itself! As a result, the party was governed by a collective leadership with a broad division of power between the Mao and Internationalist groups, a power split which was reflected in the composition of the Politburo standing committee. The nine man committee included Mao Tse-tung, Wang Ming, Chu Teh, Chou En-lai, Chang Wen-t'ien, Chang Kuo-t'ao, Ch'in Pang-hsien, Ch'en Yün, and K'ang Sheng. In this grouping Wang commanded at least four votes (his own, and those of Ch'in Pang-hsien, Ch'en Yün, and Chang Kuo-t'ao) and, if either Chou En-lai, Chu Teh, or K'ang Sheng voted with him, a clear majority. Mao, at this time, could count on the regular vote of only Chang Wen-t'ien.

The December Politburo conference accomplished Moscow's principal objective of settling the issue of party acceptance of a united front with the Kuomintang. Henceforth there would be no argument by Chinese Communist leaders, not even Mao, over the basic concept of the united front, although the policy itself was soon to be emptied of all content. Internally, the conference resulted in the division of the party along geographical and organizational lines which established the basis for the factional struggle over the next several years. Wang Ming emerged from the conference with what appeared to be a commanding position. He was in control of the newly established party organizations of north, Yangtze, and southeast China, had his own propaganda organ, the *New China Daily*, and also had command of a military force, the New Fourth Army, which, to be sure, was as yet only a scattered band of guerrillas in the mountains of Anhwei. In the Politburo itself Wang Ming's position was stronger than Mao's. On the whole, Wang and his International group seemed to have the advantage over the Mao group.

Mao, however, retained a strong position of his own. He commanded the Shen-Kan-Ning Border Area Government as well as the Eighth Route Army, both of which gave him a solid organizational basis from which to expand. In other terms, Mao retained control of both the military and state systems in the movement and a powerful voice in the standing committee of the Politburo. Geographically, too, Mao was in position to avoid direct military involvement with Japanese forces and therefore had greater freedom of action. In the Politburo, while not able to count on a majority, Mao still held the all-important post of chairman of the Revolutionary Military Committee. It was also to his advantage that the post of general secretary had been abolished, because that was the only post in the party hierarchy which was more powerful than the chairmanship of the Revolutionary Military Committee. Mao had frustrated Wang Ming's objective of claiming the position of general secretary for himself by maneuvering to abolish the post and introduce instead the system of collective leadership. The principle of collective leadership worked in Mao's favor (and worked even better when Chang Kuo-t'ao defected from the party the following April; the vacancy on the Politburo standing committee was not filled, taking one vote away from the Internationalist group). Also, one of Mao's supporters, Liu Shao-ch'i, was appointed director of the Cadres Department at the conference, a post from which he could control appointments and thus shape party organizations to his own and Mao's advantage. Finally, Mao was designated chairman of the preparatory committee to arrange for the party's Seventh National Congress, which was to convene sometime in 1938. Wang Ming was named a secretary under Mao on this committee.

It would, therefore, be at Mao's discretion when the Seventh Party Congress would be called, not Wang's.

The Two-Front War Danger Mounts

The Japanese proceeded to establish a political position in China to support the new areas which their armies had conquered. In October they set up a Federated Autonomous Government for Inner Mongolia under Princes Yun and Teh; the day following the Kwantung Army's capture of Nanking, they announced the establishment in Peking of a provisional government. On March 28, 1938, the Japanese proclaimed the establishment of the Reformed Government of the Republic of China at Nanking. The Nationalist response to these events was to convene an extraordinary National Congress at Wuchang on March 29 (the government had by this time already moved from Nanking to Hankow). The congress elected Chiang Kai-shek as director-general (*Tsung Ts'ai*) of the Nationalist Party and adopted his program for a war of resistance and national reconstruction. Calling for widespread guerrilla warfare, the congress announced an administrative decentralization of the country for purposes of local defense. The Nationalists adopted the policy of strategic withdrawal, trading space for time during which to prepare for counterattack.

While the congress convened on the 29th of March, Nationalist forces in the field struck a damaging blow to Japanese forces at Taierhchuang in southern Shantung. In a counterattack, the Japanese encircled Nationalist forces at Hsuchou and would have annihilated the Chinese units had not the latter blown a gap in the dyke of the Yellow River near Chengchow, flooding the area and preventing the Japanese from continuing pursuit. The Japanese were forced to alter their course and began to move in pursuit toward Wuhan along the Yangtze River, but progress was slow.

In addition, the eruption of a serious conflict between the Soviet Union and Japan in July caused a temporary suspension of the Japanese drive toward Wuhan and permitted the recovery of Chinese forces. A skirmish between Soviet and Japanese army patrols in the area of Lake Khassan southwest of Vladivostok (where the borders of present-day Manchuria, North Korea, and the Soviet Union join) ballooned into heavy fighting. Each side increased its forces, supporting them with heavy artillery and tanks, and each absorbed heavy casualties. The Japanese withdrew. By August 11, a settlement had been reached, with Soviet forces retaining possession of the high ground taken during the battles.

Regardless of which side initiated the skirmish (and there are widely conflicting accounts),[7] the rapid and massive Japanese buildup was interpreted in Moscow as a probing action to test the Soviet Union's Far Eastern defenses. The signing of the Munich agreement the following month, which allowed Germany to expand into eastern Europe, combined with German-Japanese talks concerning a military alliance, gave ominous significance to the Japanese military action. It brought one step nearer the possibility of the ever-dreaded combined German-Japanese attack on the Soviet Union. The Soviet Union was pinned between two aggressive powers with no effective counterbalance to deter either one except the Nationalist Government of China.

In this extremely precarious situation, the Soviet Union immediately attempted to generate Nationalist resistance against Japan to preclude any possibility of the constantly rumored rapprochement between the Nationalists and the Japanese which would totally isolate the Soviet Union. Moscow granted additional aid to the Nationalists under the nonaggression pact of the previous year and instructed the Chinese Communists to present their most conciliatory attitude toward the Nationalists. This the latter did by immediately convening the party's Sixth Plenum (instead of the Seventh Party Congress scheduled for sometime that fall), which lasted from September 28 through November 6.

The Sixth Plenum was characterized by the party's complete acceptance of the Soviet Union's policy position. Although Mao continued to differentiate his position from that of Wang Ming and the Internationalist group, internal party differences were expressed within the context of complete agreement with the united front. Hsiang Ying, for example, noted in a post-plenum report that the Comintern has issued "instructions on how China could fight for the ultimate victory in the war of resistance. The Sixth Plenum has completely endorsed and accepted these instructions." [8] Mao Tse-tung, until the previous December the one Chinese Communist leader most anxious to dispute the Soviet position, made clear the general party agreement in his opening report to the plenum, entitled "On the New Stage."

Publicly, Mao repudiated the position he himself had advocated only a few short months before; Mao praised the Kuomintang and Generalissimo Chiang profusely. "It is unimaginable," he said, "that the war of resistance could be launched and carried on without the Kuomintang." In fact, said Mao, the Chinese Communist Party "occupies a second place in the political field. . . . Unquestionably . . . the Kuomintang is playing the leading role." It was necessary for the "whole nation to give unanimous support to Generalissimo Chiang Kai-shek, the National Government, KMT–CCP cooperation, and national unity. . . . We must see to it that the prestige of Generalissimo Chiang and the National Government should not be damaged in any way. . . ." [9] In support of these blandishments, the Chinese Communists offered to join the Kuomintang in the open, provide name lists of all party members who would join, form no secret party groups inside the Kuomintang, and support Chiang Kai-shek and Chiang only as "supreme leader."

Continued wartime unity, Mao went on, augured a "bright future" for postwar China, when the Chinese Communists would support the formation of a "three-principles Republic." This future Chinese state form would be a centralized democracy based on universal suffrage and private ownership; "it will not be Soviet or Socialist."

Privately at the plenum Mao disagreed sharply with Wang Ming and the Internationalist group over the content of the united front. Wang urged the party to channel "everything through the united front." Mao disputed this conception, saying, in his concluding speech:

> The Kuomintang . . . has not allowed the united front to assume an organizational form. Comrade Liu Shao-ch'i has rightly said that if "everything through" were simply to mean through Chiang Kai-shek and Yen Hsi-shan, it would mean unilateral submission, and not "through the united front" at all. Behind the enemy lines, the idea of "everything through" is impossible, for there we have to act independently and with the initiative in our own hands while keeping to the agreements which the Kuomintang has approved. . . . We must not split the united front, but neither should we allow ourselves to be bound hand and foot, and hence the slogan of "everything through the united front" should not be put forward. . . . Our policy is one of independence and initiative within the united front, a policy both of unity and independence. [10]

At the Sixth Plenum, while disagreeing with Wang Ming's position, Mao did not attempt to label his position "total capitulationism," as he did later during the *cheng-feng* campaign. Then, Mao would resurrect this slogan and use it as the basis of his drive to eliminate the Internationalist group from leading positions within the party. At this time, since it was vital to keep the Kuomintang fighting against the Japanese, Mao tempered his remarks.

As part of its deliberations, the plenum noted the defection of Chang Kuo-t'ao the previous April and adopted a resolution expelling him from the party. Chang's personally expressed motive for leaving the party was his disagreement with Mao and others who "tried to maintain factional independence in disregard of national interests. That was why I had left Yenan and came to Wuhan." [11] No replacement was elected to fill his now vacant position on the Politburo standing committee, which was reelected at this time. Actually, by his defection Chang assisted Mao Tse-tung, for now the standing committee membership was reduced from nine to eight, which narrowed Wang Ming's voting majority.

While the Chinese Communist Party's Sixth Plenum sat, Japan increased pressure on the Chinese Nationalists to capitulate. Chiang's government, relocated in Chungking, Szech'uan, in southwest China, was almost totally cut off from outside manpower assistance. Supplies, however, were still reaching the Nationalists along three principal routes: overland, through Sinkiang from the Soviet Union and through the "Burma Road" from the west, and by sea through northern Indochina and Canton. After the Munich conference, the Japanese surmised correctly that neither the British nor the French would be willing to react antagonistically to a further Japanese thrust against China. Therefore, in order to squeeze off one of the major supply routes still open to the Nationalists, the Japanese attacked and occupied Canton on October 21. On the 25th, they completed their territorial acquisitions in China with the occupation of the Wuhan cities.

By year's end, the Japanese controlled the Yangtze River valley up to Wuhan, all of Manchuria, all major coastal cities, and had established a position in western Inner Mongolia. Some attempt had been made to establish a political framework for the conquered territories, but with minimal success. The "United Council of China," essentially a liaison committee of representatives from the Peking Provisional Government and the Nanking Reformed Government, had been established on September 22. On December 22, after Japan made public her conditions for peace in China, Wang Ching-wei left Chungking for Japanese occupied territory and announced his intention to collaborate with Japan. However, Wang's "Government of China" did not replace the "Council" until March 30, 1940.

When the Kuomintang did not collapse, but instead expelled Wang Ching-wei from the party on January 1, 1939, it became clear that Japan, by her own action, would be unable to bring about the downfall of Chiang's regime. The "China Problem" would have to be solved by events occurring outside that country, principally by means of the German advance against the colonial powers. The weaker the colonial powers became, the less support the Chinese would have and the less resistance there would be to Japan's "New Order." Therefore, the New Order was tied directly to German success. Apart from the drive to capture Nanchang, Kiangsi, in late March, and the perfunctory attempt to take Shahsi and I Chang (cities to the west of Wuhan on the Yangtze River) in May, the Japanese undertook, with two exceptions in 1944,[12] no further major offensives against the Nationalists. They continued extensive "mopping up" actions against guerrilla forces in north China and in the Yangtze valley, and air attacks against Nationalist-held cities—especially Chungking—but they concentrated on building up their armed forces for a different battle. The war in China settled into a wait-and-see effort.

In May 1939 a major military clash occurred between Japanese and Soviet forces at Nomonhon (where the Outer Mongolian People's Republic forms a salient on the Manchukuoan border). Initially a small skirmish, the fighting expanded during June, July, and August as Soviet-Outer Mongolian and Japanese-Manchukuoan legions clashed. The conflict was apparently precipitated by the move of the Japanese army in Manchuria to shift the Manchukuoan border westward to the Khalka River. The army hoped to establish a protective buffer zone for the projected railroad line which was to be constructed from Hailar to Halunarshan. Fighting raged through the summer as both sides employed aircraft and crack first-line units, but the introduction of flame-throwing tanks tipped the balance in favor of the Soviet Union. Japan admitted to 18,000 casualties; the Russians claimed more.

From the Nazi-Soviet Pact to the Fall of France

The clash at Nomonhon formed the backdrop to the Soviet-Nazi rapprochement; heavy fighting continued up to the day the pact was concluded—August 23, 1939. A final settlement of the Nomonhon incident was not reached until September 16. The Soviet-Nazi pact significantly altered the international situation. Its immediate effect was the German invasion of Poland and the embroilment of Great Britain and France in World War II. The pact gave the Soviet Union a breathing space of twenty-two months during which to build up its forces; from the way Soviet forces performed when attacked in 1941, Stalin undoubtedly expected more time than he got. Perhaps most important for the Soviet Union, the pact drove a wedge between Germany and Japan and made unlikely an alliance between them against the Soviet Union. (Discussions for just such a military alliance were in progress at the moment of the signing of the Soviet-Nazi pact and were dropped.) The pact also provided the first major impetus for a Russo-Japanese rapprochement which culminated in the Neutrality Pact of April 13, 1941, extracting the Soviet Union from involvement in war on two fronts. For the Soviets, the Soviet-Nazi pact was an undeniable stroke of strategic genius.

Sino-Soviet relations must be interpreted in terms of the new situation in the Far East. Since the Soviet Union was now less afraid of a war with Japan, it was, therefore, less important to maintain the united front in China. And, indeed, although the form and rhetoric of a united front continued from August 1939 onward, the Chinese Communists, responding to this shift in Soviet strategic priorities, vigorously began to expand into territories under Nationalist control. The result was continual, increasingly serious, armed clashes between Nationalist and Communist forces. At the same time, and for the same reasons, Chinese Communist leadership moved to redefine its public position concerning the Chinese revolution, its relations with the Nationalists, and the future form of China's government.

The Chinese Nationalists and Communists both clearly recognized the significance of the Soviet-Nazi pact for the united front. Each realized that despite what might be said publicly about it, the united front had ended. Each continued to espouse an all-encompassing united front against Japan, but the Chinese Communists embarked upon a policy of military and political expansion at the expense of the Nationalists, which the Nationalists attempted to block. From the fall of 1939 the Communist Eighth Route Army pushed directly eastward from Yenan (the Shen-Kan-Ning base) in an effort to build strength in north China, primarily in Shansi, Hopeh, and Shantung. Regular troop strength grew to around 150,000 at this time (some estimates were as high as 400,000, but this figure is doubtful). The New Fourth Army, which had been established with Nationalist permission in January 1938, also moved into the Yangtze River valley, primarily into Kiangsu and Anhwei, and quickly established north and south Yangtze commands under Chang Yun-yi and Ch'en Yi, respectively. By mid-1940 the New Fourth Army had expanded from a force of 25,000 (in late 1939) to one of between 75,000 and 100,000. It was made up principally of small units scattered over the provinces of central and southeast China (Kiangsu, Anhwei, Hupeh, Chekiang, Fukien, Hunan, and Kwangtung).

Anticipating the Nationalist reaction and attempting to place responsibility on their shoulders for the ensuing military clashes, euphemistically termed "friction," the Chinese Communists began an "anti-friction" propaganda campaign designed to depict its forces as guiltless and acting only in self-defense. On September 16, in a newspaper interview, Mao reiterated the call, made initially on September 1, to "prepare for the counteroffensive," while admitting only to measures for self-defense. "Our attitude," he said, was that "we will not attack unless we are attacked; if we are attacked, we will certainly counterattack. But our stand is strictly one of self-defense." [13]

The fact is that the period from the fall of 1939 to mid-1940 was one of intense base-building by the Communists in north and central China—an activity which went hand in hand with military expansion into these areas. It was during this period that the north and central China base areas, which had previously been nothing more than administrative expressions, reached the zenith of their development. These bases were the Shansi-Chahar-Hopeh, centered around Fup'ing county; the South Hopeh base, which, after mid-1940, was renamed the Shansi-Hopeh-Shantung-Honan border region; the Shantung base; and the Shansi-Suiyuan border region.

With this political and military expansion, the Chinese Communists were again contending with the Nationalists for leadership of the Chinese revolution. Mao Tse-tung, himself, threw out the challenge in a series of public statements made from early October 1939 through the spring of 1940. In the first, an introduction to the new internal party journal *Communist*, Mao proclaimed the party's intention to "build a bolshevized Chinese Communist Party which is national in scale, has a broad mass character, and is fully consolidated ideologically, politically, and organizationally." [14] In discussing further the party's three "magic weapons"—the united front, armed struggle, and party building—Mao went on to state that "the united front is a united front for carrying on armed struggle. And the party is the heroic warrior wielding the two weapons . . . to storm and shatter the enemy's positions." [15]

In December, the party published the textbook *The Chinese Revolution and the Chinese Communist Party*, written by Mao and "several other comrades." In it, the conception of dual revolution was resurrected in terms of the thesis of the "new democracy," along with a reassertion of the leading role of the party. Mao linked the Kuomintang by implication to the old semi-feudal, semi-colonial society, claiming the leadership of the "new democratic revolution" for the Communist party. "Except for the Communist Party," he said, "no political party (bourgeois or petty-bourgeois) is equal to the task of leading China's revolutions, the democratic and socialist revolutions, to complete fulfillment." [16]

In January 1940, Mao reinforced this position in another publication. Chapter two of *The Chinese Revolution and the Chinese Communist Party* was revised, expanded, and entitled "On New Democracy," and included as the lead article in the inaugural issue of yet another party journal, *Chinese Culture*. While ostensibly proclaiming a "liberal" program for China's future government, "On New Democracy" was a quiet declaration of war on the Nationalists. Compared with orthodox Marxism-Leninism, or even with the party's pronouncements of the Kiangsi era, Mao's statements in "On New Democracy" were, indeed, quite mild: economic and cultural policies would be relaxed; capitalism would even be "encouraged" for a time.

Compared to Mao's statements made at the Sixth Plenum in October 1938, however, "On New Democracy" was an open repudiation of his earlier position. There would be no "bright future" of cooperation between Nationalists and Communists. Gone was the self-effacing stance toward Chiang Kai-shek. The Nationalists were no longer the leaders of the Chinese revolution. The bourgeoisie was "flabby." The future Chinese state form during the period of "new democracy" would be "a dictatorship of all the revolutionary classes over the counterrevolution-aries and traitors," in which the Chinese Communist Party would play the "leading role." [17]

By March 1940, the Chinese Communists had achieved striking

success in building a position in north and central China. This was primarily because the presence of the Japanese hindered an effective Nationalist response to the Communist moves, which were undertaken in occupied territory behind Japanese lines. The process of establishing bases was the tried and true one of "armed propaganda" employed in Kiangsi days. The entry of an armed force into an area would be accompanied by the establishment of party organs and followed by the formation of "governmental agencies," which the Communists termed "democratic regimes." Under this banner party functionaries would carry out recruitment for the army, requisitioning of food and supplies, and the mobilization of manpower for other required services, both political and logistical.

Communist control, of course, was fluid and depended entirely upon the strength of the local Japanese garrison force. In inaccessible villages the Communists operated more openly than in the cities and towns controlled by stronger contingents of Japanese troops. In the latter the Communists engaged in the practice of what they called "double dealing," which was simply another name for collaboration with the Japanese. According to one post-revolutionary Communist account, the border regimes "made deals with the enemy and took advantage of the little lawful protection under enemy rule to conserve the anti-Japanese strength and protect the interests of the people." [18]

The success of the Communist expansion drive resulted in the availability of more administrative positions than there were cadres to fill them. In an effort to stretch the Communist presence in the newly created base areas and border regimes as far as possible, as well as present the appearance of the united front, the party instituted the practice of the three-thirds system. As Mao stated it in an inner-party directive written on March 6, 1940, "in accordance with the united front principle concerning the organs of political power, the allocation of places should be one-third for Communists, one-third for non-Party left progressives, and one-third for the intermediate sections who are neither left nor right." [19] Not to be misunderstood about the nature of the system, Mao went on in the next paragraph of his directive to emphasize that the party "must make sure that the Communists play the leading role in the organs of political power, and therefore the Party members who occupy one-third of the places must be of high calibre. This will be enough to ensure the Party's leadership without a larger representation."

By May, the Communist expansion offensive was in high gear. In still another directive, Mao exhorted: "Freely expand the anti-Japanese forces and resist the onslaughts of the anti-communist die-hards."

> . . . in all cases we can and should expand. The Central Committee has pointed out this policy of expansion to you time and again. To expand means to reach out into all enemy-occupied areas and not to be bound by the Kuomintang's restrictions but to go beyond the limits allowed by the Kuomintang, not to expect official appointments from them or depend on the higher-ups for financial support but instead to expand the armed forces freely and independently, set up base areas unhesitatingly, independently arouse the masses in those areas to action and build up united front organs of political power under the leadership of the Communist Party. . . . We must stress struggle and not unity; to do otherwise would be a gross error.[20]

Mao's "expansion" directive was also his latest move in the internal party struggle, which entered a new phase after the Soviet-Nazi pact. The directive itself was addressed to Hsiang Ying, political commissar and *de facto* leader of the New Fourth Army, instructing him to shift his main forces eastward to the coastal provinces and then north of the Yangtze. Mao's objective was twofold. He sought, on the one hand, to build a strong position in an area which was historically a crucial strategic battlefield, a roughly 150- by 300-mile sector bounded by the coast in the east and by the cities of Hsuchow, Nanking, and Hangchow along its western edge. On the other hand, he sought to bring the New Fourth Army more directly under his control. As part of this latter effort, in January 1940 Mao dispatched 20,000 troops of the Eighth Route Army, as he later put it, to "reinforce" the New Fourth Army's anti-Japanese activities.[21] Hsiang Ying stubbornly resisted executing Mao's directives. Their conflict was part of the larger struggle between Mao and the Internationalists, specifically Wang Ming, who commanded the New Fourth Army and the party's organizations below the Yangtze River.

The problem facing both Mao and Wang at this time of stupendous expansion of the party's forces was how to capture the allegiance of the new cadres. The decision to emphasize struggle over unity gave Mao the advantage over Wang, whose position was based on continued cooperation between the Soviet Union, the Nationalist Government, and the Communist-Kuomintang united front. In far off Chungking, Wang Ming found himself increasingly at a disadvantage as regards affecting events in north China, where the major expansion of forces was taking place. Mao, in Yenan, as chairman of the Revolutionary Military Committee, was gradually emerging as *de facto* chairman of the Politburo standing committee. It was as chairman of the Revolutionary Military Committee that he would consolidate his own position in the military and undercut Wang's control of the New Fourth Army. And it was from this position that Mao would initiate the consolidation of the party, which at this time was termed simply the "bolshevization" of the party.

In directives from Yenan, Mao called on the party to exercise vigilance against informers, traitors, and die-hards within its own ranks. Particularly in the Southeast Bureau, that is, in the one controlled by Wang Ming, all "personnel (from Party secretaries to cooks) must be strictly scrutinized one by one, and no one open to the slightest suspicion should be allowed to remain in any of these leading bodies." [22] The policy of internal scrutiny would shortly become the *cheng-feng* rectification campaign, the opening steps of which were taken at this time. Paralleling this drive was an extensive indoctrination of the party, indicated by the increasing number of party periodicals emanating from Yenan. Some of the more important "central" publications which were started at this time were: *Communist,* begun on October 4, 1939; *Chinese Culture,* in January 1940; and *Chinese Worker,* inaugurated in February 1940.

Wang Ming reacted to the challenge of Mao's expansion drive with moves of his own. In September 1939 Wang convened a conference of the South China Bureau in Chungking, attended by responsible cadres from all Communist organizations in south China. Espousing support for Mao's directive on the consolidation of the party, Wang Ming set up his own "screening" apparatus. [23] Earlier, as part of the united front policy, Wang had established "united front departments" at district, provincial, and regional levels. He now sought to tighten his grip on this organizational apparatus, for it was by means of these departments that Wang sought to capture control of the party in areas under his jurisdiction. The establishment of his own screening apparatus permitted him to install followers and remove opponents.

Wang Ming's united front departments were functionally analogous to Li Li-san's "action" committees of 1930 and suffered the same result, being paper organizations dependent wholly upon the power position of the leader. Wang lost the organizational battle with Mao, but the outcome was not decided until the "New Fourth Army Incident" of January 1941. It was at this time that Wang lost control of his military force, which determined the fate of the Internationalist group. In the meantime, however, another unpredictable turn in the international situation forced the Chinese Communists to revert once again to the tactics of the united front and gave Wang Ming his final opportunity to build an independent position within the party.

Strategic Impact of the Fall of France

German control of the entire West-European continent after the unexpectedly rapid fall of France starkly resurrected the specter, which the Nazi-Soviet pact had been designed to alleviate, if not eliminate, of a two-front war against the Soviet Union. Whatever the information Soviet leaders did or did not glean from their various intelligence sources over the next few months concerning Hitler's plans, their actions indicate that they immediately perceived the danger inherent in the strategic situation.[24] The Soviet objective, now as before the Nazi-Soviet pact, was to prevent a settlement of the Sino-Japanese war. This presumably would keep Japan mired in China and incapable of mounting a full-scale war against the Soviet Union. The Chinese Communists played a predictable role in this effort.

The Chinese Communists, pursuing a policy of unbridled expansion in a direct challenge to the Nationalists, suddenly, on July 7, announced the reversal of that policy and a return to the anti-Japanese pro-Kuomintang united front![25] The abrupt policy reversal, inexplicable in terms of the Chinese Communists' astoundingly successful expansion, was an immediate consequence of the drastic change in the international situation affecting the Soviet Union. It continued only as long as the two-front war danger persisted and was abandoned when the threat of a German-Japanese combination against the Soviet Union evaporated in December 1940. Actually, it was the Chinese Communist leadership which formally stressed unity during this period; military units in the field continued to fight.

Hitler, having made the decision to attack the Soviet Union, proceeded to link Japan into his plans without, however, informing the Japanese of his true intentions. From the end of August onward, German and Japanese authorities negotiated what shortly became the

Tripartite Pact of September 27, 1940. Despite public and official protestations by Germany and Japan that there was no intention to combine against the Soviet Union, Soviet leaders could not afford to ignore the probability that if Germany were to attack the Soviet Union, Japan would do likewise. It was on the basis of this probability—which, as it turned out, did not materialize—that the Soviet Union acted.

The key piece on the diplomatic chessboard was the Nationalist Government. Both Germany and the Soviet Union employed every means at their disposal to persuade the Nationalists to act in their respective interests. From October through November 1940 Germany attempted to mediate a settlement of the Sino-Japanese conflict. The German ambassador in China, O. P. Trautman, informed Chiang Kai-shek that Germany would guarantee the terms of any peace settlement, but, if the Nationalists refused to accept Japanese terms, Germany and Italy would formally recognize Wang Ching-wei's regime as the government of China.

On the other hand, the Soviet Union offered additional trade credits to keep the Nationalists fighting. Its minions, the Chinese Communists, although a negligible factor in determining the outcome of these international maneuvers, nevertheless faithfully supported Soviet policies by initiating an intense propaganda campaign against "capitulationism," taking the field of battle against Japan, and within ten days of the announced policy change of July 7, negotiated a plan, approved by Chiang Kai-shek, for the settlement of all outstanding issues between the Nationalists and Communists.[26] The plan, which was never put into effect, reapportioned spheres of operations, defined political controls in occupied areas, and clearly demarcated the Nationalist and Communist positions in contested areas.

The Chinese Communists took to the field against the Japanese on August 20, launching the so-called 100 regiments campaign. The campaign was not nearly as grand an affair as the name suggests; it was primarily a harassing action. The principal objectives were strategic, to force a continuation of the conflict between China and Japan, and tactical, to decommission Japanese-held railroads and motor roads in north China. In 108 days of battle, lasting through the first week in December, the Chinese Communists suffered heavy casualties proportionate to their numbers.

Concerning the settlement of all outstanding differences, the Chinese

Communists procrastinated, exchanging plans with the Nationalists and dragging out the discussions in the hope that the international situation would resolve itself. Chiang Kai-shek resolved the crisis for the Communists by rejecting the Japanese peace terms for the merger of the Chungking and Nanking regimes. Therefore, on November 13, the Japanese Imperial Conference sanctioned Wang Ching-wei's regime and on November 30 formal instruments of recognition were exchanged in Nanking. These acts were a recognition of Japan's failure to bring the war to an end. The danger of Nationalist "capitulation" had passed. The Chinese Communists, therefore, dropped all further pretense of negotiating a settlement with the Nationalists and resumed their policy of expansion.[27] This step led to the most severe clash between Nationalists and Communists to date, the "New Fourth Army Incident" of January 1941.

Part of the plan for the settlement of all outstanding issues had included the Nationalist demand that the Communists move the New Fourth and Eighteenth Group Armies (the Nationalist designation for the Eighth Route Army) north of the Yellow River into Hopeh and Chahar. On September 19 the Nationalist Government sent a telegram to Yenan ordering the move to be completed by the end of October.[28] The Chinese Communist leadership delayed until November 19 before replying. In the meantime they moved no troops. On December 8 the Nationalist Government sent another telegram, again ordering the troop transfer, but on the following day Chiang Kai-shek extended the deadline for the completion of the troop move. He set December 31 for the completion of the move across the Yangtze and January 30 for completion of the move north of the Yellow River.

Although the Chinese Communist leadership in Yenan agreed (for reasons of its own) to the transfer of the New Fourth Army northward, Hsiang Ying, the political commissar and *de facto* commander, refused to comply.[29] Instead, he began to move his troops southward with the intention of establishing a sphere of operations in south Kiangsu. In doing so, however, his forces encountered local Nationalist forces and fighting erupted on January 4. Hsiang Ying then attempted to retreat with his forces northward across the Yangtze, but was encircled by pursuing Nationalist troops. In over a week of pitched battle, the Nationalists annihilated the entire unit of 10,000 men. The Nationalist military council immediately on January 17 declared the disbandment of the New Fourth Army on the ground of a breach of military discipline. The Chinese Communist Party's Revolutionary Military Committee replied on January 20 and 22, condemning the Nationalist action as part of an extensive "anti-Communist onslaught" perpetrated by the pro-Japanese clique which sought to cooperate with the Japanese against the Communists.[30] There followed an intensive anti-Nationalist propaganda campaign in which the Kuomintang was accused of sabotaging the united front.

The New Fourth Army Incident was a windfall for Mao Tse-tung, but a stunning blow to Wang Ming, resulting in his loss of control over that military force and the party bureau which commanded it. Mao quickly took advantage of the opportunity afforded him by Hsiang Ying's intransigence and defeat; he ignored the Nationalist order to abolish the New Fourth Army and immediately assigned Ch'en Yi as commander and Liu Shao-ch'i as political commissar.[31] By early February, Mao had reorganized the party bureaus south of the Yangtze and established branch number five of the Anti-Japanese Military and Political Academy, also under Ch'en and Liu.[32] He created the Central China Bureau by merging the Central Plain Bureau (commanded by Liu Shao-ch'i) and the Southeast China Bureau (formerly commanded by Hsiang Ying). Liu was designated secretary of the combined bureau, with Ch'en Yi as director of military affairs. Jao Shu-shih was made deputy secretary.

By mid-February 1941, Mao was in the position to take a major step toward eliminating the Internationalist group entirely, his opponents having been seriously weakened by the New Fourth Army Incident. Although commanding the party's united front departments and the newspaper in Chungking, Wang Ming had lost control of two of the three principal bases of his strength: the New Fourth Army, and the party apparatus of southeast China. True, he still commanded an apparent majority in the Politburo standing committee, but the organizational bases of power in the movement—the party, army, and state apparatuses—were firmly in Mao's hands. Finally, the third element of Wang's power position, the departments of the united front, was meaningless since the policy of the united front had been abandoned by the party leadership.

PART II
The American Experience in China, 1941–1949

VI

World War II, the United States and China, 1941–1944

World War II, the ebb and flow of battle, provides the general analytical context for an interpretation of the course of events in China. Equally if not more important is American involvement, which shaped the policies of all of the participants in the conflict. In China, as elsewhere, American policy strongly affected the development and outcome of the war. Therefore, an analysis of Soviet-Chinese Communist relations must be undertaken from the perspective of the evolving wartime situation and the American impact. The war itself after the German attack on the Soviet Union and the Japanese attack on the United States may be divided into three basic periods: the strategic defensive (June 1941—November 1942); the turning point (November 1942—December 1943); the final counteroffensive (1944–1945).[1]

The Strategic Defensive

One of the major problems facing Soviet leaders after the German attack had begun on June 22, 1941 was the logistical one. Sufficient forces existed for immediate defense needs, but the question was: Could they be deployed? Despite the neutrality pact with Japan, Soviet leaders could not afford to divert troops from the Far Eastern front for defense of European Russia. It was simply too risky to assume that Japan would still not attack the Soviet Union, which Hitler was urging the Japanese to do. Besides, having signed the pact, the Japanese immediately shipped additional forces to the China mainland and mounted an intensive campaign in north China to consolidate their position in the plain. The Soviets could not afford to ignore the implications of the Japanese buildup for Far Eastern defenses. They could not be certain whether the campaign signified the establishment of a defensive position, or was merely the prelude to an attack on the Soviet Union. Japanese military activity on the China mainland after the German attack on the Soviet Union temporarily immobilized Soviet forces in the Far East.

As Hitler's forces drove toward Moscow the situation became increasingly critical for the Russians. Uncertain of Japan's true designs, the Soviets called upon the Chinese Communists, as they had the previous fall, to engage the newly reinforced Japanese divisions in combat, thereby permitting Soviet forces to be transferred to the hard pressed Western front. This time, however, the Chinese Communists refused to commit their small force against the formidable Japanese army (for which they have recently come under scathing Soviet criticism).[2] Chinese Communist troops were poorly armed, equipped and trained at this point in time and were no match for the Japanese. To have acceded to the Soviet proposals would have meant certain annihilation.

As the German attack progressed, the Soviet prospect for survival dimmed, especially after the loss of Kiev on September 19. At this juncture, whether because of intelligence supplied by Richard Sorge, head of a Soviet spy ring in Tokyo, concerning the Japanese decision to deploy their forces southward instead of northward against the Soviet Union, or because of the sheer desperation of the situation, or both, the Soviets began a frantic redeployment of Far Eastern divisions to the European front.[3] The reinforcements were sufficient to stem the German advance literally at the gates of Moscow. Of course, after December 7, 1941, when the Japanese were fully engaged by the United States, the Soviet Union would shift even larger numbers of troops away from the Far Eastern front without fear.

United States strategy in the Pacific war during the early months after Pearl Harbor was designed to stop the twin Japanese drives toward Australia and the mid-East. Although overall world strategy was to defeat Hitler first, no major American combat operations were undertaken in Europe until the North African landing in November 1942, almost one year after Pearl Harbor. But American and Allied forces were involved immediately in combat operations against the Japanese in the Philippines, South and Southwest Pacific, South and Southeast Asia. It was Japan which presented the immediate danger and which had to be confronted without delay.

The Japanese offensive during the first few months took them southeastward to the Solomon Islands in a general move to cut off United States lines of communication to Australia and westward to Burma in what threatened to become a drive to open up contact with the Germans in the mid-East. If either or both possibilities—which were not by any means slight—became realities the Allies would be placed at a serious disadvantage. The attack in the South Pacific, if successful, would have denied to the United States a crucial Pacific base—Australia—from which to launch operations against the Japanese. The linkup in the mid-East, in fact even Japanese naval command of the Indian Ocean, would have cut off India, China, and the Soviet Union from the Allies[4] and possibly furnished the Axis powers with a vital petroleum supply.

The American response, given extremely limited resources in the early stages of the war, was to meet both Japanese thrusts, but in different ways. The United States threw the force of its crippled Pacific Fleet into the South Pacific and fought a rearguard action with its garrisons in the Philippines. Early results were mixed. Although Philippine resistance ended in Japanese victory in early May, that same month saw the U.S. Navy repulse a Japanese invasion force attempting to land at Port Moresby in New Guinea in the battle of the Coral Sea. Control of Port Moresby would have given the Japanese a staging area from which to dominate the east coast of Australia and sever communications between Australia and the United States.

The American counterthrust in Burma was of a quite different order, involving an attempt to combine the meager resources of the British in India and the Nationalist Chinese for the defense of Burma. By early 1942, the Japanese had been highly successful in the Indian Ocean, achieving naval superiority in the Bay of Bengal and generating apprehension that a thrust further westward was imminent.[5] Indeed, Japanese and German leaders discussed the possibility of a linkup at Suez, but in mid-May, after taking Burma, the Japanese informed their European allies that their major effort would be at Midway in the central Pacific to reduce an American buildup there.[6] The Japanese therefore declined the opportunity, which would not arise again, to make a strategic connection with German forces.

In the attack on Pearl Harbor the Japanese had crippled the American navy; at Midway, they intended to eliminate it completely. Up to this point in the war, the Japanese fleet had been all-conquering, their only setbacks having been the "standoff" in the Coral Sea and the consequent aborted invasion of Port Moresby. In June 1942, at Midway, the westernmost point of the Hawaiian Island chain, the Japanese fleet suffered a stunning reversal from which it never fully recovered. Although American forces were still inferior to the Japanese in firepower, information obtained as a result of breaking the Japanese secret codes gave the U.S. Navy a decisive edge in battle. Japanese productive capacity was inadequate to replace the loss of four aircraft carriers, their pilots and planes. Thereafter, although the Japanese fleet remained a formidable force, relative naval superiority shifted to the United States because of the higher production rate of war matériel.

Earlier in the year, as Japan moved into Burma, the American countermove was to send a military mission to the Nationalist Government, now located in Chungking, Szech'uan. In command of the mission and the theatre, which was termed the China-Burma-India theatre, or CBI theatre, was General Joseph Stilwell. The mission's principal objective was to keep open ground communications between China and the Allies, but its larger purposes were, first, to keep China in the war and, second, to establish a position from which to thwart a possible Japanese move toward Suez. The Japanese decision not to advance westward eliminated CBI as a major theatre. Thereafter, in terms of prosecuting the war, the only possibility for CBI to become an important command area was in the event of an Allied landing on the China mainland, an eventuality which never materialized. Being a low priority theatre, perhaps the lowest of the war zones, had its impact on the second major American purpose—to keep China in the war—a purpose made doubly difficult by the failure to maintain ground communications between China and the Allies. When the Japanese captured Burma in May 1942, China was cut off from ground contact with the outside world and remained so until early 1945, when the Burma Road was reopened. Some tonnage was flown into Chungking by air over the Himalayas (the famous Hump route), but the bulk of those supplies went to U.S. forces operating in China. President Roosevelt sought to compensate the Nationalist Government with American dollar loans and by treating China as one of the major powers.

Chiang Kai-shek, Mao Tse-tung, and World War II

The Nationalist Government viewed the Soviet-Japanese Neutrality Pact of April 13, 1941 with dismay if not alarm as both signatories vowed to respect the territorial integrity of those areas under their respective control over which China had long claimed suzerainty—Manchukuo and Outer Mongolia. While the Soviet Union immediately reassured the Chinese that there would be no change in Soviet policy toward China as a result, the neutrality pact clearly violated the Soviet-Chinese nonaggression pact of 1937, which stipulated that in the event either party were attacked by a third party the signatories would "neither directly nor indirectly aid the third party or parties through the entire conflict." [7]

The German attack on the Soviet Union changed the picture considerably for Chiang Kai-shek. Soviet involvement in a European war foreclosed the possibility of a Soviet-Japanese settlement at Nationalist expense, meant less Soviet support for the Chinese Communists, and opened the possibility for reasserting Nationalist influence in Sinkiang. The offsetting factor was the abrupt termination of Soviet aid. Nor was it yet clear what the Japanese would do now that the Soviet Union was fully engaged elsewhere. Would Japan seize the opportunity to attack the Soviet Union in combination with Germany, or continue the attempt to bring the China war to a conclusion? Japan's surprise attack on Pearl Harbor resolved this issue while at the same time bolstering Chiang Kai-shek's hopes for victory.

From the point of view of Chiang Kai-shek, the sudden entry of America into the war carried with it the prospect not only of victory over Japan but also of the survival of the Nationalist Government, weakened after four years of conflict. Even though the initial effect of Japanese victories was to leave the Chinese more isolated than ever, it was rightly presumed that the United States would assume the main burden of fighting the Japanese, relieving pressure on the beleaguered Nationalists. Furthermore, the anticipated assistance China would receive from America would serve to strengthen the Nationalist Government. Chiang would presumably be in a position to hold together the diverse groups which composed his government, as well as be able to deal more forcefully with the Chinese Communists, whose fate up to this point had largely been a function of friendly relations with the Soviet Union. However, as it turned out, the United States found itself unable to deliver sufficient material aid during the first two years of the war and, once able, proved unwilling in the face of changing wartime priorities.

The intensive Japanese military operation in north China known as the "three-all campaign" (kill all, burn all, destroy all), begun immediately following the signing of the neutrality pact, gravely worried Soviet leaders and severely crippled the Chinese Communists.[8] Under heavy pressure from superior Japanese forces, the Chinese Communists were forced to withdraw from the plain to the Shansi plateau and the mountainous areas of Shantung. In fact, the period from the spring of 1941 through the summer of 1942 witnessed a great constriction of the area under Communist control, bases and border governments in the north China plain becoming once again, as they were before 1939, mere skeletal organizations. Not until after August 1942, when the Japanese shifted forces out of China to meet the American buildup in the South Pacific at Guadalcanal, did the pressure ease on the Chinese Communists, although they did not immediately perceive the change.

It was under the demoralizing impact of Japanese power in north China that Mao Tse-tung resumed his struggle with the Internationalists. Forced to decentralize Communist forces in the face of Japanese power, Mao used this development to advantage in the internal struggle with his opponents. Reducing operations against the Japanese in scope and intensity (10 percent against the Japanese, 20 percent to protection of the bases, and 70 percent to expansion of political influence), Mao continued to build the apparatus with which he aimed to purge his internal opposition. From mid-April onward, he laid the groundwork, initiating two broadly based "investigation" campaigns, one by the party and one of the party.[9] These campaigns had only just begun when international developments took another dramatic turn.

The German attack on the Soviet Union forced Mao to delay temporarily the execution of his plans as the Soviet Union, in dire straits, called upon the Chinese Communist Party to send its forces into action against the Japanese in north China. Mao refused to comply with the Soviet proposal, recognizing that an attempt to combat the well-armed Japanese would be suicidal. Mao took a risk, a small one, in refusing to honor the Soviet request, knowing that in the short run his opponents were too scattered to capitalize on it. His decision, however, made it all the more necessary to eliminate those in the party who could be expected to attempt to turn this choice against him if given the opportunity. Other factors, too, dictated a policy of momentary caution. Since the New Fourth Army Incident of the previous January, Mao had been moving to gain control of his opponent's organizations. The appointment of his own men to command the New Fourth Army and the reorganization and centralization of the party bureaus in China south of the Yangtze River, also manned by his appointees, had generated considerable conflict within party ranks. In fact, the changes had generated a potentially explosive situation as party members in these organizations were refusing to comply with the center's, that is, Mao's, directives.

In attempts to bring the internal party situation under control, Mao issued a barrage of directives beginning in late June against those who were undermining party "unity." [10] In the June directive prohibiting unprincipled controversies it was stated that some people were substituting "personal stands for the correct Party stand" and refusing to act through "regular organizational channels." The July 1 Politburo decision placed even stronger emphasis on the need for party loyalty. Indeed, it constituted a warning to those who defied the party central. "Certain tendencies," it was noted,

> if left unchecked . . . may give rise to factional groups and factional activities in open defiance of the party. . . . Besides, the individuals harboring these tendencies, if left uncorrected, will also destroy themselves.

Liu Shao-ch'i, in a lengthy speech on July 2, reiterated these themes, condemning splittist organizational activities, the emergence of petty-bourgeois individualism versus proletarian collectivism, and "liberal" political behavior, which was defined as refusal to obey the central's directives. Finally, the August 1 party decision directed the entire party to begin the collection of materials and the creation of investigation committees principally concerning the enemy, but also relating their efforts to the July 1 directive, that is, to the question of party loyalty. In essence, Mao had issued a set of rules for ideal party behavior and at the same time, under the pretext of investigating the enemy, established the rudimentary organizational basis for the internal party purge which followed.

Mao Gains Command of the CCP

If the German attack on the Soviet Union caused Mao to hesitate with his plans, then Japan's attack on the United States spurred him to act. Mao, just as Chiang Kai-shek, knew that it would be American arms which would defeat Japan and that he could concentrate on his principal problems of securing control of the party and building the Communist position *vis-à-vis* the Kuomintang. First came the internal problem. As Chinese Communist forces were pressed onto the defense by the Japanese, the central leaders had begun to recall high-level cadres to Yenan, ostensibly to prepare for the long-delayed Seventh Party Congress. Mao, recall, had been named chairman in December 1937 of the preparatory committee for the Seventh Party Congress and he appeared to be exercising his prerogative at this time. Instead of convening the congress, when some one thousand "delegates" had assembled in Yenan Mao initiated the *"cheng-feng"* rectification campaign. Whether Mao had used the congress as a ruse to bring cadres to Yenan, or whether he actually intended to convene it and unknown circumstances forced a sudden change, is moot. He had assembled a large number of high-ranking personnel in his own power base and proceeded to launch a far-reaching campaign which resulted in the removal of his major opponents and their supporters from the top positions in the party. The "party rectification" or purge continued for over three years, resulting in the virtually complete reorganization of the CCP and its capture by Mao Tse-tung and his faction.

First, Mao reorganized the Central Party School at Yenan, assuming the chairmanship. Then, on February 1, in a major speech to the school's assembled cadres, who were also the "delegates" for the projected congress, Mao announced the "rectification of three styles" from which derives the term *cheng-feng*.[11] There was, Mao declared, "something incorrect in the approach in our study, in the style in our party work, and in the tendency in our literary work."[12] In this way he unveiled the major themes of the party purge. Rectification of study meant establishment of Mao's "thought" alongside that of Marxism-Leninism within the party; rectification of party work meant the centralization of the party under Mao's control; and rectification of literary work meant subordination of literary efforts to the party's political objectives,[13] primarily the revision of party history to legitimize Mao's rise to power.

Broadly speaking, the *cheng-feng* campaign passed through four stages. The first was a two-month "rectification" of the high-ranking party cadres assembled in Yenan. A second stage, broader in scope, revolved around an ideological remolding effort of the party organization in the

Shen-Kan-Ning border area. It consisted of an initial reading period from late April through late May, intensive study and discussion through the summer, followed by a period of review and examination in September. The third stage, beginning in September, marked a significant shift in the campaign, as Mao Tse-tung undertook to restructure the party's entire organizational base. The fourth stage began in the spring of 1944. Mao's speech "Our Study and the Current Situation" signaled the end of the party purge and the beginning of the imposition of Mao's interpretation of the party's history to sanction his own ascendancy.[14] It was not completed until the Seventh Congress of the party convened in April 1945.

During February and March the *cheng-feng* campaign was conducted solely among the "delegates" to the Central Party School in Yenan. The school became the focal point of the movement over the next three years as cadres were called back from the field to participate in rectification. On April 3 the Central Committee passed a resolution to extend the campaign to the entire party, which in practice meant initially the Shen-Kan-Ning border region.[15] The guerrilla base areas where Japanese pressure was greatest were less directly affected by the rectification movement during its early stages. The organizational means by which the campaign was carried out was the "study," or "checkup," committee. Formed in all party organizations, it was Mao's instrument for purging and remolding the party.

If during the period February-September 1942 Mao emphasized ideological remolding, from September onward through the spring of 1945 he carried through the restructuring of the entire party from top to bottom, unit by unit. The Central Politburo's September 1 "decision on centralized leadership and readjustment of relations among party organs in the anti-Japanese base areas" intertwined the reorganization of the party with the *cheng-feng* campaign.[16] To understand fully the magnitude of the change which followed, recall that since 1928 the Chinese Communist Party had generally succeeded in establishing separate party-state-military structures in the areas under its control. Disrupted during the Long March, when they were restored afterward Wang Ming and his supporters had gained a strong position in them. Now, after seven months of "rectification," Mao sought to disestablish the institutional structure and reconstruct it in his own way with men of his own choosing. The September 1 decision was thus a crucial act in this plan.

The decision's principal thrust concerned the reorganization of the party at the local and regional levels. The public slogan for this drive, announced a week later on September 7, was "picked troops and simplified administration." [17] At the local level and in the guerrilla areas the party center ordered the abolition of all party, state, and military organizations on the ground of "disharmonious relations." In their stead, a unitary, all encompassing "party committee," much like that of the party front committee of Ching Kang Shan days, would be formed to serve all of the functions of the former tri-institutional apparatus. The fact that they were to be party committees was not to imply that only party cadres would compose them; selected cadres from both military and government organs as well as party organs were specifically included.

The reorganization, of course, meant that all who controlled the former organizations would no longer hold positions in the party unless they were appointed to the new party committees. No cadre could assume a leading position in the new apparatus unless and until he had undergone "ideological re-education" and "three-style rectification." In other words, only cadres acceptable to Mao Tse-Tung would be appointed to staff the new apparatus. The Central Committee reserved to itself the prerogative of appointing cadres to the party's regional bureaus and their branches. At this level, not even the formality of rectification was observed. The centralization process, which is what the reorganization amounted to, enabled Mao to stack the party committees and the higher party regional bureau posts with his own supporters, not the least of whom were military cadres. As chairman of the Revolutionary Military Committee, Mao had long since built a strong position in the Red Army, especially in the Eighth Route Army and since January 1941 in the New Fourth Army as well.

The major result of the *cheng-feng* campaign was Mao's capture of the Communist Party leadership and the displacement of the Internationalist group from positions of real power in the party. The Internationalists remained in the party—even retaining seemingly high posts in some cases—but without effective power. Wang Ming, for instance, the leader of that group, continued as a member of the Central Committee, but was excluded from the Politburo and appointed to the principalship of a girls' school in Yenan[18] to indicate his actual removal from a position of influence in the party. Mao's essential strategy for capturing power was to destroy the party's institutional components and then to construct a new apparatus staffed with his own supporters. The *cheng-feng* campaign was the means to that end.

Mao did not achieve this tremendous victory simply by the force of his personality, but rather by building a winning coalition of forces within the party. Indeed, it was principally by virtue of a mutually beneficial alliance with Kao Kang, party secretary of the Shen-Kan-Ning border region, that Mao achieved his conquest of the party and defeated the Internationalist group. Kao, as chief of the Northwest Party Bureau, gave Mao and his supporters access to the Shen-Kan-Ning border region and the cooperation necessary to carry through the purge of the Internationalists. In return for supporting Mao, Kao was promoted to a position of importance in the party hierarchy, indeed, to a position of greater power than Wang Ming. In the summer of 1943, the Central Committee passed the directive "Summation of the Experience of the Northwest Bureau's High-Ranking Conference." [19] The report extolled Kao Kang for pursuing "a correct line," condemning Wang Ming as a "sectarian." Later, at the Seventh Party Congress in April 1945, Kao was promoted to the party Politburo while Wang Ming was formally dropped from that body, although retaining a position in the Central Committee.

But this gets us somewhat ahead of the story. Overshadowing the power struggle within the Chinese Communist Party, but directly affecting the fortunes of the Chinese Communist movement, was the war itself and the policies which were formulated by the leaders of the Allied coalition to bring it to an end. It is to this which we must now turn.

World War II, the Turning Point

After a year of defensive operations the Allied coalition took the initiative in late 1942 with the North Africa landings in the west and Guadalcanal in the Pacific. More important, the production-shipping crisis which had persisted throughout the first year had been resolved. America began to produce war matériel at a rate which exceeded the combined efforts of both Germany and Japan.[20] Beginning in January 1943 at the Casablanca conference and culminating at Tehran in December, Allied leaders undertook to plan the counteroffensives against the Axis powers. Implicit in the operational plans which took shape over the course of the year were strategic choices concerning the balance of forces that would be present at war's end. Indeed, in the conferences of this year, particularly the Cairo-Tehran conferences of November-December, agreements were made regarding the strategic disposition of Allied power which set the broad conditions for the course of the postwar conflict in China and the fate of the Chinese Communist movement.

Early in the war Allied planners had envisaged five possible avenues of attack against Japan: the northern Pacific route from the Aleutians; the Central Pacific route across the many island groupings; the South Pacific route along the Solomon Islands-New Guinea-Philippines axis; the Southeast Asian route, India-Malaya-South China; and the Burma-South China route. It had been assumed from the start that a foothold on the China mainland itself would be a necessary prerequisite to waging the final offensive against Japan. China would provide the bases from which bombing of the Japanese main islands could be carried out and the manpower with which to defeat the Japanese armies on the continent. Planned access to the China mainland was by all of the routes noted above, except the northern Pacific route. Over the course of 1943 three factors—the ebb and flow of battle, improvements in military capability, and strategic alignments within the Allied coalition—shaped the choice of route along which to press the final counteroffensive.

The tide of battle shifted dramatically against the Axis forces from mid-1943. In Europe, Germany's desperate gamble to knock the Soviet Union out of the war failed at Kursk-Orel (July 5–12), and Soviet forces promptly developed a sustained counteroffensive on the eastern front. During the same week Allied forces swept across the Mediterranean from North Africa into Sicily, precipitating the collapse of Italy, which surrendered in September. Although it would be another year before the massive cross-Channel attacks would begin, the Allies had clearly assumed the strategic initiative. The same was true in the Pacific. July saw the opening of major operations in the South and central Pacific. In a two-prong, mutually reinforcing series of operations, American forces moved along the Solomon Island-New Guinea chain. A second major offensive drive opened in the Marshall and Gilbert Islands in the central Pacific. The success of the Pacific operations, particularly those in the central Pacific, was an important factor affecting the choice of further operations against Japan and, combined with advances in war-making capacity and international agreements made by Allied leaders, the role of China in the war.

In September 1943, the Japanese revised their overall war strategy trading space for time to prepare a counterstroke. They moved to retract their forces to an inner defense zone bounded by Burma, the East Indies, the western tip of New Guinea, the Marianas and the Carolines, the Bonin and Kurile islands, and the China mainland. Within this zone, they sought to secure interior lines of communication and transportation, and with the time gained put all available resources into the production of air power and, to a lesser extent, antisubmarine craft. They hoped thereby to gain an offsetting air capability and to reduce heretofore staggering shipping losses. Japanese shipping losses during the first two years totaled almost four billion tons and they had lost air superiority. Japan's leaders expected the Allies to advance along two axes, the Solomon Islands-New Guinea line toward the Philippines and through Burma onto the China mainland, before commencing an attack on the main islands. The retraction to the inner zone was designed in part to meet these anticipated offensives. They seem to have considered that U.S. naval operations in the central Pacific posed no immediate threat—a consideration which led them to embark upon a costly gamble against advancing American forces.

In November, hoping to stem the American advance toward Bougainville in New Guinea, the Japanese high command took a calculated risk that no rapid move would be made in the central Pacific. Plagued by a shortage of aircraft, they transferred carrier-based aircraft to the island airfields in the battle zone, massing the bulk of then available aircraft (200 already in the area plus 173 from the carriers) on the ground. It was a disastrous move. Prior to the Bougainville operation, American forces destroyed the enemy's airfields and his massed planes. The consequences were nothing short of catastrophic for the Japanese. Stripping the planes from the carriers made them useless and no match for the U.S. Fleet, which, at that moment, was heavily involved in the growing operations of the central Pacific. Not only did the Japanese suffer a major defeat in New Guinea, the loss weakened the Japanese navy's ability to respond to the growing danger in the central Pacific. Matériel losses were virtually irreplaceable at the time when the American production rate of war material had become unmatchable under the best of conditions. Thus, by the end of 1943 the Japanese were on the defensive and reeling, but by no means defeated.

The American strategy also became clearer. There would be no further frontal assaults on heavily fortified enemy positions. Instead, strong positions would be isolated and by-passed while a chain of stepping-stone positions was constructed. The strategy was popularly conceptualized as island-hopping and the most fruitful area in which to island-hop was the vast central Pacific, which the Japanese were progressively incapable of defending. In this strategy the decisive combat element became the navy's carrier strike force. It may well have been the existence of a strong fleet which ultimately determined the final strategy of conquest.

Less visible but equally dramatic in impact, American military capability reached almost overwhelming proportions during 1943. In terms of both rate of production and technological innovation America's efforts far outstripped those of its opponents. Two examples—ships and planes—will suffice to illustrate the point. Although the Japanese throughout the war sunk per year roughly the same amount of tonnage, by 1943 U.S. ship-building had reached full capacity and America was able to replace nearly twice the tonnage sunk by the Japanese. In addition, the U.S. Navy had developed the concept of the self-sustaining carrier strike force, which gave virtually unlimited range and mobility to naval and air power. The carrier force consisted of groups of fast carriers accompanied by their own supply ships, tenders, oilers, hospital facilities, and amphibious craft for assault operations.

In terms of aircraft production, by mid-1943 American factories were producing some 10,000 planes a month, better than three times the combined total of the Germans and Japanese at that point in time. Moreover, American aircraft designers had developed what was termed the very long range bomber, or VLR. The best of these, the B-29, had an effective mission range of fifteen hundred miles, extending the distance from which bombing missions could be carried out against the Japanese mainland and expanding the number of possible bases from which to undertake raids. In terms of military successes and capability, then, the United States was reaching a level of high achievement when the critical conferences of Cairo and Tehran convened during November-December 1943.

Cairo-Tehran-Cairo

The three conferences of Cairo (I and II) and Tehran constituted a genuine watershed in World War II. The decisions reached at the
conferences shaped the broad strategic parameters of the final phase of
the struggle against the Axis powers and set the stage for the postwar
conflict. During the conferences, President Roosevelt made agreements
with each of the conference participants. The agreements, however, were
mutually exclusive regarding American commitments to China and, as
events transpired, ultimately worked to the disadvantage of the weakest
of the participants, Chiang Kai-shek.

At the first Cairo conference (November 22–26) Roosevelt and Chiang
Kai-shek made four important agreements apart from the formal Cairo
declaration promising the restoration to China of Manchuria, Formosa,
and the Pescadores after the war.[21] These included three regarding the
prosecution of the war and one on the postwar relationship of the United
States and China. On the former, Roosevelt committed himself to
supporting a major Allied combined land, sea, and air offensive in North
and South Burma in the spring of 1944 to break the blockade of China,
and the arming and training of ninety Nationalist divisions. Chiang
Kai-shek, on his part, would settle the Communist issue by bringing
them into his government. On the latter postwar issue, Roosevelt agreed
to support China against "foreign aggression," that is, the Soviet Union,
after the war by jointly occupying with China to the exclusion of all
other powers the Port Arthur-Dairen naval complex in Manchuria.[22] The
President's commitment portended the introduction of American combat forces on the mainland as well as the buildup of Chinese forces in
conjunction with the general concept of developing a platform from
which to launch the final offensive against Japan. Explicit here was an
American military presence on the mainland when the war ended.

At Tehran (November 27–December 2) President Roosevelt partially,
but in a critical manner, nullified his agreements with Chiang Kai-shek.
At the first plenary session on the 28th, there appeared to be no change
in the plans made regarding China at Cairo. Roosevelt informed Stalin
of those plans, noting that

> our one great objective was to keep China in the war, and for this purpose an
> expedition was in preparation to attack through North Burma and from

Yunnan province. . . . In addition, amphibious operations were planned south of Burma to attack the important Japanese bases and lines of communications in the vicinity of Bangkok. . . . The aims of these operations [were] . . . (1) to open the road to China and supply that country in order to keep it in the war and (2) by opening the road to China and through increased use of transport planes to put ourselves in position to bomb Japan proper.[23]

Stalin's reply to the President, in fact, his first formally recorded substantive remark, was to reiterate the confidential pledge made to Secretary of State Hull the previous October at the Moscow conference of foreign ministers that the Soviet Union intended to enter the war against Japan once Germany was finally defeated.

Two days later, on November 30, Roosevelt contravened his agreement with Chiang concerning American postwar assistance against the Soviet Union in Manchuria. In a general discussion of warm water ports for the Soviet Union as a part of the overall postwar settlement, Stalin noted that "there was no port in the Far East that was not closed off, since Vladivostok was only partly ice-free. . . ." Roosevelt replied that "he thought the idea of a free port might be applied to the Far East . . . and mentioned Dairen as a possibility." Stalin answered that "he did not think that the Chinese would like such a scheme," to which Roosevelt rejoined that "he thought they would like the idea of a free port under international guaranty." Stalin concluded with the comment "that would not be bad. . . ."[24] The exchange indicated that the President had moved from the position of joining with China to keep the Soviet Union out of Manchuria to one of guaranteeing a Soviet presence, which was what was meant by the term "international guaranty."

The Tehran discussions not only affected the postwar alignment of forces, but, more importantly, directly affected Allied wartime strategy. After the conference, Roosevelt and Churchill returned to Cairo, where the British leader argued strenuously and successfully against the large-scale Burma campaign on the ground that since the Soviet Union had agreed to enter the Pacific war the entire rationale for a China base was lost. Soviet participation in the north, Churchill held, combined with the strong U.S. thrust across the central Pacific, would provide far better bases from which to prosecute the war against Japan than would any position established as a result of the Burma operation.

Churchill adamantly refused to commit British resources to the Burma operation. He suggested instead that Chiang be given the option of a minor operation in the spring or of waiting until the fall for a major offensive. Churchill's motives are obscure, but he apparently sought to scuttle the Burma plan in order to divert the amphibious landing craft earmarked for that operation to the Mediterranean. A possible longer range motive might have been the British desire to reorient America's Pacific strategy in a Southeast Asian direction, which would facilitate the reestablishment of Britain's prewar position in Asia. As planned, the Burma operation threatened to bypass all of Southeast Asia and Churchill may have opposed it on these unstated grounds.

Whatever Churchill's motives, which are not germane to the argument, the result was that President Roosevelt agreed to the cancellation of the amphibious phase of the Burma offensive (operation Buccaneer) and the transfer of the landing craft for the spring of 1944, thereby dramatically altering the strategic disposition of forces that would be present on the mainland for the final phase of the Pacific war. Instead of the presence of a sizable American ground force in China (the Cairo I decision), or the presence of both American and Russian forces (the Tehran decision), the major result of Cairo II was that only the Soviet Union would have a strong military force on the mainland of China for the final phase of the war against Japan.[25] Roosevelt's agreement with Chiang Kai-shek had been reduced to two elements: the promise to arm and train ninety Nationalist divisions and Chiang's "contingent" promise to settle the Communist problem. As China became less important as a military factor in the war the American position on the ninety divisions commitment became increasingly vague. Ultimately, the United States would arm and train parts of thirty-nine divisions by the time the war ended.[26]

President Roosevelt had failed to uphold any of the three commitments he made to Chiang Kai-shek at Cairo. He canceled the Burma operation for the spring of 1944, went back on his promise to support China against the Soviet Union after the war, and failed to make good his pledge to arm and train ninety Nationalist divisions. Despite reneging on his part of the bargain, however, the President persistently pressed Chiang personally and through his emissaries to reach a settlement with the Chinese Communists.

The Final Counteroffensive and America's "China Policy"

The agreements of Cairo-Tehran give only a glimpse of the larger pattern of relationships President Roosevelt sought to build in hopes of insuring a stable postwar world. To develop in detail the President's foreign policy would be far too broad a subject for this book, but it is necessary to adumbrate it in order to proceed with the analysis of the struggle for power in China. The essence of Roosevelt's plan was the establishment of a Soviet-American axis around which a stable, harmonious world could be built. The President believed that if the Soviet Union were provided with a secure international position with all legitimate claims fulfilled, its leaders would no longer incline toward an aggressive, expansionistic policy, but would cooperate with the United States in maintaining the peace.[27]

The Soviet Union's claims and requirements, discussed to one degree or another at Tehran (and later), constituted the removal of surrounding threats to Soviet power, particularly Germany and Japan, the establishment of "friendly" governments around her periphery, and access to warm water ports. Friendly governments, of course, meant coalition governments composed of Communist and non-Communist representatives. That the creation of coalition governments was the Soviet objective in Eastern Europe seems reasonably beyond dispute. That President Roosevelt attempted to promote the establishment of a coalition government in China has been obscured by the course of events both during and after the war—events which culminated in the victory of the Chinese Communists, the creation of an antagonistic relationship between the Chinese People's Republic and the United States, and the resultant furor inside the United States itself over the issue of "who lost China."

President Roosevelt's policy was to seek the creation of a coalition government in China—one in which the Nationalists would occupy the leading role—in the context of an overall settlement with the Soviet Union. Following the Cairo-Tehran conferences, Roosevelt sought by promise and threat to mount sufficient pressure on Chiang Kai-shek (evidently anticipating that the Soviet Union would do likewise with the Chinese Communists) to induce a willingness to form a coalition government. Chiang Kai-shek would only enter into a coalition if he could be certain of being the stronger partner and at Cairo the President had assured him of American support. The point is that Chiang's willingness to reach a settlement with the Communists was contingent upon the material demonstration of American assistance.

The Allied conferences of 1943 had produced a series of decisions which in their totality indicated that a major effort would soon be made by the Allies in Burma to break the blockade of China. In fact, an entirely new theatre of operations, the Southeast Asian Command, had been created amid much publicity and, combined with intense Allied activity in the area, suggested strongly that an offensive would shortly be forthcoming. The Japanese responded to these indicators by shifting reinforcements into Burma. Whether planned or not, Allied activity in Burma served to divert Japanese resources from the main point of attack in the Central Pacific. In any case, the Japanese moves were also consistent with the earlier decision taken in September to consolidate an inner defense zone whose main strong points would be Burma and the Philippines-Formosa-China coast triangle.

The large-scale Allied Burma offensive, of course, in the meantime had been canceled. The Japanese, however, had begun an offensive directed at Imphal, India, which forced reductions in Hump tonnage to China and threatened the Assam pipeline as well. Despite his cancellations of the Burma campaign, President Roosevelt prodded Chiang Kai-shek to commit his Yunnan forces, which the U.S. had been equipping, into Burma to meet the Japanese thrust. Chiang refused to commit his forces in Burma without an accompanying major Allied offensive, warning at the same time that the Japanese could be expected to mount a large-scale operation in east China to secure their own lines of communications.[28]

Twice Chiang replied to the President's entreaties by pointedly referring to the Cairo agreement, saying "you doubtless recall that at Cairo I . . . emphasized the fact that I am ready to send the Yunnan troops to Burma at any moment that large-scale amphibious landing operations can be effected at strategic points. . . ." [29] Again in March he replied in the same vein. "At Cairo I told you that as soon as the British began large scale amphibious operations along the Burma coast, our main forces would launch a vigorous attack on Burma with all their might." [30] Finally, in early April, the President removed these grounds from Chiang, saying that the Yunnan forces "should not be held back on the grounds that an amphibious operation against the South Burma coast is necessary prior to their advance. Present developments negate such a requirement. . . . I do hope you can act." [31]

Chiang Kai-shek did not himself reply to the President's message, but his chief of staff, Ho Ying-ch'in, on April 14, gave formal approval for the commitment of Chinese forces into Burma. It was an unfortunate choice for Chiang to have made, although he had been pressured tremendously by the President. Within days it became clear that, just as Chiang had predicted earlier, Japanese troop movements in central China were the beginning of a major offensive, the first such offensive, operation ICHIGO, they had attempted in China since American entry into the war. Moreover, Chiang's best forces were now engaged in Burma with no possibility of extricating them from that conflict for use in east China.

By the end of April 1944 the situation appeared to be critical. Chiang's best troops were committed in Burma while the Japanese were striking at vital points in China. Their offensive threatened the B-29 airfields at Kweilin and at Liuchou in Kwangsi province. If sufficient logistical support could be mustered, there seemed little that could stand in the way of a drive directly to Chungking which might have knocked the Nationalists out of the war. At least this was the estimate of American intelligence. (Actually, this intelligence was erroneous. The Japanese never intended to knock the Chinese out of the war with the ICHIGO campaign. Their main effort was to capture the airbases and secure a firm defensive position from which to meet the anticipated thrust from the central Pacific.)[32]

Nationalists and Communists Negotiate

The developing military crisis in China was the background for further attempts to settle differences between Nationalists and Communists. Earlier in the year, on January 16, 1944, Mao Tse-tung had suggested that talks resume. Little progress had been made in settling the problems facing the two parties since the New Fourth Army Incident of January 1941, although Chiang had noted at the Kuomintang's Eleventh Plenum of the Central Executive Committee in September 1943 that "the Chinese Communist problem is purely a political problem and should be solved by political means." [33] Both parties having indicated a readiness to discuss their differences, representatives of each met in early May

(4–11) at Sian, resuming talks which would continue—sometimes fitfully—throughout the course of the war. During the Sian sessions the Chinese Communists stated their position, which embodied three fundamental points. They demanded "legal status" for their party under Chiang Kai-shek's "Program of Armed Resistance and National Reconstruction." In return, they would be willing to reorganize their troops into four armies of twelve divisions and redesignate the Shen-Kan-Ning Border Government as an administrative area under jurisdiction of the National Government.[34]

The Nationalist Government stated its own position approximately one month later, on June 5. The Nationalists were in accord with the Communist proposal to redesignate the Shen-Kan-Ning Border Government into an administrative area, but, while agreeing to the reorganization of Communist troops into four armies, they would only sanction ten divisions instead of twelve as the Communists requested. The major difference appeared over the issue of the Chinese Communist Party itself. Avoiding the term "legal status," the Nationalist position paper noted that "Party affairs for the duration of the war should be conducted in accordance with the 'Program of Armed Resistance and National Reconstruction,' while after the conclusion of the war . . . a People's Congress should be convened to adopt a constitution and enforce constitutional government." [35] The Nationalists were unwilling to grant legal status to the Communists, instead deferring that possibility until after the war and the establishment of a constitutional government. As a concession, however, they offered to release Communist prisoners.

At the meeting where the Nationalists presented their position, the Communist representative, Lin Tsu-han, handed the Nationalist representative, Wang Shih-chieh, an additional list of demands, dated June 4, which indicated a hardening of the Communist position. The Communists now requested that the Nationalist Government "adopt democracy" and "recognize the legal status of the Chinese Communist Party," permit the reorganization of Communist forces into five armies of sixteen divisions, recognize the Shen-Kan-Ning Border Government as a legally constituted government under Communist control, lift the military blockade of Communist areas, allocate military supplies to the Communist forces, and permit Communist political activity in Nationalist areas (in return for which the Communists would be prepared to allow the Nationalists the same privilege in the Shen-Kan-Ning area).[36]

To complicate matters further, on June 6 the Communists replied to the Nationalist proposal of June 5, stating that the difference between the Nationalist position and the Communist proposals of June 4 [!] was too great. For whatever reason, perhaps the growing military crisis, the Chinese Communists clearly had decided not to pursue the negotiations with the Nationalists at this time and therefore simply muddled the issue. There followed several exchanges of communications between the two parties during June with no result. Negotiations between the two parties had reached an impasse.

At this juncture, on June 20, President Roosevelt's vice president, Henry Wallace, arrived in Chungking, having traveled by way of the Soviet Union, for three days of intensive discussions with Chiang Kai-shek.[37] The discussions in virtually their entirety were devoted to exploring ways and means of settling the Communist problem. The essence of Wallace's statements was that the United States would act as a "friend," that is, a mediator between the Communists and Nationalists, but could not be a "guarantor" of any agreement reached between China and the Soviet Union.[38] During the talks, Wallace repeatedly made the point that without a settlement between China and the Soviet Union no lasting solution to the Chinese Communist problem could be reached. In dealing with the Chinese Communists, Wallace urged Chiang to reach some "lower level" understanding with them on the use of military force in north China against Japan that might provide the basis for broader cooperation in the future. Wallace also requested—a request reinforced by the arrival of a radiogram from the President on the same subject—that Chiang permit the United States to send a military observer group to Yenan.

Chiang agreed to permit the dispatch of an observer team to Yenan, but was visibly reluctant to accept Roosevelt's formula for dealing with the Communists. He castigated the Chinese Communists as men without "good faith" and desiring the breakdown of resistance to Japan, which would strengthen their position. The Communists realized, Chiang declared, that if the war ended with the Nationalist Government still in command, they would stand little chance of emerging victorious. Regarding Sino-Soviet relations, Chiang modified the position he had taken at the Cairo conference, to which he referred several times. At Cairo, recall, Chiang had sought to obtain American support against the Soviet Union. To Vice-President Wallace, Chiang said that he now understood why Roosevelt had "changed plans at Tehran" and stated his willingness to "go more than half-way in reaching an understanding with the Soviet Union," if the United States could "bring about" and "sponsor" a meeting between the two countries. Chiang also noted that the Chinese Communists were an internal problem, yet he would "nevertheless welcome the President's assistance." Toward this end Chiang asked whether the President could appoint a personal representative. Chiang "lacked confidence" in General Stilwell, who, he said, did not understand political problems and whose military judgment had been faulty.

During his visit with Chiang, the vice president did not see Stilwell nor was any member of his staff invited to participate in the talks.[39] After his departure from Chungking, in a radiogram to the President sent on June 28, Wallace recommended that Stilwell be recalled and that some other general officer be appointed who would merit the confidence of the Generalissimo. Further, Wallace urged that the President send a permanent personal representative through whom direct contact could be maintained between the two leaders. Finally, regarding the military situation, Wallace noted that the President should take "determined steps" to stem the collapse of the east China front or risk China's loss as an American base. The situation, Wallace hastened to add, was not by any means hopeless and given Chiang's eagerness for American military aid and guidance there seemed good prospects that he "would probably inaugurate reforms in China's internal political structure" if "wisely approached." [40]

Shifts in American Policy Emphasis

The larger significance of the Wallace mission was that it marked a shift of emphasis in attempts to bring Nationalists and Communists together. In the initial months after Tehran the emphasis lay on reaching a broadly based political-military settlement, as evidenced by the unsuccessful talks at Sian and Chungking. Through Wallace, President Roosevelt suggested a more limited approach, a "lower level" understanding regarding the unification or coordination of the Chinese fighting effort in the field. These efforts to achieve military cooperation were made through General Stilwell until he was recalled in October of 1944. After his recall, Roosevelt returned to the earlier idea of a broader political as well as military settlement, which he sought to achieve through the mediation of his personal representative to Chiang Kai-shek, General Patrick Hurley.

Wallace's message containing the recommendation to recall Stilwell came at a time when the President and his close advisors were on the verge of making the contrary decision. The vice-president was not privy to the President's grand policy design; he had merely served the immediate purpose of shifting emphasis in the larger attempt to bring about a coalition in China. The President therefore ignored his recommendation because he now sought to achieve lower level military cooperation between Nationalist and Communist forces by placing an American officer in command of all Chinese forces. He chose Stilwell partly because he was already in place, partly because he seemed acceptable to the Communists, if not to the Nationalists. Perhaps for that very reason he could not be considered personally biased in favor of Chiang Kai-shek.

Before broaching this proposal to Chiang Kai-shek, General Marshall radioed Stilwell requesting his opinion on the proposed plan. Stilwell replied that the situation in China was indeed desperate but not unsalvageable. However, he would accept the job of commanding China's armed forces only on condition that he be given "complete authority." Such a condition, he thought, could only be achieved if the President sent a "stiff message" to Chiang. To repair the military situation, Stilwell saw "only one chance," which was:

> to stage a counter-offensive from Shansi . . . attacking through Loyang toward Chengchow and Hankow. . . . The Communists should . . . participate in Shansi, but unless the G-mo makes an agreement with them, they won't. Two years ago they offered to fight with me. They might listen now.[41]

Stilwell's reply to Marshall's query confirmed in the President his thought to continue with him. In fact, Stilwell became the vehicle through which the unification of Nationalist and Communist forces was attempted until his recall in the fall of 1944.

On July 6, the President sent his proposal to Chiang, gravely noting that "the critical situation which now exists, in my opinion calls for the delegation to one individual of the power to coordinate all of the allied military resources in China, including the communist forces." [42] The one individual was General Stilwell. Chiang promptly replied to the President's message two days later, saying that he agreed "in principle" to Stilwell's appointment, but that there must be a "preparatory period" before it was placed into effect. In the meantime, Chiang hoped that the request made to Vice-President Wallace for the dispatch of a "personal representative" could be acted upon. Chiang's stated rationale for requesting such an appointment was "to adjust relations between me and General Stilwell."

In messages of July 13 and 14, President Roosevelt replied. He accepted Chiang's request for the appointment of a personal representative, but noted that the selection of the appropriate person would take time and urged Chiang to appoint Stilwell on the ground that "some calculated political risks appear justified when dangers . . . are so serious." [43] In his second message, July 14, the President focused entirely on the Communist issue. He noted with "particular satisfaction" that only political means would be employed to settle the Communist problem and "welcomed" Chiang's expressed desire for improved relations with the Soviet Union. The President felt that a conference between the two countries "would be greatly facilitated if a working arrangement had been reached beforehand between the Chinese Government and the Chinese Communists for effective prosecution of the war against the Japanese in North China." [44]

Chiang Kai-shek procrastinated for nine days before answering the President's message and when he did reply, on July 23, it is apparent that he had had second thoughts about placing Stilwell in command, particularly before a personal representative would be appointed. Restating his willingness to appoint Stilwell in principle, Chiang now sought to protect himself by laying down three conditions. First, he stated that he could not agree to place the Communist forces under Stilwell's command until they had first declared their willingness to obey the government; secondly, Stilwell's authority must be specifically delineated; thirdly, control over lend-lease should pass to the Chinese Government.[45] It would be exactly one month before President Roosevelt would reply to this latest message. In the meantime, the rush of events in China was leading rapidly to crisis.

China Crisis—Japanese and American

On August 8, after nearly three weeks of difficult fighting against gallant Chinese resistance, Heng Yang fell to the Japanese, opening the way to airfields of Kweilin and Liuchou in Kwangsi province. The defeat at Heng Yang precipitated a plot, long in developing, by dissident elements within the Kuomintang. The day after the fall of the city, on the 9th, Marshal Li Chi-shen delivered a message to the U.S. Consulate at Kweilin in which he requested American support for a move to supplant the Nationalist Government of Chiang Kai-shek with a Southwest Government of Joint Defense. To be headed by Li, who during the northern campaign of the late twenties had been Chiang's chief of staff, its stated aims were to establish a democratic form of government under the Kuomintang, bring about national unity and closer cooperation with the Allies. The United States was careful not to become involved in this plot and it soon fizzled out. Moreover, Pai Chung-hsi and Li Tsung-jen, major Nationalist leaders who were not in Chiang's clique, refused to support the dissident elements.

Meanwhile, in the United States the President and his staff were settling upon the man to be the personal representative of the President to Chiang Kai-shek. The man selected was General Patrick Hurley, who had had a long and distinguished record of non-partisan service earlier during the war. Hurley had been entrusted with several diplomatic missions by the President, the latest of which had been to make the arrangements for Chiang's stay at Cairo. In that capacity he had made a favorable impression upon both Chiang and Stilwell,[46] who welcomed his appointment. The President's message of August 23 confirmed Hurley's appointment, but the bulk of his radiogram was devoted to a renewed effort to persuade Chiang to place Stilwell in command of all Chinese forces. To reassure Chiang that his own power would not be reduced in any way, the President stated that he would be relieving Stilwell of authority over lend-lease, although he did not proffer it to Chiang as demanded in his three conditions.

In a following message to Chiang, the President noted that Hurley's instructions were as his personal representative "to coordinate the whole military picture under you [and] . . . to iron out any problems between you and General Stilwell." [47] Hurley's task, until Stilwell's recall in late October, was to concentrate chiefly upon the establishment of a military, not a political, settlement. After his arrival in China on September 6—a trip made via Moscow—Hurley prepared an agenda for Chiang which clearly reflected his conception of the task he was to fulfill. Presented to Chiang on September 12, the agenda contained the following ten points:

1. The paramount objective . . . is to bring about the unification of all military forces . . .
2. to cooperate with China in bringing about closer relations and harmony with Russia and Britain . . .
3. to unify all military forces under the command of the Generalissimo . . .
4. to marshal all resources in China for war purposes . . .
5. to support the Generalissimo's efforts for political unification on a democratic basis . . .
6. to submit present and postwar economic plans for China . . .
7. to define the authority of General Stilwell as Field Commander . . .
8. to define Stilwell's authority as Chief of Staff to the Generalissimo . . .
9. to prepare for presentation a diagram of command . . .
10. to discuss future control of lend-lease.[48]

Before this agenda could be taken up in any substantive manner, the issue of General Stilwell exploded and altered both the American policy emphasis and its mode of execution. Hurley, Stilwell, and Chiang had together produced the proposed orders placing Stilwell in command of Chinese forces. The orders were in the Generalissimo's hands, although not yet signed by him, on September 15. At this juncture, however, the course of events again impinged to turn Sino-American relations topsy-turvy. The Burma situation had reached another crisis.[49] Chiang had requested Stilwell to send those Chinese forces under Stilwell's command, which had shortly before taken the town of Myitkyina, into a diversionary attack on Bhamo, south of the town of Lung Ling. It was a "request" because Chiang's authority did not extend beyond China's borders and both Myitkyina and Bhamo were located in Burma.

Lung Ling, a town astride the Burma Road but located in Yunnan, was under attack. Chiang feared that unless the Chinese garrison there was reinforced or a diversion created elsewhere to draw off Japanese reinforcements, Lung Ling would fall, leaving open an unrestricted route of access to Kunming. Chiang punctuated his request to Stilwell with the threat that unless troops were sent he would withdraw his forces from Lung Ling. (Actually, although unknown either to Stilwell or Chiang at the time, the Japanese were in no condition to push their offensive in Burma and were in the process of cutting back their strength there.) Stilwell refused Chiang's request and claimed that withdrawal of Chinese forces from Lung Ling would mean abandonment of the North Burma campaign and loss of control of the Burma Road! This was an extraordinary response to Chiang's request. Stilwell did not grasp Chiang's point, instead interpreting his request as the kind of "interference" he would have to contend with as commander of Chinese forces. In a message to Marshall, Stilwell demanded that the army chief use strong language in setting Chiang straight.

The upshot of this was a presidential message, which Marshall himself apparently drafted and which the President signed and sent on September 16.[50] Stilwell delivered the message to Chiang Kai-shek personally on the 19th in the presence of Hurley, who attempted to dissuade him from delivering it on the ground that Chiang was about to sign the orders appointing Stilwell to command. The message hinted strongly that unless Chiang appointed Stilwell "in unrestricted command of all . . . forces" the United States might end its support of Chiang Kai-shek![51] The impact of the message was multiplied by virtue of the fact that it was delivered in the presence of several high-ranking Chinese generals, revealing to them that the United States was not irrevocably committed to the person of Chiang Kai-shek.

Chiang's response to the presidential message was on September 25 to demand Stilwell's recall and replacement. Roosevelt replied on October 5, agreeing to relieve Stilwell from his position as Chiang's chief of staff but to retain him as commander for the completion of the Burma campaign. Chiang Kai-shek reacted sharply to this latest suggestion by giving the President on October 9 a general review of the development of China policy both strategically and tactically since the Cairo conference. His policy review was a direct criticism not only of Stilwell but of the President himself.

> At the Cairo Conference, commitments were finally made by the representatives of the United States and Great Britain which appeared to insure the kind of Burma campaign which I could approve. Unhappily, those commitments were abandoned shortly after I left Cairo. General Stilwell then came to me and announced that he proposed to proceed with a limited offensive in north Burma. I again warned him of the consequences, stating specifically that I feared the project would be difficult and costly, and would engage all of China's limited resources at a time when this would be dangerous. He treated my warning lightly, and intimated that if I maintained my attitude, China would be suspected of wishing to withhold any real contribution to the Allied cause. At length I consented to his employing the Ramgarh troops which were entirely American trained and equipped and with the clear understanding that these forces were all that would be forthcoming.

It was not long before my warning was substantiated. The moment obstacles were encountered in Burma, General Stilwell began to use every sort of pressure to induce me to commit additional forces. I shall not enter into details. It is enough to say that by the beginning of May, the Burma campaign had drained off most of the properly trained and equipped reserves in China. At the same time, it had greatly reduced the incoming supply tonnage so that during critical ensuing months it was impossible to strengthen the military position in any area within China. It was not until June that the Hump tonnage, exclusive of the B-29 project, again reached the January level.

As I had feared, the Japanese took advantage of the opportunity thus offered to launch an offensive within China attacking first in Honan and then in Hunan. Owing to the Burma campaign, no adequately trained and equipped reinforcements were available for these war areas. Owing to the effect of the Burma campaign on the Hump tonnage, supplies were not forthcoming for the Chinese armies stationed in Honan and Hunan. The forces brought to bear by the Japanese in their offensive in east China were six times as great as those confronting General Stilwell in north Burma, and the consequences of defeat were certain to outweigh in China all results of victory in the north Burma campaign. Yet General Stilwell exhibited complete indifference to the outcome in east China; so much so that in the critical days of the east China operations, he consistently refused to release Lend-Lease munitions already available in Yunnan for use in the east China fighting. Prior to June 1944 with the exception of the Yunnan Expeditionary Forces, the entire Chinese Army did not receive a single rifle or piece of artillery from American Lend-Lease. . . . In all, excepting the Yunnan Expeditionary Forces, the Chinese armies have received 60 mountain guns, 320 anti-tank rifles and 506 bazookas.

In short, we have taken Myitkyina but we have lost all of east China. . . . I am wholly confident that if the President replaces General Stilwell with a qualified American officer, we can work together to reverse the present trend and achieve a vital contribution to the final victory.[52]

Hurley sent Chiang's message to the President, adding comments of his own to the effect that there was no issue between Chiang Kai-shek and the President except Stilwell. Thus ended Stilwell's role in China. On the 18th he was recalled and he left China on the 27th. General Albert Wedemeyer took command of the China theatre, which was now split off from the Burma-India theatre, on October 31.

Renewed American Efforts Toward Unification

The recall of General Stilwell marked still another shift in American policy toward China, which from June had been to achieve a lower level working military agreement between Nationalist and Communist forces under General Stilwell. With Stilwell's recall the President shifted emphasis toward achievement of a political as well as military agreement in China, a task which he conferred upon General Hurley in early November.[53] After receiving his instructions from the President, Hurley flew to Yenan for a conference with Communist leaders. While there, he was instrumental in formulating a "five-point proposal," which Mao Tse-tung signed (as did Hurley, who signed as "witness"). The November 10 "five-point proposal" focused on the establishment of a coalition government.

1) Communists and Nationalists will work together for the unification of all military forces in China for the immediate defeat of Japan and the reconstruction of China.

2) The Nationalist Government is to be reorganized into a coalition National Government embracing representatives of all anti-Japanese parties and non-partisan political bodies. The National Military Council is to be reorganized into the United National Military Council consisting of representatives of all anti-Japanese armies.

3) The coalition government will support the principles of Sun Yat-sen.

4) All anti-Japanese forces will observe and carry out the orders of the coalition National Government and its United National Military Council and will be recognized by them. The supplies acquired from foreign powers will be equitably distributed.

5) The coalition National Government of China recognizes the legality of the Nationalist Party of China, the Chinese Communist Party, and all anti-Japanese parties.[54]

The Nationalist reaction to the five-point proposal was that Hurley had been "sold a bill of goods." They could not accept it, instead drafting a "three-point plan" which was presented on November 22.

1) The National Government agrees to incorporate, after reorganization, the Chinese Communist forces in the National Army and give recognition to the Chinese Communist Party as a legal party.

2) The Communist Party undertakes to give over control of all their troops to the National Government through the National Military Council to which the National Government will designate Communist representatives.

3) The aim of the National Government to which the Chinese Communist Party subscribes is to carry out the Three People's Principles of Dr. Sun Yat-sen.[55]

The difference in the two positions was clear. The Communists desired reorganization of the National Government into a coalition in which they would be equal partners with the Nationalists. The Nationalists declined reorganization but were willing to incorporate the Communists into the government—afer taking control of their armed forces. Surprisingly, Chou En-lai's initial reaction to the government's three-point counterproposal of November 22 was that although the Communist party could not give up the principle of coalition government, the government's proposals were acceptable for the present.[56] On December 8, however, just before leaving Chungking for Yenan, Chou reversed his position, declaring that the government's proposal was now unacceptable.[57] Despite Hurley's immediate objection and repeated efforts to bring the two parties back together, the Communists' only reaction was to raise additional demands as preconditions to the resumption of negotiations. For example, in his telegram of December 28, Chou declined participation in "abstract discussions" and demanded that the government release all political prisoners, withdraw all forces surrounding Communist areas, abolish all oppressive regulations, and cease all secret police activity.[58]

What had taken place? The Communists had reversed their stand, but why? The question perplexed Hurley, who on November 30 had been appointed Ambassador. It was not until late in December, however, that he discovered what had caused the Communist turnabout. The American OSS (Office of Strategic Services) had contacted the Chinese Communists without the knowledge of either Hurley or Wedemeyer, proposing "to provide complete equipment for up to 25,000 guerrillas," for small-scale disruptive action behind Japanese lines in north China, in which some U.S. forces would also participate.[59] It was this plan which appears to have prompted the Chinese Communists to break off negotiations with the Nationalists.

In effect, the OSS plan provided the Communists with the incentive to frustrate any attempt at coalition, giving not only American recognition but weapons. The Communists themselves apparently believed that the United States was inclined to deal with them directly and went so far as to propose that Mao Tse-tung and Chou En-lai travel to Washington, D. C., for a personal meeting with President Roosevelt! The Communists sought not only to bypass the Nationalists, but also Ambassador Hurley himself and deal directly with the President of the United States. They were encouraged in this naive belief by the Foreign Service officers stationed in Yenan, who insisted that Hurley did not genuinely represent American policy.[60]

The hopeless muddle was at last ironed out when Wedemeyer, who was the person through whom the Communists hoped to communicate directly to the President, informed Hurley of their actions. Hurley and Wedemeyer thereupon each set down rules of conduct for the personnel under their respective commands, although not equally successfully. Wedemeyer simply prohibited any sort of negotiations with the Communists on the part of military officers under his command, ending further involvement between the U.S. military and Chinese Communists. Hurley was less successful in restricting the actions of the Foreign Service officers. The ambassador also communicated with the Chinese Communist leaders in January, setting straight the lines of authority and encouraging the Communists to resume negotiations with the Nationalists. It being made clear that the U.S. would not deal with the Chinese Communists at the expense of the National Government, Chou En-lai returned to Chungking on January 24 for another, this time more productive, round of negotiations.

In ensuing discussions the Nationalists offered to include Communist representatives in a "war cabinet" of seven to nine men which would "act as the policy-making body of the Executive Yuan for the duration of the war." [61] Further, Chiang Kai-shek offered to appoint a three-man commission consisting of one Nationalist, one Communist, and one American officer to make recommendations regarding the reorganization, reequipping and supplying of Chinese Communist troops, and to appoint an American officer as commander of all Communist troops for the duration of the war. The Communist response to this proposal was to insist upon the abolition of party rule and the formation of a coalition government. If this could be agreed upon the Communists would turn over control of their forces, but Hurley declared that he had no authority to make such a commitment for the United States.

At this juncture, Chiang asserted that he would, according to the will of Sun Yat-sen, call a meeting for May 4 to initiate steps toward the drafting of a constitution, the abolition of one-party rule, and the establishment of constitutional government. Chiang's declaration brought the Communists around to a more constructive mood. If the constitutional process were initiated without Communist participation, they would not expect to obtain a favorable result for themselves. Therefore, Chou En-lai indicated a willingness to compromise and on February 3, representatives of both parties produced a proposal which "would make action possible." [62] They agreed to convene a Political Consultative Conference (instead of a constitutional congress) to consider steps to establish constitutional government and to formulate a common political program, a plan for military unification, and the form in which non-Kuomintang party members could participate in the existing National Government.

The Communist reaction to the February 3 proposal was favorable; the Nationalists', dubious. Hurley, as middleman, wearily strove to make each party palatable to the other. At that very moment, however, events were transpiring in far-off Yalta, where the President would have his last meeting with Stalin before Roosevelt died, a meeting which would have direct repercussions on the negotiations between Nationalists and Communists in China.

VII
The United States,
the Soviet Union,
and China, 1945

The struggle between Nationalists and Communists in China was an international event not in any sense confined to the territorial limits of the Asian mainland. Their conflict affected a larger Soviet-American effort to create a post-war balance of power. The general objective which the United States and the Soviet Union sought was the creation of a China which would not become a dangerous threat to the stability of the Far East and to the eastern flank of the Soviet Union. The specific means toward this end was the creation of a coalition government of Nationalists and Communists. The formative phase of the Soviet-American effort proceeded from the Yalta Conference of February 1945 and continued—despite the death of President Roosevelt, the principal architect of the policy—through the end of the year, when General George C. Marshall was appointed special representative to China.

Yalta, Outline for the Postwar World

At Yalta, February 4 through 11, 1945, President Roosevelt began the process of fleshing out his design for the postwar world. As described briefly in the previous chapter, the President sought to establish a secure international position for the Soviet Union, which, he felt, would predispose Soviet leaders to cooperate in maintaining the peace. At Yalta, the President took concrete measures to achieve his objectives by entering into agreements for the establishment of a postwar world organization, the United Nations, and of strong Soviet territorial positions in both Europe and Asia. A full-length discussion of the

European aspect of the Yalta conference is beyond the scope of this book. Suffice it to note that the Soviet Union obtained Allied agreement for the establishment of a strong position in eastern Europe in addition to achieving the division of Germany.[1]

The provisions regarding the Soviet Union's position in Asia were equally far-reaching, but kept secret for exactly one year. In the secret agreement, the Soviet Union agreed to enter the war against Japan "two or three months after Germany has surrendered and the war in Europe has terminated." In return for this contribution she would receive the Kurile Islands, the *status quo* in Outer Mongolia, which amounted to recognition of Soviet hegemony, South Sakhalin and adjacent islands, and control over port and rail facilities in Manchuria. It was "understood, that the agreement concerning Outer Mongolia and the ports and railroads [in Manchuria] . . . require[d] concurrence of Generalissimo Chiang Kai-shek." For his part, President Roosevelt agreed to "take measures" to obtain Chiang Kai-shek's "concurrence," while the Soviet Union expressed its "readiness to conclude with the National Government of China a pact of friendship and alliance . . . to render assistance to China with its armed forces for the purpose of liberating China from the Japanese yoke." A treaty would be necessary to legalize the Soviet gain, the Yalta agreement having no power in that regard. Finally, the "heads of the three Great Powers agreed that these claims of the Soviet Union shall be unquestionably fulfilled" and that "the preeminent interests of the Soviet Union shall be safeguarded." [2]

The Soviet Union's larger strategic purpose was the creation of a postwar world in which real or potential threats would be removed. In the Far East, this meant the emasculation of Japan and the establishment of a weak China, which would ensure Soviet control over the traditionally contested areas of Manchuria and Korea. This strategy was not incompatible with the American one of creating a secure international position for the Soviet Union—at least not in the short run and as long as a cooperative effort could be maintained. For the short run both strategies meshed in the concept of a coalition government for China, which would in fact if not in name preclude the development of a Chinese government hostile to the Soviet Union. Stated obversely, a coalition government would ensure the establishment of a "friendly" government on which the Soviet Union could exercise a strong influence through the instrumentality of the Chinese Communists, who would control the border area, especially Manchuria.

The common features of the Soviet and American Far Eastern strategies were thus the creation of a strong Soviet position in Manchuria and the establishment of a coalition government for China. Success, however, depended greatly upon the acquiescence of the one member of the wartime coalition absent from the Yalta gathering and most directly concerned—Chiang Kai-shek. Both the United States and the Soviet Union had during the course of the previous year in various ways expressed support for Chiang and the National Government, indicating that the Nationalists would play a dominant role in the coalition government.[3] Chiang, too, had repeatedly declared his willingness to enter into a coalition with the Communists, to reach a political settlement with his long-time antagonists. Yet, even if the Nationalist leader did go through with the establishment of a coalition government, there was little likelihood that he would unhesitatingly accept the powerful position envisaged by Roosevelt and Stalin for the Soviet Union in Manchuria after the war, a position which seriously compromised Chinese territorial integrity. The cruel irony was that Chiang had led the Chinese government in a seven-year-long war against the Japanese over precisely the issue of China's territorial integrity and during that war unsuccessfully had sought American support to prevent the Soviet Union from penetrating Manchuria. At Yalta, the American president had agreed to "take measures" to secure Chiang Kai-shek's "concurrence" on precisely that which the latter had striven to avoid.

Since Chiang Kai-shek was unlikely to surrender willingly the concessions contained in the Yalta agreement, it would be necessary to create the conditions which would make refusal difficult, if not impossible. For the time being, therefore, Chiang would not be told. As to when he would be informed, Stalin stated: "when it was possible to free a number of Soviet troops in the west and move twenty-five divisions to the Far East . . . it would be possible to speak to Marshal Chiang Kai-shek about these matters." [4] In other words, when the Soviet Union was in a position to back up paper gains in Manchuria with force, Chiang would be informed of the secret agreement made at Yalta.

But there was perhaps an equally compelling and related reason for secrecy. At Yalta, the United States had agreed to begin stockpiling supplies (operation Milepost) which the Russians deemed necessary to carry out the invasion of Manchuria.[5] These supplies would be shipped in the bottoms of Soviet or neutral country vessels across the Pacific and the Sea of Japan into eastern Siberian ports, principally Vladivostok and Nakhodka. The route would pass directly through Japanese waters within sight of the home islands! If the Japanese learned of the Soviet plan to enter the war, breaking the neutrality pact, they would undoubtedly attempt to prevent the stockpiling of supplies. This was a compelling argument for the maintenance of secrecy. For the time being, therefore, the Yalta agreement on the Far East would be kept secret. Or would it?

The Immediate Repercussions of Yalta

Although it was intended to be kept a closely guarded secret, within days the American Ambassador to China, Hurley, learned that a Soviet-American agreement on the Far East had been made, although he was uncertain about its contents.[6] He was sufficiently disturbed to leave Chungking for Washington on February 19, eight days after the conclusion of the Yalta conference. In Washington, the President himself showed Hurley the actual text of the Yalta agreement. In three separate meetings between them, Hurley persuaded the President that the agreement was sufficiently ambiguous to require further specification.[7] Roosevelt then instructed Hurley to travel to London and Moscow to discuss clarification of the agreement with Churchill and Stalin.[8] Hurley departed for London on April 2 as the President's personal representative.

In London he received Churchill's public affirmation that Great Britain would support the American policy of unifying all Chinese forces and assisting in the creation of a free, unified and democratic China. While en route to Moscow on April 12, Hurley learned that the President had died. He immediately cabled Truman, his successor, offering his resignation, which was not accepted. Truman informed Hurley that he would uphold all of Roosevelt's commitments, instructing him to continue on with the mission which the late President had assigned to him.[9] Hurley then proceeded to Moscow for the discussion with Stalin, who gave his assurance that he, too, would support the American policy. Stalin urged, however, that Chiang Kai-shek not be informed of the Yalta accord until he gave the signal, in a month or two.[10] Hurley concluded his mission, reporting the results fully to President Truman after his return to Chungking on April 19.

Efforts to keep Chiang Kai-shek ignorant could have been spared. The evidence strongly suggests that he, too, had learned or deduced most of the items contained in the Yalta agreement shortly after the conference. In fact, it may have been Hurley's conversation with Chiang that prompted Hurley to return to Washington in the first place.[11] The National Government immediately began to prepare its position, letting it be known that proposals for a twenty-year Sino-Soviet treaty were being drawn up for T. V. Soong, the foreign minister, to carry with him to Moscow.[12] It was, of course, vital for the Nationalists to determine precisely what the American role would be in the evolution of postwar Sino-Soviet relations. Chiang Kai-shek therefore instructed Soong to see the President.

On March 6, Soong sent a telegram to Hurley, who was still in Washington, requesting a meeting. The message was terse, betraying no hint that the Chinese were apprised of the Yalta agreement. The message simply read:

> Generalissimo desires me make quick trip to Washington to discuss international and economic problems with President. Will you kindly ascertain if this will be agreeable to President.[13]

Acting for the President, Hurley replied on March 9 and attempted to put off a meeting between the President and Soong with the transparent excuse that the "time between now and the San Francisco Conference [scheduled to open on April 25] is too short to allow for useful consultation." Moreover, Hurley continued, if the President met with one foreign minister it "might lead to misunderstandings on the part of other interested foreign ministers and complicate things." [14]

Soong was not to be deterred and on the next day, the 10th, he sent a telegram to Harry Hopkins in which he made explicit that his purpose for a meeting with the President was to discuss the secret agreement made at Yalta.

> . . . I feel that . . . obtaining the President's advice now is most vital to China. I would come as Acting Prime Minister and not as Foreign Minister. . . . The President has already seen the Prime Ministers and the Foreign Ministers of the Big Three at Yalta. Since China was not present, I know it

will help our war effort here and the future relations of the four sponsors of the San Francisco conference if I come now. There are especially some secret matters that should probably better not be raised at the San Francisco conference that it would help very much to discuss in advance. . . . China's situation is one of desperate crisis directly affecting our military plans. We feel that never has it been so important that we obtain the President's advice now about our joint strategy, and this includes our relations with Soviet Russia, the Communists and plans we have for dealing as best we can with our desperate economic problems. I would not come to ask for a loan or for embarrassing decisions but to consult the President and his top advisers with, we believe, the future of China and Asia at stake.[15]

There is no record available of the U.S. reply, but it must have been negative, because Soong's visit was put off until after the San Francisco conference. One thing is certain. The Chinese government knew enough about the Yalta agreement to make further attempts at secrecy meaningless. The one aspect about which Chiang Kai-shek continued to be ignorant was the American role. In fact, the one false assumption which Chiang seems to have made was that the United States would become formally involved in support of China against the Soviet Union when the war ended.

Chiang Initiates and Mao Responds to "Constitutional Government"

Although Chiang received no satisfaction in his attempt to gain fuller information about Yalta from the United States, he was sufficiently aware or apprehensive about the implications of the Soviet-American agreement to initiate his own plans. Speed was of the essence for Chiang, for the sooner a settlement was reached and constitutional government established, the stronger the Nationalists' position in it would be. The Chinese Communists were quite weak at this stage of the war. On March 1, Chiang announced that the National Assembly would convene the coming November 12 to begin the process of inaugurating constitutional government for China. Once it was inaugurated, all political parties would be equal; until that time, however, the National Government reserved the right of ultimate decision and final responsibility, although it was willing to admit the Chinese Communist and other parties to participation in the government.

Whether or not the impetus for Chiang's act was his concern over the Yalta agreement, his March 1 speech set the terms for the further contest for power with the Communists. By declaring that the National Assembly would convene on November 12, 1945, Chiang had not only begun the contest but set the time limit for its conclusion. At this point the advantage was his; initiating the game before reaching agreement with the Communists left control in his hands. The objective was to command a majority of delegates to the National Assembly. The number of delegates would be determined principally by the extent of area and population under control. The ensuing struggle between Nationalists and Communists would therefore be to establish claim to territories currently not under either party's direct control. But simply laying claim to territory would be insufficient; it would also be necessary to form local government structures, which would control the delegate selection process on the local level. By retaining ultimate control of the National Government, Chiang retained command of the power organ which would exist until the National Assembly convened and therefore play a decisive role in determining the ultimate political structure. To him remained the prerogative to appoint officials to reclaim areas. These officials, in turn, would organize local administrations—the key to the delegate selection process.

The Chinese Communists reacted to Chiang's initiative on March 9, condemning the whole idea of a National Assembly as a "deceitful, China-splitting" device, which Chiang was using to exclude them from participation in the political process. The Kuomintang, accused the Communists, had not the least sincerity in carrying out democratic reforms and, under the circumstances, "leaves no basis on which negotiations . . . can be continued." [16] It appeared at this juncture that any chance for a negotiated settlement between the two parties had been lost. The talks were broken off and even the ever optimistic Ambassador Hurley paused to remark that it was "most difficult to be patient" at a time when unity was "so desperately needed." [17] It would not be long, however, before both sides reaffirmed their desire to continue negotiations. These affirmations came at the Seventh CCP and Sixth KMT congresses.

The Seventh Congress of the Chinese Communist Party convened on April 23 and continued through the 11th of June. From the opening report delivered by Mao Tse-tung on coalition government it was evident that the party had shifted its position of March 9. The Chinese Communist Party was now proclaimed "ready to reopen negotiations" with the Kuomintang,[18] and participate in the political process, with reservations, on Chiang Kai-shek's terms. At the same time, Mao set forth an initial "bargaining position" for negotiations with the Nationalists, and, while upholding fundamental Communist objectives, suggested that for the foreseeable future Communist and Nationalist programs were compatible. Mao did not dispute the plan to convene the National Assembly; he now accepted it. He focused his remarks on the interim political body which would rule until the National Assembly convened. That body would determine in large part who would gain control of the territories currently under Japanese occupation. For this reason it was vital to be included in the government which would be in power when Japan was defeated. Mao therefore proposed the establishment of a provisional coalition government, which would include the Communists. It would:

> carry out democratic reforms, surmount the present crisis, mobilize and unify all the anti-Japanese forces of the country and coordinate effectively with the Allies in military operations, thereby defeating the Japanese aggressors and liberating the Chinese people from their clutches.[19]

"After that," said Mao, "we should . . . convene a national assembly and form a permanent democratic government, which will also be a coalition. . . ."

A major portion of Mao's report was devoted to establishing a favorable "bargaining position" for the Chinese Communists in negotiations with the Kuomintang, by exaggerating Chinese Communist strength. First, Mao claimed vast areas under Communist "liberation," disputing the words of "some people . . . that China's liberated areas consist mainly of the Shen-Kan-Ning border region [population 1.5 million]. This is a misconception." In actuality, Mao claimed,

> China's liberated areas under the leadership of the Chinese Communist Party have now a population of 95,500,000. They cover a region from Inner Mongolia in the north to Hainan Island in the south; almost wherever the enemy goes, there he finds the 8th Route Army, the new 4th Army or some other people's forces operating. This vast portion of China consists of nineteen major liberated areas, covering the greater or lesser parts of the

provinces of Liaoning, Jehol, Chahar, Suiyuan, Shensi, Kansu, Ninghsia, Shansi, Hopeh, Honan, Shantung, Kiangsu, Chekiang, Anhwei, Kiangsi, Hupeh, Hunan, Kwangtung and Fukien. Yenan is the guiding center for all these liberated areas.[20]

This was a gross exaggeration of Chinese Communist strength. Roughly 340 million people lived in the nineteen provinces Mao named. Twelve of the nineteen named were under undisputed Japanese control; these twelve alone contained over 300 million people. Although the Chinese Communists had "liberated areas" in these twelve provinces, they did not have threateningly large forces in them. Strong Communist positions in north China in particular would undoubtedly have prompted a reaction from the Japanese. However one defines the terms *liberated areas* and *control,* throughout the war there was no demonstrated existence of vast and powerful liberated areas up to the moment that Mao made his claim. Certainly, Communist guerrilla groups roamed behind Japanese lines, and were designated by province of operation, but to equate this with any sort of "control" over huge population groups would be a distortion of the term. The remaining seven provinces Mao named, even assuming complete Communist control, contained only a total of 35 million people.[21] Mao himself noted that in three of these, the Shen-Kan-Ning border region, the heart of the Communist territories, the Communists controlled a population of 1.5 million in a total population of 17 million. This would mean that the bulk of the 94 million people whom the Communists claimed to control were somewhere in Japanese occupied territory. Stated another way, Mao claimed that roughly one out of every 3.5 people in Japanese occupied territory was under Communist control.

The claim of controlling 95.5 million people provided the basis for a more important assertion. In his speech, Mao went on to say that

in all the liberated areas . . . governments based on cooperation between the Communists and representatives of other anti-Japanese parties as well as people without party affiliation, i.e., local coalition governments, have been or are being elected by the people.[22]

It was on the basis of an exaggerated claim to control of vast areas and populations combined with the assertion that local coalition governments were being formed in these areas that Mao sought to justify

Communist participation in a coalition government with the Kuomin-tang. Mao also claimed to have a Red Army of 910,000 men, a militia of 2.2 million men, and party membership of 1.2 million. Based on a population of 95.5 million, such figures were not out of line, but, if the Communists controlled only small pockets of territory beyond the 1.5 million of the Shen-Kan-Ning border region, then clearly Communist strength was exaggerated. (The best U.S. intelligence estimates at that time pegged Communist troop strength at 475,000 men and 207,000 rifles. Chiang Kai-shek's own estimate set Communist troop strength at just over 300,000.)[23]

In essence, Mao, in his speech, had accepted the Nationalist challenge and simultaneously made the first Communist move. Thereafter, Communist-Nationalist negotiations would be played out against a background of attempts by each party's military forces to gain hold of and set up local governments in as much of formerly Japanese-occupied territory as they could.

The "Victory" of Mao Tse-tung

The congress acted upon three other issues of importance, which need to be discussed. The delegates deliberated on the party's current and prospective military position, adopted a new party constitution, and elected a Central Committee and Politburo. Chu Teh gave the report on the military situation, which apparently was never made public. Liu Shao-ch'i presented in two parts a report on the new party constitution, which was adopted by the congress. In essence, the new constitution ratified the structural changes made in the party during the *cheng-feng* campaign and legitimized the "thought of Mao Tse-tung" coequally with Marxism-Leninism as providing the guiding principles for all party work. The congress named Mao Tse-tung chairman of the party and "elected" forty-four full members to the Central Committee and thirty-three alternate members. In itself, the list of Central Committee members tells nothing of the decisive change which had taken place in the Chinese Communist party leadership. It is only when the members of the Politburo, or Presidium, are noted that the extent of Mao's triumph over the Internationalist group, against which he had struggled for so many years, becomes evident.

The Seventh Congress was indeed a "congress of victory" for Mao and his supporters, who emerged in formal command of all top posts in the party at this time. The fifteen-member Politburo, with no exceptions, was manned by Mao's men; the Internationalists were totally excluded. Wang Ming, the recognized leader of the Internationalists, experienced the most dramatic change of fortune, dropping from the Politburo to the Central Committee. Kao Kang, Mao's ally, made perhaps the most rapid rise in status, moving from obscurity (near death in 1936 until spared by Mao's arrival) to a position in the Politburo (thirteenth of fifteen).[24]

In broadest terms, the Seventh Party Congress signified the ascendancy of Mao's group over all others, principally the Internationalists. The subsequent history of Chinese Communist politics is primarily the story of the conflict which evolved among the members of the Mao group over position and policy. It is a story which unfolds after the victory of the Chinese Communists over the Nationalists in 1949.[25] At the time of the Seventh Party Congress the CCP appears to have achieved its highest degree of "solidarity" ever, albeit it was a unity imposed by one group over the rest of the party. The decisiveness of Mao's victory was most clearly reflected in the "Resolution on Some Questions in the History of Our Party," adopted at the Seventh Plenum of the CCP Sixth Congress on April 20, just before the convocation of the Seventh Party Congress. The lengthy resolution was the history of the party as told by Mao Tse-tung, designed to give historical sanction to his rise to power in the party and to discredit the Internationalist group as being unworthy of leadership.[26]

While the Chinese Communist congress was in session, the Nationalists convened their Sixth Congress from May 5 through 21. Convened partly to respond to the Communist congress and partly because the war in Europe was over, the Nationalists, after reelecting Chiang Kai-shek *Tsung Ts'ai* (general leader) of the party, reconfirmed November 12 as the date on which the National Assembly would open. In this the congress rejected the Communist proposal to postpone the National Assembly until after Japan had been defeated. However, in a resolution on the "Communist problem" the Nationalists expressed the desire to seek a political solution "through discussion." [27] The congress also passed laws to give legal status to all political parties, including the CCP, to conduct popular elections for local government in all "free China," that is, unoccupied China, and to remove all KMT party presence from military units and schools. Finally, the crucial question of membership in the National Assembly was to be referred to the People's Political Conference, "on which it is anticipated that all parties will be represented." [28]

In other words, the Kuomintang appeared inflexible on the matters of convening the National Assembly and remaining in control of the government until that time. It did leave open the door to the CCP to have a voice in the delegate selection process to the National Assembly, which would be discussed at a meeting of the People's Political Conference (PPC). Pursuant to the congress, the Nationalists appointed a "committee of seven" (consisting of representatives of the Kuomintang, the Democratic League, and an independent) to negotiate with the Chinese Communists, who were obdurate in refusing to participate in the PPC. On July 1 the committee flew to Yenan, returning four days later with the CCP's reply. The Communists proposed that the convocation of the National Assembly be postponed and that the government summon a political conference of all major political parties in China, ostensibly preparatory to forming a provisional coalition government.[29]

The PPC convened two days after the return of the committee on July 7 and sought to effect a compromise with the Communist proposals. Principally, the PPC resolved to leave the date for opening the National Assembly to the discretion of the government, meeting in effect one of the two Communist proposals. Nothing, however, was said of convening a political conference; the PPC simply reiterated the desire to give the fullest representation to all classes of people in the Assembly and ensure freedom of political action to all political parties in the proposed elections for local self-government.[30] Meanwhile, between American and Russian leaders, decisions were being made which would directly affect the course of the contest for power between the Nationalists and Communists.

Gnawing Doubts Weaken the Prospects for Soviet-American Cooperation

World War II had ended in Europe and Soviet leaders had immediately turned their war machine eastward for the final thrust at Japan. The twenty-five divisions Stalin had mentioned to FDR at Yalta, plus an additional five, were already on the move. (Seventy divisions ultimately would participate in the Soviet invasion of Manchuria.) Most of the vital lend-lease tonnage promised by the United States to support the offensive was already in place. It was now an open secret that the Soviet Union was preparing to enter the Pacific war. The new Truman administration, at the approaching moment of truth, was gripped by the apprehension that Stalin suspected a change of heart on the part of the Americans and, if so, would not himself carry out his end of the bargain.[31]

And what of the American position? Truman had committed himself to fulfill the Yalta executive agreement. He was therefore bound to secure Chiang's compliance for the Soviet gains. Chiang had not yet been officially informed of that agreement and time was growing short. If secrecy concerning the Yalta provisions had become pointless, continued American refusal to inform Chiang of them could only be interpreted by the Chinese as Soviet-American complicity to their detriment.

To assure and be reassured, Truman sent Harry Hopkins to Moscow for conversations with Stalin. By selecting Hopkins, who with General George C. Marshall, the Army Chief of Staff, was thoroughly familiar with Roosevelt's policies (indeed they had been instrumental in formulating them), Truman hoped to demonstrate the continuity between the two American administrations. It was a supreme effort on Hopkins's part, for he literally roused himself from his deathbed to make the trip (he succumbed in late January 1946 after months of hovering on the edge of death). Nevertheless, at the end of May he flew off to Moscow. His talks with Stalin (May 26–June 6), in which Ambassador Harriman participated, covered the entire range of questions relating to Soviet-American relations.[32]

Hopkins reaffirmed Truman's pledge to carry on Roosevelt's commitments; Stalin declared the Soviet Union's continued adherence to all agreements. Both proclaimed their determination to carry through the agreements made regarding China. As to when Soviet forces would be ready to enter the Pacific war, Stalin informed Hopkins that they would be prepared to begin operations on August 8. Stalin agreed that it was now time to communicate the Yalta provisions to the Chinese government. However, he said, perhaps in an effort to apply pressure on the Chinese through the Americans, Soviet forces would not enter the war until a treaty had been concluded between China and the Soviet Union. T. V. Soong, China's foreign minister, would be called to Moscow before July 1 to begin negotiations. Finally, Stalin declared his support of

Chiang Kai-shek as the only man qualified to lead China and disavowed any territorial ambitions either in Manchuria or Sinkiang. To emphasize his point, the Soviet leader offered to permit Nationalist representatives to organize local civil administration in those areas which Soviet forces occupied during their invasion of Manchuria.

On June 15, Hurley formally informed Chiang of the Yalta accords. The day before, the Soviet ambassador had detailed the conditions of Soviet entry to Chiang without direct reference to the Yalta accord, or to the assurances which Stalin had given Hopkins concerning Chinese territorial integrity. When Hurley spoke, therefore, Chiang was apprised of every facet of the Yalta agreement except the American role. His revelation that the United States was committed to support the strong Soviet position in Manchuria at China's expense staggered Chiang visibly.[33] His response, after he had regained his composure, was to make three counterproposals, the principal thrust of which was to commit the United States and Great Britain formally to any settlement in the Far East and to support of China. He proposed that the U.S. and Britain become parties to any Sino-Soviet agreement; that all four powers jointly use the Port Arthur naval base; and that all four powers, rather than solely Russia and China, discuss the transfer of Sakhalin and the Kuriles to the Soviet Union.

In sum, in his first two proposals Chiang sought to return to the position of Cairo I, when Roosevelt had promised American support of China against the Soviet Union in Manchuria, including an American physical presence in Port Arthur.[34] His third proposal was the elementary one that the disposition of Japan's territories was not a matter for the Soviet Union and China alone to decide, but should be shared by both the U.S. and Britain. At this time, however, Chiang was singularly unsuccessful. The United States would not consent to any of his proposals. Chiang was informed that the U.S. would not become a party to the Sino-Soviet treaty, nor would it consider joint use of a naval facility in Port Arthur. The American government would uphold fully the Yalta agreement.[35] As events evolved, although the American position altered somewhat, it remained within both the spirit and letter of the agreement. Not so the Soviet Union.

The United States government had kept Stalin informed of the discussions between Hurley and Chiang. Therefore, when Soong reached Moscow in late June for negotiations for the Sino-Soviet treaty, Stalin knew exactly what the United States would and would not do for China and demanded far more than was contained in the Yalta provisions. A week of hard bargaining left Stalin and Soong far from agreement, the differences centering on the extent of the Soviet controlling position in Manchuria, especially control of the railroad system and port of Dairen. Finally, it was agreed to recess negotiations until after Stalin's return from Potsdam. Soong returned to Chungking as Stalin departed on the 14th of July for Potsdam, the third and final wartime meeting among the big three.

By the time American leaders arrived at Potsdam, earlier apprehension began to be tinged with grim determination to force the Soviet Union to adhere to its pledges. The aggressive behavior of the Russians in Europe following the termination of hostilities convinced President Truman and his chief advisors that the Soviet Union's "expanding demands" would find expression in the Far East as well.[36] The trouble was, despite the enormous naval power then being brought to bear on Japan, the United States was not in a position to counterbalance a Soviet ground thrust into Manchuria. In the absence of a countervailing American presence the Soviet Union might be tempted to exceed the terms of the Yalta agreement. Therefore, at Potsdam the American leadership initiated through diplomatic and military means an effort to limit the Soviet Union to the position agreed upon at Yalta, while encouraging the Chinese to stand firm against Soviet pressure to relinquish concessions beyond those contained in the Soviet-American agreement. The American effort failed. Within one week of the Japanese surrender, the Soviet Union had not only extracted greater gains from the Chinese government than had been agreed upon, but Soviet forces were in position in Manchuria to exert a powerful if not decisive influence upon the subsequent course of events.

Bolstered by the news of a successful test of the atomic bomb, President Truman, in his first meeting with Stalin on the 17th of July, asked for and received oral assurances from the Soviet leader that the "open door" policy would apply to all of Manchuria and that Dairen, as provided in the Yalta agreement, would be a "free port."[37] The introduction of the concept of the "open door" for Manchuria was a clear deviation from the policy conceived by Roosevelt and that agreed upon at Yalta. It constituted a demand for an American presence in Manchuria, which Roosevelt had expressly rejected. A principal Soviet objective was the exclusion of the big powers, including the United States, from Manchuria. Truman's demand therefore must have come as something of an unpleasant surprise. It may have prompted the kind of response that Stalin made. In informing Truman of the status of treaty negotiations with the Chinese, Stalin declared that the Soviet Union was being "more liberal" than required by the Yalta terms, which, he said, called for the "restoration of Russian rights," that is, the position prior to the Russo-Japanese war of 1904. The Soviet Union "would have had that formal right, but . . . had not insisted upon it." The Chinese, Stalin complained, "did not seem to be aware of the big picture." [38]

The major disagreement between the Russians and the Chinese during their negotiations was over the management of the port of Dairen, each side wanting to control it. From Stalin's remarks it seemed to American leaders that the Soviet Union would not budge, prompting Ambassador Harriman to propose that the United States participate in the management of the port as a means of settling the disagreement.[39] Although the United States did not formally offer such a compromise to the Soviets at Potsdam, the idea of establishing an American presence in Manchuria seems to have underlain the policy shift initiated at this time.

On the 23rd, the President sent a forceful message to Chiang Kai-shek, in which he stated: "I asked that you carry out the Yalta agreement but I had not asked that you make any concession in excess of that agreement." [40] Truman's message was clearly conceived to bolster Chiang in his negotiations with the Russians, indicating the limit to which he was expected to go. The President also initiated efforts to bring American military might to bear on the Chinese mainland. On the 21st and 26th, the Joint Chiefs of Staff sent messages to U.S. field commanders instructing them to be prepared for imminent action. In the first, a message to MacArthur, the Joint Chiefs of Staff advised that it might "prove necessary to take action within the near future on the basis of Japanese capitulation, possibly before Russian entry." [41] In the second, to MacArthur and Nimitz, a tone of urgency was injected.

Coordination of plans for the procedure to be followed in the event of Japanese governmental surrender is now a pressing necessity. . . . In such event immediate naval occupation of critical parts of Japan is desirable. . . . It also appears to Joint Chiefs of Staff that it would be highly desirable for similar procedure to be followed on the Asiatic mainland in following order of priority: Shanghai, Fusan in Korea, Chefoo, and Chingwangtao [sic.] on the Manchurian border. Also that preliminary landings on Asiatic Continent might best be carried out by Marines. A landing at Taku to permit the blocking of the critical communications points of Peking-Tientsin would be more desirable than at Chingwangtao but probably is impractical from the viewpoint of naval craft. The Joint Chiefs of Staff do not desire to become involved in the campaign in China on the mainland other than by air, but it is considered highly desirable to seize the ports in order better to facilitate the reoccupation of the country by Chinese forces.[42]

Immediately after the Potsdam conference, Truman gave further diplomatic support to China. On August 5, Harriman was authorized to state to Stalin that the United States: (1) believed that the Chinese had met the terms of Yalta and the Russians should not insist on more; (2) proposed a joint Soviet-American agreement reaffirming the open door in Manchuria; (3) opposed any arrangement which would include Dairen in the Soviet military zone. On the last point, Harriman was further instructed to note that the United States preferred "free port" status for Dairen under Chinese administration, but would not object to the supervision of the port by an international commission composed of U.S., Soviet, British, and Chinese representatives.[43]

A subtle but unmistakable shift had occurred in American policy. In effect, Truman's attempt to give greater support to China in Manchuria against the Soviet Union—to the extent of participating in the management of the port of Dairen—resembled in its principal aspects Chiang Kai-shek's proposals of June 15, when he was officially informed of the Yalta agreement by Ambassador Hurley! At this point, however, the pace of events was far too rapid to bring about any basic change, although the effort was made.

On August 6 the atomic bomb was dropped on Hiroshima. On the 8th the Soviet Union declared war on Japan. The Soviet move must have come as a surprise to American policymakers, who expected Soviet entry somewhat later. At Potsdam, Stalin had told Truman twice that the Soviet Union would be prepared to enter "by the middle of August"[44] (although he had earlier given Hopkins the date of August 8). Moreover, the oft-stated precondition for Soviet entry, conclusion of a Sino-Soviet treaty, had not yet been fulfilled. If American leaders hoped to get the jump on the Soviet Union by bringing the war to an end before they were prepared, then the gambit failed, although the Japanese indicated their readiness to surrender on August 10, the day after the second bomb had been dropped on Nagasaki.

Meanwhile, Sino-Soviet negotiations had resumed (August 7–14). Encouraged by Truman's expressions of support, the Chinese representatives at first stood firm. Stalin insisted on Soviet control of Dairen and after the Soviets threatened to give assistance to the Communists, Chiang instructed his negotiators to give in to Soviet demands. In return for written Soviet assurance not to assist the Chinese Communists, Chiang agreed to include Dairen in the Soviet military zone and to give greater Soviet control over the Manchurian railway system. Stalin had won, overcoming American assurances of support for the Chinese. When the treaty was announced on August 14, Stalin informed Harriman that a joint Soviet-American statement was unnecessary and declined further discussion of it. But this takes us slightly ahead of the story.

Japan's decision to surrender set the stage for an extraordinary American attempt to forestall complete Soviet dominance of Manchuria. On August 11, the Joint Chiefs instructed MacArthur and Nimitz of the following:

> The President desires that such advance arrangements as are practicable be made to occupy the Port of Dairen and a port in Korea [Seoul] immediately following the surrender of Japan if those ports have not at that time been taken over by Soviet forces.[45]

If American ground forces could reach Dairen before the Soviets did, the United States would be in a position to counterbalance the Soviet presence and insure that the terms of the Yalta agreement would be fulfilled. This, of course, was precisely the argument which Chiang Kai-shek had made as far back as the Cairo conference and that Truman had also come to appreciate. Although the President's August 5 instruction to Harriman was an attempt to express that appreciation in policy terms, the broad lines of policy sketched by Roosevelt were already too far advanced to be reshaped easily. Within a week the order was canceled. Soviet forces had won the race for Dairen and for sole control over Manchuria.[46]

The Effort to Stabilize Manchuria

The problem for the United States was how to achieve both a strong Soviet position in Manchuria and the establishment of Chinese sovereignty there. The danger lay in the possibility that if the Soviet Union obtained an overwhelmingly powerful position in Manchuria, Stalin might decide to create a separatist regime based on the Chinese Communists, thus dividing China, rather than work out the complex Rooseveltian scheme of a weak but territorially integrated China. The United States sanctioned a strong Soviet and Chinese Communist presence in Manchuria, but not a separatist Communist regime which would exclude the Nationalist Government. Hence the race for Dairen, which, if successful, would have made it easier to insure a Nationalist presence in Manchuria and the establishment of a *proforma* sovereignty.

On the other hand, policy toward the Nationalist Government was equally complex. Chiang Kai-shek was not a puppet to whom the United States could dictate policy. Although he had indicated his willingness to enter a coalition government with the Communists, he sought to establish hegemony over all of China, including Manchuria, and his forces would destroy the Communists if the opportunity arose. This complicated the American position. The task was to create the conditions under which a coalition government was the desirable alternative. Paradoxically, because the Communists were the weaker party, it involved strengthening the Communists, particularly in Manchuria, otherwise no basis for a coalition would exist. This set of extraordinarily complex and interlocking objectives helps to explain the seemingly contradictory American policy in the fall of 1945, in which the United States sought to assist the Nationalists to reoccupy coastal China, but not Manchuria. The United States would render assistance to Chiang to recover Chinese territory, but not if it would contribute to conflict with the Communists. The net effect of the policy was to permit the Chinese Communists to secure a foothold in Manchuria, while giving the Nationalists a similar opportunity in the north China plain area.

On the 15th the announcement of the Sino-Soviet Treaty was made. The following day, Chiang Kai-shek invited Mao Tse-tung to Chungking to settle the differences between their two parties. Mao hesitated at first until the publication of the full terms of the Sino-Soviet treaty on the

25th. Then he assented. In the meantime, as an inducement, Hurley had offered personally to escort the Chinese Communist leader to Chungking in an American aircraft, an offer which was accepted. Thus on August 28, Mao Tse-tung arrived in Chungking for negotiaions with Chiang Kai-shek, which took place against a background of conflict as each side's forces moved to establish a presence, however tenuous, in as much previously occupied territory as possible.

Five meetings were held over forty-one days. The final communique, published on October 11, was in no sense an indication that both sides had reached a fundamental solution. On the contrary, the communique reflected a broad agreement on the terms of the continuing struggle. The discussions themselves ranged over the gamut of political, military, and territorial questions facing the protagonists and preliminary agreement was reached in each area. The principal achievement of the talks concerned the delimitation of the territory under each party's respective control and the areas to be contested. It was implicitly agreed that the area south of the Yangtze River would be undisputed Nationalist territory, while the Shen-Kan-Ning border region would likewise be Communist territory.

The Chinese Communists agreed to "demobilize their anti-Japanese troops now deployed in Kwantung, Chekiang, southern Kiangsu, southern Anhwei, central Anhwei, Hunan, Hupeh, and Honan (not including northern Honan), and that such troops as are to be reorganized will be gradually evacuated from the said areas, to be concentrated in the liberated areas north of the Lung-Hai railway and in northern Kiangsu and northern Anhwei." [47] Agreement on this measure permitted each side to concentrate its forces for the struggle over the contested areas. Disputed territory was China north of the Yangtze and east of the Peking-Hankow Railroad, roughly the north China plain area. Manchuria did not come under formal deliberation, since it was already covered in the Sino-Soviet Treaty of August, although in reality it, too, was already a disputed area. In fact, the two principal areas in which the civil war was fought out and decided were Manchuria and the north China plain.

Secondly, both parties agreed that the ultimate goal was the establishment of a constitutional government and that the steps toward this end would be convocation of a Political Consultative Conference (as the Communists had demanded the previous July), in which all interested political parties would be represented, followed by convocation of the National Assembly to inaugurate constitutional government. There was no agreement on the number of delegates to attend the assembly, nor the respective political strengths each party would wield in the government. These issues would be determined by the extent of territory—local governments—each party controlled at the time the National Assembly convened, but general procedure was agreed upon.

The issue on which no agreement was reached was on the establishment of local governments in the liberated areas, that is, those areas formerly under Japanese occupation, which each party sought to claim. The Communists put forth several proposals, in an effort to negotiate Nationalist acceptance of a Communist political presence, principally in the north China areas. In addition to the Shen-Kan-Ning area, the Communists specified eleven provinces (Jehol, Chahar, Hopeh, Shantung, Shansi, Suiyuan, Honan, Kiangsu, Anhwei, Hupeh, and Kwangtung) and four major cities (Peking, Tientsin, Tsingtao, and Shanghai). The government responded to the Communist foray with the argument that its appointed provincial-level officials should take office so that the "recovered areas may be restored to normalcy at the earliest possible moment," [48] after which elections would be held at all levels. No agreement being reached on the disposition of local political power in the formerly Japanese-held areas, the issue was referred to the Political Consultative Conference (PCC) for further discussions. In effect, the issue of control was left to be decided on the field of battle, since it was basic to the question of the respective strengths each party would wield in any future government. In fact, while the discussions were in progress, Communist and Nationalist forces were clashing over the establishment of positions in the disputed areas, including Manchuria.

The Soviet Union, the United States, and China

The Soviet Union sought to establish the position of dominance in Manchuria expressed in the Yalta accords and to maintain it through the instrumentality of the Chinese Communists. The difficulty for them was that not only were the Chinese Communist forces relatively weaker in numbers, arms, and training than Nationalist forces at this time, there was literally no Communist presence in Manchuria to serve as a foundation on which to build. Time was necessary. Soviet policy upon entry, therefore, centered on hindering Nationalist recovery of Manchuria and creating the conditions for the buildup of Communist strength. As insurance, to guard against the possibility that the Nationalists with American help might move quickly into and occupy Manchuria, Soviet forces began to strip it of vital military and industrial equipment. In weeks, Manchuria was denuded of its capital plant, ensuring that the area could not be turned quickly to advantage against the Soviet Union. (No stripping accompanied Soviet occupation of North Korea, suggesting that Soviet fear of the early loss of Manchuria was a primary consideration.)

The Soviet invasion itself was important in facilitating Chinese Communist entry into Manchuria. Soviet entrance removed the blocking presence of the Japanese forces there. Accompanying Soviet forces entering Manchuria from the north and east was a several-thousand man Chinese Communist baggage-train armed force, which rapidly began to build military positions and set up administrations in small towns in the northern and eastern parts of Manchuria. A third invasion force thrust across Inner Mongolia, northern Hopeh province and into southern Manchuria via Liaoning province. It was this force which first encountered Chinese Communist troops under Lin Piao marching in the same direction, at Changchiak'ou, and provided rail transportation to speed the Chinese Communist journey.[49] Within a month, both the Chinese Communist regulars under Lin and the baggage-train Communists under Chou Pao-chung had set up rudimentary administrative apparatuses in many of the smaller towns and cities of Manchuria. Lin's forces were concentrated in the south, while Chou's men were stationed close to Soviet borders. Working without interference from the Nationalists, who were still excluded from the area, by December all Communist forces—close to 150,000 strong—were merged under the leadership of Lin Piao and administrative structures were functioning in four of Manchuria's nine provinces. This achievement was in no small part due to the efforts of the Soviet Union in assisting Communist work and preventing Nationalist entry—the latter a story best recounted in terms of American policy during these months.

American policy toward China in the immediate aftermath of the Japanese surrender centered around the effort to transport Nationalist troops into north China to fill the vacuum created by the end of hostilities. It was consistent with the earlier unsuccessful effort to bring

American power up to but not in conflict with Soviet power in Manchuria. The stated rationale for assisting Nationalist troops in their movement northward was to liberate former Japanese occupied territory and to facilitate the repatriation of Japanese to their homeland. In fact, U.S. forces repatriated nearly three million Japanese, military and civilian, en masse within the following year, complicating the already chaotic situation. But initially the Japanese retained control of many areas until Nationalist units relieved them.

All lend-lease aid to China had ceased by August 22, except that which was necessary to facilitate the tasks of territorial recovery. Chiang had been informed of the termination and had requested additional U.S. assistance. By mid-September, the President and his policy advisers had completed their review of China's needs, which they conceived as a limited program designed

> to assist China in the development of armed forces of moderate size for the maintenance of internal peace and security and the assumption of adequate control over the liberated areas of China, including Manchuria and Formosa.[50]

In essence, the President's decision was to provide the "equipment and supplies to complete the 39-division program" [51] initiated during the war as part of lend-lease. Although by August 23 all thirty-nine had sufficient weaponry to engage in combat operations, the program had been less than half completed. Twenty of the thirty-nine divisions had approximaely 80 percent of their full complement of arms, while twenty-three had had only incidental U.S. training. However, no replacement system, which would include the organization to train and condition troops, not to mention resupply them, was offered in the President's program.[52]

The President stated the essential caveat for American assistance:

> Having in mind statements by the Generalissimo that China's internal political difficulties will be settled by political methods, it should be clearly understood that military assistance furnished by the United States would not be diverted for use in fratricidal warfare or to support undemocratic administration.[53]

His statement indicated clearly that the United States assistance was limited and not designed to lead to a military confrontation with the

Chinese Communists, nor to support an "undemocratic" government. The transportation of Nationalist troops was continued under this blanket assurance, as was the deployment of the U.S. Marines in early October to the Peking-Tientsin area. However, although a feeble effort was made, the United States declined to assist Chinese forces in the reoccupation of Manchuria and in mid-November, through Wedemeyer, advised Chiang against the attempt to recover that area.[54] Instead, he was advised to consolidate his position in the north China plain, and to forgo the attempt to occupy Manchuria. Chiang dissented from this advice and insisted that the U.S. assist him to recover Manchuria as it had committed itself on paper to do and to which, by treaty, the Soviet Union concurred.

On October 6, U.S. naval forces attempted to land Chinese troops at the Soviet occupied port of Dairen, but were flatly refused entry with the transparent excuse that it was a commercial port and not to be employed for military purposes. This despite the fact that by the treaty just concluded between the Russians and the Chinese the Nationalists had full rights not only to access but to administer the port! The U.S. protested diplomatically but took no action. Half-hearted and unsuccessful attempts were made by American naval forces to land troops at two other ports, Yingk'ou and Hu Lu Tao in Liaotung Bay, to the north of Dairen, where there were no Russians—only hostile Chinese. The entire futile exercise consumed the better part of a month before the Chinese forces were put ashore at Shanhaikuan, far to the south and outside Manchuria proper. China's best troops sailed to and fro in the Bay, unused and unusable, in a delay which lost valuable time. In the weeks that they were aboard American vessels, the Chinese Communists rushed into Manchuria unhindered to secure positions there.

Nationalist forces, finally disembarked on November 1, were forced to enter Manchuria through the narrow corridor of Shanhaikuan, where they encountered an estimated 25,000 Communist forces which harassed the Nationalists but made no attempt to engage them in full-scale battle. At this stage, the Communists were still militarily inferior to the Nationalists and therefore avoided battle, satisfied merely to delay their advance. By the end of November Nationalist forces had managed to secure a foothold in the southern end of Manchuria, at Chinchow, but had been restrained from occupation of the rest.

Meanwhile, the Soviet Union indicated its readiness to begin the withdrawal of forces from Manchuria. Already overdue, they were scheduled to withdraw completely by December 3. The Nationalists requested a further delay at this point, fearing that precipitate Soviet withdrawal would give control of key towns and cities to the Communist forces already in the vicinity. The Nationalists now needed more time to prepare to take over from the Russians as soon as they departed. The United States agreed to transport Nationalist troops by air into Manchuria (the Russians had actually suggested this in November),[55] but delays had been costly to the Nationalists. The Chinese Communists had beaten the Nationalists and, with the invaluable assistance of the Soviet Union, were deep in the process of creating a position of strength there.[56] When the first major test came in the spring of 1946, however, despite the delays to the Nationalists and advantages given to the Communists, the latter were still no match for Nationalist power. But events occurring in far-off Washington once again critically affected the unraveling of the China tangle.

The Appointment of General Marshall

Ambassador Hurley had departed for Washington from Chung-king on September 22 for medical treatment. In Washington he encountered a situation different from that which he had been accustomed to. Under President Roosevelt, Hurley had been the President's special representative and had personally been involved in the discussion although not the formulation of high policy. It was in the capacity of the President's personal emissary (and friend) that he initially undertook his assignment in China. After Roosevelt's death, Truman significantly altered the role which Hurley subsequently played. To a marked degree, the new President relied on the established organization, the State Department, for the execution of foreign policy. Hurley, consequently, was relegated to the role formally assigned to him as Ambassador to China—executor of policy and no longer confidant of the President. Unhappy in this reduced role and dissatisfied with what he considered to be a distortion of Roosevelt's policies, he resigned.[57]

President Truman appointed General George C. Marshall as his special representative to China on the same day that Hurley resigned.[58] The appointment of Marshall was fitting, since he had been one of the principal architects of the policy being pursued. In fact, in discussing his appointment, Truman instructed Marshall to assist the Joint Chiefs in the composition of his own directive. In discussion with high level government officials, opinion was clearly divided over the course American policy should take in the event of complications. On December 9, Marshall conferred with State Department officials, Secretary Byrnes, Undersecretary Dean Acheson, and John Carter Vincent. In response to the question: What should the U.S. do if Chiang refused to cooperate and the Communists did, Byrnes replied: "in this case the Central Government would be informed that the assistance which we could otherwise give to China would not be given. . . . "[59] Two days later, on the 11th, Marshall met with the President, Byrnes, and Admiral Leahy. In a broader ranging discussion of the strategic consequences of failing to support the Generalissimo, even in the event he proved unwilling to cooperate with the U.S., Marshall noted that:

> if the Generalissimo, in his [General Marshall's] opinion, failed to make reasonable concessions, and this resulted in the breakdown of the efforts to secure a political unification, and the U.S. abandoned continued support of the Generalissimo, there would follow the tragic consequences of a divided China and of a probable Russian resumption of power in Manchuria, the combined effect of this resulting in the defeat or loss of the major purpose of our war in the Pacific.[60]

At this point, both the President and the Secretary of State agreed that "we would have to back the Generalissimo to the extent of assisting him to move troops into North China in order that the evacuation of the Japanese might be completed." [61]

On the 14th, Marshall met again with the President and Acheson, seeking to obtain full clarification of what the American response would be, particularly in light of the possibility that Chiang might not see it in his interest to cooperate with the American policy. The issue was resolved in the following way, in Marshall's words:

> In the event that I was unable to secure the necessary action by the Generalissimo, which I thought reasonable and desirable, it would still be necessary for the U.S. Government, through me, to continue to back the National Government of the Republic of China—through the Generalissimo within the terms of the announced policy of the United States Government.[62]

Both the President and Undersecretary fully agreed with this position.

The decision to back the Generalissimo regardless of the outcome of the mediation effort was to be kept secret, as was the kind of support which Marshall was to give. His ace was the authority to transport Nationalist troops into north China—under the stated rationale of evacuating Japanese troops—in order to place them in sufficient strength to manage whatever conflict situation might arise. This was the greatest of powers he could be delegated outside of being able to grant actual military assistance. It meant that Marshall could ensure that the Nationalists had superior forces in any military engagement with the Communists. (As it turned out, the opposite was the need. The Nationalists proved far superior to the Communists, and Marshall's problem became how to restrain, not to assist them.)

Thus General Marshall was named President Truman's special representative to China. His appointment was welcomed by all sides, Nationalist, Communist, and Russian. The Russians immediately responded to the announcement of the appointment by making a sharp turn in their administration of Manchuria. After the announcement of Marshall's appointment, the Soviets began to treat the Nationalist officials in Changchun and Mukden with marked cordiality, the opposite of the manner they had treated them previously. Notices were posted in the streets prohibiting further criticism of Chiang Kai-shek and favorable commentary was solicited. The Soviets were clearly preparing to give Marshall a chance to bring about the culmination of the policy which the Soviet Union and the United States were jointly, if hesitatingly, pursuing.

On December 15, President Truman delivered a formal statement of policy toward China in connection with Marshall's departure. Truman stated that the United States recognized the National Government of China as "the only legal government in China" and "the proper instrument to achieve the objective of a unified China." [63] Therefore the United States had been assisting and would continue to assist the National Government in the disarming and evacuating of the Japanese, for which purpose the U.S. Marines were in China. Beyond this, the President stated, "United States support will not extend to U.S. military intervention to influence the course of any Chinese internal strife." [64]

The President called for a cease-fire and convocation of the Political Consultative Conference, both of which had been items raised by the

Communist and Nationalist representatives who had continued the discussions initiated in August. The President also declared that if the Nationalist Government "as an interim arrangement" were "broadened to include other political elements in the country" and "all armed forces in China integrated effectively," the United States "would be prepared to assist the National Government in every reasonable way to rehabilitate the country." [65] The stage was now set for the application of the policies which had evolved during the war and particularly during 1945. Marshall's task, as the President's representative, would be to bring about a reasonable settlement between Nationalists and Communists which would result in the formation of a coalition government for China.

VIII
Strategies in Conflict, 1946–1949

The "civil war" in China was the consequence of a National-Communist failure to reach a political settlement. In the ensuing all-out military conflict from mid-1946, decisions made by Soviet and American leaders critically affected the course of battle. At a time when the United States chose to withhold military assistance from the Nationalists, the Soviet Union energetically bolstered the Communists. In particular, the failure of the American leadership to appreciate the larger significance of the Soviet decision, structural limitations of the Nationalist state, and the strategic importance of building a stable military balance on the mainland were crucial factors leading to the defeat of the Nationalist Government and the exclusion of the United States from the China mainland. The Nationalists themselves bear as mighty a responsibility for defeat as the Communists do for victory, but both Chiang Kai-shek and Mao Tse-tung acted within the broader policy parameters set by the United States and the Soviet Union.

Marshall Arranges a Settlement, December 22–March 11

The Marshall mission to China was an effort to achieve a political coalition between Nationalists and Communists as a part of the larger postwar settlement between the Soviet Union and the United States. Nationalist relative military superiority greatly complicated the problem. Although the United States was committed to the restoration of China's territorial integrity, defeat of the Communists would endanger the larger policy of establishing a strong Russian position in East Asia—to which the United States was also committed. The solution was the establishment of a coalition government in which the Chinese Communists would dominate Manchuria and thereby guarantee continued Soviet hegemony over the region.

Upon his arrival in China, Marshall moved to arrange for a cease-fire and to convoke the Political Consultative Conference. Within a few weeks he had achieved both objectives. Both sides reached agreement for a cease-fire January 10, which came into effect on the 13th. The agreement called for the establishment of an executive headquarters in Peking to oversee the cease-fire through the dispatch of three-man teams consisting of one Nationalist, one Communist, and one American member. The cessation of hostilities order applied to all areas except China south of the Yangtze River and Manchuria. In these two areas the National Government was permitted to transport troops as part of its effort to restore Chinese sovereignty to formerly occupied territories. The cease-fire applied essentially to the north China plain area (from the Yangtze River to Manchuria) and it was to this area that the agreements reached at the Political Consultative Conference primarily related.[1]

The Political Consultative Conference convened on the same day the cease-fire was signed and continued through the remainder of January. Nationalists and Communists, spurred on by the tireless efforts of General Marshall, concurred on the steps necessary to establish a coalition government for China. It was agreed to establish a provisional coalition government, which would command supreme state power until the National Assembly met, integrate all military forces into one national army, convene a national assembly whose function would be to inaugurate constitutional government for China, and compete politically for control over local government organs.[2]

The National Government would be broadened to include non-Kuomintang members, becoming, in effect, a provisional coalition government. The State Council, with Chiang Kai-shek at its head, would become the highest political body in the land. The council was to be composed of forty members, twenty Kuomintang and twenty non-Kuomintang members, including an undetermined number of Communists. The State Council would rule until the National Assembly convened to establish constitutional government for China.[3] Preliminary agreement was also reached at this time on the integration of Nationalist and Communist military forces (final agreement was not achieved until February 25). An intricate troop reduction schedule and location chart were drawn up. It was projected that within eighteen months, China's many armies would be reduced to sixty divisions of one integrated National Army, in which a ratio of five Nationalist to one Communist

Army would be maintained. Party control over the army would be abolished, while civil control over the military would be established.[4]

The question of establishing China's permanent government was dealt with in separate resolutions on the National Assembly, draft constitution, and on local and provincial political organs.[5] In the resolution on the National Assembly, it was agreed to convene that body on May 5, 1946, some five months hence. Chiang Kai-shek consented to enlarge the total number of delegates to the assembly to 2,050. Delegates would be selected according to three different criteria: 1,200 were to be elected on the basis of geographical and vocational distribution; 700 were apportioned among the various lesser parties and other "social leaders"; 150 were simply allocated to Taiwan and Manchuria.[6] The criteria for determining delegates was curious in one principal regard—the apportionment to Manchuria of only 75 seats, which clearly underrepresented that area. With a population estimated in 1946 to total 36,569,252,[7] according to the ratio of delegates to population (roughly 1:220,000), Manchuria alone should have received a total of at least 180 delegates. Chiang Kai-shek clearly downgraded the weight of Manchuria in the National Assembly, in anticipation of the likelihood that the Chinese Communists would have a strong position there.

The issue of local government was crucial in determining which party would ultimately control the National Government. Agreements on this question were contained in the resolution on the program for peace and national reconstruction.[8] Containing nine sections and one annex, the resolution covered various topics from education to overseas Chinese. Section III, "political problems," and the annex were the key sections dealing with the procedures for establishing local power. In section III.6 the Kuomintang agreed to permit "popular elections" at the provincial, district, and county levels. Recall that during the discussions between Chiang and Mao the previous autumn, the question of local elections had been a point of disagreement.[9] Although the Nationalists now agreed to popular elections, they sought to ensure control over the process. In Section III.7 it was stipulated that any district which had attained self-government must carry out "national administrative matters . . . under the supervision and control of the National Government." Section III.8 noted that "regulations issued by the Provincial and District Governments must not contravene the laws and decrees of the Central Government." Finally, point one in the annex contained the provision that "in those recovered areas where the local government is under dispute the status quo shall be maintained until a settlement is made according to articles 6, 7, 8 of Chapter III on Political Problems." [10]

Control over provincial and local governments would determine each party's respective political weight in the projected national coalition government. The provisions regarding the establishment of local self-government were fundamental to the success of the coalition effort. Even more important, the seven provinces of the north China plain lying between the Yangtze and Manchuria—Shansi, Hopeh, Hupeh, Honan, Shantung, Kiangsu, Anhwei—contained approximately 200 million people, or 44 percent of China's 450 million people! [11] These seven provinces alone would contribute almost half of the delegates to the National Assembly. Therefore the contest for control over the north China plain area would be crucial in determining Communist and Nationalist shares in the coalition government.

Except for deliberations regarding military reorganization, which continued until the end of February, the Political Consultative Conference concluded its activity on January 31. By all appearances the agreements reached constituted a major triumph for the American mediation effort in general and for General Marshall in particular, as well as marking an important step forward in the quest for peace and unity in China. The agreements, of course, did not mean an end to struggle, but rather set the rules for continued contention. Combined with the cease-fire agreement, the PCC resolutions were designed to channel further struggle between the Nationalists and Communists into the political, rather than the military, arena.

On February 26, the day after the military reorganization plan was completed, Marshall, in a telegram to the President, requested his recall "about March 12." The general intended to make personal representations to Congress and to the private financial community on behalf of China's enormous needs. His request was approved by President Truman the next day.[12] Before his departure, Marshall arranged to make a final inspection trip throughout the north China plain area. Leaving Peiping on March 1, General Marshall, accompanied by Chou En-lai and Chang Chih-chung, covered 3,000 miles in five days, visiting field team headquarters in Tsinan, Hsuchow, Hsinhsiang, Taiyuan, Yenan, and Hankow.[13] In Yenan, Marshall met with Mao Tse-tung, to whom he made a direct personal appeal for peace. Mao assured Marshall that the Chinese Communist Party would "abide wholeheartedly" by the terms of all agreements reached between them and the Nationalists.[14]

Upon his return to Peiping, Marshall sent a report of his impressions to the President in which he expressed unguarded enthusiasm for the possibilities of success. He described the work of the American officers on the various field teams scattered throughout China as "amazing," "astounding," and "splendid" and noted that "we are now ready to start on the demobilization and reorganization." [15] Unfortunately for General Marshall and the entire American mediation effort, not to speak of the policy which had evolved since the middle of the war, events were already taking place which would shortly lay waste to this sanguine prospect.

Despite the January cease-fire agreement, both sides had continued to move troops, the Communists across Jehol and Chahar into Manchuria and the Nationalists into the same areas to block them. The towns of Chihfeng and Tolun in these two provinces were principal staging areas for the Communists and continual skirmishing took place in this region between the contending forces. The Communists had, in fact, been successful in building up their troop strength in Manchuria, by land through the Chihfeng–Tolun route and by sea from ports in Shantung. By mid-February, according to a CCP press release of February 14, "the Manchurian people have organized a Manchuria Democratic Joint Army nearly three hundred thousand strong disposed in areas not garrisoned by the Soviet Army or evacuated by the Soviet Army in Manchuria." [16] Whether this was exaggerated or not, the Communists had succeeded in building a position of some strength in Manchuria, considering the fact that they had been almost totally excluded from the area since 1931 while it was under Japanese rule. Quite clearly, the Chinese Communists had not "abided wholeheartedly" by the cessation of hostilities agreement regarding Manchuria; nor, for that matter, had the Nationalists in unsuccessfully seeking to prevent the Communist move.

The impending crisis in Manchuria had not gone unobserved by the American side. The second secretary of the embassy in Chungking, Raymond Ludden, on March 9, sent a memorandum to Marshall noting the increasing hostility of the Communists toward the Nationalists on the issue of Manchuria, particularly since the issuance of the February

14 statement. He spoke with apprehension about the possibility of Communist "collusion" with the Soviet Union.[17] Marshall, too, saw the problem and sought to obtain Chiang's agreement to send the field teams into Manchuria (heretofore they were in north China only). Chiang agreed.[18] Marshall, en route to Washington, wrote to the President that "so far no measures have been taken to suppress the fighting and the struggle for favorable position in Manchuria," a situation which he viewed as "far more difficult than in North China." [19] Even as Marshall sent off his message, the initial steps toward open conflict were being taken.

Chiang Kai-shek Takes the Initiative

Marshall's departure came at a most inauspicious time. Soviet occupation of Manchuria had as one of its side effects the prevention of any large-scale armed conflict between Nationalists and Communists there. From March 7, the Soviet Union initiated an unannounced withdrawal from the southern portion of Manchuria, including Mukden and Ssup'ingchieh, key junction towns lying along the South Manchurian Railroad between Dairen and Ch'angchun. (The Soviets began the evacuation of Ch'angchun on March 26, but retained forces in Dairen and in the northern half of Manchuria throughout the civil war.)[20] Hard upon the heels of departing Soviet forces, the Chinese Communists rushed to build fortifications in preparation against the anticipated Nationalist attempt to occupy the area (as they were entitled to do by the terms of the Sino-Soviet treaty). The Communists made little effort to take Mukden, which the Nationalists occupied, but moved in force into the rail junction of Ssup'ingchieh.[21]

The Soviet withdrawal and the Chinese Communist move came at a time when the Kuomintang Central Executive Committee was in session (March 1–17). In the absence of General Marshall's restraining influence, the Nationalists decided to occupy the towns evacuated by Soviet forces, engaging whatever Communist forces they might encounter. Their plan was to recover the province of Liaoning and that part of Kirin below Ch'angchun and to the west of the Sungari River. Principal targets in their drive were to be the towns of Ssup'ingchieh, Yung Chi, and Ch'angchun—all located along the South Manchurian Railroad.[22] They began to move forces out of Mukden on March 19, proceeding slowly up the rail line, and encountered negligible resistance until they reached within a few miles of Ssup'ingchieh, about 80 miles north of Mukden.

Each side reinforced its position. The Nationalists sent troops by sea to Shanhaikuan, by rail from there to Mukden, and from Mukden on foot. By the end of March six armies were already in Manchuria and five more en route. While the Communists were building up their own forces (American estimates credited the Communists with over 80 regiments in Manchuria), their representative to the executive headquarters in Peiping importuned the United States to prevent transportation of additional Nationalist forces.[23] They were, however, adamant against the dispatch of field teams to Manchuria.[24] The day after Soviet forces completed their evacuation of Ch'angchun, on April 16, Communist forces attacked and overwhelmed the small Nationalist garrison there and occupied the city on the 18th. That day General Marshall arrived back in China.

By the 24th of April, Nationalist forces, spearheaded by the American trained First Army under General Tu Li-ming (Tu Yü-ming), had surrounded Ssup'ingchieh on three sides. Though encountering stiff resistance from Communist forces throughout the area, they commenced the battle for the city. In over three weeks of fierce fighting both sides suffered heavy casualties, the Communists employing some artillery and tanks manned by Japanese crews, the Nationalists employing artillery and air strikes.[25] By the middle of May, although outnumbered, Nationalist forces had dealt the Communists a stunning defeat.[26] On the 19th, Nationalist forces took Ssup'ingchieh and continued in pursuit of the Communists' troops, which, under command of Lin Piao, were retreating north toward Harbin and east toward the Korean border. By June 1 it appeared that Nationalist forces would pursue and destroy all Communist forces in Manchuria; they had captured Ch'angchun and were moving swiftly toward Harbin. At this point, General Marshall obtained Chiang Kai-shek's agreement to a truce, which began on June 6. But this takes us somewhat ahead of the story, for the May–June period was perhaps the most critical in the history of the civil war, if not in the struggle for power in China.

By early May it was clear that the battle would go against the Communists; the Nationalists simply possessed the superior force. Imminent defeat and its implications for continued Soviet hegemony in Manchuria gave rise to a reappraisal of policy. Soviet strategy was to control Manchuria at all costs, to the exclusion of all other powers, including the United States. Such had been Russian and then Soviet strategy since the turn of the century, when the significance of the area had first been recognized. If that objective could be realized within the context of cooperation with the United States, that is, in the establishment of a coalition government for China in which the Communists would dominate Manchuria, so much the better.

With Nationalist forces on the verge of destroying the Communist position in Manchuria and with the United States formally demanding the application of the "open door" principle to Manchuria, that is, an American presence, the possibility of not achieving Soviet objectives was great—either through the failure or a change of American policy. It might prove necessary for the Soviet Union to abandon the cooperative enterprise and give direct support to a separate Chinese Communist regime in Manchuria. The preferred alternative was a "peaceful" solution. Therefore, in early May, Stalin invited Chiang to meet with him to settle the disposition of Manchuria—to agree to the exclusion of American influence there.[27] Chiang declined Stalin's invitation, a decision which forced a policy change for the Soviet Union. From June 1946 onward, the Soviet Union pursued the unilateral policy of building Chinese Communist strength in Manchuria, declining further attempts at genuine cooperation with the United States.

Chiang fully realized the magnitude of his decision. He knew that the refusal to meet with Stalin was directed not only at the Soviet Union but at the United States as well! In discussing the issue later, Chiang noted that "it was no longer possible for China and the United States to work out a joint policy towards Soviet Russia." The National Government, he said, had decided to "go it alone, if necessary, in resisting Soviet aggression," and would not accept the "neutralization of China" through the "establishment of a coalition government." [28] It was, of course, American policy to achieve this very objective and both General Marshall and President Truman urged Chiang to accept Stalin's invitation.[29] Chiang had taken a calculated risk, if not a dangerous gamble. He knew that a refusal to meet with Stalin would mean that the Soviet leader "might become even more overt in his support of his Chinese puppets' subversive activities," but hoped that the United States would perceive that it was in its larger security interests to support the Nationalists against the Soviet Union in Manchuria.

In point of fact, whether it was known to Chiang or not, on June 1 the State-War-Navy Coordinating Committee (SWNCC) had sent to the Secretary of State an extensive memorandum considering "the implications bearing upon the security of the United States in the present and potential Manchurian situation." [30] The memo postulated a complete reversal of the policy which the United States had been pursuing since Tehran. The three salient points were:

> With or without . . . physical incorporation into the U.S.S.R., a Manchuria integrated into the Russian economy would prove a grave threat to the United States as well as to China. The resulting self-sufficiency of the U.S.S.R. in the Far East would, taken together with her western industries, place under the control of the Soviet Union the greatest agglomeration of power in the history of the world. To counter this probable long-range Soviet program the United States must adopt a policy aimed at the orientation of the people of Manchuria in the direction of China and at the integration of Manchuria into the Chinese economy. . . . Such a program must remain a Chinese responsibility, but the United States should inform the Chinese Government of its vital interest therein and of its willingness to assist. . . .

> It is felt that communism is in opposition to the basic Chinese way of life and that the present Communist party in China has won a following, not because of real devotion of the people to Communist doctrines emanating from Moscow, but rather because of . . . popular opposition to the reactionary and oppressive one-party rule of the Kuomintang. For that reason, the United States should give every encouragement to middle-of-the-road groups . . . and should continue its efforts to convince the National Government of the vital necessity for broadening its base of participation.[31]

SWNCC requested that the conclusions of the paper be transmitted immediately to General Marshall for comment, before submitting the "paper to the President for approval as definitive U.S. policy."

America's Failure in China

If General Marshall replied to the SWNCC memorandum, there is no record of it in the recently published diplomatic papers of the Marshall mission. American policy, however, did change in the second half of 1946, but in the direction opposite to that expressed in the memorandum; and the impetus for that change came from General

Marshall, reinforced by the views of Acting Secretary of State Dean
Acheson. Marshall rejected the proposed policy course, instead per-
sisting in the conviction that a cooperative policy with the Soviet Union
was still feasible—despite abundant evidence to the contrary. Perhaps
Marshall realized that unless the Nationalists were curbed, civil strife,
with the Soviet Union fully in support of the Chinese Communists,
would be the inevitable consequence. For whatever reason, Marshall
appears to have lost perspective by his direct involvement in the
day-to-day events. Like a hero in a Greek tragedy, he groped toward his
goal blinded to the fact that the Soviet Union fundamentally had
changed its policy.

When Marshall returned to China on April 18, the battle for
Ssup'ingchieh was in high gear. He immediately attempted to persuade
the Nationalist Government to terminate the battle. On the 22nd of
April, Marshall declared to Yu Ta-wei, Chiang's representative, that the
National Government "cannot support a great war. It is not going to be
supported by Americans. . . . The Communists have very strong
positions in Manchuria and on this basis it has even been suggested that
National forces *abandon* Manchuria." [32] Eighteen days later, as the
Nationalist forces were decimating the "strong positions" of the Commu-
nists, Marshall altered his line of argument. Instead of abandoning
Manchuria, he now proposed "the concentration of National troop
strength in the southern portion of Manchuria" from Mukden southward. The National Government, Marshall went on, should permit the
Communists to occupy "the area to the west of Harbin and toward
Manchouli." [33]

At this point, as the tide of battle turned decisively in the Nationalists'
favor, Chiang offered an alternative solution. On the 11th of May, Yu
Ta-wei proposed that Nationalist armies be deployed not only in the
southern portion of Manchuria, but, "as a symbolic gesture," in Harbin
and along the railroad toward Manchouli, precisely the obverse of the
General's own proposal of the day before. Marshall's reply to this was
that "he would not be a party" to such negotiations, declaring that "if
the situation in Manchuria is not resolved, then there inevitably soon
would be civil war in North China; that there would be no coalition
government; and that all previous agreements would be vitiated." [34]

Victory brought boldness on the part of the Nationalists. Toward the
end of May, Chiang became increasingly disinclined toward compro-

mise. In return for his agreement to a Marshall proposal that the executive headquarters occupy and manage the city of Ch'angchun until Nationalists and Communists worked out military and political agreements for Manchuria,[35] Chiang required three agreements. He wanted the January cease-fire and the February troop reorganization plans to apply to Manchuria and wanted Marshall to "guarantee" Chinese Communist good faith and adherence to them. The January cease-fire permitted the unopposed movement of Nationalist troops into Manchuria to "restore Chinese sovereignty"; the February troop reorganization plan called for a reduction of Communist strength to a ratio of 3:15 divisions; and by the term "guarantee" Chiang meant that Marshall set and supervise a "time limit" within which the Chinese Communists would execute the agreements. The alternative was for Nationalist forces to occupy strategic centers in Manchuria.[36] Chiang sought to consolidate the strong position he had won on the battlefield.

Marshall, clearly exasperated and also apprehensive at the prospects of failure, hardened his own approach toward Chiang. On the 29th, he sent a message to Chiang, who was in Mukden, threatening to withdraw from mediation unless the fighting in Manchuria were immediately terminated.

> The continued advances of the Government troops in Manchuria in the absence of any action by you to terminate the fighting . . . are making my services as a possible mediator extremely difficult and may soon make them virtually impossible.[37]

The next day in conversation with Chou En-lai, Marshall noted that Chiang in Manchuria was "in a situation where his generals could talk to him and [he] General Marshall could not." Chou, himself fully aware that time was growing short, noted that "at that moment they were standing at the turning point in China's history." [38]

Quite literally, Chou En-lai had been correct. The Soviet Union had at this historical moment decided to forgo further efforts at cooperation and begin in earnest to build the Chinese Communists into a fighting force which could hold its own against the Nationalists. The first genuine indication of the change, received with some degree of puzzlement by Marshall, who failed to recognize it for what it was, was another conversation with Chou on June 23. For the first time in their many

discussions together, Chou accused the United States of pursuing a
"double policy" in China, attempting to mediate on the one hand, while
supporting the Kuomintang on the other hand.[39] Instead of perceiving
their real purpose, Marshall took the remarks personally and attempted
to refute them.

From early June onward, although talks continued—indeed, the
Manchurian truce began on the 6th—their purpose had been altered.
Particularly for the Communists, "negotiations" simply became a means
of buying time during which they could prepare for the battlefield. The
truce talks during June reveal this theme. Initially a two-week cease-fire,
the truce period was extended through the end of the month and then
into July as negotiations continued. Bargaining from an inferior position,
the Communists sought a restoration of the *status quo* in Manchuria, but
Chiang would have none of it. He had won on the battlefield and strove
to reap the political rewards of his victory. Chiang demanded Nationalist
occupation of Manchuria from Harbin southward, leaving only Heilungchiang province, which adjoins the Soviet Union, to the Communists. He wanted Nationalist control of Shantung, particularly the port
cities of Chefoo and Weihaiwei, which the Communists had employed as
embarkation points to Manchuria. Finally, he sought Communist
agreement for the restoration of rail communications and Nationalist
troop increases to replace the soon to depart U.S. Marines.[40]

At first there was no agreement, then preliminary accords were
reached. Subject to final approval by their respective parties, it was
eventually agreed that rail communications would be restored and that
American officers on the three-man truce teams would have the power of
final decision in the event of dispute. A cease-fire for Manchuria was also
arranged on June 26. Finally, the Communists agreed to withdraw from
most of the areas they held in north China on the condition that the
Nationalists not occupy and overturn the local governments already
functioning. This would still ensure Communist control in determining
the choice of delegates to the National Assembly. But on this issue,
despite Marshall's vigorous support of it, negotiations broke down,
particularly over control of heavily populated north Kiangsu province.
Despite Marshall's last-minute attempt to produce a compromise
between the two positions and despite proclamations by both sides on
July 1 that the cease-fire would continue indefinitely, Communists and

Nationalists prepared for a military showdown. Marshall opposed but could not prevent the coming clash.[41]

On the 4th of July, Chiang announced that the National Assembly, which had been postponed in May because the Communists refused to submit a list of their delegates, would now convene on November 12. Three days later, on the 7th, both the Soviet Union and the Chinese Communists simultaneously issued manifestoes denouncing the United States and its support of the Nationalist Goverment.[42] Moscow's decision was now public, confirmed by the sudden change in the behavior of the Chinese Communists.[43] Yet, at this very moment, the American leadership was moving in the direction of generating even greater pressure on the Nationalist Government, seemingly blind to the change in Soviet policy and its implications for the United States in China.

On July 2, Marshall sent a message to Dean Acheson asking for his and Vincent's "reactions" to present developments and those that "might soon and suddenly arise." Marshall complained that "I am so closely engaged and so close to the trees that I may lack perspective." [44] Two days later they replied. Acheson and Vincent, who drafted the reply, saw two possibilities: stalemate, or civil war. Stalemate, they believed, might "bring wiser counsels to the fore on both sides," but if it were due to Kuomintang "intransigence," then "material support from this country could be withheld." If civil war develops, "all material support during civil war could be withheld." If, on the other hand, "Soviet support of the Communists becomes a factor, we should make a complete assessment . . . to determine whether there is a real threat to our national security. . . ." [45] Marshall was thus supported by Acheson and Vincent in the State Department in the position that the Nationalist Government should and could be restrained by withholding material support. "Stalemate" was precisely the course chosen when conflict erupted once again in mid-July.[46]

Chiang had decided that further negotiations were fruitless and sent his forces into battle. From early July, Nationalist armies moved onto the offensive, clearing the north China plain area. In the course of the next two and a half months, success followed success as Chiang's troops defeated the Communists in encounter after encounter. By mid-September, Chiang had gained control of the major rail links in the north China area and had bottled Communist forces up in the mountainous areas of central Shantung and Shansi. Two further advances were under way in west Shantung and in north Kiangsu when they were suddenly halted. What had happened? The communists, hurt and reeling under the relentless drives of Nationalist forces, were demanding an immediate cease-fire through Chou En-lai (September 21) and Marshall himself was also importuning Chiang to terminate the offensive at the same time, but it was a more serious discovery that prompted Chiang to halt.[47]

In an effort to curb Chiang's advancing forces, the American leadership—principally Marshall and Acheson—made a fateful decision. An embargo was placed on the delivery of military materiel to the Chinese government, an act which was designed to coerce Chiang to comply with American policy. On July 23, Marshall received a cable from Washington informing him of the Chinese government's request for export licenses to purchase 150 million rounds of 7.92 surplus rifle ammunition, 700 million rounds of small arms ammunition and 40,000 steel castings for machine-gun barrels. General Marshall's man in Washington, Colonel Marshall S. Carter, then declared:

> On all of these requests this office has been approached for clearance, and I have continued to stall. It may be anticipated that further intensive activity along the foregoing lines will occur. Please verify my assumption that until the situation clears, shipment of military end-use items to China obtained from any source should continue to be deferred. A consideration is also that the Chinese may go to British, Belgians, Russians or other sources if turned down by U.S. State Department is prepared to intercede with these other sources to prevent shipments if desired.[48]

Marshall wired back a rather curious remark. He stated that he had "no objection" to the Chinese "purchase" of equipment and ammunition, provided "it is stipulated that *delivery* . . . can be withheld by the United States should that course appear to be in the best interests of the United States." [49]

This position was duly made official by the Acting Secretary of State Dean Acheson, who, in a letter to General Littlejohn of the War Assets Administration, stated that there would be "no objection . . . to sales of military items of equipment and ammunition, providing there is appended as part of the sales agreement the following proviso":

> It is the desire of the United States Government that these munitions be destined for an integrated and representative National Army under a

coalition government. It is to be understood by the Chinese Government that if at the time for delivery, it appears to be in the best interests of the United States, this contract can be terminated by the United States. . . .[50]

Under this specious pretext the United States withheld military materiel from the Chinese government, effective from July 29, 1946. Although the embargo was officially lifted the following May 26, no U.S. granted ammunition was shipped from the United States until November 1948![51] Nor did the British provide any ammunition, following the U.S. lead and denying all Chinese government requests.[52] It is unknown whether the Chinese government was able to obtain ammunition from other sources, but the United States refused to grant export licenses under the ludicrous rationale that such materiel was not destined for an integrated, that is, Nationalist and Communist, army! Although the Nationalist government-operated arsenals were producing ammunition to meet part of their needs, it was not enough. The importation of ammunition was necessary to satisfy both current and reserve requirements for any contemplated large-scale offensives. The impact on Chiang Kai-shek, when he learned of the embargo, was far-reaching.

The Nationalists were initially unaware that an embargo had been placed. It was not until August 30 that they received the first denial of an export license. At that time Marshall disclaimed any responsibility and intimated that the denial was only temporary, to indicate that the United States meant business. Chiang's representative, General Yu Ta-wei, first broached the subject to Marshall in a meeting.

GEN. YU: . . . I would like to show you a message I have just received concerning orders we placed for some one hundred thirty million dollars worth of ammunition needed, and which we had hoped to buy from the United States. This message indicates that the requisitions were approved all the way up, but in the last analysis the State Department disapproved granting the necessary export license. The reason . . . was that the ammunition was intended for a representative National Army under a coalition government. This is the first really major evidence of restricting United States aid to China and it will naturally put our Government in a very difficult position.

GEN. MARSHALL: I am much interested in seeing this message, although I had nothing to do with it. I anticipated, and so told you, that it was just a matter of time before such a step would be taken. I have been in a position right along to stop this, and to stop that, but I have refrained from doing so in an effort to do everything possible to reach a solution for the peace of China. This transaction about the ammunition exports has apparently been handled in Washington without any reference to me. I am glad that it was for it confirms exactly what I have been telling you and the Generalissimo for some time.[53]

General Marshall was being less than candid with General Yu by stating that the transaction was made "without any reference" to himself. The first denial had an immediate effect. The same day Marshall extracted agreement from Chiang for the creation of a special group of five, to be headed by the newly appointed ambassador to China, Leighton Stuart, "to pave the way for the formation of the Coalition State Council." Presumably, if progress were achieved toward this end, aid would be restored.[54] Stuart's group of five failed to produce any positive results; the Communists continued to stall. On September 19, Chiang learned that the export licenses would be denied indefinitely. In another meeting with General Yu, Marshall

confirmed that the announced policy had been issued on a high level. . . . General Marshall added that he was investigating the status of the 7.92 ammunition since there was some question raised as to its availability in the United States. General Yu Ta-wei terminated the meeting. . . .[55]

The news that no further U.S. military assistance was forthcoming forced Chiang to make a fundamental and fatal change in his strategy. Except for current operations deemed essential, such as the Kalgan campaign, which continued until Nationalist forces captured the city on October 12, Chiang was required to adopt the defensive strategy of holding key points. His alternatives, given reduced ammunition reserves, were either to pull back and relinquish outright positions gained, or to attempt to hold possession. Further offensives no longer possible, Chiang chose the alternative of holding positions won earlier. Hopefully, a defensive stance in which far less of his ammunition reserves would be expended could be supported from China's own arsenals, several of which were in Manchuria. Of course, defeat of the Communists under such a strategy was now out of the question. The most which could be hoped for was to stave off attacks, while attempting to build up weapons and ammunition stocks from domestic production. Chiang's turn to a defensive strategy was designed to gain time to build strength.

Marshall achieved his objective through the imposition of the embargo.[56] Chiang terminated offensive actions against the Communists and declared his willingness to negotiate a settlement. Marshall's success, however, contained the seeds of America's failure, for the Chinese Communists were no longer interested in reaching a negotiated settlement in which their position would be weak. Instead, disdaining all offers of a truce, they demanded Nationalist withdrawal to positions held on January 13 in China proper and June 7 in Manchuria.[57] Marshall himself, meeting with Chou En-lai in Shanghai, was baffled and disheartened by the Chinese Communist response. Declaring his efforts at mediation "futile," Marshall said to Chou, clearly embittered by Chou's words:

> I told you some time ago that if the Communist Party felt that they could not trust to my impartiality, they merely had to say so and I would withdraw. You have now said so. I am leaving immediately for Nanking. . . .[58]

All further attempts to reach a peaceful settlement were futile, including that of the "third party group" of minority party leaders. Chiang was left with no choice but to proceed with the convocation of the National Assembly on November 15—three days late because of a final last-minute effort to reach agreement—and the formal establishment of constitutional government for China. Chiang's political victory was hollow, for his military position, although his forces controlled more territory than ever before, was overextended and Chinese Communist military power in the meantime had grown. Chiang simply did not possess the means to maintain the Nationalist position in the face of the growing power of the Chinese Communists. His struggle for power in China ground toward its now inexorable conclusion.

In view of the continued intransigence of the Chinese Communists, who publicly rejected the National Assembly as a direct violation of the PCC agreements,[59] Marshall requested his recall. Upon his return to the United States, on January 7, 1947, Marshall attempted to explain to the American public the reasons for his failure. The "greatest obstacle to peace," he said, was the "almost overwhelming suspicion" with which each party viewed the other, spurred by the antagonism of a "group of reactionaries" in the Kuomintang and "dyed in the wool Communists" in the Chinese Communist Party. The impasse to which Marshall himself had arrived was revealed in several guarded references to changes in Chinese Communist policy which Marshall appeared to find incomprehensible. The Communists, Marshall said, "did not . . . appear [irreconcilable] last February." He noted that "the course which the Chinese Communist Party has pursued *in recent months* indicated an unwillingness to make a fair compromise. Now the Communists have broken off negotiations. . . ." [60] General Marshall made no mention of the Soviet Union; yet, as he must have known by this time, the change in Chinese Communist tactics was directly linked to the Soviet Union's decision to forgo further attempts at cooperation with the United States.[61]

The Soviet Achievement in China

From mid-1946, the Soviet Union assiduously undertook to strengthen the Chinese Communist position in Manchuria. The Chinese Communists themselves contributed greatly to the effort; together they built the political-military-economic base which ultimately led to victory. Theirs was no easy task, for the Chinese Communists had been badly mauled up to that time by Nationalist forces. It was necessary virtually to rebuild Communist forces from the ground up. There can be no question that the rapid Chinese Communist recovery from the telling defeat at Ssup'ingchieh would have been impossible to accomplish as quickly as it was had it not been for Soviet assistance. By early spring of 1947 the Chinese Communists were ready to take the initiative against the Nationalists. They were immeasurably assisted by events which led to a further serious erosion of Nationalist strength.

Through the month of June 1946 and into early July the Chinese Communist leadership met, producing on July 7 a new policy decision. Although knowledge of the decision is firm, the "July 7 resolution" itself is unavailable.[62] As mentioned above, the publicly distributed "July 7 manifesto" clearly indicated a change in policy as did its simultaneously issued Soviet counterpart statement. Both denounced the United States and demanded American withdrawal from China.[63] The party leadership decided to reshuffle its leading personnel in Manchuria. P'eng Chen, first party secretary of the Northeast Bureau, was replaced by Kao Kang, formerly second secretary. The leadership formally adopted Mao's earlier proposal to "build stable base areas in the Northeast." [64]

In line with its decisions, the party moved to improve its administrative and military organizations to facilitate the mobilization and training of troops for the Red Army. Harbin was the location of Chinese Communist headquarters at this time.[65] Renewed emphasis was placed on land reform and recruitment campaigns as cadres scoured the Manchurian countryside for manpower. By the end of the year the Chinese Communists had taken giant strides toward the establishment of a base which could support an all-out conflict with the Nationalists. Soviet assistance in this effort was indispensable, establishing and maintaining the logistical base for the Chinese Communists. The administrative center for the Soviet effort was Chiamussu, in the extreme northeast corner of Manchuria. The "new Yenan," as it was termed, straddled the rail and river systems connecting all of Manchuria with the Soviet Union, principally Khabarovsk and Vladivostok. Soviet personnel operated the rail and river systems for the Chinese Communists, while Soviet crews repaired damaged rail and river equipment and trained the Chinese Communists in their use and maintenance.

The most decisive Soviet contribution centered on the reconstruction of Lin Piao's Fourth field army. The chaotic condition of the Communists' base in Manchuria in mid-1946 following the defeat at Ssup'ing-chieh was openly admitted by Lin Piao himself:

> . . . in the northeast . . . there is not yet the wide base of popular support for the movement that there was . . . in north China. In the northeast, the people are not yet prepared to maintain the secrecy for us that they do inside the Great Wall.[66]

The condition of the Red Army was equally unsatisfactory. As late as July 1946, the U.S. chairman of field team 35, which was operating in Manchuria, considered the Communist force observed there to consist of "hardly more than a collection of irregulars of the lowest order," with little or no training or equipment.[67] Yet in less than six months, Lin Piao suddenly materialized in Manchuria with a force estimated at upwards of 300,000 men and challenged the Nationalists for control of all Manchuria.

Although the Chinese Communists supplied the bulk of the manpower for their forces, the Soviet Union provided a trained segment of it. In fact, former party leader Li Li-san surfaced in 1946 as liaison between Soviet and Chinese Communist parties, and played a key role in this venture.[68] Sometime in the winter of 1946–47, Li arranged for the transfer of 100,000 North Korean troops into Lin Piao's army, in addition to supplies.[69] Troops, military advisors, Japanese equipment including tanks and crews, artillery, quartermaster and medical supplies, all were a part of the substantial Soviet effort to build a viable Communist force in Manchuria.[70] In fact, artillery and tanks may have been the critical contribution which the Soviet Union made, for the Nationalists were progressively unable to match this type of weapons escalation after the embargo came into effect and therefore were at a serious disadvantage, particularly as they attempted to hold the key cities.

During succeeding months, the Soviet Union transferred to the Chinese Communists 1,226 artillery pieces, according to Chinese Communist sources (the Soviet Union has recently claimed to have turned over 1,800 pieces), and 369 tanks (the Soviets claimed over 700).[71] The great majority of the equipment was of Japanese origin, captured when the Soviet Union invaded Manchuria. Gradually, the Chinese Communists mastered the employment of artillery, in particular, reversing an earlier Nationalist superiority.[72] As the Nationalists increasingly took stationary defense positions, Communist artillery played an ever vital role in their offensives.

By the end of 1946, as the Marshall mission reached its depressing end, Communist forces began to take their first probing steps in Manchuria and north China. On November 12, 1946, January 5, February 21, and March 7, 1947, Lin Piao's rebuilt Northeast Army made successive attempts to cross the Sungari River; all failed, but each took its toll on Nationalist strength. On January 19, Nieh Jung-chen, in north China, thrust his forces eastward from west Hupeh-south Chahar, severing rail communications between Paoting and Shihmen. On February 1, Mao proclaimed the approach of a "new high tide of the Chinese revolution" and urged the Communists "to make every effort to step up the building of our artillery and engineer corps."[73] The Communists were now prepared to move in force.

The Truman Doctrine and American China Policy

As February drew to a close, American leaders determined upon a major change in policy. On March 12, in a move which had been under consideration for several weeks, President Truman addressed both houses of Congress to announce a major policy change for the United States. He declared that the United States would give immediate assistance—military and economic—to Greece, which was threatened with imminent Communist conquest, and to adjoining Turkey as well. The President expressed the decision to aid Greece and Turkey as part of a larger general foreign policy stance: the United States would henceforth "support free peoples who are resisting attempted subjugation by armed minorities or by outside pressures." [74]

Although Chiang Kai-shek had known that a major policy change was in the offing, the President's words must have seemed like the answer to his most fervent prayers, for they clearly implied a reversal of American policy toward China. He responded immediately by ordering his forces into action on the 14th, and on the next day convened the Third Plenum of the KMT's Central Executive Committee, which proclaimed a formal break with the Chinese Communists and adopted a decision to "suppress the armed rebellion." [75] Believing that the United States would once again begin to supply his forces with the needed equipment and ammunition, Chiang reversed his defensive strategy to undertake a final offensive against the Chinese Communists. He was soon disappointed, both in the American response and in the military offensive.

Dean Acheson, appearing before the House Foreign Affairs Committee, gave the first indication of the effect the "Truman doctrine" was to have on China policy. Opposing any military assistance to China, Acheson declared that "the Chinese Government is not in a position at the present time that the Greek Government is in. It is not approaching collapse. It is not threatened by defeat by the Communists. The war with the Communists is going on much as it has for the past twenty years." [76] If news that there would be no change in American policy were not disheartening enough, Chiang soon discovered that his offensive had brought little success beyond the capture of an undefended Yenan on March 19. In fact, as Chiang's forces marched, they encountered the beginning of a large-scale Communist offensive in Manchuria, Lin Piao's fifth and this time successful attempt to cross the Sungari River.

Toward the end of April 1947, Communist forces were in action on a broad front. Supporting attacks to complement Lin's drive were in progress in north China and in southern Manchuria. In north China, Liu Po-ch'eng drove against the Peking-Hankow Railroad, threatening the

Nationalist Government's major communications and supply line, while other diversionary attacks in the southern sector of Manchuria, Jehol, and Shensi also occurred. On May 13, Lin Piao, concentrating a force of 400,000 men and 200 artillery pieces, began a general offensive aimed at capturing Ssup'ingchieh and Mukden.[77] By the end of June, although Nationalist forces had withstood the offensive and retained control of both cities, they, along with the Communists, had suffered extremely heavy casualties. More important, the Communists had crossed the Sungari River, securing advantageous positions from which to carry the struggle to the Nationalists.[78]

Alarmed at the power of the Chinese Communist offensive, the United States lifted the embargo on arms shipments to China and permitted the National Government to purchase 130 million rounds of 7.92 ammunition. This enabled the Nationalists to restore a portion of the reserves expended in stopping the spring Communist offensive, but was insufficient to allow them to conduct a counteroffensive. The U.S. Marines, as they began their withdrawal from north China in April, also turned over their ammunition stores, some of which could be employed immediately.[79] Although no change in policy was officially contemplated (Marshall had replied on July 6 to Chinese Nationalist requests for large-scale American assistance that the Chinese must help themselves),[80] on July 9 the President sent Lt. Gen. Albert C. Wedemeyer on a fact-finding mission to China to assess the "political, economic, psychological, and military situations—current and projected." [81]

Wedemeyer spent two months in China and Korea surveying conditions there. On September 19, he submitted to the President his report, which was immediately suppressed by Secretary of State Marshall. The primary reason for the suppression of the Wedemeyer report was that its author had strongly criticized the concept and execution of the China policy being pursued by the U.S. government. Wedemeyer called for long-term U.S. support of China against the Soviet Union and the Chinese Communists to prevent the loss of Manchuria. This was precisely the recommendation of the State-War-Navy Coordinating Committee of the year before, which had also been rejected. Wedemeyer suggested establishing a U.N. trusteeship over Manchuria as a possible means of avoiding its loss. (Marshall later cited this proposal as the reason for suppression of the report.)[82] The thrust of the report, however, was to call upon the United States to give "moral, advisory, and material support to China." The means to this end were the immediate supply of ammunition and military equipment.[83]

Wedemeyer's report led to a general policy review which continued through the winter of 1947–48 and provided the basis for the China Aid Act of April 1948. The salient point of the policy review is that it resulted in no significant change in policy. The basic strategic conception evolved during World War II of providing for strong Soviet and Chinese Communist positions in Manchuria remained unchanged. The difference was that where it had been necessary to hedge Nationalist power in the earlier years, it was now necessary to buttress the Nationalists in some degree. The policy which emerged from this conception was reflected in the China Aid Act. As formulated by Secretary of State Marshall, the China Aid Act eventually provided 400 million dollars in aid to the Nationalist Government, the great bulk of it economic. Had it not been for strenuous opposition from segments of Congress, which allocated 125 million of the total as a "special fund" to be used as the Nationalist Government saw fit, none of the 400 million could have been employed to obtain military supplies.[84] In fact, Marshall's argument was that tendering economic aid would release Nationalist funds so that the Chinese government could purchase on its own necessary military equipment, rather than have the United States grant such aid. Marshall sought to avoid tying the United States too closely to the Nationalists and to the charge that America was directly supporting the Nationalists in civil war.[85]

Meanwhile, the Chinese Communists had resumed the offensive in Manchuria. In this sixth drive, Lin Piao sought to envelop Mukden in a giant pincer movement and destroy Nationalist forces throughout the northeast. Battlefield developments, however, forced a change of plan. Encountering stiff Nationalist resistance at Ssup'ingchieh and Mukden, Lin diverted his main thrust toward Kirin (Yung Chi). A Nationalist counter drive into Ch'angchun threatened the Communist rear line of communications, forcing a withdrawal from Kirin. By November 1947, another standoff had been reached in Manchuria, but, this time, a standoff which had perceptibly weakened the Nationalist overall position. Chiang Kai-shek was now forced to concentrate his forces in three large pockets at the cities of Ch'angchun, Mukden, and Chinchow.[86]

Communist efforts in north China had produced similarly important gains, resulting in the establishment of strong positions on the periphery of the north China plain in Shantung and in the Tapieh Mountains in Honan. As the spring of 1948 rolled around, the prospects for the Nationalists grew dimmer. The months of March and April saw consecutive Communist successes at Loyang (March 14), Yenan (April 5), and, at the end of April, Weihsien, a strategically located city in Shantung. The loss of Weihsien was particularly alarming. Not only was an ammunition shortage the critical factor in the Nationalist loss, the loss itself led to the creation of a Communist wedge between Nationalist forces in Manchuria and those in north China, making virtually impossible the reinforcement of the forces in Manchuria.[87]

The serious situation facing Nationalist forces prompted some responsible U.S. officials in China to attempt to shore up the government's defenses in north China. Armed with the knowledge that Congress had passed the China Aid Act, Ambassador Stuart, Admiral Badger, commander of U.S. naval forces in the western Pacific, and Roger Lapham, head of the Economic Cooperation Administration mission, went on an inspection tour of north China in June to determine the possibility of defending north China, particularly the Peiping-Tientsin area. They conducted a thorough assessment of Nationalist forces, under General Fu Tso-yi. General Fu had eleven well-trained armies under his charge. Of these, however, four were fully armed, three poorly equipped, and four totally unequipped.[88] The spirit, loyalty, and high morale of Fu's troops persuaded Stuart, Badger, and Lapham that the United States should furnish the necessary arms and ammunition to supply all eleven of Fu's armies in an effort to stabilize a defense of north China, and ultimately to open up a relief corridor to beleaguered Nationalist forces in Manchuria.

Although their request for assistance—a total of 16 million dollars—was sent in and approved by the Joint Chiefs of Staff at the end of the first week in July, no supplies reached Tientsin until November 29, almost a full five months later. The shipment that did arrive on November 29, constituting 10 percent of the request, or 1,210 tons, came from Japan, not the United States. The final twist occurred when it was discovered that most of the arms on board were useless, since much of the equipment was missing necessary parts.[89] General Fu's telegram to Admiral Badger upon receipt of the defective equipment needs no commentary:

> The above-mentioned weapons are not in good condition, and for the most part cannot be used. I do not know how or why these weapons were forwarded in an incomplete state.[90]

The belated effort on the part of American officials in China to build a defense of north China failed. General Fu's forces held out until January 1949, when, rather than face alone the full brunt of Communist force coming down from Manchuria, he surrendered on the 22nd of that month.

Victory of the Chinese Communists

The effort to bolster Nationalist defenses in north China came as the Communists resumed their final and victorious offensive in Manchuria and elsewhere in north China. In mid-September, Ch'en Yi's Third Army attacked Tsinan, capital of Shantung province. Within ten days Nationalist forces were vanquished, a critical factor in defeat being the defection of the 84th division to the Communists. Capture of Tsinan gave the Communists for the first time control of a major city and its arsenal.

Shortly after the victory in Shantung, the Communists began what became the final drive for Manchuria. Having earlier in the summer surrounded Chinchow, the southernmost strategic city in Manchuria, which controlled access to the region, Lin Piao on October 8 opened his offensive. Preceded by a massive two hundred gun artillery barrage to soften up Nationalist defenses, Lin's forces attacked the city from three sides.[91] By the 15th, Chinchow had fallen, sealing the fates of Nationalist forces in Ch'angchun and Mukden, which were unable to break through to Chinchow. By November 2—through defeat and defection—the Communists had conquered Manchuria, giving them control of the entire military-industrial base from which to carry on the struggle.[92] Within days Lin began wheeling his forces southward into north China for the decisive battles to come.

As long as the National Government could sustain its military position, the impact of other important factors, such as skyrocketing inflation due to growing shortages of food and goods, the reduction of morale, and corruption of government officials, all could be borne without too much hardship. But as the tide of battle noticeably began to turn against the Nationalists, these factors came to have an ever greater effect, accelerating an already disintegrating situation. Popular criticism naturally focused sharply on the government and its leaders, who were, after all, responsible for the plight of the citizenry.

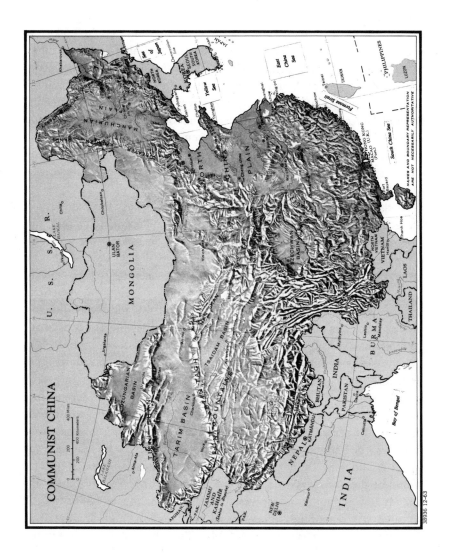

COMMUNIST CHINA

38936 12-63

As Manchuria fell to Lin Piao's forces, the Ambassador in China, Stuart, sent message after message to Secretary of State Marshall, inquiring whether there was to be any change in U.S. policy in view of the rapidly deteriorating situation. Marshall replied in the negative. No amount of United States military or economic aid "could make the present Chinese Government capable of reestablishing and then maintaining its control throughout all China." [93] Moreover, Marshall continued, to defeat the Chinese Communists at this late date would require that the United States "virtually take over the Chinese government." Such a course of action, he said, would involve the United States in a commitment from which it would be extremely difficult to withdraw, and very probably "involve grave consequences to this nation by making of China an arena of international conflict." [94] Marshall had simply written off the Nationalist Government as a loss.

At this point, Chiang Kai-shek attempted to bypass the Secretary of State by making a direct personal plea to the President himself. The President's reply was of the same tenor as his Secretary's; he was most sympathetic with China's problems, but could not go beyond the aid programs already authorized by Congress. American policy toward China remained unchanged.[95] This latest policy review by American leaders came at a time when the most critical test for the Nationalist Government was about to begin. The decision to decline any substantial commitment to support the Nationalists was made just before the decisive series of battles known collectively as the Huai-Hai campaign.[96]

In early November, while Lin Piao regrouped his forces for an assault on Fu Tso-yi in Peiping, Communist and Nationalist forces moved into position further south in the Hsuchow area, historically a strategic battlefield. Located at the junction of major north-south and east-west rail lines (the Tsin-pu and Lung-hai railways), Hsuchow was the gateway to the Nationalist capital at Nanking and to the Yangtze River. This would be the decisive battle; no purpose would be served by conserving already low ammunition reserves. Therefore, Chiang marshalled his still considerable remaining forces, some half million, and attempted to deploy them in the Hsuchow area.[97] Mao Tse-tung sent a similar number into action under the tactical command of generals Ch'en Yi (Third Field Army) and Liu Po-ch'eng (Second Field Army).[98]

The Huai-Hai campaign was actually a series of three battles, beginning in early November and continuing through January 10, 1949.

The battles were: Nienchuang (November 6–22), Shangtuichi (November 23–December 15), and Ch'inglungchi (December 16–January 10). In the first battle Nationalist forces under Huang Po-tao clashed with attacking forces led by Ch'en Yi at Nienchuang. The Communists engaged Huang's forces before they were able to reach their assigned defensive positions around Hsuchow. A second thrust from Liu Po-ch'eng's Second Field Army coming eastward to Suhsien prevented the dispatch of Nationalist reinforcements to assist Huang. Even though effectively isolated, Huang's forces beat back savage attacks for three days in succession. In fact, after this initial phase of the battle had been completed, Huang had suffered 20,000 casualties to 100,000 for the Communists. The victory was short-lived.[99] Beginning on the 14th, the Chinese Communists renewed their attacks, supported by heavy artillery bombardment. Chiang Kai-shek was unable to replenish Huang's beleaguered forces with sufficient food and ammunition, although some attempts were made to air drop supplies to them. Nor could a breakthrough be accomplished. Eventually, Huang's forces simply ran out of food and ammunition and by November 22, the Communists had destroyed his force. Huang himself committed suicide rather than surrender.[100]

The battle of Shangtuichi was an outgrowth of the first battle, when Liu Po-ch'eng's troops struck at Suhsien to prevent the Nationalists from sending reinforcements to Huang Po-tao. Liu's forces, now bolstered by the addition of Ch'en's, encircled Nationalist forces under the command of Huang Wei at Shangtuichi near Suhsien. Two weeks of fierce fighting ensued in which Communist artillery pounded the stationary Nationalist defenders. Again no rescuing breakthrough was achieved by outside Nationalist forces and the Communists eventually cracked the defenses at Shangtuichi. Under extreme pressure, some of Huang Wei's troops surrendered; the remainder attempted to withdraw when they, too, ran out of food and ammunition, and were captured, as was Huang Wei himself.[101]

As defeat loomed larger at Shangtuichi, Chiang sought to rescue Huang Wei. On November 29 he moved forces from Hsuchow toward Shangtuichi. Unable to use the Tsin-pu Railroad, which was in Communist hands, Nationalist forces under Tu Li-ming (Tu Yü-ming) moved in a southwesterly direction along the motor road. The Communists anticipated the attempt to reinforce Huang Wei and moved quickly to encircle Tu's troops, an effort which was completed by December 16, in the vicinity of Ch'inglungchi.[102] Instead of immediately attacking Tu's forces, however, the Communists laid siege, hoping to mislead Chiang into believing that Ch'inglungchi was not a trap. Mao Tse-tung ordered the lull to give Lin Piao time to complete his preparations for the attack on General Fu Tso-yi. Mao's concern was that if Chiang felt all was lost at Ch'inglungchi he would order Fu to withdraw from Peiping to reinforce Tu's men.[103]

Mao's plan succeeded. On January 6, 1949, with Lin Piao now prepared to move against Fu Tso-yi in Peiping, Ch'en Yi and Liu Po-ch'eng began the assault on Tu's positions at Ch'inglungchi. Following an intensive artillery preparation, Communist forces using human sea tactics stormed Tu's defenses. Within four days, thwarting a breakout attempt, the Communists had destroyed Nationalist forces and captured General Tu Li-ming. The disaster at Ch'inglungchi was shortly followed by the surrender of General Fu Tso-yi at Peiping on January 22. By the end of January the Communists had defeated the Nationalists decisively. Only isolated pockets of Nationalist troops remained to face the now powerful Communist armies.

On January 8, with defeat certain, the Nationalist Government requested the American, British, French, and Soviet governments to act as intermediaries in peace negotiations with the Communists. All refused. On January 21, Chiang Kai-shek retired as president and was succeeded by Vice President Li Tsung-jen. The acting president attempted to reach some compromise with the Chinese Communists, but failed. The Communists demanded unconditional surrender. On April 15, after a three-month lull in fighting, the Communist party demanded complete acceptance of its surrender terms by the 20th, or its forces would resume the offensive and cross the Yangtze River. On the 20th, Communist forces began the crossing, encountering little opposition. The remaining Nationalist forces withdrew across the Formosa Strait to Taiwan. The Chinese Communists had conquered China.

The Chinese Revolution in Global Perspective

The Chinese revolution, like all revolutions, is sustained by a body of myth as well as fact. The fact is that the Chinese Communists under Mao Tse-tung achieved a tremendous victory in conquering the Chinese Nationalists (Kuomintang) and taking control of the fourth largest country in the world. The myths arise in explaining how it was done. Many of the myths are obvious and understandable. Mao came to symbolize the indigenous nature of the

Chinese revolution, and afterward his "genius" came to be considered responsible for victory. The mass line, ideological originality, people's war, and other elements of the revolution were attributed to Mao Tse-tung. Much of this attribution was overdrawn and uncritically accepted. With the passage of time and Mao's death, a reappraisal of the Chinese revolution and Mao's role in it is in order.

It is usual to date the Chinese revolution from the founding of the party in 1921 to the victory in 1949 and to assign to Mao Tse-tung the primary role. In fact, the decisive events of the revolution actually occurred in a relatively brief period encompassing what is termed the "civil war" of 1946-1949, and Mao assumed a dominant position in the party rather late, becoming party chairman only in 1945. But it is also true that the Chinese Communist Party was in revolt against the Nationalist government after 1927, following brief periods of collaboration between the two in 1923-1927 and again during the Sino-Japanese war after 1937; and Mao was an influential figure in the party long before 1945.

In a real sense, the political influence of the Communists always exceeded their actual strength. In fact, until the "civil war" the Nationalist government decisively bested the Communists in every test of strength. The Communist defeat in 1934 when the Nationalists drove them from their Kiangsi stronghold and onto the year-long 6,000-mile Long March reduced the Red Army to militarily insignificant numbers. Although the CCP had increased its forces substantially by World War II, the Communist redoubt in Yenan contained no arms industry, and as late as 1945 the Communist forces were estimated to have no more than 200,000 rifles. How, then, does one explain the Communist victory in 1949 and Mao's role in it?

Perhaps the most prevalent myth is that the Chinese revolution was an indigenous affair on which external forces had but marginal impact. However, the fact that both Chinese Communists and Nationalists received essential military materiel from the Soviet Union and the United States, respectively, suggests strongly that external factors played more than a marginal role. Indeed, when analyzed in terms of relative aid programs and in a global context, the outcome of the Chinese revolution may be seen as a function of the conflict of Soviet and U.S. strategies in the Pacific during the "cold war." Even less does it appear that the victory of Communism in China was inevitable.

The Cold War and the Chinese Revolution. The agreements made between the Soviet Union and the United States during World War II at

Tehran and Yalta were designed to establish the postwar balance of power in the emerging bipolar international structure. The breakdown of the postwar settlement and the rapid transition from peace to cold war saw the outbreak of conflict in Europe, the Mid-East, and the Far East as the Soviet Union and the United States moved to adjust and consolidate their global positions. Soviet efforts to establish control over peripheral areas took the form of the creation of a tier of "friendly" regimes that would function as buffer zones between the Soviet and U.S. camps. It is within the context of the disintegration of Soviet-American cooperation and the shift to unilateral action on both sides that the Chinese revolution must be interpreted.

In fact, if one defines the beginning of the cold war as the first significant policy departure from the wartime agreements, the dramatic shift in Soviet policy in mid-1946 offers a defensible case for considering the conflict in Manchuria as an early—if not the initial—shot of the cold war. The question is, What particular event or series of events precipitated the breakdown of the Far Eastern portion of the postwar settlement, leading directly to the victory of the Chinese Communists? Soviet long-term strategy was to prevent the integration of Manchuria into China proper, just as, it should be noted, it had been Japanese strategy earlier. The United States, on the other hand, had committed itself in 1943 at Cairo to the restoration of Chinese territorial integrity. The compromise that Stalin and Roosevelt subsequently worked out at Tehran and Yalta meshed the two states' objectives insofar as it was possible to do so. The compromise would include support for Chinese territorial integrity and the formation of a coalition government in which the Chinese Communists would participate on the basis of a strong territorial position in Manchuria. A strong Chinese Communist position in Manchuria would fulfill the Soviet Union's objective of a *de facto* separation of Manchuria from China proper, and a coalition government would, at least formally, fulfill the U.S. objective of supporting China's territorial integrity. Chiang Kai-shek accepted these arrangements on the assumption of continued U.S. military aid beyond the wartime period and in the belief that he could maintain a dominant political position in a coalition government.

The Chinese Communists and Nationalists, after several false starts during the war, took an important step toward this solution at the Political Consultative Conference in January-February 1946 when they agreed to establish a coalition government; General George Marshall was the instrumental figure in working out all of the necessary political and military arrangements. The precise position of the Communists in Manchuria had not been negotiated at this time, but Soviet occupation of the area served to prevent the outbreak of hostilities there and provided the Communists with the opportunity to build a position of strength while the Nationalists were excluded. By the end of February 1946, when the negotiations between Communists and Nationalists were completed, it appeared that the United States and the Soviet Union had both achieved their objectives in China.

The decisive test of the Communist-Nationalist agreements and of United States-Soviet cooperation came the following month when the Soviet Union began to withdraw from Manchuria. Both Communist and Nationalist forces rushed to take control of now open positions, and a major battle ensued around Ssup'ingchieh, a rail junction between Shenyang and Ch'ang ch'un, in which the Nationalists delivered a stunning defeat to the Communists. Following up their advantage toward the end of May, Nationalist forces began an advance northward in an effort to consolidate control of the bulk of the region.

The victorious Nationalist advance and the reduction of Communist forces dramatically altered the military balance of forces in China and endangered the strategies pursued by the Soviet Union and the United States. The responses of Moscow and Washington to the changed situation in Manchuria would affect decisively the outcome of the Chinese revolution. Stalin, at this juncture, proposed a summit meeting with Chiang Kai-shek to negotiate a settlement, but Chiang declined. His refusal, combined with apparent U.S. inability to influence the Nationalist leader, led to a major change in Soviet policy. From mid-1946 onward, the Soviet Union disdained further cooperation with the United States in the Far East and pursued instead a unilateral policy of support for the Communists, hoping through them to preserve by military means the minimum objective of a buffer zone in Manchuria.

The key signal was the change in Soviet arms policy toward the Chinese Communists. Through the spring of 1946, including the battle of Ssup'ingchieh, Communist forces employed small arms almost exclusively in clashes with the Nationalists, concentrating in the main on hit-and-run, mobile tactics. In early 1947, however, Chinese Communist forces in Manchuria, strengthened and re-equipped by the Soviet Union, began to employ heavy weaponry in increasingly conventional and large-scale offensive operations.[104] In particular, the skilled use of artillery and tank warfare, combined with human-sea tactics, proved to be the decisive combat elements in every remaining battle of the Chinese "civil war."

That the Soviet Union armed and equipped the Chinese Communist armies is no longer in dispute, although at the time such assistance was vehemently denied. It is the timing of the supply of tanks and artillery that was important for the Chinese revolution. The Soviets turned over large quantities of light weapons to the Chinese Communists soon after their entry into Manchuria. They appear not to have turned over tanks or artillery in any volume at that time, for coordinated use of such weaponry by the Communists was not detected in the critical battle of Ssup'ingchieh in the spring of 1946. According to Soviet sources, the Russians turned over to the Chinese more than 1,800 pieces of artillery and 700 tanks.[105] (The Chinese claim the figures were 1,226 for artillery and 369 for tanks.[106]) In either case such large amounts of equipment should forever dispel yet another myth—that Mao led a guerrilla army to victory over Nationalist forces. Although neither the Soviets nor the Chinese have revealed exactly when the weapons transfers occurred, it is clear that they must have taken place in sufficient time for use in early 1947 when the Communists first went onto the offensive. (There is also the myth that the Chinese Communists obtained the bulk of their equipment from defecting Kuomintang forces. The first large-scale defection of Kuomintang forces—that of the 84th Division in September 1947—was too late for purposes of the myth.)

Assuming a minimum period of six months for equipment deliveries and the training of Communist forces, the Soviet decision to escalate was probably made sometime in mid-1946 for effective battlefield operation by early 1947. But more was required than artillery and tanks. The logistical support mechanism for conventional warfare had also to be introduced. Recent Soviet sources date this development from the latter half of 1946. The Soviets augmented Chinese forces with 100,000 North Korean troops and set up the administrative and support organizations to facilitate the training of these and Chinese units.[107] Harbin and Chiamussu, cities under Soviet control in northwestern and northeastern Manchuria, were the twin control centers. Chinese Communist headquarters was located at Harbin; Chiamussu was known as the "New Yenan."[108] Mao Tse-tung, it may be noted in passing, was not in Manchuria during this period. He remained in Yenan, and although he sent instructions to the leadership in Manchuria, there is little relevance between the instructions and the course of events. The crucial decisions were taken by the Soviets in conjunction with the Chinese Communists in Manchuria, chief among whom was Kao Kang, who after victory would be an early challenger of Mao's. These facts raise serious questions about Mao's actual role in the decision to settle the Communist-Nationalist struggle on the battlefield rather than at the negotiating table. His role is unclear at best.

The Soviet Union constructed the logistical base necessary to support an all-out, conventional war with the Nationalists. It included extensive rail and river transport systems, repair and damage-control mechanisms, and medical apparatus, most of which was maintained and operated by Soviet personnel.[109] Gradually, the Chinese Communist forces mastered the tactical use of equipment that they had never before employed.

U.S. Policy in China. U.S. policy in China originally was based upon the assumption that a political solution was possible and desired by the Communists. Toward this end, U.S. leaders, particularly General Marshall, applied pressure on Chiang Kai-shek to terminate military operations in Manchuria. Obtaining agreement for a cease-fire in June 1946, the United States moved to balance what it assumed were the respective military capabilities between the Communists and Nationalists by imposing an arms embargo on the Nationalists. The embargo had an immediate impact on Chiang Kai-shek's strategy. Without an assured source of supply the Nationalists could not continue their offensive actions against the Communists, and they moved into defensive positions.

Chiang's shift to the defensive, by the way, relates to still another myth regarding the Communist victory: that the Nationalists lost because they failed to take the offensive against the Communists, preferring instead to remain in the cities. This "wall psychology," it is said, largely accounts for Nationalist failures on the battlefield. Of course, with hindsight it becomes clear that Nationalist forces, which had been on the offensive through the spring and summer of 1946, were ordered into defensive positions only when the United States imposed the embargo and their ammunition stocks were in danger of being exhausted.

The hope of maintaining good relations with the Soviet Union appears to have had a controlling effect on U.S. policymakers. For example, John Carter Vincent, director of the Office of Far Eastern Affairs, in a memorandum to Secretary of State Marshall dated February 7, 1947, declared: "Without sacrificing any legitimate national interest, it is our purpose to prevent China from becoming a major irritant in our international relations, particularly with the USSR. . . . A unified China is, from our point of view, a means toward an end rather than an end in itself. In short, we are following policies in China to achieve a larger objective."[110] Marshall repeated this position almost verbatim in a memorandum to Secretary of War Patterson on March 4, stating:

"Without sacrificing any legitimate national interest, including our security, it is important to prevent China from becoming a dangerous irritant in our international relations, particularly with the USSR."[111]

At this point, events in China became clearer. As Communist forces began to show significant military strength, U.S. leaders realized that the problem was not how to restrain the Nationalists—the point of the embargo—but how to re-establish a military balance now that the Nationalists were rapidly becoming the inferior force. The Truman Doctrine announced on March 12, 1947, had a predictable effect on the course of the struggle. Chiang Kai-shek, understanding that U.S. leaders had been undecided about policy toward China, interpreted the Truman speech as a signal that Washington had decided to resume support for the Nationalists. He quickly ordered his forces onto the offensive, assuming that U.S. supplies would soon be forthcoming. To his profound dismay, the administration changed only the form of its policy, not its essence.

Lifting the embargo in May, the United States permitted the Nationalist government to purchase with its own funds limited quantities of military arms and ammunition, but no large-scale resumption of U.S. military aid followed. The issue of U.S. aid to China has led to still another myth about the defeat of the Nationalists, that the United States provided the KMT with some $2.8 billion that Chiang either squandered inefficiently or turned into personal profits for himself and his "clique." Records recently declassified show beyond a shadow of a doubt that this was not the case.[112] In fact, from the imposition of the embargo on 29 July 1946 through November 1948—despite the lifting of the embargo in May 1947—no U.S. grant aid, especially ammunition, was sent to the Nationalist government. True, the U.S. Marines left behind 6,500 tons of ammunition that KMT forces picked up, and the KMT purchased some military goods once the embargo was lifted.

Aid to the KMT was clearly inadequate and was understood by U.S. leaders to be so. For example, at a meeting on June 26, 1947, of the secretaries of state, war, and navy (the SWNCC), Secretary of State Marshall declared that "the immediate and urgent problem to be decided is what are we to do about rearming the Chinese Nationalist army. . . . *The Army is beginning to run out of ammunition* and it appears that we have a moral obligation to provide it inasmuch as we aided in equipping it with American arms."[113] Despite the lifting of the embargo and this clear understanding of the Nationalist predicament, no U.S. military aid went to Nationalist forces. In fact, Secretary Marshall himself was instrumental in blocking congressional

efforts to provide Chinese forces with the necessary funds with which to purchase arms and ammunition! The China Aid Act finally passed as a rider to a
European aid package in March 1948. Yet even at that point there was ample
time and opportunity for the United States to provide sufficient aid to the
Nationalist government to prevent defeat at least, if not to turn the tide. The
decisive battles for Manchuria and North China that determined the outcome
were yet to occur. The administration did nothing.

Anyone who examines the historical record cries out for an explanation of
these bizarre events. U.S. leaders were not blind, dumb, or befuddled. They
understood perfectly that the failure to supply arms and particularly ammunition would inevitably lead to a Nationalist defeat. The equation was simple
and straightforward; the Nationalist-Communist conflict had been reduced to
a large-scale test on the battlefields of Manchuria and North China. What is
the answer? Clearly, the U.S. government decided against becoming involved—
even as an arms supplier—on behalf of the Nationalist government, with full
knowledge of the consequences. There can be no doubt about this. The question remained: Why? Were there crypto-Communists in the U.S. leadership
who secretly worked for the triumph of Communism in China? No, that is
still another simplistic myth trumpeted by the extreme political right.

The answer derives from the United States–Soviet relationship, about
which U.S. leaders were so concerned and which they perceived as central to
U.S. policy toward China. By the spring of 1947 the United States was no
longer the formidable power it had been during World War II. The U.S. Army
had been demobilized from its wartime high of eighty-nine divisions to
fifteen divisions. The air force had been pared down from 217 active air
groups to just 2; a similar fate had befallen the navy. Moreover, although the
United States possessed the atomic bomb, it had only a handful of them in
1947 and limited ability to deliver those weapons on Soviet targets. In any
case, there was clearly inadequate military capability in being with which to
contemplate a major conflict with the Soviet Union, let alone World War III.

The Soviet Union, on the other hand, continued to maintain formidable
ground forces even though its air and sea arms were clearly inferior to the
pared-down U.S. forces and even though the Soviet state was still barely on
the road to recovery from its ruinous participation in World War II. In the
opening stages of any full-scale conflict along Soviet borders, Soviet power
would be superior to that of the United States—even though in any long war
the United States would be able to marshal overwhelming forces, as it had
just demonstrated in World War II.

The Truman Doctrine itself was only a form of declaratory rhetoric. Although Truman clearly stated that "it must be the policy of the United States to support free peoples who are resisting attempted subjugation by armed minorities or by outside pressures," suggesting that the United States would quickly move to rearm and re-establish military superiority over the Soviet Union, nothing of the kind occurred. In fact, defense expenditures remained at constant low levels (between $11 and $12 billion), while the strength of the army continued to fall, from fifteen divisions in 1947 to ten in early 1950.[114] The answer to why the United States declined to continue support for the Nationalist government must be sought in the larger strategic framework of the U.S.-Soviet relationship, its future prospects and anticipated evolution.

The United States declined to support the Nationalist government because the probable outcome of such support would lead to a significant accretion in strength for the Soviet Union. U.S. support for the Nationalist government would prolong the "civil war" and inevitably result in a division of China like that of Korea and Germany. North Korean and East German economic resources were being integrated into the Soviet power grid; the same would presumably be true of the Soviet-controlled portion of a divided China, which would include the vast Manchurian heavy industrial complex. Such a division of China would have dangerously strengthened the Soviet Union vis-à-vis the United States. On the other hand, any prospect of victory for the Nationalist government would have entailed a major commitment by the United States, raising the specter of a global conflict with the Soviet Union before the United States was fully prepared for it. In effect, the U.S. leadership took the calculated risk that a territorially integrated China—even one under a Communist leadership—would ultimately be governed by national interests rather than ideological commitments, and so it declined to extend support to the Nationalist government of China.

PART III
The Sino-Soviet Relationship, 1949–1968

IX

The Soviet Union and the Chinese People's Republic, 1949–1959

Four dynamic conditions provide the framework for the analysis of Sino-Soviet relations during the first decade of the newly constituted Chinese People's Republic (CPR). First were the strategic situations facing both nations at the outset; second was the evolving domestic political situation in the CPR; third was the death of Stalin and the ensuing succession struggle in the Soviet Union; and fourth was the growing Sino-Soviet estrangement over the issue of China's strategy of development.

Strategy of Conflict

The end of World War II saw the resolution of a major strategical issue which had plagued the Soviet Union for the previous decade and more. That issue was the two-front war danger posed by Germany and Japan. Between 1945 and 1949, however, that danger had been resurrected in the general context of a Soviet-American "cold war," in which both West Germany and Japan were allied with the United States. The primary Soviet objective on both European and Asian fronts was to establish clearly defined "camps"—a definite alignment of nations behind the cold war protagonists. The means chosen to achieve the desired ends were conflict situations which would fix international relationships in both parts of the world. In Europe, the Berlin blockade functioned as the catalyst solidifying the newly created Soviet political structure. In Asia, the Korean war served the identical function.[1]

The major strategical problem confronting Soviet leaders in Asia was how to exclude the United States from the mainland. The lines between the Soviet and American "spheres" had by no means been drawn, in particular with regard to the newly established Chinese People's Republic. The threat to the Soviet Union lay precisely in the possibility that the United States might establish diplomatic relations with the Chinese regime, thereby gaining access to the Asian mainland. Given the then-existing state of military technology, an American position in China would imperil the Soviet heartland. In the late 1940s, there were disquieting aspects to American behavior which impelled the Soviet Union to act to preclude any possibility of a Sino-American rapprochement.

From the spring of 1949 the United States gave the unmistakable impression that it was disentangling itself from the relationship with Chiang Kai-shek's vanquished regime and preparing a position from which recognition of the Chinese People's Republic could follow. The U.S. "White Paper," released on August 5, 1949, provided the political rationale for the eventual shift, blaming the defeat of the Nationalists on Chiang Kai-shek, who, it was claimed, had lost the mandate of the people. The embassy remained open, although the ambassador had returned to the United States. Finally, in a formal statement of policy, President Truman, on January 5, 1950, clearly indicated that the United States would not interfere in a Communist attempt to take Taiwan.[2]

It was the United States' own reduced military power and withdrawal from South Korea in late 1949 which provided the opportunity for the Soviet Union to attempt a low-risk high-return catalytic venture. Due to the rapid demobilization of United States armed forces after the war, by 1950, excluding naval and air forces, there were only five divisions in the United States, four on occupation duty in Japan, and slightly more than one in Europe. All were under strength and unfit for combat. The divisions in Japan were at 60 percent of strength; of those in the United States, only the 82nd Airborne Division and part of a Marine division were combat ready.[3] Such reduced ground-force capability, combined with the emergence of a defense concept which placed heavy reliance upon the deterrent effect of a nuclear armed bomber strike force, led to a reevaluation of the American strategic position. The result of the reevaluation for the Far East was the decision, expressed by Secretary of State Acheson on January 12, 1950, that the defense perimeter in the Pacific would henceforth exclude both Korea and Taiwan.[4]

Indeed, by the fall of 1949 American forces had already begun a withdrawal from South Korea, a step paralleled by the Soviet Union in North Korea. As American troops were withdrawn, they attempted a modest buildup of Republic of Korea (ROK) forces. The ROK army was expanded from 65,000 to 98,000 and total forces from 114,000 to 154,000. No tanks, artillery, or support-combat aircraft were included in the U.S. military aid package.[5] The ROK army was supplied with light arms sufficient for constabulary duty, which left them at a distinct disadvantage *vis-à-vis* the army of North Korea, supplied by the Soviet Union with heavy equipment. In fact, when the attack came, it was made by 110,000 men armed with 1,400 artillery pieces and 126 tanks.[6]

In retrospect, the Soviet plan was probably worked out during the eight weeks Mao Tse-tung and entourage spent in Moscow, December 16, 1949 to February 18, 1950.[7] It was to have consisted of a Soviet-backed North Korean attack on South Korea, followed closely by a Chinese Communist attack on Taiwan. The plan appeared to be risk-free for all parties. The Soviet Union would not become openly involved; nor would North Korean and Chinese Communist forces expect to encounter anything but light resistance from the inadequately armed and trained South Korean and Nationalist forces. Moreover, all would benefit. Korea would be unified under the Communists, the civil war would be concluded in China, and the United States would be excluded from the Asian mainland.

The actual course of events seriously compromised the Soviet scheme, but critical decisions taken by the United States at the turning point of the Korean War provided the Soviet Union with a second opportunity to recoup its miscalculation. On June 27, two days after North Korean forces initiated their offensive, the United States decided to interpose the Seventh Fleet between Taiwan and the mainland, thus preventing the Chinese Communist attack on Taiwan. During the two-week period between June 10 and 24, the Chinese Communists had increased the buildup of forces in Fukien province adjacent to Taiwan from slightly more than 40,000 men to about 156,000.[8] These troops had undergone amphibious training exercises.[9] From mid-May other forces—the 20th, 26th, 27th, 38th, 50th, and 56th armies—had deployed in the Shanghai area, presumably as a strategic reserve. The 39th and 40th armies were positioned in south China for the same purpose.[10] However, when the Seventh Fleet moved into the Taiwan Straits, the 38th and 40th armies redeployed to Manchuria, while the 27th and 39th armies moved to the

Shantung peninsula.[11] The attack on Taiwan no longer feasible, the Chinese Communists moved their forces northward for whatever contingency might develop in Korea.

In Korea, after a month and a half of bloody planned withdrawals to the southern tip of the peninsula, United Nations Forces established and maintained a defensive perimeter at Pusan. In the first week of August, these predominantly American forces, now supplied with heavy equipment, won their first major engagement. At this point in the conflict the United States made two decisions which permitted the Soviet Union to recover from the unanticipated turn of events. The first was to alter the objective. From restoration of the *status quo,* the unification of all Korea by U.N. forces[12] became the objective, as stated by the United States representative to the United Nations, Warren Austin, on August 17, 1950. The second decision followed the brilliant Inchon landing and envelopment on September 15, which decisively turned the tide of battle. With North Korean forces in full flight and disintegrating, the United States decided to pursue the enemy with American forces in a drive north of the 38th parallel to achieve the newly stated goal of Korean unification.

These two decisions forced a Chinese Communist response. After the appearance of the Seventh Fleet, the Chinese had carefully avoided involvement with American forces. Their inaction placed the entire burden of the conflict on Soviet shoulders; Soviet policy now took on the appearance of a crude power play to achieve a Communist takeover of South Korea. Most important, it did not alter the strategic relationship between the United States and Communist China. Indeed, early in the conflict (July 13), Indian Prime Minister Nehru proposed the admission of Communist China to the United Nations and the return of the Soviet representative to the U.N. as a means of achieving a solution of the Korean problem. The United States rejected this proposal on the ground that Communist China's admission to the United Nations and the aggression in Korea were separate issues.

When the tide of battle in the Korean War turned and the United States called for the unification of Korea under United Nations auspices and proceeded to employ primarily U.S. forces in the drive to the Yalu River, the Chinese Communists became alarmed. Had solely ROK troops been employed in the drive to reunify the country (there is considerable question, however, as to the feasibility of their use at this time) it would have placed a self-limiting constraint on the action. However, the use of American forces, combined with the openly hostile statements made by the theatre commander, General Douglas MacArthur, implied the possibility, if not probability, of an extension of the conflict into Chinese territory.

When the Chinese Communists intervened the Soviet Union achieved its principal strategic objective—that of excluding the United States from the mainland. Although the *status quo ante* was restored in Korea, Chinese Communist intervention in the conflict established the adversary relationship between the United States and the Chinese People's Republic, which existed until 1972. For the United States it meant the beginning of a two decade-long isolation from the mainland and only a marginal and passive role in influencing the course of events.

The Establishment of the Chinese People's Republic

The Korean War not only affected the course of early Sino-Soviet relations, but helped to shape Chinese domestic politics as well. On the eve of victory, the Chinese Communists were an entity comprising essentially five large relatively independent armies and a highly developed central party apparatus. Of course, in each of the army systems there existed a parallel party command structure. In fact, the commanders of each army were both the military and the party leaders.[13]

The initial civil-administrative structure of the Chinese People's Republic derived directly from the military situation as it evolved during the civil war. At that time there were seven "liberated" areas, each of which was ruled by a military control committee: Northeast, Inner Mongolia, East China, Northwest, North China, Chungyuan, and Chiungya, a small area in Kwangtung province. As all China was occupied after the defeat of the Nationalists this schema was extended to cover the entire country. Inner Mongolia became an autonomous area; North China was placed directly under the Peking government; the Northeast (Manchuria) and East China (Shantung and the east coast) became "Great Areas." Chungyuan was made a province and renamed P'ingyuan, and Chiungya was amalgamated into Kwangtung province. As troops moved outward from the central areas, the Northwest, Southwest, and Central South "Great Areas" were established. The status of the Great Areas, of which there were five, was formalized in three laws promulgated by the central government: the Organic Law of the People's Central Government (September 27, 1949), the Cabinet Ordinance on appointments and dismissals (November 28, 1949), and the Organic Law of the Great Administrative Areas' Governments (December 16, 1949).[14]

The field armies occupied regions which corresponded to the Great Areas, but each army's power position was balanced by a "trade-off" of military units with other field armies. The Korean War temporarily upset this arrangement as two-thirds of the People's Liberation Army units eventually saw action in the conflict, but the balance was restored afterward. The system of counterbalancing field armies bore the following general outlines. Lin Piao's Fourth Field Army units were assigned to the Northeast and to Central South. All units of the North China Field Army, except three corps, were returned after the war to the North China command (Peking). Those three were assigned to the Southwest, East, and Northeast regional commands. Ho Lung's First Field Army returned to Sinkiang, but one unit was assigned to Central South. Liu Po-ch'eng's Second Field Army returned to the Southwest, but one unit remained in the Northeast and two others were reassigned to Central South. Of Ch'en Yi's Third Field Army, six corps returned to East China, but one corps remained in the Northeast, while two others were assigned to North China. These units remained in these locations until the outbreak of the Great Proletarian Cultural Revolution.[15]

The Peking governmental structure was initially established in September 1949 with the promulgation of the Organic Law and Common Program of the Chinese People's Political Consultative Conference, and the Organic Law of the Central People's Government of the Chinese People's Republic. The Government Council, headed by Chairman Mao Tse-tung and six vice-chairmen, Chu Teh, Liu Shao-ch'i, Kao Kang, Soong Ching-ling, Li Chi-shen, and Chang Lan, held supreme state power. Below the Government Council stood five additional organs, all presumably equal in rank—the Cabinet, Military Council, State Planning Committee, Supreme Court, and Procurator-General's office. These five organs functioned directly under the Government Council and wielded not only executive but legislative power.

Theoretically the Government Council held the power of appointment in the Great Areas, but in practice the regional military commanders and party leaders were vested with central government authority. The Great

Areas' governments, for the most part, functioned independently of the central governmental apparatus. The only direct link between the two was in the Northeast, where Kao Kang concurrently held party, state, and military posts in both regional and central governmental structures. Of course, the party's own organizations served to ensure a continuity of policy, but the party's presence varied according to region. For example, in 1950, before the Chinese Communists entered the Korean War, the distribution of party members was roughly as follows: of a total of 5.8 million, 1 million were in the People's Liberation Army; 3.4 million nonmilitary were in Northeast, East, and North China; and only 1.4 million (including military) were in the vast areas of Central South, Southwest, and Northwest.[16]

The Politics of Centralization

The primary domestic task of the Chinese Communist leaders after victory was the creation of a centralized institutional structure. China's leaders knew and acted on the premise that the decentralized arrangement of Great Areas was temporary until a central apparatus could be constructed for the entire country. The problem was: how to combine the several separate but obviously interrelated political-military systems of the Great Areas into one national structure. An already existing but rudimentary central apparatus complicated the problem. The interplay between the Great Areas and Peking was the essential reality governing the development of domestic politics during the first decade. The leaders sought to establish positions for themselves which would guarantee their inclusion in the central structure as it took shape. The underlying dynamic of Chinese Communist leadership politics was, therefore, the contest for control of the emerging central institutional structure.

Tension between the center and the regions was evident from the start. For example, as early as March 1950, Peking transferred the taxing power of the Great Areas' governments to itself but, because of resistance by regional leaders, as well as an inadequately functioning central collection system, part of this authority was returned to the Great Areas the following year in May.[17] The first step taken by the central government to abolish the Great Areas altogether occurred during the Korean War. In November 1952 Peking decreed that civil rather than military rule should prevail over the Great Areas.[18] At this time the titles were changed from Great Areas People's Governments to Great Areas Administrative Councils and the councils were made subordinate to Peking. The ministries of the Great Areas' Governments were also reduced in status to departments or offices and some were placed directly under jurisdiction of the ministries in Peking.[19]

With the end of the conflict in Korea, Communist China's leaders were free to concentrate on the establishment of a national, central apparatus. Beginning in 1954, restructuring of party, state, military, and economic organizations was carried out at all levels.

The structural changes directly affected the political fortunes of the highest-ranking leaders of the Chinese People's Republic. In January 1953 it had been announced that a People's Congress would be convened at an early, but unspecified, date to approve the first constitution of the Chinese People's Republic.[20] The congress actually convened over a year and a half later (September 1954), suggesting disagreements among the top leaders over the form and substance of the proposed reorganization of the state structure.

As early as 1953, several high-ranking leaders had become disaffected with Mao's plans and formed a coalition against him and others in top positions. This was the so-called anti-party alliance of Kao Kang and Jao Shu-shih. The coalition consisted of more than Kao and Jao. Numbered among their supporters, with varying degrees of commitment, were Chu Teh, P'eng Teh-huai, T'an Chen-lin, Chen Pei-hsien, possibly T'ao Chu, several other important figures in the Northeast and East China party and state organizations, and members of the Russian leadership.

The Kao-Jao episode is an example of coalition politics in action. Several groups, initially based in the political systems of the Great Areas, vied for positions in the soon-to-be-reorganized state structure. Mao Tse-tung's group was only one, but clearly the dominant one, in this political constellation. As chairman of the constitution-drafting committee and leader of the existing central apparatus, Mao had a strong voice in shaping the future structure of the state. The main outlines of the struggle within the leadership now seem clear. A new state structure was to be built at the expense of the Great Areas and the military establishment. The entire existing apparatus was to be scrapped and a new central structure erected. The result would be fewer command positions at the regional level. Competition for positions in the central structure was therefore keen. For those who controlled the centralization process, the opportunities to exclude real or potential political opponents were great.

Mao Tse-tung sought to undercut Kao Kang's growing power in Manchuria by attempting to remove him from his geographical base and absorb him into the central leadership. The November 1952 meeting of the Central Government Council, which reduced the power of the Great Areas, also established the State Planning Committee. Kao Kang was named chairman of the committee, whose location was in Peking.[21]

The November decisions constituted the opening shots in the struggle between the Kao-Jao and Mao groups. Kao responded by seeking to persuade or pressure Mao to relinquish one of his leadership positions, either the top party or state post. He was unsuccessful. A later party resolution condemned Kao's "anti-party alliance" and claimed that Kao and Jao by conspiratorial means sought "to split our Party and to overthrow the leading core—the long tested Central Committee of the Party headed by Comrade Mao Tse-tung—with the aim of seizing the suspreme power of the Party and the State." [22].

Although the party resolution condemning Kao and Jao was published in 1955, action was taken against them much earlier, probably soon after January 1954. From that date on, Kao Kang's whereabouts is unknown.[23] In February 1954, at the Central Committee's Fourth Plenum, Liu Shao-ch'i gave the first official hint that a crisis existed when he said that there were those who "looked on their own region or department as 'personal property or an independent kingdom'" and charged that "those who cause dissension and stir up factionalism will be 'fought mercilessly'; they will be subjected to severe punitive action and will eventually be expelled from the Party." [24] By this time Kao and Jao had probably already been defeated.

To the extent that the events can now be reconstructed, Kao called for the replacement of several top leaders. His choice for the chairmanship of the state post, the post Mao would most likely have given up if it had become necessary to surrender one position, was Chu Teh, the revolutionary war hero and founder of the Red Army, who was known to be dissatisfied with his subordinate status under Mao. In 1959 Lin Piao accused Chu Teh, among other things, of wanting to become chairman in place of Mao. Kao himself planned to fill two other positions:

"General Secretary or Vice Chairman of the Central Committee of the Party and the Premier of the State Council." [25]

Kao Kang supported his claims with the "theory of two parties," one the party of the revolutionary bases and army and the other the party of the white areas—those areas controlled by the Nationalists during the war.[26] Kao argued that the party was the creation of the army and, therefore, those who represented the party of the revolutionary bases should receive preferential consideration over those who represented the party of the white areas. This interpretation of party history struck directly at Liu Shao-ch'i and Chou En-lai, who had spent much of the war years in the white areas and who occupied the very posts to which Kao aspired.

Kao also managed to obtain at least tacit support from P'eng Teh-huai, the Korean War hero. (Some charges appeared during the Cultural Revolution which actually attributed to P'eng the leadership of the Kao-Jao coalition.) Kao failed to obtain the support of one other key military man, Lin Piao. Lin declined to support Kao and Jao, instead siding with Mao, Liu, and Chou, for which he was well rewarded. At the meeting which passed the resolution condemning the opposition coalition, Lin (and Teng Hsiao-p'ing, about whom more will be said below) was elected to the Politburo in the twelfth position of thirteen.[27] Later that year he was promoted to marshal, along with nine others including P'eng Teh-huai, who evidently managed to shift away from Kao's group in time.

The reasons for Lin's decision to support the Mao group against Kao are undoubtedly numerous, but the history of Lin's and Kao's relations provides part of the answer. Kao became second secretary of the Central Committee's Northeastern Party Bureau in 1940, but until 1948 played a subordinate role in that area's affairs. The land reform carried out after 1945 in Manchuria was actually the work of Lin Piao, not Kao Kang. It was only after the collapse of Nationalist forces in 1948, when Lin moved his troops south toward T'ientsin and Peking late in that year, that Kao assumed control of Manchurian affairs. Even though part of Lin's forces returned to Manchuria after 1949 (and part was assigned to Kwangtung), Kao remained in command.[28] The elimination of Kao Kang was therefore in Lin Piao's direct interest.

Teng Hsiao-p'ing also played a role in the defeat of the challenge from the Kao-Jao coalition. Teng led the attack against Kao and Jao at the

March 1955 meeting, for which he was promoted to the Politburo, but he also evidently opposed this group earlier. Teng's role centered on his opposition in the State Planning Committee to Kao's demands for preferential treatment of the Northeast in the allocation of economic resources. Kao argued that the Northeast had a "special character," being more economically advanced and therefore deserving high priority.[29] This was in opposition to the view of the Mao group that while the Manchurian industrial base was to be maintained, as was the East China base, higher priority should be given to North and West Central China for the industrial development of those parts of the country. This is a probable reason for Jao Shu-shih's decision to support Kao Kang, for Jao was chairman of East China as well as a member of the State Planning Committee. East China, too, was to receive fewer resources relative to other areas.[30]

The contest over resource allocation in the State Planning Committee suggests that that body was one of the principal organizational vehicles for the Kao-Jao coalition. The subsequent history of the committee and its members strongly supports this hypothesis. Membership in the committee included Kao Kang, chairman; Teng Tzu-hui, vice-chairman; Lin Piao, Jao Shu-shih, Ch'en Yün, Teng Hsiao-p'ing, Li Fu-ch'un, Po I-po, P'eng Chen, Huang K'o-ch'eng, Liu Lan-t'ao, Hsi Chung-hsün, Chang Hsi, An Chih-wen, Ma Hung,, Hsüeh Mu-ch'iao, and P'eng Teh-huai.[31] P'eng Teh-huai's appointment to the committee seems to have been largely honorific, since he was in Korea at this time.

Mao Tse-tung was not a member of the committee, but managed to obtain sufficient support from the majority of its members to defeat the Kao-Jao group there. If promotions of committee members can be interpreted as political reward for supporting Mao, then it is clear who Mao's supporters were. The promotions of Lin Piao, Teng Hsiao-p'ing, and P'eng Teh-huai have already been noted. Huang K'o-ch'eng was named a general of the People's Liberation Army. P'eng Chen became mayor of Peking. That same month, January 1953, Teng Tzu-hui, Ch'en Yün, Po I-po, Hsi Chung-hsün, and Liu Lan-t'ao were all named to the constitution-drafting committee with Mao Tse-tung. In addition, Ch'en Yün was given the chairmanship of the Economic and Finance Committee of the Cabinet when that committee replaced, in function, the State Planning Committee. The State Planning Committee itself was disestablished and reorganized as the State Planning Commission under the Cabinet, losing its formerly independent and equal status. Li Fu-ch'un was named chairman of the commission.[32] By this reckoning, at least eleven of the seventeen members of the committee supported Mao.

Stalin's Death and the Succession Struggle

The issue of the allocation of resources leads directly to the question of the Soviet role in Chinese affairs. Before he died, Stalin followed the policy of concentrating Soviet aid in the Northeast in order to influence decisions in the area close to Soviet borders, particularly Korea. Consequently, Stalin dealt directly with Kao Kang as well as with Mao Tse-tung. During the initial negotiations for the Sino-Soviet treaty, Kao preceded Mao to Moscow, signing a separate agreement between the USSR and the Manchurian People's Government. Whatever else he did, Kao permitted the Soviets to exercise a strong influence in Manchuria. Russians administered the Manchurian railway and river systems, controlled ports and airfields, and directed the reconstruction of the area's industrial base. Hence, the later charge that Kao had maintained "illicit relations with foreign countries" had considerable substance from Mao Tse-tung's point of view.

Stalin's death affected Soviet policy toward Manchuria drastically and Kao Kang's position fatally. The succession struggle and its outcome provide the perspective for analysis of subsequent Sino-Soviet relations. Immediately after the dictator's death, both Malenkov and Khrushchev strove to obtain the support of the Chinese Communists for their respective candidacies. Malenkov was prepared to perpetuate the Stalinist policy of favoring Manchuria. Khrushchev, in his drive for the support of Mao Tse-tung, recognized that Stalin's Manchurian policy was a liability and turned that knowledge to political advantage.

In the early months after Stalin's death the Chinese supported Malenkov. In March 1953, in an article eulogizing Stalin, Mao expressed this support, saying "we profoundly believe that the Central Committee of the Communist Party of the Soviet Union and the Soviet Government, headed by Comrade Malenkov, will certainly be able to continue the work of Comrade Stalin." [33] That issue of *Pravda* contained a picture of Stalin, Mao, and Malenkov ostensibly taken after the conclusion of the Sino-Soviet treaty negotiations in February 1950.[34] In fact, the picture had been altered from the original photograph published in February 1950, in which Malenkov was only one of nineteen members of the Chinese and Russian delegations witnessing the signing of the treaty.[35] In the 1953 version all but Stalin, Mao, and Malenkov were excised!

Over the course of the following year, however, Mao's support shifted from Malenkov to Khrushchev. The key event was Khrushchev's and Bulganin's trip to Peking in September 1954 to sign another aid agreement with the Chinese. Khrushchev offered grants and long-term credits amounting to 520 million rubles, agreed to expand the volume of equipment deliveries for industrial projects covered in previous agreements, yielded Soviet holdings in the four Sino-Soviet joint stock companies established by the 1950 treaty, announced plans for the construction of two railroads linking China to the Soviet Union (one through Outer Mongolia and the other through Sinkiang), and agreed to the withdrawal of Soviet forces from Port Arthur by May 1955.[36] The battle lines of the Soviet struggle for power were indicated by the fact that Khrushchev was accompanied to Peking by Bulganin, the chairman of the Council of Ministers, while the Premier (Malenkov) and the Minister of Foreign Affairs (Molotov) remained in Moscow.

Economic assistance undoubtedly helped Khrushchev gain the support of the Chinese, in particular the Mao group, but it was his position on strategic defense policy, coupled with his willingness to withdraw the Soviets from their position in Manchuria (and therefore from support of Kao Kang!), which decisively turned them away from Malenkov. Malenkov, at the Nineteenth Party Congress in 1952, following Stalin's initiation of the "soft line" toward the West, asserted that "in peaceful competition with capitalism the socialist economic system will prove its superiority over the capitalistic system more and more vividly year by year." [37] After Stalin's death, Malenkov stated that a third nuclear world war would result in the destruction of world civilization and therefore there were "no objective impediments" to the improvement of Soviet-American relations. He shortly moved toward a settlement of the Korean conflict, saying that a "new epoch" had begun. He saw China as a "mighty stabilizing factor" in Asia. Malenkov's "new course" also affected domestic policy; no longer would heavy industry receive top priority. Now light industries and food industries would develop "at the same rate as heavy industry."

Khrushchev, although later championing "peaceful coexistence," in early 1954 took a position almost diametrically opposite Malenkov's. The Soviet Union, he said, should not merely avoid war but should actively deter it through a strong military posture. A nuclear world war would only result in the destruction of capitalism, not of world civilization. The Sino-Soviet relationship he saw as a "powerful factor in the struggle for peace in the Far East." [38] Domestically, Khrushchev called for continued stress on heavy over light industry at the expense of the consumer sector.

It was obvious which of these two positions Mao and his followers preferred. The Malenkov position implied acceptance of the *status quo,* while Khrushchev's hard line indicated a far greater willingness to honor a strategic commitment to China. Early in 1955 Mao publicly endorsed Khrushchev's position that nuclear war would mean not the destruction of the world, but only of capitalism, and on the eve of the Twentieth Party Congress the following year, Mao said in a telegram that "the great successes of the USSR in foreign and domestic policy in recent years are inseparable from the correct leadership of the well-tried Central Committee of the CPSU [Communist Party of the Soviet Union] headed by Comrade Khrushchev." [39] But this gets us somewhat ahead of the story.

The Khrushchev-Bulganin trip to Peking in September 1954 came at a time when Mao's power was greatly circumscribed. The National People's Congress had just ended (September 15–28), resulting in the reorganization of not only the state but the military, economic, and party structures, and the radical redistribution of political power among the Chinese leaders.

At the congress, Mao gave no major report, opening and closing the ceremonies with a few words. Until 1954, as official head of the Central People's Government, Mao had had the power of "1) enacting and interpreting the laws, promulgating decrees and supervising their execution. . . . 2) annulling or revising any decisions or orders of the Government Administrative Council not in conformity with the laws. . . . 3) ratifying . . . treaties and agreements . . . with foreign countries. . . . 4) dealing with questions of war and peace, appointing the Premier, members of the Cabinet, and all other important officials." [40] Under the new structure, as Chairman of the Chinese People's Republic, Mao's powers were severely limited by the Standing Committee, whose chairman was Liu Shao-ch'i.[41] The Chairman could promulgate laws and decrees only "in accordance with the decisions of the Congress, or, when not in session, of its Standing Committee" (article 40). He could not annul or revise any decision or order of any government organ. He could ratify treaties with foreign states only "in accordance with the decisions of the Standing Committee" (article 41).

Nor had Mao independent power to make appointments to any post. The Chairman of the Republic "appoints or removes the Premier, Vice-Premiers, Ministers . . . in accordance with the decision of the Congress or its Standing Committee." The only power which Mao exercised independently of the Standing Committee was command of the armed forces (article 42), and this, too, was qualified. Finally, the Chairman of the Republic had no veto power over the decisions of the Congress and its Standing Committee. The Standing Committee enacted decrees, interpreted laws made by the Congress, supervised the Cabinet, the Supreme Court, and the Presecutor-General's office. It had the power to annul laws, and appoint vice-premiers and ministers. When the Congress was not in session, the Standing Committee assumed its prerogatives relating to the negotiation of treaties with foreign countries, proclamation of war and so forth (articles 31–33).

Essentially what had taken place in the state reorganization was that the Standing Committee was interposed between Mao and the major administrative organs of the new state structure. The Standing Committee became responsible for supervision of the day-to-day workings of the Cabinet, the Defense Council (even though Mao retained command of the armed forces), the Supreme Court, the office of the Prosecutor-General, and the general office. In sum, the reorganization of the state saw Mao Tse-tung's power severely limited.

The military apparatus was also radically restructured. The six military regions were replaced by thirteen smaller military regions. The large field armies were broken up and their thirty-five or so component units were each designated as field armies and placed directly under control of the newly established (state) Ministry of Defense and (party) Military Affairs Committee. The redesignated military units remained in place, but the many regional commanders and the marshals (after 1955) were brought to Peking. The military reorganization stripped military, and therefore political, power from regional commands and centralized it in Peking. The restructuring of the state organization also had its effect on the shape of the party. When the Great Areas were abolished the party's regional bureaus were also reorganized, the line of command now running from Peking directly to the provincial level party organizations.

The results of the major restructuring of Chinese state, military, and party organizations saw significant redistribution of political power among the top leaders. Among these, two were completely removed from authority (Kao Kang and Jao Shu-shih), several others advanced in the new power structure (Lin Piao, Liu Shao-ch'i, Teng Hsiao-p'ing, P'eng Teh-huai), some made no apparent gains (Chou En-lai, Chu Teh), and one suffered a partial eclipse of power, but retained a dominant position (Mao Tse-tung). In the next phase, some of those who had colluded with Mao against the challenge of Kao Kang and had been promoted for their service used their positions to obtain even greater power at Mao's expense. The thrust came at the Chinese Communist Party's Eighth National Congress, the first to be held since the establishment of the Communist regime. It saw a further realignment of political forces and the erosion of the position of Mao Tse-tung. It followed the politically explosive Twentieth Party Congress of the Soviet Union, to which we must first turn.

Twentieth Party Congress of the CPSU and Its Aftermath

Khrushchev's secret speech denouncing Stalin, delivered at the Twentieth Party Congress, was a bombshell for the leadership of all the world's Communist parties, especially the Chinese. The events surrounding the decision to give the speech, and its significance, are complex matters open to varying interpretations. It appears that Khrushchev planned to end collective leadership and to assume Stalin's mantle himself, but he met with strong eleventh-hour opposition. The previous September, Khrushchev had approved a reissue of Stalin's *Short Course*, and on the anniversary of Stalin's birthday, December 21, the Soviet press published photographs and editorials lauding the departed leader. These events suggested a continuation of the "cult of the individual." [42]

The decision to turn against the Stalin image, or personality cult, was apparently made sometime in January 1956. In retrospect, a key indicator that an anti-Stalin move was under way came at the conference of historians that took place in Moscow in late January. There an open clash occurred between the academic and the *apparatchik* historians when the Deputy Editor-in-Chief of the historical journal *Problems of History*, E. M. Burdzhalov, launched a broadside attack against the falsification of Soviet history. He singled out for special criticism the party histories of the Ukraine and Transcaucasia, and Stalin's *Short Course.*[43] The Ukraine and Transcaucasia had been Khrushchev's responsibility ever since 1937. Criticism of these histories was implied criticism of the responsible party leader; moreover, indirect reference was made to the purge of the former party chief, Kossior, whom Khrushchev had replaced. Mention of the *Short Course* also implied criticism of Khrushchev, who had released it for republication only a few months before.[44] Both criticisms were repeated by Mikoyan in his public report to the Twentieth Party Congress.[45]

At the congress the 1,436 delegates received a set of documents which contained, among other things, Lenin's "testament," in which he warned against the "immense power" that the "rude" Stalin had arrogated to himself, and also advised enlarging the Central Committee as a means of ensuring collective leadership.[46] If there was anyone for whom these documents constituted a threat, it was Khruschev. It was he who sought to fill the position left by Stalin's death, and his own "rudeness" was well known. Moreover, it was Khrushchev who sought to bring collective leadership to an end.

Khrushchev delivered the main report to the congress and spoke of Stalin's passing in warm, emotional language ("death tore Joseph Vissarionovich Stalin from our ranks").[47] Ten days later, Khrushchev made a complete turnabout. He declared in the famous secret speech that "Stalin . . . used extreme methods and mass repressions. . . . Stalin showed in a whole series of cases his intolerance, his brutality, and his abuse of power." [48] At the same time he attempted to exculpate himself from guilt in the Kossior affair by denying any knowledge of Kossior's arrest and purge until after the fact. He also called for the compilation of a new party history to replace the *Short Course.*[49]

Apparently Khrushchev had attempted to suppress the speech, which, judging from its detailed content, had been in preparation for some time. When he found that he could not suppress it, he decided to read it himself rather than permit someone else to do so. This was necessary to save his own position. Khrushchev faced a dilemma. If he did not read the speech, he would very likely lose his own position, since the attack on Stalin would also be taken as an implied attack on Khrushchev. If Khrushchev did read the speech, he would probably save his own position, but at the cost of incalculable consequences to the total system.

Khrushchev chose to read the speech, and thereby saved himself—at least in the short run. But the larger consequence of his attack on Stalin was to set in motion the fragmentation of Stalin's empire, of which the subsequent revolutions in Poland and Hungary were but a part. Whatever the motive, Khrushchev's indictment of Stalin—the cult of the individual, mass repression, terror, suppression of minority peoples, and so forth—was an implied indictment of every Communist party leader, of the system that Stalin had built, and of the men who operated it.

To Mao Tse-tung, the anti-Stalin speech must have come as a terrific surprise. Since he was the ranking member of the Communist world outside Russia, the speech could be interpreted as being aimed at him. Moreover, he must have suspected that Khrushchev had turned away from his earlier understanding with Mao and his followers. His suspicions were strengthened in the months that followed the congress as Stalin's appointees in the eastern European satellites were replaced one by one. Moreover, Khrushchev began to sound more and more like Malenkov, placing emphasis on the necessity of avoiding a general war, reducing investment in heavy industry, increasing production of consumer goods, and renewing emphasis on disarmament and peaceful coexistance. Finally, at the Eighth Party Congress of the Chinese Communist Party there were indications that Mao himself had become a target.

Eighth Party Congress of the Chinese Communist Party

The first and second sessions of the Eighth Party Congress, which convened eighteen months apart (September 1956 and May 1958), reveal several marked power shifts among the top leaders of the party. At the first session, Mao's position as head of the party was seriously undercut, both ideologically and organizationally. Again, as in 1954, aside from making brief opening remarks, Mao made no major address to the congress. Liu Shao-ch'i delivered the important political report and Teng Hsiao-p'ing the report on the revision of the party constitution. At the congress, both men made significant advances in the political hierarchy.

Ideologically, collective leadership was emphasized over the role of the leader. This was undoubtedly in part a reaction to the de-Stalinization campaign begun by Khrushchev earlier in the year. At this first session

the Marxist-Leninist basis of the Chinese Communist Party was emphasized; the reference incorporated into the 1945 party constitution to the
"thought of Mao Tse-tung" was omitted. Organizationally, several key
changes took place. The Central Committee was enlarged from 64 to 97
members and the Politburo from 13 to 17 with 6 candidate members.
There had been no candidate member category previously. Two new
organizations were established for the Central Committee and Politburo,
which clearly reflected the rise in status of Liu and Teng and the further
weakening of Mao.

Liu Shao-ch'i had assumed the chairmanship of the Standing Committee of the reorganized state structure in 1954, his payoff for support of
Mao against the challenge of Kao Kang. He now became senior
vice-chairman of another newly established organ, the Standing Committee of the party Politburo. Since 1949 Standing Committees had
existed only at the provincial level. The first six men in the Politburo
composed the Politburo Standing Committee. They were: Mao, chairman; Liu Shao-ch'i, senior vice-chairman; Chou En-lai, Chu Teh, Ch'en
Yün, and Teng Hsiao-p'ing. The seventh man was Lin Piao, who did not
become a member of the Standing Committee until May 1958, when
altered political circumstances enabled Mao to enlarge the Standing
Committee and bring him in. Clearly, if Chu Teh or Ch'en Yün, for
instance, sided with Liu and Teng on any issue, it would have been
impossible for Mao to obtain a majority vote.

Teng Hsiao-p'ing also advanced in rank at the first session. Placed at
the head of the Secretariat of the Central Committee, Teng was charged
with "attending to the daily work of the Central Committee," [50] a newly
assigned function for that body. At every level of organization—from the
national down through the provincial, local, branch, and including the
factory level—there now existed twin party control mechanisms, standing committees and secretariats, commanded by Liu Shao-ch'i and Teng
Hsiao-p'ing.[51]

It was at this time that the party's leaders made the decision to
establish the "first and second lines," which apparently relate to the
distinction between policy and command. (In a speech given in October
1966 Mao asserted that it had been his idea to establish the "two lines"
so that Liu and Teng could preside over important conferences and take
charge of the party's daily operations.)[52] Viewed in terms of the conflict
hypothesis, Mao's "idea" connotes an attempt to preserve a policy-

making prerogative for himself while relinquishing the power of command to Liu and Teng, rather than an attempt to develop some sort of succession mechanism. If so, then Mao was correct in charging in this 1966 speech that Liu and Teng were establishing "independent kingdoms" in an organizational sense, like Kao and Jao before them, and that it was for this reason that it had been necessary to initiate the Great Proletarian Cultural Revolution. Mao was acknowledging that he had lost the power to ensure that his policies would be carried out. The Great Proletarian Cultural Revolution was necessary for him to regain control of the state and party leadership.

After the 1956 session of the congress had ended, Mao moved to bolster his sagging political position. Four major developments mark his efforts. First, Mao managed to purge the party and state apparatuses, particularly at the provincial level. His speech "On the Correct Handling of Contradictions Among the People," delivered in February 1957, initiated and provided the justification for his step. In it Mao spoke of the need to "supervise the party," implying that the party could err, and of "contradictions arising from the bureaucratic practices of certain state functionaries in their relations with the masses." [53] Second, the speech itself represented Mao's first move in a longer-run drive to reestablish his image as supreme leader, one who stands above the party. In actuality, the contest for control over the mass media was joined at this time. Third, following and perhaps accompanying the personnel shifts during 1957, the party as a whole assumed direction of the offices of the "state functionaries." The "rectification campaign," or purge, which permitted Mao to identify if not eliminate opposition, took place at a time when domestic policy took a sharp swing to the left. This leftward shift got under way in mid-1957, despite the moderate economic program proposed at the Eighth Party Congress's first session the previous September.[54] The shift was reflected in public statements. For example, Po I-po, chairman of the State Economic Commission, told the National People's Conference in June that China must reduce her "reliance on foreign countries." Others saw a break-neck pace of economic development as the "only way out" for China.[55]

Fourth, at this time it is possible to detect a shift away from support of Khrushchev. There is considerable uncertainty about the extent of the change, but the Chinese appear to have moved to the support of Khrushchev's opposition, the Malenkov-Molotov-Kaganovich group, which unsuccessfully attempted to unseat Khrushchev in mid-1957.[56] In this context, the Sino-Soviet defense conference held in Moscow in October of that year, and the Moscow meeting of twelve Communist parties which followed in November and which Mao himself attended, bore all the earmarks of an attempt to reconcile diverging positions. Despite the conclusion of an "agreement on new technology for national defense," which the Chinese now claim included the supply of a sample atomic bomb,[57] the conferences only papered over the differences between the two countries.

After the Twentieth Party Congress of the CPSU, Mao Tse-tung had faced a dilemma. He had supported Khrushchev because the latter had indicated a willingness to assist in China's development. But as Khrushchev consolidated his position in the Soviet Union, he seemed less inclined to support Mao. Although the agreement on "new technology" was signed in November 1957, no new credits were forthcoming from the Soviet Union after that date (with one exception to be discussed below). It is now apparent that Mao and Khrushchev had become estranged. After 1957, Soviet exports to China were on a cash basis, a step which placed the Chinese in an increasingly awkward economic position.

The Chinese recognized that if this situation were permitted to drift, the entire program of rapid industrialization, geared to and dependent upon Soviet aid, would inevitably grind to a slow walk. China would find it harder and harder to maintain current rates of development, let alone increase them. The Chinese were beholden to the Russians for plans, technical assistance, spare parts, and, most of all, for oil. By restricting credits, the Russians were in a position to make China an economic and even a political satellite, effectively controlling its rate of economic growth and freedom of political action.

The debate among the Chinese leadership over the issue of military power most clearly illustrates the alternatives as they developed for the Chinese. In the early 1950s, Soviet aid was essential to China and the Chinese had no choice but to accept Soviet terms. The kinds of materials and know-how required to build a modern industrial and military establishment were unavailable elsewhere. But while helping establish the basis for a modern economic system, Stalin attached certain strings to Soviet aid. He supplied weapons, but not all the means to make them. Of course, the Russians could not prevent the Chinese from ultimately building an independent economic system, but to the extent that the Chinese were dependent upon the Soviet Union, the Russians could affect China's rate of growth.[58]

The Soviet succession struggle after Stalin's death gave the Chinese an opportunity to raise the question of redefining the Sino-Soviet relationship. This was undoubtedly part of the reason for Khrushchev's and Bulganin's trip to China in September 1954. The next few years saw the gradual phasing out of Soviet military aid and training programs. By late 1956 the Chinese were flying their first Chinese-manufactured MIG jets, and the army had become a reasonably well-equipped light infantry force.[59] By then, Chinese military men were already deep in debate over the need for China to acquire her own nuclear weapons. Actually, the debate was never over whether to acquire nuclear weapons, but only how and when. Some advocated increased resource allocation to heavy industry as a means of establishing an autarkic military establishment and providing the basis for China's own nuclear program. Others argued for continued reliance on the "expedient measure of placing orders with foreign countries" to obtain needed materials.[60] The implied question in both of these positions was: what role would the Soviet Union play? At this stage of the relationship, advocates of both positions would continue to depend heavily on the Soviet Union for support, but, depending on the course chosen, for different kinds of support. It was not yet a question of "with or without" the Soviet Union.

The de-Stalinization campaign, the failure of the so-called anti-party group to oust Khrushchev, and the growing Sino-Soviet estrangement led to a restructuring of the alternatives open to the Chinese leadership. The choices now facing the Chinese leaders were either to go along with the Russians in the hope of restoring the former relationship at some future date, or to strike out independently—to break the bonds of Soviet economic and political domination. Both choices contained difficulties. To stay with the existing relationship left the Chinese open to the danger of falling further under Soviet domination, even though they gained some Soviet aid in the process. The other choice, to break away from Soviet controls, meant an inevitable period of dislocation and perhaps even chaos until the Chinese could switch to alternative sources of supply and restructure the economy. In these choices were planted not only the seeds of the Sino-Soviet split, but also the Great Proletarian Cultural Revolution.

The issue, then, was: how should the Chinese respond to the dilemma posed by the Russians? One wing in the party, headed (as we now know) by Liu Shao-ch'i, favored continued cooperation with the Soviet Union—staying with the alliance and hoping that China would be able to avoid becoming an economic and political satellite. The other wing, led by Mao Tse-tung, made the decision to strike out on an independent course. The decision was made at the second session of the Eighth Party Congress, held from May 5 through 23, 1958.

Great Leap Forward: The Choice for Independent Action

The tone of the second session differed sharply from that of the first. The congress communique carried in the *People's Daily* of May 25 called it a *"cheng-feng* reform session." Indeed, the expulsion of eight members of provincial party standing committees, two members of provincial party committees, and one member of a provincial party secretariat were announced. The communique also noted the existence of "anti-party groups" among the highest ranks of party members in several provinces and said that several party provincial leaders were under investigation for "regionalistic" and "nationalistic" activities.[61]

At the first session in September 1956, the creation of the Politburo Standing Committee saw the transfer of power from the Politburo to the Standing Committee, in which Mao had been unable to outvote his opponents. At the second session Mao, presumably as a result of the purge of the lower level party organizations, was able to enlarge the Politburo and the Politburo Standing Committee. Added to the Politburo at this time were K'o Ch'ing-shih, party First Secretary of Shanghai city; T'an Chen-lin, member of the Central Committee Secretariat; and Li Ching-ch'uan, party First Secretary of Szech'uan province. Added to the Politburo Standing Committee was Lin Piao.

Whether or not the addition of three men affected the power relationship in the Politburo, the addition of Lin Piao to the Politburo Standing Committee gave Mao at least a four-to-three voting edge in that body, assuming that Mao, Lin, Chou En-lai, and either Ch'en Yün or Chu Teh voted together. This voting edge was sufficient for Mao to obtain a favorable decision at the second session on his program of the three red banners—the General Line, the Communes, and the Great Leap Forward.[62]

The Great Leap Forward symbolized China's, in particular Mao's group's, determination to break free of Soviet controls, to disengage the Chinese economy from the Soviet, and to reject what the Chinese have since asserted were "unreasonable demands designed to bring China under Soviet military control." [63] Ostensibly, the purposes of the Great Leap were to catch up with Great Britain economically and to move into the stage of full communism ahead of the Soviet Union. More realistically, it was to prepare the ground for China's development independent of the Soviet Union. By all conventional economic standards, the Great Leap was an immense failure. Backyard furnaces, the mobilization of millions of people as a substitute for capital, the agricultural communes, the decentralization of industry—all became an enormous fiasco.

Politically, for Mao Tse-tung, the results were mixed. By the decision of the congress, Mao set China on a new policy course which would be extremely difficult to alter and which in fact continues to this day. For Mao, personally, the results were less satisfactory. The almost immediate and obvious failure of the Great Leap gave Mao's opponents the necessary political leverage to deprive him of his position as chairman of the Republic (one of the objectives which Kao Kang and Jao Shu-shih had sought to achieve a few years earlier).

It seems clear that Mao did not step down voluntarily and that he apparently exerted all his efforts in an attempt to garner sufficient support to beat off the challenge at the Sixth Plenary session of the Eighth Central Committee, which was held in Wuchang from November 28 to December 10, 1958. The plenum communique, issued one week after the close of the session on December 17, pointedly noted that Mao had personally "prepared for the Plenary session," calling two meetings— one from November 2 through 10 and a second from November 21 through 27.[64] Evidently, he failed to convince a majority that he should not step down. According to the communique, the "plenary session approved the proposal of Comrade Mao Tse-tung not to stand as candidate for Chairman of the People's Republic of China for the next term of office." [65]

Mao's principal opponent, Liu Shao-ch'i, assumed the chairmanship of the Republic. Indicative of the Soviet Union's attitude toward Mao and his policies was the fact that, as soon as Mao had been excluded, the Russians (in an agreement negotiated by Chou En-lai, who had flown to

Moscow in January 1959) quickly extended additional economic aid to China, agreeing to build thirty-one more industrial plants.[66] The agreement was signed on February 7, 1959. Liu subsequently, very quietly and without fanfare, attempted to undo Mao's policy of the Great Leap. He began to dismantle the backyard furnaces, recentralize industry, and deemphasize the mass mobilization of labor and the agricultural commune program. He was only partly successful in this effort, but from this point onward, as Mao said in a later talk, Liu and Teng Hsiao-p'ing began to treat him as if he were already dead.

The policy decision to embark upon the Great Leap is a watershed in the political history of the Chinese People's Republic. During the first decade, Chinese Communist politics was not characterized by struggle between two "factions." Various groups contended. By splitting them, pitting one against another, and allying himself with one against another, Mao managed to remain leader of the single most powerful group and in overall control, even though he came precipitously close at times to losing supremacy. He was never above the political struggle; he has always been deeply involved in it. His political preeminence has been directly related to his ability to build his own political machine and to prevent the coalescence of opposing coalitions. The Great Leap policy decision marked a fundamental change in the nature of Chinese Communist leadership politics, which began to polarize. The polarization process became increasingly apparent during the succeeding seven years and culminated in what has become known as the Great Proletarian Cultural Revolution.

X

The Polarization of
Communist Politics, 1959–1965

The decision to take the Great Leap transformed the nature of Sino-Soviet relations and of Chinese leadership politics. The following six years witnessed a widening of the breach between the two powers and the increasing polarization of Chinese domestic politics. Increasingly, a primary issue which acted as the implicit touchstone for coalescing domestic factions was China's relationship with the Soviet Union. Indeed, major policy considerations were ultimately reducible to whether the choice involved cooperation or conflict with the Soviet Union—a choice which became painfully explicit in the foreign policy "debate" of 1965.

The growing institutional sophistication of the Chinese People's Republic had led to the rise of men to positions of decision-making power from which they were able to pursue policies of benefit to themselves and their organizations. The result was the formulation and execution of incompatible and even contradictory policies through separate institutional apparatuses. The Great Leap marked the beginning of what became a continually escalating institutional conflict among leaders of state, military, party, and other *ad hoc* organizations. The period 1959 to 1965 is therefore one of institutional flux characterized by attempts of various leaders to capture existing organizational apparatuses and to create new ones at both national and sub-national levels.

The Great Leap, in addition to constituting a rupture in economic relations with the Soviet Union, was a first attempt to destroy the very institutional system which Mao Tse-tung had helped to create, but of which he had lost control. The story of Mao's gradual loss of command of state and military apparatuses—even as they were being built—was discussed in the previous chapter, as was the struggle for control over the party. In the Great Leap, Mao sought to redress the imbalance of political power against him through the mechanism of the institutionally self-contained commune. Through it, he hoped to bypass the existing state, military, and party structures between the party center and the commune—the regional, provincial, and district organizations. The policy struck at the leaders of the institutions which Mao sought to leapfrog and its failure roused them to action. The group most seriously affected by the Great Leap, the military, responded earliest and most vigorously.

The Military Response to the Great Leap

If successful, the Great Leap would have emasculated the military "establishment." The break with the Soviet Union meant the end of the military modernization program, which depended on Soviet military assistance. In addition, Mao had attempted to create a military force which he could employ for political purposes by greatly expanding the militia in 1958 as part of the commune plan. The issue of party control of the militia was discussed in the December 10, 1958, party resolution, the same meeting at which it was decided that Mao would not stand for reelection to the chairmanship of the state. The connection of these events suggests the possibility that Mao agreed to step down from the state post in return for acceptance of his commune and militia proposals. The militia was to be an independent military organization, the armed instrument of the self-supporting commune, which was directly responsible to the party center, that is, to Mao Tse-tung.[1] By January 1959 the militia reportedly included 220 million men and women, or something like one-third of China's total population! How effective it was as a political instrument was another matter.

The response of the military establishment came directly from its chief, the Minister of Defense, P'eng Teh-huai, who was supported by the heads of all major military departments as well as by other important leaders.[2] P'eng had just returned from a trip to eastern Europe, where he had had discussions with Khrushchev in Tirana, Albania. Apparently encouraged by the Soviet leader, P'eng leveled an attack on Mao's policies at an enlarged Politburo conference at Lushan (July 2 to August 1, 1959). P'eng focused his criticism entirely on the "excessiveness," "shortcomings," and "errors" of the Great Leap and the communes, terming them the result of "petty-bourgeois fanaticism" and of being "dizzy with success." These "leftist mistakes," he said, derived from a misapplication and exaggeration of the principle of "putting politics in command" and a misunderstanding of the "socialist laws of planned and proportionate development." [3]

Mao Tse-tung withheld his rejoinder to P'eng and the military establishment until the Eighth Plenum of the CCP, which he convened immediately afterward (August 2 through 16). Evidently, Mao could not count on a majority at the enlarged Politburo conference, but could in the Central Committee meeting of the Eighth Plenum, at which seventy-five full and seventy-four alternate members of the Central Committee and fourteen non-Central Committee members were present. In a stirring speech, Mao admitted that "we've made a mess of things. This is good. The more said about the mess the better." He noted that "we are said to have departed from the masses, but the masses still support us." Returning the challenge to the military leadership, Mao asserted that the loyalty of the PLA rank and file was to him personally.

> If we deserve to perish, then I will go away, go to the countryside to lead the peasants and overthrow the government. If you the Liberation Army don't follow me, I'll go find a Red Army. I think the Liberation Army will follow me.[4]

After extensive and heated argument, Mao and his supporters emerged victorious in the struggle with the military establishment. The final resolution of the plenum, dated August 16, labeled P'eng and his followers a "right-opportunist anti-party clique" seeking to sabotage the dictatorship of the proletariat. At an enlarged Military Affairs Conference in September, P'eng and those who backed him were removed from their positions, although not all at the same time.[5] In the shuffle of personnel, Mao obtained a command position in the military apparatus through Lin Piao, who became Minister of Defense in place of P'eng Teh-huai.

Later Red Guard revelations and captured military documents indicate that P'eng Teh-huai had indeed consolidated a firm grip on the military apparatus through the Ministry of Defense. He had weakened party control over the military by reducing the number and role of the party committees in army units, fought the buildup of the militia as an independent military force, and opposed the policy decision to build a modern national defense system independent of the Soviet Union.[6] In short, P'eng Teh-huai had repudiated the policy of "going it alone." The failure of the Great Leap provided the opportunity for him to attempt to reverse that policy; hence his attack on Mao Tse-tung at Lushan. His attack failed and Mao was able to capture the Ministry of Defense, or at least a part of it sufficient to begin his own campaign to build a political position within China's armed forces.

Breach in Sino-Soviet Relations

Mao Tse-tung's victory in his confrontation with the military establishment, although not by any means complete, henceforth shaped the nature of the political struggle both inside China and with the Soviet Union. Mao was sufficiently powerful to frustrate all attempts to reestablish closer relations with the Soviet Union; as a result the Russians terminated their nuclear assistance program, pulled out all their technicians in mid-1960, and cut off all further aid. The hardening of positions was further reflected in public commentary. In an article published in *Hung Ch'i* on April 16 entitled "Long Live Leninism," the Chinese labeled Russian arguments in favor of peaceful coexistence "absurd," while Khrushchev, during his speech to the conference of Communist parties in Bucharest on June 21, 1960, replied that the Soviets "do not intend to yield to provocations and to deviate from the general line of our foreign policy . . . laid down by the Twentieth CPSU Congress and approved in the Declaration of the Communist and Workers' Parties adopted in 1957." [7]

Over the next two years Mao intensified the indirect ideological polemics with the Soviet Union. Worsening relations with the Soviets was not only consistent with his policy of independent action, but was also a method of isolating his internal opponents, who favored closer cooperation. This was the dual significance of the many letters, communiques, and statements that passed between the two countries. Peking attacked "revisionist" Yugloslavia (meaning the Soviet Union), while Moscow countered by attacking "doctrinaire" Albania (that is, China). The purpose of the dispute from China's point of view was to establish an independent Chinese ideological position to parallel China's evolving political independence. Principal areas of disagreement concerned the character of the present epoch, of war, peace, the transition to socialism, the unity of the international Communist movement, and the rules regulating relations among Communist parties. On each question the Chinese attempted to establish their position as "orthodox" Marxist-Leninists, while labeling the Soviet position as "revisionist." [8] On the basis of such theoretical arguments the Chinese Communists asserted their leadership of the world Communist movement and justified their attempts to establish "Maoist" parties parallel to, or in place of, existing Communist parties around the world.

Khrushchev countered Mao Tse-tung's ideological gambit at the Twenty-second Party Congress of the Soviet Union, which was convened in October 1961. He set forth a new theoretical conception of the "party of the whole people" and the "state of the whole people." One of the Chinese Communists' objectives during the polemical exchange had been to institutionalize the Soviet leadership position, possibly in order to make it vulnerable to attack on doctrinal grounds. The concept of the "party and the state of the whole people" shifted the grounds of the argument from relatively narrow doctrinal ones to a broader plane of societal development. The Soviet claim became that they were farther ahead on the path to communism.[9] Since all other Communist regimes, including the Chinese, would have to follow the same path, the Soviet position of leadership was, therefore, historically sanctioned and not subject to attack on doctrinal grounds. The following spring (1962) Soviet and European "Marxists" began to debate the long-buried concept of the "Asiatic mode of production." The discussions, which continued until Khrushchev's fall from power in 1964, implied that the Chinese were not only not socialist, but were actually heading into a blind alley of societal development. The Soviets were laying the grounds for the contention that Chinese society under Mao's leadership had regressed into a more primitive stage of development rather than progressing toward socialism.[10]

Economic Crisis and Organizational Conflict

Domestically, after establishment of the Great Leap, party leaders struggled to determine economic policy and to gain control of the administrative apparatus. Primarily as a result of popular resistance to the Great Leap, unfavorable climatic conditions, and the withdrawal of

Soviet assistance, China's economy moved to the brink of collapse. Adjustments to the commune program were necessary and Liu Shao-ch'i, now chairman of the state apparatus, pushed through major modifications. Between December 1958 and August 1959 the commune organization was virtually dismantled although lip service continued to be given to the commune as a "good thing." In essence, the commune became a federation of collective farms in which the basic administrative unit was the individual collective instead of the commune.

In April 1959, the Seventh Plenum returned individual garden plots to the peasants and granted them permission to raise livestock. Private production meant private purchase and sale; in other words, it meant the restoration of a rural "free market," without which the economy could not function. Pre-commune structures reappeared. The household was reinstated as the basic unit of society, personal property was returned to households, free food supplies were curtailed, and families were again permitted to prepare their own food.[11]

Mao Tse-tung called a halt to the retrenchment program after his victory over the military establishment in August 1959 at the Eighth Plenum. Following the harvest, a drive began to reestablish the commune system. The mess halls were reopened, many private plots were recollectivized and the rural free market was abolished. Mass labor was again mobilized for use in large-scale irrigation and other rural projects, including hog raising, fertilizer collection, and vegetable growing. The results were disappointing. The consequence of diverting large numbers of rural workers away from field and crop work was that there was a severe shortage of labor for the spring harvest. Despite concerted efforts (and partly because of a second consecutive year of unfavorable weather) the later 1960 spring harvest was poorer than that of 1959.[12]

The prospects for the coming fall were equally grim. Combined with the withdrawal of Soviet aid and technicians in June, China faced an unprecedentedly serious economic crisis. In an effort to retain control in the countryside, a Central Work Conference decided in July–August to reestablish the party's six regional bureaus, which had been abolished in 1954. To alleviate the growing food shortage, China terminated food exports and began importing grain. Another poor harvest in the fall of 1960 revealed the stark inadequacy of these measures as the winter brought reports of widespread undernourishment, famine, and resultant grumblings against the regime.

Liu Shao-ch'i's response to the desperate economic situation was to convene the Central Work Conference, an *ad hoc* organization, by means of which he could communicate policy directly to those who would administer it, primarily the party *apparatchiki,* or bureaucrats.[13] In fact, the Central Work Conference seems to have been the mechanism Liu employed to strengthen his hold on the party organization at all levels. Recall that Liu and Teng Hsiao-p'ing had, since the Eighth Party Congress of 1956, commanded the standing committees and secretariats, respectively, in the party apparatus from the central committee down to the lowest levels.[14] The Central Work Conference was a way of assembling some or all of these men and addressing them directly.[15] Nineteen such conferences were held between 1960 and 1966. At the start, Liu clearly determined the agenda and probably also the attendance, but by the fall of 1962 Mao asserted his preeminence.

From January 1961 through the first half of 1962 Liu Shao-ch'i initiated the formulation and execution of policy for both agricultural and industrial sectors. In January 1961, for instance, at the Ninth Plenum of the party, Liu pushed through basic changes in economic priorities. Agriculture was given first priority, becoming the "foundation," while industry was assigned the role of "leading factor," a reversal of previous priorities. New industrial investment was cut back and reallocated to the agricultural sector, where it was badly needed. Also, the plenum announced the decision to establish the six regional bureaus of the party. In the course of 1961, Liu convened three Central Work Conferences (in March, May, and August) which dealt with problems of the economy, primarily agricultural. The "60 articles" on Communes were adopted, which reversed policy toward the communes once again. In December 1961 a conference of party secretaries in charge of industrial affairs formulated the "70 articles" on industry, which revised downward industrial targets.

The first public clash between Liu Shao-ch'i and Mao Tse-tung occurred in January 1962.[16] The occasion was an enlarged Central Work Conference, a "five-level" cadres conference attended by 7,000 representatives from central, regional, provincial, district, and *hsien* levels. In giving an overall view of the state of the nation, Mao is reported to have said that in general "the situation is very favorable," but vigilance must be maintained against infiltration by the bourgeoisie, whose actions increase the possibility of a capitalist restoration. He urged the masses to prevent such an eventuality by close supervision of China's "class enemies." [17]

At the meeting, Liu Shao-ch'i spoke out against Mao, attacking as well the policies of the previous few years.[18] "In saying that the situation is very favorable, the Chairman refers to the political situation, since the economic situation cannot be described as very favorable but is very unfavorable." In fact, Liu went on, "our economy is on the brink of collapse." Referring to Mao's policies of the three red banners, which he saw as "a historical lesson," implying that it had been dispensed with, Liu explained that the difficulties of the recent past were brought about "30 percent by natural calamities and 70 percent by manmade disasters." The Great Leap had thrown things "off balance" and the communes had been set up "prematurely." In a line of argument that sounded like a repetition of P'eng Teh-huai's criticisms of over three years before, Liu said that it might take eight or ten years to make the necessary "readjustments." He saw the coming decade as a "transition period" during which "any method" to spur production would be "good enough," including the resurrection of the rural free market. In fact, strictures against private production and sale were greatly relaxed at this time.

At the same meeting, Liu also put forward the view that "opposition to Chairman Mao is only opposition to an individual; those sharing P'eng Teh-huai's viewpoint, so long as they are not guilty of treason, may be vindicated; it is not an offense for anybody to speak his mind at Party meetings." [19] Finally, he exhorted the intellectuals to "vent your spleen and air your views." [20] Whether the attribution is correct or apocryphal, literary criticism of Mao Tse-tung and his policies—particularly the Great Leap, communes, and the dismissal of P'eng Teh-huai—reached a crescendo during the spring of 1962.[21] Undoubtedly, worsening economic conditions prompted criticism, but Liu's effort to strengthen his political position was surely a factor.

Mao Tse-tung and the PLA

Mao's victory over the military establishment gave him an organizational context in which to act. It marked the beginning of his long-range program to build a strong position in the army, which was largely successful. Command of the military apparatus permitted Mao to enter into a protracted contest for control over party and state institutions, particularly at the sub-national levels. From 1954 through 1959 Mao had retained the chairmanship of the party, but had lost control of the military and state institutions in virtually their entirety, and of much of the party apparatus below the national level. The defeat of P'eng Teh-huai in 1959 marked the first step in Mao's drive to recapture control of these organizations. Before he could move against opponents—united more by common interest than by thought of a grand conspiracy against Mao's person—it was necessary first to consolidate a firm position in the military—a difficult and extensive undertaking.

Although he won the high command posts of the military establishment in 1959 with Lin Piao's appointment as Minister of Defense, there is some question of the extent of Mao's victory inside the Ministry itself. After P'eng's fall, three vice-ministers were dismissed and the total number of members increased from eight to ten, giving Mao and Lin the opportunity to appoint five men to the Ministry.[22] Despite the new appointments, it appears that a stalemate existed in the Ministry. If the captured documents contained in the *Bulletin of Activities* are representative of the organizational vehicle through which Lin Piao operated after 1959, he transmitted few orders as Defense Minister, instead issuing important policy directives from the office of the party Military Affairs Commission.[23] From Mao's point of view, given the strength of the organization built by P'eng over the previous five years, a stalemate in the Ministry of Defense was not an undersirable situation at this time. The Ministry of Defense had played a prominent role since 1954 in the military modernization effort. It would have been extremely difficult to force desired policy changes through this channel. For the political task of building a loyal pro-Maoist military force, Lin employed other channels, the party Military Affairs Commission and the General Political Department of the Ministry of Defense.

The Military Affairs Commission had acted primarily in a policy-making capacity before 1959; afterward under Lin Piao it broadened the scope of its functions to include the execution as well as the creation of policy. Most important, Mao and Lin held a clear majority in the committee, which they lacked in the Ministry of Defense. At least seven of the ten members of the Military Affairs Commission could be counted on to support their policy initiatives. Mao chaired the Military Affairs Commission; Lin Piao was its senior vice-chairman.[24] It was this command position that permitted the "Maoization" of the People's Liberation Army which followed.

Army Corps, Regional Forces, and Militia

The military was organized into three elements: main force units—the thirty-five army corps; regional forces—the independent divisions and regiments, border defense units, and garrison forces; and the militia. In each of these elements, Mao Tse-tung, through his Defense Minister, Lin Piao, carried out three basic policies: purge of undesirables, recruitment of new party members, and the intensive indoctrination of all in the "Thought of Mao Tse-tung." While the methods employed varied slightly in each case, the objective was the same: the establishment of a reliable "Maoist" party group within the military at every unit level, which would place overall control of the military apparatus in Mao's hands.

Dominance of the Military Affairs Commission gave Mao and Lin virtually automatic and immediate command over approximately one half of the army—the army corps, which were controlled directly by Peking. Even though placed in military regions, regional commanders exercised command over main force units only with central permission. They were concentrated in the northeast along the Sino-Soviet and Korean borders, the east coast adjacent to Taiwan, and the central south along the Vietnam border, and considerations of national defense primarily dictated their deployment. Authority to command, however, did not make command a reality. P'eng Teh-huai, during his tenure as Defense Minister, had built a thoroughly professional military establishment at the army corps level which would be transformed with difficulty. Lin Piao made no immediate effort to dislodge army commanders from their positions during the early stages of his program. Instead, he concentrated on building a loyal "Maoist" force among the rank and file, with heavy emphasis on indoctrination in the "Thought of Mao Tse-tung" (TMTT).

Under the cover of an intensive Mao-thought indoctrination campaign, Lin Piao conducted a purge of undesirable elements, focusing his efforts at the company level, the army's "basic unit."[25] The "four good" and "five good" companies campaigns were part of this program. Simultaneously, he initiated a drive to expand the party's organization in the army. Where P'eng had reduced the party's presence in army units to one man per unit, Lin expanded it to several-man party committees. Collective leadership was stressed. The role of the political commissar was restored and increased. A vast party recruitment campaign netted 229,000 new party members among the rank and file and the Communist Youth League conducted a parallel recruitment drive.

The command structure of the regional forces differed considerably from that of the army corps and required a different approach. The military regional commander controlled the forces in his region, except, as noted, the army corps. Therefore, at regional, district, and sub-district levels, it was the regional commander who directed the movements and activities of the independent regiments and divisions, border defense units, and garrison forces.[26] In his efforts to secure control over these forces, which constituted the other—less heavily armed—half of the People's Liberation Army, Lin again sought to secure command authority from above while developing loyalty from below.

His problem was complicated by the fact that the provincial party first secretary, in the majority of cases, held authority over the regional commander. Therefore, the problem for the Mao-Lin group was not simply one of ensuring command of the regional forces, but of gaining control of the provincial party apparatus as well. In addition to establishing the prerogatives of the central authorities to command divisions and regiments of regional forces directly, and conducting an extensive "Thought of Mao Tse-tung" indoctrination campaign among the rank and file, Mao and Lin initiated a major, long-term plan to gain control of the provincial party apparatus.[27] It was a plan, however, which had *not* succeeded by the time that Mao decided to launch the Great Proletarian Cultural Revolution.

Lin Piao's difficulties were compounded because the party opposition, presumably Liu Shao-ch'i and Teng Hsiao-p'ing, were taking steps of their own.[28] While Mao and Lin were attempting to strengthen their control over the regional military apparatus, Liu and Teng were busily securing party control over that apparatus. From 1961 onward party first secretaries were appointed concurrently as first political commissars to military posts at regional, district, and sub-district levels. Such appointments did not prevent Mao from gaining a strong position in the regional forces, but did hinder his employment of them. To a much lesser extent there occurred the appointment of district commanders to provincial party committees, but, in any case, such appointments did not include political authority.

Mao now maneuvered to gain control of the provincial party apparatus by packing the provincial committees, and he used the militia in this effort. During the Great Leap Mao had sought to create a militia which was independent of the military. After gaining control of the military in 1959, however, he reversed that policy, seeking to return the militia once again to its role as a reserve of the regular military establishment. Indeed, he attempted to employ the militia as a Trojan horse for political power. In a campaign to build up the militia, the district military (provincial level) commanders were to direct militia activities, sending "work teams" to assist in the establishment of liaison committees and militia departments in their respective party organizations.[29] Militia cadres were instructed to carry out their activities under the leadership of local party committees from provincial levels downward.

> All militia activities must be conducted under the united leadership of local Party committees, and the personnel must become excellent staff members for the local Party committees.[30]

Beginning in the early spring of 1961, when Liu began appointing provincial first party secretaries concurrently as first political commissars to military districts, Mao sought to establish, through the militia, a working link between the military and the party organizations at provincial and sub-provincial levels.[31] His next step was the creation of political departments in the party-based militia offices and the assignment of political cadres to militia units. As the largest single, although not well developed, organization in the countryside, the militia was established as a political department in the provincial party headquarters. This department was the wedge by which the regular military would enter into and play an increasingly important role in the provincial party apparatus. The main thrust of this trend would not occur until 1964; in the meantime both groups girded for the next clash, which came in the fall of 1962.

Struggle for the Provincial Apparatus, Phase I

Throughout the early spring and summer of 1962, top-level discussions were under way concerning national budget allocations. Senior economic officials viewed the economy as being in "a time of emergency" and the budget "several hundreds of millions of dollars in the red." Basic construction investments were slashed and some projects already under way were dismantled. In efforts to foster economic recovery in the countryside, Teng Tzu-hui, director of the party's rural work department, and others proposed dividing the land according to individual households and fixing state output quotas on that basis.[32] Although a practical policy in view of the extreme economic deterioration, it carried deep implications for the entire political system of the regime. If adopted, such a policy would result in not only the final repudiation of Mao's commune system, but also the formal acceptance of a capitalist system for peasant producers. It would mark the end of the "three red banners" of Mao Tse-tung.

At a central work conference in August Mao reacted, as he had the previous January, by raising the issue once more of a capitalist restoration. Positing the continuation of class struggle between proletariat and bourgeoisie, Mao refused to compromise the essentials of a socialist system as he conceived it and rebuked those willing to contemplate making the state directly dependent upon the individual producers, by implication eliminating the commune system. Ch'en Yün, Li Fu-ch'un, Li Hsien-nien, Po I-po, and Teng Tzu-hui came under personal criticism. One important decision of the conference was to dismiss Teng Tzu-hui as director of the party's rural work department.[33]

Mao moved onto the offensive at the Tenth Plenum of the Central Committee, held from September 24 through 27, 1962. The plenum approved Mao's policies in three general categories: internal politics, economics, and Sino-Soviet relations.[34] At the plenum, Mao continued to emphasize the class struggle between the supporters of capitalism and the supporters of socialism. The plenum communique noted that "this class struggle inevitably finds expression within the Party." [35] Perhaps as one manifestation of that struggle, several new appointments and dismissals were made. Huang K'o-ch'eng and T'an Cheng were dismissed from their posts in the Central Committee Secretariat and Lo

Jui-ch'ing, Lu Ting-yi, and K'ang Sheng were appointed to that body.[36] In a step possibly related to these personnel changes, Mao abolished formally the "two lines" established at the Eighth Party Congress in 1956 and resumed an active executive role in the policy-processes, a role which became evident in the Socialist Education Movement that followed.[37]

The plenum decided to launch a Socialist Education Movement in city and countryside, a decision related to the general objective of continuing the policy, first adopted at the Ninth Plenum in January 1961, of developing the economy with "agriculture as the foundation and industry the leading factor." The core of the program was the further consolidation of the people's communes, the strengthening of the party control commissions at all levels, and the "planned interchange" of important leading cadres of party and government organizations at various levels.[38] The genesis of the Socialist Education Movement was contained in article ten of the "Resolutions on the Further Strengthening of the Collective Economy of the People's Communes and Expanding Agricultural Production," which stated:

> In order to strengthen the leadership in agricultural work, the collective economy of the people's communes, and the basic-level party work in villages, the Central Committee and the party conmittees of provinces, cities, and autonomous regions must select cadres . . . to go out to districts, counties, and villages and participate in work for long periods of time. At all organizational levels of the communes, the cadres must be given training and assistance in raising their political level and their competence as workers.[39]

Throughout the fall and winter of 1962–1963, spot-testing of the new program was carried out in several provinces. In February, at a Central Work Conference, Mao urged the nationwide application of the Socialist Education Movement on the basis of the testing experience. Under his direction, in May, the Central Committee produced a draft resolution "On Some Problems in Current Rural Work," which became known as the "first ten points." [40] The resolution constituted Mao's first concerted attempt since the Great Leap to formulate and apply policy in the non-military sector and to carry the struggle to "those in authority who were taking the capitalist road."

Mao's objective was to capture the provincial and communal party apparatus. He sought to employ the Socialist Education Movement to shake up, then presumably reestablish, the rural leadership according to his own liking. The cadre structure in the countryside was essentially divided into two categories, higher and lower, each separate but obviously related. The higher cadre organization was the provincial apparatus, which consisted of provincial, district, and *hsien* organizations. The lower organization was the commune and consisted of the communes, production brigades, and production teams. In the "first ten points," Mao attempted to establish opening positions in both structures which would later permit him to affect the recomposition of the leadership. Literally applying the slogan "to grasp revolution from both ends," Mao employed the system of downward transfer, or *"hsia fang,"* from the top and established the "poor and lower-middle peasant committees" at the bottom.

Concerning the application of pressure from above, Mao stated:

> We hope to succeed within three years in having all the Party secretaries in the rural Party branches throughout the country devote themselves to participation in production labor. If we succeed in having one-third of all the secretaries in the Party branches join in the production labor during the first year, we will have scored a great victory.[41]

In the lower organization, the poor and lower-middle peasants, just as in the days of land reform during the early fifties, were "the only ones to rely upon." They were the "social foundation" on which to build up socialist enterprises in the rural areas. Therefore, poor and lower-middle peasant committees would be set up at levels of the "commune, the brigade, and the production team." Their function would be to assist and oversee the work of the commune and brigade administrative committees.[42]

In essence, Mao planned to transfer cadres from the provincial structure into the communal, from the higher to the lower level organizations. He urged that the great masses of cadres, "especially the cadres on the four levels of *hsien*, commune, brigade, and production team," join in productive labor "on a long-term basis."[43] Such movement of cadres, of course, would result in vacancies in the provincial apparatus, vacancies which Mao could fill with his own men. At the same time, establishing the poor and lower-middle peasant committees created a potential avenue through which Mao's supporters could rise to positions of authority in the lower, or communal organizations. The initial effect of the "first ten points," if implemented, would have been to loosen the party apparatus in the countryside, heretofore controlled by Mao's opponents.

Struggle for the Provincial Apparatus, Phase II

After observing the course of the "first ten points" for a few months, the party *apparatchiki* quickly reacted, attempting to preserve the integrity of the provincial structure, which was threatened by the "planned interchange of important leading cadres." In a Central Committee directive of September 1963, drafted under the supervision of Teng Hsiao-p'ing and termed the "later ten points," the party strove to deflect the thrust of the Socialist Education Movement away from the provincial apparatus and contain it in the communes.[44] Where Mao had sought to build positions in both provincial and communal structures, the "later ten points" sought to minimize the impact of the movement on the provincial apparatus and regulate it in the communes.[45]

The higher level cadres in the provincial, district, and *hsien* organizations were instructed to *lead* the movement by organizing and training "work teams," which they would then send into the lower level organizations—commune, production brigade, and team. The work teams were to serve as "staff" to the lower level cadres (Article II.4). At the same time, these leading cadres were to conduct a party "rectification campaign," or purge of dissident elements, to ensure strong leadership (Article VIII). The downward transfer of cadres would occur only in the communes, production brigades, and teams (Article I.10). Once in the lower level organizations, the work teams were also to carry out party reform (Article VIII), the effect of which was to neutralize, if not to disrupt, the activities of the poor and lower-middle class peasant committees.

Mao Tse-tung reacted to the problems in the higher and lower level organizations in turn. His response to the effective insulation of the provincial apparatus was to turn to the People's Liberation Army (PLA). In the general context of a nationwide campaign launched February 1, 1964 to emulate the People's Liberation Army, Mao attempted to establish an organizational framework which would give him political leverage inside the provincial party committees. The "learn from the PLA" campaign saw the creation of new political departments, modeled after the army's political departments, in industrial and commercial enterprises throughout China. Simultaneously, Mao set up an Industrial Communications Political Department and a Trade and Finance Department in the Central Committee of the Chinese Communist Party. Shortly thereafter the party's regional bureaus and provincial party committees were instructed to set up analogous departments inside their own organizations [!] to oversee those already functioning in their provinces.[46]

The "learn from the PLA" campaign represented an oblique maneuver to penetrate the provincial party apparatus. During the campaign Mao created the rudiments of a new political organization, with financial and communication links from the central committee down through the region and province to individual industrial and commercial enterprises. Moreover, the new organs were staffed primarily with army cadres, who were either previously demobilized or transferred while on active-duty status. Excluded from the provincial apparatus, Mao sought to gain access by creating new organizations based on the PLA. By mid-1964, therefore, the military input to the provincial party committees now included organizations staffed by regular army cadres as well as militia personnel.

At a Central Work Conference and Politburo Standing Committee Conference in June 1964, Mao pushed through the "Organizational Rules of Poor and Lower-Middle Peasant Associations," which constituted an attempt to expand the role and function of the poor and lower-middle peasant committees.[47] It was his response to his party opponents' attempt to hamstring these committees. Seeking an organization which would "respond actively to the call of the party and Chairman Mao," the "Rules" established the basis for a nationwide poor and lower-middle peasants' association. The association was to have organs at national, regional, provincial, hsien, municipal, and basic levels. At each level, peasant congresses would elect representatives. A national standing committee would give "unified leadership to the work of the peasant associations throughout the whole country" (Article V). The "Rules" also contained a provision for the establishment of poor and lower-middle peasant "work committees," which were a transparent attempt to counter the impact of the "work teams" established in the "later ten points" of the previous September. Mao further called upon the poor and lower-middle peasant organizations to engage in

> managing the commune as one of their own regular, important jobs . . . [and to] assist public security departments in strengthening the supervision and reformation of landlords, rich peasants, counterrevolutionaries and bad elements. (Articles XIII, XV)

The "learn from the PLA" campaign and the "rules" for poor and lower-middle peasants clearly increased the pressures for conflict in the countryside. The party *apparatchiki* waited only until September before issuing a counter document. This was the "revised later ten points," drafted under the supervision of Liu Shao-ch'i himself.[48] Liu strove to lodge control of the entire Socialist Education Movement firmly in the hands of the higher or provincial party committees. The instrument of control was the work team, which no longer would act merely as "staff" of the basic-level cadres as stated in the "later ten points," but would now thoroughly dominate all action. "The whole movement should be led by the work team" (Article II.3). In fact, it was stipulated that "to launch the Socialist Education Movement *at any point requires* the sending of a work team from the higher levels."[49]

Both Mao Tse-tung and his opponents had manipulated the rules of the movement and altered the functions of their respective organizations. Each had sought to counter the moves of the other in order to gain advantage. In the "revised later ten points," Liu had deftly out-maneuvered Mao. By means of the "work teams," as stated in the directive, "a new force should be built up during the movement." Indeed, that is precisely what was happening. The work teams were organs formed and trained by higher level or provincial party leaders, which meant that control over the Socialist Education Movement remained firmly in the hands of the *apparatchiki,* whose loyalty was to Liu Shao-ch'i and Teng Hsiao-p'ing. Their advantage, however, was short-lived.

At the Central Work Conference convened in December 1964 and continued through the first two weeks of January 1965, Mao Tse-tung managed to reformulate to his advantage the prescriptions for the Socialist Education Movement as they had evolved up to that time. In what must have been a stormy series of meetings, Mao criticized Liu's administration of the Socialist Education Movement, clearly defining the nature of the movement now as embodying nothing less than the contradictions between socialism and capitalism.[50] Lifting a corner of the veil obscuring Mao's true intentions, article II of the Twenty-Three Articles, the document produced by the conference, stated that the Socialist Education Movement was really a vast class struggle against "those people in positions of authority within the Party who take the capitalist road." The struggle would be carried on against all who opposed socialism wherever they might be, "even in the work of provincial and Central Committee Departments"! [51]

The Twenty-Three Articles eliminated the distinction between higher and lower level organizations; the issue was nothing less than the purging and remolding of the party apparatus at all levels. Article XVI, for example, noted that in "speaking of a single *hsien*, both during and after the Four Cleans Movement the work of training a party leadership nucleus must be gradually done." Then in language harsh even by Cultural Revolution standards, the question of power was raised:

> . . . where leadership authority has been taken over by alien class elements or by degenerate elements who have shed their skin and changed their nature—authority must be seized, first by struggle and then by removing these elements from their positions. In general, the question of their membership in the Party should be resolved later. In cases which are especially serious, these elements can be fired from their posts on the spot, their Party membership cards taken away, and they may even, if need be, be forcibly detained. Counter-revolutionaries, landlords, rich peasants and bad elements who have wormed their way into the Party must all be expelled from the Party.[52]

Terminological distinctions between city and countryside were also abolished. The Twenty-Three Articles explicitly instructed that the Socialist Education Movement, which had been termed the "Five Anti Movement" in the cities, would henceforth be termed the "Four Cleans Movement" in both city and countryside.[53]

Article XI dealt with the question of time, and revealed the time period which Mao Tse-tung believed to be available to him in carrying out his plans. It was stipulated that "three years will be needed to complete the movement throughout one-third of our country. Within six or seven years, the movement will be completed throughout the whole country." However, Mao would not have the luxury of six or seven years, or even three years, for that matter, to rid himself of his opponents. Already events were developing on the political horizon outside of China which would force Mao, once again, to accelerate abruptly the pace of action. To appreciate the nature of the political factors impinging upon Mao at this juncture, it is necessary to discuss the question of the fall of Khrushchev.

The Fall of Khrushchev and Vietnam

The most widely accepted explanation of Khrushchev's fall is that it was caused by his failures in domestic policy and by differences with colleagues over questions of party power. Khrushchev did suffer several serious policy reversals in both agriculture and industry. His virgin lands program failed dismally and his increased emphasis on chemical and plastic industries at the expense of heavy industry had not met with anticipated results. He had also divided the Communist party into industrial and agricultural hierarchies and this, too, had not worked well. In the months before his ouster, moreover, there were indications that he was preparing new "heresies" in the industrial and agricultural organizations.[54]

These factors, whether taken separately or together, do not account for the peculiarity of Khrushchev's ouster. It was a sudden move, done secretly and in his absence. Moreover, few substantive changes were made in Khrushchev's policies immediately after his dismissal except that the party was structurally reunified. According to party statutes adopted in 1961 (and since revised), Khrushchev could not have sat in the Presidium for more than three terms (twelve years) unless reelected for a fourth term by a three-fourths majority of the Central Committee voting by secret ballot.[55] He assumed the position of First Secretary in September 1953; this meant that he could have been ousted by a dissident minority in September 1965, when the time came to vote his fourth term. Instead, Khrushchev was removed one year beforehand, which suggests that something happened that precluded a wait of a year and required immediate action.

That something, it seems, was an unexpected development in the Vietnam War and the need of a major policy change toward the Chinese People's Republic. Since the Great Leap of 1958, the implications of which the Soviets recognized for Sino-Soviet relations, Khrushchev had sought to bring about a leadership change in China. He evidently felt that the Soviet Union could apply sufficient pressure to effect either the removal of Mao Tse-tung himself or changes in the leadership which would result in a return to cooperation with the Soviet Union. His plan included carefully conceived moves at state, ideological, and party levels, and was to culminate at a conference of the world's Communist parties in December 1964.

On the state to state level, Khrushchev attempted to isolate the Chinese. The two most obvious events in this connection were the Taiwan Straits crisis of 1958 and the Sino-Indian border war of 1962. In each case Khrushchev declined to support the Chinese, instead adopting what in effect was an anti-Chinese position. The ideological wheels, as previously noted,[56] had been set in motion in 1962 when Soviet scholars began to debate the long-buried concept of the "Asiatic Mode of Production." Finally, on the party to party level, Khrushchev assiduously built support among the world's Communist parties and implicitly threatened the Chinese with exclusion from the world movement. He may have felt that the threat of exclusion would prompt the pro-Soviet group inside the Chinese Communist Party to act against Mao. (They, in fact, did so but were unsuccessful, as will be shown below.)

The world conference of Communist parties was scheduled to open in December 1964 but developments in Vietnam upset Khrushchev's timetable. It appears that Tonkin Gulf became his Waterloo, setting in motion a sequence of events that culminated in his ouster. In essence, Khrushchev's China policy interfered with his attempts to aid Hanoi and, in the face of a mounting international crisis requiring the unity of the Communist world, it led his colleagues to force him from power.

The "Tonkin Gulf incident" occurred on August 2 and 4, 1964, at a time when the Viet Cong were on the verge of victory in South Vietnam. In less than a week a massive deployment of American military power began. On August 6, Secretary of Defense McNamara reported that reinforcements of various kinds were moving into the area.[57] Two days later the United States Congress overwhelmingly passed a resolution authorizing President Johnson to employ "all necessary measures . . . to prevent further aggression." [58] Khrushchev, too, reacted quickly to the incident. On August 5, the Soviet representative to the United Nations presented a resolution inviting North Vietnam to send an emissary to discuss the issue.[59] On the 7th, Hanoi appealed to the signatories of the

1954 Geneva Agreements on Indochina to check "U.S. preparations to invade its territory." [60] And on the following day, the Soviet Union assured Hanoi of full support, demanding that the United States "immediately stop military actions against the Democratic Republic of Vietnam." [61] Khrushchev apparently hoped that debate on the Tonkin Gulf incident at the United Nations would freeze the deployment of American power long enough to permit the Viet Cong to win. But Hanoi itself rejected the plan to send a representative to the United Nations, maintaining, instead, that only the 1954 Geneva Conference signatories could deal with the question.[62]

It was at this point that Khrushchev's China policy began to get in the way. When Hanoi rejected the United Nations filibuster plan, Khrushchev's only alternative was to neutralize the American deployment with Soviet aid to North Vietnam. In order to do so, however, he needed land access across China. There was no question of attempting to aid Hanoi exclusively by sea. The recent Soviet adventure in Cuba had precipitated a dramatic confrontation with the United States and Soviet leaders were unquestionably reluctant to place themselves in a similarly exposed position again. A safe transportation route across China was necessary to provide effective assistance to Hanoi. But Khrushchev's refusal to alter his policy toward China, or, perhaps, the Chinese price for land access, or both, persuaded his colleagues to depose him rather than risk an open break with China at a time when unity was necessary. Thus Khrushchev fell from power sometime between October 12 and 14, 1964.

For five weeks after Khrushchev's fall, an uneasy truce prevailed in Sino-Soviet relations. Chou En-lai led a Chinese delegation to Moscow for the October Revolution celebrations to assess the impact on Soviet policy of Khrushchev's removal. The new Soviet leaders, Leonid Brezhnev and Aleksei Kosygin, evidently proposed to let the dust of the American elections settle until it became clear what the United States would do. In addition, they suspended their side of the polemics and postponed the December conference of the world's Communist parties.[63] Evidently unwilling to wait and see, the Chinese resumed criticism of Soviet policy, after a brief silence, with an editorial in *Red Flag* on November 21 entitled "Why Khrushchev Fell" labeling Soviet policy as "Khrushchevism without Khrushchev."

The Soviets, however, did not reply in kind. Desperately needing

274

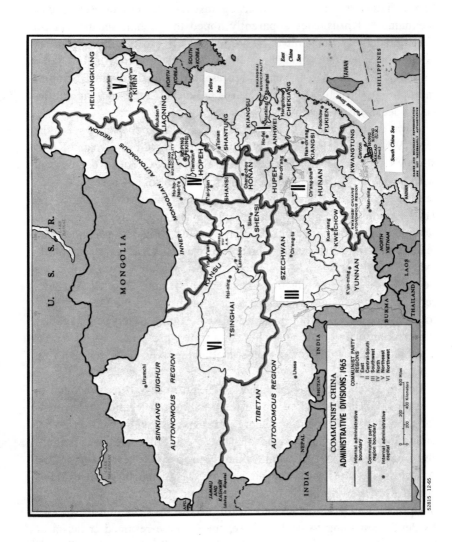

COMMUNIST CHINA,
ADMINISTRATIVE DIVISIONS, 1965

COMMUNIST PARTY
REGIONS
I East
II Central-South
III Southwest
IV North
V Northeast
VI Northwest

Internal administrative
boundary

Communist party
region boundary

Internal administrative
capital

0   200   400 Miles
0   200 400 Kilometers

52815 12-65

transit rights across Chinese soil, they responded with a call for "united action," a demand which was the central point of Kosygin's visits to Peking in early February 1965 en route to Hanoi and Pyongyang. Kosygin's plea was made all the more urgent by the fact that on the very day he arrived in Hanoi, the United States began the bombing of North Vietnam. The new leadership appeared willing to subordinate its quarrels with the Chinese in order to arrive at an agreement on defense of Vietnam. In a televised speech reporting his trip, Kosygin stressed "socialist internationalism" and the duty of all socialist states to unite in the face of the imperialist challenge, and he minimized the differences between socialist states as natural and stemming from historical factors.[64]

By the end of March the issue of transit rights had been settled. The Chinese granted the Soviet Union minimum transit requirements and by early April Soviet equipment was rolling across Chinese territory.[65] The month of April, however, saw the stakes in Vietnam raised higher by both the Soviet Union and the United States. On the 3rd of April the Soviet Union delivered the first of two notes requesting additional rights on Chinese soil (reportedly, in addition to permission to send 4,000 Soviet personnel across China to Vietnam, the Russians called for a meeting with the Chinese and Vietnamese).[66] On April 7 the President of the United States made a statement of policy. In a speech at Johns Hopkins University, President Lyndon B. Johnson stated that the United States "must be prepared for a long continued conflict" in Vietnam.[67] That month the United States augmented its forces in Vietnam by 15,000 men. On the 17th the Soviet Union delivered a second note to the Chinese, this time requesting (as far as can be determined) the use of two airfields in southwest China, the right to station 500 men there, an air corridor and air passage rights.[68]

Kosygin's trip to Peking, the American escalation of the conflict, and insistent Soviet demands for closer cooperation created intense political pressures in Peking, which in turn precipitated a lengthy and heated foreign policy "debate" within the Chinese leadership.[69] The issue, clearly crystallized by the events of the previous month, was: should China intervene in Vietnam and, if so, on what basis? The Soviet notes implied that transit rights were no longer adequate. Would China consent to act as a base area, perhaps even become directly involved? The ensuing debate over whether or not to intervene in Vietnam revealed the extent to which the polarization process of the previous years had rent the Chinese leadership, particularly over the crucial issue of Sino-Soviet relations. For the pro-Soviet group within the Chinese leadership, however, the crisis over Vietnam presented an unparalleled opportunity to advance arguments for reconciliation, which, if achieved, would greatly strengthen their own positions *vis-à-vis* the Mao group, and perhaps lead to their permanent ascendancy.

Of the several leaders involved in the debate, the principals were the Chief of Staff, Lo Jui-ch'ing, who put forth the pro-Soviet position, and the Minister of Defense, Lin Piao, who presented the Maoist position. On May 7, the anniversary of the victory over Germany in World War II, Lo Jui-ch'ing gave a speech in which he argued in favor of reconciliation with the Soviet Union as the most effective means to assist a fraternal ally, the Democratic Republic of Vietnam.[70] Lo envisaged the likelihood of a Sino-American conflict as a consequence of Chinese involvement in Vietnam. To prepare for this, he argued, China needed to adopt a strategy of "active defense," which required a modern, professional military force-in-being. This in turn implied the need for a closer relationship with the Soviet Union, since it would only be by such means that China could obtain the necessary supplies in a short time.

The Maoist position was stated most forcefully by Lin Piao in a speech given on the anniversary of the surrender of Japan, September 2, 1965.[71] In it, Lin took the Maoist line of independent action. He stated that China would assist revolutionaries everywhere to the extent that she could, but they must provide their own solutions by employing Mao Tse-tung's principles of "people's war." Rejecting direct intervention, Lin argued that there was little probability of a Sino-American conflict. In effect, Lin opted for "passive defense." If China were attacked, he said, the response would be a people's war. Under such circumstances, there was no need for a rapprochement with the Soviet Union.

The upshot of the debate, which reached its climax in early September, was that China rejected the proposed intervention in Vietnam. Mao Tse-tung and his supporters declined involvement in any direct sense, particularly with Chinese combat forces.[72] However, in the course of the debate, the nature of the problem facing the Chinese had altered significantly. When the discussions over China's role began in the spring of 1965, the United States had just over 30,000 troops in Vietnam, but U.S. forces were restricted to constabulary duties. On June 27 American forces began combat operations for the first time and by the end of November troop strength in Vietnam had surpassed 184,000; American forces had taken the offensive! Mao Tse-tung thus faced still another crisis. He had won a battle with his internal opponents, but he had not won a war. Inevitably, the issue of "united action" would arise again in the course of further increases (clearly implied by the rapid American buildup during 1965), particularly if the war turned against the Communists. In this eventuality, the probability was that Mao and his supporters would be unable to stem the voices urging direct intervention in Vietnam and closer cooperation with the Soviet Union. The implications for his own dominance should this course of events occur were ominous. It was this threat to his own political position which led him to initiate what we have come to know as the Great Proletarian Cultural Revolution.

XI
The Great Proletarian Cultural Revolution
I: The Mounting Crisis, 1965–1967

Beginning in the fall of 1965 and continuing for over three and one-half years, Mao Tse-tung convulsed China in revolutionary paroxysm. Partly because of the means he chose, but primarily because he could not fully anticipate the reaction to his policies, Mao's assault on "those in authority taking the capitalist road" shook the Chinese polity and threatened his own preeminence. The course of events was marked by sudden changes in policy and intermediate objectives and forced increasing reliance upon military participation, which brought success of one kind only to create problems of quite another order. Although Mao achieved his primary goal of removing his opponents from positions of power at the center, control over the provincial party apparatus eluded his grasp. The Great Proletarian Cultural Revolution was in essence the struggle over the manner in which political reconstruction of the provinces would proceed and which groups would rule.

The Decision to Initiate the "Cultural" Revolution

Sometime in the early fall of 1965, Mao Tse-tung decided that the threat to him implicit in the Soviet Union's call for unity over Vietnam precluded the continuation of his plan for gradual recapture of power in the provinces. To preserve his own position, it would be necessary first to remove those in the central committee who favored a policy of unity. His method would be an extension of the one he had employed previously—the creation of *ad hoc* extra-legal organs to penetrate the established structure. Initially, Mao needed to capture the central media and military command posts. These would permit him to control and shape the flow of information and enable him to use without obstruction the centrally commanded army corps, if necessary. As Lin

Piao bluntly put it at a Politburo meeting the following May, when he spoke of Mao's actions as necessary to prevent a *coup d'état:*

> . . . seizure of political power depends upon gun barrels and inkwells. . . . We . . . must take concrete measures of action in order to prevent it from coming into being. . . . Otherwise, once the opportune time comes, a counterrevolutionary coup d'état will occur; once we have a natural calamity, or once a war breaks out, or Chairman Mao dies, this political crisis will come,
>
> When the civilian and the military are coordinated, public opinion and gun barrels are in their hands, then a counterrevolutionary coup d'état can occur at any time. If a general election is needed, people can be called to cast ballots. If armed uprising is needed, the armed forces can immediately be dispatched. Whether it is a parliamentary coup d'état or a military coup d'état, they can accomplish it.[1]

Mao's immediate targets would be Lo Jui-ch'ing, who "controlled military power," P'eng Chen, who "controlled the General Secretariat," Lu Ting-yi, "commander in chief of the cultural and ideological war front," and Yang Shang-k'un, head of "confidential affairs, intelligence, and liaison."[2] All four would fall before the major opponents, Liu Shao-ch'i and Teng Hsiao-p'ing, would be ousted during the fall of 1966.

Moving against unsuspecting opposition, Mao initiated his plan at a Central Work Conference and Politburo Standing Committee session which met during September and October. At the conference Mao called for criticism of Wu Han, vice-mayor of Peking and author of several works implicitly critical of Mao's policies. Toward this end, a five-man "cultural revolution group" was appointed to study the class struggle on the cultural and ideological fronts and report its findings to the Politburo Standing Committee. P'eng Chen, mayor of Peking and first secretary of the Peking party apparatus, under whose wing writers critical of Mao, including Wu Han, had been protected, was named head of the group. This assignment constituted the first step of Mao's plan to entrap P'eng Chen. After the conference, Mao withdrew from public view to Shanghai, where he planned the next phase of the campaign. Remaining in seclusion, Mao ostensibly was preparing an "article" for publication.[3]

In early November, Mao Tse-tung moved again, this time on both international and domestic fronts. On November 11, the article "Refutation of the New Leaders of the CPSU on United Action" appeared in

People's Daily and *Red Flag*, indicating that the issue of cooperation with the Soviet Union over Vietnam had been decided and clearing the way for Mao to concentrate on his domestic opposition. At the same time, on November 10 in Shanghai's *Wen Hui Pao*, Mao opened an attack on the "cultural" front, which was triggered by Yao Wen-yuan's critical article, "On the New Historical Drama, the Dismissal of Hai Jui." Yao's article generated an outburst of criticism against major writers, playwrights, and later even high party officials, like Chou Yang, who were in charge of literary affairs. It constituted a challenge to those who publicly but indirectly opposed the "Thought of Mao Tse-tung."

Perhaps the most critical step taken during the preliminary stage of the Great Proletarian Cultural Revolution was Mao's removal of Lo Jui-ch'ing, chief of staff of the PLA and vice-chairman of the Military Affairs Committee.[4] At a Central Committee "conference," convened by Mao in Shanghai on December 8, Lo was subjected to severe criticism. Chou En-lai himself reportedly examined him "many times" in an effort to "help" and to "reeducate" him. A work group was set up to investigate Lo's errors, which were further exposed at a "conference on political work in the army and among the ranking cadres of the Party and the Army." Apparently arrested in early March, Lo was held "under the direct supervision of the Central Committee" from March 4 through April 8, 1966, during which time "face to face" struggle was conducted against him. Throughout, Lo Jui-ch'ing remained "extremely hostile to the thought of Mao Tse-tung." On one occasion, March 18, he sought to commit suicide by jumping from an upper story of the building in which he was being held. He injured himself in the attempt, but survived.

While Mao Tse-tung was marshalling his forces in Shanghai, his opponents were active in Peking, now thoroughly aware that the level of the struggle had been raised to the Central Committee. Perceiving an opportunity to outmaneuver Mao in his absence from Peking, Liu Shao-ch'i convened a Politburo Standing Committee meeting in early February to consider the P'eng Chen Committee's report. Termed the "February Outline Report," it was approved on February 8 and disseminated on the 12th. P'eng, who evidently drafted the report without consulting K'ang Sheng, Mao's man and a member of the five-man cultural revolution group, sought to "channel the political struggle in the cultural sphere into so-called pure academic discussion." [5] In an obvious slam at Mao Tse-tung, the "report" noted:

. . . we must not behave like scholar-tyrants who are always acting arbitrarily and trying to overwhelm people with their power . . . we should guard against any tendency for academic workers of the Left to take the road of bourgeois experts and scholar-tyrants.[6]

On March 28, Mao Tse-tung sharply criticized the "outline report," clearly stung by its contents. "It was wrong to draft this outline," he said. Reacting to the criticism contained in the report, Mao said, "those who detain and suppress the manuscripts of the leftists and shield the anti-communist intellectuals are 'big academic overlords,' and the Propaganda Department of the Central Committee is the demon king's palace. We must knock down the demon king and get rid of the demons!"[7] Mao, in replying to the "outline report," broadened the scope of his attack to include Lu Ting-yi, who was director of the Propaganda Department, as well as Minister of Culture. It would take less than two months to depose Lu Ting-yi, once P'eng Chen was out of the way. The same would be true of Yang Shang-k'un, the fourth of Mao's initial targets, liaison and recording secretary for the Central Committee Secretariat.

In the meantime, on March 26, Liu Shao-ch'i had departed for a state visit to Pakistan and Afghanistan, remaining out of the country until April 19. His absence gave Mao the opportunity to take formal action against P'eng Chen. At a meeting of the Central Committee Secretariat on April 9–12, attended by Chou En-lai and K'ang Sheng but not Mao Tse-tung, K'ang "systematically criticized and repudiated a series of grave mistakes made by P'eng Chen."[8] Despite P'eng's attempts to defend himself by maintaining that he had no intention of opposing Chairman Mao, the secretariat's members decided to draft a notice for the purpose of repudiating the "outline report" and to set up a new cultural revolution drafting group for the approval of Mao and the Politburo Standing Committee.

A few days later, on April 18, the PLA became publicly involved in the struggle at the top for the first time. The editorial in *Liberation Army Daily* flatly charged that the corrosive literature of the "anti-Party black line" in the literary world would inevitably have a deleterious effect on the military. The following day Liu Shao-ch'i returned to Peking, setting the stage for a major confrontation between the Mao and Liu groups, which occurred from May 4 through 18.

Mao Tse-tung Takes the Offensive

Mao Tse-tung summoned the party's leaders for an enlarged Politburo Standing Committee Conference in Hangchow, outside of Shanghai, which opened on May 4. To ensure against unwanted disruption, he "dispatched personnel and had them stationed in the radio broadcasting stations, the armed forces and the public security systems." [9] During the succeeding two weeks, the Liu and Mao groups battled over two issues: P'eng Chen's "February Outline Report" and the "errors" of Lo Jui-ch'ing. On the 16th of May, the Mao group emerged victorious from this conference, obtaining approval of four important measures. First, the "February Outline Report" was repudiated on the ground that it obscured the "sharp class struggle" taking place, violated the "basic Marxist thesis" that all class struggles are political struggles, and turned the political struggle into an "academic discussion." Secondly, "P'eng Chen alone, usurping the name of the Central Committee," was blamed for the outline's contents. The four other members of the group, particularly K'ang Sheng, were absolved of all culpability. Thirdly, the conference decided to dissolve the group of five and set up a new group, "directly under the Standing Committee of the Politburo, in charge of the cultural revolution." Finally, both P'eng Chen and Lo Jui-ch'ing were removed from posts of responsibility.[10]

Mao Tse-tung's triumph in the May confrontation laid the basis for the next step to be taken against his opponents inside the central committee as well as carrying the "cultural revolution" to the country as a whole. Creation of the Cultural Revolution Group directly under the Politburo Standing Committee gave Mao the instrument he could use to shape a political apparatus independent of the party, which would then be directed to attack the party at every level of operation. Headed by Mao's wife, Chiang Ch'ing, and including K'ang Sheng, Ch'en Po-ta, Yao Wen-yuan, and Chang Ch'un-ch'iao, the new "group of five" in charge of the cultural revolution would function as the mobilizing and directing agent for cultural revolution groups throughout the country later in the year. The dismissal of Lo Jui-ch'ing allowed Mao and Lin Piao the unhindered use of the army corps and P'eng Chen's removal opened the way for the capture of the Peking apparatus, which came in early June, and with it control of the national media organs.

Both groups prepared for the clearly imminent showdown. Stationing troops at key points in and leading to Peking, Maoist forces took control of the city. On June 1, a *People's Daily* editorial entitled "Sweep Out All Monsters and Ghosts" hinted that a major change had occurred in the city; three days later it was confirmed with the announcement of the reorganization of the Peking municipal committee, headed by new first secretary Li Hsueh-feng. Liu Shao-ch'i and his supporters immediately responded to Mao's act. Convening a Central Work Conference, Liu attempted to gain control of the forces Mao was unleashing by sending out party work teams to provinces to channel the ferment into non-destructive areas. Both Mao and Liu were repeating to a great extent the methods each had employed during the Socialist Education Movement earlier. Mao urged the creation of "mass organizations" in the schools, which he hoped to use against the party; Liu sent the party's "work teams" to protect the party apparatus.

The purge of the Peking organization included the purge of the top officials of Peking University. Coupled with the announcement on June 2 that admission to higher schools would be suspended for six months, it signaled activists in the provinces to emulate the pattern observed in Peking through the press. Soon officials in charge of the schools and newspapers in virtually every province began to topple. But results in the provinces were mixed. Nothing like the wholesale purges in Peking occurred, which may be attributed primarily to the appearance of the party's work teams, sent out by provincial party headquarters. The work teams limited the scope of the movement, making scapegoats in the cultural field in order to protect the ultimate target, the provincial party leaders themselves.

Although Mao immediately cautioned against the excessive use of the work teams,[11] it took him over a month and a half before he could place a check on their activities. His opportunity came at a Central Work Conference which convened from July 20 and continued through the end of the month. At the meeting of July 22, which included the party's regional secretaries as well as members of the Central Cultural Revolution Group, Mao made the following remarks:

> The most important thing is to change our method of dispatching work groups so that the revolutionary teachers and students of the schools and those taking a neutral position may form cultural revolution groups to lead

the great cultural revolution. Only they understand the schools' affairs. The work groups do not. Some work groups have created disturbances.

Since the work groups have played an obstructive role in the movement, can we carry out the task of struggle and transformation? . . . In school affairs . . . it is necessary to rely on the internal forces within the schools. It won't do to rely on the work groups, nor on me, nor on you, nor on the provincial committees. To carry out struggle and transformation, it is necessary to rely on the units of the schools themselves, but not the work groups.

Can the work groups be changed to function as liaison personnel? They will be given too much power if they are converted into advisers. One alternative is to call them observers. Some work groups are obstructive to the revolution but some are not. Those work groups which obstruct the revolution will inevitably become counterrevolutionary.[12]

Six days later, on the 28th, Mao issued, through the Peking Municipal Committee, the Central Committee's decision to abolish the work groups, which were "no longer capable of meeting the . . . revolutionary demands" of arousing the masses to topple those in authority taking the capitalist road in universities, colleges, and schools. As soon as the work groups were abolished, schools were instructed to form a "temporary or preparatory committee to make preparations for the election of the cultural revolution committee of the whole school." [13] Once the cultural revolution committee was established it would have the authority to conduct the cultural revolution in its own institution and elsewhere, if necessary.

Mao was now prepared to confront his opponents. He had succeeded in creating what in effect was a personal apparatus, based on his "thought" and independent of the party, in all of the higher schools in the country. Still inchoate, the nucleus nevertheless had been created. At the same time, he had stripped power from the work groups, the instruments of his opponents. Presumably, the final task of attacking and capturing the provincial party and state apparatuses would occur with minimal opposition. Therefore, the Central Work Conference, which decreed the abolition of the work groups, determined to convene the Eleventh Plenum of the Chinese Communist Party. The plenum, which opened on August 1 and continued through the 12th, represented the culmination of Mao Tse-tung's drive to oust his opponents in the Central Committee and laid the ground rules for the campaign to take command of the provincial power structure.

Ultimately, a party congress (the Ninth) and a National People's Congress (the Fourth) would have to be convened to give formal sanction to the acts of the Maoist group against Liu Shao-ch'i and others. Such congresses would, in turn, require assembling delegates from the provinces. Since Liu's strength lay principally in the party, state and, to some extent, the military apparatuses in the provinces, no decision made at the top could be permanent unless the basis of Liu's strength were removed. Therefore, the extension of the struggle to the provinces was necessary for Mao Tse-tung to make his solution stick in the center. At this stage of the struggle, Mao's intention was to gain control of the provincial power structure, not to destroy it. The shift to the policy of destroying the provincial apparatus would occur only in January 1967, when it became apparent that Mao could not oust Liu's supporters from the apparatus.

The Great "Proletarian" Cultural Revolution— Initial Strategy

The means Mao Tse-tung employed in the cultural revolution were the classic ones of divide and rule combined with piecemeal assault on isolated positions. He applied this principle and tactic at every level of the party, state, and military apparatuses in a relatively bloodless fashion, considering the magnitude of the endeavor, but not without violence. At the Eleventh Plenum, Mao and his opponents hammered out the procedural guidelines for the ensuing round of battle, adopting on August 8 the "Decision of the CCP Central Committee Concerning the Great Proletarian Cultural Revolution." [14] The resolution, comprising sixteen points, starkly reflected the organizational methods which had characterized the struggle to date; Mao relied on *ad hoc* mass organizations, while Liu acted through the party's apparatus.

A narrow victory for Mao in the Central Committee, the Eleventh Plenum signaled the extension of the struggle to the entire country and to all levels of the power structure. If the struggle during the "socialist education campaign" had been restricted to the commune structure in the countryside and schools, the sixteen-point decision shifted it to the "big and medium cities," where the "key points" of attack were to be "cultural and educational units and *Party and government leadership organs*" (point XIII). [15] Indeed, as stated in point V, "the focus of this movement is on the purge of those powerholders within the Party who take the capitalist road."

The resolution reflected the narrowness of Mao's victory in a curious way, by the inclusion of contradictory instructions, which represented the strengths of both the Mao and Liu groups. In this composite resolution, however, Mao's position clearly dominated. Employing the technique once again of *ad hoc* mass organizations, Mao gained acceptance for the creation of "cultural revolutionary groups . . . committees and . . . congresses" as *permanent* mass organizations, the "power organs of the proletarian cultural revolution" (point IX). Once established, these "forces should be concentrated on attacking a handful of extremely reactionary bourgeois rightists and counterrevolutionary revisionists. Their . . . crimes must be fully exposed and criticized, and they must be isolated to the maximum extent" (point V).

Exposure and criticism of the handful was precisely what Liu Shao-ch'i and his supporters were determined to minimize, if not prevent, and the resolution reflected their intentions. Point VI noted that "the minority must be protected because sometimes truth is in the hands of the minority." Point XI stipulated that "criticism by name in the press must first be discussed by the Party committees at the corresponding levels, and in some cases approved by the higher Party committees." Finally, in point XIII, the right of the "party committee" was asserted concerning the issue of integrating the "cultural revolution" with the Socialist Education Movement.

Despite efforts of the Liu group to lodge control of the cultural revolution in the hands of the "party committees," as they had during the socialist education campaign, Mao Tse-tung succeeded in isolating the leaders of the state and party apparatuses "to the maximum extent." Point XIV forbade the provincial party leaders from employing either the military or economic forces under their control in the cultural revolution. Point XIV also contained Mao's "guarantee that the cultural revolution and production will not impede each other," provided that the masses were "fully" mobilized and "satisfactory arrangements" were made. "It is wrong," continued the resolution, "to set the great cultural revolution against the development of production." Most important, point XV prohibited the use of military force. The "cultural revolutionary movement and the socialist education movement in the armed forces" would be conducted by Mao's organs, the Military Affairs Commission and the PLA's General Political Department.

The effect of these stipulations was to restrict, at least on paper, the kinds of responses beleaguered provincial party leaders could make to Mao's initiative. Although the "broad masses of workers, peasants, and soldiers, revolutionary intellectuals and revolutionary cadres constitute the main force. . . . Large numbers of revolutionary youngsters . . . have become brave vanguards . . . firmly launching an attack against those open and covert bourgeois representatives" (point II). In other words, the workers, peasants, and soldiers in the provinces, whom the provincial party leaders could mobilize in their defense, were to remain outside the sphere of direct and widespread involvement. Their role was differentiated from that of the "brave vanguards," who, consisting almost totally of students acting under Mao's direction, would attack the presumably supine provincial party leaders. The legitimation of their actions was contained in point XVI. The "guide of action" would be the "thought of Mao Tse-tung," which was to be "regarded as a compass to the cultural revolution." Finally, the party committee themselves, "at various levels must abide by the successive directives of Chairman Mao."

The sixteen-point resolution of the Eleventh Plenum laid the ground rules for the assault on the provincial power structure, but only dimly and implicitly reflected the political infighting and strategic maneuver of which it was the product. In a major political change, the plenum's assembled leaders voted to enlarge the Politburo Standing Committee from seven to eleven members. Added were T'ao Chu, Ch'en Po-ta, Li Fu-ch'un, and K'ang Sheng. Within the enlarged standing committee, Liu Shao-ch'i was demoted from position number two to position number eight and T'ao Chu promoted to position number four. In a related move, Sung Jen-ch'iung, boss of the party's Northeast Regional Bureau was promoted to alternate status on the Politburo. These decisions alone constituted a substantial victory for Mao, who now commanded a clear majority in the enlarged standing committee. The promotions of T'ao Chu and Sung Jen-ch'iung were a *mariage de convenance* by which Mao divided his opponents.[16]

The principal danger in Mao's plan to attack the entire provincial power structure was the possibility, if not the likelihood, of broad-based armed defiance of the party center in Peking. There was no certainty that regional and provincial leaders would willingly suffer removal from entrenched positions of power. Mao had to take precautions to prevent the formation of regional opposition, which would most likely coalesce around the strong regional party secretaries, all of whom commanded significant military forces. For example, although the first secretary of each of the six regional bureaus had no formal provincial party post, he was first political commissar of one of the military regions under the jurisdiction of his bureau.[17] At a minimum, the regional bureau itself included the first and second secretaries from each of the provincial party committees in its region. The first secretary of the provincial party apparatus also was political commissar to the corresponding military district. Therefore, each regional bureau leader, in addition to having direct control of military forces at the regional level, could exercise control at the district level, too, through the provincial secretaries subordinate to him in his bureau.

It was imperative that Mao Tse-tung disestablish the regional apparatus before proceeding with the attack on the provincial power structure. The difficulty was that before the Eleventh Plenum Mao controlled only one, the North China Bureau, of the six regional party bureaus. This he had secured in June when he captured Peking. The East China Bureau, being without a chief, Mao disregarded for the time being, but the remaining four bureaus (Northwest, Northeast, Southwest, and Central South) represented immediate threats. Mao's achievement at the Eleventh Plenum was to divide the four regional bureaus by "allying" (temporarily) with two of the regional secretaries, T'ao Chu and Sung Jen-ch'iung.[18]

Mao's "alliance" with the Northeast and Central South bureau leaders, if it can be termed that, was an important strategic victory, for it precluded the possibility of the development of "northern" opposition based on the Northeast regional bureau as well as a "southern" opposition based on the Central South regional bureau. Moreover, by controlling Manchuria, north China, and the Central South area, which consisted of the Wuhan and Canton military regions and the provinces of Honan, Hupeh, Hunan, Kwangsi, and Kwangtung, it left possible only one opposing regional combination—Southwest and Northwest.[19] (See map of China's military regions and party regional bureaus.) Because of this preoccupation with preventing the development of regional opposition, the considerable difficulties which quickly developed in the Southwest, Northwest, and East China areas never became insurmountable problems. In fact, because of the early immobilization of *all* the regional bureaus as functioning organs, no significant regional, as opposed to provincial, opposition to Mao Tse-tung ever evolved during the cultural revolution. With no significant exceptions the principal problems which occurred during the cultural revolution were all restricted to *provincial* dimensions, although at times provincial crises threatened to spill over and become regional ones.

In the long run, of course, by virtue of the vital importance of the Northeast and Central South regions, Mao could not afford to bank on a "permanent alliance" with the first secretaries there. He would be forced to take command of these areas himself, or at least split them up, to prevent any one leader from controlling an entire region. Perhaps it was for this reason that Mao gave roles at the center to both Huang Yung-sheng of the Central South and Ch'en Hsi-lien of the Northeast regional bureaus. They would act as counterweights to both T'ao Chu and Sung Jen-ch'iung. For the moment, however, the situation at the top was well in hand. It would now be possible to begin the assault on the provincial power structure, without undue fear of immediate regionalization.

The Red Guards, Mao's Student Left

University and higher school students had been involved in the Cultural Revolution since early May 1966.[20] Initally, they held struggle meetings to criticize Wu Han and other literary figures. Their criticism was all long-range, affecting none of them personally. After the May 16 circular criticizing P'eng Chen, students were encouraged to criticize local authorities. Their teachers became targets. In early June the dismissal of P'eng Chen and sharp newspaper attacks on other high party officials in Peking signaled students to emulate these acts in their own localities. The presence of the party's work teams, however, muted the ferocity of student criticism and diverted the main thrust away from local party officials. Despite this, by the end of July, "cultural revolution groups" had been organized by the activist groupings which had emerged in virtually every higher school more or less spontaneously from the struggle-criticism activities of the previous months.

The Eleventh Plenum's sixteen-point resolution exhorted the "brave vanguards" to further criticism of party leaders, but provided no specific

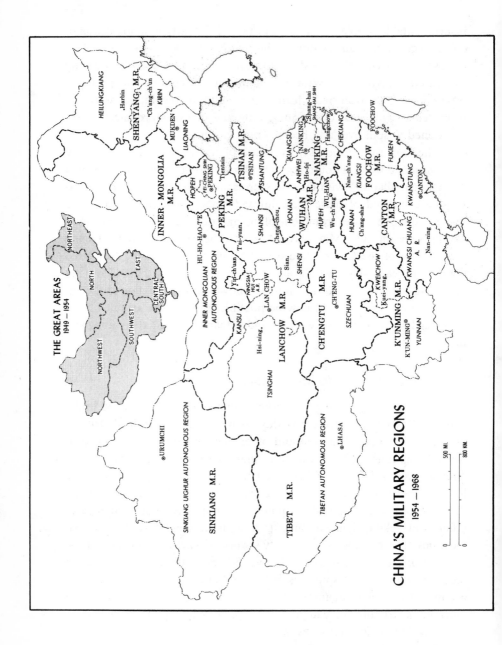

THE GREAT AREAS
1949 – 1954

NORTHEAST

NORTH

EAST

CENTRAL
SOUTH

SOUTHWEST

NORTHWEST

HEILUNGKIANG

Harbin

SHENYANG M.R.

Ch'ang-ch'un

KIRIN

MUKDEN

LIAONING

INNER - MONGOLIA
M.R.

HU-HO-HAO-T'E

HOPEH

PEI-CHING SHIH

PEKING

Tientsin

PEKING
M.R.

T'ai-yuan

SHANSI

Cheng-chou

SHANTUNG

TSINAN

TSINAN M.R.

HONAN

KIANGSU

NANKING

ANHWEI

Ho-fei

NANKING
M.R.

SHANG-HAI SHIH

Shang-hai

Hangchow

CHEKIANG

FOOCHOW

FOOCHOW
M.R.

FUKIEN

Nan-ch'ang

KIANGSI

CANTON

KWANGTUNG

CANTON
M.R.

WUHAN
M.R.

HUPEH

Wu-ch'ang

WUHAN

HUNAN

Ch'ang-sha'

KWEICHOW

Kuei-yang,

KWANGSI CHUANG
A. R.

Nan-ning

Sian,

SHENSI

INNER MONGOLIAN
AUTONOMOUS REGION

Yin-ch'uan

NINGSIA
HUI
A.R.

LAN CHOW

LANCHOW
M.R.

KANSU

Hsi-ning,

TSINGHAI

CH'ENGTU
M.R.

CH'ENG-TU

SZECHUAN

K'UNMING M.R.

K'UN-MING

YUNNAN

URUMCHI

SINKIANG UIGHUR AUTONOMOUS REGION

SINKIANG M.R.

TIBET M.R.

TIBETAN AUTONOMOUS REGION

LHASA

CHINA'S MILITARY REGIONS
1954 – 1968

500 MI.

800 KM.

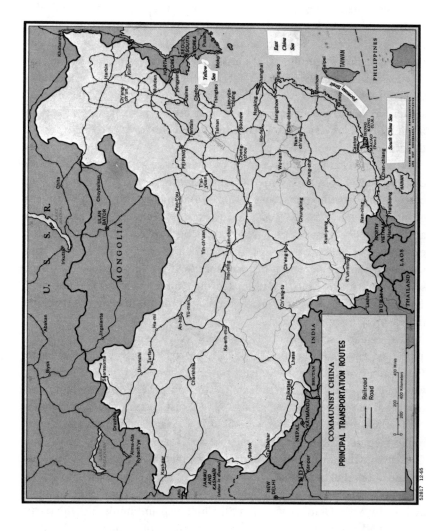

COMMUNIST CHINA
PRINCIPAL TRANSPORTATION ROUTES

Railroad
Road

0   200   400 Miles
0   200   400 Kilometers

NAMES AND BOUNDARY REPRESENTATION
ARE NOT NECESSARILY AUTHORITATIVE

52817 12-65

guidelines as to how this should be done. Many groups formed, but
membership and organization of any particular group remained ill-
defined and fluid. The method of organizing the students remained a
problem until August 18, when Mao Tse-tung, at a mass student rally
and review before T'ien An Men in Peking, accepted the armband of a
student group which called themselves "Red Guards." This symbolic act
expressly indicated approval of the name, method, and actions of this
particular student group. The message was clear. All should become
"Red Guards." Mao's symbolic act, combined with specific instructions
that only the most revolutionary students (the "five kinds of red"
students)[21] could participate, gave greater organizational cohesion, even
though the "five red students" comprised only about 10 percent or less of
the student body of any given school.

From August 23 until the end of October these student groups moved
out of the schools and into the cities smashing the "four olds" (old
customs, habits, thoughts, and culture) and merged with other student
groups. Street by street, "Red Guard" groups of students systematically
and repeatedly terrorized all who could be labeled one of the "black
elements," or backward classes. By early September, as the groups from
various schools coalesced, it became specifically acknowledged that their
sole authority was Mao Tse-tung and their direction was his "thought."
The party's officials at provincial, municipal, and university levels came
increasingly under suspicion.

The "great exchange of experiences" was one of the "five great
activities" in which the students participated.[22] It involved traveling to
Peking and other cities. The transportation system, both rail and bus,
was made available to the students for this purpose, as were lodging and
meals, at no expense. Beginning on August 18 and lasting through
November, nine mass rallies were held in Peking, involving some eleven
million student Red Guards who came from all over China to see
Chairman Mao and the new second in command, Lin Piao. On the way
to and from Peking, as well as in their home areas, these groups of
students participated in attacking the "four olds." The result of their
actions by early October was that all China was in tumult. Yet the party
leaders had managed to "deflect the spearhead" of student attacks from
themselves by cooperating in no small measure with them and in many
instances organizing student groups of their own as a protective measure.
Thus, by the time that Mao convened a Central Work Conference on

October 8, 1966, most provincial party leaders had suffered considerable fright, but had lost little actual power.

At the Conference, attended by the secretaries of the party's regional bureaus, provincial, district, and *hsien* committees, Mao threatened his listeners, stating plainly that the previous two months of the cultural revolution had not yet produced the results that he had hoped for. He noted that "at the last meeting [Eleventh Plenum] I did not have any confidence at all. I said that my instructions might not necessarily be carried out, and, as I had expected, many comrades still failed to understand them adequately." [23] Continuing, Mao said:

> If, upon your return, you still do things according to the old rules and regulations, maintain the status quo, oppose one group of Red Guards and let another group of Red Guards protect you, I think things will not change and the situation will not take a turn for the better. Naturally, we cannot ask too much. Not all the broad masses of cadres of the Central Committee's bureaux, provincial Party Committees, district Party committees and hsien Party committees will see the light. There are always some people who fail to arrive at a right perception of things, and a few will take the antagonistic stand. But I believe that the majority can be won over. [24]

In closing, Mao noted that "the time is too short, and we are not mentally prepared for the new problems." Whether the "new problems" Mao referred to were those he faced because of the intransigence of the party secretaries or those he was about to create for them is not clear from the text. In any case, the cultural revolution moved into a new stage after the October Central Work Conference, the last such assemblage of party secretaries to be held.

After the conference, Mao altered both the scope and depth of the Red Guard assault, hoping to place sufficient pressure upon the party secretaries to topple those who would not shift to Mao's side. On November 3, Lin Piao in a speech reported in *People's Daily* declared that "all the masses" should "criticize the Party and government at all levels." Later in the month, the workers and peasants, whom the party sought to isolate from the struggle earlier, were now specifically enjoined to enter the fray. At the same time the "five red" criterion for Red Guard membership was dropped, increasing student participation. This meant the rapid expansion of the student assault organizations, which heretofore had been relatively small. The "revolutionary groups" were now augmented greatly in size and were more diverse in composition. The month of December saw the formation of cultural revolution groups and other mass organizations in factory, commune, and commercial enterprises, as well as the amalgamation of various student groups. Mao and his supporters in Peking were clearly building a large shock force of the masses which they hoped would simply overwhelm the "power holders" in the party apparatus.

Despite the fact that the month of December revealed the arrest of P'eng Chen (December 4) and the publication through wall posters of the "confessions" of Liu Shao-ch'i and Teng-Hsiao-p'ing (December 25), party officials in the provincial apparatuses showed no inclination to surrender to the frantic and sometimes hysterical groups which stormed their headquarters. In fact, by the end of the year, most party officials had surreptitiously matched the buildup of "Maoist" forces among the masses with those of their own. Peking referred to this development as "using the Red Guards to attack the Red Guards" and "waving the Red Flag to oppose the Red Flag," but there was little Mao and his men could do about it. For the most part, the formation of groups to counter "Mao's forces" was spontaneous. It was dangerous to remain isolated, a fact which ordinary citizens soon discovered. Spontaneously, "self-protection" groups arose to dot the countryside. Many of these were sponsored by local party officials as a self-defense measure. By this time virtually everyone realized that, as one student in Kwangtung put it, "we were involved in a real power struggle between Mao Tse-tung and Liu Shao-ch'i. . . . We knew in a general way that we would probably be mobilized for even more intense activities in the future. We were prepared to await the new signals from Peking. . . ." [25] The "more intense activities" were not long in coming, the first signals appearing at the turn of the year.

The Attempt to "Seize Power"

By the end of the year the rampaging Red Guards and Revolutionary Rebels presented a confusing spectacle in China's large and medium-sized cities. Although Mao had succeeded in building an attack force of students, workers, and peasants, the party's provincial leaders had responded with similar methods to build self-protection units of their own. Pitting Red Guard group against Red Guard group, their tactic was to broaden the scope of the conflict and to muddle things by involving greater and greater numbers of workers and peasants in the struggle. In addition to encouraging those who had been "sent down" previously to return to the cities, the provincial party leaders enticed workers and peasants to leave their posts in factories and communes to go to the cities. This tended to clog the rail and bus lines, making it difficult for the Maoists to use them. The net effect of the injection of thousands of workers, peasants, and students into what was already a chaotic situation was incredible disorder. Although the Maoists were nowhere defeated by such tactics, they were not victorious. The result was a stand-off in the cities.

A level of conflict and chaos was acceptable, even desirable—if Mao and his supporters could control and channel it in the intended direction. Toward this end, concerted efforts were made to limit the numbers entering the cities and to point the Maoist revolutionaries toward the party offices and prevent them from diffusing their energies in what were from Mao's viewpoint unproductive activities. To forestall workers' and peasants' inundation of the cities, Peking issued on December 15 a directive which urged the rural masses to participate in the cultural revolution, but "in their localities and under the single leadership of the cultural revolution committees of communes and brigades in their localities." [26] Similarly, the students were enjoined to desist from "exchanging experiences" and ordered to return to their own schools. On December 31 Peking issued still another circular instructing the PLA to provide short-term (two to three weeks') military and political training for revolutionary teachers and students of universities and middle schools.[27] The school itself would be the physical site for the PLA's activities and the principal type of instruction would be "formation training," which would enable the Maoist groups to coordinate rapid movement in groups. Indoctrination in the major documents of the cultural revolution would accompany the physical training.

Shanghai, a key "demonstrator" city in Mao's plans, was particularly chaotic, prompting him to act there first. On the 4th of January, Maoist revolutionary rebel forces led by Chang Ch'un-ch'iao, a member of the Central Committee Cultural Revolution Group, took over the party and newspaper offices in the city. Four days later, a mass rally was held in Peking whose major purpose was to announce publicly the overthrow of China's Khrushchev, Liu Shao-ch'i, and his chief collaborators. The surprise addition to the list of those overthrown was T'ao Chu, who only four months before had been promoted to the number four position on the Politburo Standing Committee! His fall coincided with a strong Maoist move in Canton to oust the members of T'ao's apparatus there. That the events in Shanghai and Peking were interconnected quickly became clear. On the next day, January 9, *People's Daily* exhorted Mao's legions to emulate the example shown in Peking by "seizing power" in the provinces and routing out all of the henchmen of China's Khrushchev, and on the 11th, the Shanghai power seizure was held up to the nation as a "brilliant example" of "correct policy." [28] The next few days saw the Mao group in Peking simultaneously urging the masses on while funneling them against the party offices in the provinces.

Of course, the provincial party leaders sought to turn the mass movement to their own advantage, which Mao strove to prevent. On January 11, the same day that Shanghai was publicly held up to be the example for genuine revolutionaries all over China to follow, Peking issued three "notices" condemning the tactics of the opposition. Decrying what they called "economism," the Maoists excoriated the small handful of "capitalist roaders," who were "corroding" the masses with material benefits, using "money to win over the revolutionary masses." Unless we concentrate on strengthening "our own revolutionary fighting will," the notification stated, it will be easy for the small handful to "utilize" the masses for their own ends.[29]

> At present, a handful of Party persons in authority taking the capitalist road, for the sake of undermining the great proletarian cultural revolution and *shifting the target of struggle,* have instigated the workers, peasants and organ cadres, who have been hoodwinked into supporting them for the time being, to leave their production or work posts and come to Peking or make their way into big cities. These capitalist roaders have even fomented strikes and instigated the *masses who do not understand the actual situation* to flock to the banks and withdraw their deposits by force. All revolutionary comrades must . . . firmly oppose this way of doing things.[30]

> By various means of economic bribery, they try to lead some of the masses onto the evil road of economism. . . . They incite some of the masses to demand promotion and wage increases and to freely demand [from] the state . . . money and material supplies.[31]

It was immediately obvious that merely issuing notices would be insufficient, so Mao increased the level of force and degree of involvement of the public security forces and PLA, a decision which created a minor crisis in Peking. The chaos made it increasingly difficult to distinguish a genuine from a sham revolutionary. It became apparent that not all groups which assaulted and ousted party officials were pro-Maoist. The attacks on radio stations were a case in point. It being vital to ensure control over the mass media, Mao instructed the local military forces to take over all broadcasting stations, regardless of who controlled them. The revolutionary masses were encouraged to attack the stations, thereby deposing incumbent party officials, but they were then ordered to "pull out at once," giving place to the local PLA, which would operate them. The army, in turn, would rebroadcast only those programs originating in Peking, which enabled Mao to transmit directives to the masses while at the same time precluding the radio stations from being used to mobilize opposition to him and his supporters.[32]

Since the command to "seize power" had been issued on January 9, the level of violence had risen alarmingly. Concerned that the movement was beginning to spread out of control and therefore to his disadvantage, Mao instructed the public security forces to become more directly involved by moving to protect the revolutionary left and damp down the level of violence. A *Chung Fa* (central issue) of the 13th declared that the public security forces must protect "the revolutionary masses and their organizations."

> Armed struggle is strictly banned. It is unlawful to attack the revolutionary mass organizations or to assault or detain the revolutionary masses. . . . Offenders . . . who have committed serious offenses and those manipulating things from behind the scenes . . . must be punished according to law.[33]

The revolutionary masses were also called upon to "assist and supervise" the public security organs themselves to ensure that they should carry out their functions and "uphold revolutionary order." Implicit in the *Chung Fa* was the recognition that respect for Mao's "thought" had evaporated and had to be enforced. It was deemed to be an "active counterrevolutionary deed" punishable under the law to write or shout reactionary slogans or to vilify Chairman Mao and his close comrade in arms, Lin Piao.

Crisis in Peking over Greater PLA Involvement

Mao recognized that the public security forces were inadequate to perform the task of channeling the masses toward the desired targets. In fact, despite official decrees, the majority of the public security personnel of the larger cities moved to support the conservative groups against the revolutionaries.[34] Therefore, on the 14th, in a move which had been under discussion for several days, Mao ordered increased participation by the PLA in the struggle. The question of greater involvement by the PLA created a minor crisis at the top in Peking. Apparently, many high-ranking military leaders had gone along with Mao's scheme on the understanding that the military would not become directly involved, but balked when he sought to raise the level of PLA participation in early January. The January crisis over the role of the military in the cultural revolution was the first of five such crises (the other four occurring in April and August 1967, March 1968, and the spring of 1971).

Each crisis, except the last, was resolved in favor of an increased role for the military and each decision resulted in a reshuffle of the military leadership in Peking. In January the issue was over the use of the military to guard key points in Mao's effort to restrict the scope of the movement and direct it squarely against the party offices. The head of the PLA Cultural Revolutionary Group, Liu Chih-chien, who was appointed the previous May, 1966, opposed this decidedly more open role for the military, but was overruled. In consequence, he was dismissed and replaced by Hsü Hsiang-ch'ien. The group itself was enlarged at this time and Chiang Ch'ing, Mao's wife, named to it as advisor.[35] The reorganization was made public in wall posters in Peking on January 12 as the PLA's organ, the *Liberation Army Daily*, attacked the "power holders inside the army taking the capitalist road." Wall posters at this time also carried attacks on Ho Lung and other high-ranking military leaders, who had been opposed to the decision.

The upshot of this first crisis was a compromise. Mao obtained greater participation for the PLA in guarding key points, but in return he would attempt to keep the military out of direct conflict with the masses.[36] The January 14 "notification," issued down to the *hsien* and regimental levels, stated that the local PLA would henceforth assume the responsibility "for guarding the local radio stations, prisons, warehouses, roads and bridges"; the masses were not allowed "to encircle, attack, and occupy and sabotage these places." [37] In fact, "hereafter, no person or organization may attack the organs of the People's Liberation Army," which not only was charged with making preparations for war and national defense, but also was assigned the new task of "defending the great proletarian cultural revolution." Events were now moving so quickly, however, that active defense of the cultural revolution became necessary in less than a week after the promulgation of the "notification."

That significant groups within the military leadership were reluctant to accede to direct PLA involvement is apparent from the high turnover in their ranks during the cultural revolution. The reasons are also clear. The possibilities for clashes with the aroused masses were limitless, as was the prospect for potentially widespread civil conflict between army units. As long as military dissidence did not reach the point of open defiance and challenge to the legitimacy of the party center, isolated cases of dissidence among the military leadership were an acceptable risk for Mao Tse-tung to take. For Mao, the alternative was the loss of political power. Therefore he pushed the military into greater and greater involvement in the cultural revolution. Where the directive of the 14th left open the date when the army would assume responsibility for guarding certain places, a directive of the 19th called for immediate action. It declared:

> It has now been discovered that there are bad people inciting the pillage of warehouses. The Central Committee hereby decided that *troops must be dispatched at once to exercise military control* over all important granaries and warehouses, prisons, and other important units which must be protected. . . . [38]

As Mao edged the army toward total involvement in his plans, the need for its participation became more urgent. The call for power seizures by the Maoist revolutionaries had caused tremendous confusion in the provinces. Throughout China, but particularly in the area of the East China Bureau, which Mao had discounted earlier, the Maoists had had little success in storming the provincial party apparatus. Not only had incumbent leaders held on through one subterfuge or another, but the burgeoning strife threatened to develop into a regional problem as distinct from separate provincial conflicts. Anhwei, Chekiang, Kiangsi, and Fukien constituted a solid block of linked provinces. Excluding the province of Shantung, the entire East China regional bureau was spiraling out of control. It became necessary to "solve" the problem of incipient regionalism there, particularly because these provinces included a total of seven army corps (roughly 275,000 men) and 165,000 troops in the regional forces. The emergence of organized regional opposition there would constitute a direct threat to the survival of Mao Tse-tung and had to be dealt with swiftly.

In response to the East China situation, which Mao may have felt was only a forerunner of things to be expected in the near future, he pushed the reluctant military leaders into full involvement in the cultural revolution. It may be surmised that Mao himself moved far more precipitately than he should have at the time, a conclusion which derives support from the zigzag course of events during the last week in January. On January 21, Mao instructed the PLA of Anhwei province to "support the broad masses of the left," [39] which it was hoped would forestall the disintegration of the Maoist position in East China. Fearing the worst, two days later the order was applied to all of China and to the entire PLA, both regional and army corps forces. The directive of January 23 stated flatly the future policy which would govern the army's role in the cultural revolution:

> From now on, the demands of all true revolutionaries for support and assistance from the army should be satisfied. The so-called "non-involvement" is false, for the army was already involved long ago. The question therefore, is not one of involvement or non-involvement. It is one of whose side we should stand on. . . . The PLA should actively support the revolutionary Leftists.[40]

Transmitted to every soldier in the PLA, the directive instructed army commanders to "send out troops" when "genuine proletarian Leftists ask the army for help." By the same token, "counterrevolutionary organizations . . . must be resolutely suppressed." If the army met with resistance in carrying out its duties, it was instructed to "strike back with force." The army was not to side with the handful of party power holders "who persist in the bourgeois reactionary line" and not be "an air raid shelter" for the opposition.

There was great difficulty with the directive. It did not specify precisely how army commanders could identify "genuine proletarian Leftists" from among the many revolutionary groups making that claim. Actually, the directive could not have been more specific than it was. Mao's first objective at this point was to commit the military to his side, the "revolutionary left." Once committed, the manner of their involvement could be specified later with greater precision. Still, the way in which commanders responded to the directive must have created a quandary for Mao Tse-tung. Given the firm but general order to support groups which they could not easily identify, many commanders tended to respond to the demands of the party political commissars, from whom they had taken orders all their professional lives.[41] Indeed, party officials demanded their support. At best, some commanders declared support for the "left," but actually did nothing. At worst, commanders responded to the demands of their party superiors, the provincial party secretaries, and stepped in to support them or their surrogates. In most cases, the effect of the "support the left" order was to frustrate the takeover of the provincial party apparatus by the Maoists.

Within days, Mao perceived danger in the general order for PLA intervention and strove to restrict PLA involvement, for the most part, to regional forces and to reserve use of the army corps for a later date. In certain troublesome areas, the armed forces were instructed to postpone the cultural revolution altogether, while in others the top levels of the army command were to carry out a cultural revolution, but troops were to be left undisturbed. This latter action was aimed directly at the Southwest and Northwest bureaus, which Mao split by decree. Two orders issued on January 28 contained these instructions. The first declared that:

> . . . the great cultural revolution movement in the military regions on the first line of defense against imperialism and revisionism (Tsinan, Nanking, Foochow, Canton, Kunming and Sinkiang) and the Wuhan Military Region . . . *should be postponed for the time being. . . .*[42]

In terms of the party's regional bureau system, the order included all of Central South (the Wuhan and Canton military regions) and East China (Tsinan, Nanking, Foochow) bureaus and parts of the Southwest (Kunming) and Northwest (Sinkiang) bureaus, effectively splitting the latter two. It pointedly demonstrated Mao's continued concern with the development of regional opposition and his determination to prevent it. The order also left Mao free to deploy troops in the North China and Northeast China bureau commands, which were not restricted.

The second order of the 28th sought to immobilize certain military commands *outside* the "postponed" area, while leaving their troops untouched by the effects of the cultural revolution. The order stipulated that *at the command level* "in armed forces units where the great cultural revolution has been launched, there should be big contending, big blooming, big character posters, big debates. . . . Earnestly promote civil struggle, [but] resolutely oppose struggle by brute force." The situation below the command level was quite different. Those units were to engage only in "positive education," not the "big contending" and so forth. The order declared:

> Armies, divisions, regiments, battalions, companies, and special units designated by the Military Commission must resolutely adopt the policy of positive education, so as to facilitate the strengthening of war preparedness, take care of national defense, and protect the great proletarian cultural revolution.[43]

It is not known which "special units" were "designated" by the Military Commission, presumably those in the North and Northeast areas, but the effect of the two orders was to place severe restrictions on the use of the army in the Southwest and Northwest regional bureau areas, shaking up their command organizations. Mao had postponed the cultural revolution at both command and troop levels in the military units of certain areas, essentially the Central South and East China regional bureaus. This permitted the regional and district commanders in those areas to act in defense of the cultural revolution. Most important, Mao kept the army corps from direct involvement. At this stage only the regional forces would be employed; the army corps would constitute Mao's trump card, to be used when all else failed.

Mao Alters the Theoretical Basis of the Cultural Revolution

The introduction of the PLA in late January indicated that Mao's "revolutionary rebels" had failed in the task of seizing power.

Greater military involvement, however, required a redefinition of the form and content of political power. Initially, Mao had hoped to gain control of the provincial power structure without extensive and overt military assistance. The provincial party was to have been elected by the masses employing the method of "extensive democracy," thus eliminating party bosses. Accordingly, Mao had elaborated a theoretical basis for the new order which contained no rationale for inclusion of the military. This was the concept of the "Paris Commune," which had been introduced as early as March 1966 in the party's theoretical journal, *Red Flag,* and discussed in the press through the summer. The Eleventh Plenum gave formal sanction to the concept in point number IX of the sixteen-point resolution, which noted that members of the various cultural revolutionary groups were to be "fully elected as in the Paris Commune." As late as New Year's Day 1967, *Red Flag* contained the call for the establishment of people's communes after the Paris example, indicating that it was indeed the political model which Mao hoped to use to justify his "democratic" takeover of the provincial party apparatus.

Mao's principal reason for employing the concept of the Paris Commune was that it provided an historical precedent for a successful revolution by armed masses without a party and without an army. The failure of the "masses" and the introduction of the army on a vast scale rendered the Paris Commune concept inappropriate. It had to be changed, because of the danger that Mao's opponents would attempt to use the concept against him by justifying the exclusion of the army! In searching for a new conceptual model, Mao reverted to the CCP's own revolutionary history dating back to Kiangsi days and resurrected the old concept of the revolutionary military committee, whose preparatory organ would be the military control commission.

As in early January, Shanghai and Peking were again used as "model cities." Shanghai was employed to indicate that the Commune concept would be phased out and from Peking came the signals for three new concepts, the three-in-one alliance, the revolutionary committee, and the military control committee. On February 4 the Shanghai Commune had been established, but in less than two weeks, as the full implications of military participation became clear, it had been discredited by Mao Tse-tung himself. On the 13th, a wall poster carried Mao's comment that he thought it undesirable for China to become "an association of People's Communes." [44] Also, in a widely publicized speech delivered to

Shanghai rebel leaders at this time, Chang Ch'un-ch'iao bluntly declared the necessity for a party organization and the end of the People's Commune concept.

> With the commune inaugurated, do we still need the Party? I think we need it because we must have a hard core, whether it is called the Communist Party or a social democratic party . . . In short, we still need a party.
> . . . . . .
> Let the Shanghai People's Commune be changed to Shanghai Municipal Revolutionary Committee! [45]

On the 24th of February, the Shanghai Commune was transformed into the Shanghai Revolutionary Committee, setting a prominent example for the rest of the country that the Commune concept was out. In Peking, meanwhile, events were occurring which indicated the way the revolutionary committee was to be achieved.

In Peking on February 10 and 11 two events took place which clearly signaled the new policy. On the 10th in *People's Daily* an article appeared proclaiming a successful power seizure in Heilungchiang and the establishment of the first provincial revolutionary committee. The event reportedly occurred on January 31. The method employed was the combination of "three sides into one" and was described in the following manner:

> The revolutionary rebels, acting in accordance with concrete conditions in the struggle here and carrying out the party policy in a clear-cut way, have united with the principal leading members in the Provincial Party Committee who have carried out Chairman Mao's correct line and the provincial leading members of the People's Liberation Army united in the area to weld the three sides into one in the seizure of power. [46]

The "three way alliance," as it soon came to be called, was the basis of the new policy of revolutionary committees. Where the Commune offered no place for party and military representation, the three-way alliance specifically included both of them. But how was the new policy to be enacted? Who would determine which representatives of the many rebel groups and party cadres would participate in the alliance?

The answer to this question came the very next day when Peking issued a proclamation announcing that the Peking garrison of the PLA had taken over the city's Public Security Bureau and "set up the Military Control Committee . . . to enforce military control." The tasks of the committee were:

> to consolidate the dictatorship of the proletariat, firmly suppress all counter-revolutionaries, preserve revolutionary order, firmly support and protect the proletarian revolutionaries, and defend the great proletarian cultural revolution.[47]

In other words, the military through military control committees would determine the composition of political power in the provinces. The fact that it was the Peking garrison forces which took over Peking further indicated that local military forces would form the military control committees, not the PLA's army corps.

The postulation of the three-in-one combination meant a reduced role for the revolutionary rebels, who were now required to settle their differences and form "great alliances." Once united, an almost insuperable task in itself, representatives would be drawn from the alliances for inclusion in the new political structure, the revolutionary committees, which were composed of three elements: military, old cadres, and revolutionary rebels. In succeeding months, the military attempted to knock together the various contending rebel groups while Peking negotiated with representatives from the provinces to form the revolutionary committees. The shift from the Paris Commune concept to the revolutionary committee provoked another crisis in the party leadership which became known as the "February Adverse Current."

The issue was: what respective political weights were to be assigned to the revolutionary rebels and to the old line cadres in the revolutionary committees? The failure of the rebels to oust the party bureaucrats and increased reliance upon the military caused great concern among a segment of the Mao group which sought a counterweight to the military in the old line cadres. Led by T'an Chen-lin, but including eight other high ranking leaders,[48] this group argued for greater weight to cadre representation in the revolutionary committees to balance that of the military. T'an may even have sought the exclusion of the rebels altogether from the new political structure on the ground that they had failed and could not form an adequate counterweight to the military. Mao refused to increase the political weight of the cadres for that would be nothing less than a restoration of the "bourgeois-reactionary line" of Liu and Teng.[49] It would amount to the restoration of power to the party bureaucracy, against which Mao had been fighting all along. Determined to prevent this at all costs, Mao proposed instead a ratio of one military, one cadre, and one rebel to govern the composition of the revolutionary committees. This solution apparently satisfied all but T'an, who continued to object and was purged.

While succeeding in preventing a restoration of the status of the old cadres, Mao used the February incident in an attempt to place a check upon local military commanders, perhaps as a way of assuaging those in the leadership who were concerned about military dominance. After the incident occurred (February 17, 1967),[50] wall posters in Peking noted that T'an Chen-lin had suppressed rebel groups in the agricultural and forestry departments under his jurisdiction. Rebel groups in the provinces immediately began to whip up propaganda campaigns against "local T'an Chen-lin's," who were suppressing them, that is, the local military commanders. In Canton, for example the rebels termed their campaign the "March black wind," to refer to the February Adverse Current's expression in their province.[51] The net effect of the campaigns was initially to inhibit some military commanders in their harsh treatment of rebel groups, but soon to provoke others into over-reacting with force.

The Mounting Crisis, February–March 1967

The seize power order of January 9, which triggered conflicts between "radical" and "conservative" rebel organizations for control over the provincial party apparatus, soon spilled over to include assaults on broadcasting stations, newspaper offices, public security departments, warehouses, and local military units. In early January, recall, the PLA was ordered to maintain the security of these installations. Later when the PLA was called upon to enter the fray, "support for the left" came into conflict with the maintenance of security. The more radical rebel groups tended to be the ones which occupied the installations that the army had been instructed to guard. The ensuing struggles gave the impression that the army had sided with the "conservative" rebels against the "radicals." But this was misleading.

Actually, most local military commanders attempted to carry out orders to pull together the "grand alliances" of diverse rebel groupings, even while coming into conflict with the more radical of them in the course of maintaining control over key installations. The military commanders naturally tended to favor those rebel groups they could most easily manipulate, in some cases creating rebel groups of their own to facilitate the establishment of grand alliances. It would be erroneous to assume that a given commander's support for a "conservative" rebel group automatically placed him in opposition to Mao Tse-tung in Peking. The overwhelming majority of military commanders attempted to carry out their orders without becoming unduly involved in the political struggle. That commanders suppressed many "Maoist" rebel groups is obvious enough, but to conclude from this that the military as a group was therefore opposed to Mao is not only faulty reasoning but misses the main point of the policy decision of January 21, 1967.

The function of the revolutionary rebels changed dramatically the instant it was decided to call in the PLA to play an active part in the cultural revolution, but the altered role for the rebels was not immediately obvious from the initial order. It was not until February 10 and 11, when the "three-in-one" and "military control committee" concepts were announced, that the new rebel role became clearer. Nor did the new role for the rebels signify that conflict between radical and conservative rebel groups would become less severe. On the contrary, the struggle became even more intense as rebel groups competed with each other to dominate the grand alliances and fought even more tenaciously against the commanders who sought to forge alliances from antagonistic rebel elements.

This mounting conflict accounts for the fact that until the beginning of the final week in February, apart from the "showpiece" revolutionary committee established in Heilungchiang on January 31, only Kweichow could boast the establishment of a provincial revolutionary committee (February 14). Fourteen other provinces had announced "power seizures," [52] which Peking claimed were "false" and refused to recognize, and in half a dozen others the situation was critical and struggle rife.[53] Even as Shantung and Shanghai announced the establishment of revolutionary committees on February 23 and 24 respectively, the situation elsewhere had acutely deteriorated. In every province rebel groups were in conflict with one another and with local military forces. For the most part there was no widespread armed conflict at this time, but in a few places armed struggle did erupt as a result of the local military commander's zeal in forcing grand alliances onto opposed rebel groups, setting the stage for another policy crisis in Peking.

As it happened the worst cases occurred in provinces of the three regional bureaus over which Mao had had little direct control: East, Southwest, and Northwest China, and in Honan and Hupeh, the provinces of the strategically crucial Wuhan military region of the Central South Bureau.[54] In the area of the East China Bureau, with the exception of Shantung province, all of the remaining five provinces were in ferment during February and March, with Fukien, Kiangsi and Anhwei the worst. In Fukien, a group of "rebels" had stormed the local military headquarters twice during late January and had "deliberately seized army cadres . . . [and] inflicted corporal punishment on them." [55] Considerable tension developed as "incidents" increased through February and March. In Anhwei a "false" power seizure had occurred on January 26 and in struggle between rebels the military became involved, suppressing one group and arresting its leaders.[56] Tension mounted here, as well. In Kiangsi widespread violence had broken out in early January and continued unabated through the next two months. The local military commander ousted the first secretary of the party provincial committee and on February 26 announced a power seizure and the formation of a revolutionary committee. Peking, however, refused to recognize the act as legitimate.[57] East China was in chaos.

In the area of the Southwest Bureau, Mao had managed to achieve a measure of stability in Kweichow in February, but in both Szech'uan, long-time power base of the first secretary of the bureau, Li Ching-ch'uan, and Yunnan factional fights increased in number and intensity through the early spring. In the provinces of Honan and Hupeh, which composed the Wuhan Military Region, severe factional strife occurred throughout the spring of the year. The Wuhan military commander, Ch'en Tsai-tao, stated publicly in early March that there had been "bitter struggles" in the region, requiring early and continuous military participation.[58]

It was in the Northwest Bureau region, however, that armed conflicts between rebel groups and the local military forces reached such proportions that a new crisis developed in Peking regarding the military's role in the cultural revolution. Even though Mao had terminated the cultural revolution in Sinkiang in early February,[59] thus reducing the magnitude of the problem in the Northwest, the situation in Tsinghai escalated out of control in late February. The deputy commander of the Tsinghai provincial military district, Chao Yung-fu, had squeezed out the party secretary, Liu Hsien-ch'uan, and proceeded to suppress rebel organizations. On February 23 Chao's troops fired on the rebels *en masse,* killing some two hundred persons and wounding over two thousand.[60]

The Chao Yung-fu "incident," as Peking referred to it, prompted what might be called an agonizing reappraisal of the role of the regional forces in the cultural revolution. It seemed apparent that the regional forces were proving incapable of dealing with the many tasks which they had been assigned. In addition to maintaining order and providing minimum security the additional tasks of pulling together grand alliances and constructing new organs of political power were simply proving to be beyond the capabilities of these forces. In late March, Mao Tse-tung and his supporters faced the question of what to do next. Should the cultural revolution be brought to an end at this point, short of Mao's goals? Should it be pushed forward, applying whatever force was necessary to achieve a successful conclusion? In either case, what role would the army corps standing in reserve play? In early April, after thrashing out the issues with top commanders, a decision was reached. The cultural revolution would not be halted half-way; it would be "pushed forward to the very end."

XII
The Great Proletarian Cultural Revolution
II: Protracted Crisis, 1967–1968

The question facing the Chinese Communist leaders in the early spring of 1967 was whether to bring the cultural revolution to an early conclusion or to carry it through to the end. The decision reached was to push on with the cultural revolution, a decision which precipitated bloody armed conflict throughout China for the next two years and sporadic violence after that. Only the direct and massive intervention of the People's Liberation Army kept provincial-wide outbreaks from spreading into wider civil strife. Continued instability and the inability to establish a satisfactory provincial apparatus required ever increasing inputs of main force military units. The result was that by the middle of 1968 China's national defense capabilities had been seriously reduced. In order to guard against possible external attack by the Soviet Union, China's leaders brought the cultural revolution to a premature conclusion in the latter months of 1968.

"Carry the Cultural Revolution Through to the Very End"

The Tsinghai bloodbath of late February had been only the most extreme example of a phenomenon which had occurred with increasing frequency during February and March following the introduction of the regional military into the cultural revolution. The military commanders in virtually every province had tended to support the less radical of revolutionary rebel groups. The result was that although "great alliances" were formed and the nuclei for provincial revolutionary committees established, Mao's political interests were not being served. The natural outcome of the "support the left" policy as it was being applied was the reentry of the old cadres to positions of dominance inside the new structures. It was this trend which precipitated a new crisis in the Central leadership in late March.

In the face of the mounting crisis the leadership became embroiled in a dispute over the course to follow. The failure of Mao's revolutionary rebels to seize power or to unify into "great alliances," and the increasing level of chaos and hardship, prompted several leaders in the Central Committee and PLA cultural revolution groups to advocate the early termination of the cultural revolution. Mao and his supporters had superior guns, however, and emerged victorious in yet another leadership conflict, purging the dissenters and embarking upon a more vigorous but less hasty attempt to capture power in the provinces.

In a speech delivered to a visiting Albanian military delegation in early April Mao revealed that some leaders wanted to bring the cultural revolution to an end. "This question is being discussed in the Central Cultural Revolution Group," he said. "Some think the suitable time is the end of this year, others favor May next year. But the matter of time must also be subject to the law of class struggle." [1] The upshot of this "discussion" was a victory for Mao and his supporters, who thereupon sent the struggle into what Mao termed its "fourth phase," a protracted effort which involved not only "the question of [political] power seizure," but also the "ideological seizure of power from revisionism and the bourgeoisie." Mao clearly admitted that initial attempts to bring victory in the provinces had failed and that a longer-run policy was being set into motion.

> The Center repeatedly urged the formation of revolutionary great alliances after the January storm, but to no avail. *Later it was found that this was a subjective wish which did not conform to the objective law of class struggle,* because the different classes and political forces of different factions would still stubbornly seek self-expression, and . . . would fall apart again even if they were united in the alliances. *So what the Center now does is simply to urge, not to help speed up, the formation of alliances.* The method of speeding up the growth of rice by pulling at the stems will not do. The law of class struggle will not change according to anyone's subjective wishes.[2]

Mao's new policy consisted of "urging" the formation of great alliances, after which he would make another strike for political power in the provinces. As part of the new hands-off attitude, the regional military forces were to be instructed to step aside from the struggle which would inevitably accompany the merging of factions. To ensure that the regional military would respond positively to the Center's policy, Mao played his trump card, the army corps, which were to be deployed to prevent the conflict from growing to uncontrollable dimensions. The decision to inject the army corps into the struggle engendered great opposition within the military leadership, undoubtedly on the ground that to do so would leave China vulnerable to external attack. Mao weathered this storm as he had so many others by compromising with the moderates and excluding the unyielding in both party and military. He placated the moderates by assuring them that the army corps would not become politically involved but would, in effect, play the role of pacification units preventing further conflict. Secondly, partly to mask the fact that China's first line army units were being redeployed for domestic political purposes, Mao initiated a voluminous propaganda campaign in late March which continued at fever pitch for the next two years. In it for the first time in the open press (as apart from wall posters) Liu Shao-ch'i and his now numerous "accomplices" were savagely attacked.

Mao removed those unalterably opposed to him. These included Hsü Hsiang-ch'ien, head of the PLA cultural revolutionary group appointed only a few months before in January, and three others in that group, T'an P'ing-tzu, Hu Ch'ih, and Ho Ku-yen, all men in charge of communications work.[3] The PLA cultural revolution group was reorganized with a triumvirate at the top consisting of Hsiao Hua, who was named acting head of the group, Yang Ch'eng-wu, acting chief of staff since Lo Jui-ch'ing's fall, and Hsieh Fu-chih, newly appointed member and current Minister of Public Security. Two men were also dropped from the Central Committee cultural revolution group. Liu Chih-chien, who had been removed as head of the PLA cultural revolution group in January, was now removed from the Central group entirely, as was Hsieh T'an-chung, head of cultural affairs in the General Political Department of the Ministry of Defense.

The Order of the Military Commission of the CCP Central Committee, which Mao described as "very good," was issued on April 6. It prohibited the district commanders from making arbitrary arrests, declaring revolutionary organizations "reactionary," and acting independently in their relations with mass organizations.

When it is absolutely necessary to declare them reactionary organizations and repress them, *approval must first be obtained from the Center.* . . . Before taking any important action, a report should be made to the Central Cultural Revolution Group and the All-PLA Cultural Revolution Group and their advice sought.[4]

Above all, shooting was forbidden; any form of corporal or "disguised" corporal punishment was also similarly prohibited. In short, the *regional* military forces were instructed to end their direct involvement with the revolutionary mass organizations.

While urging the rebels to unite, Mao attempted once more to defuse the explosive potential of burgeoning factional organizations. On April 8 *People's Daily* set forth a new formula by which every member of a revolutionary unit or organization would be judged. Contracted to the characters *"tou-p'i-kai"* (struggle-criticism-transformation), all rebels would henceforth be required to undergo criticism—self-criticism experiences in terms of which the general repudiation of Liu Shao-ch'i and others would serve as the criterion. Periodically, beginning later in April, Peking issued proclamations reiterating a February order prohibiting travel by any individual except with permission of the Central Committee and directing the return of all individuals to their original organizations.[5]

Under cover of the intensive propaganda campaign, Mao sent all or parts of at least eleven army corps into the most serious trouble spots to prevent further escalation of fighting. From late March onward, army corps became involved in ten provinces and four generally troubled areas.[6] Troops were sent to the three regions where conditions had been unsettled earlier—East, Northwest, and Southwest China. In addition, a fourth area—the Central South region—required the presence of an army corps. The growing disturbances in these regions threatened to develop into precisely that which Mao most feared, the coalescence of a regional opposition; this was a primary reason for involving the army corps.

From late March onward, Mao and his supporters in Peking attempted to achieve political solutions on a province by province basis as the situations in these provinces reached a flash point. The Center published decisions on certain provinces without prior consultation with the individuals involved, as in Inner Mongolia and Szech'uan. For the most part, the general procedure became the adoption of one of two methods. Either the Central Committee sent representatives to a disturbed province, for example, Chou En-lai's trip to Canton April 14–18, or provincial groups were received in Peking to negotiate a settlement. Afterward, the Center would publish a "decision" on the concerned province which, following the earlier prescription for a "three-way alliance," publicly identified those revolutionary mass organizations, old cadre groups, and military leaders who enjoyed the Center's support and those who did not. Most of the directives included the appointment of a preparatory committee to lay the groundwork for the formation of a provincial revolutionary committee. Paradoxically, the immediate result of Mao's new policy as it came into focus during the spring of 1967 was increased chaos and violence, not the reverse.

Failure of Mao's Policy and Increase in Violence

Mao strove to curtail the spiral of violence developing during early spring and provide a respite during which he could mobilize his forces for yet another attempt to seize power in the provinces. His policy was too little too late. Although he succeeded in establishing a revolutionary committee for Peking on April 20, the situation had already deteriorated farther than he had realized, for no other province or municipality followed Peking's example. The revolutionary groups had already polarized to such an extent that it proved impossible to unite them into grand alliances. Therefore, calling off the regional military forces and inciting the masses with the intensive anti-Liu propaganda campaign had the opposite effect from that intended. Instead of cooling down the situation in the provinces, it incited groups, particularly in already troubled areas, to further violence. In many cases, revolutionary groups intensified their attacks on military installations!

Throughout May the number of killed and wounded mounted as the use of weapons multiplied. By the end of the month, armed incidents had occurred in virtually every province, autonomous region, and large municipality, but Szech'uan and Inner Mongolia were the most serious problems. In Szech'uan, despite the presence of the 50th Army corps, sent from Manchuria, violent disturbances occurred in the major urban areas of Ch'engtu, Ip'in, and Chungking involving the use of rifles and machine guns. On April 14, a separate "notification" was issued concerning the situation in the Ip'in area and a month later, on May 7, a more encompassing directive was issued for Szech'uan as a whole. In it the Peking leadership relieved Li Ching-ch'uan and the top Szech'uan party and military leadership from their regional party and military posts.[7] Chang Kuo-hua, party and military chief of Tibet, was instructed to assume control of Szech'uan and begin the preparation of a revolutionary committee for the province.

In Inner Mongolia a similar "decision" was published on April 13 which publicly branded Ulanfu, long-time chief of the area, "the party person in authority taking the capitalist road," who was to be "openly exposed." [8] Liu Hsien-ch'uan, who had been given "full power" earlier to return order to Tsinghai after the Chao Yung-fu incident in February, was named Commander of the Inner Mongolian Military District and Wu T'ao, ousted secretary of the party committee, was restored to his former position. The two men were instructed to set up a preparatory committee for the establishment of a provincial revolutionary committee.

While Mao acted to contain the fighting in Inner Mongolia and Szech'uan, the situation in the East China and Central South regions deteriorated rapidly. Mao was forced hurriedly to bring the military, or at least a selected portion of it, into the struggle once again to prevent further breakdown of a situation which now saw frequent use of weapons in factional fighting and open brigandage. A "circular" of June 7 ordered that "no organization or individual" could henceforth arrest anyone, steal or destroy official documents, disturb state property, or engage in armed struggle under pain of strict punishment.

> To prevent counterrevolutionary elements from taking advantage of this trend [toward breakdown] . . . *all garrison forces and PLA forces dispatched from Peking* shall take responsibility for the implementation of each of the above items.

In other words, as he had done so often in the past, Mao had used the developing crisis to do what he had previously assured his comrades he would not do. In this case, the army corps "dispatched from Peking" were now to become more directly involved. Initially, it had been thought that their mere presence would be a brake on violence. Now the army corps and garrison forces were instructed to *enforce* order by apprehending and punishing lawbreakers.

Ironically, in attempting to resolve one type of crisis, Mao set the conditions for still another more dangerous development. If the April 6 order generally restrained or removed the PLA regional forces from direct involvement in the cultural revolution, the June 7 "circular" contained a loophole through which they could legitimately reenter the struggle. Although Mao had limited the participation of regional forces to urban "garrison forces," their inclusion provided the opportunity for those regional commanders whose responsibilities included large municipalities to involve themselves directly in the cultural revolution once again. Aided by "*all* revolutionary organizations" which were to "set examples," the "garrison forces and dispatched PLA forces [had] . . . the right to arrest, detain, and punish the leaders and the wirepullers in an offense." [9] In fact, this is precisely what one such regional commander, Ch'en Tsai-tao, did, leading to the extremely explosive affair known as the "Wuhan incident."

From the beginning Wuhan had been the scene of clashes among literally hundreds of rebel groups. Between February and April Ch'en Tsai-tao, as had other commanders elsewhere, supported the "left" by suppressing the most radical groups. The order of magnitude was indicated by one estimate in which it was noted that during that period "more than 300 'revolutionary rebel groups' throughout the province of Hupeh were branded 'counterrevolutionary' and over 10,000 people arrested." [10] Although the situation eased somewhat after the issuance of the April directive restraining the regional forces, immediately after the promulgation of the June 7 circular the intensity of clashes picked up. Given the authority once again to "arrest, detain, and punish," Ch'en resumed his support of the strong paramilitary organization named the "Million Heroes." This organization was composed of several rebel groups, demobilized troops from one of Ch'en's own independent divisions (the eleventh independent division under the command of Niu Huai-ling), public security forces of Wuhan, and other elements of the established order. These were arrayed against another composite rebel group, the "Three Steels." By late June clashes between the two large groups had become increasingly bloody. In Wuhan alone between June 16 and 24, 350 had been killed and over 1,500 wounded. [11]

To make matters worse a similar sequence of events had taken place in Honan, the province immediately to the north of Hupeh. Chengchow, the main city and key rail junction, had also been the scene of serious clashes and by late June it, too, exhibited extreme disorder. Honan and Hupeh together composed the Wuhan Military Region, which was the key link between Peking and South China and an area, which, according to Lin Piao, Mao and his supporters had found particularly difficult to penetrate.[12] Further chaos in this region would hinder north-south movement from Peking, reducing the Center's ability to respond quickly to crises that developed in the various regions. Therefore, the chaos and disorder in Wuhan, in particular, had to be brought to an end as quickly as possible.

Earlier, Peking had sent Hsieh Fu-chih and Wang Li, two members of the Central Committee's Cultural Revolution Group, to Yunnan and Szech'uan to manage factional disputes.[13] These men were subsequently instructed to proceed to Wuhan en route to Peking, where they arrived on July 14.[14] Chou En-lai, who had preceded Hsieh and Wang to Wuhan, attempted to resolve the difficulty in that city. He informed Ch'en Tsai-tao that he, as commander of the military region, had made mistakes in supporting the left and instructed him to rehabilitate the "Three Steels" as a revolutionary mass organization, brand the "Million Heroes" a conservative group, and bring about a "great alliance" of the two feuding groups. Chou then left the city, delegating further management of the dispute to Hsieh and Wang. On July 19, at a meeting between the Wuhan region command and concerned persons, Wang Li issued a four-point directive to Ch'en Tsai-tao ordering him to rehabilitate two large revolutionary organizations—the Three Steels and the Workers' General Headquarters—label the Million Heroes "conservative," and publicly acknowledge that the military district command had committed "errors." [15]

Whatever the reasons, an angry group from the Million Heroes refused to accept Wang Li's directive and took matters into their own hands, abducting both Hsieh and Wang and holding them incommunicado for several hours.[16] If the commander of the region, Ch'en Tsai-tao, did not support their action, he did nothing to stop them. Wang was severely beaten and one of his entourage killed. News of the "incident" in Wuhan quickly spread, presenting Mao and his supporters with a serious problem, which was not primarily how to handle the events in Wuhan, but what they portended. Successful open defiance by the Wuhan military command would be interpreted by other military leaders as weakness of the Center. Unless Peking demonstratively showed its strength in Wuhan and decisively dealt with those involved, then other commanders also might be tempted to test the strength of Peking.

Mao appears to have panicked momentarily in the face of this realization and to have overreacted. Fearing that the defiance of the Wuhan leaders would be emulated, Mao immediately sent Chou En-lai back to the city with air and naval support. The East China fleet steamed up the Yangtze River, anchoring off the city while planes parachuted several airborne units into the city. These troops forcibly disarmed and broke up the Million Heroes' organization. In short order Hsieh and Wang were on their way to Peking, followed a few days later by Ch'en Tsai-tao and the leaders of the Wuhan military command, who were required to "confess" their errors. A heroes' welcome was staged in Peking for Hsieh and Wang, which was clearly intended to suggest a Central triumph; the immediate policy reaction, however, demonstrated apprehension regarding the regional commanders.

In the initial panic during the Wuhan incident, Peking had summoned the principal military commanders to the capital. Pressured by the "left wing" in the Central Cultural Revolution Group, Mao acceded to a policy of arming the revolutionaries and directing them against the military. *People's Daily* on the 20th called for the revolutionary masses to "drag out the handful of power holders in the army" and on the 22nd Chiang Ch'ing urged the revolutionaries to adopt a stance of "attack by reasoning, defense with force." [17] At the same time, Central leaders armed a few rebel organizations in Peking and Shanghai. The reasoning behind the decision was undoubtedly to prevent any repetition of the Wuhan syndrome elsewhere and the growth of provincial into regional incidents. The almost immediate result of the order to arm the left was a precipitate increase in the level of armed conflict between rebels and military. Rebels immediately stormed arms depots and arsenals and even took weapons from troops. In the ensuing conflicts the military got the worst of it because, except for "garrison forces and dispatched PLA forces," the entire army was still under the restrictions of the April 6 hands-off, no-shooting order.

To Whom the Leading Role, Rebels or Soldiers?

Mao succeeded in preventing the link-up of potentially dissident forces by the stop-gap measure of directing the armed revolutionary rebels against the regional commands, but the increased level of violence and number of casualties suffered by military forces provoked strenuous opposition among Mao's top military leaders. They undoubtedly demanded either disarming of the rebels or release from the April 6 restraints or both. At this critical juncture during the first week of August, two groups pressed for mutually contradictory policies in what seems to have been a vicious encounter. Wang Li, hero of Wuhan and close confidant of Chiang Ch'ing, supported by several members of the Central Committee Cultural Revolution Group, argued for continuation of the expedient policy of late July. He urged that the armed revolutionary rebels become the primary vehicle for achieving the objectives of the cultural revolution in place of the military. His alleged grounds were that:

> . . . 90 per cent of the leadership in the armed forces is conservative, 7 to 8 per cent is Rightist, and only 1 to 2 per cent is revolutionary.[18]

The military leaders in the PLA Cultural Revolution Group vehemently opposed the proposition that the leading role in the cultural revolution be delegated to the armed rebels, although they seem not to have been unified over the precise extent to which the military should continue to be entangled. Given the clear-cut choice of power to armed rebels or to the military, Peking's military men reached the obvious conclusion. However, they divided over the manner in which the power should be exercised by the military. Events of the 8th and 9th of August reveal that the top leadership had resolved the debate over "to whom the leading role" by devising a compromise of sorts between the two positions. Mao and his top leaders decided that the army and not the armed rebels would continue to be the instrument in the cultural revolution, but that all independent initiative would be withdrawn from field force commanders and centered in Peking. Literally all problems large or small would henceforth be decided by the Central leaders. As for the rebels, it was decided to arm on an experimental basis selected revolutionary rebel groups, which, however, would be subordinate to, and function under, the orders of the local military commanders.

On August 9, Lin Piao drove home the main guidelines for field commanders in an important policy speech given at a reception for Tseng Ssu-yü and Liu Feng, the newly appointed commanders of the Wuhan military region, Ch'en Hsi-lien, commander of the Mukden military region, Liu P'ei-shan, first political commissar of the Foochow military region, Cheng Wei-shan, commander of the Peking military region, and Wu Fa-hsien, commander of the Air Force.[19] These men represented the key regions of Central South, Northeast, East, and North China. Although Mao was not present, members of the Central Committee Cultural Revolution Group included Ch'en Po-ta, K'ang Sheng, Chiang Ch'ing, Hsieh Fu-chih, Wang Li, Kuan Feng, and Ch'i Pen-yü. To preclude the possibility of "another Ch'en Tsai-tao," Lin stipulated three guidelines to be followed. First, commanders were to study local conditions carefully so that they were well acquainted with the various mass organizations. Second, commanders were ordered to:

> . . . seek instructions from and report to Chairman Mao, the Central Committee, and the Cultural Revolution Group of the Central Committee. We must not have the idea that we need not report to the Central Committee so long as we ourselves understand the situation. Nor must we have the idea that we need not seek instructions from the Central Committee because the matter can be dealt with by us since it is so small or because we ourselves are intelligent enough to deal with the matter. . . . We should seek instructions . . . on all matters, big and small.[20]

To emphasize his point, Lin reiterated, "don't act on your own because you think your ideas are right or you are clever. This I must say again and again, and it is the most important of the three ways."

The third point concerned the method of distinguishing Maoists from non-Maoists. "You must divide people into Left and Right," Lin declared, "not according to whether they attack the military district, but according to whether they protect or oppose Chairman Mao." He continued:

> We must resolutely stand on the side of Chairman Mao, on the side of the Left, and on the side of the masses. We must not judge a group as to whether it is a leftist or rightist one simply on the basis of whether the class status of its members is pure or not, whether it has many or few Party members or many or few cadres. Class status must be examined, but it is not everything. The main thing is to see what line is followed.[21]

The "rightists" must be divided and won over, and their leaders dragged out "in the spirit of Chairman Mao's directives." Above all, however, continued Lin, "the masses must not be suppressed." Those cadres who make "mistakes," he said, "should be sent to receive training in accordance with Chairman Mao's instructions." In a final admonition to his listeners, Lin cautioned:

> Lest you should make mistakes, may I remind you once more of the three ways, especially the second one. Things should rather be done a bit slowly . . . and must not be done in a hurry. If they are delayed for a few days, the sky would not fall.[22]

On the next day, the Central Committee issued "several decisions" concerning the problem of Kiangsi. Point five of the document revealed the decision concerning the future role of the revolutionary rebels.

> In districts where opportunity is ripe, revolutionary masses should be armed under the guidance of the preparatory group. For the time being research and preparations for putting this into effect will be made in the Nanchang and Fuchou areas. *The reason for arming the revolutionary masses is to help the PLA* protect state property and maintain revolutionary order. Guns and ammunition should not be supplied to the conservatives under any excuse.[23]

The revolutionaries would be armed, on an experimental basis, but only "to help the PLA," not to become the main force in the cultural revolution. The slogan "drag out the handful of power holders in the army" was dropped, and Wang Li with his supporters suffered the predictable consequences. They were purged from their positions and efforts were made to ferret out all those with whom they had been linked. Wang Li, Kuan Feng, Mu Hsin, and Lin Chieh, all members of the Central Committee Cultural Revolution Group, were dismissed from their positions. To signal this major decision, Mao issued his directive "Give Back Our Great Wall" to indicate that the army would no longer come under attack.

Although the army would continue to function as the main bulwark, Mao took safeguards to insure that those regional commanders of dubious reliability would comply with Central directives. He ordered additional army corps to take over all or parts of eleven military commands, bringing the total number of army corps involved in the cultural revolution to at least twenty.[24] This was a major decision for the leadership to make and one which some military leaders, notably Hsiao

Hua, acting head of PLA Cultural Revolution Group, refused to accept. Undoubtedly, these men repeated the argument broached earlier about denuding China's defenses, this time with greater force. With over half of China's first line corps entangled in "defense of the cultural revolution," how could she meet an external threat? Mao's response, one may believe, was that unless the army corps were deployed there would be no China left to defend, at least not one under the current leadership.

During the debate over greater employment of the army corps, Hsiao Hua evidently had countered with the proposal that the task of supervising the regional forces be assigned to the Public Security Forces, but this alternative was forcefully rejected by Hsieh Fu-chih, former Minister of the Public Security Forces, who noted that:

> We have not found a single instance where public security, procuracy and judicial systems support the proletarian revolutionaries. Of course, individually speaking, everywhere there are persons who support the Leftists. But, in terms of the organization as a whole, all support the conservatives. In big cities, 80 percent of county public security bureaus support the conservatives whether they have had revolts or not and whether the power has been seized or not.[25]

The upshot of the debate was that Mao carried the day and his opponents were purged from their positions in the PLA Cultural Revolution Group. Those dismissed were Hsiao Hua, Hsu Li-ch'ing, Li Man-ts'ung, and Kuan Feng. Appointed to replace these men were Wu Fa-hsien, head of the air force, Ch'iu Hui-tso, General Rear Services chief, Yeh Ch'un, Lin Piao's wife, and Chang Hsiu-ch'uan, head of the navy political department.[26] With the exception of Yeh Ch'un, all the new men were military leaders whose primary areas of responsibility were at the national defense level.

While removing his opponents, Mao attempted to reduce the likelihood of an external aggressor's acting on the knowledge that China's defenses were being seriously compromised by creating an extraordinary diversion which screened the events. Beginning on August 11 and continuing through that month, attacks were carried out not only on foreign embassies in China, particularly the Soviet and other Communist embassies, but the British legation in Hong Kong was set afire and Red Guards stormed China's own Foreign Ministry(!), "dragging out" the foreign minister, Ch'en Yi, and making a spectacular issue of his "errors." [27]

After almost a month of experiment with arming the rebels, the leadership reached a major decision concerning the future role of the revolutionary rebels. It was decided to terminate "struggle by force." In the weeks since the Wuhan incident it had become clear that arming the rebels simply complicated the overall situation. Combined with the decision to continue with the military as the main force in the cultural revolution, arming the rebels was counterproductive as it created a force basically antagonistic to the military. The rebels were extremely difficult to control. Therefore, Mao and his supporters rammed through the decision to disarm the rebels entirely and gave the task of promulgating this decision to Chiang Ch'ing, the central leader who had been publicly identified with the policy of arming rebel groups. In a speech given on September 5, which was recorded and subsequently widely disseminated as the authoritative statement of the new policy decision, Chiang Ch'ing set forth the following points:

> The Central Committee is tackling the problems province by province, and city by city in the case of those large cities.
>
> Now in various provinces the case is generally like this: Talks are being held through arrangements made by the Central Committee, and although there have been reversals in some individual places, reversals are a normal phenomenon.
>
> Now we come to the second question—the army. Sometime earlier, there was this wrong slogan: Seize a "small handful in the army." As a result, "a small handful in the army" was seized everywhere and even the weapons of our regular troops were seized. . . . Let us not fall into the trap. The slogan was wrong. . . . We can only talk about dragging out the handful of Party capitalist roaders in authority and nothing else.
>
> The slogan of seizing the small handful in the army is wrong, and it has produced a series of undesirable consequences.[28]

At the end of her speech, Chiang Ch'ing read a Central Committee order on control of weapons which was issued that same day. The order called for a movement to "support the Army and cherish the people." The main point was repeated several times:

> No mass organization or person, no matter to which group they belong, is permitted to steal weapons, ammunition, equipment, vehicles, munitions or

materials from the PLA nor to steal weapons, ammunition, equipment, vehicles, munitions or materials from the munitions stores or scientific enterprises. They are not permitted to steal weapons, ammunition, equipment, vehicles, munitions or materials from trains, vehicles or boats. No outside unit is allowed to occupy military commands or Army camps.[29]

The PLA was instructed to collect all weaponry, using persuasion first in dealing with those in possession of stolen materials. "If this is ineffective they should fire warning shots in the air." If this doesn't work:

> . . . they may announce that the theft was a counterrevolutionary action and should . . . arrest the small number of bad elements among the leaders of the group. . . . If these people resist the PLA has the right to counterattack in self-defense.[30]

The speech and disarmament order represented a major shift in the course of the cultural revolution, which became manifest in the fall of 1967. The short-lived "experiment" of using selected armed rebel groups "to help the PLA" had not worked. The role of the revolutionary rebels had been curtailed because the range of possible developments and consequences virtually had dictated this course of action.

The Attempt to Construct a Civil-Military "Balance"

Until the Wuhan incident Mao had been willing to tolerate a high level of chaos and wait for a Maoist "core" to develop and provide new leadership for the provinces. The Wuhan incident forced a change of plans, convincing him of the overriding need for the rapid establishment of an administrative structure to harness the political and military forces in the provinces. Mao feared the consequences implied in the Wuhan "mutiny," that other regional military commanders would follow suit. Hence he sought some means of placing a check upon the power of the regional commanders. The decision to send in additional main force units to take over troublesome military districts was part of the answer, arming selected revolutionary rebel units the other part; but the latter had proved infeasible.

The new means employed to check the military was to speed up the formation of provincial revolutionary committees. Mao hoped that a civil structure in the provinces would serve to counterbalance and eventually to supersede the military's position in the provincial power structure. Paradoxically, the chief builder of this new administrative apparatus would be the regional military forces themselves. Once it was built, of course, the separation of civil and military functions could be effected, but that was in the future. In the short run, each revolutionary committee would be dominated by military men, to be sure, but there would also be "civilian" functionaries on each committee, an as yet undertermined mix of old cadres and revolutionary rebels, which would act to balance the presence of the military.

Mao's decision to use the old, experienced cadres instead of the rebels in the drive to reestablish an administrative structure for the provinces provided mute but dramatic testimony to the magnitude of the post-Wuhan political crisis as viewed in Peking. All along, Mao had strenuously resisted the arguments of those who, like T'an Chen-lin, had urged the employment of the cadres to counter the military. Now, at last, he had grudgingly acceded. He could no longer afford the luxury of "waiting" for a Maoist revolutionary core to form in the provinces. The civil structure had to be restored in the shortest possible time. It was the decision to proceed with the rapid establishment of the revolutionary committees that in fact determined the mix of cadre and rebel. The old cadres were experienced and could be employed immediately, while the rebels, for the most part, had not yet even forged great alliances, let alone developed the necessary expertise to participate in the administration of the new political structure Mao sought to build. The result was that through the fall and winter of 1967–68 the rebels were systematically and intentionally excluded from important positions in the provincial political organs.

The medium used to form the new revolutionary committees was the "Mao Tse-tung Thought Study Class," in which provincial representatives of old cadres, revolutionary rebels, and military leaders were brought together either in Peking or in the concerned province, or sometimes in both places. At these "classes" Central leaders including the highest personages, such as Mao Tse-tung himself, Chou En-lai, K'ang Sheng, Chiang Ch'ing, and others, would exhort the provincial representatives to unite. The representatives of the revolutionary rebel groups would form "grand alliances," after which representatives from all three elements would form the "three-way alliance." Only after successful completion of the "course" would the group be permitted to return to its home province to establish a revolutionary committee. Following this general procedure, eleven additional provincial and municipal revolutionary committees were formed between November 1, 1967 and March 24, 1968, bringing the total to eighteen.[31]

Anticipating an adverse reaction from excluded rebel groups, Mao and his supporters attempted to reduce the problem in both quantitative and qualitative terms. In efforts to siphon off as many rebels as possible schools were reopened in September and students were urged to return to "make revolution in the schools," rather than to study.[32] It was hoped that the numerical size of the rebel groups would be diminished by this measure. At the same time, the Central leadership employed both cajolery and threats to minimize further the opposition of disgruntled rebel groups to the new political apparatus being set up in the provinces. As an organizational alternative, the party and youth organizations were revived and aspiring individuals were urged to seek membership. This would further weaken the independent rebel organizations. It was stressed, however, that the leaders of the revolutionary committees would hold real power, not the party. The question of party leadership in the provincial power structure was, in Hsieh Fu-chih's words, "to be mentioned later." [33]

Threats ranged from denunciation of "extremism" in the press to televised public trials and executions. An article by Yao Wen-yuan, member of the Central Cultural Revolution Group, in September launched an extensive campaign against what was called the "ultra 'left'." [34] Yao attacked T'ao Chu for his "pseudo-leftist" role as former head of the Central Committee's Propaganda Department, but more importantly named a heretofore unknown group, the May 16 corps, as a current perpetrator of T'ao's undercover activities. Whether or not such a group ever existed, subsequent Red Guard publications contained accusations against several alleged ringleaders of the organization. These included Wang Li and Kuan Feng, former members of the Central Cultural Revolution Group who had already been purged. It seems that the drive against the machinations of members of the May 16 corps was a clear signal that extremism would no longer be tolerated and that those associated with such policies—even in the very center of the proletarian dictatorship—would be eliminated. Wang Li and Kuan Feng thus served as scapegoats for the new policy.

At the other end of the spectrum, the leadership revived public trial rallies on an extensive scale. Not since the early and mid-fifties, when Peking required a demonstration that it would tolerate no further disorder, had the method of public trials and executions been used. The reintroduction of such trials in late August clearly indicated that the regime would treat those who refused to bend to its policies in the same harsh manner. During the critical period of late August 1967 to April 1968, the official Chinese press reported numerous public trial rallies attended by large numbers of people, sometimes as many as 250,000, of "counterrevolutionary elements." In some cases public executions were televised.[35]

The larger, more encompassing theme carried in the official press during the fall and winter was the personal and continuous involvement of Mao Tse-tung himself in all questions. In the context of an alleged trip made by Mao through the North, East, and Central South China regions in late September, Mao's "great strategic plan" and his "latest instructions" were continuously publicized throughout the country. Beginning in November, the press talked optimistically of the final battle and decisive victory and the convocation of the Ninth Party Congress by the spring of 1968. In the "latest supreme instructions" of September 26, Mao is reported to have said:

> The situation is highly favorable. In the whole country, the problems of seven provinces have been solved and those of eight other provinces have been basically solved, and effort should be made to solve the problems of another ten provinces (five in southern China and five in the north) this year. . . . Problems of the whole country should be solved basically and the whole situation put into the normal track before the Spring Festival.[36]

A month later, Hsieh Fu-chih noted that "judging from the situation in Peking, it is possible to hold the [Ninth] congress in May or June [1968]." [37] These hopeful forecasts concerning the rate of progress on the formation of provincial revolutionary committees, which determined when the Ninth Party Congress could be held, were not borne out by events.

Instead of a projected twenty-five provinces having revolutionary committees by the end of 1967, only six provinces plus the municipalities of Peking, Shanghai, and Tientsin had proclaimed them. It was only with the start of the new year that the pace picked up. Two revolutionary committees were formed in January, four in February, and three more in March. The increased pace was accompanied by a revival of violence as disaffected rebels, excluded from positions in the revolutionary committees, increasingly rejected these committees as well as their efforts to bring dissident groups under control. The press referred more and more to the need to bring "factionalism and anarchism" to an end, even while it praised the new committees. There was no further talk of convening a congress.

Representative of the views of those rebel groups left out in the cold politically was the program of the Hunan Provincial Proletarian Revolutionaries Great Alliance Committee, abbreviated as the *Sheng Wu Lien*.[38] In a lengthy pamphlet entitled "Whither China?" the rebel leaders attacked the Hunan revolutionary committee as just "another kind of bourgeois rule of bourgeois bureaucrats" made up by "the old provincial party committee and the old military district command." The rebels were bitter about their exclusion from the committees and particularly so about the decision to bring back the old cadres. In their view, only the form of political power had changed, not its content. The old cadres, they claimed, along with the old party provincial committee and the military district committee, simply had changed their titles to revolutionary committees or preparatory groups for revolutionary committees.[39] The rebels demanded "radical change . . . from below." The Hunan *Sheng Wu Lien* was not the only disaffected rebel group overtly or covertly opposing the revolutionary committees; there were others in practically every province.[40] The cohesion of such groups varied with the province and while the power each group had was minimal, still, such groups provided foci for the attraction of those who were excluded from a share in the provincial power structure.

Cultural Revolution on the Verge of Success

By the early spring of 1968, then, two trends were clearly observable on the cultural revolution scene. The first and more obvious trend was the apparently successful formation of provincial revolutionary committees, which, by the end of March, had reached a total of eighteen. The creation of a functioning administrative apparatus in the provinces accomplished the primary objective of stemming further deterioration of the military situation following the Wuhan incident.

This success was partly offset by the necessity of bringing in the old experienced cadres to run the new apparatus and shunting aside the revolutionary rebels. The rebels simply rebelled, opposing the formation of revolutionary committees, a development which was confined for the most part within provincial boundaries. From the perspective of the central leaders, rebel-caused disorders were an acceptable price to pay to forestall the military rebellion which seemed imminent after the Wuhan incident. Having overcome the greater danger of an army revolt, central leaders turned to the lesser problem of growing "factionalism and anarchism" in the provinces.

The question facing the leadership in February–March 1968 was how to deal with those rebels who had been excluded from the revolutionary committee. Mao Tse-tung proposed to undercut the growing opposition of the rebel groups—which had been his own creation—by giving them a greater collective share in the revolutionary committees. Several top leaders, led by acting chief of staff Yang Ch'eng-wu, opposed this course of action, proposing the continuation of the existing policy for the revolutionary committees. Yang and his supporters, Yü Li-chin and Fu Ch'ung-pi, Air Force Political Commissar and commander of the Peking PLA garrison respectively, were defeated in this policy struggle and removed from office. According to Lin Piao's post-mortem of the affair they were "wrong and . . . in a minority." [41] Such are the bare outlines of the "Yang Ch'eng-wu affair." The underlying motives and generative impulses are at best murky and it is possible to propose only a tentative hypothesis at this time.

Part of the decision to restore the civil-military balance the previous fall included renewed emphasis on the role of the Central Committee in the policy-making process and the relative decline of both the Central Committee Cultural Revolution Group and PLA Cultural Revolution Group. The CCCRG had suffered considerably through the purges of its membership during the cultural revolution, and the latest of those purges, that of Ch'i Pen-yü in mid-February, left that organization with only five members. [42] A worse fate befell the PLA Cultural Revolution Group. Sometime during the late fall of 1967 (November–December) the PLA Cultural Revolution Group had been quietly dissolved and replaced by a "management group" (*pan shih tzu*). [43] The effect of this decision was to remove several military leaders from the high political councils and give greater weight to the civilian component in the policy-making process.

Yang Ch'eng-wu's opposition to Mao's call to allocate a greater political share to the rebel component in the provincial revolutionary committees appears at bottom to represent his attempt to arrest the further deterioration of what he conceived to be the PLA's proper political role. From accounts linking Yang with a "rightist reversal of verdicts" it would seem that he favored the continuation of the previous policy of relying on the old cadres to staff the revolutionary committees. He sought unsuccessfully to bolster his position with the appointment of "men with whom he had close ties" to important positions in Peking.[44] Instead, his current rivals, Wu Fa-hsien, Huang Yung-sheng, Hsü Shih-yü, Han Hsien-ch'u, and Hsieh Fu-chih, moved into stronger positions.[45] Huang Yung-sheng, in fact, succeeded Yang Ch'eng-wu as chief of staff of the People's Liberation Army.

Following Yang's dismissal, the new policy was inaugurated, accompanied by a new surge of violence in the provinces. Between early April and the end of May, six provinces established revolutionary committees and in four of these a discernible increase occurred in the ratio of rebel to cadres and military men. The first two committees established during the period reflected the earlier policy of military dominance. In Hunan (formed on April 8) and Ninghsia (April 10) the respective ratios of rebel:cadre:military were 2:4:8 and 1:1:6. In the succeeding four committees, however, there was a distinct increase in rebel representation. In Anhwei (April 18) the ratio was 4:3:8; in Shensi (May 1) 6:2:9; in Liaoning (May 10) 7:6:11; and in Szech'uan (May 31) 8:7:7.[46] In other words, Mao was succeeding in his attempt to broaden rebel participation in the provincial revolutionary committees.

The Szech'uan revolutionary committee at the end of May was the twenty-fourth to be established, leaving only five provinces to complete the task of establishing revolutionary committees for all of China. Yet no other revolutionary committees were set up after May 31. Instead, in a 180 degree policy turnabout, the PLA from early June onward began to move forcibly against the rebel organizations which Mao had just recently unleashed! On July 3 and 24 Peking issued strongly worded "notices" calling for the "immediate" end to armed struggles, the return of all weapons to the PLA, the resumption of the flow of railway traffic and material to Vietnam, and the punishment of the "small handful" hoodwinking the masses.[47] At the same time the army began the task (to be continued well into the following year) of rounding up the more intractable rebels and cadres and shipping them off to PLA camps to learn how to "forget self" and to "study" the Thought of Mao Tse-tung. The result was widespread armed clashes between rebel groups and military units. Some of the bloodiest conflict to occur at any time during the cultural revolution took place during the policy reversal of June and July.

Finally, on the early morning of the 28th, Mao held an interview with five rebel leaders representing the largest mass organizations in Peking. In what was reportedly a lengthy and acrimonious session Mao vented his exasperation at the rebels' inability to achieve settlements in the provinces.[48] Mao had publicly declared at different times that revolutionary committees would be established over all of China, first, by the end of 1967, then later by the spring of 1968. Neither target had been met. Unmistakably, Mao's meeting with the rebels signaled a major decision to bring their role in the cultural revolution to an end. What had happened? Why had Mao and his top leaders suddenly reversed themselves after seeming on the verge of triumph? Why had the cultural revolution been halted abruptly in mid-stride?

The Decision to Terminate the Cultural Revolution

Mao and his supporters had successfully hidden from the outside world the extent to which China's national defenses had been weakened during the cultural revolution. Still, they realized that it was only a matter of time before this condition would be perceived and possibly tested by a hostile neighbor, namely the Soviet Union. In other terms, external perception of China's weakness would constitute the time limit for the cultural revolution. Several events occurred during the spring and summer of 1968 which strongly suggested that the Soviet Union's leaders not only had perceived China's state of unreadiness but had decided to prepare to take action, the nature of which, however, was undisclosed. The first indication of a change in the Soviet position came in April with the publication of the first of what became a series of six articles on the "events in China." [49] Timed to coincide with preparations for the World Congress of Communist Parties, scheduled to open in June (the same conference which had originally been scheduled for December

1964), the articles constituted a strong attack on Mao Tse-tung and his policies and laid the political basis for a formal break. The essence of the Soviet position developed in the articles but clearly spelled out in the very first one was that Mao had destroyed the Communist party and replaced it with a military dictatorship suffused with the cult of Mao Tse-tung. Alluding to the coming world congress, the Soviet author called for a "collective rebuff" to Mao Tse-tung and "practical international aid to the forces in China which remain loyal to Marxism-Leninism and resist Maoism." [50] The implications in this argument were ominous.

More serious were Soviet military activities. Since 1965, the Soviet Union had gradually built up the number of divisions and logistical service components in the Soviet Far East. By the spring of 1968 the Soviets reportedly had in place close to half a million combat troops with an equally sized logistical complement. In addition, Outer Mongolian military power was augmented both in terms of troop strength and missile implacement. Although the incidence of border clashes had risen in proportion as the buildup along the border progressed, the Soviet and Chinese press played down the potentially explosive significance of the clashes.

In terms of their implications for China, the events in Czechoslovakia were most foreboding, providing Chinese leaders with a current case study in Soviet problem-solving techniques. Beginning in May, the Soviets openly mobilized their armed forces in an effort to intimidate the Czech party leadership into accepting Soviet demands. "Joint military maneuvers" on Czech territory as part of the Warsaw Pact operations were to be held to "test cooperation and commands under conditions of modern warfare and to improve the combat readiness of troops and staff." [51] At the end of the month, Soviet troops and tanks entered Czech territory for the maneuvers. Accompanying these troop moves, Soviet press commentary justified the Soviet position and action in terms which sounded strangely similar to terms used to denounce China at about the same time.[52]

The point was inescapable. If the Soviet Union were willing to employ a combination of political and military pressure against the Czechs, was it not conceivable that they would do the same against the Chinese? However unlikely China's leaders may have considered actual military intervention by the Soviet Union, both the propaganda and the military buildup in the context of the Czech crisis could not be ignored. In view of China's extremely weak national defense position due to the deep involvement of her main force units in the cultural revolution, the mounting Soviet threat presented Mao and the central leadership with a painful dilemma. To continue the cultural revolution would leave China exposed to outside aggression and to terminate it would leave Mao's objectives unfulfilled. The decision reached by the leadership was to bring the cultural revolution activity to a conclusion—to terminate the cultural revolution for the time being—and to devote all efforts toward the buttressing of China's defenses.

The decision to shore up border defenses to meet the growing Soviet threat required a rapid shift in domestic policies, a shift which, under the circumstances, was accomplished with remarkable dispatch beginning during the month of August. It was necessary to begin the process of extracting the main force units from their domestic political involvement and return them to their defense positions. On August 1 the *People's Daily* editorial demanded "absolute obedience" to the PLA. On the 5th the same organ declared that there was only one command post, the proletarian headquarters of Chairman Mao. All other claimants to authority were false; there could not be "many centers" of power. Meanwhile, the PLA crackdown on the rebels continued, but a new group was introduced to assist the military in its job. On the 5th of August Mao gave a gift of mangoes received from a Pakistani delegation to a new group of Tsinghua University, a group called a "Worker-Peasant Mao Tse-tung Thought Propaganda Team."

Mao's symbolic act signaled the appearance on the political scene of an organization which partially assumed duties heretofore performed by the main forces of the PLA. Regional military units provided military support for the teams,[53] permitting the extraction of main force units from their involvement on the domestic scene. Delegation of authority over the teams to the provincial revolutionary committees further confirmed the jurisdictional shift and also served to facilitate the release of main force units from their domestic chores. On the 15th of August, perhaps to assert a degree of doctrinal orthodoxy in the face of Soviet claims to the contrary, the "leading role" in the cultural revolution was now assigned to the working class as represented by the Mao Thought Propaganda Teams. The leading role of the working class became a prominent theme in the press. Yao Wen-yuan, member of the Cultural

Revolution Group and author of the article attacking Wu Han, which in 1965 had signaled the beginning of the cultural revolution, confirmed the basic policy shift. In another article which appeared in late August, Yao severely criticized the Red Guards and revolutionary rebels for their ineptitude. They must submit to "revolutionary discipline," he said, and learn from the working class, which must lead "in everything." [54]

Meanwhile, between August 13 and September 5 the remaining five provinces announced the formation of revolutionary committees. The new policy adopted in the spring of a more equitable balance among rebels, cadres, and military was adhered to in each case, although the committees were clearly imposed from above by the military commanders on the spot and not formed through struggle as they were earlier. In Yunnan, whose committee was formed on August 13, the rebel:cadre: military ratio was 8:7:7; in Fukien, formed August 19, the ratio was 7:4:9; in Kwangsi, formed August 26, it was 8:2:9; and in Sinkiang and Tibet, formed on September 5, the ratios were 4:5:7 and 12:5:10.[55] Peking demanded the rapid completion of the revolutionary committee system and would brook no further delay. By September 5, 1968 China had turned "all red."

The abrupt policy reversal was met—as could be anticipated—by considerable resistance from the rebels and, as before, the leadership employed a carrot and stick policy. On the one hand, Central leaders spoke of the positive achievements made by the Red Guards during the early and middle stages of the cultural revolution, but that a new stage had been reached in which they must follow and no longer lead. For example, at a rally in Peking on September 7 celebrating the establishment of revolutionary committees throughout China, Chiang Ch'ing said:

> At the command of our great leader Chairman Mao, the working class, that main force, ascended the stage of struggle-criticism-transformation of the superstructure on July 27. The People's Liberation Army gave it backing. The young Red Guard fighters and all teachers and staff who are willing to make revolution should welcome this act of the working class and follow its leadership. We must not allow the few bad elements to make trouble.[56]

On the other hand, provincial leaders were much less conciliatory in both word and deed. "Intellectuals" would be "welcomed" only if they accepted reeducation by the workers. If they were "willing to serve the workers, peasants, and soldiers," then there might be "hope for them and they have a future." [57] At the same time, provincial military forces continued to gather up and deport thousands of young people, both rebels and cadres, to the countryside. Even though violent armed clashes were common during this time, the youthful rebels stood little chance against trained military forces. The youths were installed in "cadre schools," where they were subjected to "fierce class struggle and intense manual work." [58]

"Unity and Strength Under Chairman Mao and Vice-Chairman Lin"

The dual thrust of regime policy throughout the fall and winter of 1968 was the consolidation of "all-round victory" in the cultural revolution and China's preparedness to meet any external challenge. The latter theme was expressed in several different but unmistakable ways. Chou En-lai, speaking at the September 7 rally noted above, hinted broadly that the reason for the policy shift was the increased threat of external attack. In discussing the trials and tribulations of U.S. imperialism and Soviet revisionism, Chou stated:

> It is . . . certain that our proletarian socialist revolution is advancing to world-wide victory. However, before the advent of victory, the enemies throughout the world will surely put up last-ditch struggles and launch counter-attacks. Therefore, our present Great Proletarian Cultural Revolution is a most extensive, thorough-going and all-round political and military mobilisation. Should enemies from abroad dare to invade China, we will . . . wipe them out.[59]

It was clear which enemy the Chinese considered the more dangerous. Throughout the fall, Chinese leaders stressed China's readiness to meet the Soviet buildup along the Sino-Soviet and Sino-Mongolian borders. Moreover, they specifically related the Soviet invasion of Czechoslovakia in August to the border problem. On September 16, in a protest note to the Soviet embassy in China, the Chinese claimed that Soviet aircraft had intruded into China's airspace 119 times in 1968 and that between August 9 and 29 twenty-nine intrusions had occurred over the border province of Heilungchiang alone. Soviet "provocations" were expressly linked in the note with the invasion of Czechoslovakia.⁶⁰ Later that month, Chou En-lai bluntly accused the Soviet Union of "stepping up armed provocations against China."

> In coordination with U.S. imperialism, it is energetically forming a ring of encirclement against China by stationing massive troops along the Sino-Soviet and Sino-Mongolian borders and, at the same time, it is constantly creating border tension by even more frequently sending planes to violate China's air space.⁶¹

The Chinese leadership sought to discourage any challenge by displaying military strength, political unity, productive capacity, and quietly beginning war preparations. On National Day, contingents of soldiers from "outposts of coastal and frontier defenses" marched past the Gate of Heavenly Peace, while both Lin Piao and Chou En-lai in speeches averred China's defenses were "stronger than ever." ⁶² Two weeks later, the leadership secretly convened its Twelfth Plenum, which continued through the end of the month. It was attended by the top party leadership, "members" and alternate members of the Central Committee, "all members" of the central cultural revolution group, "principal responsible comrades" of the revolutionary committees and PLA. Unity was a dominant theme. The plenum communique noted that

> This was a session of mobilization for the seizure of all-round victory in the great proletarian cultural revolution, a session on unprecedented unity in the whole party under the leadership of the proletarian headquarters with Chairman Mao as its leader and vice-chairman Lin as its deputy leader.⁶³

Although both Mao and Lin reportedly spoke, their words were not made public. The session upheld as "correct" the Eleventh Plenum decision to initiate the cultural revolution, Mao's "proletarian revolutionary line, his great strategic plan . . . the series of important instructions . . . and vice-chairman Lin's many speeches. . . ." The communique contained the announcement that "ample ideological, political, and organizational conditions have been prepared for convening the Ninth National Congress of the Party . . . at an appropriate time." The plenum formally expelled Liu Shao-ch'i from the party and dismissed him from all posts "both inside and outside the party."

Finally, a draft of the CCP's new party constitution was circulated among those in attendance for discussion. It specifically named Lin Piao as Mao's successor.

During November and December the Chinese leadership quietly accelerated the decentralization of Chinese society in preparation for invasion while at the same time loudly trumpeting the economy's ability to satisfy all production targets. The effort was closely analogous in form to the decentralization of the Great Leap period, but, of course, it was undertaken at this time for entirely different reasons. Increasingly, references to terms such as "people's war" and "Yenan" found their way into the press descriptions of educational, economic, and political activities. Commune authority was established over rural schools. *People's Daily* of November 13 praised a Kansu middle school for pursuing an educational policy reminiscent of the "anti-Japanese military and political college in Yenan." Inner Mongolia provincial radio broadcasts spoke of "people's war" in the general context of the struggle to establish the revolutionary committee, but the use of such terms was meant to prepare the population for what could come.[64] Exaggerated production targets and output figures appeared in the press. In Hunan, the provincial press spoke of production brigades raising production goals as much as 25 percent, and in Heilungchiang output during the cultural revolution was said to have increased by several times over production during 1963–1965.[65]

The Chinese leadership pushed forward with preparations for the Ninth Party Congress. There were reports of provincial congresses of revolutionary committees coupled with insistent demands that the party be rebuilt, infused with new blood, and transformed into a militant vanguard of the proletariat. At the highest level, Peking reopened the Warsaw talks with the United States government, which presumably would serve as a communication channel in the event hostilities erupted between the Russians and Chinese.[66] Sporadic incidents continued to occur primarily in the Sinkiang and Manchurian border areas. Each side studiously ignored them in the press. On December 2, 1968 *Izvestia* did quote General Losik, newly appointed commander of the Soviet Far Eastern Military Region, as saying that "military maneuvers had taken place in the East of the Soviet Union." No further details were given. By year's end the situation along the border was filled with tension, but the

Chinese leaders were already well on the way to reestablishing defense positions weakened earlier. None too soon. In early March, 1969, the situation would erupt into armed conflict leading to the most severe crisis in the crisis-studded relationship between the two countries.

The Soviet Legacy

In the course of almost two decades, the Chinese People's Republic evolved from a decentralized, regionally focused state into a highly centralized, if still somewhat disordered, polity. The course of that evolution was marked and indeed continues to be marred by a major systemic flaw—the absence of an institutionalized leadership selection mechanism. A primary legacy of the historical relationship with the Soviet Union, this flaw is a major determinant of the continuous conflict that characterizes Chinese Communist politics. Without an institutionalized mechanism to determine who holds power, no limits are placed upon the quest for power. The cultural revolution itself was in this sense a logical, if not inevitable, escalation of that struggle. A secondary legacy was the creation of a leadership cadre with strong sympathies for the concept of world revolution as preached from Moscow. Indeed, as we shall see, the death of Mao and the return to power of Teng Hsiao-p'ing would result in the reinstatement of the vast majority of party leaders whom Mao had purged. Even though Mao had doubled the size of the Chinese Communist Party during the cultural revolution (to 38 million members), the party leadership would once again revert to those who came to power during the years of close ties with the Soviet Union. Mao's hope of cultivating a new generation of revolutionary successors would accompany him to the grave.

PART IV
The Evolution of U.S.-China Relations, 1969–1980

XIII
China in a Tri-Polar World, 1969–1973

The threat of armed conflict with the Soviet Union persuaded the Chinese leadership to bring the cultural revolution to a premature conclusion in order to bolster China's defenses. The year 1969 witnessed a major confrontation between China and the Soviet Union in which Soviet leaders went so far as to threaten China with nuclear bombardment. Propaganda statements to the contrary, the confrontation drove each power to seek better relations with the United States. The stakes were of the highest magnitude. For the Soviets, the split with China raised the possibility of an anti-Soviet coalition between the Chinese and the Americans that would adversely affect Soviet security not only in the Far East but throughout the world. The Chinese, on the other hand, needed to improve their strategic position and to develop alternative sources of developmental assistance from the non-Communist world. Internal instability, however, evidenced by the challenge of Lin Piao and the return to power of Teng Hsiao-p'ing, left the question of China's strategic orientation open for the time being (even though arrangements were being made to establish a working relationship with the United States over the problem of Vietnam).

The Soviet Union Probes China's Defenses

Ever since the Great Leap Forward, Soviet leaders have sought to resume close relations with the Chinese. Khrushchev employed various means toward this end but succeeded only in driving the Chinese and Russians further apart. His successors, Brezhnev and Kosygin, pursued the same policy objective much more forcefully. Before the cultural revolution, a pro-Soviet group existed within the Chinese leadership, which gave the Soviet Union a means of exerting considerable leverage upon the internal decision-making process.[1] Indeed, it was the Soviet call for "united action" over

Vietnam in 1965 that galvanized members of this group into action. They unsuccessfully strove for a resumption of close Sino-Soviet ties over the issue of aid to North Vietnam. One early result of the cultural revolution was the elimination of the pro-Soviet group from the Chinese leadership.

From 1966 onward, Soviet leaders perceived themselves unable to influence the Chinese decision-making process from within. In response they increased the Soviet presence along the Chinese border in an effort to intensify pressure on the Chinese leadership from without, and certain events during the cultural revolution made it possible for the Soviets to use this border tactic frequently and to advantage. It had become clear by mid-1968, if not earlier, that Mao had significantly weakened China's defenses by employing main force units in pursuit of internal political victory. Thus China was quite vulnerable to intensified Soviet military and political pressure. The ultimate Soviet objective was not war but the creation of enough pressure to force the Chinese to return to their earlier relationship with the Russians.

Throughout 1969 the Soviets applied pressure along each of the three main sectors of the Sino-Soviet border—Manchuria, Mongolia, and Sinkiang. The Manchurian sector was the first to reach a flash point: on 2 March a border incident occurred at Damansky (Chen Pao) Island in the Ussuri River. The river forms part of the border along the eastern edge of Manchuria, and the island is virtually equidistant from the two major Soviet cities of Vladivostok and Khabarovsk. The armed exchange resulted in an undisclosed number of Chinese dead and, according to varying reports, between thirty and forty Soviet soldiers killed.[2] Each side immediately denied responsibility for the incident and blamed the other side, but it was clear that the incident was a direct result of the prior Soviet buildup on the border.

A second, more violent incident occurred two weeks later in the same area, involving upwards of two to three thousand men on each side, tanks, and artillery. Clashes also occurred in the far western province of Sinkiang. The Chinese successfully matched the Soviet effort in both these cases. But Chinese leaders could not fail to see the analogy between their situation and that of Czechoslovakia, in which escalating border activity had preceded invasion—an analogy, in fact, to which Soviet leaders were soon to draw attention. During the crisis, the Canadian Communist party newspaper *Canadian Tribune* published an article by Wang Ming, a former member of the CCP Politburo and Central Committee who since 1957 had been living in the Soviet Union. The article, "China: Cultural Revolution or Counterrevolutionary Coup?" represented the situation in China as a struggle between "two lines"—the "Marxist-Leninist" and the "anti-Marxist Maoist."[3] Focusing on Mao's attempt to "smash the Chinese Communist Party," the article took much the same line of argument that the Soviets had employed earlier in the Czech case, leaving no doubt as to its implication and raising the possibility of a "Marxist-Leninist" alternative in China under Wang Ming. But although the border probes combined with related political activity like Wang Ming's article may have been designed to disrupt or otherwise influence the Chinese Communist Party's Ninth Party Congress, they failed.

The Ninth Party Congress convened secretly on 1 April 1969 and continued through 24 April. The congress was clearly staged to show internal unity in the face of external threat. No new internal policies were announced aside from the decision to continue to "consolidate" the gains made during the cultural revolution. The cultural revolution itself was seen to have been "absolutely necessary and most timely." Stress throughout was laid on the necessity of preparedness for war. In the only speech reported in the press, Lin Piao, Mao's newly designated successor, declared, "We must make full preparations against their [the Soviet Union and the United States] launching a big war and against their launching a war at an early date, preparations against their launching a conventional war and against their launching a large-scale war."[4]

Privately, Mao said he was determined not to allow China to be provoked into war against the Soviet Union. At the secret First Plenum following the congress on 28 April, he declared,

> When the other side strikes in at us, we will not strike back out at them. We will not invade others. I say we will not be provoked. We will not invade others, even if we are tempted to do so. But if they invade us, we must deal with them. Whether to strike a big or small blow is up to you. If you want to strike a small blow, border areas will do. If you want to fight big, I suggest room be made for such a battle. China is not a small land. The enemy will not get any advantages. I believe he will not be able to come in.[5]

Although the leadership that emerged from the congress was heavily studded with military men—a phenomenon that is usually interpreted to mean army dominance of the political scene—the presence of the military also suggested that the army was not only behind the party but also able to defend the nation.

In June 1969, when the World Congress of Communist Parties met, an intensification of Soviet military pressure along the Mongolian sector of the Sino-Soviet border became apparent. Although the Russians had hoped to mobilize Communist support at the World Congress for their position in the conflict with the Chinese, they encountered stubborn opposition from Romanian and Yugoslav leaders.[6] Instead of publicly rebuffing the Chinese, the congress specifically rejected any proposals to expel Peking from the world Communist movement. Still, rumors about an extension of the Brezhnev Doctrine to China were rampant, particularly after Brezhnev virulently attacked the Chinese in his speech to the assembled body and set forth the concept of Asian collective security.[7]

Immediately following the congress, Tsedenbal, party leader of the Mongolian People's Republic, a Soviet satellite, declared that "our party will continue to wage a resolute struggle against the subversive and splitting activities of Mao Tse-tung's group in China, which . . . [has] broken with the principles of Marxism-Leninism."[8] The implication of Tsedenbal's statement was that Inner Mongolia, bordering on Outer Mongolia, would become a pressure point. A news leak of an increase in Soviet troop strength in Outer Mongolia, the emplacement of additional missiles, and the assignment of a new Soviet commander with expertise in rocketry further heightened this impression.

Sinkiang, China's westernmost province bordering on the Soviet Union, became a focal point during August, and armed clashes occurred frequently. On 19 August, the Chinese issued an official protest charging the Soviet Union with the responsibility for as many as 429 border incidents in the previous two months.[9] Chinese protests were now accompanied by visible signs of defense preparations. Officials moved to relocate industry, accelerate excavation projects for air defense, mobilize the militia, and hold meetings throughout China to prepare the population for the worst. On the Soviet side of the frontier the deployment pattern was equally obvious. Great stocks of military materiel—rockets, artillery, transport equipment, fuel, and food— were moved into place. Soviet troops were in evidence all along the border, including the Mongolian sector. Both sides were openly preparing for combat.

The death of Ho Chi-minh on 3 September provided an opportunity for contact between Soviet and Chinese leaders. Premier Kosygin, on his return from Ho's funeral, stopped off in Peking to hold discussions with Premier Chou En-lai on 11 September. The usual communique noted that they had held a "frank conversation," but the talks were inconclusive. On 16 September an article by Victor Louis, unofficial Soviet channel to the West, appeared in the *London Evening News,* entitled "Will Russian Rockets Czechmate China?" The article moved the 1969 crisis to its highest point, clearly indicating that the Soviets were prepared to take aggressive action against China as they had against Czechoslovakia. Louis made three points: First, there was no reason why the Brezhnev Doctrine should not be applied to China; second, Soviet rockets stood aimed and ready to destroy China's nuclear center at Lop Nor, Sinkiang; and third, clandestine radio broadcasts indicated a "degree of unification of anti-Mao forces" that "could produce a leader who would ask other Socialist countries for fraternal help."

The twin threats of Soviet military intervention and nuclear bombardment brought the Chinese to the bargaining table. On 7 October the Chinese issued an official statement declaring that they were entering negotiations out of fear that "a handful of war maniacs" in the Kremlin would "dare to raid" China's nuclear installations: "There is no reason whatsoever for China and the Soviet Union to fight a war over the boundary question."[10] "Negotiations" began in Peking on 20 October, but soon stalled. Although the two parties reached no settlement of the border issue, the Soviets gradually moderated their extremely aggressive public posture of the previous six months, and tension seemed to ease somewhat along the border. For now the external crisis had passed.

The Continuing Struggle in Peking: The Challenge of Lin Piao

Mao had transformed the nature of Chinese politics during the cultural revolution in more ways than the obvious. In particular, the shift to the revolutionary committee form was a very significant move, but one that would not become apparent until the turmoil of the cultural revolution had largely subsided. Adoption in early 1967 of the "three-in-one alliance" concept for the revolutionary committee (revolutionary masses, the military, and the old party cadre) was tacit admission that Mao had failed to achieve his initial objective of eliminating the power bases of Liu Shao-ch'i and Teng Hsiao-p'ing and had therefore failed to gain control of the provincial power apparatus. In the original formulation (see Chapter XI) Mao had sought to lodge power solely in the hands of the revolutionary masses, stripping power from the entrenched old party and military bureaucracies; the decision to employ selected old party cadres and the military in the new apparatus implied that the bases of their strength had been preserved and that, given the proper combination of circumstances, they could return to positions of power.

In short, to maintain some degree of cohesion in China, Mao had been forced to broaden the scope of political participation. Henceforth, the dynamics of Chinese politics would center around the effort to manipulate the composition of the revolutionary committees and provincial party committees, especially the standing committees of these bodies. From 1969 until his death in September 1976, generally speaking, the revolutionary masses constituted a base of support for Mao Tse-tung, just as the military and the cadres did for Lin Piao and Teng Hsiao-p'ing, respectively. (There were obviously crossovers in each category, cadres who supported Mao or Lin, military men who supported Mao or Teng, and rebels who supported Lin and Teng.) The first clear manifestation of the new political dynamics occurred in the context of Lin Piao's challenge to Mao Tse-tung.

Mao Tse-tung had skillfully employed the Soviet threat to his advantage, but the threat came back to haunt him. Initially it had facilitated a reduction in the numbers and influence of military officers on the standing committees of the revolutionary committees. When the Soviet threat moved from a potential to an actual one as military clashes on the Sino-Soviet border increased in frequency in early 1969, it was Lin Piao who turned the threat to political advantage at the Ninth Party Congress. The congress was managed exclusively from the top, with delegates selected by so-called democratic consultation rather than by any sort of balloting process. Lin Piao parlayed the national defense issue into his formal designation as successor to Mao Tse-tung, as well as into a formidable body of support in the Politburo.

Mao Tse-tung emerged from the congress with a clear majority in the five-man Politburo Standing Committee, the highest decision-making body. On it were Mao, Chou En-lai, K'ang Sheng, Ch'en Po-ta and Lin Piao; there appeared to be a four-to-one voting edge for Mao over Lin. The Politburo itself was another matter. It would seem that Mao's supporters were a minority of the Politburo's twenty-one members. The ten in Mao's voting bloc were Mao, Chou, K'ang, Ch'en, Chiang Ch'ing, Chang Ch'un-ch'iao, Yao Wen-yuan, Hsieh Fu-chih, Li Hsien-nien, and Ch'en Hsi-lien. In Lin's group were Lin, Huang Yung-sheng, Wu Fa-hsien, Ch'iu Hui-tso, Yeh Ch'un, Li Tso-p'eng, Liu Po-ch'eng, Tung Pi-wu, Yeh Chien-ying, Chu Teh, and Hsü Shih-yü.

Mao's minority position within the Politburo may well explain why he did not press for the establishment of provincial party committees after the Ninth Party Congress. Another obvious reason for delay was the continuing Soviet threat, which intensified over the course of 1969. The failure to begin the re-construction of the party apparatus for well over a year and a half after the congress, however, suggests that the Politburo balance was changing to Mao's further disadvantage. Although the immediate crisis with the Soviets was re-solved in October with the decision to resume border talks, the larger issue of how to deal with the Russians evidently persuaded some in the leadership to support Lin Piao. Such support could only have meant a willingness to agree to greater military representation on the provincial party committees than Mao could accept. So he blocked action on the basis of his command of the Politburo Standing Committee.

The Second Plenum of the Chinese Communist Party

By the late summer of 1970, Lin Piao had strengthened his position sufficiently to take the initiative against Mao Tse-tung. At the Second Plenum (23 August–6 September) Lin Piao proposed that the position of state chair-man be re-established (it had been abolished following the purge of Liu Shao-ch'i) and that Lin himself become chairman.[11] Although Mao's position was weakened by the defection of Ch'en Po-ta, who supported Lin's proposal, Mao still had sufficient voting strength in the Standing Committee (three out of five) and possibly in the Politburo (nine out of twenty-one) to block this move.[12] Lacking the votes to reinstall himself as chairman, which he had been up to 1958, Mao managed to gain a standoff with Lin; the chairmanship of the state would not be re-established.

There may have been other grounds for this step. As Liu Shao-ch'i had not been removed legally from the chairmanship, re-establishment of the position would have required formal action by the National People's Congress before anyone else, including Mao, could assume it. Mao would probably have had to rely increasingly heavily on the old party cadres as the conflict with Lin Piao deepened; re-establishing the state chairmanship was an unnecessarily risky course of action to pursue at this stage. It was possible that one of Mao's opponents would gain that post.

In a related move, Lin promoted the theoretical concept of Mao Tse-tung's "genius" in an attempt to set Mao above and apart from the state and party apparatuses. Mao fully appreciated the significance of this action, as he had himself employed the concept to justify taking action outside the existing institutional framework by means of *ad hoc* political bodies. The revolutionary masses, cultural revolution groups, and the like were but the latest examples of Mao's use of this tactical device. The issue here, however, was control over the party apparatus that was about to be re-established, and Mao avoided the pitfalls of the "genius" tactic by countering with the view that "a genius cannot succeed by himself . . . a genius must rely on the Party."[13]

The draft constitution produced by the plenum contained several points that would, on paper at least, preserve Mao's position both at the center and in the provincial revolutionary committees. Mao's supreme position was formally emphasized in Article 2. "Chairman Mao is the great leader of the people . . . the head of the proletariat of our country, the supreme commander of all armed forces of the whole nation." Lin Piao's new status was also formally inserted in the draft. Vice-Chairman Lin was "Chairman Mao's close comrade-in-arms and successor, the deputy commander of all armed forces of the whole nation."[14]

The plenum also resolved in Mao's favor the crucial issue of control of the delegate selection process for the Fourth National People's Congress (to be held at an as yet undisclosed date). Article 3 stipulated that deputies would be selected by means of "democratic consultations and elections," which meant that control of the selection process would remain at the center, presumably in Mao's hands. Article 11 contained a provision that precluded packing the revolutionary committees to Mao's disadvantage: Not only were the revolutionary committees to apply the three-in-one combination to representation among the Red Guards, cadres, and the military, but the same rule was to be applied to the young, the middle-aged, and the old. If literally applied, these two rules would guarantee, at a minimum, one-third representation for the revolutionary masses—and, of course, for Mao Tse-tung. Finally, through state protection of the continued use of the tactics of "great blooming, great contending, big-character posters, and great debate" (Article 13), Mao's influence on the revolutionary committee structure could be maintained.[15] It would be precisely in these areas, together with a few others, that the final constitutional draft of 1975 would be altered most when the Fourth National People's Congress convened.

Of more immediate significance was the plenum's decision to proceed with the re-establishment of the provincial party structure, which had lain in a shambles since 1967. Fully realizing that Lin Piao was in a position to extend his influence in the provinces, Mao attempted to counter by strengthening his position at the center. According to his own account, he adopted three measures: "One was to cast stones, one to blend with sand, and one to dig up the cornerstone."[16] Casting stones was a reference to the purge of Ch'en Po-ta, which Mao accomplished through his majority in the Standing Committee of the Politburo. Blending with sand was Mao's attempt to add several of his supporters to the Military Affairs Committee, diluting Lin's influence in that body. Digging up the cornerstone meant reorganizing the Peking Military Region; Mao achieved this reorganization by the end of the year by removing Li Hsueh-feng, Hopei provincial head, and Cheng Wei-shan, Peking military area commander.

Mao's success in his three measures failed to offset the growth of Lin Piao's strength in the newly forming provincial party committees. Of the eight committees in existence by the end of January 1971, four were led by Mao's supporters. But these numbers were misleading.[17] Of the more than ninety Standing Committee members on the eight committees,[18] twenty were military men, ten were party cadres, and only four were representatives of the revolutionary masses—and three of the four were on the Shanghai committee.[19] The other stood alone on the Anhwei party committee. Clearly, Mao's interests were not being served—even though several of his supporters occupied important positions, they were isolated.

A few days later, on 31 January, Mao put out the call for staffing the provincial party committees according to the rules for the revolutionary committees—equal representation among the old, the middle-aged, and the young—indicating clearly that the first eight committees had not been so staffed. His call went unheeded. Between the end of January and 20 March, seven additional party committees were established, with the same results as in the first eight. Of a total of one hundred additional Standing Committee members, twenty-one were military, thirteen were old party cadres, and only two were representatives of the revolutionary masses (one each in the Kirin and Shensi party committees).[20]

With fifteen party committees now established and Lin Piao in a strong position, Mao Tse-tung was forced to make a major decision. The alternatives were grim. Even if he could gain control of the remaining fourteen party committees, an unlikely prospect, Mao would still be in a minority position. On the other hand, Mao faced the probability that Lin would rise to supreme power on the basis of enduring military control if he was able to strengthen his position further in the provinces, where party committees had yet to be formed. Mao desperately needed additional support, especially from the old party cadres, to counterbalance Lin's growing strength, and in his extremity Mao issued a bid to obtain the support of Teng Hsiao-p'ing!

Mao had anticipated this eventuality. In early 1967, when forced to broaden the scope of political participation by including both the military and the old party cadres along with the revolutionary masses in the three-in-one alliances, Mao began to de-emphasize direct criticism of Teng, focusing instead solely on Liu Shao-ch'i. By the end of 1967 references in the central media to the "Liu-Teng group" had virtually disappeared in favor of the phrase "Liu Shao-ch'i's clique." Indeed, the last official criticism of Teng occurred on November 23, 1967, in the party journal *Hung Ch'i.*

The first subtle indication that Mao was seeking Teng's support came in late February when an article appeared in the central media explaining the correct application of the "Ta Chai" principle and noting that it was "not necessary to level rich and poor."[21] Thus, when Mao announced a major change in agricultural policy on March 21, there could be no mistaking its significance. The essence of the policy change was the restoration of private incentive to the peasantry, a sharp reversal of the earlier application of the "Ta Chai system" of compensation in proportion to political loyalty. Private plots, which Mao had consistently opposed since the Great Leap Forward, would once again be encouraged, as would private breeding of poultry and pigs. The term "Ta Chai" would continue to be used, but now it would have entirely new content. In effect, Mao moved to reintroduce the economic practices advocated by none other than Liu Shao-ch'i and Teng Hsiao-p'ing, a concession that clearly signaled Mao's interest in re-establishing political relations with the latter (Liu Shao-ch'i having died in the meantime). To underscore his sincerity, Mao proceeded to rehabilitate one of Teng's protégés, Chao Tzu-yang, of Kwangtung province, who had been purged during the cultural revolution as a "capitalist roader." In May Chao was appointed a secretary to the Inner Mongolian provincial party committee.[22]

The "Lin Piao Incident"

Once Mao had opened the door to Teng Hsiao-p'ing, he initiated action against Lin Piao. In early April at a Central Committee "briefing meeting" attended by ninety-nine responsible persons from central, local, and military units, Chou En-lai made public the purges of Ch'en Po-ta, Li Hsueh-feng, and Cheng Wei-shan and "handed down" written criticisms of five of Lin Piao's key supporters.[23] All members of the Politburo, they were Yeh Ch'un, Lin's wife and office manager; Huang Yung-sheng, chief of the general staff; Wu Fa-hsien, commander in chief of the Air Force; Ch'iu Hui-tso, director of the Rear Services Department; and Li Tso-p'eng, First Political Commissar of the Navy. Each of these leaders would suddenly and mysteriously vanish along with Lin Piao himself in the September "Lin Piao incident."

The April meeting also saw the making of an important foreign policy decision. It was decided to acknowledge publicly the improving relationship with the United States—a step vehemently opposed by Lin Piao, who urged the continued use of the formula that placed China in opposition to both superpowers. The issue was not whether to establish a relationship with the United States. That had already been accomplished in 1969 (see next section). Rather the question was, Should it be revealed? Lin's opposition was understandable enough. Public acknowledgment of the American connection would serve to undercut the basis of Lin's political hold on the party committees: There would be less urgency over the Soviet threat and therefore less need for military domination of the political apparatus. Under the changed circumstances Mao could hope to re-establish party control over the military.

The upshot of the matter was the extension of an invitation to the U.S. table tennis team, then on tour in Japan, to visit the People's Republic of China. The team's visit was followed in mid-July by the stunning announcement that President Nixon's chief national security advisor, Henry Kissinger, had surreptitiously flown to Peking and met with Chou En-lai and that the American President himself would travel to China for a formal state visit early the following year!

Certainly at this point, if not earlier, Lin Piao must have realized that Mao was mobilizing forces against him. Yet he had grounds for optimism. From the April meeting until August 19, when the last of the provincial party committees was established, Lin's position continued to improve. The growth of his strength was unchecked and seemingly uncheckable, despite all that Mao and his supporters could do. For example, after the April meeting, for the first time since the onset of the cultural revolution (and possibly before), Chou En-lai began to send cadres of the central state apparatus into the provinces to assume leading positions in an effort to give added weight to the civilian bureaucracy against the military—to no avail. Furthermore, in those party committees established after the April meeting, only one, Tibet, included a single representative of the revolutionary masses.[24] By mid-August, in other words, Lin Piao's men, despite a significant increase in cadre representation, thoroughly dominated the standing committees of the entire provincial party apparatus. Of the 405 total standing committee members of all twenty-nine party committees, 94 were military men, 56 were old party cadres, and only 7 were members of the revolutionary masses.[25]

The establishment of all the provincial party committees by late August set the stage for the final act in the contest between Mao Tse-tung and Lin Piao for control of the central power structure. On the night of September 12-13, 1971, nine people were aboard a British-made Trident jet (one of three then owned by the Chinese) that departed from Peking and headed northward toward the Soviet Union. The plane crashed at Altan Bulak, a missile base in Outer Mongolia some three hundred miles due north of Ulan Bator on the Soviet–Outer Mongolia border. Neither the Chinese, the Soviet, nor the Outer Mongolian press made any mention of the plane crash until the Soviet news agency Tass reported it eighteen days after the event.

Virtually the entire top Chinese leadership went into seclusion for several weeks, suggesting that a major political crisis was under way. A week before China's national day, October 1, it was officially announced that the traditional military parade would not be held, although local celebrations would be permitted as in previous years. In the past, the leaders had always observed the parade from atop T'ien An Men (Gate of Heavenly Peace). Cancellation of the event added fuel to the speculation that all was not well and that, for one reason or another, the leadership could not appear together. The initial surmise was that Mao was either seriously ill or dead, but he soon reappeared in public, meeting with Emperor Haile Selassie of Ethiopia on October 8. Chou En-lai also continued to appear in public, but Lin Piao and the top military brass were conspicuously absent. Moreover, others began to undertake duties normally performed by Lin and the other missing generals—Wu Fa-hsien, Huang Yung-sheng, Ch'iu Hui-tso, and Li Tso-p'eng. For example, Marshal Yeh Chien-ying, vice-chairman of the party's Military Commission, was much in evidence. In November, at a ceremony celebrating the founding of the Albanian Communist party, he was listed fourth behind Mao, Chou, and Chiang Ch'ing, Mao's wife; Lin's name was omitted.

By mid-October, persistent reports were filtering out from the mainland that Lin Piao and the others "were finished" because they had plotted unsuccessfully against Chairman Mao.[26] Rumors were rife that Lin and his supporters had failed in an attempt to assassinate Mao and had sought to flee China aboard the plane that crashed in Outer Mongolia. It was the Soviets, however, who definitely linked Lin and the plane. In a news release on January 1, 1972, Soviet medical experts stated that they were "reasonably certain" that two of the nine bodies aboard the crashed jet were those of Lin Piao and his wife, Yeh Ch'un.[27] They also noted that all nine of the bodies aboard the aircraft were "bullet-riddled," implying that all had perished before the crash. What had happened? Had there been an argument in flight among the passengers? Or had they been placed aboard the aircraft dead? Even more mystifying was the unconfirmed report that not one but two aircraft penetrated Outer Mongolian airspace on the night of September 12–13 and that one had returned to China. Whatever the facts, there was sufficient ambiguity about the events to cause serious misgivings regarding the obvious deductions.

In late July 1972 the Chinese officially acknowledged Lin's death in the September plane crash; Mao Tse-tung himself informed visiting statesmen of Lin's fate.[28] According to the report, Lin had opposed Mao on two crucial issues, restoration of civil leadership over the military, which was the issue of control of the provincial party apparatus, and the move to normalize relations with the United States. With the party leadership against him, so the official version went, Lin plotted to assassinate Mao and to establish a military dictatorship. Failing in his endeavor, Lin sought to flee to the Soviet Union, where he hoped to secure refuge with tape recordings of conversations between President Nixon's national security advisor, Henry Kissinger, and top Chinese officials.[29]

The official version of Lin Piao's demise was altogether too pat and fitted Mao's political needs too neatly to be accepted entirely. It justified the purges that followed and that allowed Mao to regain a secure position. There is little question that Lin Piao lost out in a struggle with Mao and that he perished, but there was no reason for Lin to attempt a *coup d'état* against Mao, unless in self-defense. Lin had already won control of the provincial party apparatus, had a majority in the Politburo, and was Mao's officially designated successor. Rather, the evidence suggests that the situation was reversed. It was Mao who needed to eliminate Lin in the only way left open to him after having failed to best Lin in the game of organizational politics. Mao himself later periodized the final stage of the struggle against Lin Piao in his "A Summary of Chairman Mao's Talks with Responsible Comrades of Various Places during His Inspection Tour (Mid-August–September 12, 1971)."[30] Mao's "inspection tour" was undoubtedly a last-ditch effort to marshal support for the decision to purge Lin and his supporters. The grounding of all aircraft and the cancellation of all military leave immediately prior to the purge insured that Lin and his supporters would be isolated and enabled Mao to remove them from power without undue interference.

The immediate results of the "Lin Piao incident" were extremely beneficial to Mao Tse-tung, particularly within the central power structure. Lin's demise left Mao apparently in complete command of the Politburo Standing Committee and the Politburo itself. Although Yeh Chien-ying was shortly promoted to membership in the Politburo Standing Committee, Mao, Chou, and K'ang Sheng had a majority vote. The situation in the Politburo was even better. Lin had held a twelve-to-nine majority before the "incident"; now, with his removal and that of his five supporters and Ch'en Po-ta, Mao's minority position was transformed into a commanding nine-to-five majority.[31] On Mao's side were the same nine men who had made up his group at the Ninth Party Congress, except for Ch'en Po-ta; only Tung Pi-wu, Liu Po-ch'eng, Chu Teh, Yeh Chien-ying, and Hsü Shih-yü remained in opposition. The story in the central military apparatus was equally dramatic. Of the thirty-two officers purged, twenty-five had clear ties to Lin Piao.[32]

The "Summary of Chairman Mao's Talks with Responsible Comrades" was issued as a Central Committee document on March 17, 1972, in the wake of the Lin Piao purge and constituted yet another signal to Teng Hsiao-p'ing. As a Central Committee document the summary reflected the sentiments of the party leadership as well as Mao personally and made Teng's acceptability clearly apparent. Referring to the party's "ten major line struggles," the document mentioned the names of all of Mao's major opponents since the establishment of the Chinese Communist Party in 1921 except Teng; only an indirect reference was made to Teng in the phrase "Liu Shao-ch'i and company." In the conclusion of the summary yet another gesture was made: "The Great Cultural Revolution dragged out Liu Shao-ch'i, P'eng, Lo, Lu, and Yang, which was a great achievement. But there were losses. Some good cadres have not yet been rehabilitated. . . . It is the tradition of our party that when a person makes a mistake, he must conduct self-criticism and be criticized; mistakes are allowed to be corrected."[33]

The obvious question was this: With Lin Piao gone, why did Mao still need Teng Hsiao-p'ing? True, Mao had succeeded in purging Lin and regaining a majority in the Politburo as well as removing many of Lin's men from the central military apparatus. He had not yet, however, been able to regain command of the provincial party structure. For this task Teng's support remained vital. Mao would probably succeed in removing many if not most of the military from the party apparatus on the grounds of association with Lin Piao's allegedly traitorous behavior. But it would be impossible to administer the provincial apparatus effectively without the cadres; the revolutionary masses were still incapable of performing this function by themselves, if indeed they ever would be given the opportunity.

In the eighteen months following the "Lin Piao incident" major changes occurred in the composition of the provincial party committees. A marked increase in the number of party cadres took place, combined with a reduction in the weight of the military in the committees. In August 1971 military men occupied the first secretaryships in twenty-one of the twenty-nine provincial party committees. The ratio was similar for the positions of secretary and deputy secretary. By the early spring of 1973, military men held first secretaryships in only thirteen provincial parties, while cadre representation had increased from eight to twelve; four first secretaryships were undetermined. An increase in cadre representation also occurred at the secretary and deputy-secretary levels.[34] Mao simultaneously proceeded to undermine Lin's residual influence by appointing members of the Second and Third Field armies in place of members of the Fourth Field Army, Lin's old command. The net effect of the changes was to reduce the influence of the military as a homogeneous bloc in the provincial party apparatus, in particular virtually eliminating that of the Fourth Field Army.

To reduce the role of the military in the party Mao was forced to increase the strength of the cadres. This change brought closer the day when the cadres as a group would seek if not demand representation in the highest decision-making councils. In other words, by the early spring of 1973, the conditions had been created for Teng Hsiao-p'ing's return to power. What was required was the opportunity. It came about as a result of the apparent failure of Mao Tse-tung's policy of cooperation with the United States in Southeast Asia.

Peking, Washington, and Moscow

The Chinese relationship with the United States centered on a coincidence of interests both at the strategic level—the need to counterbalance the growth in Soviet power and assertiveness—and at the regional level—the desire to achieve a mutually beneficial settlement of the conflict in Southeast Asia. The *quid pro quo* that evolved in 1969 thus included subtle Chinese assistance in establishing a military balance in Southeast Asia, which facilitated the satisfactory withdrawal of U.S. ground forces, and U.S. support of the People's Republic against the increasingly ominous threat emanating from the Soviet Union. Until the spring of 1971, the outline of the new relationship could be perceived only dimly. At the public level, Peking showed its willingness to establish contact with the new Nixon administration by expressing a desire to reopen the Warsaw talks,[35] and the United States moved unilaterally to relax restrictions on trade with and travel to China. Such steps revealed little of the deeper elements that, by the spring of 1971, would produce Henry Kissinger's visit and the announcement that President Nixon would come to Peking.

As President Nixon saw it, the initial crucial step taken on the Chinese side was the decision to reduce the volume of Soviet war materiel traversing the Chinese railroad network to North Vietnam. In 1966 the Soviets and the Chinese were sending roughly equal amounts of materiel to Vietnam. Beginning in early 1969 the Chinese reduced their share by 60 percent; they were then supplying only one-fourth as much as the Russians.[36] The drawdown of the supply effort across the Chinese railroad system substantially reduced the level of combat activity North Vietnam could generate. Easing the withdrawal of U.S. forces not only made less onerous for Washington the task of establishing a military balance in Southeast Asia; it reduced the potential of a two-front conflict for China. As U.S. troops withdrew from Vietnam, Peking in turn redeployed forces positioned in south China northward to strengthen its defenses against the Soviet Union.

Once the China link had been established, the President proceeded to interdict the remaining routes of access to Vietnam: Sihanoukville, Cambodia, and the Haiphong port complex. The opportunity for the first came with the deposition of Sihanouk on March 18, 1970. Lon Nol, upon taking power, immediately closed the port of Sihanoukville, provoking a North Vietnamese military operation designed to overthrow his regime and reopen the port. The combined U.S.-South Vietnamese drive into the border sanctuaries in early May blocked the North Vietnamese offensive and kept Sihanoukville closed. Closure of the port severely crippled the Soviet Union's supply effort to North Vietnam, for well over one thousand tons of supplies per month were being shipped to the North Vietnamese via Sihanoukville.[37] From mid-1970 onward, with the sharp reduction of supplies along the Chinese rail system and the closure of Sihanoukville, only the Haiphong port complex remained open to Soviet use, and it, too, would be closed during the Easter offensive of 1972.

The Laotian crisis of early 1971 further revealed the extent—and the limits—of the Sino-American rapprochement. The focus of both countries' efforts was re-establishment of the fragmented structure of Indochina as created by the Geneva Conference of 1954. That objective required a military balance that involved neither victory nor defeat for North Vietnam and survival for South Vietnam. Thus, in the Laotian operation (Lam Son 719) in February, when South Vietnamese forces experienced initial successes in battle, the Chinese moved quickly to bolster North Vietnam with substantial military assistance for the first time since 1969, sending a high-level military delegation to Hanoi to secure the agreement. Having ensured that the essential structural balance would be maintained, the Chinese backed off. They neither followed up the North Vietnamese counterattack, which routed the forces of Saigon, nor threatened direct intervention.

At the height of the crisis of operation Lam Son 719, on 25 February 1971, the President in his state of the world message referred to China as the People's Republic for the first time and called for a new dialogue between the two countries. The Chinese responded by inviting the U.S. table tennis team to China in April and in an interview with Edgar Snow, Mao Tse-tung indirectly extended an invitation to President Nixon himself. Finally, the announcements of 15 July that Kissinger had secretly visited China and that the President would do so early the following year overshadowed the events in Laos.

Soviet leaders were acutely conscious of U.S. success in interdicting the logistics routes to North Vietnam. In addition, the decision to carry out the buildup of troop levels along the Chinese border strained the capacity of the Trans-Siberian Railway and required increased reliance on the long and exposed sea route from the Black Sea port of Odessa through the Dardanelles, the Suez Canal, and Bab El Mandeb, across the Indian Ocean, and through the Malacca Straits before reaching the ports of Sihanoukville and Haiphong. The closure of the Suez Canal during the 1967 Arab-Israeli war was a severe blow to Soviet efforts to maintain North Vietnamese fighting capabilities. It forced the rerouting of Soviet transport ships around Africa, transforming a seven-thousand-mile journey between Odessa and Haiphong into a fifteen-thousand-mile one. When first the Chinese and then the Cambodian routes were squeezed off, the Russians, sometime in the summer of 1970, decided to change their China strategy in response to that of the United States.

The Soviet leadership formally adopted a counterstrategy at the Twenty-fourth Party Congress in March 1971. Publicly stressing the détente theme, the Soviets moved to strengthen their position in each of the five regions on the Eurasian land mass in which Soviet and U.S. power compete: East Asia, Southeast Asia, South Asia, the Middle East, and Europe. Their objective was to reduce tension on the Western or European front so as to permit action in each of the other areas. Movement toward a settlement of the Berlin question was the means chosen to reduce tension in Europe. In the Middle East, the death of Nasser the previous September complicated the Soviet position, but strenuous efforts were made to legitimize by treaty the Soviet position in Egypt, as well as to strengthen it in Syria, Iraq, and Somalia. In East Asia, the Soviets made concerted efforts to wean Japan away from an improved relationship with the People's Republic of China (PRC). Although Japanese-Soviet discussions had been going on for some time, new impetus was given to consideration of a final peace treaty and other issues that had blocked progress, such as the northern islands question and various joint projects for exploitation of natural resources in Siberia and increased trade.

South and Southeast Asia constituted the double main thrust of Soviet geopolitical activity in the months following the Twenty-fourth Party Congress. In retrospect it is clear that the South Asian situation presented an opportunity for both the Soviet Union and India to restructure the regional balance to their mutual advantage and to the disadvantage of Pakistan, the PRC, and the United States.[38] By the spring of 1971, in part due to the previous extension of a $1 billion, five-year economic aid program from the Soviet Union and in part due to the internal crises then rocking Pakistan, India had established clear military superiority over Pakistan.

The re-establishment by Pakistani troops of control of the main population centers in East Pakistan by May did not seriously redress that imbalance, but Indian leaders may have feared that the opportunity to move against their neighbor was beginning to slip away. Further, the dramatic change in United States–PRC relations, revealed in mid-July, had to be interpreted by India as also involving Pakistan, with which both powers had a security relationship (even though the United States had not been generous with military aid to Pakistan since the embargo of 1965 and PRC aid was comparatively meager). In any case, Indira Gandhi moved to conclude the treaty for which Moscow had been pressing since 1969 and with renewed vigor following the Twenty-fourth Party Congress.

The 9 August 1971 treaty established the essential conditions that permitted India to attack and dismember Pakistan. The strategic role of the Soviet Union in the conflict was to check action by the PRC and the United States. In the United Nations the Russians vetoed two resolutions sponsored by the United States, thus blocking action in the Security Council until after India had achieved its main objective. In strategic-military terms the Soviets threatened Peking with military action if the PRC should enter on Pakistan's side against India and deployed some thirty-five ships in the Bay of Bengal in an effort to neutralize the United States. India emerged from the conflict the unrivaled power on the Asian subcontinent, surrounded by weak states. The Soviet Union, too, moved a step closer to its larger objective of effectively encircling China. The partition of Pakistan removed a pro-Chinese buffer state and replaced it with a pro-Indian and pro-Soviet one, Bangladesh.

Perhaps the most crucial decision made in Moscow at this time was to conclude the current round of struggle in Southeast Asia and prepare the best possible bargaining position for North Vietnam. Realizing that a North Vietnamese victory was impossible because of Sino-American cooperation, Soviet leaders stepped up the flow of arms supplies to Vietnam via the remaining Haiphong route for a final, full-scale assault on the south. The North Vietnamese offensive, which began in late March 1972, after President Nixon returned from Peking but before he departed for the Moscow summit, was designed to achieve the best possible bargaining position for Hanoi. U.S. leaders who had observed the increased supply effort following the Twenty-fourth Party Congress anticipated the offensive, but its ferocity and scale took them by surprise. In addition to hastening to ship in tanks and anti-tank weaponry to counter the initial shock of North Vietnamese tank tactics, President Nixon ordered the mining of the Haiphong harbor complex—an act aimed directly at the Soviet Union and the impending summit.

Most important, in terms of the President's strategy of interdicting the logistics routes to North Vietnam, the offensive provided the opportunity to close off the remaining route of access to Hanoi. Thereafter, the only materiel received by the North Vietnamese was the sharply reduced flow of supplies still trickling overland from China, an amount insufficient to permit continuation of the offensive. The offensive failed, and the cutoff of supplies combined with the intensive bombing in December finally persuaded the North Vietnamese to sign the Paris Peace Accords the following January (1973).

For Peking the accords appeared to represent the achievement of its long-term objective of fragmenting the region to prevent the emergence of a major threat in the south. While North Vietnam retained *de facto* control over Laos, a weak buffer state, Cambodia and South Vietnam would continue to occupy a containing position. The United States, too, appeared to have accomplished a major strategic victory by successfully extricating itself from what only a few short years before had been a hopeless, open-ended involvement. At the same time, Washington preserved for itself a seemingly defensible position on the Southeast Asian mainland. Sino-American cooperation had dealt the

Soviet Union and its ally North Vietnam a stunning defeat—or so it appeared.

The peace accords were never put into effect. It quickly became apparent that neither Moscow nor Hanoi had the slightest intention of honoring the provisions of the agreement, as they immediately, flagrantly, and grossly violated restrictions on the buildup of troops and equipment levels in the South. It also became clear that, contrary to its repeated pledges of support, the United States would neither extend war materiel to South Vietnam at a level sufficient to counterbalance the North Vietnamese effort nor in any other substantive way attempt to deter Hanoi from completing an outright military conquest of South Vietnam.

Whether the American decision—and there is little question that the United States deliberately cut off support to the government of South Vietnam—was taken in response to the growing domestic "Watergate crisis" that soon engulfed the administration, or whether it was the planned second stage of some larger strategy to withdraw U.S. power entirely from the Southeast Asian mainland, the effect on the Chinese political scene was immediate.

The Maoist leadership had not expected the sudden turnabout in what had been a brilliantly executed American policy—in which the Chinese had played a key role. When informed of the change, probably by Henry Kissinger himself during his trip to Peking in mid-February 1973, the Chinese were thrown immediately into a serious and prolonged policy crisis.[39] If in the evolution of the Sino-American relationship cooperation in establishing a military balance in Southeast Asia had been an integral part of Chinese strategy, then the failure of the United States to maintain that balance had to raise questions about the validity of Mao's strategic course. In fact, the intensive effort by Chinese leaders from the spring of 1973 to justify Mao's policies suggested that they were coming increasingly under fire both from within Mao's group and from those currently out of power.[40] Indeed, beginning in the spring of 1973 and continuing for the next three and a half years, those who opposed the Maoist strategy, led by Teng Hsiao-p'ing, increasingly voiced their opposition. It appeared that they would succeed in reversing the course charted by Mao Tse-tung of improving relations with the United States.

XIV
The End of the Maoist Era, 1973–1976

The period from the spring of 1973 through Mao's death in the fall of 1976 was one of geostrategic uncertainty compounded by a sharp internal power struggle. The failure of the United States to maintain the Paris Peace Accords over Indochina produced a major and prolonged policy crisis in Peking, precipitating the return to power of Teng Hsiao-p'ing, the staunchest remaining opponent of Mao Tse-tung. Teng's return led to an intense policy reappraisal regarding (1) China's developing relationship with the United States, (2) Indochina, where long-term objectives were on the verge of failing, and (3) the Soviet Union, which had re-entered the Chinese political picture with an offer to normalize relations once again. On the internal scene, Mao Tse-tung, in his final year, sought to predetermine the outcome of the inevitable, already apparent succession struggle by selecting his successor, Hua Kuo-feng, and by purging Teng Hsiao-p'ing a second time.

The Return to Power of Teng Hsiao-p'ing
and Moscow's Offer

The crisis in the Chinese leadership surfaced in the spring of 1973. Mao Tse-tung's strategy of employing the United States to counterbalance Soviet pressure as well as to help re-establish a dominant Chinese position in Southeast Asia appeared to be failing as the precipitous American withdrawal from the region got under way. Those Chinese leaders who had disagreed with Mao's course of action from the beginning and had been purged as a result were the first to demand and receive a hearing. Beginning in April 1973 with the reinstatement of Teng Hsiao-p'ing, debate grew over the question of how to respond to the immediate and longer-term problems posed by the unanticipated U.S. decision. Teng's reappearance came on the occasion of a state dinner for the deposed Cambodian premier, Prince Sihanouk, suggesting that the Cambodian issue was related to his return.[1] In the policy debate that followed, the familiar pre-cultural revolution antagonism between Mao Tse-tung and Teng Hsiao-p'ing resurfaced. Questions were raised in the Chinese press regarding Washington's value as a "trustworthy partner" and the United States was accused of violating the original cease-fire agreement on Vietnam.[2] The result was that further improvement of relations with the United States (which may not have been possible from the American side in any case because of turmoil in the United States over Watergate) was deferred while the leadership determined a response to the immediate problem posed by the now inevitable North Vietnamese conquest of South Vietnam.

Unable to maintain a fragmented Indochina without the cooperation of the United States, Peking moved unilaterally to establish its own client state in Cambodia to counterbalance the imminent emergence of the Socialist Republic of Vietnam. Peking's need to forestall North Vietnamese domination of all Indochina led paradoxically to the resumption of large-scale military and technical assistance to Hanoi after the Tenth Party Congress in August. Chinese assistance focused Hanoi's efforts on South Vietnam, giving Peking the time and the opportunity to establish the Kampuchean People's Republic under Pol Pot in Cambodia.

As Chinese leaders were reaching a decision on the Indochina problem, the Soviet Union in mid-year began a sustained effort to re-establish friendly relations with the People's Republic of China. The Russians, too, had been taken by surprise by the American withdrawal but quickly perceived the policy crisis in Peking. They inferred that Teng Hsiao-p'ing's return raised the possibility of a strategic reversal. To act on that possibility, however, required a major readjustment in the policies Moscow had been pursuing since the Twenty-fourth Party Congress of 1971, particularly with regard to Japan.[3] In the two years since the congress, Soviet-Japanese economic negotiations had entered a new stage, specifically focusing on several very large development projects in Siberia, including Tyumen oil and Yakutia natural gas and coal. By early 1973 the principal obstacles to completion of negotiations were the territorial problem (four islands of the Kurile chain off the northern coast of Hokkaido that the Soviet Union had seized following World War II and that Japan still claimed) and Japanese reluctance to provide long-term, low-interest loans to finance the projects.

In January 1973, however, perhaps in response to American urging, Japan's Prime Minister Tanaka undertook a major new initiative, for the first time specifically separating the northern islands issue from economic relations.[4]

Tanaka justified his action by the premise that goodwill built through economic cooperation would eventually lead to resolution of the territorial question. The initial Soviet response was receptive but disbelieving, and Moscow sought reassurances on the availability of long-term, low-interest loans. A letter from Tanaka to Brezhnev of March 8, reaffirming the Japanese proposal and suggesting a visit to Moscow, produced an enthusiastic Soviet response. The Soviet press acclaimed the Tanaka initiative as a breakthrough in Soviet-Japanese relations and Brezhnev extended an invitation to the Japanese prime minister to visit Moscow later in the year (late August was the date eventually chosen) for substantive deliberations.[5] In other words, by the spring of 1973, Soviet hopes of establishing a major new economic relationship with the Japanese, which would draw Japanese capital into Siberia and away from China, appeared on the verge of realization.

Contrary to expectations, however, the Soviets did not follow through on the Japanese initiative. Instead, Moscow reversed itself in early June and actively discouraged further progress in negotiations for the remainder of the year. On June 6, the Soviet ambassador to Tokyo, Oleg Troyanovsky, postponed the Tanaka visit on the grounds that late August would be "inconvenient," the conventional diplomatic term for a change of plans, yet the very next day Moscow invited a broadly based Japanese Diet delegation to visit the USSR at the time of the previously scheduled Tanaka trip![6] Making plain the reversal, Moscow moved in late August to discourage Japanese interest in the Siberian projects by increasing the amount of the loan required for Japanese participation and reducing the return Japan was to receive. The maximum amount of crude oil Japan was to obtain from the Tyumen oil project, for example, was reduced from between 40 and 50 million tons annually to 25 million tons. The change in Soviet policy toward Japan was clearly not a function of their bilateral relationship, which had just then entered a promising stage. What persuaded Moscow to forsake an objective so long and eagerly sought was the turmoil in Peking. The Soviets viewed the growing policy debate in the Chinese capital as a great opportunity—perhaps the first genuine opportunity in years—to bring the rancorous relationship with their former ally to an end.

The turnabout in Soviet policy, although it confused the Japanese, was fully consistent with the decision to seek an improvement in relations with China. Timing was the key to Soviet actions. A strong move toward Japan could be read in Peking as an effort to contain China (which it was originally intended to be). The Soviets wanted to avoid giving that impression, which would only provide Mao and his supporters with greater leverage in their expected efforts to thwart any reconciliation scheme. Therefore, Moscow put off negotiations on the economic issue, instead pressing Japan to sign a peace treaty and to declare adherence to the Asian Collective Security System that Moscow had been proposing for years. Originally designed as a means of containing China, the scheme was flexible enough to include China in a general defense system to counter U.S. power in the Pacific. As an inducement, the Soviets now indicated a willingness to discuss the northern islands issue (something they had not been prepared to do previously), contingent upon Japan's adherence to the collective security system. The implication was that Moscow would be equally forthcoming on territorial issues with Peking.

Having deferred the move toward Japan, Moscow in mid-June 1973 made a secret demarche to Peking, offering the Chinese a non-aggression pact.[7] At the same time, Moscow's leaders publicly developed the Asian Collective Security System concept to make it more palatable to the Chinese. Two new principles were added: the right of each country to determine its own social and economic growth patterns and the right of each member country to control the disposition of its natural resources.[8] On August 24, the day the Tenth Party Congress secretly convened in Peking, *Pravda* and *Izvestia* carried front-page editorials extolling the benefits of the system. Brezhnev himself, in major speeches in August at Alma Ata and in September at Tashkent, gave prominence to the twin themes of Sino-Soviet relations and the Asian Collective Security System.[9] It was in the Tashkent speech on September 23 that the Soviet leader revealed for the first time publicly that Moscow had offered the Chinese a non-aggression pact the previous June. The major reversal of Soviet policy toward Japan combined with the carefully crafted and secret offer to China clearly indicated Moscow's seriousness of purpose.

The Chinese response, given by Chou En-lai in his speech to the Tenth Party Congress, was skeptical but not unreceptive. Castigating the Soviet revisionist ruling clique, Chou noted: "Recently, the Brezhnev renegade clique have talked a lot of nonsense on Sino-Soviet relations. It alleges that China is against relaxation of world tension and unwilling to improve Sino-Soviet relations."[10] Rejecting this allegation, Chou went on to suggest what the Soviet Union could do to improve things:

Why don't you show your good faith by doing a thing or two—for instance, withdraw your armed forces from Czechoslovakia or the People's Republic of Mongolia and return the four northern islands to Japan? . . . Must China give away all the territory north of the Great Wall to the Soviet revisionists in order to show that we favour relaxation of world tension and are willing to improve Sino-Soviet relations? . . . The Sino-Soviet controversy on matters of principle should not hinder the normalization of relations between the two states on the basis of the five principles of peaceful co-existence. The Sino-Soviet boundary question should be settled peacefully through negotiations free from any threat.[11]

If Chou En-lai's response was not entirely positive, events at the congress gave the Soviets grounds for continued hope. The realignment of the top leadership at the congress suggested strongly that disagreement continued over China's strategic orientation and that the issue would continue to be discussed.

In the aftermath of the purge of Lin Piao and his supporters, the Politburo Standing Committee had been reduced to three: Mao, Chou, and K'ang Sheng (Yeh Chien-ying was added later). The new Standing Committee included these four men and five additions. Two old hands, Tung Pi-wu and Chu Teh, and three "young" leaders, Wang Hung-wen, Chang Ch'un-ch'iao, and Li Teh-sheng, were added to make up a nine-man Standing Committee. In terms of voting alignment Mao held a majority of six votes out of nine: himself, Chou En-lai, K'ang Sheng, Wang Hung-wen, Chang Ch'un-ch'iao, and Li Teh-sheng versus Yeh Chien-ying, Tung Pi-wu, and Chu Teh.

Mao Tse-tung's two-thirds majority in the Standing Committee was duplicated in the Politburo itself. In addition to the six men noted above, Mao's fourteen supporters in the Politburo included his wife, Chiang Ch'ing, Hua Kuo-feng, Chi Teng-k'uei, Wu Teh, Ch'en Hsi-lien, Wang Tung-hsing, Ch'en Yung-kuei, and Yao Wen-yuan. In Teng Hsiao-p'ing's camp, in addition to the three opponents of Mao already mentioned, were Teng himself, Wei Kuo-ch'ing, Hsü Shih-yü, and Liu Po-ch'eng. The Central Committee also underwent a marked change in its composition. Military representation dropped severely, from 127 at the Ninth Party Congress to 63; there were 76 representatives from the "revolutionary masses" and 40 from the ranks of the party cadres. Among the old party cadres rehabilitated and elected to the congress, however, were many staunch opponents of Mao's, such as Li Ching-ch'uan, T'an Chen-lin, and Ulanfu.

That Mao Tse-tung's hold on the provincial party apparatus remained tenuous was indicated in the main speeches given at the congress by Wang Hung-wen and Chou En-lai. Wang, in his speech on the revision of the party constitution, emphasized several features of party life normally taken for

granted.[12] Most striking was the seemingly unnecessary stress on the preeminence of the party central organs over lower organs. Wang repeatedly
stressed that all other organs must "accept the party's centralized leadership."
The party and the party alone must decide. The party "must not be replaced
by a 'joint conference' of several sectors." At the same time tolerance of
differences of view was also stressed. Wang stated:

> There are still a small number of cadres, especially some leading cadres,
> who will not tolerate differing views from the masses inside or outside the
> Party. They even suppress criticism and retaliate, and it is quite serious in
> some individual cases. In handling problems among the people, party
> discipline absolutely forbids such wrong practices as resorting to "suppres-
> sion if unable to persuade, and arrest if unable to suppress."[13]

While Wang Hung-wen warned party leaders not to suppress criticism,
Chou En-lai, in his "Report to the Tenth National Congress," exhorted party
members to "dare to go against the tide." Raising what was perhaps the most
bedeviling issue, Chou noted that Chairman Mao constantly taught that

> It is imperative to note that one tendency covers another. . . . The struggle
> against Liu Shao-ch'i's revisionism covered Lin Piao's revisionism. There
> were many instances in the past where one tendency covered another and
> when a tide came, the majority went along it, while only a few withstood
> it. Today, in both international and domestic struggles, tendencies may
> still occur similar to those of the past, namely, when there was an alliance
> with the bourgeoisie, necessary struggles were forgotten and when there
> was a split with the bourgeoisie, the possibility of an alliance under given
> conditions was forgotten. It is required of us to do our best to discern and
> rectify such tendencies in time. And when a wrong tendency surges towards
> us like a rising tide, we must not fear isolation and must dare to go against
> the tide and brave it through.[14]

The question that must immediately have sprung to the minds of his
listeners was: Does opposition to Lin Piao include Teng Hsiao-p'ing? And if
so, was Teng Hsiao-p'ing building a majority against which the party must
dare to go? The concept of "going against the tide" introduced here explicitly
urged going against the majority. Were Mao and Chou anticipating the strengthening of Teng's position and preparing the ground for opposing it? Did the
concept signal the regime's willingness to tolerate open disagreement over

policy? In foreign affairs, did the alliance with the bourgeois United States still require certain "necessary struggles" that had been forgotten?

However one answers these questions, it is clear that the Tenth Party Congress was anything but a united gathering. It was rather a hasty convocation of quarreling leaders confounded by the turnabout in American policy and pressed strongly from within and from without by those who had all along opposed the Maoist strategy. In the period between the Tenth Party Congress and the Fourth National People's Congress held in January 1975, Mao's opponents gained in strength. Indeed, it began to appear that as the Maoist era drew to a close, the Chinese leader's policies might not outlive the leader himself.

From the Tenth Party Congress to the Fourth National People's Congress

Three significant sequences of events occurred following the close of the Tenth Party Congress that indicated the continuation of a high-level policy crisis in Peking and that, in retrospect, were the beginning of a concerted rear-guard political action by Mao Tse-tung. First, a redistribution of control over the military regions occurred, most probably to cushion the impact of the appointment of several of Teng Hsiao-p'ing's newly rehabilitated supporters; second, the news media carried on an extensive criticism campaign designed to limit the degree of support Teng could muster; and last, the media gradually and defensively began to reveal the principal issues and personalities in conflict within the leadership.

The reassignment of commanders of eight of the eleven military regions[15] in late December, which on the surface appeared to be an attempt to strip political power from powerful regional commanders, also began the process of redistributing power in the military regions between supporters of Mao and supporters of Teng. Several men who had been removed during the cultural revolution and who presumably were thus Teng's men were appointed to key posts. These included Yang Yung, Ch'in Chi-wei, and Pai Ju-ping. The shuffling of military region commanders can be seen in this light as reflecting Mao's continuing concern to retain a strong hold on the crucial military regions of the Northeast, North, East, and Central South, where virtually all of the PLA's main force units were deployed. Thus Mao sent Li Teh-sheng out of the Politburo Standing Committee to command the Shengyang military region in the northeast, Ch'en Hsi-lien from Shengyang to command of the

Peking military region, Chi Teng-k'uei to Peking as first political commissar, Tseng Ssu-yü to command the Tsinan military region, and Yang Teh-chih to command the Wuhan military region. Teng Hsiao-p'ing made obvious gains in the south. Hsü Shih-yü and Wei Kuo-ch'ing were sent to the Canton military region as commander and first political commissar, respectively, and Ting Sheng was assigned from Canton to Nanking to make room for Teng's man, Chao Tzu-yang, who would replace him as first secretary of the Kwangtung provincial party committee later in the spring of 1974.[16]

The separation of military officers from concurrent party positions may also have reflected an agreement to restrict the policy debate to the highest party levels, excluding the military as far as possible. Thus the reassignment of Li Teh-sheng to command the Shenyang military region took him out of Peking and out of the Politburo Standing Committee. Li's transfer reduced Mao's margin in the Standing Committee to five to three, although he remained in the Politburo where the balance remained fourteen to seven. Li's departure also meant that of the eight men then on the Politburo Standing Committee, only one, Chang Ch'un-ch'iao, had direct control over a military force, as first political commissar of Nanking.

Second, Mao Tse-tung sought to limit support for Teng Hsiao-p'ing by means of extensive propaganda campaigns and other devices that clearly identified the unacceptable and required payment of at least lip service by all parties to the issues raised in the propaganda campaign. The criticize Confucius–criticize Lin Piao campaign was the centerpiece of the media propaganda effort. A joint *Red Flag–People's Daily–Liberation Army Daily* editorial on New Year's Day announced the coming campaign, which began in *People's Daily* on February 2, 1974. Although criticism of Confucius had been a running theme in the newspapers for several years, linking the Confucius issue with Lin Piao was new. The criticism of Confucius had at its core the idea of avoiding a reversal of relationships. In the Maoist view of China's past, Confucius represented those who wished to revert from the feudal to the slave-holding stage of development (in the Marxian unilinear scheme of historical development—primitive, slave-holding, feudal, capitalist). Similarly, in the Maoist view Lin Piao also wished to revert to an earlier set of relations by reaffirming the initial alliance with the Soviet Union. The campaign as a whole constituted a definition of the unacceptable and an implicit admonition to stay on the present policy track. As Lin Piao had already been dead for more than two years, the campaign was obviously aimed at a current leader who had similar predilections; that leader was, of course,

Teng Hsiao-p'ing. After a strong beginning, however, the campaign began to fade by mid-year, reflecting further change in power relations at the top.

Following the Tenth Party Congress, Peking conveyed to the Soviet leaders the message that any suggestion of a dramatic improvement in relations was premature at best. Chou En-lai gave the first signal in an interview with *New York Times* reporter C. L. Sulzberger in late October.[17] Chou declared that "there was no point in" the Soviet offer of a non-aggression pact, as the very definition of such a pact included avoiding the threat of force as well as the actual use of force. "Since the Russians didn't agree on that, what would be the point of a . . . non-aggression pact?" The expulsion of six Soviet diplomats in January on espionage charges, coinciding with the beginning of the anti-Confucius, anti–Lin Piao campaign, was a further signal that no change in relations was in the offing. The decisive turn occurred when Teng Hsiao-p'ing, the leader with whom Soviet leaders believed they could deal, publicly began to take a pro-American stand, declaring that there was positive value in a continued U.S. presence in Asia, supporting Japan on the northern islands question and the temporary necessity for continued U.S.-Japanese security ties, and taking a stand critical of the Soviet Union.[18]

When it became obvious to Moscow that there was no hope for an improvement in the relationship with Peking, the Soviets reversed policies toward Japan once again! Their response was to criticize Teng Hsiao-p'ing publicly by name and to return to the policy pursued before Teng came back into power—the attempt to establish strong economic ties with Japan.[19] Thus, in early 1974 the Soviet Union began to de-emphasize the need for a peace treaty with Japan and Japan's adherence to the Asian Collective Security System, instead stressing once again the need for immediately expanding economic cooperation. The new Soviet policy succeeded. In April Japan agreed to extend $1.05 billion in Export-Import Bank credits for the exploitation of Yakutia coal and natural gas and Siberian forestry development.

The third development noted in this period was the effort to communicate directly to the people, albeit in the time-honored Aesopian manner universally employed in the Communist world, the issues in dispute as well as the positions of important actors. Two articles in *Hung Ch'i* (Red Flag), both by the party historian Lo Ssu-ting, were particularly representative of this type of communication. The first appeared shortly after the Tenth Party Congress in November. Addressing the Confucius issue, the author recounted a period in the history of the Ch'in dynasty in which the legalist Fan Sui proposed the policy of "keeping friendly relations with distant states and attacking nearby states."[20] Although Fan became prime minister, he was "sitting on top of a volcano which could erupt at any time." In the face of the intransigent old aristocrats whose influence was still powerful, Fan Sui wavered in his conviction and, because of illness, was asked to return the seal of office.

The parallel was, of course, not perfect, but it was highly suggestive of the issues and personalities in dispute. The allusion to the contemporary situation was unmistakable, for the issue then before the leadership was precisely China's strategic orientation toward the United States and the Soviet Union. The reference to an ill and wavering premier could have been meant to exert pressure on Chou En-lai, who was certainly ill and may have been vacillating over the correct course to pursue. Any lingering doubt that the article was important was dispelled later in April 1974 when it was reprinted in the English-language *Peking Review* at the time when Chou En-lai began to decline attendance at state functions. Shortly thereafter he retired to the hospital.

In November 1974 Lo Ssu-ting's second "historical" article appeared. This one was about the Sung period and the political reformer Wang An-shih.[21] Wang, the anti-Confucianist, advocated the reconquest of the lost northern territories, but Ssu-ma Kuang, the Confucianist, followed a policy of capitulationism. To make the analogy with the contemporary situation clear, at the end of the article the author spoke of Lin Piao and his willingness to "surrender to Soviet revisionism." Less than two weeks later *People's Daily* also printed an essay on Wang An-shih arguing the same point unmistakably in the contemporary context, hinting broadly that the principal issue in the high-level policy debate was indeed China's strategic orientation.[22] On the twenty-first of November a second article appeared in *People's Daily* making the same points.

By the time the Fourth National People's Congress convened secretly in mid-January, it was apparent that the propaganda campaigns had not achieved the desired results. The events that took place immediately preceding and during the congress revealed that the position of Mao Tse-tung and his supporters had deteriorated further. During the preparatory meetings of the congress the Second Plenum of the party met (8-10 January). The terse post-plenum communique divulged a most significant change in the composition of the top leadership: Teng Hsiao-p'ing had been elected to membership of the Politburo Standing Committee and Li Teh-sheng had been dropped. That change reduced Mao's advantage in the highest decision-making body to the narrowest of margins, five to four. This, of course, assumed that Chou

En-lai would continue to vote with Mao. On the other hand, although Teng remained in the minority, he could now act from a position of high authority.

The Fourth National People's Congress, too, produced a series of surprises that worked to Mao's disadvantage. Organizationally, Mao received no formal state post. The chairmanship of the People's Republic, having been abolished during the cultural revolution, was not re-established. Nor, of the members of the Politburo Standing Committee, did Wang Hung-wen obtain an appointment in the state apparatus. On the other hand, all of the other members of the Politburo Standing Committee were appointed to key positions. Chu Teh was named chairman of the Standing Committee of the Congress, with K'ang Sheng and Tung Pi-wu as deputy chairmen. Chou En-lai, although he was seriously ill and made only a brief appearance at the congress, retained the premiership of the State Council; Teng Hsiao-p'ing and Chang Ch'un-ch'iao were named first and third vice-premiers, respectively. Yeh Chien-ying assumed the Ministry of Defense post. Teng and Chang also became chief of staff of the PLA and chief of the General Political Department of the PLA, respectively, at this time.

The Standing Committee of the Congress, whose chairman was Chu Teh, was studded with rehabilitated cadres purged during the cultural revolution.[23] Mao Tse-tung was better represented, however, on the State Council, headed by premier Chou En-lai. Aside from Teng Hsiao-p'ing, who was first vice-premier, the next six vice-premiers listed were Mao's supporters: Chang Ch'un-ch'iao, Li Hsien-nien, Ch'en Hsi-lien, Chi Teng-k'uei, Ch'en Yung-kuei, and Hua Kuo-feng. Of a total of thirteen members, then, one could count at least seven supporters of Mao, if Chou was included,[24] although Teng held the number two slot just after Chou.

There were significant changes in the state constitution. Perhaps most important were changes in Mao's personal role in the relation of party to state and in the redefinition of the state. The 1970 draft designated Mao Tse-tung by name as "the great leader of the people of all nationalities in the whole country . . . the chief of state of the proletarian dictatorship of our country [and] . . . the supreme commander of the whole nation and the whole army."[25] The 1975 constitution left out all reference to Mao as a person, instead vesting these powers in the chairman of the CCP Central Committee. Although Mao currently held the chairmanship, theoretically at least, the constitutional formula resolved the issues of power that would arise once the Great Helmsman died. Compared with the 1970 draft, which also identified Mao's thought as the sole infallible guide, Article 2 of the 1975 constitution placed emphasis instead on "Marxism-Leninism–Mao Tse-tung thought" as the theoretical basis for action.[26] The 1975 state constitution subordinated the state formally to the party. All state and military powers were placed under party control; conversely, it was the right and duty of all citizens to support the leadership of the party. The new constitution also changed the nature of the state from a people's democracy, as stipulated in the 1954 constitution, to "a socialist state of the dictatorship of the proletariat led by the working class and based on the alliance of workers and peasants."[27]

There were other differences between the 1975 constitution and the 1970 draft. Where the 1970 draft called for the revolutionary committee to be made up equally of rebels, cadres, and military, as well as of old, middle-aged, and young, Article 11 of the 1975 version stated simply that state organizations "must be a three-in-one combination of the old, the middle-aged and the young." Moreover, the revolutionary committees now became "the permanent organs of the local people's congresses and . . . local people's governments at various levels."[28] Where in the 1970 draft the state protected the use of big-character posters, great debates, and so forth as "forms of mass struggle," Article 13 of the 1975 constitution noted that these were specifically designed "to help consolidate" the leadership of the party over the state.

Finally, it was decided to amalgamate the functions and powers of the legal organs. The functions and powers of procuratorial organs would henceforth be exercised by the organs of public security at various levels (Article 25). In effect, the policeman now became both prosecutor and judge in China's legal system, and the person in charge of the public security apparatus was given great powers. (It would be the newly appointed head of the security apparatus who would succeed Chou En-lai as premier.) Appointed at the congress to that position, of course, was Hua Kuo-feng. Yet the strong representation of Teng and his supporters in the state apparatus, Teng's own rise to Politburo Standing Committee status, and the passage of a state constitution that all but excluded Mao Tse-tung from that important sector of power placed Teng Hsiao-p'ing in an ascendant position. Teng's rise also made Mao's absence and dissociation from the party plenum and people's congress understandable.

Internal Change and Foreign Policy Stagnation

The reshuffling of the top leadership was reflected in the foreign policy shift that occurred at this time. Chou En-lai, in his report on government, set forth China's position within the context of the theory of three worlds that Teng Hsiao-p'ing had introduced the previous April in his speech at the United Nations.[29] In this theory, the United States and the Soviet Union occupied the First World; the developed nations of Europe and Asia, the Second World; and the developing nations of Asia, Africa, and Latin America, the Third World. China was placed as a developing nation in the Third World. The theory permitted China to assume a position roughly equidistant between Washington and Moscow, which, in effect, meant to draw away somewhat from the United States. It also allowed China to establish closer relations with Europe and Japan quite independent of any relationship with the United States and with the developing nations of the Third World as well. This was the position Chou En-lai developed in his speech.

China, he said, should enhance "unity with the countries and people of Asia, Africa and Latin America and resolutely support them in their struggle to win or safeguard national independence, defend their state sovereignty, protect their national resources and develop their national economy."[30] Declaring China's support for the countries and peoples of the Second World against "superpower control, threats and bullying," he said: "We support the efforts of West European countries to get united in this struggle. We are ready to work together with the Japanese Government and people to promote friendly and good neighborly relations."[31] With regard to the United States, Chou declared that "there exist fundamental differences between China and the United States." Owing to the "joint efforts of both sides," he explained, relations between the two countries had "improved to some extent" in the last three years and would continue to improve, "so long as the principles of the Sino-American Shanghai communique are carried out in earnest."

If Chou's remarks indicated a cooling of relations with Washington, the previous harsh tone was absent from his words for Moscow. Aside from a single mention of "Soviet social imperialism" making "a feint to the East while attacking in the West," his references to the Soviet leadership were quite moderate in tone, particularly when contrasted to earlier Chinese statements. Chou referred to the Sino-Soviet ideological conflict as a "debate." The "Soviet leading clique," he said, "betrayed Marxism-Leninism, and our debate with them on matters of principle will go on for a long time."

> However, we have always held that this debate should not obstruct the maintenance of normal state relations between China and the Soviet Union. The Soviet leadership have taken a series of steps to worsen the relations between the two countries, conducted subversive activities against our

country and even provoked armed conflicts on the border. . . . They . . . refuse to do anything about such matters as the disengagement of the armed forces of the two sides in the disputed areas on the border and the prevention of armed conflicts; instead they talked profusely about empty treaties on the non-use of force against each other and mutual non-aggression. . . . We wish to advise the Soviet leadership to sit down and negotiate honestly, do something to solve a bit of the problem.[32]

Obviously, Chou's remarks were not to be taken as a personal statement, but as the agreed position of the leadership. The subtle shift in policy thus reflected the change in the balance of political forces within the leadership. In any case, Chou's admonition to the Soviet Union's leadership to "do something to solve a bit of the problem" came in the wake of an unsuccessful Chinese attempt to respond positively to Moscow's previously proffered non-aggression pact. In late 1974 the Chinese indicated their willingness to accept Moscow's offer, contingent upon Soviet concessions on certain Chinese border claims and upon the withdrawal of Soviet troops from the border area.[33] In this context the Chinese leadership's cool reception of Henry Kissinger in late November was meant as a signal to Moscow. It was, however, perplexing to the U.S. secretary of state.

Kissinger arrived seriously prepared to negotiate further improvement in Sino-American relations, including concessions on the Taiwan question. The Chinese stunned and confused the secretary of state by declining to negotiate! Indeed, Mao did not receive him, and his visit with Chou En-lai in the hospital was terminated after only thirty minutes even though the ailing premier appeared in good condition. Kissinger later noted that the formerly loquacious premier's manner during the meeting was "strangely guarded."[34] The terse four-sentence communique issued upon his departure marked a low point in the three-year relationship between the two countries. In any case, Peking's cautious handling of the U.S. secretary of state while attempting to move toward Moscow came to naught, because the Soviets now refused to enter into any discussions until the Chinese side gave up all "preconditions."[35] What brought about the abrupt change in Soviet behavior? The Soviets, too, perceived the alteration in the Chinese leadership balance, but having concluded that any further efforts would be premature, decided to await its further evolution. It appeared that Teng Hsiao-p'ing and his supporters were moving into the ascendant and would soon be in a position to negotiate from strength, perhaps following Mao's death. So Moscow temporized.

Moscow's deferral turned out to be, in retrospect, a miscalculation, however sound the logic behind it. In the months following the Fourth National People's Congress, even though U.S.-China relations continued to sour and even though Teng Hsiao-p'ing's position improved as the internal leadership conflict intensified, relations with Moscow remained on the same level as before. Indeed, it appeared that China's policy toward the First World, that is, toward Washington and Moscow, was completely immobilized. The governing factor was the intensification of the power struggle at the top, the initiative for which came from Mao Tse-tung. Shortly after the congress ended, Mao re-emerged from his self-imposed isolation somewhere in the south of China (his whereabouts had not been precisely known) to respond to the challenge of Teng Hsiao-p'ing.

Mao Tse-tung's move was to trigger renewed dispute over the theoretical issue of the conflict between the proletariat and the bourgeoisie.[36] In a *People's Daily* editorial written under the pseudonym of Liang Hsiao, he argued the continuing necessity to impose the dictatorship of the proletariat over the bourgeoisie, "people like Lin Piao," who would restore capitalism if they came into power. The question "Who were the bourgeoisie?" was addressed directly by one of Mao's allies, Yao Wen-yuan, in an article in the March issue of *Red Flag*. The article was broadcast nationwide several times on 28 February.[37] Picking up Mao's theme, Yao struck out at "people like Lin Piao," who were the "old bourgeoisie." Yao offered two verses from Mao's favorite novel, the *Dream of the Red Chamber*, as a further guide to the identification of the bourgeoisie. The first was about the wolf who, saved by a man, turned and devoured him. The second was about the "evil man" who married into a rich family, then treated his wife shabbily. Although no names were used, the themes referred implicitly to Teng and his supporters. It was they who had been saved and now sought to devour their benefactors. Many rehabilitated old hands were the ministers in charge of the state apparatus, giving the economy a consumerist and therefore "bourgeois" orientation. Yao Wen-yuan concluded his article with yet another veiled reference to Teng Hsiao-p'ing. Citing Mao's letter to his wife, Chiang Ch'ing, written at the outset of the cultural revolution prior to Teng's initial purge, Yao noted Mao's warning against the danger that "rightists" would grab power. [38] The terms "bourgeois" and "rightist" were those with which Mao had castigated Teng Hsiao-p'ing and Liu Shao-ch'i ever since the late 1950s. The references were unmistakably clear to any politically conscious Chinese reader.

Meanwhile, in mid-March came further reinforcement of the foreign policy shift noted at the Fourth National People's Congress. Chiang Ch'ing, in a speech delivered to foreign affairs cadres, attempted to explain in class terms the failure of U.S. foreign policy in Southeast Asia and to exonerate Peking from any complicity. Focusing on Henry Kissinger as an "adventurer and a defeatist" to explain the failure of Washington's nerve, she revealed that in the talks between the two countries' leaders

> Kissinger hinted at the view that the United States has the intention of abandoning the Asian Pacific region. . . . We feel that Kissinger is unable, in the final analysis, to depart from the limitations of a bourgeois politician. His basic perspective is restricted by the class interests which it defends, and consequently, he can neither comprehend nor solve the various types of contradictions which are now emerging from the new and complex international situation.
>
> We will not be like the imperialists of the United States or the Soviet revisionists who have abandoned friends who have come through thick and thin with them, and we definitely will not conduct behind-the-scenes dealings with superpowers for our own benefit or sell out our friends.[39]

In her entire speech, the above reference to the "Soviet revisionists" was only one of three to the Soviet Union—and in two of the three the Soviet Union was linked with the United States. The general import of Chiang Ch'ing's speech was to de-emphasize further the Washington connection.

Despite the mounting criticism of the bourgeoisie's return to power, Teng Hsiao-p'ing's position strengthened measurably over the course of the next several months. His strength grew mainly as a function of a major shift of power within the Politburo Standing Committee—the deaths of three of its members: Tung Pi-wu, K'ang Sheng, and most importantly, Chou En-lai. The Second Plenum in January 1975 had shaved Mao's advantage in the Standing Committee to five to four; Tung Pi-wu's death in early April increased his majority to five to three and, if anything, negatively affected Teng Hsiao-p'ing. The most significant events surrounded Chou En-lai's incapacitation and death.

Chou En-lai had entered the hospital in late June 1974, but he continued to receive visitors until September 1975 and, as noted above, appeared briefly at the Fourth National People's Congress in January 1975 to deliver his report on the work of the government. The presumption is that after September 7, 1975, the date of his last public appearance,[40] Chou became too ill to participate in the political process. After that date, Teng Hsiao-p'ing began to substitute for Chou at state functions on a regular basis. Chou's incapacitation meant that Mao's advantage in the Standing Committee was reduced still further, from five to three to four to three by September 1975. Furthermore, there was some question at this time of Wang Hung-wen's loyalty to Mao Tse-tung as well, making Mao's voting edge in the Standing Committee tenuous at best and opening up a power vacuum at the very top of the Chinese Communist Party leadership.

For Teng Hsiao-p'ing the summer of 1975 was the beginning of a period of maximum political power, as Chou's illness became an asset. As long as Chou En-lai was alive but incapacitated Teng was premier in fact if not in name. Indeed, during the fall there occurred a sharp increase in appointments of old Teng supporters, particularly in October immediately following Chou's departure from the political scene.[41] The death of K'ang Sheng in December further increased Teng's advantage, leaving the Politburo Standing Committee evenly balanced at three to three—if, that is, Wang Hung-wen voted with Mao Tse-tung. In this context, the "Water Margin campaign," which began in early September at the time of Chou's departure, can be interpreted as Mao's attempt to place some constraints upon Teng's freedom of action.

The September issue of *Red Flag* contained five articles all condemning the ancient popular novel *Shui Hu Chuan* (Water Margin Chronicle).[42] The novel recounts the swashbuckling adventures of a band of noble bandits, to whom Mao had referred approvingly in earlier years. A *People's Daily* editorial on September 4 launched a nationwide campaign to criticize the novel, buttressed with quotations and commentary from Chairman Mao, who now offered a revised opinion. The editorial depicted Sung Chiang, the novel's hero, as a capitulationist who, having infiltrated the peasant bandit army and seized the leadership, surrendered to the emperor even while pretending to resist him. In short, the editorial concluded, Sung Chiang was a revisionist who surrendered at home and capitulated to foreign enemies. It is clear in retrospect that the Water Margin campaign was designed to direct further criticism at Teng Hsiao-p'ing, the revisionist, in the hope of preventing or at least retarding his drive to power.

Late in the year the two divergent political tendencies represented by Mao and Teng, the struggle between two lines that the Chinese press never tired of trumpeting, came more clearly into focus. While Mao made every effort to cement the American connection, Teng was there to stall. Mao received what seemed like a constant stream of important visitors from the United States.

Secretary of State Henry Kissinger visited in October, President Ford in December.[43] Following Ford's visit came David and Julie Eisenhower's trip at the turn of the year (December 28–January 12), followed a month later by former President Nixon himself on the fourth anniversary of his historic 1972 visit. Mao had sent one of China's newly acquired Boeing 707s to Los Angeles to transport the former president, the first time that the People's Republic had provided transportation for any foreign visitor. Mao spent almost two hours with President Ford and more than an hour and a half with Richard Nixon. Teng, of course, now either was present when Mao received visitors formally or held separate meetings with them himself. President Ford's visit, potentially the most productive, came to nothing and was described by the U.S. side as "a holding action"—all it could have been under the circumstances.[44]

At the end of the year, just after the conclusion of the Ford visit and on the eve of the Eisenhowers' arrival, a most unusual event occurred, for which Teng Hsiao-p'ing was widely believed responsible. On December 27, the Chinese government suddenly announced that crew members of a Soviet helicopter, which had been downed after penetrating Chinese airspace in Sinkiang province in the far northwest twenty-one months before, would be released.[45] From March 1974 (when the intrusion occurred) until that moment, the Chinese government had consistently maintained that the crew were "spies" and would be treated as such. Instead, the government publicly acknowledged that it had erred. The crew was feted lavishly and given a remarkably friendly sendoff to Moscow. Coming when Teng's political ascendancy had become seemingly irreversible, it conveyed clear signals both to Washington and to Moscow. Indeed, David Eisenhower, upon his return to the United States, published an article in the *Wall Street Journal* in which he identified Teng Hsiao-p'ing for American readers as the one Chinese leader who could improve Sino-Soviet relations.[46] Regardless of the foreign policy implications of the helicopter crew's release, the death of Chou En-lai, which occurred during the Eisenhowers' visit, trained all attention on domestic politics to the virtual exclusion of all else for the remainder of the year.

The Death of Chou En-lai and
Designation of Mao's Heir

Chou En-lai's death in early January 1976 did not affect the balance of power at the top—his incapacitation the previous September had already done so. The six-man Politburo Standing Committee was evenly split.[47] On one side were Mao Tse-tung, Chang Ch'un-ch'iao, and Wang Hung-wen; on the other were Teng Hsiao-p'ing, Yeh Chien-ying, and Chu Teh. Chou's death forced the issue of his replacement; it would be necessary now to appoint a new premier. If the new premier came from within the ranks of the Standing Committee the voting balance would not be tipped one way or the other, but control of the state apparatus would be involved. If Teng Hsiao-p'ing obtained the premiership, as virtually everyone expected, it would formalize the current condition—he would then be premier in name as well as in fact. On the other hand, if one of Mao's people were appointed—Chang Ch'un-ch'iao was most likely—then clearly Teng would lose control of the state apparatus and suffer a setback in his drive to power.

In the event, the Politburo Standing Committee deadlocked, neither side being willing to accede to the other. It was Mao Tse-tung who, a few weeks later in late January, skillfully circumvented the Standing Committee impasse by appointing Hua Kuo-feng as "temporary and acting" premier.[48] Hua, an unknown even though he had been a Politburo member since 1973, had moved up in the Communist Party hierarchy during the cultural revolution as one of the revolutionary masses, or one of Mao's men. His appointment as chief of the Public Security Ministry at the Fourth National People's Congress in January 1975 had placed him in a strong position in the state apparatus. As party chairman, Mao Tse-tung had the authority to make temporary appointments without submitting his decisions to formal vote, although in this case the Standing Committee and possibly even the Politburo were consulted. Hua appeared to be the most acceptable compromise candidate among those on the Politburo whom Mao could have chosen. Hua's "temporary" appointment did not include a position on the Standing Committee, which remained split.

Appointing Hua Kuo-feng solved, even if only temporarily, the immediate problem of ensuring that the important post of premier was held by an ally of Mao's, but not the longer-range problem of succession. Nevertheless, Mao had placed his supporter in a position from which he could contend for the party chairmanship, even if he was not a strong figure in his own right. For Mao the significant question was how to manipulate the balance of forces in the leadership, particularly in the Standing Committee, to improve Hua Kuo-feng's chances in the coming succession struggle. The principal contender for Mao's mantle was obviously Teng Hsiao-p'ing, who now was also in a strong position from which to capture the chairmanship of the party once

Mao passed from the scene. Therefore, Mao intensified the criticism of Teng Hsiao-p'ing in an effort to discredit and mobilize opposition to him.

Charges against Teng now appeared one after another. The first came in an article by Liang Hsiao in *People's Daily* on January 28, just after Hua had been appointed acting premier. "The anti-Party gang of Lin Piao," it was said, "publicly announced that they intend to enter into 'secret talks' with Soviet revisionists."[49] In mid-February Teng was also charged with rendering class struggle secondary instead of as the "key link" while placing emphasis on stability and unity and on promotion of the economy, particularly the four modernizations. Stability, unity, and class struggle were Mao's "three directives," which Teng was accused of "twisting."[50] In late February Mao amplified an earlier quote regarding the three directives to make clear his point: "What [does Teng mean by] taking the three directives as the key link? Stability and unity do not mean writing off class struggle; class struggle is the key link, and everything else hinges on it."[51] By early March it was obvious to the most casual reader of the newspaper that Teng Hsiao-p'ing was Mao's target, even though his name had not yet been mentioned. An article by Ch'ih Heng on March 2 in *People's Daily,* also carried in the March issue of *Red Flag,* stated:

> The unrepentant man on the capitalist road; who was at the origin of the rightist wind of reversal of verdicts, is the man who opposed collectivization and communization, who wanted redistribution of the land, who said "a cat may be white or black; if it catches mice it's a good cat"; later he opposed the great cultural revolution, repressed the movement of the masses and wanted reversal of verdicts and restoration.[52]

A week later *People's Daily* carried another editorial based on a "recent instruction of Chairman Mao." It, too, spoke of a single person:

> That person who blew the rightist wind to reverse verdicts, who before the great cultural revolution followed the revisionist line of Liu Shao-ch'i, who in the past has several times resisted the socialist revolutionary movement; the man on the capitalist road who was criticized during the cultural revolution but did not repent . . . this man has never been a Marxist.[53]

By early March, although rumors were now rife that Teng's ouster was imminent, the public criticism seemed to have little visible impact on him.[54] Teng was reported to have said defiantly, "I fell once; why be afraid of falling a second time?"[55] In late March at a mass meeting convened by Wu Teh, first party secretary of Peking and Mao's ally, Teng adamantly refused to undertake "self-criticism," retorting, "I'm an old man and my ears aren't good. I can't hear anything you are saying."[56] Nevertheless, even though *People's Daily* declared Teng to be "completely isolated," he remained unshaken.[57] Clearly, Mao would need to resort to more stringent measures to oust his formidable antagonist.

Mao Tse-tung's opportunity came in early April during the Spring Festival, when the dead are honored. For several days in early April people had been going to T'ien An Men Square to place commemorative wreaths, primarily in honor of Chou En-lai, at the Monument of the People's Heroes. According to the official account, "a handful of class enemies under the guise of commemorating the late Premier Chou . . . engineered an organized, premeditated and planned counterrevolutionary political incident."[58] Speeches were made, leaflets distributed, poems and slogans posted—many inflammatorily anti-Mao and pro-Teng—resulting in the outbreak of scuffles between supporters of the two. The agitation culminated on the morning of April 5 when a day-long riot broke out as the local police sought to remove the many wreaths that by now were heaped around the monument. Counterrevolutionary "hooligans," so the official account went, "savagely beat up" those who sought to resist them. Several vehicles were overturned and set on fire during the day, and the PLA barracks building located in the southeast corner of the square was ransacked and set on fire. At six-thirty in the evening the Peking party secretary, Wu Teh, delivered a speech directing the crowd, which at its height approached 100,000 people, to disperse, and three hours later he sent several thousand public security police and militia to clear the square, bringing an end to the "incident."

Whether it was Mao or Teng who "engineered . . . organized, premeditated and planned [the] . . . incident," it was Mao Tse-tung and his supporters who used it to advantage. The T'ien An Men riot provided Mao with the opportunity simultaneously to strengthen Hua's position and to deal a severe setback to Hua's chief rival, Teng. While the capital was still reverberating from the events, the Politburo met and on April 7 released two resolutions, both passed "on the proposal of . . . Chairman Mao."[59] The first promoted Hua Kuo-feng from "acting and temporary" to permanent status as premier and appointed him to the Politburo Standing Committee as "first vice-chairman." The second dismissed Teng Hsiao-p'ing "from all posts both inside and outside the Party."

How did Mao Tse-tung bring off this extraordinary accomplishment? Party convention dictated that all votes be presented publicly as "unanimous," but votes were taken and won by Mao and his supporters. Given the unusual circumstances surrounding the vote, the question that arises is: What kind of voting majority is required to promote into and dismiss from the Politburo Standing Committee? It would appear from the lineup in the nineteen-member Politburo that a two-thirds majority, rather than a simple majority, is required for such action. Furthermore, dismissal from the Standing Committee would seem to require not only a two-thirds majority in the Politburo, but the same margin in the Standing Committee as well. Based on these assumptions, an examination of the events immediately following the T'ien An Men riot reveals that Mao held a temporary two-thirds majority in both bodies that enabled him to gain passage of the resolutions on Hua and Teng.

A key element in the explanation is the absences of Yeh Chien-ying and Liu Po-ch'eng from Peking when the crucial Politburo meetings were held. Yeh had resigned his post as minister of defense in protest against Mao's decision to attack Teng Hsiao-p'ing in February, at which time he returned to his home in Kwangtung province near Hong Kong.[60] Liu Po-ch'eng had been ill for some time and also away from the capital. Yeh's absence, in particular, gave Mao a three-to-two advantage in the Standing Committee and, with Liu also gone, a twelve-to-five edge in the Politburo itself. Voting with Mao were Hua Kuo-feng, Chang Ch'un-ch'iao, Wang Hung-wen, Chiang Ch'ing, Yao Wen-yuan, Wang Tung-hsing, Chi Teng-k'uei, Ch'en Hsi-lien, Wu Teh, Li Teh-sheng, and Ch'en Yung-kuei. Voting against were Teng Hsiao-p'ing, Chu Teh, Li Hsien-nien, Hsü Shih-yü, and Wei Kuo-ch'ing.

Even if one assumes that Hua Kuo-feng would not have been able to vote on an issue involving his own promotion, the eleven-five breakdown would still have been sufficient for the two-thirds requirement, so long as Mao could keep his supporters from splitting their vote. This, then, explains Hua's elevation to the Standing Committee. Hua's promotion to the Standing Committee, combined with Yeh Chien-ying's absence, in turn explains the dismissal of Teng Hsiao-p'ing. Hua's entry gave Mao a temporary four-to-two majority in the Standing Committee and a more than sufficient twelve-to-five advantage in the Politburo itself, with Hua Kuo-feng now voting against Teng in both bodies. On the basis of the two-thirds requirement neither Hua's promotion nor Teng's dismissal would have been possible had Yeh Chien-ying been present.

Ironically, although Yeh's absence gave Mao the opportunity to act against

Teng, the unusual circumstances probably account for the fact that his victory was incomplete. In the resolution expelling Teng, Mao linked his antagonist's "latest behavior" to the T'ien An Men incident[61] and declared that his "problem" had "turned into one of antagonistic contradiction," that is, one that is irresolvable by political compromise. Nevertheless, Teng was permitted to retain his party membership "so as to see how he will behave in the future."[62] In other words, Mao had succeeded in dealing his chosen successor's chief rival a serious but only temporary setback, for the door was left open for yet another rehabilitation.

Dissolution of the Maoist Coalition

Up to this point, Mao Tse-tung had managed to hold together his diverse leadership coalition, including its "radical" element. The Politburo decisions of April 7 in particular could not have been made had the so-called Gang of Four been in opposition to Mao.[63] Yet even as Mao was elevating his chosen successor to a position of preeminence, his coalition began to crumble. Teng's dismissal reduced the Politburo by one from nineteen to eighteen members. Mao held a twelve-to-six edge there and a four-to-two advantage in the Standing Committee, Yeh Chien-ying having returned to Peking by mid-April.[64] Maintenance of this advantage required the continued cohesion of Mao's coalition, which divided over the issue of the succession.

The crucial sequence centered on the "three instructions" Mao Tse-tung gave to Hua Kuo-feng on April 30. Following a meeting between Mao and New Zealand Prime Minister Robert Muldoon, which Hua attended, Mao wrote: "Carry out the work slowly, not in haste"; "Act according to past principles"; and "With you in charge, I'm at ease."[65] Mao surely understood the political significance of these words, which in effect conferred upon Hua Kuo-feng the status of heir-designate. Hua certainly did, for he "promptly transmitted" the first two of the three instructions to the Politburo in the presence of the Gang of Four, but reserved the third instruction "with you in charge, I'm at ease" for later use as his trump card.[66]

Mao Tse-tung's "three instructions" precipitated a crisis in his coalition leading directly to its division—even though he quite naturally sought to prevent it, to no avail.[67] Suspecting that there was more to Mao's "instructions" than the two Hua reported to the Politburo, Chiang Ch'ing and her supporters attempted immediately to lay the basis for repudiating any last will and testament that might some day emerge. On May 5, *People's Daily* reprinted an earlier article by Liang Hsiao that criticized "class enemies" for fabricating the "premier's will" and the chairman's "instructions." Although couched in terms of the now revitalized campaign to criticize Teng Hsiao-p'ing, the criticisms had broader relevance in the context of the "three instructions" Mao had just given to Hua Kuo-feng.

On June 15 the Chinese Foreign Ministry announced to foreigners in Peking, but not to the Chinese people, that Mao Tse-tung would no longer receive visiting dignitaries.[68] Mao had weakened gravely, and over the next few weeks a form of collective leadership began to function. For example, Chu Teh received the president of Madagascar, Didier Ratsiraka, on June 12 (which had occasioned the Foreign Ministry's announcement), but Hua Kuo-feng also held discussions with him. The leadership followed the same procedure with the Australian prime minister, Malcolm Fraser, on June 21.[69] Mao's incapacitation removed him from effective political life from that point onward, extinguishing the force that had held together the "Maoist" coalition.

The impact of Mao Tse-tung's incapacitation was not immediately discernible. If anything, it enhanced Hua Kuo-feng's position in the Standing Committee, for Chang Ch'un-ch'iao and Wang Hung-wen needed Hua's support to ensure a three-to-two majority over Chu Teh and Yeh Chien-ying. The balance in what was now a seventeen-member Politburo was also critically affected by Mao's departure, the voting edge for the "Maoist group" declining to eleven to six. The event that completely altered the political dynamics of the Chinese leadership and triggered the coalescence of a new factional alignment in the Standing Committee and Politburo was Chu Teh's sudden death on July 6.

On the surface, Chu Teh's death increased the Mao group's advantage in the Standing Committee to three to one and ensured its continued dominance. But appearances were deceiving, for Chu Teh's death actually made Hua superfluous to Chang Ch'un-ch'iao and Wang Hung-wen, the two members of the Gang of Four on the Standing Committee, as they no longer needed his vote for a majority over Yeh Chien-ying. They now saw him as an obstacle to their own ambitions. Hua was now not only dispensable, but dangerous, for if he shifted toward Yeh Chien-ying, together Hua and Yeh could block any proposals Chang and Wang might make in the Standing Committee. In fact, over the next several months a major realignment occurred in both the Standing Committee and Politburo centering around precisely the evolution of a *mariage de convenance* between Hua Kuo-feng and Yeh Chien-ying. The regrouping was largely obscured at the time by the major earthquake of

July 28 and its extensive aftershocks, which demolished the city of Tangshan, some one hundred and seventy-five miles east southeast of Peking near the coast, and in which nearly three quarters of a million people perished.[70] In retrospect, the evolution of a coincidence of interests between Hua and Yeh was suggested by the prominent role that Hua, with extensive military support, played in the relief effort that continued for several months.

To citizens of the People's Republic of China with a penchant for symbolism the Tangshan earthquake portended dynastic change as their leader for over a quarter of a century neared his final breath. On the evening of September 9, the Peking government announced Chairman Mao's death in a "message to the whole party, the whole army and the people of all nationalities throughout the country." The Chairman's death released political forces held in check till then in the system forged and tempered by the leader himself. No successor could lay claim to the charismatic mantle of "Maoism," nor was there anyone capable of holding together the system Mao had built. With Mao gone, his attempt to realign China's geostrategic orientation with the United States and to establish a line of domestic political continuity with his selection of Hua Kuo-feng would be put to the test. The first question to be addressed was, of course, the issue of a new party chairman.

The succession struggle would pass through three rather distinct stages similar to those that had occurred earlier in the Soviet Union and in Romania.[71] Death of the leader would lead to a brief period of collective leadership, then to a more or less evenly balanced but unstable coalition and then to rule by a single leader once again, even if that condition could be described as *primus inter pares*. Without an established succession mechanism, which Mao himself had refused to create, the People's Republic of China now inevitably commenced a lengthy period of intense political infighting that also involved high-level disagreement over China's foreign policy position. Mao's legacy thus would be to spark as far-reaching a political revolution over the succeeding four years as any the Chairman had instigated during his lifetime.

XV
The Struggle for Succession, 1976–1978

In the two years after Mao's death the Chinese leadership underwent a virtual revolution. Domestically, following the fall of the Gang of Four, a three-way struggle developed among Hua Kuo-feng, Yeh Chien-ying, and Teng Hsiao-p'ing. Teng, rehabilitated a second time in the summer of 1977, then began a successful drive for power that saw him eclipse Hua Kuo-feng by the end of the following year. These internal changes occurred against the backdrop of equally, if not more, significant international developments. In 1978 two grand coalitions began to coalesce in Asia—the United States, Japan, and the People's Republic of China, on the one hand, and the Soviet Union and the Socialist Republic of Vietnam on the other. Teng's successful rise to power thus occurred in the midst of a rapidly changing domestic as well as international environment.

The Fall of the Gang of Four

Mao Tse-tung's death on September 9, 1976, opened up the question of selection of a new party chairman and revealed the extent of the factional realignment that had taken place in the Politburo. In the month following Mao's death the issue of who would be the new party chairman was fought out between Hua Kuo-feng, Mao's chosen successor, and Chiang Ch'ing, Mao's widow. Yet, even while these two and their respective supporters contended, they also colluded on a matter of joint interest. It was in the interests of both the Hua and Chiang groups to prevent Teng Hsiao-p'ing from exerting any direct influence on the outcome of their struggle. Therefore, both continued to press the anti-Teng campaign that had dominated the press since his ouster in April, except that Chiang Ch'ing and her supporters gave it a significant twist. Selecting one of Mao's "instructions" to Hua, Chiang Ch'ing altered the phrase "act according to past principles" to "act according to principles laid down."[1] Presumably, this arcane maneuver would not only keep pressure on Teng, but also forestall any move Hua might be contemplating against Chiang Ch'ing and her allies, the Gang of Four.

In an atmosphere thick with tension, at the end of September the Politburo met to select a new chairman. Supporters of both the Hua and Chiang Ch'ing groups put forward their candidates for the top party post, but neither side could marshal the necessary majority.[2] If we break down the sixteen-member Politburo[3] into the three groups identifiable immediately after Hua's emergence as party chairman in October and assume that something like this breakdown was already in existence in late September, then the Politburo division when the first standoff vote took place was:

Hua Kuo-feng	Yeh Chien-ying	Chiang Ch'ing
Wang Tung-hsing	Li Hsien-nien	Chang Ch'un-ch'iao
Chi Teng-k'uei	Liu Po-ch'eng	Wang Hung-wen
Wu Teh	Wei Kuo-ch'ing	Yao Wen-yuan
Ch'en Hsi-lien	Hsü Shih-yü	
Li Teh-sheng		
Ch'en Yung-kuei		
7	5	4

In this three-way division it is readily apparent that neither of the principal candidates could gain a simple majority, let alone a two-thirds majority, if the remaining two groups were opposed. What is also obvious is that it was the Maoist coalition that had divided over the issue of succession.

The initial clash revealed that the Politburo balance was heavily weighted against Chiang Ch'ing and her supporters. Realizing the impossibility of gaining Politburo approval for her candidacy, the regime later claimed, Chiang Ch'ing and her group prepared plans for a *coup d'état*.[4] The official exposé notwithstanding, the available evidence is contradictory and inconclusive. It may be true that the Gang planned a coup, but it was Hua Kuo-feng, with the support of Yeh Chien-ying, who actually executed one. The actual date, place, time, and circumstances of the "arrest" of the Gang of Four vary from account to account, but a common thread connects them all—Hua's initiative.[5] One account claims that on October 4, Hua Kuo-feng sent troops to seize the four, who were meeting at a resort town several miles outside of Peking.[6] In this version one or more of the gang were killed and Wang Tung-hsing was wounded while attempting to protect Chiang Ch'ing. A second ac-

388 The Evolution of U.S.-China Relations

count states that the four were arrested on October 6 and subjected to "investigation in solitary confinement."[7] In this version all of the Gang were alive and unharmed, although several guards may have been injured during the arrest. Still a third account avers that Hua called a Politburo meeting on October 7 and "detained" Chiang Ch'ing, Chang Ch'un-ch'iao, and Yao Wen-yuan when they entered the meeting room.[8] In this version Wang Hung-wen, who refused to attend the meeting, was wounded attempting to leave his place of residence by troops of unit 8341 under the command of Wang Tung-hsing.

Reports of troop movements on both sides were also associated with the coup. Prior to October 6, Hsü Shih-yü, Canton military region commander and Politburo member, sent troops to occupy Shanghai, capturing the Gang's power base.[9] At the same time, Hua Kuo-feng, with Yeh Chien-ying's full agreement, called the 112th division of the 38th army back to Peking from Tangshan, where it had been sent for post-earthquake support duties.[10] Under the command of deputy commander Hsü Heng-lu, the 112th reportedly arrived in Peking only "a few hours" ahead of Mao Yuan-hsin's tank division moving into the suburbs of Peking in support of Chiang Ch'ing.[11] According to this account, troops of the 112th division arrested the Gang. According to Yeh Chien-ying, the "8341 unit carried out the task" of arresting the four, after Hua Kuo-feng "personally talked with Comrade Wang Tung-hsing."[12] Wang Tung-hsing, on the other hand, declared that "Marshal Yeh was personally on the scene, directing the operation."[13]

The theme common to all of these accounts is that sometime between October 4 and 7 Hua Kuo-feng moved to arrest Chiang Ch'ing and her supporters, that military and security forces were involved, perhaps on both sides, that shooting occurred, and that one of the Gang was shot.[14] By the morning of October 7 the deed had been done. The arrest of the Gang reduced the Politburo Standing Committee to two men, Hua and Yeh, and the Politburo to twelve. Under these circumstances, for the next several months, the Politburo would function as the supreme decision-making body.

Later on October 7 Hua, Yeh, and Wang Tung-hsing each delivered reports on the "fall" of the Chiang Ch'ing group to the Politburo.[15] Although the Politburo "unanimously supported the resolute action initiated by Hua Kuo-feng," he was not made chairman of the party at that meeting. It would be two weeks before Hua's election to the chairmanship of the Chinese Communist Party would be announced on October 21 (although the resolution was dated October 7), suggesting that the two-week period following the ouster of the Gang of Four, as they were now formally termed, was one of intense negotiation, perhaps even bargaining, before the final decision was made in Hua's favor.[16]

The "Selection" of Chairman Hua Kuo-feng

Three issues appear to have been central in the negotiations between the Hua and Yeh groups that led to Hua's designation as chairman of the party and, concomitantly, chairman of the Military Commission. First was the legitimacy of Hua's claim to be Mao Tse-tung's chosen successor; second was the issue of Teng Hsiao-p'ing's reinstatement; and third was the question of revising economic priorities. The first two issues were resolved by the ninth or tenth of October.[17] Between then and the thirteenth, Central Committee members were contacted for their approval of the arrangements,[18] although no formal plenary meeting was convened, and between the thirteenth and the twentieth party leaders worked out substantive revision of the five-year economic plan.[19]

In support of his legitimacy, Hua Kuo-feng produced the third of Mao's "three instructions," which he had reserved for the occasion, the six-character phrase "with you in charge, I'm at ease." The instruction, handwritten by Mao himself, showed unquestionably that Hua was his designated heir, but that alone did not automatically confer the chairmanship.[20] Strong objections were raised by Hsü Shih-yü and Wei Kuo-ch'ing of Yeh Chien-ying's group, two leaders who were also long-time supporters of Teng Hsiao-p'ing. If a later criticism by those two leaders is at all indicative of their stand in early October, the argument they set forth against Hua's candidacy took the following form. In response to Hua's claim based on Mao's instruction, Hsü and Wei asserted that the party and state constitutions contained "specific provisions . . . about how the party chairman is elected":[21] "No matter how glittering these six characters are, they represent at most Chairman Mao's personal intention and are by no means a reflection of the views of the party, the armed forces, and the people."[22]

Yeh Chien-ying, acting as kingmaker and supported by Li Hsien-nien, interceded to produce an acceptable compromise. In return for Hua Kuo-feng's agreement to reinstate Teng Hsiao-p'ing and to make major revisions of economic policy, Yeh and Li voted with Hua's group of seven to produce more than the necessary two-thirds majority—nine to three[23]—in the now twelve-member Politburo. Why did these two leaders support Hua's claim to the chairmanship? First, Hua's solid block of support, consisting of Wang Tung-hsing, Chi Teng-k'uei, Wu Teh, Ch'en Hsi-lien, Li Teh-sheng, and Ch'en Yung-kuei, precluded any one of the Yeh group from obtaining the eight votes necessary to become chairman. Second, it was after all "Chairman Mao's personal intention" that Hua Kuo-feng succeed him, as even Hsü Shih-yü and Wei Kuo-ch'ing admitted. Perhaps most important was the issue of continuity, which Mao's "instruction" represented. Support of Hua would facilitate a smooth transition to the post-Mao era. Open contention for the chairmanship and the leadership instability it would produce would only encourage attempts at intervention by outside forces. Therefore, to prevent internal disintegration, forestall external pressures, and retain control of the decision-making process, Yeh and Li supported Hua for the chairmanship.

What of the compromise agreement to reinstate Teng Hsiao-p'ing? Clearly Hua's concession on this question gained the acquiescence of Hsü Shih-yü and Wei Kuo-ch'ing, but what of Yeh and Li? Hua's appointment as chairman of the party and Military Commission, and his continued control of the premiership and the internal security apparatus, placed him formally in a stronger position than Mao had ever held! It was probably the need to develop a counterweight to the formidable power Hua was acquiring that persuaded Yeh, if not Li, to support demands for Teng's return to active political life. A final consideration was their own positions, which would certainly be enhanced by the role of mediator, not to mention the increase in allocations to the economy in general and the military in particular as a result of the five-year plan revisions. These considerations explain Yeh's promotion to the number two position in the party hierarchy and Li Hsien-nien's promotion to number three.

Yet if the party leadership reached an acceptable compromise in selecting Hua as chairman, some, notably Hsü Shih-yü and Wei Kuo-ch'ing, steadfastly maintained that the new leadership arrangement was only temporary. In their view

Comrade Hua Kuo-feng assumed the position of party chairman and chairman of the military council without convening the national congress and without even consulting the plenary meeting of the central committee. That was only an expedient, the outcome of the struggle against the anti-party gang of four. The party, the armed forces, and the people understand this. But it is wrong for us to stress that the elevation of Comrade Hua Kuo-feng to the party chairmanship was based on Chairman Mao's six-character written instruction: "You do things, I feel assured."[24]

Hua Kuo-feng paid a stiff, but acceptable, price for the chairmanship. While agreeing to rehabilitate Teng Hsiao-p'ing, however, he did not commit himself to a specific timetable for Teng's return and continued to permit criticism of Teng to appear in the press. (The increasingly insistent public demands by members of Yeh's group through the spring of 1977 for Teng's early reinstatement lend support to this deduction.[25]) At the same time, Hua had accepted the need to revise the five-year plan, which the Gang had opposed. Thus, he endorsed the full implementation of the four modernizations, and although key decisions appear to have been taken on wage policy, military modernization, and the degree of reliance on importation of foreign technology, it would be months before these decisions would be finalized and made public.

The agreements on Teng Hsiao-p'ing's rehabilitation and on revision of economic policy represented future dangers for the new party chairman. Although Hua Kuo-feng had accepted the requirement that China move forward on its industrialization program, he himself was not the most obviously qualified person to lead China on that path. The most qualified leader was clearly Teng Hsiao-p'ing, who had advocated the heavy industrialization course since the mid-1950s and who commanded not only the expertise in that field, but also the allegiance of many trained cadres. On the other hand, Hua's not inconsiderable advantage lay in his occupation of all of the top positions in the regime, while Teng Hsiao-p'ing, for the time being, was still out of power.

Hua Kuo-feng, Yeh Chien-ying, Teng Hsiao-p'ing— Triumvirate Inchoate

In the months following the selection of Hua Kuo-feng as chairman, a three-way contest similar to that which had evolved after Mao's incapacitation began to unfold. The contestants were Hua, Teng, and Yeh, each employing different tactics to similar ends. Hua sought to delay the return of Teng for as long as possible and in the meantime strove to improve his image as Mao's successor and to broaden his power base. Teng, of course, by his own action and with the assistance of his supporters, sought to be reinstated as quickly as possible. Yeh, while generally supporting Teng's rehabilitation, took the opportunity to strengthen his own hold on the military apparatus as well as to work to improve his general political position. Central to each man's efforts was the promotion of supporters to positions of power at lower levels.

While delaying the reinstatement of Teng, Hua sought to preempt Teng's policy ground by identifying himself prominently with the new industrialization course. Hua had issued memorandum number twenty-one in late November declaring that Teng's reinstatement would be discussed at the Third Plenum, the date for which had yet to be set.[26] Having dealt with the Teng problem for the moment, Hua proceeded to build an image for himself as a qualified successor to Mao Tse-tung and a man fully capable of leading China onto its modernization path. His opening gambit on this issue was the announcement in December of a Central Committee decision to publish the fifth volume of Chairman Mao's *Selected Works*.

Volume Five would cover the period of the mid-1950s, which encompassed the first modernization debate over the issue of China's future economic development. The one speech singled out for immediate and separate publication and extensive quotation in the media was entitled "On the Ten Major Relationships," delivered on 25 April 1956 but hitherto unpublished and unknown in its entirety outside of high party circles.[27] In the speech, Mao discussed two alternate paths of economic development, which could lead to the construction of a heavy industrial base. He said:

> There are . . . two approaches to our development of heavy industry: one is to develop agriculture and light industry less, and the other is to develop them more. In the long run, the first approach will lead to a smaller and slower development of heavy industry, or at least will put it on a less solid foundation. . . . The second approach will lead to a greater and faster development of heavy industry and, since it ensures the livelihood of the people, it will lay a more solid foundation for the development of heavy industry.[28]

Publication of the speech showed that Mao Tse-tung had clearly anticipated the development of a heavy industrial base once the foundation had been laid in the light industrial and agricultural sectors. It also shattered the notion that he was a simple agrarian revolutionary with no concept of the modernization process. Finally, the issues Mao raised in 1956 were precisely those that the current leadership was then in the process of considering.

Hua Kuo-feng closely identified himself with Mao's position and the implied idea that the time had come for China to emphasize construction of a heavy industrial base. At the same time, he identified Teng Hsiao-p'ing as having opposed this developmental strategy from the beginning. He did this by publishing an article by Mao, penned, it was indicated in an editorial note, in 1971, but suppressed by the Gang of Four.[29] Titled "The Fundamental Way Out for Agriculture Lies in Mechanization," the article pointedly illustrated the differences between Mao and Liu Shao-ch'i (and implicitly Teng). Referring to the debate of the 1950s, the article noted that Mao in 1955 had taken the position that collectivization should precede mechanization, while Liu had taken the opposite stand. Adopting Liu's position would have entailed continued heavy investment in the industrial sector, which would have to supply the tractors to mechanize agriculture at the expense of the consumer sector. In 1955 Mao had also declared that not only should collectivization precede mechanization, but mechanization—even though initially deferred—would be completed "in the main" within twenty-five years, that is, coincidentally, by 1980. Aside from the implication that no major modifications were necessary in this developmental strategy worked out by Mao Tse-tung, Chinese leaders reading the article knew perfectly well that Liu and Teng were the two leaders who had opposed Mao's strategy, even though Teng's name was not mentioned.

Through the first half of 1977 Hua Kuo-feng participated prominently in a series of conferences in an effort to highlight his managerial expertise in economic matters. The series began with the national conference on agriculture at Tachai (December 9-27, 1976) and concluded with the national conference on industry at Taching (April 20-May 13, 1977). In between there were numerous other conferences on subjects ranging from air defense to finance and banking. Yeh Chien-ying also participated in these meetings, his name usually being ranked just one notch below Hua's, but occasionally, as at the Taching conference in May, he actually played a more prominent role.[30] Throughout the spring, however, the issue of Teng Hsiao-p'ing's reinstatement cast a shadow over events.

In early January, for several days surrounding the anniversary of Chou En-lai's death, wall posters appeared in Peking demanding Teng Hsiao-p'ing's immediate rehabilitation.[31] In a Politburo meeting later that month, as a result of an investigation conducted by Yeh Chien-ying, it was decided to downgrade Teng's indictment by Mao as a case of "antagonistic contradiction" to one of a "contradiction among the people."[32] The former permitted no rehabilitation; the latter meant that Teng's problems were rectifiable. Although the way was now formally cleared to reinstate Teng, the Politburo disagreed on the posts that he should be given. Therefore, Hua directed that each of the two hundred-odd Central Committee members give written opinions on Teng's case.[33]

The timing of Teng Hsiao-p'ing's return would be at Chairman Hua's direction.[34] Requiring each Central Committee member to provide a written opinion on the matter would—aside from further delaying matters—give Hua a much more precise tally of Teng's strength in the Central Committee by identifying potential supporters and opponents. By early March the polling of the Central Committee had been completed, and the Politburo convened specifically to decide on Teng's case. In a meeting lasting two weeks (approximately March 7-21) and marked by "hard bargaining," the Politburo agreed to restore Teng to his former posts.[35] Hsü Shih-yü, Wei Kuo-ch'ing, and Li Hsien-nien argued forcefully for his appointment to the premiership, in addition to his previous posts, but equally determined opposition led by Peking Mayor Wu Teh and Ch'en Hsi-lien forced a retreat from this demand.[36] Hua Kuo-feng retained the premiership, but Teng would be reappointed to the posts of member of the Politburo Standing Committee, first vice-chairman of the State Council, and chief of the Army General Staff—top positions in the party, state, and military hierarchies. It was undoubtedly their failure to secure the premiership for Teng that prompted Hsü Shih-yü and Wei Kuo-ch'ing to write the strong letter criticizing Hua Kuo-feng cited above.[37]

The decision of the March Politburo meeting triggered an acceleration of the struggle for control of the provincial party secretaryships to build support for the upcoming Third Plenum and Eleventh Congress. Up to this point, only four new appointments had been made in the provinces since Hua Kuo-feng's selection as chairman. Three of the four—Huo Shih-lien, who was appointed to Ninghsia in January, and Chiao Hsiao-kuang and An P'ing-sheng, who were appointed in February to Kwangsi and Yunnan, respectively—were Teng Hsiao-p'ing's men. The fourth appointee was Admiral Su Chen-hua, who took over the Shanghai party apparatus in October 1976 and probably supported Yeh Chien-ying, if anyone. Both Hua and Yeh perceived that if the trend in appointments continued, the composition of the Central Committee would gradually be altered to Teng's advantage, and they joined forces to block Teng's advance.

Yeh Chien-ying's greater involvement in power politics marked a significant change from his earlier political role. Elsewhere I distinguished between power seekers and power holders in Chinese politics.[38] The former were continuously involved in building and maintaining their power bases both in the center and in the provinces; the latter were essentially executors of policy, who, whether by choice or circumstance, did not challenge the leader, Mao Tse-tung. I identified Chiang Ch'ing and Yeh Chien-ying as power holders, not power seekers. In the main that characterization was accurate for as long as Mao Tse-tung exerted primary control over Chinese politics. Once Mao passed from the political scene and his coalition dissolved, both Chiang Ch'ing and Yeh Chien-ying became—by circumstance if nothing else—heavily involved in power politics. The change with respect to Chiang Ch'ing was immediately apparent due to her prominent even if unsuccessful role in the first stage of the succession crisis following Mao's demise. Yeh Chien-ying, on the other hand, initially assumed the less visible role of behind-the-scenes kingmaker. From the spring of 1977 onward, however, Yeh began to play a more vigorous role as a power seeker, in a manner perhaps analogous to that of Lin Piao when he was thrust into a political position during the cultural revolution.[39]

In the spring of 1977 at least eleven provinces churned in turmoil as Hua Kuo-feng and Yeh Chien-ying sought desperately to counter Teng Hsiao-p'ing's growing influence. By the end of March, six provincial secretaryships had changed hands in a flurry of activity; three secretaries could be identified as supporters of Teng's, while two backed Yeh and one, Hua. T'an Ch'i-lung, who became first party secretary in Tsinghai, Wang En-mao in Kirin, and Hsu Chia-t'ung in Kiangsu were Teng's men. T'ieh Ying in Chekiang and Liu Kuang-t'ao in Heilungchiang were Yeh's; Ma Li in Kweichow was Hua's. Wan Li's appointment to Anhui in early May and Chao Tzu-yang's ability to hang onto his position in Szechwan, where he was under fire, further strengthened Teng's position. In June, just a month before the Third Plenum, Hua and Teng each managed to install one more supporter into power, Mao Chih-yung in Hunan and Sung P'ing in Kansu, respectively. By this tentative reckoning, since becoming party chairman the previous October, Hua Kuo-feng had managed to place only two supporters into provincial secretaryships and Yeh Chien-ying had placed three, while Teng Hsiao-p'ing had inserted eight, not counting Chao Tzu-yang, who had assumed the Szechwan party leadership in December 1975.

Accompanying the political struggle was a hard-hitting campaign of press criticism, which, although more apparent in the central media, occurred in the provincial press as well. Being formally out of power, Teng had no direct access to the central press organs, but open and frequent criticism of Hua surfaced in the regional press. For example, in the southwest, Teng's long-time political base, the press conducted a virulent anti-Hua campaign in which the party chairman was denounced as "double-faced and mean."[40] Hua Kuo-feng held the advantage in the central media, where he authorized sustained campaigns directly condemning the Gang of Four and indirectly criticizing

Teng Hsiao-p'ing. The primary vehicles for Hua's attack were several "historical" articles recounting the succession to Lenin in the Soviet Union during
the 1920s. In each article the basic point was to establish Hua as Mao's successor in the same way that Stalin succeeded Lenin and to brand the Gang
of Four explicitly and Teng Hsiao-p'ing implicitly as part of the "opposition,"
much as Stalin had maneuvered Kamenev, Zinoviev, Rykov, and Trotsky into
that position. The "succession" articles appeared in *People's Daily* on March
19 and March 30, during and following the Politburo meetings discussed
above. The publication in *Ming Pao* in April of a March exchange of letters
between Teng and Hua revealed a much different picture.[41] In his letter,
Teng declared: "I firmly welcome Mr. Hua as chairman of our party. I firmly
support the crushing of the "gang of four" by the party central committee
under Chairman Hua. I am well and I ask Chairman Hua to send me to the
front line [of work]."[42] Hua, in his reply, said that "you have made mistakes
and you should be criticized. . . . [but] you are not responsible for the
Tienanmen Square incident. Not only will you be sent to the front line, but
to the firing line [of work]."[43] Teng's declaration of support for Chairman
Hua and Hua's exoneration of Teng from any responsibility for the T'ien
An Men incident cleared the way for Teng's formal reinstatement to all posts
at the Third Plenum.

Teng Hsiao-p'ing's Return to Power
and Peking's Uneasy Coalition

The Third Plenum convened from July 16 to July 21, 1977, and
passed three important resolutions.[44] Hua, Yeh, and Teng each spoke at the
plenum, which was attended by all of the Politburo members (except Liu
Po-ch'eng, who was noted as absent on sick leave), alternate Politburo members, members of the Central Committee, and principal leading comrades of
several localities and army units. The plenary session agreed with the Politburo decision to convene the Eleventh Party Congress "before the due date,"
endorsed the agenda for the congress, and "discussed and in general approved"
the political report, the report on the revision of the constitution, and the
draft of the revised party constitution.

The first item was adoption of the "resolution confirming the appointment of Comrade Hua Kuo-feng as Chairman of the Central Committee of
the Communist Party of China and Chairman of the Military Commission of
the Central Committee of the Communist Party of China." The plenum

"expressed full support" for the 7 October 1976 Politburo resolution appointing Chairman Hua "in accordance with the arrangements made by the great leader and teacher Chairman Mao" and agreed that Chairman Hua was Chairman Mao's "good student and successor." The October resolution was "entirely correct," winning the "warm support of the whole party, the whole army and the people of all nationalities in the country." As its second official act, the plenum adopted the "resolution restoring comrade Teng Hsiao-p'ing to his posts." The plenum, "after earnest discussions," expressed "complete support" for Hua's suggestion made at the Central Work Conference in March that the Third Plenum "take an official decision so that Comrade Teng Hsiao-p'ing could resume work."[45]

Finally, the plenum unanimously adopted the "resolution on the anti-party clique of Wang Hung-wen, Chang Ch'un-ch'iao, Chiang Ch'ing, and Yao Wen-yuan," noting the "entirely correct" resolute measures taken by Chairman Hua in "shattering" their clique. The Gang was condemned on a long list of charges. Their anti-party activities were traced back to the "early period of the Great Proletarian Revolution when they worked hand in glove with Lin Piao and company" to oppose Mao Tse-tung. They attempted to "overthrow Comrade Chou En-lai"; they "feverishly attacked and fabricated accusations against Comrade Teng Hsiao-p'ing"; they "bitterly hated and wildly opposed" Mao's decision to appoint Hua Kuo-feng premier; and they "attempted to overthrow Comrade Hua Kuo-feng." After "tormenting" Chairman Mao when he was on his deathbed, once he died they "plotted to overthrow the party central committee headed by Comrade Hua Kuo-feng and bring about a counter-revolutionary restoration."

Hua Kuo-feng's intent at the plenum was to obtain official party sanction for his chairmanship and to remove the Gang from any future role in political affairs, but the most important resolution, and also the briefest, was that restoring Teng Hsiao-p'ing to his former posts. Teng's reappointment to the Politburo Standing Committee, in particular, was a change of major significance, yet not quite in the manner envisaged by outside observers. Teng stepped into a Standing Committee that had been doubled in size, in which, it seemed, he could not automatically count on holding a majority. In fact, the opposite was true. In what must be interpreted as a crucial if unheralded change, the Politburo had voted to promote Wang Tung-hsing and Li Hsien-nien to the Standing Committee in late May.[46] Liu Po-ch'eng's continuing illness and absence, combined with a shift in Yeh Chien-ying's vote, made the promotions possible, providing a greater than two thirds (seven-to-two) majority to Hua's group (assuming that neither Wang nor Li could vote on their own promotions).

Hua Kuo-feng	Hsü Shih-yü
Yeh Chien-ying	Wei Kuo-ch'ing
Ch'en Hsi-lien	
Chi Teng-k'uei	
Wu Teh	
Li Teh-sheng	
Ch'en Yung-kuei	

The addition of Wang Tung-hsing and Li Hsien-nien to the Standing Committee altered the voting pattern in that now five-member body, strengthening Hua's position with the addition of Wang, but more importantly, placing Yeh in position to continue as balancer between Hua and Teng. By siding with Hua and Wang on specific issues, Yeh could tip the balance in their favor even if Li Hsien-nien supported Teng. On the other hand, by siding with Teng and Li, Yeh could tip the balance toward them. At the Eleventh Party Congress that followed, Hua, Yeh, and Teng would each strengthen his own position further, but none independently would yet be able to build a decisive advantage over the other two.

The Eleventh Party Congress convened August 12-18, 1977, amid amplified attacks on the Gang of Four.[47] Of major significance was the addition of ten new men to the Politburo. It would appear that Hua managed to add only Ni Chih-fu to his group, while Yeh and Teng each profited handsomely. To Yeh's group were added Hsü Hsiang-ch'ien, Nieh Jung-chen, Chang T'ing-fa, Yu Chiu-li, Fang Yi, and Su Chen-hua. To Teng's were added Ulanfu, Keng Piao, and P'eng Ch'ung. Even if this is only a rough approximation of accretions to their respective strengths, the balance in the now twenty-three-member Politburo stood thus:

Hua Kuo-feng	Yeh Chien-ying	Teng Hsiao-p'ing
Wang Tung-hsing	Li Hsien-nien	Hsü Shih-yü
Ch'en Hsi-lien	Hsü Hsiang-ch'ien	Wei Kuo-ch'ing
Chi Teng-k'uei	Nieh Jung-chen	Liu Po-ch'eng
Wu Teh	Chang T'ing-fa	Ulanfu
Li Teh-sheng	Yu Chiu-li	Keng Piao
Ch'en Yung-kuei	Fang Yi	P'eng Ch'ung
Ni Chih-fu	Su Chen-hua	
8	8	7

It is apparent from this breakdown, however tentative, that the Hua and Yeh groups together held a greater than two-thirds majority over Teng and his supporters in the Politburo. But if Teng did not gain a dominant position in the Politburo and continued to be hedged in in the Standing Committee, he did obtain an important concession from Hua Kuo-feng. Hua relinquished his post as minister of public security to one of Teng's men, the former public security chief of Szechwan, Chao Ts'ang-pi.[48]

Between the Eleventh Party Congress and the Fifth National People's Congress (NPC), which convened in late February 1978, the organizational maneuverings for position continued. During these months five Central Committee members, including two provincial first secretaries, were removed. Wu Kuei-hsien dropped from sight after she attended the first anniversary ceremony of Mao's death; Liu Hsing-yuan, Chengtu military region commander, was replaced by Wu K'o-hua in October; and Kuo Yu-feng, director of the PLA's Organization Department, was replaced by Hu Yao-pang in December 1977. Two provincial secretaries who lost their positions were Saifudin in Sinkiang and Liu Kuang-t'ao in Heilungchiang. Yang Yi-ch'en replaced Liu Kuang-t'ao in December and Wang Feng took over as party boss in Sinkiang in January, even though the ousted Saifudin would be re-elected as an NPC standing committee member the next month.

In preparation for the Fifth NPC the leadership convened the fourth session of the Fourth NPC on October 23-24, 1977.[49] It was decided to convene the Fifth NPC in the spring following the re-election of all of the provincial revolutionary committee leaderships. The process commenced with the election of the Hunan provincial revolutionary committee on November 16, 1977, and concluded with the election of the Kiangsi committee on February 18, 1978, as all twenty-nine provincial revolutionary committees had completed their tasks.[50] On that day the Second Plenum of the party convened, granting Hua Kuo-feng "expanded powers" and setting the stage for the opening of the Fifth National People's Congress, February 26-March 5.[51]

How much the struggle during these months affected the balance within the Politburo Standing Committee is difficult to determine, but judging from the results of the Fifth NPC, it appeared that a combined effort by Hua Kuo-feng and Yeh Chien-ying blocked Teng Hsiao-p'ing's drive to power. Of the issues surrounding the Fifth NPC the most divisive was the question of whether or not to reinstitute the position of chairman of the state, or the "presidency."[52] Other vital posts to be filled or changed were the premiership and the chairmanships of the Defense Ministry and State Planning

Committee. It was generally assumed that Teng would either obtain the re-established presidency or be named premier and that his supporters would fill other top posts.

But Teng suffered a startling and unexpected reverse. Not only was it decided not to reinstitute the presidency, Teng was not accorded the premier-ship either—Hua Kuo-feng retained it. In addition, the *pro forma* head of state post, the chairmanship of the Standing Committee of the People's Congress, went to Yeh Chien-ying, who, in turn, relinquished his chairmanship of the Defense Ministry to his supporter Hsü Hsiang-ch'ien.

Yet another of Yeh's supporters, Fang Yi, assumed command of the committee on science and technology, and Yeh's ally, Li Hsien-nien, obtained the appointment of Yu Chiu-li to the chairmanship of the State Planning Committee. Clearly the biggest winner at the Fifth NPC was Yeh Chien-ying, who placed several supporters in key posts, but Hua Kuo-feng also made gains and managed to retain control of the premiership. The biggest loser was Teng Hsiao-p'ing, who was excluded from any position of direct control in the state apparatus. But Teng's setback was only temporary. As the international situation coalesced during 1978 and China moved toward normalization of relations with Washington and war with Vietnam, Teng's political fortunes took a decided turn for the better. By the end of the year his star was once again on the rise.

The Soviet Decision to Increase
Military Pressure on China

At the end of March, following the Fifth NPC proceedings, *Peking Review* published an article revealing and rejecting Moscow's most recent effort to normalize relations.[53] The Soviet note of February 24, delivered on the eve of the Fifth NPC, called upon the two countries to issue a "joint statement on the principles of mutual relations" as a means to "advance the cause of normalization of our relations." The Chinese side decided to publish the full text of the Soviet letter "so that all who are interested in Sino-Soviet relations may know the truth." In rejecting this latest Moscow offer, the Chinese declared that the Soviet Union "went back on the understanding reached by the Premiers of the two countries" in September 1969, which was "spelled out in specific measures." To illustrate their point, the Chinese described the Soviet offers of 1971 and 1973 as well as the current effort as "singing the same old tune": "How can the Chinese people be expected to believe that a hollow statement on the principles of mutual relations . . . is of any real worth and not a propaganda stunt?"[54] While noting that since the smashing of the Gang of Four Moscow had carried on continuous "attacks on the domestic and foreign policies of our country in a vain attempt to make us alter the revolutionary line of Chairman Mao," the Chinese had missed the significant change that occurred at this time and would result in a quantum intensification of pressure on the People's Republic of China.

Several disparate sequences of events—in the strategic weapons balance between Moscow and Washington, in Southeast Asia, and in Peking itself— had coalesced by early spring of 1978 in a way that led the Soviet leadership to conclude that only a major intensification of pressure on the Chinese carried any hope of improving relations. This conclusion was made possible by a qualitative change in the strategic weapons balance between the Soviet Union and the United States. In the late fall of 1977 Moscow succeeded in achieving a major, and to U.S. policymakers, unexpectedly early, break- through in ballistic missile guidance systems. The breakthrough, which U.S. leaders had not expected Moscow to achieve until the mid-1980s, enabled the Soviet Union to mount a serious threat to Minuteman, the U.S. land-based intercontinental ballistic missile force, in the near term. The almost immedi- ate effect upon the United States was to heighten the inclination to avoid crises that was already apparent in the new Carter administration and to ac- celerate U.S. efforts to consolidate those geopolitical positions that could be expected to come under attack, particularly in the Middle East and the Far East. For Moscow, realization that a favorable shift in the strategic balance was under way led rapidly to the general decision to seize the initiative and to prepare for moves in the Middle East, in Afghanistan, and in Southeast Asia. This last reflected a larger decision regarding China.

Soviet leaders had assumed that Teng Hsiao-p'ing, having consistently opposed Mao Tse-tung throughout his career (despite his somewhat ambiguous behavior between 1973 and 1976), was the one leader with whom they might reach some sort of accommodation, and they hoped for his return to a top position after Mao's death.[55] But in ensuing months, even though extensive reshuffling of the top leadership cadre had occurred and Teng's position had visibly strengthened, he had not assumed a top post. When the Eleventh Party Congress in August of 1977 confirmed Hua Kuo-feng as party chairman, if not a few months earlier, Moscow began to prepare the ground for the ap- plication of greater pressure on China through increasingly active involvement in Hanoi's ongoing drive to conquer Kampuchea. The reconfirmation of Hua's position as premier and Teng's continued exclusion from any formal top posts at the Fifth National People's Congress foreclosed any possibility of improvement in Sino-Soviet relations under current conditions. The die was cast.

In Indochina, as both the Kampuchean and Vietnamese regimes moved to consolidate their respective territories after coming to power in 1975, initially cool relations between the two countries soon deteriorated so that by the spring of 1976 border clashes were commonplace.[56] Hanoi mounted two large but inconclusive punitive expeditions against Kampuchea the following year, the first in April 1977 and the second in December 1977 and January 1978. Up to this point, Hanoi had also sought to gain China's acquiescence in its domination of the region by diplomatic means, but without success. By the early spring of 1978 it was clear to the leaders in Hanoi that although the Socialist Republic of Vietnam had succeeded in establishing a dominant position in Laos—a treaty of peace and friendship had been signed the previous July—incorporation of Kampuchea into Vietnam's sphere of influence would be impossible without a major use of force. This course of action, however, would most certainly provoke Chinese counteraction and require Soviet assistance to deter Peking from frustrating Hanoi's designs. A coincidence of interest between Hanoi and Moscow thus had emerged by the spring of 1978.

Moscow's decision to support Hanoi in its attempt to conquer China's client state ran directly counter to Peking's long-term strategy in the region. A Vietnamese invasion of Kampuchea would leave Peking with no recourse but to intervene militarily to protect its client state. The unacceptable alternative was to stand idly by and witness the emergence of a Hanoi-dominated Indochina closely allied to Moscow, a region in which Peking would have little influence and which would constitute a continuing threat to China's southern flank. It was therefore a foregone conclusion that Peking would take military action against Hanoi once all other options to maintain Kampuchean territorial integrity had been foreclosed.

Moscow's role would be to supply Hanoi's war needs and, as in the Indo-Pakistani conflict of 1971, to deter Peking from taking action that would defeat Moscow's ally.[57] Certainly, considerable goodwill would accrue from Hanoi's success, but Moscow's objectives were more complex than the simple notion of building goodwill within the socialist camp. The emerging favorable strategic weapons balance, combined with Hanoi's determination to secure control of Kampuchea and Indochina proper, offered the Soviet leadership an unparalleled opportunity to generate pressure on the Chinese in the hopes of interrupting Peking's rapprochement with Washington. Moscow's longer-range objective was to create new conditions for reaching an accommodation with Peking, or failing that, to lock the People's Republic into the vise of a vastly more threatening situation of threats on two fronts, thereby partially neutralizing the threat to the Soviet Union from the east.

In retrospect, Moscow's decision was signaled by Hanoi's sudden crackdown in March on Chinese enterprises in Vietnam and the deportation of several hundred thousand Chinese from the cities to so-called new economic zones in the countryside. Among other things, the removal of the overseas Chinese from the Vietnamese body politic eliminated a potential fifth column in the Vietnamese rear in the event of a major conflict between Vietnam and China. Nationalization of all property in May also hit the overseas Chinese community especially hard. This step led directly to a sharp deterioration of relations with Peking, as the Chinese media mounted a vituperative propaganda campaign excoriating Vietnam's treatment of the overseas Chinese population. Later in the summer both sides withdrew their respective ambassadors, and Peking shut its side of the border to all but official traffic.

Beginning in early April and continuing through August of 1978, Hanoi conducted its most extensive military operations against Kampuchea to date, driving up to twenty miles into Kampuchean territory.[58] The Vietnamese also began openly training ethnic Khmer soldiers as part of the Kampuchean United National Front for National Salvation. In June Hanoi entered the Soviet-controlled Council for Mutual Economic Assistance, reportedly to bolster a sagging economy. Finally, beginning in July Vietnam moved to upgrade air and air defense positions in the north, construct border fortifications, and conduct a campaign of repeated provocations along the Chinese border.[59]

Strategy, Counterstrategy, and Normalization

On the broader chessboard of international politics, the Sino-Japanese-American "entente" began to take shape in the summer of 1978. U.S. leaders, correctly perceiving the change in Soviet policy, moved to complete the normalization process with regard both to Sino-Japanese and Sino-American relations before a major conflict could occur to prevent it. President Carter's national security advisor, Zbigniew Brzezinski, traveled to Peking in early May to initiate the process, the first part of which was concluded with the signing of the Sino-Japanese peace and friendship treaty on August 12.

Perhaps suspecting the purpose of Brzezinski's visit, the Soviets precipitated the largest military clash on the Sino-Soviet border since 1969: A Soviet unit supported by eighteen naval craft penetrated two and a half miles into PRC territory along the Ussuri River. A few days later, Moscow declared that a "mistake" had been made, but offered no apology.[60]

In the first week of August Vietnamese military units stepped up operations against Kampuchea, bolstered by a massive new Soviet airlift of supplies and advisors.[61] A *Pravda* commentator noted with satisfaction that Soviet-Vietnamese relations were "becoming filled with new content."[62] The Chinese, on the other hand, interpreted Soviet actions to mean that Moscow was "pushing" Hanoi into a "large-scale invasion of Kampuchea"[63] and responded by beginning preparations for conflict between China and Vietnam as well as between China and the Soviet Union. Arrangements for normalization thus moved parallel to stepped-up preparations for military action on China's northern and southern borders. In particular, Peking's need to build a counterweight to Moscow forced a softening of its bargaining position *vis-à-vis* Washington, whose leaders took the advantage thus proffered. On September 19, President Carter became directly involved in the normalization process, meeting with PRC Liaison Office Chief Chai Tse-min and stipulating that, as a fundamental condition of normalization, the United States would continue to sell certain defensive weaponry to Taiwan after abrogation of the United States–Republic of China mutual defense treaty—a position the Chinese accepted.

In the meantime, Teng Hsiao-p'ing traveled to Pyongyang, North Korea, in September; on the same trip he inspected Manchurian defenses. The purpose was to neutralize Pyongyang and to shore up China's northern defenses in anticipation of a Soviet attempt to deter Peking by generating military pressure on the Sino-Soviet and Sino–North Korean borders. That done, the Chinese began deploying the first of twenty-seven divisions as well as several hundred combat support aircraft in the Sino-Vietnamese border area. The September deployment indicated that the decision to intervene had already been made, and its size suggested a major military campaign. The exact nature and timing of the strike, however, would ultimately depend upon Peking's ability, alone or in concert with allies, to neutralize the Soviet Union.

At this point, Moscow entered the picture once again, signing a treaty of peace and friendship with the Socialist Republic of Vietnam on November 3, 1978.[64] The treaty put Peking and Washington on notice that any military move against Vietnam would have to take into account Moscow's public pledge of support to Vietnam. At the same time and for the same reason—Moscow's now more evident deterrent posture—Hanoi redoubled its efforts to topple the Pol Pot regime in Kampuchea. On December 3, Hanoi announced that the Kampuchean National United Front for National Salvation had been formed; the announcement was accompanied by a sharp escalation of incidents along the Sino-Vietnamese border.

Before Hanoi could move into the final phase of its military campaign against Kampuchea, the United States and the People's Republic of China announced on December 15 their decision to exchange ambassadors and extend formal articles of recognition on January 1, 1979.[65] The announcement preempted any Soviet hope of forestalling normalization by means of the Vietnamese-Kampuchean conflict and, to some degree, also neutralized the Soviet-Vietnamese peace and friendship pact of November 3. Nevertheless, if it had any operational impact on Vietnamese war plans, the normalization announcement advanced the timetable for the Vietnamese attack, which began on December 25, one week before formal recognition between Washington and Peking was scheduled to occur.

Meanwhile, the evolving international situation had its impact on internal Chinese politics. The earlier momentum built by Teng Hsiao-p'ing, which had produced the combined effort by Hua Kuo-feng and Yeh Chien-ying to block Teng's advance at the Fifth NPC, continued through 1978. But differences among the leaders over the advisability of invading Vietnam, the terms of normalization with the United States, and the pace of China's modernization program brought about a realignment of power among the three men. In particular, a split between Hua Kuo-feng and Yeh Chien-ying and the latter's support for Teng as the conflict with Vietnam became unavoidable opened the way for a significant increase in Teng's power.

Between the Fifth NPC and mid-November, Hua Kuo-feng held the upper hand on each of the three issues. He was in control of the normalization process with the United States and had determined the pace of China's modernization program. His position on the war issue during these months is more difficult to assess, but if the views he expressed in January just prior to the conflict are any indication, then he opposed taking military action against Hanoi. In mid-January, he declared that China should "oppose big as well as small hegemonism and defend itself against threats from the outside, not by arms, but by diplomatic means."[66] Hua appeared to view normalization of relations with the United States primarily as a means of facilitating China's modernization, the timetable for which he accelerated. Since the

Fifth NPC Hua had consistently advocated that the four modernizations be completed "at an early date," by which he meant that "the first eight years are the key to accomplishing the four modernizations in 23 years, that is, by the year 2000."[67] Presumably, accelerating the pace of modernization would channel resources into the capital plant sector and away from current defense expenditures, a feature congruent with opposition to military action, which would require considerable investment in the defense sector at the expense of the other sectors.

Teng Hsiao-p'ing's positions during this period were markedly different. As with Hua, his views on normalization and modernization were clearer than that on the war issue until early in 1979. Teng took a pessimistic stand regarding China's ability to modernize by the end of the century, much less complete the basic requirements within eight years, which Hua claimed was possible. His clearest statement on the subject came during a press conference in Tokyo on October 25. Comparing the relative levels of development of China and Japan, he said that it would be difficult for China to reach Japan's present level by the end of the century "let alone [Japan's] level 22 years from now."[68]

During the same press conference, Teng took an inflexible position on normalization, continuing to hold that it was dependent upon satisfaction of three conditions: U.S. derecognition of the Republic of China, abrogation of the mutual defense treaty, and withdrawal of troops from the island. Teng also declined to commit himself to a peaceful approach to the settlement of the Taiwan question after normalization. A week later, Teng gave a similar assessment, this time to Japanese journalists in Peking. He expressed a pessimistic view of the negotiations then under way with Washington and declared that "China was in no hurry" to reach a final settlement.[69] Finally, on November 6, in talks with Thai premier General Kriangsak, Teng continued to insist on fulfillment of the three conditions and declined to offer a statement on the peaceful settlement of the Taiwan issue.[70] Teng's statement in Bangkok came two days after the United States had presented its final draft on normalization to the Chinese government.[71] Up to the last minute, therefore, Teng's position remained obdurate and inflexible.

Favoring the attack on Vietnam implied and required greater allocation of resources in the military sector for current requirements. Teng's argument for slower-paced modernization was thus consistent with greater spending for defense. In this context Teng viewed normalization as a means of deterring Moscow as well as acquiring access to military technology from the United

States and its allies. Indeed, on the eve of the announcement to establish diplomatic relations with the United States, he declared that "normalization depended on whether the United States was prepared to act irrespective of what the Soviet Union might think."[72]

The Rise to Power of Teng Hsiao-p'ing

Thus, up to mid-November 1978, Hua Kuo-feng and Teng Hsiao-p'ing openly differed on the issues of normalization with the United States and the pace of China's modernization, even if their views on the coming conflict with Hanoi were murky. It was also apparent that, up to this time, Hua Kuo-feng was in control of the policy-making machinery in Peking, while Teng expressed reservations about policy. The following six weeks, however, marked a fundamental reversal of relative political strength between the two leaders. The decisive sequence commenced with Teng's return from his trip to Thailand, Singapore, and Malaysia (November 5-14) and culminated with his assumption of control of the policy-making mechanism and domination of the three issues discussed above.

Although the exact chain of events is unclear, enough data exist to allow a tentative reconstruction. Teng Hsiao-p'ing returned from his Southeast Asia trip to discover that Hua Kuo-feng and his supporters, subsequently identified variously as the "oppositionists," the "whatever faction," or the "everything faction,"[73] were meeting to coordinate their efforts against him. Teng immediately convened the Central Work Conference, which remained in session until the opening of the Third Plenum on December 18. It was the Central Work Conference that produced a major swing in the respective fortunes of Hua and Teng. Evidently for reasons of factional activity, Hua was given a reprimand and at least five and possibly as many as seven of his nine supporters were "suspended," formal action being taken on the suspensions at the Third Plenum (December 18-22, 1978).[74] Those suspended could "no longer take part in meetings and discussions or in making decisions, but they still retain[ed] their party positions and government posts."[75] All of Hua's group, they were Wang Tung-hsing, Ch'en Hsi-lien, Ch'en Yung-kuei, Chi Teng-k'uei, Wu Teh, Ni Chih-fu, and Li Teh-sheng. The first three were also placed under house arrest. The suspensions, which apparently were for three months, produced a dramatic shift in the Politburo and Politburo Standing Committee balance, greatly eroding Hua's position and strengthening those of Teng and Yeh. Even if we assume that only five of Hua's supporters were excluded from "making decisions," Teng with the support of Yeh Chien-ying held thirteen votes to Hua's five, more than enough to meet the two-thirds voting majority requirement postulated earlier. Teng's coup may have persuaded Li Teh-sheng to shift his allegiance from Hua at this time. (See previous chart of Politburo groupings.) Wang Tung-hsing's suspension also meant his removal from the Standing Committee and gave Teng, Yeh, and Li Hsien-nien a clear three-to-one edge in that body as well.

That the Chinese leadership had entered a period of crisis in the second half of November is generally acknowledged by all observers of the Chinese political scene. American and Soviet China watchers, not to mention President Carter himself, spoke openly of a crisis. U.S. reporters noted the upsurge in critical wall poster commentary on Hua Kuo-feng and his allies, particularly Wang Tung-hsing, and even in criticism of Mao Tse-tung himself.[76] Soviet analysts in Peking interpreted events as a "power bid by Teng," anticipating that "a major reshuffling of personnel will probably take place in the supreme organ of the CCP. It is most likely that some of Hua's faction will be removed to the benefit of Teng's faction. . . . The outcome of the Hua-Teng conflict . . . could arrive at any moment."[77] Finally, President Carter, during his news conference on November 30, observed that "the attitude of China, the domestic situation in China, has changed, and we watch it with great interest."[78] Even through the mangled syntax came the conclusion that a significant change had occurred within the Chinese leadership.

By the end of the month Teng had clearly assumed the central leadership role. In an interview with the visiting chairman of the Japanese Democratic Socialist Party, Teng declared that "the time had come to correct action taken by the Chinese Politburo after the Tienanmen incident. . . . The decision that followed the Tienanmen incident was wrong," he said, "this must be corrected."[79] There had been, of course, two decisions taken immediately following the T'ien An Men incident, one purging Teng and the other appointing Hua permanently to the premiership and to the Politburo Standing Committee. Teng had already been restored to all of his posts at the Third Plenum, which, at the very least, implicitly repudiated the T'ien An Men resolution purging him. Unless there was still some formal action required, which was doubtful, his remarks could have meant only that he wished to have "corrected" the resolution promoting Hua! He was immediately required to "clarify" himself. The next day in another interview, Teng formally denied any aspirations to Hua's position, saying that he "had refused an offer to take over Mr. Hua's other job as prime minister" the previous year.[80] The official interpretation of the T'ien An Men incident itself was reversed from its original depiction as "counter-revolutionary" to "completely revolutionary."[81]

Teng Hsiao-p'ing's decisive role in the last stages of the normalization process now also became evident. In an interview with *Washington Post* correspondents Rowland Evans and Robert Novak, Teng assumed the spokesman's role on normalization, reversing his position on Taiwan, making no mention of the three conditions, and declaring that "Taiwan could maintain its own non-communist economic and social system under unification with the mainland."[82] A few days later he reiterated the view that Taiwan would have "special status," while taking a positive view of the negotiations then in the concluding stage with Washington. "Only when we normalize relations," he said, "will peace, security and stability be brought to this part of the world."[83] As negotiations on the final terms for normalization of relations neared their conclusion, the United States insisted that the defense treaty with the Republic of China on Taiwan be terminated in accordance with the treaty provisions, that is, one year's notice should be given of intent to terminate. In other words, there would be no abrogation of the treaty. In addition, the United States indicated its intention to continue sales of defensive arms to Taiwan following termination of the treaty.

On December 5, Teng Hsiao-p'ing called on U.S. Liaison Office Chief Leonard Woodcock to convey Chinese acquiescence, even if "very reluctantly," in the U.S. position.[84] The final obstacle was the issue of Taiwan's future unification with the mainland. On December 13, Teng Hsiao-p'ing and Woodcock met again and agreed on procedure. The United States would issue a statement regarding its expectations of a peaceful resolution of the Taiwan question; the Chinese would not contradict this statement. Two days later, Washington and Peking issued statements agreeing to recognition and the establishment of diplomatic relations on January 1, 1979. The joint communique expressed the common objective of opposing hegemony "in the Asia-Pacific region or in any other region of the world" and reducing "the danger of international military conflict." On Taiwan, the communique acknowledged the Chinese position that "there is but one China and Taiwan is part of China" while reaffirming Washington's intention to "maintain cultural, commercial, and other unofficial relations with the people of Taiwan."[85]

The establishment of formal diplomatic relations, which had eluded the two countries for thirty years, was achieved by finessing the Taiwan issue in a compromise that was largely formal in the short run and for the long run offered largely promises. For while the United States withdrew diplomatic recognition from Taipei and reduced its military position on the island, it also continued to provide military support for the Taiwan government, which made any early military takeover by Peking illusory. Economic relations with the thriving island nation continued virtually unaffected through existing commercial channels. Peking would have to remain content with the short-run *status quo* and only the future prospect of integration of the island with the mainland, although it reserved the right to use force if that became necessary. The normalization announcement preceded by a few days the opening of the CCP's Third Plenum on December 18, at which Teng Hsiao-p'ing made a major advance over Hua Kuo-feng in his now seemingly ineluctable drive to power.

XVI
Whither China?
The Uncertain Future,
1978-1980

Beginning with the Third Plenum in December 1978 and culminating in mid-December 1980, Teng Hsiao-p'ing gradually and, it seems, inexorably, consolidated his position within the Chinese Communist Party. He accomplished this primarily at the expense of Hua Kuo-feng, forcing the designated heir of Mao Tse-tung first to step down from the premiership and then to give up his party chairmanship. Teng successfully challenged Hua, in the main gaining acceptance of his views on issues as diverse as the interpretation of PRC history, China's modernization, war with Vietnam, and relations with Washington and Moscow. Indeed, the final month of 1980 appeared to mark a decisive turn in Chinese leadership politics as Teng, once the purged outcast, came full circle to capture the reins of power from Hua, who, at least for the time being, literally dropped from sight.

The Third Plenum of the Chinese Communist Party

Following the announcement that relations with Washington would be normalized on January 1, the Chinese leadership convened the Third Plenum, December 18-22, 1978.[1] After five days of hard bargaining, the Hua and Teng camps produced a final communique, revealing, however obliquely, the significant power shift that had taken place at the pinnacle of power in Peking. In form, the Third Plenum's communique resembled the sixteen-point resolution of the Eleventh Plenum of the Ninth Party Congress of August 1966[2] on the eve of the Great Proletarian Cultural Revolution. Both documents were products of compromise between two roughly equal groups, but whereas the sixteen-point resolution represented Mao's triumph over Teng Hsiao-p'ing and Liu Shao-ch'i, the Third Plenum communique marked Teng's ascendancy over Mao's successor, Hua Kuo-feng. Even though Hua succeeded in establishing his views on certain matters in the communique,

Teng clearly had moved into a commanding position. The principal issues and personalities under consideration—if not in dispute—were the leadership question, including the personalities of Teng and Hua; the interpretation of China's history and of Mao's role in shaping that history; and China's economic modernization program.

Teng Hsiao-p'ing strengthened his position at all levels of party power, in the Politburo Standing Committee, the Politburo, and the Central Committee. Ch'en Yün, a specialist on economic matters, a Central Committee member since 1934 and Politburo Standing Committee member between 1956 and the cultural revolution, when he fell out of favor with Mao Tse-tung, was named to the Politburo Standing Committee once again, this time as a supporter of Teng's. Ch'en reportedly criticized Hua at the plenum for excessive "worship" of Mao Tse-tung and "hasty" action with regard to the question of modernization.[3] Ch'en's appointment to the Standing Committee gave Teng an overwhelming four-to-one majority in that body (Teng, Yeh Chien-ying, Li Hsien-Nien, and Ch'en Yün versus Hua). (Wang Tung-hsing was suspended and could not vote in support of Hua. In fact, the plenum removed Wang from his posts as director of the administrative office of the CCP Central Committee, first vice-president of the Central Committee party school, and political commissar of special unit 8341.[4])

Three of Teng's supporters were added to the Politburo: Hu Yao-pang, Chou En-lai's widow Teng Ying-ch'ao, and Wang Chen. Hu's appointment was particularly significant. A longtime ally of Teng's, Hu was placed in charge of the secretariat of the Central Committee, the same position to which Teng had been appointed in 1956 and which conferred great power over personnel matters. The three new faces, together with Ch'en Yün, increased the membership of the Politburo to twenty-six (Politburo member Su Chen-hua was ill and incapacitated. He would die in February 1979). Nine men were also added on a provisional basis to the Central Committee; their appointments were subject to confirmation by the coming Twelfth Party Congress. All victims to one degree or another of the cultural revolution and therefore in all likelihood predisposed to support Teng, they were Huang K'o-ch'eng, Sung Jen-ch'iung, Hu Ch'iao-mu, Hsi Chung-hsün, Wang Jen-ch'ung, Hung Huo-ch'ing, Ch'en Tsai-tao, Han Kuang, and Chou Hui.

The Third Plenum represented the initial phase of a general all-out attack by Teng Hsiao-p'ing on the Maoist interpretation of the history of the People's Republic of China. If successful, Teng would be able not only to solidify his position, but also to set China on a policy course of his own choosing. It was only partly clear in the final communique that Teng had attempted to divide the history of the People's Republic into two periods, with the Eighth Party Congress of 1956 the dividing line. He deemed the earlier period "correct" and the later one marred by a series of errors perpetrated by Mao Tse-tung that led to the "catastrophe" of the cultural revolution. This interpretation accorded with the history of Teng's personal relations with Mao Tse-tung, as the split between them had occurred at the time of the Eighth Party Congress, and would allow Teng to argue for a reversion to the "correct" policies adopted before Mao set China on the course of the Great Leap Forward. It would also justify driving out of power those whose fortunes subsequently rose in association with Mao. Such a reinterpretation of Chinese history incidentally paralleled Soviet interpretations and in this subtler, even if limited, sense would raise the prospect of an improvement in relations with the Soviet Union based upon a common understanding of China's past.[5]

The general schema for an attack on all that Mao represented found its initial formal expression at the Third Plenum. The communique revealed Teng on the offensive and Hua attempting to close off areas vulnerable to attack, such as Lin Piao and the Gang of Four or the role of Mao Tse-tung and the cultural revolution, in addition to engaging Teng on the main current policy question of China's modernization. Both men inserted statements in the communique praising themselves as leaders responsive to the will of the people. For example, in extolling Hua's capabilities, the communique read: "Comrade Hua Kuo-feng's call of 'solve the problems while stabilizing the situation' and 'further emancipate our minds, be more courageous and resourceful and step up the pace' has found a warm response in the hearts of the people." Teng, on the other hand, made a broader effort to exonerate himself from all past political blame, to tar Lin Piao and the Gang of Four with the brush of "errors," and to leave open the possibility of later connecting others to Lin and the Gang. To wit:

> The session points out that in 1975, in the period when Comrade Teng Hsiao-p'ing was entrusted by Comrade Mao Tsetung with the responsibility of presiding over the work of the Central Committee, there were great achievements in all fields of work, with which the whole party . . . army . . . and the people . . . were satisfied. . . . Comrade Teng . . . waged tit for tat struggles against interference and sabotage by the gang of four. The gang arbitrarily described the political line and the achievements of 1975 as a "right-deviationist wind to reverse correct verdicts." This reversal of history must be reversed again.[6]

Hua desperately attempted to halt the effort to reverse the "reversal of history." In three separate places in the communique, he argued that "now is the appropriate time to take the decision to close the large-scale nation-wide mass movement to expose and criticize Lin Piao and the gang of four. . . ." His tactic was to "shift the emphasis of our party's work and the attention of the whole people of our country to socialist modernization." Teng accepted the general proposition to "shift the emphasis . . . to socialist modernization" (although he would engage Hua on the details here, too), but he persisted in arguing that although the campaign against Lin and the Gang "has fundamentally come to a successful conclusion . . . in a small number of places and departments the movement is less developed [and] still needs some time to catch up and so cannot end simultaneously. . . ."[7]

Hua Kuo-feng went on to argue that the shift from the anti-Lin, anti-Gang campaign to emphasis on China's modernization effort was "of major significance for fulfillment of the three-year and eight-year programmes for the development of the national economy and the outline for twenty-three years" and for the four modernizations in general.[8] Teng Hsiao-p'ing's response to Hua's accelerated economic program was to argue that "whether or not we can carry this general task to completion, speed socialist modernization and on the basis of a rapid growth in production improve the people's living standards significantly and strengthen national defense—this is a major issue which is of paramount concern to all. . . ."[9] Reflecting Teng's ambivalence, although the plenum participants "discussed arrangements for the national economic plans for 1979 and approved them in principle," the plenum decided that the State Council should "submit them after revisions to the second session of the National People's Congress to be held next year for discussion and adoption."[10]

Teng Hsiao-p'ing's attack on Mao came through unmistakably in the communique as caveats against Hua's effort to establish the continuing relevance of Mao's thoughts and policies: on his leadership role, his economic conception of China's modernization process, and on the wisdom of the cultural revolution. On the question of Mao's general leadership, "The session emphatically points out that the great feats performed by Comrade Mao Tsetung in protracted revolutionary struggle are indelible. Without his outstanding leadership and without Mao Tsetung thought, it is most likely that the Chinese revolution would not have been victorious up to the present. . . . Comrade Mao Tsetung was a great Marxist. . . ."[11] Teng's response was to add that "it would not be Marxist to demand that a revolutionary leader be free of all shortcomings and errors." On Mao's economic thought, the "session holds that the fundamental policy put forth in the report 'On the Ten Major Relationships' which Comrade Mao Tsetung made in 1956 . . . is an objective reflection of economic law and also an important guarantee for political stability of society. This report still is significant for guidance today."[12] The counterpoint to this argument followed in the next sentence:

> While we have achieved political stability and unity and are restoring and adhering to the economic policies that proved effective over a long time, we are now, in the light of new historical conditions and practical experience, adopting a number of major new economic measures, conscientiously transforming the system and methods of economic management, actively expanding economic cooperation on terms of equality and mutual benefit.

On the cultural revolution and other matters, it was Teng Hsiao-p'ing's view that "the session had a serious discussion on some major political events which occurred during the Great Cultural Revolution and certain historical questions left over from an earlier period. It holds that satisfactory settlement of these questions is very necessary for consolidating stability and unity"[13] and facilitating the shift of focus of all work to the four modernizations. Hua Kuo-feng's reaction was to differentiate between Mao's purpose in initiating the cultural revolution and the actual course that it took. Moreover, he contended that whatever shortcomings and mistakes there had been should be summed up as "experience and lessons" that would unify the party. Above all, there should be no haste in dealing with these matters. Thus, the communique read:

> The Great Cultural Revolution should . . . be viewed historically, scientifically and in a down-to-earth way. Comrade Mao Tsetung initiated this great revolution primarily in the light of the fact that the Soviet Union had turned revisionist and for the purpose of opposing revisionism and preventing its occurrence [in China]. As for the shortcomings and mistakes in the actual course of the revolution, they should be summed up at the appropriate time as experience and lessons so as to unify the views of the whole party and the people of the whole country. However, there should be no haste about this.[14]

If Teng Hsiao-p'ing had been outmaneuvered by that formulation, he did succeed in inserting caveats in the text, namely, that "shelving this problem will not prevent us from solving all other problems left over from past history" and, in Section 3, that "historical questions must be settled in accordance with the principle consistently advocated by Comrade Mao Tsetung, that is, seeking truth from facts. . . ." The admonition to seek truth from facts was, of course, the principle publicly and consistently espoused by Teng Hsiao-p'ing—even if it had originally been one of Mao's own ideas. Finally, in Section 4, Teng inserted another favorite maxim: "The session puts a high evaluation on the discussion of whether practice is the sole criterion for testing truth, noting that this is of far-reaching historic significance in encouraging comrades . . . to emancipate their thinking."

Finally, in undoubted reference to the suspension penalties that the plenum had meted out to Hua's supporters, the view was expressed that

> just as a country has its laws, the party should have its rules and regulations. Observance of party discipline by all party members and party cadres is a minimum requirement for restoring normal political life in the party and the state. Leading party cadres at all levels should take the lead in strictly observing party discipline. Disciplinary measures should be taken against all violators of party discipline with no exception, so that there is a clear distinction between merits and faults. . . .[15]

In a related action, the plenum decided to establish a one-hundred member Central Commission for Inspecting Discipline, to be headed by Ch'en Yün, whose "fundamental task" was to "enforce party rules and regulations and develop a good party style."

Teng Hsiao-p'ing's ascendancy over Hua Kuo-feng at the Third Plenum would not have been possible without the active support of Yeh Chien-ying and his followers. Together the two groups marshaled the necessary votes to gain effective control of the policy-making process. Hua was able to register his own positions with some force in the communique undoubtedly partly because he was after all still party chairman and partly because of the manner in which Teng and Yeh had achieved their majority by suspending virtually all of Hua's supporters. Hua's perception that the cards were stacked against him also explains why he took the initiative in laying "stress on the importance of collective leadership in the party Central Committee" in an effort to prevent any further concentration of forces to his disadvantage.[16]

A key question is, What accounts for Yeh Chien-ying's shift once again to support of Teng Hsiao-p'ing after having cooperated with Hua Kuo-feng earlier in the year at the Fifth National People's Congress to block Teng's advance? Yeh's unusual turnabout cannot be explained solely in terms of the data contained in the communique. His name is mentioned only once as one of the vice-chairmen of the Politburo Standing Committee. The veiled references to the dispute over the pace of modernization held greater relevance for Yeh and the institutional interests that he as a military man represented. He could not have favored Hua's proposed course of rapid modernization at the expense of current defense spending. Furthermore, for the same reasons, Yeh could not have looked with favor upon Hua's opposition to military operations against Vietnam. Thus, it was the twin issues of modernization and war as they developed over the second half of 1978 that split Yeh Chien-ying and Hua Kuo-feng and prompted the military leader's shift to Teng, whose positions on these issues were much more compatible with his own.

The issue of war with Vietnam quite naturally found no explicit expression in the Third Plenum's communique. The communique referred simply to the fact that "the plenary session discussed the international situation and the handling of foreign affairs, reaching the view that [the] foreign policy of the party and the government was correct and successful." The communique also noted that although China had had "new and important successes" in developing the international united front against hegemonism "the grave danger of war still exists. We must strengthen our national defense, and be prepared to repulse at any moment aggressors from any direction."[17]

The War with Vietnam:
Lesson That Backfired Or Signal to Moscow?

The question of intervention against Vietnam, including the role China's new ally, the United States, might play, was obviously explored in great detail at the plenum. Immediately afterward, Peking commenced alert and evacuation procedures along the Sino-Soviet border as well as continued its buildup along the Sino-Vietnamese border. On the twenty-fifth, the day Hanoi's large-scale invasion of Kampuchea began, a *People's Daily* editorial intoned: "Hanoi has gone far enough. . . . Don't complain that we didn't warn you in advance." The editorial warning also came two days after a major armed clash on the Sino-Vietnamese border in which nine Chinese border guards were killed.

The multipronged Vietnamese invasion, supported by extensive air support and directed by Soviet and Cuban advisors, proceeded along all of the major routes of access into Kampuchea. Within two weeks, by January 7, Phnom

Penh had fallen to Vietnamese forces, and the west coast port of Kampong Som was under heavy attack. In the east, by January 19, Hanoi's forces had secured the Mekong River between Phnom Penh and the Vietnamese border. Hanoi's armies had overrun most of Kampuchea in a blitzkrieg-like operation that lasted little more than a month, but that left Vietnamese forces strung out and overextended at many points. Despite Hanoi's insistent claims of victory, Pol Pot's forces had been staggered but not routed and had reverted to guerrilla warfare tactics after initial heavy setbacks. Concentrating on cutting Hanoi's line of communications, Pol Pot's scattered forces were still actively engaging the enemy, although they were clearly on the defensive by late January and in danger of total collapse.

Meanwhile, in Peking, Teng Hsiao-p'ing now assumed command of the planned attack against Vietnam. It was under these political circumstances and against the background of the imminent military collapse of Peking's client, Pol Pot, that Teng Hsiao-p'ing undertook a visit to the United States (January 28-February 5, 1979). His trip was clearly intended, at least in part, to elicit from the American leadership the extent of the support that Peking could expect to receive when it moved into action against Vietnam. In an important speech shortly after his arrival in Washington, Teng declared that "our two countries are duty-bound to work together to maintain the peace," leaving clear the implication to U.S. leaders that he sought American support for the coming strike at Hanoi (and conveying the impression to Soviet leaders that he already had it).[18]

The most important and self-evident question that Teng wished to put to the U.S. leadership was: Would Washington act to neutralize Moscow if the Soviet Union actively threatened intervention against China while Peking's forces were engaged in Vietnam? Although Washington would extend diplomatic support, the answer, no matter how delicately phrased, was no, which helps to explain the curious nature of the "lesson" Peking then attempted to teach Hanoi. Although the United States called for "two withdrawals" after the conflict had begun—withdrawal of Chinese forces from Vietnam and withdrawal of Vietnamese forces from Kampuchea—Washington made it clear that the United States would not attempt to deter the Soviet Union. During the conflict in late February, amid reports of Soviet troop movements toward the Chinese border, U.S. spokesmen said plainly that a Soviet strike on China's northern border "would not be of direct concern to the United States."[19] This was, of course, a one-hundred-and-eighty-degree turn from the public stance the United States adopted during the 1969 Sino-Soviet confrontation!

In light of the U.S. refusal to support China in a strategic sense, the analogy between Teng's Washington visit and Khrushchev's 1958 visit to Peking is thought-provoking. Then, as the Chinese were preparing for what came to be known as the Taiwan Straits crisis, Mao Tse-tung asked Khrushchev if the Soviet Union would deter the United States when Peking moved against Taiwan's positions on Quemoy and Matsu. The Soviet leader's answer was no. Mao then employed what was probably an anticipated rejection by Khrushchev to demonstrate to wavering colleagues inside the Politburo that the People's Republic could not rely upon the Soviet nuclear deterrent to achieve its geopolitical objectives. The refusal of the Soviet Union to extend its nuclear shield to protect China was part of the argument that Mao had used to justify breaking relations with the Russians. In the current case, the intriguing strategic question was this: Was Teng Hsiao-p'ing engaged in a similar maneuver with the United States to prepare the ground for normalization of relations with the Soviet Union?

Even if Teng in this case anticipated a negative American answer, he nevertheless expressed great bitterness after his departure. In Japan, on the way back to Peking, Teng was highly critical of U.S. policy. He said that he could not complain while a guest in the United States, but having left, he could say what he thought. "The Soviet Union," he remarked, "will never be impressed by halfway positions."[20] On the other hand, the United States "is allowing the Soviet Union to place a lot of pawns on the world's chessboard. . . . things cannot be allowed to go on this way."[21] Indeed, on February 8, upon his return, Teng convened and presided over a meeting of the Politburo Standing Committee and, on the twelfth, a meeting of the Military Commission, at which the final decision was taken on the moment to strike Vietnam as well as on the nature of the strike, which would have to be made without American support.[22] The leadership placed Hsü Shih-yü in charge of the invasion forces, with Yang Teh-chih as deputy commander and Chang T'ing-fa as chief of staff. Li Teh-sheng was named commander of the northern front in his home area of Manchuria. It was also decided to deploy an additional 200,000 troops in the border area to support the 300,000 already in place.[23]

Chinese strategy in Southeast Asia for a generation had been to promote fragmentation in order to preserve Chinese domination of the region. Given the imminent prospect of the utter failure of that strategy in the Soviet-supported Vietnamese invasion of Kampuchea, the last remaining area of significant Chinese influence, the only type of "lesson" that would have been consistent with long-term Chinese strategy was one that forced Vietnam to withdraw from Kampuchea. Yet the Chinese offensive against Vietnam (February 17–March 16, 1979) did not come remotely close to accomplishing that objective. Despite the mobilization of more than 500,000 troops and 800 aircraft and an initial attack on twenty-three points along the border from Laichau in the west to Langson in the east, from the Laotian border to the Gulf of Tonkin, no objective commensurate either with Peking's long-term strategy or the size of the military buildup was achieved.

Were the Chinese simply engaged in a punitive spoiling action to demonstrate China's capability to strike at Hanoi if it so desired? If so, it was certainly not cost effective and in fact demonstrated the opposite, as the Soviet Union quickly moved to reinforce Hanoi as well as to increase its own presence in the country. In less than a month of actual fighting the Chinese absorbed combat losses of 28,000 killed and 43,000 wounded, and the Vietnamese suffered nearly three times more fatalities than the Chinese. Yet Peking failed to engage, let alone destroy, even a single main force Vietnamese division, encountering only regional forces during the month-long campaign. It is true that Hanoi, with Soviet air and seaborne transport assistance, began to redeploy three main force combat divisions from South Vietnam to the Hanoi area in early March following the Chinese seizure of Langson. This was because the Chinese entry into Langson on March 5 after a fierce week-long battle opened the door to a direct attack on Hanoi itself.[24] At this juncture, however, the Peking leadership declared that all military objectives had been met and announced the beginning of withdrawal from the country, a withdrawal the Chinese would complete substantially by March 16.

Clearly, the Chinese leadership under Teng Hsiao-p'ing deliberately chose not to undertake an offensive powerful enough to achieve the strategic objective, even when, following the battlefield victory at Langson, that objective became a real possibility. In the absence of a countervailing U.S. posture toward the Soviet Union, Moscow's deterrent proved to be decisive. Yet the Chinese leadership knew all this *before* the attack. What purpose, then, was the limited strike designed to achieve? Given the failure to maintain the fragmentation of Indochina either in cooperation with the United States or unilaterally, the invasion was an apparent effort to move toward the strategic objective by the only means remaining—direct negotiation with Moscow. If so, it was an effort that the Chinese undertook in early April in conjunction with the official notification to terminate the 1950 Sino-Soviet treaty of friendship and alliance.

A few weeks earlier, however, immediately following Peking's withdrawal from Vietnam, the Hua and Teng groups tangled again in a series of political skirmishes lasting through the month of April. Details are sketchy, but it seems that Hua Kuo-feng and his supporters, including those whose suspensions had ended, pressed Teng on several issues, prominent among which were his conduct of the just concluded war with Vietnam, the democracy movement, economic policy, the Third Plenum's treatment of Mao, and the terms for normalization of relations with Moscow. Although forced into several compromises, Teng emerged from this latest test of strength in an even stronger overall position than before.

Signaling the end of their suspensions, the Chinese press on March 12 publicized the participation of Ch'en Hsi-lien, Chi Teng-k'uei, Wu Teh, and Li Teh-sheng in a tree-planting ceremony in Peking. It was the first time that they had appeared in public for three months.[25] Wang Tung-hsing would also reappear later in March after a similarly lengthy absence.

Teng and the PLA leadership were forced to defend their conduct of the war against charges that the conflict had had negative effects and should not have been fought at all. Their response came in commentaries published in both *People's Daily* and *Liberation Army Daily* on March 26. The defense was that the strike at Vietnam was a "just war," a "counterattack," and that it "would not do if we had not fought it."[26] Furthermore, they contended that the attack provided "a very good review of our frontier defenses, our economic construction and national defense as a whole."[27]

If Teng successfully weathered the attack on his conduct of the war, he was less successful on the democracy issue. Hua and his supporters attacked the democracy movement on grounds that the unbridled human rights campaign was the result of an "excessive" emancipation of minds, which, in their view, was counterproductive if not "rightist and revisionist."[28] The result of this challenge was that Teng agreed to restrict the scope of the campaign. Toward the end of the month, public notices were posted in major cities prohibiting wall posters, slogans, and so forth "in public places other than those designated for such purpose."[29] To Hua's charges that Teng's handling of the economy reflected poor planning and produced a foreign exchange shortage, Teng and his allies responded vigorously. Li Hsien-nien, in an interview on March 4, implicitly criticized Hua for "mishandling" the economy. He went on to declare that the current ten-year economic plan was "too huge to be practicable" and that it had been worked out by "impatient comrades" and was under reconsideration.[30] The result of their discussions was the decision to "readjust, reform, consolidate and improve" the economy. In other words, the pace of economic construction would be slowed further compared to the economic programs announced by Hua the previous year at the Fifth National People's Congress.

Hua and his supporters called into question the decision of the Third Plenum regarding Mao Tse-tung. They claimed that the plenum had "negated Chairman Mao" and "chopped down the banner" of Mao's thought by publicly acknowledging his errors and stressing the slogan of practice as the sole criterion of truth.[31] Teng's reply to this criticism was to label his opponents as the "two whatever" faction (whatever policies Mao had devised and whatever instructions he had issued) and to formulate a slogan of his own, the "four upholds." The four upholds were socialism, the dictatorship of the proletariat, the leadership of the party, and Marxism-Leninism–Mao Tse-tung thought. The "four upholds" amounted to a compromise reaffirmation that China's direction would not be changed, that China would not take the capitalist, revisionist road, at least in the short run—or so it seemed.

Study of the initial phase of the struggle between the Hua and Teng groups after the Third Plenum shows that from mid-March through April Teng had come under vigorous criticism for his handling of policy matters. What stands out in the record, however, is that he had weathered the storm without a significant diminution of power, even though he had to compromise on several issues. On the other hand, Hua Kuo-feng's attack, even though reinforced by those supporters who had been suspended earlier, had rebounded negatively upon him, particularly with regard to economic policy. The decision to jettison the original fast-paced modernization program in favor of a much slower-paced and less ambitious one was a serious blow to Hua. There can be little question that, although he was under pressure, Teng was in command of the reins of power throughout this period. Moreover, as far as can be determined, none of Teng's supporters lost position or power. At any rate, it was under conditions of heightened inner party strife that the Chinese leadership initiated a major move to bring about an improvement in relations with the Soviet Union.[32]

The Abortive Opening to Moscow

On April 3, 1979, Foreign Minister Huang Hua met with the Soviet ambassador to China, J. S. Shcherbakov, to give formal notice that the government had "decided not to extend the Sino-Soviet treaty beyond its expiration" date of April 11, 1980.[33] In the same communication the foreign minister "reiterated the consistent stand of the Chinese government" that differences of principle between the two countries should not hamper the maintenance of "normal state relations." "To this end, the Chinese government has proposed to the Soviet government that negotiations be held between China and the Soviet Union for the solution of outstanding issues and the improvement of relations between the two countries."[34] The Soviet government replied immediately to the Chinese note, vigorously denying any responsibility for what the Chinese charged were "violations" that had deprived the treaty of all content, but the Soviets waited for almost two weeks to respond to the offer to improve relations. The delay was prompted in large part by the fact that the Chinese offer represented a significant change from their previous position on negotiations. There was no reference to the 1969 "understanding" that the Chinese had heretofore stipulated as a precondition to negotiations.[35]

The Soviet response came on April 17 as Foreign Minister Andrei Gromyko expressed Moscow's general willingness to improve relations but sought further clarification of Peking's intentions.[36] What came, however, was not clarification but confusion. A week later, the Chinese government sent a note declaring that the 1969 understanding after all "must be implemented first prior to the holding of the proposed China-Soviet talks for normalization of their relations."[37] What had happened? First, the Chinese government offered talks without preconditions, then reversed its position to insist on them. The most plausible explanation lies in the continued unsettled conditions within the party leadership, which were evident from mid-March. It would appear that Hua Kuo-feng and his supporters temporarily marshaled sufficient support to reinsert the 1969 caveat into the Chinese offer for negotiations in order to impede them, but the caveat did not stand. On May 5 the Chinese government sent yet another note that did, indeed, clarify the situation and indicated that Teng had gained control of the negotiation process. The note mentioned the opening of formal talks and made no reference to the 1969 "understanding," instead proposing to divide negotiations into three parts: talks on improving relations; border talks (which had been occurring sporadically since 1969); and trade discussions (the two countries had continued to conclude annual trade agreements despite their acrimonious relationship).[38]

The Chinese offer included the suggestion—communicated through private channels—that the normalization of relations between Moscow and Peking be accompanied by a political solution in Indochina, that is, Kampuchea. It became increasingly clear over subsequent months that the Chinese position was to link the two questions. Moscow, on the other hand, agreed "in earnest" to improve relations with Peking, but "not at the expense of third parties," a position Brezhnev himself expressed in a speech on June 1 in Budapest.[39] Accompanying authoritative press commentary made explicit the point to which Brezhnev had alluded, namely, that no deal would be made at the expense of Hanoi.[40] On the fourth, the text of Gromyko's April 17 note to Peking was published in *Pravda*. It expressed Moscow's willingness to formulate a statement of principles governing relations between the two countries, a document that would include, among other things, a commitment to oppose "hegemony in world affairs." The note further suggested that talks get under way in Moscow in July and August.

If Moscow's agreement to proceed with talks reflected an assumption that the Chinese political situation had stabilized, it proved once again to be premature. Even though Teng had gained control of the negotiating process, Hua still possessed sufficient power to hinder if not thwart Teng's objectives. An exchange between the two that took place at this time regarding the pace of economic modernization illustrates the point. A major *Red Flag* article appeared in mid-May elaborating the economic readjustment that had been agreed to earlier, emphasizing Teng's slow development program. Criticizing "over-high targets" and stressing the need to strengthen "weak points of the Chinese economy," the author declared that there would be a "firm reduction of the huge industrial construction program launched one year ago." Priority would go to light industry and to fuel production projects in order to balance consumption and the accumulation of capital. Agriculture, too, would undergo "gradual modernization."[41]

All this was, of course, in sharp contrast to the rapid modernization program Hua had "launched one year ago" at the Fifth National People's Congress. Nevertheless, Hua stuck to his guns. In his opening address to the second session of the Fifth NPC, which convened from June 18 to July 1, he declared that there must be "steady, proportionate and high-speed development of the national economy" over the next three years.[42] In the same speech, Hua attempted to throw a monkey wrench into the upcoming negotiations with Moscow. He said, "Prospects for Sino-Soviet negotiations depend on whether the Soviet government makes a substantive change in its position." Even though the Soviet government had agreed to include the anti-hegemonism clause in the negotiations, Hua said, words were cheap; only deeds mattered. For those who could not interpret for themselves the split in the party leadership, *Peking Daily* noted that "misunderstandings and divisions . . . have come in between a certain number of comrades."[43]

Moscow reacted sharply if belatedly to Hua's taunting remark during his speech to the second session of the Fifth NPC that words were cheap and only deeds mattered. The Soviet riposte was to perpetrate an "incident" on the Soviet-Sinkiang border during a major military exercise conducted by Soviet forces in the Far East in July. On the sixteenth, twenty Soviet soldiers ambushed and killed a Chinese official inspecting pasture areas near the border.[44] Whether or not this was the sort of "deed" Hua had in mind, two days later the Chinese government informed the Soviets of their agreement to begin the Sino-Soviet talks in mid-September in Moscow.[45] A few weeks after that, on August 6, the two governments signed their annual trade agreement following several months of dilatory negotiation.[46]

That the Chinese internal scene remained unsettled came through clearly at the Fourth Plenum of the party, September 25–28, 1979. The main personnel changes occurring at the Fourth Plenum were the promotions of Teng's protégé, Chao Tzu-yang, and an old ally, P'eng Chen, to the Politburo, increasing that body from twenty-six to twenty-eight members, and the addition of twelve more people to the Central Committee. These were Wang Ho-shou, Liu Lan-po, Liu Lan-t'ao, An Tzu-wen, Li Chang, Yang Shang-k'un, Chou Yang, Lu Ting-yi, Hung Hsueh-chih, P'eng Chen, Chiang Nan-hsiang, and Po I-po. The return of the twelve, all purged by Mao during the cultural revolution, completed the process of restoring to power all those elected to the Eighth Central Committee in 1956, except for those who had died or shifted allegiance to Mao. The personnel changes measurably strengthened Teng's position of control within the leadership, further undermining Hua's already gravely weakened political position.

The main task of the plenum, as announced, was to work out the major points of a speech Yeh Chien-ying was to deliver a few days later on the national day commemorating the thirty-year history of the People's Republic. The speech constituted a significant departure from previous interpretations of China's past, marking the first dramatic step in the reinterpretation of that history, of Mao's role and responsibility, and therefore of the political fortunes of all those connected to the former chairman. In what was perhaps the only bow to Hua, Yeh declared that in the first seventeen years of the regime's history the party had pursued a "generally correct line."[47] Even though Mao had committed some errors, these had been "rectifiable." Teng's view was different. He had argued for an interpretation that characterized the entire history of the People's Republic from the Eighth Party Congress in 1956 as a leftist deviation for which Mao had been solely responsible.

The Fourth Plenum compromise, small as it was, centered on two points. First was the periodization of 1966, the outbreak of the cultural revolution, rather than the Eighth Party Congress of 1956, as the point of departure for Mao's irredeemable errors. Second was assignment of explicit responsibility for the cultural revolution, that "appalling catastrophe suffered by all of our people," to Lin Piao and the Gang of Four, rather than to Mao himself.[48] Yeh Chien-ying observed that although the cultural revolution was "launched with the aim of preventing and combatting revisionism," "the estimate made of the situation in the party and the country ran counter to reality, no accurate definition was given of revisionism and an erroneous policy and method of struggle were adopted."[49] All this, Yeh declared, was the fault of Lin Piao and the Gang of Four, who formulated and pursued an ultraleft line and attempted to seize power. The grounds were thus established for the trial these two groups would undergo in November–December 1980.

Even though it was cautiously stated, Yeh's speech represented a broadside fired at Mao and his policies, an attack best perceived by comparison of his remarks with the speech that Hua Kuo-feng had delivered to the Eleventh Party Congress in August 1977. Yeh's speech revealed graphically just how far Teng Hsiao-p'ing had come to dominate the party and its thinking in two short years. On the issue of the origins of Communism in China, Hua, in his speech, had declared unambiguously that Mao was the founder of the Chinese Communist Party.[50] Yeh, on the other hand, said that there were many originators, including Mao, Sun Yat-sen, Chou En-lai, Chu Teh, and others. On the subject of Mao's thought, while Hua attributed it to Mao alone, Yeh introduced a novel conception. Mao's thought, he said, was but the "crystallization of the collective wisdom of the party."

Hua Kuo-feng declared that the policy lines of the ninth and tenth party congresses were correct; Yeh declared that the time of these congresses was a period of "great calamity," instead averring that the Eighth Party Congress line was correct. Hua had defined the line of the Gang of Four as an "ultra-right counterrevolutionary revisionist line," but Yeh reversed this view, too, terming it simply an "ultra-left" line. Hua had placed Liu Shao-ch'i in the same category as the Gang of Four, but Yeh separated Liu from the Gang, offering a positive assessment of him in the context of his approval of the Eighth Party Congress. Finally, in contrast to Yeh's view of it as an "appalling catastrophe," Hua had taken the Maoist view that the cultural revolution had been "necessary and very timely." Comparison of the two speeches showed not only the wide gulf separating Hua and Teng on fundamental issues, but also the shift of Yeh Chien-ying away from Hua and toward Teng, for the views Yeh expressed were clearly those of Teng Hsiao-ping.

The day before the Fourth Plenum ended, on the twenty-seventh, Chinese and Soviet representatives began preparatory talks for the coming normalization negotiations. Between September 27 and October 12 five preliminary meetings were held to work out an agreed agenda. After the fourth meeting, the Chinese leadership publicly expressed surprise and dismay that no progress had occurred. In an October 8 article entitled "Negotiation on Equal Footing Is the Only Correct Way," Hsinhua, the Chinese news agency, noted the negotiating deadlock and declared, "This is something unexpected. It is only natural for those interested in improvement of Sino-Soviet relations to want to know the reason for this."[51] The Chinese side, the article continued, proposed the talks in order to bring about a "removal of obstacles" hindering their relations and to reach a "determination of the norms governing . . . relations." Indicating the Chinese seriousness of purpose, the article then declared forthrightly that "documents should be signed in the light of the results of the negotiations."

The Hsinhua article suggested strongly that the Chinese were very much interested in normalizing relations, while the Soviets were holding back. Although formal negotiations got under way on October 17 and continued until November 30, no progress was evident. After the November 30 meeting, it was decided to consider the six meetings held during this period as the "first round" of talks, which would be continued at a later date, but events would intervene to postpone whatever future talks had been planned. On Christmas Day, 1979, Soviet forces invaded neighboring Afghanistan, placing further efforts to improve Sino-Soviet relations in limbo.

The Fifth Plenum and the Fate of Hua Kuo-feng

Meanwhile, the internal struggle between Teng Hsiao-p'ing and Hua Kuo-feng moved inexorably toward a climax. The Chinese Communist Party held its Fifth Plenum on February 23-29, 1980. The results were startling. The piecemeal changes that Teng had effected over previous months now enabled him to make a major move against his principal adversary. In retrospect, three sequences of events provided clues that a dramatic turn was in the offing. The first was a major revamping of the regime's administrative structure

428   The Evolution of U.S.-China Relations

separating party from state. The second was a subtle shift in Peking's public position *vis-à-vis* Moscow and Washington, and the third was an extensive military reshuffle during January and February 1980.

One of the decisions taken at the second session of the NPC in June of 1979 was to begin the process of separating the party and state apparatuses. By the end of the year twenty-seven of twenty-nine provincial administrative units had held congresses where the revolutionary committees established during the cultural revolution were all scrapped and "people's governments" re-established.[52] Also re-established was the pre-cultural revolution system of standing committees of provincial people's congresses to oversee the work of the people's governments. While superficially rational and plausible, the power play aspect of the restructuring was apparent. In the vast majority of the cases the new appointees to the state structure were those who had held office prior to the cultural revolution. The move, engineered by Teng Hsiao-p'ing, was reminiscent of Stalin's approach in the Soviet Union; he, too, had based his power upon the state rather than the party apparatus.

The second sequence was a subtle shift in Peking's public position that hinted at playing the "American card" against Moscow in order to build greater leverage in dealing with the Soviets. Immediately following the Soviet invasion of Afghanistan the Chinese media began a campaign of scathing criticism of Moscow's actions. From early January, however, against this background noise of criticism, a more temperate approach to the Soviet question could be identified, particularly during the visit to China of U.S. Secretary of Defense Harold Brown (January 6-13). On January 3 the Chinese press reported that the People's Republic of China had been ready to improve relations with the Soviet Union until the invasion of Afghanistan occurred to preclude it.[53] Then, on the eleventh, while Secretary Brown was in China, Teng declared in a television interview that "China's . . . global strategy . . . is to strive for a comparatively long period of peaceful environment. In order to attain this aim, we have to oppose hegemonism *from all sides*."[54]

Teng's suggestion that China must oppose hegemonism from all sides implied that Peking was not locked into a rigidly anti-Soviet stance. Indeed, the suggestion was further reinforced by an unprecedented step, the retraction of a three-day old news item in which Teng had been quoted in remarks to Secretary Brown as urging the United States, China, and other friendly nations "to enter into an alliance" to counter the Soviet invasion of Afghanistan. Hsinhua said that it was withdrawing the news item because it contained "several mis-translations."[55] The substitute version was toned down considerably, quoting Teng as urging all countries to "unite and deal seriously with the Soviet policy of global expansionism."[56] Finally, on the twentieth, the Chinese Foreign Ministry issued a statement to the effect that it would be "inappropriate" to hold the second round of talks in light of the Soviet invasion of Afghanistan, further implying a temporary suspension rather than a decisive break. The impact of these items suggested that China was ever so carefully keeping its distance from Washington and its channels open to Moscow. This was in great contrast to the virtual media blitz in the United States, which held that Brown's visit signaled closer Sino-American ties and a concerted effort to oppose the Soviet Union.

The third and possibly more portentous indicator of what was to come was a series of some two dozen military command changes in January and February. Perhaps most significant, toward the end of January Peking military region commander Ch'en Hsi-lien was removed from his post and replaced by one of Teng's allies, Ch'in Chi-wei.[57] Ch'en was a Politburo ally of Hua Kuo-feng, and his summary demotion suggested that he had come under attack in the Politburo. Then, early in February two more of Teng's allies were promoted to key posts in the party-military hierarchy. Hsü Shih-yü moved to the party Military Commission, and Yang Teh-chih became a vice-defense minister of the Ministry of National Defense.[58] Finally, on the eve of the Fifth Plenum, Teng Hsiao-p'ing stepped down from his post as chief of staff of the PLA to be replaced by none other than Yang Teh-chih.[59]

The personnel changes decided upon at the Fifth Plenum were even more dramatic and far-reaching. In a bitter and acrimonious session marked by "sharp exchanges,"[60] Teng had sufficient strength to remove four of Hua's closest allies from the Politburo and to promote two of his own to the Politburo Standing Committee. The final communique announced the removal of Wang Tung-hsing, Ch'en Hsi-lien, Wu Teh, and Chi Teng-k'uei "from their leading party and state posts."[61] At the same time, Chao Tzu-yang and Hu Yao-pang were promoted to the Politburo Standing Committee, increasing the size of that body to seven. In addition to Chao and Hu, it now included Teng Hsiao-p'ing, Yeh Chien-ying, Li Hsien-nien, Hua Kuo-feng, and Ch'en Yün. The two additions combined with the removal of Wang Tung-hsing gave Teng at least a four to three majority, with Ch'en Yün's support.

The twenty-four member Politburo was also solidly packed with Teng's supporters. The groups were probably not as sharply defined as suggested by the chart below, but the chart nevertheless gives a general idea of the extent of Teng's domination of the Chinese leadership at this time.

Hua Kuo-feng	Teng Hsiao-p'ing	Yeh Chien-ying
Li Teh-sheng	Ch'en Yün	Li Hsien-nien
Ch'en Yung-kuei	Chao Tzu-yang	Hsü Hsiang-chien
Ni Chih-fu	Hu Yao-pang	Nieh Jung-chen
	Hsü Shih-yü	Yu Chiu-li
	Wei Kuo-ch'ing	Fang Yi
	Keng Piao	Chang T'ing-fa
	P'eng Ch'ung	
	Wang Chen	
	Teng Ying-ch'ao	
	Ulanfu	
	Liu Po-ch'eng	
	P'eng Chen	
(4)	(13)	(7)

Thus, it would appear that even if they were so inclined the Hua and Yeh groups would not be able to marshal even a simple majority over Teng and his supporters, who have moved to a position of virtual dominance of the Chinese Communist leadership.

Even though Teng was reproached during the proceedings for taking as hard a line against his opponents as the Gang of Four had taken against theirs, the diminutive leader would not be deterred.[62] "After serious and earnest discussions" the plenum decided "to restore the system established at the Eighth CCP National Congress." This meant applying the principle of separating the party and state hierarchies, which had already been carried out in the provinces, to the central leadership organs as well. The most significant restoration was re-establishment of the Central Secretariat under the Politburo Standing Committee.[63] Hu Yao-pang was now appointed to the post that Teng himself had held in 1956. Ten secretaries were elected to the Central Secretariat, at least eight of whom were Teng's supporters. These included Wan Li, Wang Jen-ch'ung, Ku Mu, Sung Jen-ch'iung, P'eng Ch'ung, Yang Teh-chih, Hu Ch'iao-mu, and Yao Yi-lin. Fang Yi and Yu Chiu-li, supporters of Yeh Chien-ying, were the remaining two men named to the new organ.[64]

The extent of Teng's victory at the plenum was marked by passage of a resolution to rehabilitate Liu Shao-ch'i, who, it was said, was a victim of "the biggest frame-up our party has ever known [which] must be completely overturned."[65] Similarly reflecting Teng's strength was the decision to delete from the NPC constitution Article 45, which gave citizens the right to "speak out freely, air their views fully, hold great debates, and write big-character posters." The only objective Teng and his supporters did not achieve at this time was the removal of Hua Kuo-feng from the premiership and his replacement by Chao Tzu-yang.[66] Hua's success on this point was, however, short-lived.

The events of the Fifth Plenum sharply turned the internal balance against Hua Kuo-feng, whose political base of support within the highest body was now fundamentally undermined. Hua's hold on the premiership was not publicly affected, despite rumors that a change had been under discussion, but without the support of allies in the Politburo it was only a matter of time before he would come under attack and suffer serious and perhaps irreversible damage. Indeed, in the months following the Fifth Plenum, Hua increasingly took on the appearance of a man filling a ceremonial post while actual decisions were being made by others.

Teng Hsiao-p'ing in Command of Chinese Politics

Teng, now in command, followed up his subtle hints of January with more straightforward signals of interest in balancing relations with Moscow. First Mikhail Kapitsa, the Soviet Union's most influential advisor on Chinese problems, turned up in Peking for talks in what was officially described as a "private" visit[67] the week prior to the formal expiration of the Sino-Soviet treaty. Then Enrico Berlinguer, Italian Communist party chief, arrived in Peking on April 14, the first visit by a prominent European Communist party leader in many years. His visit as a guest of the Chinese Communist Party suggested that the Italian Communist party could function as a future bridge between the Soviets and the Chinese as his predecessor, Palmiro Togliatti, had attempted to do in the 1960s.

The suggestion that ideological differences, at least, were a thing of the past occurred in other ways as well. In April Peking bookstores suddenly began offering for sale months-old copies of a Heilungchiang provincial literary journal that carried a most unusual message. The magazine commented that despite the Soviet Union's aggressive foreign policies, many Chinese "believe its internal policy is basically that of socialism" and that "the Soviet economy, science and technology have made considerable progress, and the livelihood of the people has been improved."[68] Such praise for the Soviet Union was unprecedented in recent years.

Similarly, while officials of most Western countries boycotted a reception celebrating the founding of the Red Army that was held at the Soviet Embassy in Peking on February 23 (the day the Fifth Plenum opened), Chinese officials in several provinces placed wreaths on long-ignored Soviet war memorials. One of the main ceremonies took place in the Manchurian province of Hei-lungchiang, where fierce fighting had taken place between Chinese and Soviet troops in 1969. Finally, the trade delegation that had spent several months in Moscow negotiating the annual trade agreement reported on its return that the Soviet Union's brand of heavily centralized economic planning operated quite successfully.[69] The signals could not have been clearer that the Chinese sought an improvement in relations. But still there was no perceptible change in Moscow's attitude.

Hua Kuo-feng's response to Teng's now open position of dominance was a brief and unsuccessful attempt to rebuild his ties with the People's Liberation Army leadership. Although the evidence is scanty, it suggests that Teng's coalition may have lost some of its cohesion at this time, but not sufficiently to affect his position. *Hung Ch'i* number eight, published on April 16, carried an article highlighting the slogan "promote what is proletarian and liquidate what is bourgeois" (*hsing wu mieh tzu*), a phrase that had surfaced the year before during a previous tense period in the spring but that was subsequently dropped. Now Hua, in a speech to the All Army Political Work Conference on April 29, revived the slogan, which was endorsed by several senior PLA officials, including Wei Kuo-ch'ing, head of the General Political Department and erstwhile ally of Teng Hsiao-p'ing's, and Hsü Hsiang-chien, an ally of Yeh Chien-ying's. Hsü Hsiang-chien went out of his way to declare that *hsing wu mieh tzu* was a "good slogan."[70] That senior PLA officials were concerned with more than a slogan was evident from the absence of Yeh Chien-ying, Hsü Shih-yü, and Wang Pi-ch'eng from the official ceremony posthumously honoring Liu Shao-ch'i on May 17,[71] which implied disharmony if not dis-affection within Teng's camp.

By mid-May, however, Teng and his allies had already mounted a strong counter-campaign, which succeeded in preventing Hua from re-establishing substantive ties with the PLA. Teng's campaign focused on "warlordism" and "feudalism" and included sharp criticism of the "two whatevers" and "modern superstition," the codeword for "Mao's thought." A symposium devoted to "theory" promoted by the *Kuangming Daily* on May 11–13, 1980, raised anew Teng's slogan of "practice is the sole criterion of truth" and kicked off an extensive media campaign through the summer emphasizing these themes. Although there were grounds enough for military disaffection from Teng as he began to back away from earlier promises for rapid military modernization and attempted to undercut senior PLA officers by removing them from bases of power, he managed not only to limit significant defections from his camp, but also to broaden his attack to include Hua and Li Hsien-nien, another of his erstwhile allies.

In June the new "gang of four," headed by Teng Hsiao-p'ing and including Hu Yao-pang, Chao Tzu-yang, and Ch'en Yün, took the offensive. In early June, the Teng camp mounted attacks on Li Hsien-nien, who up to this point had been the principal economic planner for the regime. Criticism of "over-ambitious targets" (for which Hua had also been criticized) led to a reshuffling of high-level economic managers. Li Hsien-nien was replaced by Ch'en Yün and Li's man Yu Chiu-li by Ch'en Yün's supporter Yao Yi-lin. Another of Li's protégés, K'ang Hsien, who was in charge of the petroleum industry, came under heavy fire for an oil rig disaster in the Yellow Sea earlier in the year and was also removed from his post.

Heretofore, Teng Hsiao-p'ing had avoided direct criticism of Mao's "er-rors"; they now became a major topic. In an interview with Yugoslav report-ers in mid-June, Hu Yao-pang stated that a document was then in preparation for party adoption that would assess Mao's mistakes, and Teng Hsiao-p'ing took up the subject several weeks later.[72] Hua Kuo-feng himself came im-plicitly under criticism as well. In a eulogy for a deceased veteran cadre on July 3, Hu Yao-pang criticized K'ang Sheng for the first time by name. Prior to this occasion, K'ang had been referred to solely as "that advisor and theo-retical authority." K'ang had been, of course, one of Mao's oldest and closest colleagues, with whom Hua Kuo-feng had also worked while head of the pub-lic security apparatus in the mid-1970s. After K'ang's death in December 1975, Hua had consistently praised him. The public attack on K'ang was therefore one not only on Mao but on Hua, too. K'ang would be purged post-humously from the party later in October.

It was a measure of Teng Hsiao-p'ing's command of the Chinese political scene that he could undertake public criticism of Mao and all that the deceased leader symbolized. Ch'en Yung-kuei, another of Hua Kuo-feng's supporters, also came under direct attack. Teng and his allies mounted a vituperative media campaign on Ch'en's misappropriation of funds and mismanagement of one of Mao's model projects, the Tachai brigade, for which Ch'en held major responsibility. As Hua had identified himself closely with what was now termed to be a "fraudulent" operation, the criticism here, too, extended by implication to Hua.

Finally, Po I-po, vice-premier and a close ally of Ch'en Yün, opened yet another line of criticism of Hua Kuo-feng and Li Hsien-nien. In a meeting with a visiting Japanese delegation in early July, Po criticized the Pao Shan steel plant as a mistake. Po's criticism of the plant, a project strongly advocated by Li Hsien-nien and highly praised by Hua, was aimed at both men. In the same meeting, Po I-po offered one of the earliest official "hints" that Hua Kuo-feng would soon step down as premier.[73] Thus by the time the Third National People's Congress session opened in late August, the stage had been set for another reshuffle of the top leadership, one that, it was widely anticipated, would now include Hua Kuo-feng's resignation from the premiership.

While the National People's Congress was meeting and before any decisions were announced, Teng Hsiao-p'ing agreed to a lengthy interview with Italian journalist Oriana Fallaci in which he set forth his and the party's new positions on major issues. Most important was the issue of Hua's position. While denying that differences existed between himself and Hua, Teng went on to say that he and "many colleagues of my age will resign from government work. And Hua Kuo-feng will not be anymore Premier of the State Council and Chairman of the party at the same time."[74] After revealing that it had been decided to appoint Chao Tzu-yang as premier, he then declared: "In fact, even the post of Chairman of the party . . . is not a lifelong post. I mean, he [Hua] cannot be Chairman for life; it is not permitted by the present system. He can serve two more terms, three, but that's all. And a decision will have to be taken also on how many terms he will serve."[75]

Teng was, of course, speaking authoritatively. The congress's communique announced that seven vice-premiers had resigned from the State Council: Teng himself, Ch'en Yün, Li Hsien-nien, Hsü Hsiang-chien, Ch'en Yung-k'uei, Wang Chen, and Wang Jen-ch'ung. All, of course, retained their party posts. In his speech to the assembled congress Hua Kuo-feng dutifully tendered his resignation as premier, basing it upon the newfound principle that a person should not concurrently hold party and state posts. On September 7, in his speech, Hua stated that the Central Committee

> has decided that, as a rule, the first secretary of a party committee should not concurrently be provincial governor, or chairman of an autonomous region. . . . This is aimed at preventing an overconcentration of power and the holding of too many posts concurrently by one person. . . . In line with this principle, I proposed to the CCP Central Committee that I cease concurrently holding the premier-ship of the State Council. The proposal has been approved by the CCP Central Committee.[76]

In Hua's case, however, it was not a matter of principle. Not only would he not hold "too many posts," he would hold none at all by the end of the year. In mid-December 1980 he suddenly dropped from sight. Western newsmen reported without contradiction from the Foreign Ministry that Hua Kuo-feng had resigned his party chairmanship under pressure from Teng Hsiao-p'ing and his allies.[77]

Hua's resignation was said to have been accepted in return for an agreement not to implicate him in the activities of the Gang of Four, whose trial was then coming to a close, and to make no charges against him for his role in suppressing the T'ien An Men demonstrations in April 1976.[78] With Hua's disappearance, Hu Yao-pang stepped prominently into Hua's former role, welcoming foreign guests, giving interviews, and making policy statements. According to Teng Hsiao-p'ing, Hu was due for a "big promotion" at the next party congress.[79] As Hu occupied the number two post, Teng's remark could mean only that Hu would become party chairman, barring any unforeseen reversal of political fortune. In fact, Hu was promoted before the next party congress, his appointment to the party chairmanship coming at the Sixth Plenum of the Chinese Communist Party, 27-29 June 1981.[80] At the same time Hua Kuo-feng formally resigned from his posts as chairman of the party and Military Commission. He retained a seat on the Politburo Standing Committee, which numbered seven: Hu Yao-pang, Teng Hsiao-p'ing, Chao Tzu-yang, Yeh Chien-ying, Ch'en Yun, Li Hsien-nien, and Hua Kuo-feng.

Implications for the Future

By mid 1981 the political succession to Mao Tse-tung appeared to have run its course. And what a course it has been. In the absence of an institutionalized succession mechanism, the four years following Mao's demise were marked by a virtual revolution in the Chinese leadership, a revolution in which Teng Hsiao-p'ing, once an outcast on the Chinese political scene, now holds sway over the man who was Mao's designated successor. His victory would seem to augur a period of internal political stability, if only because no obvious challengers are emerging from the wings. If so, that in itself would be a radical departure from the history of the Chinese Communist Party, which has been punctuated by periodic leadership crises. The more prudent judgment based upon that history would be that the destabilizing tendencies inherent in the immature Chinese political system will continue to plague

China's leaders and hinder their efforts to lift the country out of its semi-feudal morass.

In the broadest historical sense and by any objective standard of measurement, the Communist period has been a backward step in China's evolutionary experience. The Chinese political fabric has been rent with constant factional conflict. The simple fact that Mao and his supporters emerged victorious on crucial strategic issues should not becloud the reality of never-ending disagreement on vital issues at the pinnacle of power in Peking from the very foundation of the People's Republic. Indeed, since Mao's departure, factional strife has intensified rather than abated as China under Teng Hsiao-p'ing's helmsmanship moves off the course charted by Mao Tse-tung. Such persistent, fundamental disagreement reflects a most significant phenomenon—the absence of any shared broad political vision within the leadership of the best means to shape the future course of China's development. Without that common vision China's future cannot be bright.

High-level disarray has, in turn, had a profound impact on the economic means adopted to move the country forward. Alternating emphasis first on heavy industry and then on light industry and agriculture resulted in embarking on major projects only to abandon them, at times only partially completed, when a new policy was decided upon. The effect has been to confuse and disorient the population, further compounding the difficulties facing the regime. The upshot of Communist rule on the mainland of China has been to slow development, in absolute terms, to a snail's pace. When compared to the rates of progress of its neighbors, China's "development" amounts to nothing less than retrogression, with very little prospect for halting the current trend. The Chinese leadership is correct in placing China in the Third World, for backwardness is everywhere evident, notwithstanding isolated advances in areas like missile development. Under these circumstances the possibility of major structural change in China cannot be ruled out.

However, assuming the improbable—a period of internal stability until the end of the century—what are the developmental options open to the leadership? Clearly, for the stated objective of the four modernizations to be achieved substantially by the year 2000, China requires not only internal stability but external security. Furthermore, modernization presupposes external security, without which development will be difficult if not impossible. The first question, therefore, is how to obtain long-term security. Put starkly, there are three possibilities. First, China can pursue a hostile course *vis-à-vis* the Soviet Union, leaning upon the United States for the degree of security Washington chooses to provide while progressing fairly rapidly in the various developmental progeams. This option offers a relatively fast-paced modernization program, but on the other hand places China's security, especially in the short run, in the hands of the United States.

Option two is full-scale rapprochement with the Soviet Union, including re-establishment of the alliance structure of 1950 in a more equitable form. This option clearly buys what China needs most—long-term security—but at the cost of significant loss of independence no matter how nicely packaged, ideologically or otherwise. Chinese development under this option would occur more slowly but perhaps more surely. The kinds of defense costs would, of course, be far different within an alliance with the Soviet Union than in opposition to it, and such an alliance would permit greater allocation of scarce resources to domestic improvements. The loss of independence is the real and probably unacceptable cost in this option.

Option three can be characterized as the "even-handed approach" implicit in the "three worlds" thesis that Teng Hsiao-p'ing espoused at the United Nations in April 1974. In this approach China would treat both the United States and the Soviet Union more or less equally while attempting to develop stronger ties with the Second World of Europe and Japan. This option would provide greater security than option one but less than option two and would permit a moderately paced developmental scheme that would not infringe upon Peking's desire for independence. Treating Washington and Moscow even-handedly, of course, requires the normalization of relations with Moscow (as has already occurred with Washington). Drawing primarily upon the resources of Europe and Japan for basic development while acquiring as much technology as Washington and Moscow deign to provide, Peking could maximize its independence and security. Option three is therefore the position toward which the Chinese are most likely to move.

How does option three affect the U.S. position, in Asia as well as globally? U.S. strategy for the past decade has been based upon the notion of maintaining an adversary relationship between Moscow and Peking, thus diverting Soviet resources eastward to meet the Chinese threat and to that extent away from the European theater to achieve an overall balance across the entire Eurasian landmass. The objective was to offset the dramatic increase in Soviet power that has occurred in the past decade and a half and to restrict Moscow's ability to concentrate its power at any single point. From Washington's perspective, any degree of normalization between Moscow and Peking that frees the Soviets to redeploy resources once again from east to west destabilizes the overall balance and vitiates the original basis for American strategy toward China.

438   The Evolution of U.S.-China Relations

The basic contradiction in U.S.-PRC relations concerns the issue of Peking's security, which cannot be obtained by long-term hostility to the Soviet Union. Washington will attempt within limits to keep China in the adversary posture *vis-à-vis* Moscow, but it cannot and should not expect to keep the Chinese there indefinitely because it is clearly not in Peking's interest to do so. In fact, the United States has just about reached the end of the policy line in this regard. The extreme limit would be arms sales, if it were believed that such sales would persuade the Chinese to maintain the desired position. It is an illusion, however, to believe that arms sales in the amounts necessary to offset the Soviet threat will push Peking to option one, the only option available to the Chinese that is consistent with U.S. strategy. The continuing prospect thus is for an unsteady three-way relationship among the United States, the Soviet Union, and the People's Republic of China. How American leaders balance relations between the Soviet Union and the People's Republic while striving to maintain a stable equilibrium on the Eurasian landmass will continue to be the central problem, if not dilemma, for Washington policymakers for the foreseeable future.

For the Soviet Union the problem remains how to neutralize the People's Republic as a threat to Moscow's eastern flank. The Soviets may indeed have come full circle in that quest. The brief period of alliance with the People's Republic served the strategic objective by peaceful means, but Peking's decision to break with Moscow in the mid 1950s brought a turn to a more forceful approach. Since then, Moscow has applied an aggressive containment policy to bring about a reversal of Peking's position, creating pressure on China's periphery through the buildup of military power along the border and the manipulation of conflict situations between China and its neighbors. Recent events—the growth of Soviet power *vis-à-vis* the United States, strong Soviet support for the Socialist Republic of Vietnam against the Kampuchean People's Republic, the refusal of the United States to provide anything more than token support to Peking in the conflict against Hanoi, and the major change in Peking's leadership—have created a new political situation that the Soviet invasion of Afghanistan and the U.S. debacle in Iran have only accentuated. The new situation raises the possibility that Moscow may for the first time in two decades be in a position to bring about a favorable accommodation with Peking—a normalization of relations based on a more equitable arrangement than in 1950—and move a step closer to its long-range objective of neutralizing the threat in the east.

For China, the inescapable developmental future, no matter what course any Chinese leadership adopts, is for continued slippage relative to the Soviet Union, Japan, and the United States. Furthermore, the path of modernization any Chinese leadership adopts, is for continued slippage relative to the Soviet Union, Japan, and the United States. Furthermore, the path of modernization is fraught with danger for the regime. The extensive financial investment required to modernize has already generated an unacceptably high rate of inflation, threatening to nullify what has been accomplished so far. The inflationary surge, combined with an estimated deficit of US$7 billion in 1980, prompted Chinese leaders to alter the nature and scope of the program and to slow the entire process to a crawl. The current modernization program is virtually unrecognizable as the one put forward in 1978. From another perspective, modernization, by virtue of the need for better-educated and -trained personnel, introduces to the new elite ideas that go beyond the technological. The educational process may weaken if not undermine the loyalty of the new technological elite to the political goals of Communism. Creating the cadre competent enough to manage a modern state thus carries with it the danger of forging an opposition to the regime unified by a common educational background. In sum, the Chinese find themselves trapped in the infamous and intricate "Chinese box," a puzzle that may defy solution.

Notes

Part I. The Origin and Development of Chinese Communism, 1917–1941

Chapter I: To Build a Communist Movement in China, 1917–1927

1. See, for example, Chapter XI, "Dual Power," in Leon Trotsky, *The Russian Revolution*, F. W. Dupree, ed. (New York, 1959), pp. 199–209.

2. Branko Lazitch and Milorad M. Drachkovitch, *Lenin and the Comintern*, Vol. I (Hoover Institution, 1972), pp. 386–92.

3. *Sovetsko-kitaiskie otnosheniia 1917–1957* (Soviet-Chinese Relations, 1917–1957) a collection of documents (Moscow, 1959), pp. 64–65.

4. See Karl Wei, "The Founding of the Chinese Communist Party and Its First National Congress (1920–1921)," *Issues and Studies*, Vol. VII, no. 3 (December 1970), p. 48.

5. Maring instructed the Chinese Communists to this effort in April 1922 and they, after some argument, duly made it party policy the following July at the Second Hangchow Plenum. See Dov Bing, "Sneevliet and the Early Years of the CCP," *The China Quarterly*, no. 48 (October-December 1971), p. 689.

6. James C. Bowden, "Soviet Military Aid to Nationalist China, 1923–1941," in Ray Garthoff, ed., *Sino-Soviet Military Relations* (New York: Praeger, 1966), p. 46.

7. C. Martin Wilbur, "Military Separation and the Process of Reunification Under the Nationalist Regime, 1922–1937," in Tang Tsou and Ping-ti Ho, eds., *China in Crisis*, Vol. 1, book 1 (Chicago, 1968), p. 234.

8. *Military Campaigns in China: 1924–1950*, Office of U.S. Military History (Taipei, 1966), pp. 1–5.

9. "Extracts from the Resolution of the Seventh ECCI Plenum on the Chinese Situation," Dec. 16, 1926, in Jane Degras, ed. *The Communist International, 1919–1943 Documents*, Vol. II (London, 1960), p. 336.

10. Li Yun-han, *Ts'ung Jung Kung Tao Ch'ing Tang* (From Admission of the Communists to [Nationalist] Party Purge) (Taipei, 1966), pp. 472–73.

11. Soon afterward, in May, Chiang moved to restrict the Communists further. On May 15, he pushed through two party resolutions which restricted Communist participation in any single department to one-third, prohibited Communists from appointments as department heads, and required a name list of all Communist party members in the KMT.

12. Mobilization order, July 1, 1926. As quoted in F. F. Liu, *A Military History of Modern China*, p. 36.

13. *Military Campaigns in China: 1924–1950*, p. 9.

14. *Military Campaigns in China: 1924–1950*, p. 11.

15. Leon Trotsky, *Problems of the Chinese Revolution* (New York, 1931), p. 254.

16. According to T'an P'ing-shan, then head of the KMT Organization Department. See "Extracts From the Resolution of the Sixth ECCI Plenum on the Chinese Question," 13 March 1926, in Degras, II, p. 276.

17. "Extracts from the Resolution of the Seventh ECCI Plenum on the Chinese Situation," in Degras, II, pp. 343–44.

18. Ibid., p. 345.

19. "Extracts From an ECCI Statement on Chiang Kai-shek's Anti-Communist Coup," 15 April 1927, in Degras, II, p. 359.

20. "Extracts From the Resolution of the Eighth ECCI Plenum on the Chinese Question," 30 May 1927, in Degras, II, p. 383.

21. Ibid.

22. J. Stalin, "The Revolution in China and the Tasks of the Comintern," 24 May 1927, in *Works*, Vol. IX, p. 304.

23. "Extracts From the Resolution of the Eighth ECCI Plenum on the Chinese Question," 30 May 1927, in Degras, II, pp. 386–90.

24. Martin Wilbur, "Ashes of Defeat," *China Quarterly*, no. 18 (April-June 1964), p. 52.

25. See Lominadze's remarks at the Sixth Comintern Congress in *Stenograficheski Otchet Shestoi Kongress Kominterna* (The Stenographic Report of the Sixth Comintern Congress), Vol. III (Moscow, 1929), p. 469.

26. Stuart R. Schram, "On the Nature of Mao Tse-tung's 'Deviation' in 1927," *The China Quarterly*, no. 18 (April-June 1964), p. 59.

27. Hsiao, Tso-liang, "The Dispute over a Wuhan Insurrection in 1927," *The China Quarterly*, no. 33 (January-March 1968), pp. 108–122.

28. For discussion see the author's *The Comintern and the Chinese Communists, 1928–1931* (Seattle, 1969), pp. 4–22.

Chapter II: The "Soviet" Experiment, 1927–1931

1. This "scapegoat thesis," that after undertaking, according to Stalin's orders, large-scale nationwide uprisings and failing, Li Li-san was removed from the party leadership for Moscow's blunder, is expounded by Benjamin I. Schwartz, *Chinese Communism and the Rise of Mao*, chap. 9.

2. The Fifteenth Party Congress of the Soviet Union in December 1927, the Ninth Plenum of the ECCI in February 1928, the Sixth Congress of the CCP in June-July 1928, and the Sixth Congress of the Comintern in July-September 1928.

3. For the formulation of the policy see the author's *The Comintern and the Chinese Communists: 1928–1931*, chaps. 1 and 2.

4. *Stenograficheskii otchet shestoi Kongress Kommunisticheskoi Partii Kitaia* (Stenographic Report of the Sixth Congress of the CCP), Vol. 5.

5. See *The Comintern and the Chinese Communists: 1928–1931* for a detailed discussion of these years.

6. For Mao's side of this exchange, see Mao, *SW*, I, "The Struggle in the Ching Kang Mountains" and "A Single Spark Can Ignite a Prairie Fire."

7. "Kung Ch'an Kuo Chi Chih Hsing Wei Yuan Hui Yü Chung Kuo Kung Ch'an Tang Shu" (Letter of the Executive Committee of the Comintern to the Chinese Communist Party), 7 June 1929, in *Hung Se Wen Hsien* (Red Documents), Liberation Press, 1938, pp. 326–27.

8. "Lun Kuo Min Tang Kai Tsu P'ai Ho Chung Kuo Kung Ch'an Tang Te Jen Wu" (A Discussion of the KMT Reorganizationists and the tasks of the CCP), 26 October 1929 in *Hung Ch'i* (Red Flag), 15 February 1930, no. 76, sec. 4.

9. "Chung Yang T'ung Kao Ti Liu Shih Hao" (Central Circular No. 60) *Hung Ch'i* (Red Flag), 7 December 1929, sec. 4.

10. Mao, *SW*, I, "On Correcting Some Mistaken Ideas in the Party."

11. Mao, "A Single Spark. . . ."

12. Edgar Snow, *Red Star Over China* (New York: Grove Press, 1961), pp. 174–75.

13. "Chung Yang T'ung Kao Ti Ch'i Shih Hao" (Central Circular No. 70), 26 February 1930 (Bureau of Investigation Collection, Taiwan).

14. "Hsin Te Ke Ming Kao Ch'ao Yü I Sheng Huo Chi Sheng Shou Hsien Sheng Li" (A new revolutionary high tide and an initial victory in one or several provinces), *Hung Ch'i* (Red Flag), 19 July 1930.

15. "Chung Kuo Wen Ti Chüeh I An" (Resolution on the Chinese Question), passed by the ECCI Political Secretariat, 23 July 1930 in *Shih-Hua* (Truth), no. 1, 30 October 1930.

16. Ibid., sec. 4.

17. "Cheng Chih Chü K'uo Ta Hui Chi Lu" (Minutes of the Enlarged Politburo Meeting), 22 November 1930 (Bureau of Investigation Collection, Taiwan) p. 27.

18. Snow, p. 180.

19. *Chung Yang T'ung Kao Ti Chiu Shih Yi Hao—San Ch'uan K'uo Ta Hui Ti Tsung Chieh Yü Ching Shen* (The Spirit and Conclusion of the Third Enlarged Plenum) 12 October 1930, p. 2 as quoted in *The Comintern and the Chinese Communists, 1928–1931*, p. 188.

20. For a detailed discussion of this involved situation, see the author's *The Comintern and the Chinese Communist Party: 1928–1931*, chap. 9.

21. "Kung Ch'an Kuo Chi Chih Wei Ke Chung Kung Chung Yang Te Hsin" (Letter of the ECCI to the CCP Central), received 16 November 1930 in *Kuo Chi Lu Hsien* (The International Line), Bureau of Investigation, Taiwan.

Chapter III: Defeat in Kiangsi, 1931–1934

1. Two invaluable sources which provide the basic documents for the interpretation in this chapter are: Hsiao Tso-liang, *Power Relations Within the*

444 Notes for Chapter III

Chinese Conmunist Movement, 1930–1934 (Seattle, 1961) and Warren Kuo, *Analytical History of Chinese Communist Party*, book II (Taiwan, 1968).

2. See Hsiao, pp. 161–62 for a discussion of the departure date.

3. The membership of the committee was: Chou En-lai, Hsiang Ying, Mao Tse-tung, Chu Teh, Jen Pi-shih, Yü Fei, Tseng Shan, Ku Tso-lin, and Wang Shou-tao. Later in 1931 Wang Chia-hsiang and Teng Fa were added.

4. See Mao, *SW*, III, pp. 968–69, 984, 988.

5. For an elaboration of these erroneous tendencies, see Kuo, II, pp. 384–92.

6. Pavel Mif, ed., *Strategiia i takitka Kominterna v natsional'no kolonial'no revoliutsii, na primere Kitaia* (The Strategy and Tactics of the Comintern in the National Colonial Revolution, the Example of China) (Moscow, 1934), pp. 296, 300.

7. Hsiao, *Power Relations*, 172 *et passim*, for a discussion of the Congress's documents.

8. People's Liberation Army Unit Reference Book, pp. 65–69.

9. An earlier CCP historical account claims that Chu Teh was chairman, see Kuo, II, p. 380.

10. PLA Unit Reference Book, p. 69.

11. Kuo, II, pp. 413–14.

12. Statement of the CCP on the Current Situation, 1 January 1932, in Hsiao, p. 200.

13. Dated 9 January 1932, see Kuo, II, pp. 392–96 and Hsiao, pp. 200–201.

14. Cited in Kuo, II, p. 424.

15. Mao Tse-tung, "Strategy in China's Revolutionary War," *Selected Military Writings of Mao Tse-tung* (Peking, 1963), p. 99.

16. Ibid., p. 139.

17. Kuo, II, pp. 525–26, for a translation of the resolution.

18. See p. 72 below.

19. Hsiao, p. 249.

20. Kuo, II, p. 575.

21. Kung Ch'u, pp. 397–98.

22. Kuo, II, p. 575.

23. Kung Ch'u, p. 398.

24. Kung was appointed head of the south Kiangsi military region in July 1934. The following month at Yütu, the regional center, Mao arrived, stating that he was there to do work for the Soviet Government. Later that month, Kung went to Juichin for a meeting where he met Chu Teh and asked why Mao was living in Yütu, rather than Juichin. Chu Teh, with great satisfaction, replied that Mao had been punished by the party and was on probation for his role in the Fukien rebellion. *Wo Yü Hung Chün* (The Red Army and I) (Hong Kong: South Wind Publishing Company, 1954), pp. 397–98.

25. For the Tsunyi resolution, see Jerome Ch'en, "Resolution of the Tsunyi Conference," *China Quarterly* (April-June 1969), no. 40, p. 10; Mao Tse-tung, "On the Tactics of Fighting Japanese Imperialism," 27 December 1935, *SW*, I,

pp. 156–57 and "Resolution on Questions in History of Party," 20 April 1945, *SW*, IV, p. 186.

26. Mao, *SW*, III, "Our Study and the Current Situation," p. 969.

27. The fourteen-man politburo consisted of Ch'in Pang-hsien, Ch'en Shao-yü, Chang Wen-t'ien, Chou En-lai, Hsiang Ying, Ch'en Yün, Wang Chia-hsiang, Chang Kuo-t'ao, Chu Teh, Jen Pi-shih, Ku Tso-lin, Ho Ke-chuan, K'ang Sheng, and Kuan Hsiang-ying. Kuo, II, p. 565.

28. The seventeen-man presidium was composed of the following: Mao Tse-tung, chairman; Hsiang Ying and Chang Kuo-t'ao, vice-chairmen; Chu Teh, Chang Wen-t'ien, Ch'in Pang-hsien, Chou En-lai, Ch'ü Ch'iu-pai, Liu Shao-ch'i, Ch'en Yün, Lin Po-ch'u, Teng Cheng-hsun, Chu Ti-yuan, Teng Fa, Fang Chih-min, Lo Mai, and Chou Yueh-lin. Kuo, II, p. 592.

29. Hsiao, p. 281.

30. Kuo, II, p. 613.

31. Hsiao, p. 294.

Chapter IV: From the Long March to the United Front, 1934–1937

1. Kuo, Jan. 1968, pp. 39–40.

2. Kuo, "The Tsunyi Conference" (Part I), *Issues and Studies*, Jan. 1968, Vol. IV, no. 4, p. 42.

3. Ibid., p. 43.

4. Ibid., p. 46.

5. Kuo, "Twin Central Committees of the CCP" (Part I), *Issues and Studies*, March 1968, Vol. IV, no. 6, p. 40.

6. Ibid., pp. 43–45.

7. Ibid., p. 47.

8. Kuo, "The United Front" (Part I), *Issues and Studies*, May 1968, Vol. IV, no. 8, p. 43. Kao's dissatisfaction may have been the partial basis for his later conflict with Mao Tse-tung. See chap. 9, p. 226–30 below.

9. For the organizational charts, see Kuo, Warren, "The United Front" (Part I), *Issues and Studies*, Vol. IV, no. 8, May 1968, pp. 46–48.

10. *VII Congress of the Communist International: Stenographic Report* (abridged) (Moscow: FLPH, 1939), p. 173.

11. In fact, on August 1 the "joint appeal" was published by Moscow in the name of the CCP, whose leaders did not know of the existence of such a statement until some time later. Ibid., p. 288. See Kuo, "The Conflict Between Chen Shao-yü and Mao Tse-tung," *Issues and Studies*, Nov. 1968, Vol. V, no. 2, pp. 3, 5, 6.

12. Mao, *SW*, I, pp. 164–65.

13. Ibid., p. 157.

14. Intellectuals would receive preferential treatment, all petty-bourgeois elements would receive the right to vote and to hold office, their property would

not be confiscated, and investment by the national bourgeoisie was encouraged. Their property would be "protected." This was the kernel of the economic program which would become known as "new Democracy" later in 1940, after the publication of Mao's pamphlet of the same name.

15. Kuo, "United Front" (Part II) *Issues and Studies*, Vol. IV., no. 9, June 1968, p. 29.

16. See Chapter II above on 6th Congress.

17. Kuo, "United Front" (Part II) p. 33. In March 1936 an item in *Inprecorr* noted that Mao had given an interview in which he extended the "hand of friendship" to Chiang Kai-shek, if only he would cease attacking the Communists and carry the struggle against Japan (p. 378, *Inprecorr* 1936). Given Moscow's penchant for issuing statements in the name of the CCP, one must view this interview with some degree of scepticism. It was not included in Mao's *SW*.

18. Kuo, "The Zigzag Flight of Red Army Troops," *Issues and Studies*, Vol. IV, no. 10, p. 48.

19. In Nov. 1935, the Second Army had broken through a KMT encirclement at Sangchih, west Hunan. After eight months, generally following the route of the First Front Army, the Second Army reached Chang Kuo-t'ao's forces at Kantzu, Sik'ang in June 1936. Only 3,000 of the original complement of 20,000 men survived the miniature long march of the Second Army.

20. Kuo, "United Front" (Part II), p. 34. A position strongly urged by the Comintern since Aug. 1935 and in subsequent articles by Comintern personnel, in particular Wang Ming.

21. Van Min (Wang Ming), "Boryba za antiyaponski narodnyi front v kitae," Kommunisticheski International (Communist International), 1936, no. 8 and Van Min, "15 Let bor'by za nezavisimost i svobodv Kitaiskogo Naroda," Kommunisticheski International, no. 14.

22. Kuo, "United Front" (Part II) p. 48; see pp. 45–49 for the entire resolution.

23. Kuo, "Zigzag Flight," p. 48.

24. Edgar Snow, *Red Star Over China* (New York, 1961), pp. 461–62.

25. Kuo, "The Chinese Communist Party Pledge of Allegiance to the KMT" (Part I), *Issues and Studies*, Aug. 1968, Vol. IV, no. 11, p. 76.

26. Kuo, "The CCP Pledge of Allegiance to the KMT" (Part II), *Issues and Studies*, September 1968, Vol. IV, no. 12, pp. 33–36.

Chapter V: The Road to War, 1937–1941

1. For the Lochuan discussions, see Kuo, "The Conference at Lochuan," *Issues and Studies*, Vol. V, no. 1, October 1968, pp. 35–45.

2. Mao, *SW*, II, "Urgent Tasks Following the Establishment of Kuomintang-Communist Cooperation," pp. 35–45.

3. Kuo, "The Conflict Between Ch'en Shao-yü and Mao Tse-tung," Part I, *Issues and Studies*, Vol. V, no. 2, November 1968, p. 35.

4. Kuo, *Ibid.*, p. 36.
5. Kuo, "The Conflict Between Ch'en Shao-yü and Mao Tse-tung," Part II, *Issues and Studies*, Vol V, no. 3, December 1968.
6. Mao, *SW*, II, "The Situation and Tasks in the Anti-Japanese War After the Fall of Shanghai and Taiyuan," 12 November 1937.
7. For example, Ivan Krylov in *Soviet Staff Officer* (London: Falcon Press, 1951), p. 9, claims that General Blücher (Galen), commander of Soviet Far Eastern forces, "provoked" the incident, for which he was imprisoned and ultimately lost his life. The International Military Tribunal, the Far East, *Judgment*, p. 833, majority opinion was that the Japanese initiated the hostilities.
8. Hsiang Ying, "The Summation of the CCP CC 6th Plenum and its Spirit," a report delivered to the Communist Activists Conference, 31 October 1938, as quoted in Kuo, "The 6th Plenum of the CCP 6th Central Committee" (Part II), *Issues and Studies*, Vol. V, no. 7, April 1969, p. 29.
9. Mao's speech was immediately published by the Chinese Communist *New China Daily* and distributed widely in Chungking in both Chinese and English. The speech itself was omitted from Mao's works, except for a drastically rewritten segment, which appears in *SW* II under the title "The Role of the Chinese Communist Party in the National War," pp. 195–210. The original speech can be found in the journal *Liberation*, no. 57, 5 November 1938 and the English translation in the *New China Daily* pamphlet published in January 1939. It was republished in 1948 by the New Democratic Publishing Co., Hong Kong, as a pamphlet titled *On the New Stage* (Lun Hsin Chieh Tuan).
10. Mao, *SW*, II, "The Question of Independence and Initiative Within the United Front," pp. 215–16.
11. In Kuo, "The Incidents Concerning Ch'en Tu-hsiu and Chang Kuo-t'ao," Part II, *Issues and Studies*, Vol. V, no. 5, February 1969.
12. See below, pp. 145–46.
13. Mao, *SW*, II, pp. 269, 272. For his statement of September 1, see ibid., pp. 263, 268.
14. Mao, *SW*, II, "Introducing the Communist," 4 October 1939, p. 285.
15. Ibid., p. 295.
16. Ibid., p. 331.
17. Ibid., p. 351.
18. Chi Wu, *Yi Ko Ke-Ming Ken-Chu-Ti Te Ch'eng-Chang* (The Growth of a Revolutionary Base Area) (Peking: People's Press, 1958), pp. 84–86.
19. Mao, *SW*, II, p. 418.
20. Mao, *SW*, II, pp. 434, 436, no. 7.
21. Ibid.
22. Mao, *SW*, II, 4 May 1940, "Freely Expand . . .", p. 435.
23. Kuo, "The CCP Campaign for Consolidation of Party Organizations," *Issues and Studies*, Vol. VI, no. 3., Dec. 1969, p. 81.
24. Before the campaign in France had ended, Hitler told Jodl, chief of staff of the supreme command of the armed forces (OKW), "of his fundamental

decisions to take steps against this danger [the Soviet Union] the moment our military position made it at all possible." *IMT, Nuremberg*, Vol. 37, p. 638. At a Fuehrer Conference on July 21, Hitler declared his intention to attack the Soviet Union in the fall of 1940. Gerhard Weinberg, *Germany and the Soviet Union, 1939–1941*, (London: Brill, 1954), pp. 109–110. Ten days later, having learned in the meantime that an attack in the fall was infeasible, Hitler decided to attack the Soviet Union in May 1941, pending the outcome of an air bombardment of England. *IMT, Nuremberg*, Vol. 5, p. 740. The timing of Hitler's decision-making process strongly suggests Soviet knowledge of it, but is unproved and probably unprovable. In any case, the fall of France alone is sufficient to make the case for a change in Soviet policy *vis-à-vis* the Chinese Communists, who were again desperately needed to stave off the possibility of an end to the war in China.

25. See Mao, *SW*, II, "Unity to the Very End," pp. 437–39, and *Issues and Studies*, Appendix I, "Decision on the Current Situation and the Tasks of the Party," dated 7 July 1940, Vol. VI, no. 5, Feb. 1970, pp. 62–65.

26. Kuo, "Disbandment of the New 4th Army," *Issues and Studies*, Vol. VI, no. 7, April 1970, pp. 66–73.

27. "With the conclusion of Japan's agreement with Wang Ching-wei and the [Nationalists'] receipt of U.S. loans and Soviet assistance, the danger of capitulation has been overcome." *Issues and Studies*, Appendix II, "CCP Central Committee's Directive on the Current Situation and Party Policies," December 25, 1940, in Vol. VI, no. 8, May 1970, pp. 106–109. The first few pages of Mao's "On Policy," dated 25 December 1940, *SW*, II, pp. 441–49, are virtually identical to this secret directive.

28. Kuo, "Disbandment of the New 4th Army," *Issues and Studies*, Vol. VI, no. 7, April 1970, pp. 71–73.

29. Northwest Industrial University, nos. 177, 178, "The South Anhwei Incident and the Renegade Hsiang Ying," a Red Guard publication dated July 1968.

30. Mao, *SW*, II, "Order and Statement on the Southern Anhwei Incident," and "Statement by the Spokesman of the Revolutionary Military Commission of the Central Committee of the Communist Party of China to a Correspondent of the Hsinhua News Agency," pp. 451–58.

31. Ibid., "Order and Statement."

32. Kuo, "Communist Moves After the Incident in Southern Anhwei," (Part I), *Issues and Studies*, Vol. VI, no. 9, June 1970, pp. 68–69.

Part II. The American Experience in China

Chapter VI: World War II, the United States and China, 1941–1944

1. Most writers on World War II have defined the "turning point" as a battle or series of battles which decisively altered the balance of forces. Thus, some

view the battle of Moscow during the first winter as the turning point in the war; others see the battle of Stalingrad the following year, or the battle of Kursk during mid-1943 as the decisive battles. The definition of turning point I employ here is broader, embracing the facts of stemming the enemy advance, preparing for and taking the initial, limited steps of the counteroffensive. In this sense, no single battle alone was decisive, but a series of events, including domestic war production, control of the seas, air, etc., combined constituted the turning point.

2. "The Indisputable Facts of History," Radio Moscow, Chinese language broadcast, 10 May 1970. "In 1941 when the Hitlerite troops had gained temporary success and when the Soviet Union was plagued by the chaos of war, the Soviet Union and the Communist International made proposals to the CCP leadership in Yenan for concerted action to prevent Japan from attacking the Soviet Union. Mao Tse-tung openly boycotted these proposals. . . . In July 1941, the Soviet Union informed Yenan of Japan's sending of fully prepared combat troops to the mainland and requested it to take effective steps to pin down these Japanese troops and prevent them from moving towards the Soviet borders."

3. In an article acknowledging Richard Sorge's contribution to the Soviet war effort, *Pravda*, 4 September 1964, p. 1, noted that "two months" before Pearl Harbor Sorge supplied vital information detailing Japan's plans for war in the Pacific, which enabled the Soviet army to shift urgently needed reinforcements from the Far East to help stop the German advance at the gates of Moscow. *Istoriia Velikoi Otechestvennoi Voiny Sovetskogo Soiuza* (History of the Great Patriotic War of the Soviet Union), Vol. II (Moscow, 1961) pp. 240–41, notes that reinforcements from the east began arriving in the Moscow area early in October.

4. Except for limited access via Murmansk in the Soviet north.

5. The British expected Japanese landings on Ceylon and Madagasgar (!) and moved to strengthen their positions there. As it turned out, the Japanese conducted only a naval raid against Ceylon. See B. H. Liddell Hart, *History of the Second World War* (New York: Putnam, 1971) pp. 236–38.

6. See Johanna Menzel Meskill, *Hitler and Japan, the Hollow Alliance* (Chicago: Atherton, 1966) pp. 80–82, fn. 52.

7. I. F. Kurdiukov, V. N. Nikiforov, and A. S. Perevertailo, eds., *Sovetsko-Kitaiskie Otnosheniia 1917–1957*, Sbornik Dokumentov (Sino-Soviet Relations, 1917–1957, a collection of documents) (Moscow, 1959) p. 162.

8. Richard Sorge, in a statement written for the Japanese after his capture, noted that Japan's attitude toward the war between the Soviet Union and Germany "was of great concern to Moscow. . . . No other issue had had as direct a relation to my most important mission. . . ." Regarding the Japanese buildup in Manchuria following the signing of the Neutrality Pact, Sorge stated that "a correct knowledge of the scope of the mobilization and its direction (north or south) would give the most accurate answer to the question of whether or not Japan wanted war with the Soviet Union. *At the outset, the large-scale nature of the mobilization and the fact that some reinforcements were sent northward*

gave us cause for anxiety, but it gradually became apparent that it was by no means directed primarily against the Soviet Union." (emphasis supplied) Charles A. Willoughby, *Shanghai Conspiracy* (Boston, 1952) pp. 162–63.

9. See Mao, *SW*, IV, "Preface and Postscript to 'Rural Survey'," 19 April 1941 and "Reform Our Study," May 1941, pp. 7, 12.

10. Representative documents include: "Decision on the Prohibition of Unprincipled Controversies and Disputes Within the Party," The CCP South China Working Committee, June 1941, in *Issues and Studies*, Vol. VII, no. 3 (December 1970), p. 69; "Decision on the Strengthening of the Party Character," adopted by the CCP Politburo, 1 July 1941, Ibid., Appendix III, pp. 72–74; "Central Committee Resolution on Investigation and Research," 1 August 1941, Ibid., pp. 69–72. Liu Shao-ch'i, "On the Intra-Party Struggle," delivered to the Central China Party School, 2 July 1941, in Boyd Compton, *Mao's China*, pp. 188–245.

11. Cheng-tun San-feng, or Cheng-Feng.

12. Mao, *SW*, IV, "Rectify the Party's Style in Work," p. 28.

13. All party members were required to study the "twenty-two documents," which included all of Mao's important writings as well as those of Lenin, Stalin, Dimitrov, and several members of Mao's group (K'ang Sheng, Liu Shao-ch'i, Ch'en Yün); for the listing of documents see Kuo, *Analytical History of the Chinese Communist Party*, IV, appendix I, "The CCP Propaganda Department's Decision on Yenan's Discussions of the Central Committee's Decisions and Comrade Mao Tse-tung's Speeches on the Rectification Campaign," 3 April 1942, pp. 635–40.

14. Mao, *SW*, IV, "Our Study and the Current Situation," 12 April 1944, pp. 157–70. In his speech Mao proudly boasted that "factions . . . no longer exist" in the party, p. 159.

15. "The CCP Propaganda Department's Decision on Yenan's Discussions of the Central Committee's Decisions and Comrade Mao Tse-tung's Speeches on the Rectification Campaign," 3 April 1942, in Kuo, IV, pp. 635–40.

16. *Cheng-feng Wen-hsien* (Rectification Documents) (Liberation Press, 1943) in Kuo, IV, pp. 603–606.

17. Mao, *SW*, IV, "An Extremely Important Policy," pp. 94–97.

18. Boyd Compton, *Mao's China, Party Reform Documents, 1942–1944* (Seattle, 1952) xxxix.

19. In Kuo, IV, pp. 595–99.

20. See the excellent study by Louis Morton, *Strategy and Command: The First Two Years* (Washington, 1962) for a lucid account of Allied strategy during the early years of the war.

21. For the formal declaration, see *Foreign Relations of the United States, the Conferences at Cairo and Tehran, 1943* (Washington, 1961) p. 448. The Chinese memorandum of the Roosevelt-Chiang talks notes that the restoration of Manchuria included as understood "the Liaotung Peninsula and its two ports Lu Hsun (Port of Arthur) and Dairen . . ." p. 325.

22. The evidence for the Roosevelt-Chiang *quid pro quo* is inferred from two accounts, that of the President's son Elliot, in *As He Saw It* (New York, 1946) and the Chinese government's memorandum, produced in 1956, of the talks. There exists no public American record of the President's discussions with Chiang Kai-shek at Cairo.

Elliot Roosevelt was present at both Cairo and Tehran and made "notes which I took myself" (xviii) of conversations with his father, the relevant portions of which I reproduce here. At Cairo, late Thanksgiving night, the following conversation reportedly took place:

"I had heard some scuttlebutt from our own Navy's officers about landings on the coast of China. 'Oh, certainly,' said Father. 'That's quite in the cards. But much farther north than the British think will ever prove feasible. They see only a Chinese coast infested with Japanese, while we are fully aware of the fact that much of that coast is in the hands of Chinese guerrillas.' I asked if these guerrillas were the Chinese Communist troops, and he nodded an affirmative. 'Incidentally,' he said, 'Chiang would have us believe that the Chinese Communists are doing nothing against the Japanese. Again, we know differently' . . . 'Matter of fact, I was talking to Chiang . . . at dinner, a few days ago. You see, he wants very badly to get our support against the British moving into Hong Kong and Shanghai and Canton with the same old extraterritorial rights they enjoyed before the war.' I asked if we were going to give such support. 'Not for nothing,' Father answered. 'Before it came up, I'd been registering a complaint about the character of Chiang's government. I'd told him it was hardly the modern democracy that ideally it should be. I'd told him he would have to form a unity government, while the war was still being fought, with the Communists in Yenan. And he agreed. He agreed, contingently. He agreed to the formation of a democratic government once he had our assurance that the Soviet Union would agree to respect the frontier in Manchuria. That part of it is on the agenda for Teheran.' So then, if you're able to work out that end of it with Stalin, Chiang has agreed to form a more democratic government in China. And in return . . . 'In return, we will support his contention that the British and other nations no longer enjoy special Empire rights to Hong Kong, Shanghai, and Canton. That's right.' It was quite a deal, and promised good things. 'I was especially happy to hear the Generalissimo agree to invite the Communists in as part of the National Government prior to elections,' Father said." pp. 163–64.

The President's son was also present at Tehran during a conversation between the President, Stalin, and Molotov. The relevant passage reads: ". . . they were discussing the Far East, China, the things that Father had already discussed with Generalissimo Chiang. Father was explaining Chiang's anxiety to end Britain's extraterritorial rights in Shanghai and Hong Kong and Canton, his anxiety about Manchuria, and the need for the Soviets' respecting the Manchurian frontier. Stalin made the point that world recognition of the sovereignty of the Soviet Union was a cardinal principle with him, that most certainly he would respect, in turn, the sovereignty of other countries, large or small. Father went on to the other aspects of his conversation with Chiang, the promise that the Chinese Communists would be taken into the Government before any national Chinese elections, that these elections would take place as soon as possible after the war had been won. Stalin punctuated his remarks, as they were translated, with nods: he seemed in complete agreement. This was the only phase of policy that the two discussed during this interview." pp. 179–80.

The only official record of any of the Roosevelt-Chiang discussions is a "summary record" prepared by the Chinese government and made available to the U.S. government in 1956. According to the Chinese record, President Roosevelt proposed a postwar mutual assistance arrangement which would protect China "in the event of foreign aggression." Chiang agreed to place the Port Arthur naval complex "at the joint disposal of China and the United States." See *FRUS, The Conferences at Cairo and Tehran, 1943*, pp. 322–25. Chiang's urgent desire to gain American support against the Soviet Union was made manifest again a few days later in a conversation with Harry Hopkins, the President's chief adviser. The only record of that conversation is a photograph of a page of notes taken by Mr. Hopkins, which, fortunately, is available in Ibid., p. 367 facing, and which unmistakably indicates Chiang's position. Hopkins's note on the issue of a free port at Dairen reads: "C [Chiang Kai-shek] obviously does not want us to say anything about Dairen to Russia."

23. *FRUS, The Conferences at Cairo and Tehran*, p. 488.

24. Ibid., p. 567.

25. In fairness to the President, he may have contemplated a landing on the China coast from the central Pacific, as suggested by the Elliot Roosevelt account cited above.

26. On the ninety division issue, see Romanus and Sunderland, *Stilwell's Command Problems*, p. 64. On November 25, 1943, in a meeting of the President, Stilwell, and Marshall, the President stated that "the Chinese could have equipment for ninety divisions. . . ." For an indication of some of the confusion about the commitment after the President's death see *FRUS, The Conferences at Cairo and Tehran*, pp. 889–90.

27. Robert E. Sherwood, in *Roosevelt and Hopkins*, writes: "Roosevelt [at Tehran] now felt sure that, to use his own term, Stalin was 'getatable,' despite his bludgeoning tactics . . . and that when Russia could be convinced that her legitimate claims and requirements—such as the right to access to warm water ports—were to be given full recognition, she would prove tractable and co-operative in maintaining the peace of the postwar world." pp. 798–99.

28. Radio messages, Chiang Kai-shek to Roosevelt, December 9 and 17, 1943, in *Stilwell's Command Problems*, pp. 75 and 306.

29. Chiang Kai-shek to Roosevelt, 2 February 1944, Ibid., p. 301.

30. Chiang Kai-shek to Roosevelt, 27 March 1944, Ibid., p. 308.

31. Roosevelt to Chiang Kai-shek, 3 April 1944, Ibid., p. 310.

32. *Stilwell's Command Problems*, p. 316.

33. *United States Relations With China* (White Paper) p. 530. Chiang's comment may have been in reply to the Soviet Union, which in previous months had indicated renewed interest in Chinese affairs. The specific item apparently was an article by one V. Rogov, published on August 1 in the Soviet journal *War and the Working Class*, in which he asserted that the Kuomintang was preparing for armed conflict with the Chinese Communists. See Charles B. McLane, *Soviet Policy and the Chinese Conmunists, 1931–1946* (Columbia, 1958), pp. 166–69.

34. *White Paper*, Appendix 40, pp. 532–33.

35. Ibid., p. 535.

36. Ibid.

37. *White Paper*, Annex no. 43, pp. 549–59. The information on the Wallace-Chiang conversations is contained in notes prepared by John Carter Vincent, chief of the State Department's Division of Chinese Affairs at this time. Mr. Vincent apparently attended all but the first meeting between the two men, although a summary of the first discussion appears in the record.

38. As reported by Mr. Wallace the President's words were: "In as much as the Communist and members of the Kuomintang were all Chinese, they were basically friends and that 'nothing should be final between friends'." Ibid., p. 549.

39. *Stilwell's Command Problems*, pp. 375–76.

40. Ibid., p. 377.

41. Radio, Stilwell to Marshall, 3 July 1944, in *Stilwell's Command Problems*, pp. 380–81.

42. Radio, Roosevelt to Chiang Kai-shek, 6 July 1944, in *Stilwell's Command Problems*, pp. 383–84.

43. Radio, Roosevelt to Chiang Kai-shek, 13 July 1944, in Ibid., p. 386.

44. Roosevelt to Chiang Kai-shek, 14 July 1944, in the White Paper, p. 560.

45. *Stilwell's Command Problems*, p. 414.

46. *Stilwell's Command Problems*, p. 415 ff.

47. *Stilwell's Command Problems*, p. 417 n57.

48. Ibid., pp. 425–26.

49. See *Stilwell's Command Problems*, pp. 433–36.

50. Ibid., pp. 442, 447. There seems to be some question as to who actually drafted the message.

51. Ibid., pp. 444–46.

52. *Stilwell's Command Problems*, pp. 461–62.

53. There is little ground for the contention that Hurley acted independently in these matters. He reported every move directly to the President and acted on presidential authority. For example, see Romanus and Sunderland, *Time Runs Out in CBI*, p. 73 n67 for Hurley's radio message of November 7 and the President's reply. In it the President notes that a working arrangement between Communists and Nationalists was highly desirable and he authorized Hurley to say to Chiang that this was "from my point of view and also that of the Russians. You can emphasize the word 'Russians' to him."

54. *White Paper*, pp. 74–75.

55. Ibid., p. 75.

56. *China Handbook*, 1937–1945, p. 70.

57. Ibid.

58. *White Paper*, p. 77.

59. For the OSS plan, see *Time Runs Out in CBI*, pp. 249–54. There were at least two other plans inspired by U.S. military officers to utilize the Chinese Communists; see Ibid. For Hurley's account, see his telegram to the President of January 14, 1945 in *Foreign Relations of the United States, The Conferences at Malta and Yalta, 1945*, (Washington, 1955), pp. 346–51. The Foreign Service officers stationed in China also suggested ways and means to employ the Communists. For example, John Paton Davies, Stilwell's political advisor, on October 2, 1944 proposed to Stilwell that the U.S. and the Chinese Communists seize the Shanghai area, after which large quantities of captured German arms would be given to the Chinese Communists. The whole affair was to be kept secret from Chiang Kai-shek and the Chinese Communists were to be "treated as a sovereign power." Stilwell labeled this "plan Davies" and dropped it in his file. John Stewart Service, in a message to Stilwell of October 10, 1944, recommended that the United States enter into diplomatic discussions with Yenan; see *Stilwell's Command Problems*, pp. 458, 467.

60. Perhaps the real damage which the Foreign Service officers in Yenan perpetrated was in encouraging the Chinese Communists to ignore Ambassador Hurley on the grounds that he did not represent U.S. policy, which was not in fact the case. One of these men, John S. Service, maintains that position to this day; see his *The Amerasia Papers: Some Problems in the History of U.S.-China Relations* (Berkeley, 1971) 76ff.

61. *White Paper*, p. 79.

62. *White Paper*, pp. 80–81.

Chapter VII: The United States, the Soviet Union, and China, 1945

1. See *Foreign Relations of the United States, The Conferences at Malta and Yalta.*

2. *White Paper*, pp. 113–14.

3. The latest of such instances was at Yalta; see *The Conferences at Malta and Yalta*, p. 771.

4. *The Conferences at Malta and Yalta*, pp. 769–70.

5. Ibid., p. 688. See also Robert H. Jones, *Roads to Russia*, appendix A for items delivered under the Milepost agreement. The Russian demand for one million tons of supplies, 80 percent of which was actually agreed to and delivered, as a precondition to launching an attack raises considerable doubt about the strength of the Red Army in the Far East. This, in turn, erodes part of the rationale given for the Yalta agreement that the Soviet Union was so

powerful it would be able to take what it wanted in Manchuria no matter what the United States did. Following this reasoning, by eliciting a statement of Soviet claims they were thereby partially limited.

6. Hurley testimony, 21 June 1951, *Military Situation in the Far East* (Washington, D.C., 1951), "When I returned from China after I found out there was a secret agreement, I heard all kinds of rumors about what it was and how it was. . . . I left there late in February within weeks after the Yalta agreement. . . . I had already heard and my telegrams will show that I had heard that there was a secret agreement." Pt. IV, p. 2884.

7. While Hurley was in Washington, a telegram from the embassy in Chungking arrived. Prepared under the signature of George Atcheson, Charge of the embassy, it in essence called for a change in American policy involving a more tentative commitment to the National Government and the arming of the Chinese Communists. Arrival of the telegram led to a confrontation between Hurley and the Asian affairs personnel in the State Department, a showdown in which the Ambassador was fully supported by the President. The result was the transferral to other posts of those in the Chungking embassy and State Department whom Hurley felt were undermining his efforts. See Feis, *The China Tangle* (Princeton, 1953), pp. 268–73, for discussion.

8. According to Hurley, Roosevelt's words were: "go ahead ameliorate it or set it aside." Hurley testimony, 21 June 1951, *Military Situation in the Far East*, pt. IV, p. 2887.

9. Harry S. Truman, *Memoirs*, Vol. I, p. 61.

10. Summary of memorandum of the Hurley-Stalin talk prepared by the American interpreter, Mr. Edward Page, in Feis, p. 285.

11. "The Ambassador in China (Hurley) to President Truman," 10 May 1945. "Before my last visit to Washington and before I had been informed by the President of the Yalta decision pertaining to China including particularly the all-important prelude [Soviet entry and its timing], the Generalissimo had discussed with me China's position on the same problems decided upon at Yalta and had given me his attitude relating to them. He gave me, at that time, an aide memoire summarizing his position on some of the problems. Of course, the subject discussed in the prelude to the Yalta decision was not known to him. . . . I want to emphasize to you that prior to my recent visit to Washington I had discussed with Chiang Kai-shek all phases of the Chinese-Russian problem before we knew what was contained in the Yalta agreement, and since coming back to Chungking we have again thoroughly covered the same subjects. . . ." *Foreign Relations of the United States, The Far East, China, 1945* Vol. VII (Washington, D.C., 1970), pp. 865–67.

12. "The Charge in China (Atcheson) to the Secretary of State," 27 February 1945, Ibid., p. 856.

13. "The Chinese Minister for Foreign Affairs (Soong) to the Ambassador in China (Hurley), Temporarily in Washington." 6 March 1945, Ibid., p. 65.

14. "The Acting Secretary of State to the Charge in China (Atcheson)." 9 March 1945, Ibid., p. 66.

15. "The Chinese Minister for Foreign Affairs (Soong) to Mr. Harry L. Hopkins," 10 March 1945, Ibid., pp. 66–67.

16. *White Paper*, p. 85.

17. Ibid., p. 86.

18. Mao, *SW*, IV, p. 286.

19. Mao, *SW*, IV, p. 244. Later in his report, Mao restated his proposal in clearer terms: "first . . . form a provisional coalition government by common agreement of the representatives of all parties and people without party affiliation; secondly, at the next stage, through free and unrestricted elections . . . convene a national assembly which will form a proper coalition government." P. 285.

20. Ibid., pp. 259–60.

21. The remaining seven provinces were: Jehol, Chahar, Suiyuan, Shensi, Kansu, Ninghsia, and Shansi. U.S. military intelligence had identified sixteen areas in which the Chinese Communists had concentrated "regular" troops.

Shen-Kan-Ning	50,000
Shansi-Suiyuan	31,000
Shan-Cha-Ho	64,000
Shantung	70,000
Shan-Hopeh-Honan	28,000
Central Kiangsu	19,000
South Huai	21,000
North Kiangsu	23,000
North Huai	18,000
Hupeh-Honan-Anhwei	22,000
South Kiangsu	6,000
Central Anhwei	5,000
East Chekiang	4,000
East River	3,000
Hainan	5,000
Unaccounted for	31,000

Total regular soldiers, 475,000; total regulars with rifles, 207,000. See *The Chinese Communist Movement*, Lyman Van Slyke, ed., p. 180. The rough population totals of the nineteen provinces named by Mao were: (in millions)

Chekiang	21.7
Liaoning	15.2
Jehol	2.2
Chahar	2.0
Suiyuan	2.1
Shensi	9.7
Kansu	6.5
Ninghsia	.7
Shansi	11.6
Hupeh	24.6
Honan	31.8

Shantung   38.1
Kiangsi   13.7
Kiangsu   36.4
Anhwei   22.0
Hopeh   28.6
Honan   32.0
Kwangtung   32.0
Fukien   11.6

The China Handbook, 1937–1945. (New York: Macmillan, 1947), p. 2.
22. Mao, *SW*, IV, "On Coalition Government," p. 260.
23. For the U.S. estimate, see Van Slyke, *The Chinese Communist Movement*, p. 180; for the Chinese, see the *White Paper*, p. 817.
24. The Politburo:

Mao Tse-tung	K'ang Sheng
Chu Teh	Ch'en Yün
Liu Shao-ch'i	Ch'en Yi
Chou En-lai	Ho Lung
Jen Pi-shih	Hsü Hsiang-ch'ien
Lin Po-ch'u (Lin Tsu-han)	Kao Kang
P'eng Teh-huai	Chang Wen-t'ien
	P'eng Chen

In order given by the Communists the Central Committee included those in the Politburo, plus:

Lin Piao	Tseng Shan
Tung Pi-wu	Yeh Chien-ying
Kuan Hsiang-ying	Nieh Jung-chen
Ch'en T'an-ch'iu	Teng Tzu-hui
Li Fu-ch'un	Wu Yu-chang
Jao Shu-shih	Lin Feng
Li Li-san	T'eng Tai-yuan
Lo Jung-huan	Chang Ting-ch'en
Wang Jo-fei	Li Hsien-nien
Chang Yün-yi	Hsu T'e-li
Liu Po-ch'eng	T'an Chen-lin
Cheng Wei-san	Po I-po
Ts'ai Ch'ang	Ch'en Shao-yü
Teng Hsiao-p'ing	Ch'in Pang-hsien
Lu Ting-yi	

New China News Agency, Yenan, 13 June 1945.
25. After 1949 the principal conflicts occurred between the Mao group and those represented by Kao Kang, P'eng Teh-huai, and Liu Shao-ch'i, all of whom were part of the 1945 Politburo. By the year 1972, only Mao and Chou En-lai, of the fifteen-man Politburo elected in 1945, remained. See Part III this book.
26. The "resolution" became the principal guideline for writing of all party

458   Notes for Chapter VII

history, by Communist and non-Communist historians alike, until the Great Proletarian Cultural Revolution, which produced a great outpouring of new information of the history of the CCP and which required the rewriting of all Chinese Communist history. Mao, *SW*, IV, pp. 171–218.

27. *The China Handbook, 1937–1945*, p. 53.

28. *The White Paper*, p. 101.

29. Ibid., p. 105.

30. Ibid., p. 101.

31. If Stalin was privy to American high councils, he would have known that some like Grew and Forrestal were indeed raising the question about the necessity of Soviet entry into the Pacific war.

32. *Foreign Relations of the United States, The Conference of Berlin (Potsdam)*, Vol. I, pp. 21–63, for the official record of the meeting.

33. See General Wedemeyer's testimony in *Military Situation in the Far East*, Part III, pp. 2416–17 and 2431.

34. See Chapter VI.

35. "The Acting Secretary of State to the Ambassador in China (Hurley)," 18 June 1945, *Foreign Relations of the United States*, 1945, p. 907.

36. *Foreign Relations of the United States*, Potsdam, Stimson diary entry of 23 July 1945, p. 260. "Harriman . . . confirmed the expanding demands being made by the Russians. They are throwing aside all their previous restraint as to being only a Continental power and not interested in any further acquisitions, and are now apparently seeking to branch in all directions. Thus they have not only been vigorously seeking to extend their influence in Poland, Austria, Rumania, and Bulgaria, but they are seeking bases in Turkey and now are putting in demands for the Italian colonies in the Mediterranean and elsewhere. He told us that Stalin had brought up yesterday the question of Korea again and was urging an immediate trusteeship."

37. *Foreign Relations of the United States*, Potsdam, Truman-Stalin meeting, 17 July 1945, Bohlen minutes, pp. 1586–87.

38. Ibid.

39. Ibid., Harriman memorandum, 18 July 1945, p. 1240.

40. *Foreign Relations of the United States*, Potsdam, "The President to the Ambassador in China (Hurley)," 23 July 1945, p. 1241.

41. Ray Cline, *Washington Command Post*, (Washington, 1951), p. 348.

42. Joint Chiefs of Staff to MacArthur and Nimitz, No. victory out 357, 26 July 1945. CCS Decimal File 386.2 Japan Sec. 3, RG 218, National Archives.

43. Feis, *The China Tangle*, p. 330. Feis's work is a brilliant and sophisticated apologia for the Roosevelt-Truman administration.

44. *Foreign Relations of the United States*, Potsdam, Stalin-Truman meeting of 17 July 1945, p. 1585.

45. Joint Chiefs of Staff message No. WARX 48004 to MacArthur and Nimitz, 11 August 1945, CCS Decimal File 386.2 Japan Sec. 3, RG 218, National Archives.

46. Joint Chiefs of Staff message No. WARX 51482 to MacArthur and Nimitz, 18 August 1945. "In view of the reported rapid advance of the Russians into Liaotung the directive contained in WARX 48004 to make such arrangements as are practicable to occupy the port of Dairen is hereby cancelled." CCS Decimal File 386.2 Japan Sec. 4, RG 218, National Archives. I am indebted to Mr. Robert J. Doll for bringing this material to my attention.

47. *The White Paper*, p. 579.

48. Ibid., p. 580.

49. See Carroll Wetzel, "From the Jaws of Defeat; Lin Piao and the Fourth Field Army in Manchuria," unpublished doctoral dissertation, George Washington University, 1972, for a discussion of the first encounter.

50. *The White Paper*, p. 939. It is, of course, impossible to ascertain the relationship between this statement and the Soviet stripping of Manchuria, but this statement of policy includes the idea of U.S. assistance in the recovery of Manchuria, which may have prompted the Russians to act.

51. Ibid.

52. Romanus and Sunderland, *Time Runs Out in CBI*, pp. 308–73, 391, 395.

53. *The White Paper*, p. 939.

54. Ibid., p. 131.

55. Feis, p. 386.

56. Mao, *SW*, V, "Build Stable Base Areas in the Northeast," 28 December 1945. Mao urged that the Chinese Communists build base areas in north, east, and west Manchuria, declaring that "three or four years are needed to build such base areas. But a solid preliminary groundwork must be laid in the year 1946. Otherwise we may not be able to stand our ground." He cautioned against building bases in the big cities or along main communication routes, which "are or will be occupied by the Kuomintang; under present conditions this is not practicable." Areas adjacent to those occupied by the Kuomintang will be guerrilla zones. "The regions in which to build stable bases are the cities and vast rural areas comparatively remote from the centers of Kuomintang occupation." Then Mao admitted frankly that "all cadres must be made to understand that the Kuomintang will be stronger than our Party in the Northeast for some time to come and that unless our starting point is to arouse the masses to struggle . . . we shall become isolated in the Northeast . . . and indeed may . . . even fail." Pp. 81–82.

57. See Hurley's testimony in Military Situation in the Far East, Part IV, pp. 2937–38.

58. President Truman expressed "surprise" at Hurley's resignation. *Memoirs*, Vol. II, p. 66.

59. "Memorandum of Conversation, by Lieutenant General John E. Hull, War Department General Staff," 10 December 1945, *Foreign Relations of the United States*, VII, China, p. 762.

60. "Memorandum of Conversation by General Marshall," 11 December 1945, ibid., p. 768.

61. Ibid. The issue here was: who would evacuate the Japanese. On the 9th, the officers in the State Department argued that the U.S. should deal with the Communists directly in order to achieve this objective. P. 762.

62. "Memorandum of Conversation by General Marshall," 14 December 1945. Ibid., p. 770.

63. Ibid., p. 771.

64. Ibid., p. 772.

65. Ibid., pp. 772–73.

Chapter VIII: Strategies in Conflict, 1946–1949

1. *White Paper*, "Press Release on Order for Cessation of Hostilities," 10 January 1946, pp. 609–610.

2. *Foreign Relations of the United States*, The Far East: China, 1946, Vol. IX, pp. 1–177.

3. "Resolution on Government Organization adopted by the PCC, January 1946," *White Paper*, pp. 610–11.

4. "Resolution on Military Problems adopted by the PCC, January 1946," Ibid., pp. 617–19.

5. "Agreement on the National Assembly by Sub-Committee of the PCC," Ibid., p. 619 and "Resolution on the Draft Constitution adopted by the PCC, January 1946," Ibid., 619–21.

6. "Resolution on Program for Peaceful National Reconstruction adopted by the PCC, January 1946," Ibid., pp. 612–17.

7. *China Handbook, 1937–1945*, p. 737.

8. "Resolution on Program for Peaceful National Reconstruction," pp. 612–17.

9. See Chapter VII.

10. "Program for Peaceful National Reconstruction," *White Paper*, Annex, p. 617.

11. Population figures for the seven provinces are: (in millions) Shansi 11.6; Hopeh, 28.6; Shantung, 38.1; Honan, 31.8; Hupeh, 24.6; Kiangsu, 36.4; Anhwei, 22; *China Handbook; 1937–1945*, p. 2.

12. "General Marshall to President Truman," 26 February 1946, *Foreign Relations of the United States-China, 1946*, IX, pp. 444–46 and "President Truman to General Marshall," 27 February 1946, Ibid., p. 446.

13. Ibid., pp. 464–500.

14. "Minutes of Meeting Between General Marshall and Chairman Mao Tse-tung at Yenan," 4 March 1946, Ibid., pp. 501–502.

15. "General Marshall to President Truman," 6 March 1946, Ibid., pp. 510–11.

16. "Press Release Issued by Spokesman of Central Committee of the Chinese Communist Party," 14 February 1946, Ibid., pp. 450–53.

17. "Memorandum by the Second Secretary of Embassy in China (Ludden) to General Marshall," 9 March 1946, Ibid., pp. 513–16.

18. "Memorandum by General Marshall to President Truman," 13 March

1946, Ibid., pp. 541–42. It was not until March 27 that field teams were actually dispatched.

19. "Memorandum by General Marshall to President Truman," Ibid., p. 542.

20. "The Counselor of Embassy in China (Smyth) to the Secretary of State," 20 March 1946, pp. 586–87 and "The Consul General at Shanghai (Josselyn) to the Secretary of State," 26 March 1946, Ibid., pp. 600–601.

21. *Military Campaigns in China: 1924–1950,* (U.S. Office of Military History, 1966), p. 103.

22. *Military Campaigns in China, 1924–1950,* pp. 103–106.

23. "Brigadier General Henry A. Byroade to Lieutenant General Alvan C. Gillem, Jr., and Mr. Walter S. Robertson," 28 March 1946, *Foreign Relations of the United States-China, 1946,* IX, pp. 713–14 on Yeh Chien-ying's attempt to forestall Nationalist troop movements; "Memorandum by Colonel J. Hart Caughey to Lieutenant General Alvan C. Gillem, Jr.," 18 April 1946, Ibid., p. 779 for estimated Communist troop strength.

24. "Mr. Walter S. Robertson to General Marshall," 8 April 1946, Ibid., 740.

25. *Military Campaigns in China, 1924–1950,* 105–106; on Communist use of Japanese tanks and artillery, see "General Marshall to President Truman," 6 May 1946, *Foreign Relations of the United States-China, 1946,* IX, 815; for an updated account of the campaign, see Carroll Wetzel, *From the Jaws of Victory.*

26. Chiang's evaluation of the battle a decade later was that it "was the most decisive battle against the Communist troops since the Government's fifth campaign in southern Kiangsi in 1934. As a matter of fact, the Communist losses in and around Szepingchieh in 1946 far surpassed those which had forced the Reds to flee from Central China twelve years earlier." *Soviet Russia in China,* 116. It is curious that neither the *White Paper,* published in 1949, nor *Foreign Relations of the United States,* IX, published in 1972, gives emphasis to the battle of Ssup'ingchieh.

27. "General Marshall to President Truman and the Under Secretary of State (Acheson)," 12 May 1946. "Most confidentially, Generalissimo informed me today that . . . Stalin desired Generalissimo to go to Moscow immediately on completion of meeting now in progress in Paris. Generalissimo replied that the situation in China was so serious that he could not leave China at this time." *Foreign Relations of the United States,* IX, 841. On Stalin's objectives in seeking the meeting, see Chiang, *Soviet Russia in China,* 102.

28. *Soviet Russia in China,* 102–104.

29. "General Marshall to President Truman . . ." 12 May 1946, and "President Truman to General Marshall," 13 May 1946 in *Foreign Relations of the United States,* IX, 841 and 846.

30. "Memorandum by the State-War-Navy Coordinating Committee to the Secretary of State," 1 June 1946, *Foreign Relations of the United States,* IX, 933–34.

31. Ibid., 935.

32. "Minutes of Meeting Between General Marshall and General Yü Ta-wei at House 28," Chungking, 22 April 1946, IX, 789. (Emphasis supplied.)

33. "Memorandum by General Marshall to Generalissimo Chiang Kai-shek," 10 May 1946, *Foreign Relations of the United States*, IX, 824–25.

34. Minutes of Conference Between General Marshall and General Yü Ta-wei at General Marshall's House," 11 May 1946, IX, 830–32.

35. "General Marshall to President Truman," 22 May 1946, IX, 882.

36. "Madame Chiang Kai-shek to General Marshall," 24 May 1946, IX, 891; "General Marshall to Generalissimo Chiang Kai-shek," 26 May 1946, IX, 901–902; "Madame Chiang Kai-shek to General Marshall," 28 May 1946, IX, 906; "Generalissimo Chiang Kai-shek to General Marshall," 28 May 1946, IX, 907–908.

37. "Memorandum by General Marshall to the President of the Chinese Executive Yuan (Soong)," 29 May 1946, IX, 912.

38. "Minutes of Meeting Between General Marshall and General Chou En-lai at 5 Ning Hai Road, Nanking," 30 May 1946, IX, 923.

39. "Minutes of Meeting Between General Marshall and General Chou En-lai at 5 Ning Hai Road, Nanking," 3 June 1946, IX, 953. In fact, during June there were increasingly numerous instances when Chinese Communists fired upon the three-man truce teams wounding and killing American and Chinese Nationalist team members. See *Foreign Relations of the United States*, IX, pp. 1110–11; see also Ludden conversation with Soviet Second Secretary Vinogradov of June 14. Vinogradov declared that the Marshall mission had "failed," the Soviet Union was "distrustful of American Policy in the far east," and might find it necessary "actively to intervene in China." *Foreign Relations of the United States*, IX, 1046.

40. For a summary of the June negotiations, see the *White Paper*, pp. 644–46; for details, see *Foreign Relations of the United States*, IX, 985–1272; for a brilliant analysis, see the unpublished paper by H. Lyman Miller, "Nationalist Position-Building in East China: June-November 1946," May 1972, The Institute for Sino-Soviet Studies, The George Washington University, Washington, D.C.

41. *White Paper,* pp. 191 and 645–46.

42. See *Pravda,* 7 July 1946 and *Foreign Relations of the United States,* IX, pp. 1309–16.

43. The Communists began to attack the U.S. Marines, dramatizing the change in policy. In mid-July, Communist forces kidnapped seven Marines detaining them for several days before releasing them. Two weeks later an estimated 300 Communists ambushed a 41-man Marine motor convoy carrying supplies between Peiping and Tientsin. Three Marines were killed and twelve wounded. The investigation of the "incident" dragged on for months with little result. See the *White Paper*, 172 and *Foreign Relations of the United States,* IX, p. 1432ff.

44. "General Marshall to the Acting Secretary of State," 2 July 1946, IX, 1277–78.

45. "The Acting Secretary of State to General Marshall," 4 July 1946, IX, 1295–97.

46. It makes all the more curious the argument of those who claimed that the United States could not have affected the course of events by what it did, could

have done, or left undone. The principal exponent of this argument was, of course, Dean Acheson himself; see the *White Paper,* xvi.

47. "Memorandum by General Chou En-lai to General Marshall," 21 September 1946, X, 212 on the demand for immediate cease-fire. "Minutes of Meeting Between General Marshall and General Yü Ta-wei at No. 5 Ning Hai Road," 23 September 1946, X, 220–21.

48. "Colonel Marshall S. Carter to General Marshall," 23 July 1946, X, 753–54.

49. "General Marshall to Colonel Marshall S. Carter," 26 July 1946, X, 755. (Emphasis supplied.)

50. "The Acting Secretary of State to the Administrator of the War Assets Administration (Littlejohn)," 6 August 1946, X, 755–56.

51. Between April and September 1947 the First Marine Division dumped 6500 tons of ammunition for Chinese government use prior to their withdrawal from China. Only a relatively small proportion of the total was immediately suitable for use by Chinese infantry, such as the .30 calibre ammunition (2.1 million rounds) and 105 MM Howitzer shells (64,000), insignificant amounts compared to the 130 million rounds of 7.92 ammunition which the Chinese themselves purchased in June 1947 following the lifting of the embargo. The 7.92 ammunition was shipped from west coast ports on July 14 and August 11, 1947. Arrival time is unknown. See the *White Paper,* 355 and 940.

52. "The Ambassador in China (Stuart) to the Secretary of State," 30 October 1946, X, 764.

53. "Minutes of Meeting between General Marshall and General Yü Ta-wei at No. 5 Ning Hai Road," 30 August 1946, X, 108–109.

54. "General Marshall to President Truman," 30 August 1946, X, 109–110.

55. "Minutes of Meeting Between General Marshall and General Yü Ta-wei at No. 5 Ning Hai Road," 19 September 1946, X, 206–208.

56. "General Marshall to Lieutenant General Alvan C. Gillem, Jr.," 27 September 1946. "General Marshall desires that all action to complete the so-called reoccupation (of Manchuria) program that is, the supply of ammunition and combat equipment to the Chinese Government, be deferred until further notice from him." *Foreign Relations of the United States-China, 1946,* X, 761.

57. "Minutes of Meeting Between General Marshall and General Chou En-lai at General Gillem's Residence, Shanghai," 9 October 1946, X, 338.

58. Ibid., 341.

59. "Statement by the Head of the Chinese Communist Party Delegation (Chou)," 16 November 1946, *White Paper,* 683–85.

60. "Personal Statement by the Special Representative of the President (Marshall)," 7 January 1947, Ibid., 686–89. (Emphasis supplied.)

61. Marshall was kept fully informed of U.S. intelligence estimates regarding Soviet actions. On August 14, 1946, for instance, the War Department informed him that "the obvious Soviet aim in China is to exclude U.S. influence and replace it with that of Moscow. The major concern is that, should the U.S. for

any reason or reasons withdraw from China, the result would be a triumph for Soviet strategy in an area of global importance. . . . If General Marshall's mission fails, the U.S. must revert to the status of an interested bystander rather than that of an active participant in Chinese affairs. Our exclusion from China would probably result, within the next generation, in an expansion of Soviet influence over the manpower, raw materials, and industrial potential of Manchuria and China. The U.S. and the world might then be faced in the China Sea and southward with a Soviet power analogous to that of the Japanese in 1941, but with the difference that the Soviets could be perhaps overwhelmingly strong in Europe and the Middle East as well. The great difficulties in attaining our objectives in China are well recognized. However, we should preserve a position which will enable us effectively to continue to oppose Soviet influence in China even though internal strife continues. It is felt that failure to maintain this position would have the gravest effect on our long-range security interests." See "Colonel Marshall S. Carter to General Marshall," 14 August 1946, *Foreign Relations of the United States-China, 1946,* X, 27–28.

62. Yen Chung-ch'uan, "Recollection of a Period of History of Struggle Between the Two Lines in the Northeast Region After the Victory of the Anti-Japanese War," *Jen Min Jih Pao,* 3 December 1968, in *Survey of the China Mainland Press (SCMP),* no. 4315, 10 December 1968, p. 4.

63. See "Manifesto of the Central Executive Committee of the Chinese Communist Party in Commemoration of the 9th Anniversary of the '7th of July,' " in *Foreign Relations of the United States-China, 1946,* IX, 1310–16, and McLane, *Soviet Policy and the Chinese Communists,* pp. 252–56.

64. Mao, *SW,* V, "Build Stable Base Areas in the Northeast," 28 December 1945, pp. 81–85.

65. M. I. Sladkovski, "Sovetsko-kitaiskie otnosheniia posle razgroma Iaponskogo imperializma (1945–1949)" (Sino-Soviet Relations after the Defeat of Japanese Imperialism), in *Leninskaia politika SSSR v otnoshenii Kitaia* (The Leninist Policy of the USSR in Relations with China) (Moscow, 1968), pp. 130–36. See also O. B. Borisov and B. T. Koloskov, *Sovetsko-Kitaiskie Otnosheniia* (Sino-Soviet Relations), 1945–1970 (Moscow, 1971), especially pp. 28–44.

66. Lin Piao, *Principles of Combat* (Harbin, September 1946), as quoted in R. Rigg, *Red China's Fighting Hordes* (Harrisburg, Pa., 1951), p. 204.

67. Col. F. J. Culley, "Dragon Report on Conditions in Communist Area," to Director of Operations, Changchun, Manchuria, 1 August 1946, Shuang Cheng, Manchuria, in Executive Headquarters, Peiping, 1st Quarter, 1947, Section XIII, *Communist Party Views,* p. 33. It is quite likely that Col. Culley was not permitted to observe the main troop centers; still, his report carries considerable validity regarding the general state of Chinese Communist forces at this time.

68. A. T. Steele interview with Li Li-san, *New York Herald Tribune,* 28 August 1946.

69. Kiwon Chung, "The North Korean People's Army and the Party," *The China Quarterly,* no. 14 (April-June 1963), p. 109.

70. Sladkovski, *op. cit.*, 141f. The Soviets supplied the Chinese Communists through Port Arthur and North Korean ports and by rail through the Trans-Siberian railway. Soviet military advisors were positively identified with Chinese Communist troops as early as the battle of Ssup'ingchieh; see *Foreign Relations of the United States-China, 1946*, IX, pp. 780–82. See also the Joseph and Stewart Alsop article in the *Washington Post*, 20 May 1946. The Alsops claimed that 10 percent of the casualties at Ssup'ingchieh were Russian.

71. Hu Hua, ed., *Chung-Kuo Hsin Min-Chu Chu-Yi Ko-Ming Ts'an-K'ao Tzu-Liao* (Reference Materials for the History of the Chinese New Democratic Revolution) (Peking, 1957), p. 493, and Losyachin, "General Recalls Soviet Aid to Chinese PLA," Moscow radio broadcast in Mandarin to China, 3 September 1967.

72. On the issue of Nationalist superiority in artillery at Ssup'ingchieh, for example, see "The Counselor of Embassy in China (Smyth) to the Secretary of State," 4 June 1946. Smyth noted that "missionaries at Ssupingkai during fighting report action desultory during major part of battle but Communists regularly suffered telling losses from KMT artillery." *Foreign Relations of the United States-China, 1946*, IX, p. 974.

73. Mao, *SW*, V, "Greet the New High Tide of the Chinese Revolution," p. 123.

74. "Message of the President to the Congress," *Department of State Bulletin*, 16 March 1947, p. 536.

75. "Summary of the Manifesto Issued by the Kuomintang Central Executive Committee," issued 24 March 1947, in the *White Paper*, pp. 737–38.

76. "Statement of Under Secretary Acheson Before House Committee on Foreign Affairs," 20 March 1947, in *Military Situation in the Far East*, part IV, p. 2810.

77. Major General Samuel Howard, in command of the First Marine division then being withdrawn from China, stated in a conversation of 3 July 1947 with the Secretary of Defense, James Forrestal, that the Communists had begun to employ artillery on a large scale for the first time in their recent offensive. See Walter Millis, ed., *The Forrestal Diaries* (New York, 1951), p. 289.

78. *Military Campaigns in China: 1924–1950*, p. 127.

79. See footnote 51, this chapter. In a meeting with the heads of the War and Navy Departments, on June 26, 1947 Secretary of State Marshall declared that "the immediate and urgent problem to be decided is what are we to do about rearming the Chinese National Army. . . . The Army is beginning to run out of ammunition and it appears that we have a moral obligation to provide it inasmuch as we aided in equipping it with American arms." *United States Foreign Relations*, Vol. VII, The Far East, China, 1947 (Washington, 1973), p. 850. Despite the urgency in the Secretary of State's remark, the issue of arming the Nationalists dragged on for over a year from that date. There simply was too much antagonistic sentiment to the Nationalists among high-level persons in the American government to permit reversing the wheels of earlier policy. In this

connection the section "Military Aid to China" in Ibid. (pp. 785–941) contains detailed discussions among American leaders who realized the significance of low ammunition reserves as well as the implications for chances of Nationalist success and the American position in the Far East.

80. *White Paper,* pp. 251–52.

81. *White Paper,* p. 814. For the documents of the Wedemeyer mission, see *United States Foreign Relations,* Vol. VII, The Far East, China, 1947, pp. 635–784.

82. *White Paper,* p. 260.

83. *White Paper,* p. 814.

84. *White Paper,* p. 389.

85. *White Paper,* pp. 270–71. General Marshall, testimony before the Senate Foreign Relations Committee, 14 February 1947: "The thing is a very confused thing. They [the Nationalists] sent troops up to North China with only two rounds of ammunition per gun at one time and had some very bad reverses. . . . The trouble with them is that the ammunition was over in Chungking thousands of miles away where it had come over the Burma Road, and they were in North China. . . . They have had all sorts of things happen. That is a very delicate issue in this whole business because if we give them ammunition, we are participating in the civil war directly. On the other hand, if we never give them any ammunition, we have disarmed them because they have American equipment through our decision way back in 1943. So we have a very delicate thing there which I was always hoping was such that the situation would overtake the dilemma, which it has not. We have made no decision with regard to that." Quoted in *Military Situation in the Far East,* Part IV, p. 2991.

86. *Military Campaigns in China, 1924–1950,* p. 129.

87. General David Barr, commander of the Military Advisory Group in China from January 27, 1948 until January 29, 1949, asserted in a widely quoted report that "no battle has been lost since my arrival due to lack of ammunition or equipment." See the *White Paper,* p. 358. Yet first-hand accounts of the battle of Weihsien, for example, noted that "the defenders lost about 50 percent of their troops, and when the Communists overwhelmed them by their attack on that town, the defenders were not only throwing rocks, bottles, and bricks at them, but they were dropping homemade bombs out of small planes made of bottles with powder in them and ordinary caps. They just ran out of ammunition at Weihsien, and that is all there was to it." See the testimony of Admiral Oscar C. Badger, 19 June 1951, *Military Situation in the Far East,* part IV, p. 2762. Barr's assertion is placed in somewhat better context by his own testimony to the Senate Armed Services hearings cited above. Three days following Admiral Badger's testimony, General Barr stated in reference to his oft-quoted remark: "I did not observe the Chinese Nationalist forces actually in battle. I observed them out of battle on many occasions, and I inspected their training, exercised supervision over their training, and inspected some places." Ibid., p. 2959. Had General Barr observed Nationalist forces in battle he would have seen key

battles lost for precisely a lack of ammunition, see the account below of the Huai-Hai campaign.

88. *Military Situation in the Far East,* IV, p. 2745.

89. According to General Barr, "We knew beforehand this equipment would arrive incomplete." Barr went on to note that some of the missing parts were sent within a few days to General Fu's forces, but mentions no figure. Ibid., p. 2996.

90. *Military Situation in the Far East,* IV, p. 2747.

91. *Military Campaigns in China, 1924–1950,* pp. 156–57.

92. Mao, V, 265. Mao demanded a concentration of forces in an effort to take Chinchou, recognizing it as the lynchpin to control of Manchuria.

93. *White Paper,* p. 281.

94. Ibid.

95. For the exchange of letters, see the *White Paper,* pp. 888–90.

96. The *White Paper,* p. 322, describes the Huai-Hai campaign in one sentence as a minor conflict, whereas in fact it was the decisive battle of the Nationalist-Communist struggle for the mainland.

97. Estimates vary as to the number of troops engaged in the Huai-Hai campaigns. A Nationalist military history estimates 700,000 Communist and 400,000 Nationalist troops were involved; *Military Campaigns,* p. 161. A Communist source calculated some 800,000 on each side; Chang Chen, "Yeng-ming ti yu-chien, Cheng-ch'üeh ti chan-i fang-chen Hui-i Huai-Hai Chan-i" (Brilliant Anticipation and Proper Battle Strategy—an Account of the Huai-Hai Battle) *Hung-Ch'i P'iao-P'iao* (The Red Flag Waves), Vol. 15, (Peking, 1961), pp. 78–79.

98. The CCP at this time, November 1, 1948, designated their various forces into field armies, regional and guerrilla forces. Although I employed numerical designators for the field armies in this account, at this time Ch'en's forces were called the Eastern China Field Army and Liu's the Central Plains Field Army. It was not until later that they were renamed the Third and Second Field Armies; see Mao, *SW,* V, p. 266.

99. Yale Fung, *Hsü-pang Chan-i Chien-wen lu* (The Factual Report of the Hsuchow-Pangpu Battle) (Hong Kong, 1963), p. 26.

100. *Military Campaigns,* p. 163.

101. Ho Kuang-hua, "Tsai Huai-Hai nan-hsien" (On the Huai-Hai Southern Front), in Yeh Chien-ying, et al., *Wei-ta ti Chan-lueh Chüeh-chan* (The Great Strategically Decisive Battle) (Peking, 1961), p. 170.

102. Chang Chen, "Brilliant Anticipation and Proper Battle Strategy," pp. 100–102.

103. Mao, *SW,* V, p. 291.

104. See the remarks of General Sam Howard, commander, First Marine Division in China, in Walter Millis, ed., *The Forrestal Diaries,* p. 289.

105. M. Losyachin, "General Recalls Soviet Aid to Chinese PLA," Moscow Radio in Mandarin, September 3, 1967.

106. Hu Hua, *op. cit.,* p. 493.

107. Chung, "The North Korean People's Army and the Party," p. 109.

108. M. Sladkovski, *op. cit.,* pp. 130–136.

109. O. B. Borisov and B. T. Koloskov, *Sovetsko-Kitaiskie Otnosheniia, 1945–1970* (Sino-Soviet Relations, 1945–1970) (Moscow: Thought Publishers, 1972), pp. 28 ff.

110. "Director, Office of Far Eastern Affairs (Vincent) to the Secretary of State," February 7, 1947, *Foreign Relations of the United States,* Volume VII, The Far East, China, 1947, p. 790.

111. "Secretary of State (Marshall) to Secretary of War (Patterson)," March 4, 1947, Ibid., p. 805.

112. See the recently declassified materials on U.S. military aid to China, National Archives, Washington, D.C., especially the reports of Brigadier General T. S. Timberman and Ambassador Leighton Stuart in the files of the U.S. Embassy in Nanking.

113. *Foreign Relations of the United States,* Vol. VII, The Far East, China, 1947, p. 850.

114. *Economic Report of the President of the United States* (Washington, D.C.: Government Printing Office, February 1975).

Part III. The Sino-Soviet Relationship, 1949–1972

Chapter IX: The Soviet Union and the
Chinese People's Republic, 1949–1959

1. The current Soviet position on the role of the Korean war is that "before October 1949 American ruling circles held the illusion that the CCP would never ally with the socialist camp. Even after the victory of the revolution and the expulsion of Chiang Kai-shek from the continent the government of the USA still had not lost hope for the development of an anti-Soviet foreign policy in the new regime, since the Chinese [Communist] leaders awaited the development of events and did not themselves take the initiative in worsening relations with the USA. The establishment of friendly relations between the Soviet Union and the CPR in 1950 and simultaneously the decisive support for the struggle of the Korean people against American aggression demolished these hopes." M. I. Makarov, B. N. Zanegin, et al., *Vneshniaia Politika KNR* (The Foreign Policy of the Chinese People's Republic) (Moscow, 1971) p. 142.

2. In December 1949 after the Nationalists had established themselves on Taiwan, the Joint Chiefs recommended a modest military aid program to prevent the Communist capture of the island. The State Department opposed this recommendation, urging a hands-off policy. The President settled the dispute in early January 1950 when, on the 5th, he announced that "the United States . . . [does not] have any intention of utilizing its armed forces to interfere in the present situation. The United States Government will not pursue a course which will lead to involvement in the civil conflict in China. . . . The United States Government will not provide military aid or advice to Chinese forces on Formosa. . . . " Harry S. Truman, "United States Policy Toward Formosa," *Department of State Bulletin*, XXII, no. 550, 16 January 1950, p. 79. See also, *The United States and Communist China in 1949 and 1950: The Question of Rapprochement and Recognition*, a Senate Foreign Relations Committee Staff Study (Washington, 1973).

3. *Military Situation in the Far East*, U.S. Senate Foreign Relations Committee Hearings. Testimony of George C. Marshall, part I, pp. 352, 382.

4. Dean G. Acheson, "Crisis in Asia—An Examination of U.S. Policy," *Department of State Bulletin*, XXII, no. 556, 23 January 1950, p. 116.

5. *Military Situation in the Far East*, testimony of Dean Acheson, part III, p. 2010.

6. Glenn D. Paige, *The Korean Decision* (New York, 1968), p. 81.

7. In January 1950, one day after Acheson delivered his remarks excluding Taiwan and Korea from the U.S. defense perimeter in the Pacific, the Soviet representative walked out of the U.N. Security Council on the pretext of a protest against the seating of the Nationalist delegate. The absence of the Soviet

representative not only permitted the U.S. to act through the U.N., it freed the Soviet Union from being forced to condemn acts of aggression by its allies.

8. *Military Situation in the Far East,* testimony of Louis A. Johnson, part IV, p. 2621.

9. Frank Kierman, *The Fluke That Saved Formosa* (M.I.T., 1954).

10. Allen S. Whiting, *China Crosses the Yalu* (Stanford, 1960) p. 66.

11. Ibid., 67.

12. This objective was approved by the United Nations on October 7, 1950, by a vote of 47–5, eight nations abstaining.

13. In command of the field armies were: Ho Lung, First Field Army (some sources state it was P'eng Teh-huai); Liu Po-ch'eng, Second Field Army; Ch'en Yi, Third Field Army; Lin Piao, Fourth Field Army; the Fifth Field Army, or North China Field Army, was presumably under Central Command.

14. For the texts of the laws, see Albert P. Blaustein, ed., *Fundamental Legal Documents of Communist China* (South Hackensack, 1962), pp. 96–114.

15. William Whitson, "The Field Army in Chinese Communist Military Politics," *The China Quarterly,* no. 37 (January-March 1969) pp. 1–30.

16. *Jen Min Jih Pao (People's Daily),* 1 July 1950.

17. *China News Analysis,* no. 43, 9 July 1954 (Hong Kong), p. 5.

18. *Hsin Hua Yueh Pao (Hsinhua Monthly),* December 1952 (Hong Kong), p. 3.

19. Ibid.

20. *China News Analysis,* no. 41, 25 June 1954 (Hong Kong), p. 2.

21. *SCMP,* no. 453, 15–17 November 1952 (Hong Kong), p. 20.

22. *Jen Min Jih Pao (People's Daily),* 10 April 1955.

23. The last official mention of Kao Kang occurs on January 1, 1954 when his name headed the list of guests at a banquet feting the visiting Soviet Minister of Metallurgy, I. F. Tevosyan. *SCMP,* no. 719, 1–4 January 1954 (Hong Kong), p. 18.

24. *Jen Min Jih Pao (People's Daily),* 18 February 1954.

25. Ibid., p. 6.

26. Ibid.

27. *China News Analysis,* no. 80, 22 April 1955 (Hong Kong), p. 2.

28. Ibid., p. 6.

29. *Jen Min Jih Pao (People's Daily),* 5 April 1955.

30. Jao Shu-shih was also director of the Organization Department of the Central Committee from 1953 and was accused of having "actively carried out activities to split the party" in this capacity. Afterwards, the Organization Department was dissolved and replaced by a Control Department. For Jao's indictment, see "National Conference of the Communist Party of China, March 21–31, 1955," *Current Background (CB),* 1 April 1955, p. 4.

31. *SCMP,* no. 453, 15–17 November 1952, p. 20.

32. Biographical data was obtained from *Chung Kung Jen Ming Lü* (Who's Who in Communist China) (Taipei, 1967).

33. *Pravda,* 10 March 1953.

34. Ibid.

35. Ibid., 15 February 1950.

36. *Sino-Soviet Relations, a collection of documents 1917–1957,* pp. 284–308.

37. Malenkov, Georgi M., "Report of the Central Committee" in Leo Gruliow, ed., *Current Soviet Policies: The Documentary Record of the Nineteenth Party Congress and the Reorganization After Stalin's Death* (New York, 1953), pp. 105–106.

38. Quoted in Hsieh, p. 24.

39. Quoted in Polaczi-Horvath, *Khrushchev, the Making of a Dictator* (Boston, 1960), p. 193.

40. Organic Law of the Central People's Government, article 7; promulgated 29 September 1949, in *Fundamental Legal Documents.*

41. Organic Law, National People's Congress, article 20; promulgated 28 September 1954, in Ibid.

42. See Paloczi-Horvath, pp. 183–84.

43. See Merle Fainsod, "Historiography and Change," in John Keep, ed., *Contemporary History in the Soviet Mirror* (New York, 1964). Over the next fifteen months, Burdzhalov came under continuous criticism, but it was not until after the ouster of the so-called anti-party group in June 1957 that he was fired.

44. See Paloczi-Horvath, p. 187.

45. See Leo Gruliow, *Current Soviet Policies* (New York, 1957), Vol. II, pp. 87–88.

46. Ibid., pp. 211–12.

47. Ibid., p. 55.

48. Ibid., p. 188.

49. Ibid.

50. "Mao Tse-tung's Talk at a Central Work Meeting," 25 October 1966, *Facts and Features*, Vol. II, No. 9, 19 February 1969 (Taiwan), pp. 25–27.

51. On the establishment and functions of the Politburo standing committee and Secretariat, see article 37 of the 1956 party constitution. For their establishment at various levels of the organizational hierarchy, see articles 41, 46, 49. *Fundamental Legal Documents,* pp. 79–88.

52. "Mao Tse-tung's Talk at a Central Work Meeting," 25 October 1966.

53. Mao Tse-tung, *On the Correct Handling of Contradictions Among the People* (Peking, 1960), pp. 5, 59.

54. Chou En-lai, in his "Report on the Proposals for the Second Five-Year Plan for Development of the National Economy" (16 September 1956), said that "First, we should, in accordance with needs and possibilities set a reasonable rate for the growth of the national economy and place the Plan on a forward-looking and completely sound basis, to ensure a fairly balanced development of the national economy." *Eighth National Congress of the Communist Party of China* (Peking, 1956), Vol. I, p. 272.

55. Donald S. Zagoria, *The Sino-Soviet Conflict, 1956–1961* (Princeton, 1962), p. 68.

56. Carl A. Linden, *Khrushchev and the Soviet Leadership, 1957–1964* (Balti-more, 1966), pp. 180–81, cites Khrushchev's radio speech of July 19, 1963, in which he "accused his Chinese foes of 'poking their noses' into CPSU internal affairs and seeking the overthrow of his leadership. . . . " No date is mentioned by Khrushchev for the Chinese action, but the only attempt to oust Khrushchev up to that point in time was the attempt of the so-called anti-party group in 1957.

57. *The Origin and Development of the Difference Between the Leadership of the CPSU and Ourselves* (Peking, 1963), p. 26.

58. Raymond L. Garthoff, "Sino-Soviet Military Relations, 1945–1966," in Raymond L. Garthoff, ed., *Sino-Soviet Military Relations* (New York, 1966), p. 86.

59. Ibid., p. 87.

60. Hsieh, pp. 34–62, gives a fascinating analysis of discussions among military men in which the alternatives set forth above are implicit.

61. *Jen Min Jih Pao (People's Daily)*, 25 May 1958.

62. *China News Analysis*, no. 231, 6 June 1958 (Hong Kong), p. 6.

63. *The Origin and Development of the Differences* . . . , p. 26.

64. "Communique of the Sixth Plenary Session of the Eighth Central Committee," 17 December 1958, in Robert R. Bowie and John K. Fairbank, *Communist China 1955–1959*, Policy Documents With Analysis (Cambridge, 1962), p. 484.

65. Ibid.

66. David Floyd, *Mao Against Khrushchev* (New York: Praeger, 1963), p. 260.

Chapter X: The Polarization of Communist Politics, 1959–1965

1. See John Gittings, *The Role of the Chinese Army* (Oxford, 1967), pp. 213ff on the militia and party control as opposed to PLA control.

2. In support of P'eng were: Huang K'o-ch'eng, Chief of Staff; T'an Cheng, Director of the General Political Department; Hung Hsueh-chih, Director of the General Logistics Department; Hsiao K'o, Director of the General Training Department; Wan I, Director of the Equipment Department; Teng Hua, in command of the Northeast military region; Chang Wen-t'ien, Vice-Minister of Foreign Affairs; Chou Hsiao-chou, First Secretary of the Hunan Provincial Party Committee; Chu Teh, and several other lesser military figures.

3. For P'eng Teh-huai's "Letter of opinion," and selected Red Guard criticism, see "The 'Wicked' History of P'eng Teh-huai," *Current Background*, no. 851, 26 April 1968.

4. Mao Tse-tung's Speech at the Eighth Plenary Session of the CCP's Eighth Central Committee, *Issues and Studies*, Vol. VI, no. 7 (April 1970) pp. 80–86.

5. Lo Jui-ch'ing replaced Huang K'o-ch'eng as Chief of Staff; Hsieh Fu-chih moved into the post of Minister of Public Security vacated by Lo. Ch'iu Hui-tso became Director of the General Logistics Department, replacing Hung Hsueh-

chih. T'an Cheng, however, was not removed from the directorship of the General Political Department until the following year, when Hsiao Hua replaced him. For the periodization of the meetings surrounding the Eighth Plenum, see Parris Chang, "Research Notes on the Changing Loci of Decision in the Chinese Communist Party," *The China Quarterly*, no. 44 (October-December 1970), p. 189.

6. "Settle Accounts with P'eng Teh-huai for his Crimes of Usurping Army Leadership and Opposing the Party" (part II), 29 August 1967, *SCMP* 4007, 12–13 and J. Chester Cheng, ed., *The Politics of the Chinese Red Army* (Stanford, 1966), p. 68.

7. Quoted in David Floyd, *Mao Against Khrushchev* (New York: Praeger, 1963), p. 279.

8. For a survey of the ideological dispute, see Floyd, *Mao Against Khrushchev,* passim.

9. *The Road to Communism: Documents of the 22nd Congress of the CPSU, October 17–31, 1961* (Moscow, 1961). See also Franz Michael, "Who Is Ahead on the Way to Communism?" *Communist Affairs,* Vol. 4, no. 6 (November–December 1966).

10. For a survey of these discussions, see the author's "Soviet Historians and China's Past," *Problems of Communism,* Vol. 17, no. 2 (March-April 1968), pp. 71–75.

11. Marion R. Larsen, "China's Agriculture Under Communism," in *An Economic Profile of Mainland China* (U.S. GPO, February 1967), Vol. 1, p. 220.

12. Ibid.

13. Parris Chang in "Research Notes . . . " points out that this was not the first occasion on which *ad hoc* meetings had been called, although previously all such meetings seem to have been called by Mao, who exercised this prerogative as chairman of the Central Committee.

14. See Chapter IX above, p. 236–38.

15. Parris Chang discusses the issue of attendance, which apparently varied according to the agenda. "Research Notes. . . . " See especially, 170–171.

16. "A Chronicle of Events in the Life of Liu Shao-ch'i," *CB,* n. 834, 17 August 1967, p. 20.

17. "An Epoch-Making Document," joint *Hung Chi-Chieh Fang Chun Pao* editorial, New China News Agency, 16 May 1968.

18. "A Chronicle of Events . . . ," pp. 20–21.

19. *CB,* no. 842, "Chronology of Events on the Cultural Front in Communist China," p. 4.

20. Ibid., p. 21.

21. See the article by Merle Goldman, "The Unique 'Blooming and Contending' of 1961–62," in *The China Quarterly,* no. 37 (January-March 1969) pp. 54–83, for a discussion of literary developments. See also "Chronology of Events on the Cultural Front . . . ," *CB,* no. 842.

22. Huang K'o-ch'eng, Hsiao K'o, and Li Ta were dismissed. Of the five

vice-ministers appointed in 1959, only one, Liu Ya-lou, can be positively identified as a supporter of Lin Piao. Three of the remaining four, Ch'en Keng, Sü Yü, and Hsü Shih-yü, were long-standing members of the Third Field Army with no history of a close affiliation with Lin Piao. The last, Lo Jui-ch'ing, was clearly not one of Lin Piao's supporters. The continuing five vice-ministers were all appointed in 1954. They were: Hsiao Ching-kuang, Hsü Kuang-ta, T'an Cheng, Liao Han-sheng, and Wang Shu-sheng. Of these, Liao Han-sheng was a man of the First Field Army and probably not a supporter of Lin Piao. Wang Shu-sheng, on the other hand, although originally of the Second Field Army, after 1949 served with the Fourth Field Army and therefore, presumably, was a supporter of the new Minister of Defense. If survival of the purge of the Ministry is any indicator, the remaining three also supported Lin Piao.

23. *The Politics of the Chinese Red Army,* passim. Of the 151 items contained in the volume, this author noted only two as having their origin in the Office of the Ministry of Defense (pp. 713, 722) and these were approved by the party's Military Affairs Committee. Thirty-one items originated directly from MAC or had its approval. Numerous directives were issued through the General Political Department (GPD), which, of course, was part of the Defense Ministry, but the making of policy clearly occurred outside the Ministry. It appears that MAC and the GPD were the primary organizational vehicles which Lin used at this time.

24. The eight standing members of MAC were: Ho Lung, Nieh Jung-chen, Lo Jui-ch'ing, Hsiao Hua, Yeh Chien-ying, Hsü Hsiang-ch'ien, Lo Jung-huan, and Liu Po-ch'eng.

25. "Directive of the General Political Department on Carrying Through the Instructions of the Central Authorities to Conduct a Movement for the Suppression of Counterrevolutionaries in Society and the Liquidation (Purge) of Counterrevolutionaries in the Party," in *The Politics of the Chinese Red Army,* pp. 25–28.

26. It is quite likely that Peking controlled border units stationed at sensitive points. For an in-depth exposition of these intricate relationships, see the unpublished dissertation of Harvey Nelsen, "An Organizational History of the Chinese People's Liberation Army, 1966–1969," on file at George Washington University, 1972.

27. In March 1961 it was deemed the prerogative of the central authorities "in time of emergency . . . to make cross-level commands," which meant that central "headquarters can directly command divisions and regiments." See "Comrade Yang Ch'eng-wu's Talk at the Special Conference of Signal Units in the Entire Army," in *The Politics of the Chinese Red Army,* p. 544.

28. See R. L. and H. F. Powell, "Continuity and Purge in the PLA," *Marine Corps Gazette,* LXII, no. 2 (February 1968) p. 23.

29. "We Must Do Substantial Work in Building Up the Militia," in *The Politics of the Chinese Red Army,* pp. 559–64, and "The Nanking Military Region Organizes a Unit for Coordinating Militia Work," Ibid., p. 565.

30. "We Must do Substantial Work . . . ," p. 564.

31. "Endorsement and Transmission by the Military Affairs Commission of the Preliminary Summing-up of the General Staff Department of the Mobilization Department Concerning Execution of Duties by the Work Teams During the Last Four Months," 23 March 1961, *The Politics of the Chinese Red Army*, pp. 378–84.

32. "Liu Shao-ch'i's Self-Criticism Made at the Work Conference of the CCP Central Committee," 23 October 1966, in *Issues and Studies*, Vol. VI, no. 9, June 1970, pp. 94–95.

33. Teng, who was reassigned deputy director of the state planning commission under Li Fu-ch'un, proposed the system of *Tse Jen T'ien*, or individual responsibility for the land allotted to the peasantry. "Liu Shao-ch'i's Self Criticism . . . ," p. 95.

34. Although it is known that Mao discussed the question of Sino-Soviet relations at the plenum and that those relations entered a new state after the plenum, the plenum communique offers only veiled hints to the retrospective eye about "modern revision."

35. "Communique of the 10th Plenary Session of the 8th Central Committee of the CCP," *CB*, no. 691, 5 October 1962, p. 4.

36. Ibid., p. 1. Eighty-two members and 88 alternate members of the Central Committee and 33 persons drawn from other Central Committee departments, provincial, municipal, and autonomous regional party committees attended.

37. "Mao Tse-tung's Talk at a Central Work Meeting," 25 October 1966, *Facts and Features*, Vol. II, no. 9, 19 February 1969, pp. 25–27.

38. "Communique of the 10th Plenary Session . . . ," p. 1.

39. Document no. IV in C. S. Chen and G. P. Ridley, *Rural People's Communes in Lien-Chiang* (Stanford, 1969) p. 87.

40. In Richard Baum and Frederick C. Teiwes, *Ssu-Ch'ing: The Socialist Education Movement of 1962–1966* (Berkeley, 1968), appendix B.

41. Ibid., article IX, p. 68.

42. Ibid., articles V and VII, pp. 62–65.

43. Ibid., article IX, pp. 67–69.

44. Ibid., appendix C, "Some Concrete Policy Formulations of the Central Committee of the Chinese Communist Party in the Rural Socialist Education Movement," pp. 72–94.

45. Although the directive approved, according to Central Committee instructions of 1957, *hsien* level cadre participation in rural collective labor, "the summoning of commune-level cadres for meeting by business departments at the *hsien* level must first be approved by the *hsien* committee." Ibid., article VII. For an analysis of the classifications and methods of "downward transfer" (*hsia fang*), see Wang Hsio-wen, "An Analysis of Peiping's 'Send Down' Movement," *Issues and Studies*, Vol. I, no. 6 (March 1965) pp. 58–68.

46. See Gittings, pp. 254–58 for discussion of the campaign.

47. Baum and Teiwes, appendix D, pp. 95–101.

48. In his "self criticism," *op. cit.*, Liu said, "in the summer of 1964, having

discovered that some articles in the 'second 10-point decision' would interfere with the free mobilization of the masses, I made some revision and the revised draft was sent out on September 18" (p. 96). For the "revised later ten points," see Baum and Teiwes, appendix E, "Some Concrete Policy Formulations of the Central Committee of the Chinese Communist Party in the Rural Socialist Education Movement," September 1964, pp. 102–117.

49. Ibid. (emphasis supplied).

50. Baum and Teiwes, appendix F, "Some Problems Currently Arising in the Course of the Rural Socialist Education Movement," pp. 118–26. Liu, in his self-criticism, *op. cit.,* stated: "By the time of the work conference of the Party Central at the end of 1964, my mistakes . . . had not been corrected. At this conference, I pointed out that the nature of the movement was the contradiction between being pure and being impure on the four questions, the overlapping of the contradiction within and without the Party or the overlapping of the contradiction between the enemy and ourselves and the contradiction among the people. Just as it was stated in the 23-point decision, the two explanations did not touch on the basic nature of the socialist education movement and hence they were not Marxist-Leninist. . . . These mistakes were rectified only after Chairman Mao personally formulated the '23-point decision' " (p. 96).

51. Ibid.

52. Article IX, p. 7.

53. Article III.

54. For a discussion of Khrushchev's "last offensive" from a Soviet perspective, see Carl A. Linden, *Khrushchev and the Soviet Leadership, 1957–1964* (Baltimore, 1966), chap. 9, *passim.*

55. *Program of the CPSU* (Moscow, 1961) chap. 3, sec. 25.

56. See above, p. 248.

57. *New York Times,* 7 August 1964.

58. Quoted in Ibid., 9 August 1964.

59. Ibid., 6 August 1964.

60. Ibid., 8 August 1964.

61. Ibid., 9 August 1964.

62. Ibid., 10 August 1964.

63. A preparatory meeting was held in March 1965, but the conference was not convened until June 1969.

64. *Pravda,* 27 February 1965.

65. *New York Times,* 2 April 1965.

66. Edward Crankshaw in *The Observer* (London) 14 November 1965, p. 5.

67. Lyndon B. Johnson, "Pattern for Peace in Southeast Asia," Department of State *Bulletin,* 26 April 1965, p. 608.

68. Crankshaw, p. 5.

69. For an extended analysis, see Uri Ra'anan, "Peking's Foreign Policy 'Debate,' 1965–1966," in Tang Tsou, ed., *China in Crisis,* Vol. II (Chicago, 1968), pp. 23–71.

70. "Commemorate the Victory Over German Facism! Carry the Struggle Against U.S. Imperialism Through to the End," *Red Flag*, 10 May 1965.
71. *Long Live the Victory of People's War* (Peking, 1965).
72. The Chinese, however, supplied rear services support in the form of supplies, skilled and unskilled labor, weapons and ammunition. See Allen Whiting, "How We Almost Went to War With China," *Look*, 29 April 1969, pp. 76–79.

Chapter XI: The Great Proletarian Cultural Revolution   I: The Mounting Crisis, 1965–1967

1. "Lin Piao's Address at the Enlarged Meeting of the CCP Central Politburo," 18 May 1966. *Issues and Studies*, Vol. VI, no. 5 (February 1970) p. 85.
2. Ibid.
3. Ibid., p. 83.
4. "Report on the Question of the Errors Committed by Lo Jui-ch'ing," *Issues and Studies*, Vol. V, no. 11 (August 1969) pp. 87–101.
5. "Circular of the Central Committee of the Communist Party of China," 16 May 1966, *CB*, no. 852, p. 3.
6. Ibid., p. 4.
7. "Counter-Revolutionary Revisionist P'eng Chen's Towering Crimes of Opposing the Party, Socialism and the Thought of Mao Tse-tung," *SCMM*, no. 640, p. 9.
8. Ibid., p. 12.
9. "Lin Piao's Address . . . ," p. 83.
10. "Circular of the Central Committee of the Communist Party of China," 16 May 1966; and "CCP Central Committee's Comment on the Transmission of the Report of the Work Group of the Central Committee Concerning Lo Jui-ch'ing's Mistakes and Problems," *CB*, no. 852, pp. 1–7.
11. As Chiang Ch'ing noted later that year, Mao Tse-tung, in June, "had forbidden the sending of work teams, but some of the Party comrades had not obeyed the order. The question is not the form of working teams but their direction and policy." *China News Analysis*, no. 642, 6 January 1967, p. 3.
12. "Address to Regional Secretaries and Members of the Cultural Revolution Group under the Central Committee," 22 July 1966, *CB*, no. 891, p. 60.
13. "Decision of the CCP Peking Municipal Committee Concerning the Abolition of Work Groups in Various Universities, Colleges and Schools," 28 July 1966, *CB*, no. 852, p. 8.
14. *CB*, no. 852, pp. 9–15.
15. Emphasis supplied.
16. See Jürgen Domes, *Die Äre Mao Tse-tung* (The Era of Mao Tse-tung) (Verlag: W. Kohlhammer, Stuttgart: 1971), p. 149.
17. Li Hsueh-feng, first secretary of the North China Bureau, was political commissar of the Peking Military Region. Sung Jen-ch'iung, first secretary of the

Northeast Bureau, was political commissar of the Shenyang Military Region. Liu Lan-t'ao, first secretary of the Northwest Bureau, was political commissar of the Lanchou Military Region. Li Ching-ch'uan, first secretary of the Southwest Bureau, was political commissar of the Ch'engtu Military Region. T'ao Chu, first secretary of the Central-South Bureau, was political commissar of the Canton Military Region. The First Secretary of the East China Bureau, K'o Ch'ing-shih, died in April 1965; his position was not filled.

18. In Mao's April speech to a visiting Albanian delegation he noted that at the Eleventh Plenum "Li Ching-ch'uan did not understand me; neither did Liu Lan-tao, when Comrade (Chen) Po-ta spoke to them, they replied; 'I do not understand in Peking, and when I return home I will understand no better! In the end, we could only leave the task of judging their behavior to the future.' "

19. Most revealing here is that only four of the PLA's thirty-five army corps were located in the Southwest and Northwest areas. The 13th and 14th army corps were stationed in the K'unming Military Region, the 54th in the Ch'engtu Military Region, and the 18th in Tibet. Regional forces in these areas, however, totaled approximately 275,000. All in all, only a small fraction of the PLA's military forces were located in these two areas.

20. Gordon A. Bennett and Ronald N. Montaperto, *Red Guard, The Political Biography of Dai Hsiao-ai* (Doubleday, 1971), have provided the most accurate treatment of the organization, development, and denouement of the Red Guards.

21. The five kinds of red students included the children of workers, poor peasants, revolutionary martyrs, revolutionary cadres, and revolutionary soldiers.

22. The other four activities were: great contending, great blooming, great power seizure, and great debate.

23. *CB,* no. 891, 8 October 1969, p. 75.

24. Ibid., p. 76.

25. Bennett and Montaperto, p. 146.

26. "Directive (Draft) of the CCP Central Committee, on the Great Proletarian Cultural Revolution in the Rural Districts," 15 December 1966, *CB,* no. 852, p. 32.

27. Ibid., "Circular of the CCP Central Committee and the State Council on Short-Term Military and Political Training for Revolutionary Teachers and Students of Universities and Middle Schools," 31 December 1966, p. 34.

28. "Message of Greetings from the CCP Central Committee, the State Council, the Military Commission and the Cultural Revolution Group to Revolutionary Rebel Organizations in Shanghai," 11 January 1967, *CB,* no. 852, p. 38.

29. "Notification by the CCP Central Committee and the State Council on Prohibiting the Corrosion of the Masses," 11 January 1967, Ibid., p. 42.

30. "Document of the CCP Central Committee, the State Council and the Military Commission," Chung Fa, no. 14, 11 January 1967, Ibid., p. 39.

31. "Notification by the CCP Central Committee on Opposition to Economism," 11 January 1967, Ibid., p. 40.

32. "Notification by the CCP Central Committee Concerning Broadcasting Stations," 11 January 1967, Ibid., p. 43. The pertinent section of the directive reads as follows: " . . . it is entirely correct and necessary that the revolutionary masses should fight against those in authority taking the capitalist road who are in control of the broadcasting stations. . . . The Central Committee has decided that the local PLA should exercise military control over all such broadcasting stations. These broadcasting stations should cease to edit and broadcast local programs and should only rebroadcast the programs broadcast by the Central Broadcasting Station. The revolutionary masses who have taken over those broadcasting stations should pull out at once. Those in authority taking the capitalist road in these broadcasting stations should be handed over to the masses, and struggle should be conducted against them away from the broadcasting stations."

33. "Some Provisions Concerning the Strengthening of Public Security Work in the Great Proletarian Cultural Revolution," Chung Fa, no. 19, 13 January 1967, Ibid., pp. 44–45.

34. See "Hsieh Fu-chih's Talk at a Struggle Rally Against Lo Jui-ch'ing," *Issues and Studies,* Vol. V, no. 12 (September 1969). In a speech given on August 7, 1967 Hsieh said: "We have not found a single instance where public security, procuracy and judicial systems support the proletarian revolutionaries. Of course, individually speaking, everywhere there are persons who support the Leftists. But, in terms of the organization as a whole, all support the conservatives. In big cities, 80 percent of county public security bureaus support the conservatives whether they have had revolts or not and whether the power has been seized or not" (p. 101).

35. The complete membership of the group was as follows:

Chairman:	Hsü Hsiang-ch'ien	Members:	Yü Li-chin
Advisor:	Chiang Ch'ing		Liu Hua-ch'ing
Deputies:	Hsiao Hua		T'an P'ing-chu
	Yang Ch'eng-wu		Hu Ch'ih
	Wang Hsin-t'ing		Yeh Ch'un
	Hsü Li-ch'ung		Wang Feng
	Kuan Feng		Ho Ku-yen
	Li Man-ts'un		Chang T'ao
	Hsieh T'an-chung		Sung Ch'un

Yi chiu liu chiu chung kung nien pao (1969 Yearbook on Chinese Communism) (Taiwan, 1969) Vol. I, part III, p. 7.

36. The PLA forces in question were the "regional forces" not the army corps, which did not become involved on a widespread basis until April, although there were isolated instances of army corps involvement before this time.

37. "Notification by the CCP Central Committee Ordering That the Spearhead of Struggle May Not be Directed Against the Armed Forces," 14 January 1967, *CB,* no. 852, p. 46.

38. "Document of the CCP Central Committee," 19 January 1967, Ibid., p. 48.

39. "Instructions on Establishment of Anhwei Provincial Revolutionary Committee," in Chien Yu-shen, *China's Fading Revolution* (Hong Kong, 1969), p. 281.

40. "Decision of the CCP Central Committee, the State Council, the Military Commission of the Central Committee, and the Cultural Revolution Group under the Central Committee on Resolute Support for the Revolutionary Masses of the Left," *CB*, no. 852, p. 49.

41. The party leaders argued that "the provincial military district was not a part of the national defense army, and that its task was mainly concerned with the localities, and its principal leadership was the provincial party committee," Harbin Radio, 6 October 1967. Others attacked, immediately sought "to seize control of the army. In the name of the provincial Party committee, they asked us to consider the so-called question of 'protecting the safety of the Party committee.' . . . The Party . . . begged us of the provincial military district to give them shelter," *Kuang Ming Jih Pao*, 25 March 1967, in *Survey of China Mainland Press (SCMP)* 3912, 5 April 1967, p. 19.

42. "Directive of the Military Commission of the Central Committee Reiterating the Carrying Out of the Great Cultural Revolution Stage by Stage and Group by Group in Military Regions," 28 January 1967, *CB*, no. 852, p. 56.

43. "Order of the Military Commission of the Central Committee," 28 January 1967, *CB*, no. 852, p. 54.

44. See also "Chairman Mao's Speech at his Third Meeting with Chang Ch'un-ch'iao and Yao Wen-yuan," given sometime before the 18th of February during the two men's visit to Peking, February 12–18, 1967, in *Translation on Communist China*, no. 90, Selections from Chairman Mao, Joint Publications Research Service, 49826, 12 February 1970, p. 44.

45. *SCMP* 4147, 27 March 1968, p. 7.

46. Ibid., 3880, pp. 1–5.

47. "Proclamation," 11 February 1967, Peking, *CB*, no. 852, p. 67.

48. According to Chou En-lai, these were: Chu Teh, Ch'en Yün, Ch'en Yi, Li Hsien-nien, Teng Tzu-hui, Yeh Chien-ying, Nieh Jung-chen, and Hsü Hsiang-ch'ien. See "Chou En-lai Talks About the 'February Adverse Current,' " *Issues and Studies*, Vol. V, no. 12 (September 1969) pp. 103–104.

49. "Central Leaders' Important Speeches (Excerpts) on Counter-Attacking the February Adverse Current," *SCMP* 4166 (April 1968), pp. 6–8.

50. "Chou En-lai Talks About the February Adverse Current," p. 103.

51. Bennett and Montaperto, pp. 177–80.

52. Honan, 1/13; Tsinghai, 1/15; Fukien, 1/11 and 2/16; Kwangtung, 1/11; Kwangsi, 1/23; Kiangsi, Anhwei, Kiangsu, and Shansi, all on 1/26; Yunnan, 1/30; Szech'uan, 2/1; Kansu, 2/6; Tibet, 2/9; Kirin, 2/19.

53. Inner Mongolia, Sinkiang, Shantung, Chekiang, Shanghai, and Hupeh.

54. For data on the provincial situations, see Jürgen Domes, "The Role of the Military in the Formation of Revolutionary Committees in 1967–68," *The China Quarterly*, no. 44 (October-December 1970) pp. 112–45.

55. "Proclamation of the Armed Force Units on the Fukien Front, Transmitted by the Military Commission of the Central Committee," 6 February 1967, *CB*, no. 852, pp. 63–64.

56. "Decision of the CCP Central Committee on the Question of Anhwei," 27 March 1967, *CB*, no. 852, pp. 113–14.

57. Domes, pp. 124–25.

58. Ibid., p. 127.

59. "Regulations of the CCP Central Committee, the State Council and the Military Commission of the CCP Central Committee," 11 February 1967, *CB*, no. 852, pp. 68–70.

60. Bennett and Montaperto, 178 and "Decision of the CCP Central Committee, the State Council, the Military Commission of the Central Committee and the Cultural Revolution Group under the Central Committee Concerning the Question of Tsinghai," 24 March 1967, *CB*, no. 852, p. 109.

Chapter XII: The Great Proletarian Cultural Revolution   II. Protracted Crisis, 1967–1968

1. "A Talk by Chairman Mao to Foreign Visitors," 18 June 1968, *SCMP*, no. 4200, p. 5. This speech is reported to have been delivered on 31 August 1967, but the terms of reference in it make it clear that Mao is speaking in early April. Mao describes the course of the cultural revolution as having passed through four phases, the last of which began with the publication of Ch'i Pen-yu's "Is It Patriotism or National Betrayal" and "The Essence of Self-Cultivation Is Betrayal of the Proletarian Dictatorship." The articles appeared on March 31. Since events forced another change of policy in late July, it seems highly unlikely that the speech could have been given in late August.

2. Ibid., p. 4.

3. T'an was editor of *People's Daily*, Hu of *Liberation Army Daily*, and Ho chief of cultural affairs in the PLA.

4. *CB*, no. 852, pp. 115–16.

5. Proclamations were issued on April 20, May 15 and 18, and June 1 and 7.

6. From late March through mid-May the following moves were made by army corps. To the Northwest, the 21st Army moved from Shansi to Shensi, sending one division into Inner Mongolia. In what probably were related moves, the 16th Army moved from Shenyang to Peking to join the 38th Army, which was already there. The 69th Army moved from Hopeh to Shansi. In the Southwest, the 50th Army, stationed in Liaoning, moved to Szech'uan at which time the 54th Army, stationed in Ch'engtu, was redeployed to Chungking. In Central-South (Canton Military Region) the 55th Army became active in its Canton location, the 47th Army moved from Kwangtung to Hunan, and the 41st Army sent one division

from Kwangtung to Kiangsi, that is, from the Central-South to the East China region. Other moves in East China included the 12th Army's move from Chekiang to Anhwei, the 20th Army's move from Nanking city into Chekiang, and redeployment of the 27th Army from Shantung to Kiangsi (one division). I am indebted to Dr. Harvey Nelson for data on the movement of army corps. See his unpublished doctoral dissertion "An Organizational History of the Chinese People's Liberation Army, 1966–1969," on file at George Washington University.

7. "Notification of the CCP Central Committee Concerning the Rehabilitation of Liu Chieh t'ing and Others in Ip'in Area, Szechwan Province," 4 April 1967, *CB*, no. 852, p. 125 and "Decision of the CCP Central Committee Concerning the Question of Szechwan," 7 May 1967, Ibid., pp. 128–30.

8. *Yomiuri* (Tokyo), 8 June 1967.

9. Ibid., emphasis supplied.

10. Chien Yu-shen, *China's Fading Revolution* (Hong Kong, 1969), p. 2.

11. Ibid.

12. "Deputy Supreme Commander Lin's Important Directive," 9 August 1967, *SCMP*, no. 4036, 6 October 1967, p. 3.

13. Hsieh Fu-chih was also Minister of Public Security and Chairman of the Peking Revolutionary Committee and Wang Li the acting chief of the Central Committee Propaganda Department.

14. It was rumored that Mao Tse-tung himself was in Wuhan at this time *in cognito* on a "tour" of China's southern provinces and narrowly escaped involvement in the incident.

15. There seems to have been some discrepancy between Chou's pronounce- ment and the four-point directive issued by Wang Li, which possibly could have been the precipitating cause for the conflict that ensued. Chou apparently did not require a public disclaimer from Ch'en Tsai-tao and the military command, but Wang Li stated that as one of his four points. Perhaps Ch'en felt that he was a victim of double-dealing.

16. For a Japanese account of the incident, see *China's Fading Revolution*, appendix I.

17. In a speech delivered late in October, Chou En-lai declared that the policy of dragging out the small handful in the army "was wrong." The central propaganda department had "made a mistake." See "Premier Chou's Speech to Representatives of the Mass Organizations of the Canton Area," *Lhasa Hung-se Tsao-fan Pao* (Lhasa Red Rebel Paper) 12 October 1967.

18. "Purge of the 'Wang, Kuan, Chi and Lin Anti-Party Group'," *Facts and Features*, Vol. I, no. 14 (1 May 1968), p. 15. These views were expressed by Wang En-yu, a member of the Wang Li-Kuan Feng group. "It took scores of Red Guards only a few days to topple a provincial Party committee secretary. They took only about a dozen days to topple a man like T'ao Chu. But the job of toppling a military district commander can't be done by even ten thousand people. It is because men of this sort have actual power."

19. "Deputy Supreme Commander Lin's Important Directive," 9 August 1967, *SCMP*, no. 4036, 6 October 1967, p. 3.

20. Ibid.

21. Ibid.

22. Ibid.

23. *Sankei Tokyo*, 15 August 1967 (morning edition).

24. The PLA's army corps became involved in at least eleven provinces and perhaps others. Those provinces which definitely reported the presence of army corps after August 1967 were: Anhwei, Chekiang, Kiangsi, Kiangsu of the East China region; Sinkiang, Shensi, Ninghsia of the Northwest; Kirin and Liaoning of the Northeast; Hunan and Honan of Central South. Earlier, of course, army corps had become involved in Szech'uan, Hopeh, Kwangsi, Kwangtung, and Yunnan, all of which indicated that main force strength was spread quite thin across the vast expanse of China by the fall of 1967 and it was no wonder that military leaders were gravely concerned about China's national defense capabilities. For a discussion of the PLA's role in the cultural revolution, see Harvey Nelson, "An Organizational History of the Chinese People's Liberation Army, 1966–69."

25. "Hsieh Fu-chih's Talk at a Struggle Rally Against Lo Jui-ch'ing," 7 August 1967, *Issues and Studies*, Vol. V, no. 12 (September 1969), p. 101.

26. *Yearbook on Chinese Communism*, 1969, part III, p. 9.

27. Ch'en was rehabilitated shortly thereafter.

28. "Important Talk Given by Comrade Chiang Ch'ing on September 5 at a Conference of Representatives of Anhwei Who Have Come to Peking," *SCMP*, no. 4069, 29 November 1967, pp. 2–5.

29. In Chien Yu-shen, *China's Fading Revolution* (Hong Kong, 1969), p. 267.

30. Ibid.

31. These provinces, in chronological order of formation, were:

Inner Mongolia	November 1, 1967
Tientsin	December 6, 1967
Kansu	January 4, 1968
Honan	January 24, 1968
Hopeh	February 3, 1968
Hupeh	February 5, 1968
Kwangtung	February 21, 1968
Kiangsi	February 28, 1968
Kirin	March 6, 1968
Kiangsu	March 23, 1968
Chekiang	March 24, 1968

32. *Peking Jih Pao* (*People's Daily*), 1 October 1967, p. 1. See also "Education Reform and Rural Resettlement in .Communist China," *Current Scene*, Vol. VIII, no. 17 (7 November 1970).

33. "Vice Premier Hsieh Fu-chih's Important Speech on Questions of 'Ninth Party Congress' and 'Party Organization'," 26 October 1967, in *SCMP*, no. 4097, 11 January 1968, p. 4.

34. For a discussion of Yao's letter and its significance, see *China News Analysis* (*CNA*), no. 680, 6 October 1967, pp. 3–7.

35. "Public Trial Rallies," *China Topics*, 20 May 1968.

36. "Chairman Mao's Latest Supreme Instructions During his Inspection Tour in Central and Southern Parts of China," *SCMP*, no. 4070, 30 November 1967, pp. 2–3.

37. "Vice Premier Hsieh Fu-chih's Important Speech on Questions of 'Ninth Party Congress' and 'Party Organization'," p. 2.

38. John Gittings, "Student Power in China," *Far Eastern Economic Review* (*FEER*), no. 26 (Hong Kong), June 23–29, 1968, pp. 648–50.

39. See "Comrade K'ang Sheng on 'Sheng-wu-lien' of Hunan," *SCMP*, no. 4136, 12 March 1968, pp. 5–17.

40. For a discussion of some of the evidence on this point, see "Underground Anti-CCP Trends," *China News Analysis*, no. 705, 26 April 1968.

41. "An Important Speech by Vice-Chairman Lin at a Reception of Army Cadres on March 25," *SCMP*, no. 4173, 8 May 1968, p. 2.

42. Ch'en Po-ta, Chiang Ch'ing, K'ang Sheng, Chang Ch'un-ch'iao, and Yao Wen-yuan.

43. *China Yearbook*, 1969, part III, p. 13.

44. "An Important Speech by Vice-Chairman Lin . . . on March 25," p. 2.

45. Wu Fa-hsien, as noted above, was head of the PLA Air Force, Huang Yung-sheng commander of the Canton Military Region, Hsü Shih-yü commander of the Nanking Military Region, Han Hsien-ch'u commander of the Foochow Military Region, and Hsieh Fu-chih formally was the chairman of the Peking municipal revolutionary committee.

46. See Domes, pp. 134–37.

47. "Notice of the CCP Central Committee, State Council, Military Commission of the Central Cultural Revolution Group," 3 July 1968, *SCMP*, no. 4232, 6 August 1968, p. 2, and "July 24, 1968 Notice," *Facts and Features*, Vol. I, no. 26, pp. 29–30.

48. Stanley Karnow, "Peking Starts Disbanding the Red Guards," 14 August 1968, *The Washington Post*.

49. "The Roots of Present Events in China," *Kommunist*, no. 6, 1968; "On the Character of the Cultural Revolution in China," Ibid., no. 7; "The Political Course of Mao Tse-tung in the International Arena," Ibid., no. 8; O. Vladimirov and V. Riazantsev, "On Certain Questions of History of the Chinese Communist Party," Ibid., no. 9; A. Kholodovskaia, "The Destruction of Trade Unions in China," Ibid., no. 10; A. Nekrasov, "On the Foreign Economic Policies of the Mao Tse-tung Group," Ibid., no. 12.

50. Ibid., no. 6, "The Roots of Present Events in China."

51. Tad Szulc, *Czechoslovakia Since World War II* (New York: Viking Press, 1971), p. 328.

52. "Situation in Czechoslovakia," *Pravda*, 24 September 1968, p. 4.

53. *People's Daily*, 27 August 1968.

54. Yao Wen-yuan, "The Working Class Must Exercise Leadership in Everything," *Red Flag*, no. 2 (25 August 1968) pp. 4–5.

55. Domes, pp. 137–42.

56. "Chiang Ch'ing's Speech at Peking Rally Marking China Turned 'All Red'," 7 September 1968 in *China's Fading Revolution*, p. 338.

57. *Wen Hui Pao* editorial, 27 September 1968.

58. *Daily Report*, 7 October 1968, B 1–3. In Honan alone over 240,000 youths were rounded up and shipped to camps to undergo "reform by labor."

59. "Excerpts from Chou En-lai's Speech at Peking Rally Marking China Turned 'All Red'," 7 September 1968, in *China's Fading Revolution*, p. 340.

60. "Sino-Soviet Border Developments 1967–1969," *China Topics*, 1 May 1969, p. 9.

61. Ibid.

62. John Gittings, "Revolution on Guard," *FEER*, no. 42, 17 October 1968, p. 149 and "The 19th Anniversary of the Founding of the People's Republic of China," 1 October 1968, *CB*, no. 865, 18 October 1968, pp. 11–15.

63. "Communique of Enlarged 12th Plenary Session of the Eighth Central Committee of the Chinese Communist Party," 1 November 1968, *SCMP*, no. 4293, 6 November 1968, pp. 12–16.

64. Inner Mongolia provincial radio, 6 November 1968.

65. Hunan provincial radio, 12 February 1969 and Harbin radio, 2 March 1969, cited in Philip Bridgham, "Mao's Cultural Revolution: The Struggle to Seize Power," *The China Quarterly*, no. 41 (January-March 1970), p. 10.

66. Although the talks would be postponed, other more secure "back channels" of communications were opened by early 1969.

Part IV. The Evolution of U.S.-China
Relations, 1969–1980

*Chapter XIII: China in a Tri-Polar
World, 1969-1973*

1. "Pro-Soviet" refers to a specific identifiable group of leaders who, when presented with a set of policy alternatives, select the alternative favorable to the Soviet position at the time. Whatever the composition of the decision-making body, whatever the policy under consideration, one of the alternatives will necessarily be more beneficial to Soviet policy interests than the others. Those leaders who opt for the alternatives more beneficial to the Soviets are therefore objectively "pro-Soviet," and over time, support of consistently pro-Soviet alternatives makes identifiable a pro-Soviet group.

2. For two reasonably balanced accounts of the initial event, see Stanley Karnow, "Red China Charges Many Soviet Raids," *Washington Post*, 4 March 1969; and Henry Kamm, "Soviets Exploiting Clash With China," *New York Times*, 13 March 1969.

3. The Soviet press agency Novosti reprinted the article in pamphlet form and distributed it widely around the world.

4. Lin Piao, "Report to the Ninth National Congress of the Communist Party of China," 1 April 1969, in *Survey of the China Mainland Press,* no. 4406 (1 May 1969), p. 42.

5. "Mao Tse-tung's Speech to the 1st Plenary Session of the CCP's 9th Central Committee," *Issues and Studies,* Vol. VI, no. 6 (March 1970), p. 96.

6. Joseph G. Whelan, *World Communism, 1967–1969: Soviet Efforts to Reestablish Control,* Committee on the Judiciary, U.S. Senate (Washington, D.C.: Government Printing Office, 1970), pp. 129–134.

7. Ibid., p. 164.

8. Novosti Mongolii, 22 June 1969.

9. "Red Chinese Protest on Border Strife," *Washington Post,* 20 August 1969.

10. Official New China News Agency (NCNA) news release, 7 October 1969.

11. "A Summary of Chairman Mao's Talks With Responsible Comrades of Various Places During His Inspection Tour," *Issues and Studies,* Vol. VIII, no. 12 (September 1972), pp. 66–67.

12. Ibid.

13. Ibid., p. 67.

14. "Revised Draft of the 'Constitution of the People's Republic of China,'" *Issues and Studies,* Vol. VII, no. 3 (December 1970), pp. 89–90.

15. Ibid., pp. 90–91.

16. "A Summary of Chairman Mao's Talks," p. 68.

17. The four were Hua Kuo-feng in Hunan, formed December 4; Chang Ch'un-ch'iao in Shanghai, on January 10; Ch'en Hsi-lien in Liaoning, on January 13; and Li Teh-sheng in Anhwei, on January 21.

18. The number of Standing Committee members on the Hunan party committee was unknown. See Chu Wen-lin, "An Analysis of 29 New CCP Committees at the Provincial Level" (Part I), *Issues and Studies,* Vol. VIII, no. 2 (November 1971), pp. 49–50.

19. These three were Chang Ch'un-ch'iao, Wang Hung-wen, and Yao Wen-yuan, who later, in collusion with Mao's wife Chiang Ch'ing, would become the Gang of Four.

20. Chu Wen-lin, "Analysis of 29 New CCP Committees" (Part I), pp. 51–52.

21. *China News Analysis* (Hong Kong), no. 839, March 26, 1971, p. 4.

22. Chu Wen-lin, "An Analysis of 29 New CCP Committees at the Provincial Level" (Part II), *Issues and Studies,* Vol. VIII, no. 3 (December 1971), p. 87.

23. "A Summary of Chairman Mao's Talks," p. 69.

24. Chu Wen-lin, "Analysis of 29 New CCP Committees" (Part I), p. 53.

25. Ibid., pp. 49–53.

26. Joseph Alsop, "Lin Piao is 'Finished,'" *Washington Post,* 10 November 1971.

27. Dev Murarka, "Soviets 'Reasonably Certain' Lin Died in Mongolian Crash," *Observer*, 2 January 1972.

28. John Burns, "Mao Confirms Lin's Death in Crash," *Washington Post*, 28 July 1972.

29. Lee Lescaze, "Lin Piao Attempt Seen to Give Russia Secrets," *Washington Post*, 14 March 1972.

30. *Issues and Studies*, Vol. VIII, no. 12 (September 1972).

31. One of Mao's men, Hsieh Fu-chih, would die in March 1972, leaving the balance at eight to five.

32. Chang Ching-wen, "Mao's Purge of Lin Piao's Faction," *Issues and Studies*, Vol. IX, no. 7 (April 1973), pp. 19–27.

33. "A Summary of Chairman Mao's Talks," p. 71.

34. Fang Chun-kui, "The Reorganization and Current Status of the CCP Provincial Committees," *Issues and Studies*, Vol. IX, no. 8 (May 1973), pp. 40–43.

35. Although the Warsaw talks were postponed, other channels were subsequently opened through France, Romania, and Pakistan.

36. "Excerpts From Unofficial Account of President Nixon's Meeting With Reporters at Guam, July 25, 1969," in U.S., Senate, Committee on Foreign Relations, *Background Information Relating to Southeast Asia and Vietnam* (Washington, D.C.: Government Printing Office, 1970), p. 320.

37. Henry Kissinger, *The White House Years* (Boston: Little, Brown and Co., 1979), pp. 241–242. The exact figures are unknown but this is believed to be a close estimate.

38. For a full discussion of the South Asian crisis, see the author's "South Asia: Imbalance on the Subcontinent," *Orbis* (Fall 1975), pp. 863–873.

39. Y.C.Y., "Henry Kissinger's Sixth Visit to Peking," *Issues and Studies*, Vol. X, no. 3 (December 1973), p. 2.

40. For example, see "Reference Materials Concerning Education on Situation," numbers 41–45, printed between 30 March and 6 April 1973 and distributed to the Kunming and Yunnan military regions, in *Chinese Communist Internal Politics and Foreign Policy* (Taipei: Institute of International Relations, 1974), pp. 120–154.

Chapter XIV: The End of the Maoist Era, 1973–1976

1. Neither Mao nor his wife, Chiang Ch'ing, attended the dinner, although a place was set for Chiang Ch'ing and it was left empty, subtly hinting that Teng's return was not looked upon favorably by Mao.

2. Henry Bradsher, "China Policy Row Portends Political Trouble," *Evening Star* (Washington, D.C.), 20 June 1973.

3. I am deeply indebted to Richard E. Kistler, of Georgetown University, whose graduate research on the subject of Soviet-Japanese relations has contributed substantially to the following analysis.

4. *Mainichi Daily News,* 17 January 1973.

5. For the Soviet reaction, see *Pravda,* 8, 9, 10 March 1973, p. 1; and *Pravda,* 22 March 1973, p. 5.

6. For the postponement, see *Asahi Evening News,* 6 June 1973; for the invitation to the Diet men, *Mainichi Daily News,* 7 June 1973.

7. Leonid Brezhnev, *Pravda,* 23 September 1973.

8. Moscow Domestic Service (in Russian), 18 August 1973 (FBIS 24 August 1973) and *Pravda,* 24 August 1973. There were four principles in all. (1) renunciation of force in relations between states, (2) respect for the sovereignty of other countries and the inviolability of borders, (3) non-interference in the internal affairs of other countries, and (4) broad development of economic and other forms of cooperation on the basis of complete equality and mutual benefit. They can be found in *Pravda* and *Izvestia,* 21 March 1973, in a speech delivered by Brezhnev.

9. *Pravda,* 25 September 1973 and FBIS, USSR, 31 August 1973.

10. Chou En-lai, "Report to the Tenth National Congress of the Communist Party of China," NCNA, 31 August 1973.

11. Ibid.

12. Wang Hung-wen, "Report on the Revision of the Party Constitution," NCNA, 1 September 1973.

13. Ibid.

14. Chou En-lai, "Report."

15. The Sinkiang and Kunming regional commands had been reshuffled a few months before.

16. For more information on the backgrounds and commands of these officers see Chu Wen-lin, "Personnel Changes in Peiping's First Level Military Regions," *Issues and Studies,* Vol. X, no. 5 (February 1974), pp. 10–18.

17. C. L. Sulzberger, "China Condemns USSR on Border Problems," *Asahi Evening News,* 31 October 1973.

18. *Asahi Evening News,* 17 January 1974; see also Teng's speech to the United Nations, *Peking Review,* no. 16, 19 April 1974.

19. *Pravda,* 25 January 1974; see also Kistler, "Japanese-Soviet Relations," p. 13.

20. *China News Analysis,* no. 963, 14 June 1974, p. 7.

21. *China News Analysis,* no. 982, 29 November 1974, p. 3.

22. *People's Daily,* 12 November 1974, p. 3.

23. See *Documents of the First Session of the Fourth National People's Congress of the People's Republic of China* (Peking: Foreign Languages Press, 1975), p. 69, for a listing.

24. Ibid., p. 73.

25. Yao Meng-hsuan, "The Fourth National People's Congress and Peiping's Future Direction" (Part I), *Issues and Studies,* Vol. XI, no. 3 (March 1975), pp. 6–7.

26. "Constitution of the People's Republic of China," adopted 17 January 1975, *People's Daily,* 20 January 1975.

27. Ibid.
28. Article 22.
29. Teng Hsiao-p'ing, speech to the United Nations, *Peking Review*, no. 16, 19 April 1974.
30. Chou En-lai, "Report on Government," *People's Daily*, 20 January 1975.
31. Ibid.
32. Ibid.
33. Victor Zorza, "Clues to Kissinger's Peking Failure," *Washington Post*, 5 December 1974.
34. Joseph Lelyveld, "China's Attitude on U.S. Assayed," *New York Times*, 19 December 1974.
35. Zorza, "Clues."
36. *People's Daily*, 9 February 1975.
37. Yao Wen-yuan, "On the Social Basis of the Anti-Party Clique of Lin Piao," *Red Flag*, no. 3, March 1975.
38. See also *China News Analysis*, no 993, 14 March 1975, pp. 6-7.
39. "Chiang Ch'ing's Speech to Foreign Affairs Cadres," *Chinese Law and Government*, Vol. IX, no. 1-2 (Spring-Summer 1976), pp. 49-61.
40. *China News Analysis*, no. 1019, 7 November 1975, p. 2.
41. See the very informative article by Li Ming-hua, "The Chinese Communist Leadership Reorganization," *Issues and Studies*, Vol. XII, no. 3 (March 1976), pp. 37-56. Teng's impact was also apparent on Chinese foreign policy. In Angola, for example, Peking had supported Daniel Chipenda's Front for the National Liberation of Angola (FNLA) from mid-1974 but withdrew from the field beginning in July 1975. If the United States and the People's Republic had pursued "parallel" policies in Angola through mid-1975, as is generally believed, Peking's subsequent withdrawal cannot be so described. Regardless of other reasons adduced to explain Peking's policy change, it occurred coincidentally with Teng's ascendancy in the summer of 1975. Chou's incapacitation in September immeasurably strengthened Teng's hand and facilitated China's complete withdrawal from Angola.
42. See *China News Analysis*, no. 1018, 24 October 1975, and no. 1022, 5 December 1975, for further discussion.
43. H.D.S. Greenway, "China Tie Intact as Kissinger Departs," *Washington Post*, 24 October 1975; and Lou Cannon, "Ford, Mao Talk Nearly Two Hours," *Washington Post*, 3 December 1975.
44. Ibid.
45. *People's Daily*, 28 December 1975.
46. David Eisenhower, "Notes from a China Trip," *Wall Street Journal*, 20 February 1976.
47. The split was officially revealed in a *People's Daily* editorial on 17 February 1976.
48. H.D.S. Greenway, "Peking Acts on Premier," *Washington Post*, 7 February 1976.

49. *People's Daily*, 28 January 1976.

50. *People's Daily*, 17 February 1976.

51. *People's Daily*, 24 February 1976. The original was carried in *People's Daily*'s New Year editorial: "Stability and unity does not mean that there is no longer class struggle." See the interpretation of John M. Newman, "Year of the Dragon: The Succession to Mao Tse-tung," *Asian Affairs*, Vol. 5, no. 6 (July-August 1978), pp. 363-364.

52. *People's Daily*, 2 March 1976.

53. Ibid., 10 March 1976.

54. *New York Times*, 11 March 1976.

55. *People's Daily*, 17 March 1976.

56. Kyodo News Agency (Tokyo), 13 April 1976.

57. *People's Daily*, 21 March 1976.

58. "Texts on Peking Changes and Account of Disturbance," *New York Times*, 8 April 1976; and *Peking Review*, 9 April 1976.

59. *Peking Review*, 9 April 1976.

60. Fox Butterfield, "Peking Indicates Senior Aide Is Out As Defense Chief," *New York Times*, 18 April 1976.

61. It would later be suggested that he had been behind the incident. See *Peking Review*, 14 May 1976, p. 14.

62. *Peking Review*, 9 April 1976, p. 3.

63. The Gang of Four were Chang Ch'un-Ch'iao, Wang Hung-wen, Chiang Ch'ing, and Yao Wen-yuan. Their votes were essential for Hua's promotion and Teng's dismissal, as a look at the Politburo and Standing Committee votes will attest. Of course, after their defeat in the succession struggle in October, every effort would be made to show the Gang's opposition to Mao as far back in time as possible.

64. Butterfield, "Peking Indicates Senior Aide Is Out."

65. *Peking Review*, 24 December 1976, p. 8.

66. Ibid.

67. The reference here is to the Politburo meeting that CCP documents date 3 May 1975. In the context of the April 30 "instructions" and explosive aftermath, the meeting referred to as having taken place in 1975, or one very much like it, must have taken place in early May of 1976. Mao's warning plea, "Do not form a gang of four! Do not do that! Why do you still want to do it?" constituted his final attempt to forestall the breakup of his coalition. Furthermore, in the current leadership's effort to discredit the Gang of Four all references to Mao's warnings against forming a gang are to the period 1974-1975 when that was not a crucial issue, while totally ignoring the year 1976 when it was. For the regime's position, see the *People's Daily-Red Flag-Liberation Army Daily* joint editorial, 24 October 1976 and Hua Kuo-feng's political report to the Eleventh Party Congress, *Peking Review*, 26 August 1977, pp. 26-27.

68. *China News Analysis*, no. 1048, 23 July 1976, pp. 1-2.

69. Ibid., pp. 3-4.

70. Ibid., no. 1054, 17 September 1976, pp. 3–4.

71. The successions to Lenin, Stalin, Khrushchev, and Gheorghiu-Dej in Romania all moved through the same stages, although the political dynamics and the timing of each were obviously different. See Myron Rush, *Political Succession in the USSR* (New York: Columbia University Press, 1955) and J. F. Brown, "Rumania Today, I: Towards Integration," *Problems of Communism*, Vol. 18, January-February 1969, pp. 8–17.

Chapter XV: The Struggle for Succession, 1976-1978

1. *Peking Review*, 24 September 1976, p. 10; and John Newman, "Year of the Dragon: The Succession to Mao Tse-tung," *Asian Affairs*, Vol. 5, no. 6 (July-August 1978), pp. 361–393.

2. It was evidently at this meeting that Chiang Ch'ing castigated Hua with the remark that he was "incapable" of leading the party; Hua countered with the reply that he was "very capable" and "knew how to solve problems." Tanjug Domestic Service, 15 October 1976.

3. Chu Teh's death had reduced the Politburo to sixteen members.

4. See Wang Hsueh-wen, "The 'Gang of Four' Incident: Official Expose by a CCPCC Document," *Issues and Studies*, Vol. 13, no. 9 (September 1977), pp. 46–58. For an account of the trial, see Li T'ien-min, "The Trial of the Lin Piao and Chiang Ch'ing Cliques," *Issues and Studies*, Vol. 17, no. 1 (January 1981), pp. 19–26.

5. See Newman, "Year of the Dragon," pp. 385ff., for additional versions of the arrest.

6. *United Press International* (UPI) (Hong Kong), 15 October 1976.

7. *Ming Pao* (Hong Kong), October 1976.

8. *Agence France Presse* (AFP) (Hong Kong), 24 October 1976.

9. *United Daily News* (Taipei), 23 October 1976; see also *China News Analysis*, no. 1065, 7 January 1977.

10. *K'uai Pao* (Hong Kong), 15 April 1977.

11. Ibid.

12. *Ming Pao* (Hong Kong), 29 May 1977.

13. Ibid.

14. Yeh Chien-ying later confirmed the shooting of Wang Hung-wen. Speaking about the T'ien An Men case, Yeh noted that the Gang should not be killed, but kept as a "negative example." "Wang Hung-wen," he said, "should be criticized only after he has recuperated from his wounds." *Central Daily News* (Taipei), 13 April 1977.

15. *Ming Pao* (Hong Kong), 26 October 1976.

16. NCNA, 21 October 1976.

17. AFP (Hong Kong), 11 October 1976, reported on Peking University wall posters declaring that Hua had been "nominated" for the chairmanship on the ninth.

18. UPI (Hong Kong), 13 October 1976, noted "high level meetings" taking place in the wake of Hua's nomination. UPI (Hong Kong), 14 October 1976, declared that Hua and others had been engaged in a series of meetings "for the past few days." Kyodo (Tokyo), 14 October 1976, identified a large number of official cars at the Great Hall of the People around 8:00 p.m. the previous evening, the thirteenth, and speculated that possibly a Central Committee meeting was in progress.

19. AFP (Hong Kong), 14 October 1976, "Officials say, 'The Five-Year Plan Is Undergoing Revision.' "

20. For a different view, see Newman, "Year of the Dragon," pp. 387–388.

21. China News Agency (CNA) (Taipei), 24 March 1977. See also *Ming Pao,* 24 March 1977, for a slightly different version of this report.

22. CNA (Taipei), 24 March 1977.

23. See the Politburo breakdown noted above.

24. CNA (Taipei), 24 March 1977.

25. See Newman, "Year of the Dragon," for a survey of the campaigns critical of Teng during the spring.

26. See CNA (Taipei), 13 January 1977, for the report. The identification of the memorandum's number can be found in *Ming Pao* (Hong Kong), 14 March 1977.

27. Volume 5 itself would not appear until the summer of 1977. "On the Ten Great Relationships" was published on 25 December 1976 in *Peking Review.*

28. Ibid.

29. NCNA, 23 December 1976.

30. NCNA, 9 May 1976. Cf. Hua's and Yeh's speeches at the Taching conference.

31. AFP (Hong Kong), 7 January 1977; AFP (Hong Kong), 8 January 1977; AFP (Hong Kong), 9 January 1977.

32. AFP (Hong Kong), 16 January 1977.

33. AFP (Hong Kong), 6 February 1977.

34. Kyodo (Tokyo), 27 March 1977.

35. AFP (Hong Kong), 19 March 1977.

36. Ibid. and CNA (Taipei), 20 May 1977. The CNA report was misdated, placing a clash between Hsü Shih-yü and Ch'en Hsi-lien in February instead of March. From the context it is clear that their clash occurred during the March Politburo discussions. According to the report, Ch'en Hsi-lien asserted that "Hsu's advocacy of the rehabilitation of Teng Hsiao-p'ing was seeking [sic] his advantages." Hsü fought back, saying that, "It's none of your business whether I'm seeking my advantage. Anyway, we cannot let you alone gain advantages." It was Yeh Chien-ying who mediated between them, appealing for unity in the "greater interests of the party."

37. CNA (Taipei), 24 March 1977.

38. See Richard C. Thornton, "Teng Hsiao-p'ing and Peking's Current

Political Crisis: A Structural Interpretation," *Issues and Studies,* Vol. 12, no. 7 (July 1976).

39. Ibid., for an analysis along these lines of the "Lin Piao incident."

40. See CNA (Taipei), 14 April 1977, for the general tenor of press commentary in Hunan, Szechwan, and Kweichow. For Yunnan, see Wang Hsiao-hsien, "The Turmoil in Yunnan," *Issues and Studies,* Vol. 13, no. 12 (December 1977), pp. 41–52.

41. *People's Daily,* 19 March 1977 and 30 March 1977. *Ming Pao,* 14 April 1977. A third article appeared in *People's Daily,* 13 June 1977.

42. *Ming Pao,* 14 April 1977.

43. Ibid. Teng also sent a letter of appreciation to Hua on 10 April 1977, following the March meetings; see *Ming Pao,* 26 May 1977.

44. NCNA, 22 July 1977, "Communique of the Third Plenary Session of the Tenth Central Committee of the Communist Party of China" (adopted 21 July 1977).

45. Teng's speech at the Third Plenum is of interest, particularly as regards the responsibility for his return to power and Yeh's role as well.

> Chairman Mao used to criticize. . . . "Don't just stick together with that bunch of yours; there is bound to be trouble." . . . Had I taken heed of Chairman Mao's advice, I would not have committed errors of line and would not have been struck down at the outset of the Cultural Revolution. After I had been struck down, the Chairman again let me out to work [in 1973]. I was afraid of disappointing him. Being so anxious, I erred in my consciousness of the line of "Four Modernizations" by confusing the "key link" with "items." As a result, I let the "gang of four" grab my tail and give me a sound flogging. . . . When Chairman Mao was fatally ill, Chairman Hua and Vice-Chairman Yeh linked with the majority of leading comrades in the central committee to suppress repeatedly the ferocious bluster of the "gang of four." Otherwise the "gang of four" might have succeeded in establishing an "Ad Hoc Leading Group of the Central Committee."

For all of Teng's remarks, see "Teng Hsiao-p'ing's Speech to the Ad Hoc Forum of the Third Plenary Session," *Issues and Studies,* Vol. 13, no. 10 (October 1977), pp. 76–77.

46. As a result of their promotions, they, along with Hua and Yeh, were described in wall poster reports as the "new gang of four." AFP (Hong Kong), 28 May 1977.

47. NCNA, 19 August 1977.

48. Tanjug, 28 November 1977.

49. NCNA, 24 October 1977.

50. For the committee composition and dates of elections, see *PRC Official Activities and Monthly Bibliography* (Hamburg: Institute of Asian Affairs, March 1978), pp. 20–23.

51. AFP (Hong Kong), 23 February 1978. For the Communique of the Second Plenum, see NCNA, 23 February 1978.

52. AFP (Hong Kong), 4 December 1977, reported internal discussions

regarding the re-establishment of the "presidency" and "the problem of sharing out between the future head of state, the party chairman, and the premier."

53. "Real Deeds, Yes; Hollow Statements, No!" *Peking Review*, 31 March
1978, pp. 14-18.

54. Ibid. The 1969 understanding, according to the Chinese, was that
both "sides first of all reach an agreement on the provisional measures for
maintaining the status quo of the border, averting armed conflicts and disengagement."

55. See, for example, V. Krivtsov, "Precarious Balance," *Novoye Vremya*
(New Times), 12 August 1977.

56. For a detailed analysis of the Southeast Asian events, see John M. Newman, "Soviet Strategy in Asia, 1977-1979," *Asian Affairs* (May-June 1980),
pp. 305-334.

57. For an analysis of the Indo-Pakistani conflict from this perspective,
see the author's "South Asia: Imbalance on the Subcontinent," *Orbis* (Fall
1975), pp. 863-873.

58. *Washington Post*, 8 April 1978.

59. Marquis Childs, "Relations Between China and Vietnam," *Washington Post*, 1 August 1978.

60. Jay Mathews, "China Accuses USSR of Attacking Across Disputed
Border Region," *Washington Post*, 12 May 1978; Kevin Klose, "Kremlin
Admits Incursion into China," *Washington Post*, 13 May 1978.

61. *Washington Post*, 2 September 1978.

62. *Pravda*, 2 September 1978.

63. *People's Daily*, 17 September 1978.

64. *Pravda*, 4 November 1978.

65. *New York Times*, 16 December 1978.

66. *Asahi Shimbun*, 15 January 1979. For a more optimistic interpretation of Hua's position *vis-à-vis* Teng, see John Newman, "The Chinese Succession Struggle: Sino-American Normalization and the Modernization Debate,"
Asian Affairs (January-February 1979), pp. 184-186.

67. *Peking Review*, no. 13, 31 March 1978, p. 12. See also his speech to
the Fifth NPC, *Peking Review*, no. 10, 10 March 1978.

68. *Washington Post*, 26 October 1978.

69. Ibid., 7 November 1978.

70. AFP (Hong Kong), 7 November 1978.

71. Newman, "The Chinese Succession Struggle," p. 178, and Cyrus R.
Vance, speech on Sino-American normalization, in U.S., Department of State,
U.S. Policy Toward China, July 15, 1971-January 15, 1979, Selected Documents No. 9 (Washington, D.C.: Government Printing Office, January 1979),
p. 55.

72. Kyodo (Tokyo), 29 November 1978.

73. "Whatever" and "everything" referred to the views of Hua's people
that whatever and everything Mao had said had to be followed.

74. *South China Morning Post*, 31 March 1979. The *Morning Post* item

identifies five men, Wang Tung-hsing, Ch'en Hsi-lien, Ch'en Yung-kuei, Wu Teh, and Ni Chih-fu, but wallposters associated Chi Teng-kuei and Li Teh-sheng with them, as well. See, for example, FBIS, Soviet Union, 1 and 7 December 1978, C 1.

75. *South China Morning Post,* 31 March 1979.

76. *Baltimore Sun,* 17 November 1978.

77. FBIS, Soviet Union, 28 November 1978, pp. C 1-2.

78. U.S., Department of State, *U.S. Policy Toward China,* p. 44.

79. *New York Times,* 27 November 1978.

80. *New York Times,* 28 November 1978.

81. *Peking Review,* no. 47, 24 November 1978, p. 6.

82. *Washington Post,* 28 November 1978.

83. *Washington Star,* 4 December 1978.

84. Rowland Evans and Robert Novak, *Washington Post,* 18 December 1978.

85. *New York Times,* 16 December 1978.

Chapter XVI: Whither China? The Uncertain Future, 1978-1980

1. NCNA, 23 December 1978.

2. See Chapter XI for an analysis of the sixteen-point resolution.

3. *Free China Weekly,* 1 April 1979, p. 3.

4. Chang Chen-pang, "Chinese Communist Party Organization and Leadership under Hua, Yeh and Teng," in Tsai Wei-ping, ed., *Struggling for Change in Mainland China: Challenges and Implications* (Taipei: Institute of International Relations, 1980), p. 42.

5. O. B. Borisov and B. T. Koloskov, *Soviet-Chinese Relations, 1945-1970* (Bloomington: Indiana University Press, 1975), especially Chapter 5, section 3.

6. NCNA, 23 December 1978, section 3.

7. Ibid., section 1.

8. Ibid.

9. Ibid.

10. Ibid., section 2.

11. Ibid., section 4.

12. Ibid., section 2.

13. Ibid., section 3.

14. Ibid., section 4.

15. Ibid., section 5.

16. Ibid., section 5.

17. Ibid., section 1.

18. *Wall Street Journal,* 30 January 1979.

19. *Christian Science Monitor,* 28 February 1979.

20. *New York Times,* 8 February 1979.

21. *Washington Star,* 8 February 1979.
22. Agence France Press (Hong Kong), 20 February 1979.
23. Ibid.
24. *New York Times,* 16 March 1979.
25. Hsinhua, 12 March 1979.
26. *People's Daily, Liberation Army Daily,* 26 March 1979.
27. *Liberation Army Daily,* 18 March 1979.
28. Chang Chen-pang, "Chinese Communist Party Organization and Leadership under Hua, Yeh and Teng," pp. 42-43.
29. *Free China Weekly,* 1 April 1979, p. 3. The Peking city notice appeared on 29 March.
30. Ibid.
31. See FBIS, PRC, 7 June 1979, pp. R 1-7.
32. For a different view regarding the respective positions of Hua and Teng during this period, see Lyman Miller, "Chinese Political Debate Since The Third Plenum," *FBIS Analysis Report,* 1 August 1979.
33. Hsinhua, 3 April 1979.
34. Ibid.
35. See Chapter 13 for discussion.
36. *Pravda,* 18 April 1979.
37. Kyodo, 25 April 1979.
38. Kyodo, 15 June 1979.
39. FBIS, Soviet Union, 4 June 1979.
40. See the article by I. Alexandrov, *Pravda,* 11 July 1979.
41. AFP (Paris), 14 May 1979, in FBIS, PRC, 15 May 1979, p. L 8.
42. Hsinhua, 18 June 1979.
43. AFP (Hong Kong), 4 June 1979.
44. Kyodo, 24 July 1979.
45. Kyodo, 18 July 1979.
46. Hsinhua, 6 August 1979.
47. Hsinhua, 29 September 1979.
48. Ibid.
49. Ibid.
50. Hua Kuo-feng, speech to the Eleventh Party Congress, *Peking Review,* August 1977.
51. Hsinhua, 8 October 1979.
52. "Reorganization of China's Provincial Governments," *FBIS Analysis Report,* 6 March 1980, p. 4.
53. Kyodo, 3 January 1980.
54. FBIS, PRC, 11 January 1980 (emphasis supplied).
55. Linda Matthews, "China Softens Report on U.S. 'Alliance,'" *Los Angeles Times,* 12 January 1980.
56. *Washington Star,* 11 January 1980.
57. Kyodo, 23 January 1980.
58. Kyodo, 12 February 1980.

59. AFP (Hong Kong), 25 February 1980.

60. AFP (Hong Kong), 28 February 1980.

61. Hsinhua, 29 February 1980.

62. AFP (Hong Kong), 28 February 1980.

63. Hsinhua, 29 February 1980.

64. Chang Chen-pang, "Chinese Communist Party Organization and Leadership," p. 44.

65. Hsinhua, 29 February 1980.

66. Kyodo, 24 January 1980.

67. William Sexton, "Glacial Sino-Soviet Relations Turn Frosty," *Japan Times,* 23 April 1980.

68. Ibid.

69. Ibid.

70. *People's Daily,* 8 May 1980.

71. *Free China Weekly,* 17 August 1980, p. 3.

72. For Hu's remarks, see FBIS, PRC, 23 June 1980, pp. L 1-4; for Teng's see the interview with Oriana Fallaci in the *Washington Post,* 31 August and 1 September 1980.

73. For Po I-po's remarks, see FBIS, PRC, 3 July 1980.

74. *Washington Post,* 31 August 1980.

75. Ibid.

76. *People's Daily,* 7 September 1980.

77. *Washington Post,* 16 December 1980; and *Free China Weekly,* 18 January 1981.

78. For an account of the trial, see James C. Shiung, ed., *Symposium: The Trial of the "Gang of Four" and Its Implication in China,* University of Maryland, Occasional Papers/Reprints Series in Contemporary Asian Studies, no. 3, 1981.

79. *Washington Post,* 16 December 1980.

80. *Washington Star,* 29 June 1981.

Suggested Readings

Acheson, Dean. *Present At the Creation*. New York: New American Library, 1975.

An, T'ai-sung. *The Chinese Cultural Revolution*. Indianapolis, Ind.: Pegasus, 1972.

Baum, Richard, ed. *China in Ferment*. Englewood Cliffs, N.J.: Prentice-Hall, 1971.

Boersner, Dmitri. *The Bolsheviks and the National and Colonial Questions*. Geneva: Librairie E. Oroz, 1957.

Borisov, E., and Koloskov, B. *Soviet-Chinese Relations, 1945-1970*. Bloomington: Indiana University Press, 1975.

Chang, Parris. *Power and Policy in China*. University Park: Pennsylvania State University Press, 1975.

Clubb, O. Edmund. *China and Russia: The Great Game*. New York: Columbia University Press, 1971.

Cohen, Arthur. *The Communism of Mao Tse-Tung*. Chicago: University of Chicago Press, 1964.

Dittmer, Lowell. *Liu Shao-ch'i and the Cultural Revolution: The Politics of Mass Criticism*. Berkeley: University of California Press, 1973.

Domes, Jurgen. *The Internal Politics of China, 1949-1972*. New York: Praeger Publishers, 1973.

Duiker, William J. *The Communist Road to Power in Vietnam*. Boulder, Colo.: Westview Press, 1981.

Esmein, Jean. *The Chinese Cultural Revolution*. New York: Doubleday, 1973.

Feis, Herbert. *The China Tangle: The American Effort in China from Pearl Harbor to the Marshall Mission*. Princeton: Princeton University Press, 1953.

Gittings, John. *Survey of the Sino-Soviet Dispute*. London: Oxford University Press, 1968.

Griffith, William. *The Sino-Soviet Rift*. Cambridge, Mass.: M.I.T. Press, 1964.

Herring, George. *America's Longest War*. New York: John Wiley & Sons, 1979.

Hinton, Harold. *The People's Republic of China, 1949-1979, A Documentary Survey.* 5 vols. Wilmington, Del.: Scholarly Resources, 1980.

Ho Kan-chih. *A History of the Modern Chinese Revolution.* Calcutta: Books and Periodicals, 1959.

Hsiao, Tso-liang. *Power Relations Within the Chinese Communist Movement, 1930-1934.* Seattle: University of Washington Press, 1961.

Kuo, Warren. *Analytical History of the Chinese Communist Party.* 4 vols. Taipei: Institute of International Relations, 1968-1971.

Lin Piao. *Long Live the Victory of People's War.* Peking: Foreign Languages Press, 1965.

McFarquhar, Roderick. *The Origins of the Cultural Revolution: Contradictions Among The People.* London: Oxford University Press, 1974.

Mao Tse-tung. *Selected Works.* 5 vols. Peking: Foreign Languages Press, 1961 and 1977.

Michael, Franz, and Taylor, George. *The Far East in the Modern World.* 3rd ed. New York: Holt, Rinehart & Winston, 1975.

Moody, Peter. *The Politics of the Eighth Central Committee of the Communist Party of China.* Hamden, Conn.: Shoestring Press, 1973.

Nelsen, Harvey W. *The Chinese Military System: An Organizational Study of the Chinese People's Liberation Army.* 2nd ed., revised and updated. Boulder, Colo.: Westview Press, 1981.

Romanus, Charles, and Sunderland, Riley. *The United States Army in World War II, China-Burma-India Theater.* 3 vols. Washington, D.C.: Department of the Army, Office of the Chief of Military History, 1953.

Roy, M. N. *Revolution and Counter Revolution in China.* Calcutta: Renaissance Publishers, 1946.

Schram, Stuart. *Authority, Participation and Cultural Change in China.* Cambridge: Cambridge University Press, 1973.

Simmons, Robert R. *The Strained Alliance: Peking, Pyongyang, Moscow and the Politics of the Korean Civil War.* New York: Free Press, 1975.

Tang Tsou. *America's Failure in China, 1941-1950.* Chicago: University of Chicago Press, 1963.

Terrill, Ross. *Mao.* New York: Harper & Row, 1980.

Thornton, Richard C. *The Comintern and the Chinese Communists, 1928-1931.* Seattle: University of Washington Press, 1969.

Treadgold, Donald, ed. *Soviet and Chinese Communism.* Seattle: University of Washington Press, 1966.

Vogel, Ezra. *Canton Under Communism.* Cambridge, Mass.: Harvard University Press, 1969.

Zagoria, Donald. *The Sino-Soviet Conflict, 1956-1961.* Princeton: Princeton University Press, 1962.

Index

Acheson, Dean, 185, 197, 200, 201, 208, 228
Afghanistan. *See* Soviet Union, and Afghanistan
"Agrarian revolution," 12–13, 18
Agriculture, national conference on (Tachai 1976), 393
Albania, 255
Aleutians, 138
All Army Political Work Conference (1980), 432
All-China People's Government of National Defense, 89
Allied coalition, 137–138, 141, 142, 145
Altan Bulak (Outer Mongolia), 352
An Chih-wen, 237
Anhwei province, 108, 109, 180, 300, 308, 330
An P'ing-shen, 394
Anti-Japanese Military and Political Academy, 124
"Anti-Lo-Ming line," 66
"Anti-Marxist Maoist," 343
An Tzu-wen, 425
Asian Collective Security System, 364, 369
"Asiatic mode of production," 256, 272
Assam pipeline, 145
Atomic bomb, 176, 177
Austin, Warren, 230
Australia, 129, 384
Autumn Harvest Uprising, 20

Backyard furnaces, 250, 251
Badger, Oscar C., 211
Bangladesh, 359
Bengal, Bay of, 129
Berlinguer, Enrico, 431
Bhamo (Burma), 153
Bolsheviks, 3, 4
Borodin, Michael, 7, 9, 10, 13, 15, 19, 20, 22
Bougainville (New Guinea), 139
"Bourgeois revolutionaries," 5, 6, 83
Braun, Otto. *See* Li Teh
Brezhnev, Leonid, 273, 341, 363, 364, 424

Brezhnev Doctrine, 344, 345
Brown, Harold, 428
Brzezinski, Zbigniew, 403, 404
B-29, 140, 146
Bukharin, Nikolai, 11, 12, 24, 25, 27, 30, 83
Bulganin, Nikolai, 239, 240, 248
Bulletin of Activities, 260
Burdzhalov, E. M., 242–243
Burma, 129, 130, 138, 141, 142–143, 145–146, 153, 155
Burma Road, 113, 130, 153
"Butcher of China," 96
Byrnes, James F., 185

Cabinet Ordinance (1949), 232
Cairo conference I and II (1943), 140–141, 142–143, 144, 218
Cambodia, 359, 361–362. *See also* Kampuchean People's Republic
Canadian Tribune, 342
Canton (China), 13, 15, 296, 306
  Japanese occupation of, 113
  uprising, 20, 21, 22–23
Capitulationism. *See* "Total capitulationism"
Carter, Jimmy, 404, 408
Carter, Marshall S., 201
Casablanca conference (1943), 137, 138
CBI theatre. *See* China-Burma-India theatre
CCP. *See* Chinese Communist Party
Central Bureau of the Soviet Areas, 52, 53, 55
Central Circular
  Number 60, 35, 37
  Number 70, 37, 42
Central Commission for Inspecting Discipline, 416
Central issue. *See* Chung Fa
Centralized democracy, 112
Central Pacific route, 138, 146
Central Party School (Yenan), 134, 135
Central Revolutionary Military Commission, 55–56
Central South area, 232, 233
Central Soviet Area, 51, 52, 58, 62, 66, 69, 74, 76, 83

Central Work Conferences (1960–1966, 1978), 257, 258, 264, 265, 268, 269, 279, 283, 284, 292–293, 407

Chahar province, 180, 192

Chai Tse-min, 404

Chang Chih-chung, 191

Ch'angchun (Manchuria), 56, 193, 194, 198, 210

Chang Ch'un-ch'iao, 282, 295, 304, 346, 365, 368, 371, 379, 382, 384, 388, 397

Chang Fa-k'uei, 22, 36, 39, 41

Chang Hao (Lin Yu-ying), 88, 90, 93, 94

Chang Hsi, 237

Chang Hsiu-ch'uan, 322

Chang Hsüeh-liang, 15, 17, 20, 32, 33, 39, 96

Chang Kuo-hua, 315

Chang Kuo-t'ao, 27, 43, 45, 55, 58, 59, 62, 63, 77, 78, 81, 83–84, 85, 86, 87, 91, 92–94, 95–96, 98, 99, 102, 104

  as defector, 109, 113

Chang Lin, 232

Ch'angsha (China), 10, 20, 21, 42, 43

Chang T'ing-fa, 398, 419

Chang Wen-t'ien, 48, 72, 73, 79, 80, 85, 87, 88, 99, 103, 104, 105, 108

Chang Yun-yi, 116

Ch'aoch'ow (China), 22

Chao Ts'ang-pi, 399

Chao Tzu-yang, 350, 368, 395, 425, 429, 431, 433, 434

Chao Yung-fu, 309

Chefoo (Shantung province), 199

Chekiang province, 10

Ch'en Ch'ang-hao, 85, 86

Ch'en Ch'eng, 59

Chengchow (Honan province), 110, 316

Cheng-feng rectification campaign, 113, 120, 134–137, 249

Ch'engtu (Szech'uan province), 314

Cheng Wei-shan, 320, 349, 350

Ch'en Hsi-lien, 289, 319, 346, 365, 367, 371, 382, 390, 394, 407, 421, 429

Chen Keng, 99

Chen Pao. See Damasky Island

Ch'en Po-ta, 282, 287, 320, 346, 347, 349, 350, 354

Ch'en Shao-yü (Wang Ming), 37, 39, 40, 41, 46, 47, 48, 49, 52, 89, 91, 98, 105, 106–110, 111, 112, 113, 119, 120–121, 124, 136, 137, 170, 342–343

Ch'en Tsai-tao, 308, 316, 317, 318, 412

Ch'en Tu-hsiu, 6, 14, 20, 33, 81

Ch'en Yi, 62, 75, 116, 124, 212, 214, 215, 216, 232, 323

Ch'en Yün, 72, 80, 105, 108, 238, 245, 249, 264, 412, 416, 429, 433, 434

Ch'en Yung-kuei, 365, 371, 382, 390, 407, 433, 434

Chia, 68

Chiaching Mountains, 82

Chia Ling River, 82, 83

Chiamussu (Manchuria), 206, 220

Chian (China), 58

Chiang Ch'ing, 282, 298, 318, 320, 323, 325, 334, 346, 365, 375, 376, 382, 383, 386–387, 388, 394, 395, 397

Chiang Kai-shek, 7, 8–10, 11, 12, 13, 14–15, 17, 18, 19, 21, 36, 82, 131

  arrest of, 96–98

  bandit suppression campaign, 50, 59

  at Cairo conference, 141, 143, 144–145, 148–149

  and coalition government, 144–145, 146–148, 156–159, 162, 178–179, 189, 190, 200, 218

  and Communist encirclement campaigns, 69–70, 82, 96

  and consitutional government, 159, 165–166, 179–180

  as director-general of Nationalist Party, 110, 170

  and Japanese peace plan, 122, 123

  and Manchuria, 183, 193, 195, 197–198, 214, 221

  and Marshall, George C., 185–187, 197–198, 203

  retirement as president (1949), 216

  and Stillwell, Joseph, 150–151, 152, 153–155

  at Tehran conference, 142

  and united front policy, 90, 91–92, 94, 104, 112

  and Wallace, Henry A., 148

  and Yalta conference, 161, 162, 163–165, 172, 173, 175, 176, 177

  and "Yen-Feng" insurgent coalition, 38–39, 41

  Yunnan forces, 145–146, 155

Chiang Nan-hsiang, 425

Chiang Ting-wen, 96

Chiao Hsiao-kuang, 394

Chihfeng (Jehol province), 192

Ch'ih Heng, 380

Ch'ih Sui River, 81, 82

China

  civil war (1946), 208–212, 214–216. See also Manchuria, and Chinese

Communists; Manchuria, and
    Nationalists
and Germany, 101
and Japan, 3, 49, 54, 56, 57–58, 65,
    107, 130–131. *See also*
    Sino-Japanese War
map, 60–61
Marxist study groups in, 6
North, 191, 207, 208–209, 210–211
population, 191
post–World War I, 3, 5
Soviet Republic of, 54–55
students abroad, 6
See also Chinese People's Republic;
    Soviet Union, and China; United
    States, and China; Yalta Conference
China Aid Act (1948) (U.S.), 210, 211,
    223
China-Burma-India theatre (CBI), 130
"China: Cultural Revolution or
    Counterrevolutionary Coup?"
    (Wang Ming), 342
Ch'in Chi-wei, 367, 429
Chinchow (Manchuria), 65, 183, 210,
    212
Ch'in dynasty, 369–370
Chinese Communist Party (CCP) (1921)
    "armed propaganda," 26, 48, 83
    and army, 14, 15, 16, 18, 27, 28, 29,
        33, 37, 50, 51–52, 55, 56–57, 190,
        367–368. *See also* Red Army
    "bolshevization," 28–29, 50, 116, 120
    bureaus, 99, 107–108, 109, 120, 124,
        205, 241, 287–289, 293, 299–302,
        308, 315
    cadres, 266–267, 305–306, 325, 345,
        346, 348, 351, 355, 365, 439
    Central Bureau, 51, 52, 53, 55, 66
    central cadres administration, 99, 109
    Central China Bureau, 124
    Central Committee, 20, 72, 73, 84, 85,
        88, 93, 135, 136, 137, 169, 170, 235,
        245, 250, 254, 264, 265, 267, 268,
        280, 281, 284, 285, 312–313, 321,
        329, 365, 412, 425, 457 n24. *See
        also* Cultural Revolution Group
    Central faction, 47–48
    centralization, 28–29, 36, 40, 52
    Central Plain Bureau, 124
    Central South Bureau, 288, 289, 301,
        302, 308, 315
    and coalition government, 166–170,
        171, 188, 204–205. *See also* Chiang
        Kai-shek, and coalition government
Committee for Work Among White
    Troops, 88

committees, 136
constitution, 337, 348
and constitutional government,
    179–180
Council of People's Commissars, 73
East China Bureau, 288, 299–300,
    301, 302, 308, 315
factional strife, 436
First (founding) Party Congress
    (1921), 6–7
Fifth Party Congress (1927), 15, 22
Sixth Party Congress (1928), 25, 27,
    31, 36, 83
Second Plenum (1929), 31
Third Plenum (1930), 44, 45, 46
Fourth Plenum (1931), 44, 47, 48, 50,
    51
Fifth Plenum (1934), 67, 72
Sixth Plenum (1938), 111–113
Seventh Plenum (1945), 170
Seventh Party Congress (1945), 109,
    111, 134, 135, 137, 166–171
Eighth Party Congress (1956, 1958),
    242, 244–247, 249–250, 258, 265,
    413
Ninth Party Congress (1969), 285,
    327, 336, 337, 343, 346
First Plenum (1969), 343
Second Plenum (1970), 347, 348
Tenth Party Congress (1973), 362,
    366–367, 370
Third Plenum (1977), 396–398
Eleventh Party Congress (1977), 394,
    396, 398–399, 401
Third Plenum (1978), 411–417
Fourth Plenum (1979), 425–427
Fifth Plenum (1980), 427, 429
Sixth Plenum (1981), 435
French branch, 7
front line cadres, 66
general strike call (1932), 58
guerrilla forces, 25, 26, 33, 40, 42,
    52–53, 59, 83, 107, 135, 168
history of, interpretation, 236
and industrial strikes, 37
inspection committees, 28
insurrections, 20–23, 24, 25
July 7 resolution (1946), 205–206
left wing, 27, 45, 83, 92, 301, 306, 310
liberated areas, 167–169, 179, 180,
    456–457 n21
membership, 8, 233, 338
Military Affairs Commission (or
    Committee), 241, 260–261, 349
Military Commission, 287, 302, 312,
    389, 429

and Nationalist Party, 7, 8, 9, 12–13,
14, 16, 17–22, 24, 26–27, 33, 36–37,
39, 41, 49, 50–51, 53–54, 56, 57, 90,
94, 98, 99, 102, 104, 107, 115–119,
122–124, 189, 208, 216. *See also*
Chiang Kai-shek, and coalition
government; New Fourth Army,
Incident
North China Bureau, 99, 107–108,
288, 302
Northeast Bureau, 205, 288, 289, 301,
302, 309
Northwest Bureau, 137, 288, 301, 308
Organization Department, 88, 107,
108
and peasantry, 12–13, 17, 21, 26, 30,
31, 33, 37, 40, 66–67
Politburo, 27, 30–31, 33, 38, 45, 48,
52, 72, 80, 94, 98, 99, 106–107, 108,
109, 113, 133, 135, 169, 170, 245,
249, 253, 268, 279, 280, 282, 287,
350, 365, 368, 379, 387, 394,
397–399, 412, 425, 429, 430,
457 n24
power, 11, 28, 38
Propaganda Department, 281, 326
publications. *See Chinese Culture;*
Chinese Worker; Communist; Red
Flag
recruitment campaign, 262
reorganization, 51–53, 87–88, 108,
241–242
right wing, 27, 45, 83, 92, 104,
320–321
secret police, 50
South China Bureau, 120
Southeast Bureau, 107, 108, 109, 120,
124, 288, 301, 302
Southwest Bureau, 93, 308
and Soviets, 11, 17, 18, 21, 22, 25–26,
28, 29, 36, 37, 39–40, 42, 51, 52,
58–59, 62, 68, 83, 84, 104
Trade Union Movement Committee,
88
"two-parties theory," 236
and united front policy, 89–95,
97–98, 102–103, 104, 108–109, 111,
115, 121, 124
and urban areas, 26–27, 28, 29, 37,
40, 42, 43, 58
Women's Department, 88
"Workers' Guard," 9
Yangtze Bureau, 107, 108, 109
See also Chinese People's Republic;
Comintern, and Chinese Communist
Party; Internationalists; Long

March; Political commissar system
Chinese Culture (1940), 117, 120
Chinese Eastern Railway crisis (1929),
32–34
Chinese news agency. *See* Hsinhua
Chinese People's Republic (CPR) (1949)
agriculture, 257–258, 264, 265, 350,
424, 436
Cabinet, 232, 237, 241
and Cambodia, 362. *See also*
Kampuchean People's Republic
and capitalism, 264, 296
Central Government, 232, 234–235,
240
centralization, 338
constitution, 371–372, 430–431
decentralization, 337
Defense Council, 241
earthquake (1976), 385
East China fleet, 318
Economic and Finance Committee,
237
economy, 247, 248, 250, 257–259,
264, 391, 422, 436, 439
Government Council, 232–233, 235
industry, 258, 265, 436
and Japan, 358, 403, 438
and Korean War, 231
leadership, 252
legal system, 372
liberated areas, 231–232
maps, 213, 274, 290–291
military, 247–248, 253, 254–255
Military Council, 232
Military Regions, 290(map), 367–368
militia, 253, 263
Ministry of Defense, 241, 260
and modernization, 438–439
National People's Congress (1954),
234, 240, 241, 246, 285, 348, 371,
399, 428, 434
and North Vietnam, 403, 417–418,
419–421
nuclear program, 248, 255, 345
Procurator-General's office, 232, 241
public security system, 372
and security, 436–438
and Soviet Union, 229, 238–240,
246–249, 251, 252, 253, 255–256,
271–273, 275–277, 331–333,
335–336, 337–338, 341–345,
358–359, 363–365, 369, 373–374,
375, 378, 400–403, 404, 419,
422–425, 427, 428, 431–432,
437–438
Standing Committee, 240–241

State Economic Commission, 246
State Planning Commission, 237-238
State Planning Committee, 232, 235, 237
Supreme Court, 232, 241
and Taiwan, 229, 374
as Third World nation, 373
transportation routes, 291(map)
and United Nations admission, 230
and United States, 144, 231, 337, 351, 355-356, 357, 359-360, 362, 373, 374, 375, 378, 403, 405, 409, 418-419, 428, 437-438
See also Sino-Indian border war
Chinese Revolution and the Chinese Communist Party, The (Mao et al.), 117
Chinese Worker (1940), 120
Ch'ing dynasty, 3
Ching Kang Mountains, 21, 28
Ch'inglungchi, battle of (1948-1949), 215, 216
Ch'in Pang-hsien (Po Ku), 48, 49, 52, 72, 76, 79, 80, 87, 99, 108
Chin Sha River, 82
Ch'i Pen-yü, 320, 329
Chi Teng-k'uei, 365, 368, 371, 382, 390, 407, 421, 429
Ch'iu Hui-tso, 322, 346, 350, 352
Chiungya liberated area, 231
Chou En-lai
    and Central Revolutionary Military Commission, 55, 79, 85, 87
    and Chinese Communist Party, 7-8, 27, 31-32, 37, 38, 43, 44-45, 47, 48, 50, 72, 74, 79, 80, 88, 108, 236, 245, 249, 281, 314, 317, 318, 325, 346, 350, 354, 365, 366, 367, 370-371, 426
    and civil war, 201
    and constitutional government, 159
    death, 376, 378, 381
    illness, 370, 374, 376-377
    and Kissinger, Henry, 351
    and Lin Piao incident, 352, 366
    on Long March, 76
    and Marshall, George C., 191, 198-199, 204
    as political commissar, 56, 64
    and power, 242
    and Red Army, 62
    and Soviet Union, 250-251, 273, 335, 336, 344, 364-365, 369, 373-374
    and three worlds theory, 372-373
    and united front policy, 103

    and United States, 373
    wife. See Teng Ying-ch'ao
    and Yenan conference, 157-158
Chou Hui, 412
Chou Pao-chung, 181
Chou Yang, 280, 425
Ch'ü Ch'iu-pai, 20, 22, 25, 27, 43, 44-45, 47, 81
Chu Jui, 107
Chu Li-chih, 86
Chung Fa (central issue), 297
Chungking (Szech'uan province), 113, 130, 314
Chungshan (gunboat), 9
Chungyuan liberated area (P'ingyuan province), 231
Churchill, Sir Winston, 142-143, 163
Chu Teh, 28, 40, 42, 43, 55, 56, 62, 70, 73, 85, 86, 94, 102, 103, 108, 169, 242, 245, 249, 346, 354, 365, 371, 379, 382, 384, 426
    as Government Council vice-chairman, 232, 235
Class struggle, 3, 264, 279
CMEA. See Council for Mutual Economic Assistance
Cold War, 218, 227
Comintern (1919), 4
    and Chinese Communist Party, 6, 14, 20, 26-28, 29, 30-32, 33, 34, 35, 38, 39, 41, 42-48, 49, 52, 53, 54, 74, 80-81, 84, 90, 92, 93, 105, 111, 128
    Far Eastern Bureau, 51
    and Japanese invasion of Manchuria, 56-57
    Second Congress (1920), 5, 11
    Seventh Congress (1935), 88-89, 90, 91
    and Southeast Asia, 51
    See also Executive Committee of the Comintern
Communes, 249, 250-251, 253, 257, 258, 259, 264, 265-266, 269. See also "Paris Commune" concept
Communist (1939), 116, 120
Communist International. See Comintern
Communist Youth League (CPR), 262
Confucius. See Criticize Confucius-criticize Lin Piao campaign
Coral Sea, battle of, 129
Council for Mutual Economic Assistance (CMEA), 403
Council of People's Commissars, 87, 88
CPR. See Chinese People's Republic

CPSU. *See* Soviet Union, Communist
   Party
Criticize Confucius–criticize Lin Piao
   campaign, 368, 369
Cuba, 273
Cultural Revolution. *See* Great
   Proletarian Cultural Revolution
Cultural revolutionary groups, 286, 289,
   293–394
Cultural Revolution Group (CCP), 279,
   280, 282–283, 295, 311, 313, 317,
   318, 319, 320, 321, 326, 329
Czechoslovakia. *See* Soviet Union, and
   Czechoslovakia

Dairen (Manchuria), 141, 142, 174, 175,
   176, 177, 178, 183, 193
Damansky Island (Manchuria), 342
"Decision of the CCP Central
   Committee Concerning the Great
   Proletarian Cultural Revolution,"
   285–287
"Decision on Certain Problems in the
   Land Struggle" (Mao), 72
Declaration of the Communist and
   Workers' Parties (1957), 255
"Democratic centralism," 7
Democratic League (China), 171
Democratic Republic of Vietnam. *See*
   North Vietnam
De-Stalinization. *See* Stalin, Joseph, and
   personality cult
Détente, 357
Dictatorship of the proletariat, 54
Dimitrov, Georgi, 89
Dream of the Red Chamber (Tsao
   Hsueh-chin), 375
Dual power, 4, 5, 17, 26, 54
Ducroux (Serge Lefranc), 51
Dvoevlastie. *See* Dual power

East China liberated area, 231, 233, 237
Easter offensive (1972), 356
ECCI. *See* Executive Committee of the
   Comintern
"Economism," 296
Eighteenth Group Army. *See* National
   Revolutionary Forces, Eighth Route
   Army
Eighth Route Army. *See* National
   Revolutionary Forces, Eighth Route
   Army
Eisenhower, David, 378
Eisenhower, Julie, 378
Éléments déclassé, 26
Engels, Friedrich, 4

Evans, Rowland, 409
Executive Committee of the Comintern
   (ECCI), 52, 89
   Seventh Plenum (1926), 12
   Eighth Plenum (1927), 16, 17, 18, 19
Export-Import Bank, 369

Fallaci, Oriana, 434
Fang Chih-min, 75
Fang Yi, 398, 400, 430
Fan Sui, 369–370
Far East balance of power, 3, 5
Far Eastern Bureau (Comintern), 51
Fascism, 89
"Fast and close strike," 74, 80
"February Adverse Current" (1967),
   305–306
"February Outline Report" (P'eng
   Chen), 280–281, 282
February 7 Conference (1930), 37
Federated Autonomous Government
   (Inner Mongolia), 110
Feng Yü-hsiang, 6, 9, 15, 16, 19, 36, 38,
   39
First Army Corps (China), 9, 10
"First ten points," 265–269. *See also*
   "Revised later ten points"
First World, 373
"Five Anti Movement," 269
"Five kinds of red," 292, 293
Foochow (Fukien), 69, 70
Ford, Gerald, 378
Foreign Service officers (U.S.), 158
Formosa, 141, 145, 182. *See also* Taiwan
"Forward offensive line," 62, 64
Four Cleans Movement, 270
Four modernizations, 391, 406, 415, 436
"Four olds," 292
Fourth Corps, 19–20
France, 113, 115, 121. *See also* Soviet
   Union, and France
Fraser, Malcolm, 384
Fuchow (China), 58
Fu Ch'ung-pi, 329
Fukien-Kwangtung-Kiangsi area, 52
Fukien province (China), 10, 69, 229,
   308
   revolutionary committee, 334
Fukien Rebellion (1933), 69–71
"Fundamental Way Out for Agriculture
   Lies in Mechanization" (Mao), 393
Fu Tso-yi, 211, 212, 214, 216

Galen, Vasily (Bleucher), 7, 32
Gandhi, Indira, 358
Gang of Four, 383, 384, 386, 387–389,

Gang of Four, *cont.*
  393, 395, 397, 398, 426, 490 n63.
  See also New "gang of four"
General Line, 249
Geneva Agreements (1954), 273, 356
Germany, 114–115, 121, 161. *See also*
  China, and Germany; Japan, and
  Germany; Soviet Union, and
  Germany; West Germany
Gilbert Islands, 138
"Give Back Our Great Wall" (Mao), 321
"Government of China," 114
Great Areas, 231–232, 233–234, 235,
  241
Great Britain, 51, 113, 115, 129,
  142–143, 173, 202, 250
Great Leap Forward (1958–1960),
  249–250, 251, 252–255, 256–257,
  259, 271
Great Proletarian Cultural Revolution
  (1965–1968), 246, 248, 251, 262,
  277, 280, 284, 289, 295–297,
  300–335, 415, 426
  and foreign embassies, 322–323
  power organs, 286
  See also Cultural Revolution Group;
  Red Guard
Greece. *See* United States, and
  Greece
Gromyko, Andrei, 423, 424
"Group of five," 282
Guadalcanal, 132, 137

Hailar-Halunarshan railway, 114
Haile Selassie (emperor of Ethiopia),
  352
Haiphong (North Vietnam), 356, 357,
  359
Han Hsien-ch'u, 330
Hankow (China), 110
Han Kuang, 412
Hanyang arsenal (Wuhan), 10
Harbin (China), 56, 194, 206, 220
Harriman, W. Averell, 172, 175, 176,
  177
Harvest (1960), 257–258
"Hegemonism from all sides," 428
Heilungchiang province, 56, 199, 304,
  307, 335, 337
Heng Yang (China), 151–152
Hiroshima (Japan), 176
Hitler, Adolf, 121
Ho Chang-kung, 86
Ho Chi-minh, 51, 344
Ho Kai-feng, 99
Ho Ku-yen, 312

Ho Lung, 19, 33, 40, 58, 59, 62, 63, 75,
  77, 78, 84, 94, 103, 232, 298
Ho Meng-hsiung, 39, 40, 43, 44, 45–46,
  47
Honan province, 15, 20, 59, 180, 211,
  308, 316
Hong Kong, 51, 322
Hong Kong Strike Committee, 9
Hopeh province, 180, 181
Hopkins, Harry, 164, 172, 176
Ho Ying-ch'in, 10, 21, 146
Hsia fang, 266, 267
Hsia Hsi, 59
Hsiang Chung-fa, 27, 31, 45, 47, 48, 51
Hsiang River, 77
Hsiang Ying, 27, 30, 55, 56, 62, 72, 75,
  80, 87, 108, 111, 119, 123, 124
Hsiao Hua, 312, 321–322
Hsiao K'o, 75
Hsi Chung-hsün, 237, 412
Hsieh Chueh-tsai, 87
Hsieh Fu-chih, 312, 317, 318, 320, 322,
  326, 327, 330, 348
Hsieh T'an-chung, 312
Hsing wu mieh tzu, 432
Hsinhua, 427, 428
Hsiyen Mountains, 77
Hsu Chia-t'ung, 395
Hsuchow (China), 214, 215
Hsüeh Mu-ch'iao, 237
Hsü Hai-tung, 86, 87
Hsü Heng-lu, 388
Hsü Hsiang-ch'ien, 40, 59, 78, 298, 312,
  398, 432, 434
Hsu Li-ch'ing, 322
Hsü Shih-yü, 330, 346, 354, 365, 368,
  382, 388, 389, 394, 419, 429, 432
Huai-Hai campaign (1948–1949),
  214–216
Hua Kuo-feng, 361, 365, 371, 382, 395,
  411, 421–422, 426, 429–430, 433
  as acting premier, 379, 383
  and Cultural Revolution, 426–427
  and Gang of Four, 387–389, 395–396,
  397, 414, 426, 435
  and industrialization, 392–393
  and modernization, 405–406, 407,
  413–414, 424
  as party chairman, 387, 388, 389–392,
  394, 395, 396–397, 398, 435
  and People's Liberation Army, 432
  as premier, 381, 384, 385, 386
  as security head, 372, 399
  and United States, 405, 407
Huang Hua, 422

Huang K'o-ch'eng, 237, 264, 412
Huang Po-tai, 215
Huang Shao-hsiung, 15
Huang Wei, 215
Huang Yung-sheng, 289, 330, 346, 350, 352
Hu Ch'iao-mu, 412, 430
Hu Ch'ih, 312
Hull, Cordell, 142
Hu Lu Tao (China), 183
Human capital, 250, 251
Hump route, 130, 145, 155
Hunan-Hupeh-Kiangsi area. *See* Central Soviet Area
Hunan province, 77, 337
  revolutionary committee, 330
Hunan Provincial Proletarian Revolutionaries Great Alliance Committee, 328
Hunan-Szech'uan-Kweichow border area, 75
Hunan-West Hupeh area, 58, 59, 62
Hungary, 244
Hung Ch'i. See Red Flag
Hung Hsueh-chih, 425
Hung Hu (Lake Hung), 59
Hung Huo-ch'ing, 412
Huo Shih-lien, 394
Hupeh-Honan-Anhwei border area, 55, 58, 59, 62
Hupeh province, 180, 308, 316
Hurley, Patrick, 150, 152, 153, 154, 155, 156, 157, 158, 159, 163–165, 166, 173, 179, 184
Hu Tsung-nan, 82, 83, 84, 85
Hu Yao-pang, 399, 412, 429, 430, 433, 435

I Chang (China), 114
ICHIGO offensive (1944), 146
Imperialism, 3, 5, 89, 376
Imphal (India), 145
Inchon landing (Korea), 230
India, 138, 145, 358–359. *See also* Sino-Indian border war
Indian Ocean, 129
Indochina, 361, 362
Indo Chinese party, 51
Industrial Communications Political Department, 268
Industry, national conference on (Taching 1977), 393
Inner Mongolia, 96, 110, 113, 181, 314, 315, 337, 342, 344
  liberated area, 231
  Military District, 290(map), 315

Internationalists, 49, 50, 52, 53, 54–55, 56, 66, 72, 73, 80, 83, 84, 85, 87, 88, 97, 99, 106, 108, 109, 111, 112, 119, 121, 124, 132, 137, 138, 169, 170
  criticism of Chinese Communist Party, 52–53
  and Red Army, 63–64, 70
I'pin (Szech'uan province), 314
Italian Communist Party, 431
Italy, 122, 138
Izvestia, 96, 337, 364

Jao Shu-shih, 234, 235, 237, 242
Japan
  as expansionist, 3, 71, 88, 100
  and Germany, 111, 114, 121–122, 127
  inner defense zone, 139, 145
  Marxist study group in, 6
  post–World War II, 227
  See also China, and Japan; Chinese People's Republic, and Japan; Sino-Japanese War; Soviet Union, and Japan; United States, and Japan
Japanese Imperial Conference (1940), 123
Jehol province, 180, 191
Jen Pi-shih, 62, 94, 103
Johnson, Lyndon B., 272, 275
Joint Chiefs of Staff (U.S.), 175–176, 177, 185, 211
Juichin (China), 50, 54, 65
July 7 resolution. *See* Chinese Communist Party, July 7 resolution
June 7 "circular," 315, 316

Kaganovich, Lazar, 246
Kamenov, Lev, 396
Kampong Som (Kampuchea), 418
Kampuchean People's Republic, 362, 401, 402, 403, 404, 405, 417–418, 419–420, 423, 438
Kampuchean United National Front for National Salvation, 403, 405
Kanchow (China), 58
K'ang Hsien, 433
K'ang Sheng, 105, 108, 265, 280, 282, 287, 320, 325, 346, 354, 365, 371, 376, 377
Kansu province, 86
Kao-Jao coalition, 234, 235, 236–237
Kao Kang, 86, 137, 170, 205, 233, 235–237, 238, 239, 242
  as Government Council vice-chairman, 232

Kao Kang, *cont.*
  as State Planning Committee chairman, 235, 237
  See also Kao-Jao coalition
Kapitsa, Mikhail, 431
Keng Piao, 398
Khabarovsk (Soviet Union), 206, 342
Khabarovsk protocol (1929), 32
Khalka River (Outer Mongolia), 114
Khassan, Lake (Soviet Union), 110
Khrushchev, Nikita, 238, 239–240, 242, 243–244, 246–247, 248, 253, 255, 256, 271–273, 341
Kiangsi-Fukien-Anhwei area, 52
Kiangsi province, 308, 321
Kiangsi provincial soviet, 37, 49, 52, 62–63, 65, 69, 74, 75. *See also* Central Soviet Area
Kiangsu province, 180, 199
Kiev (Soviet Union), 128
Kirin (Kirin province), 193, 210
Kissinger, Henry, 351, 353, 356, 357, 360, 374, 376, 378
KMT (Kuomintang). *See* Nationalist Party
K'o Ch'ing-shih, 249
Korea, 161, 177. *See also* North Korea; South Korea
Korean War (1950), 227, 229–231, 239
Kossior, Stanislav, 243
Kosygin, Aleksei, 273, 275, 341, 344
Kriangsak Chamanan, 406
Kuan Feng, 320, 321, 322, 326
Kuangchang, battle of (1934), 73, 74
Kuangming Daily, 432
Kuangyuan (Szech'uan province), 82, 83
Ku Hsun-chang, 50–51
Ku Mu, 430
Kung Ch'u, 71
Kuo Hung-tao, 86
Kuomintang (KMT). *See* Nationalist Party
Kuo Yu-feng, 399
Ku Pai, 66, 72
Kurile Islands, 161, 173, 362
Kursk-Orel battle (1943), 138
Ku T'ien conference. *See* Ninth Conference of Red Army Delegates
Kwangsi province, 152, 334
Kwangtung province, 6, 20, 22, 180
Kwantung Army (Japanese), 56, 65, 110
Kweichow province, 78, 81, 82, 307, 308
Kweiyang (Kweichow province), 82

Lake Hung. *See* Hung Hu
Lam Son 719 operation (1971), 357

"Land rectification" campaign, 66–67
Langson (North Vietnam), 420
Laos, 356, 357, 359
Lapham, Roger, 211
League of Nations, 88
Leahy, William, 185
Lefranc, Serge. *See* Ducroux
"Left exclusionism," 92
Lenin, V. I., 3, 4, 5, 11, 243
"Letter to the Hupeh-Honan-Anhwei Soviet Area" (CCP), 59
Lianghok'ou conference (1935), 83–84, 86
Liang Hsiao (pseudonym of Mao Tse-tung), 375, 380, 384
Liaoning province, 181, 193, 330
Liaotung Bay, 183
Liberation Army Daily, 281, 298, 368, 421
Li Chang, 425
Li Ching-ch'uan, 249, 308, 315, 365
Li Chi-shen, 15, 22, 152, 232
Li Cho-jan, 86
Li Fu-ch'un, 87, 237, 238, 264, 287
Li Hsien-nien, 264, 346, 371, 382, 389, 390, 394, 397, 398, 400, 412, 421, 429, 433, 434
Li Hsueh-feng, 108, 283, 349, 350
Li Li-san, 27, 28–29, 30, 31, 33, 34–48, 81, 206–207
"Li Li-san line," 28, 32, 34, 37, 39–42, 43, 44, 46, 47
Li Man-ts'ung, 322
Lin Chieh, 321
Lin Pai-chu, 73
Lin Piao, 85, 181, 235, 236, 242, 336, 346
  and Chinese Communist Party, 245, 249, 278–279, 292, 293, 297, 319, 320–321, 329, 346
  criticism of, 368, 369, 426
  incident, 351, 352–354
  as Mao's successor, 337, 343, 346, 347–349, 350–352
  as military commander, 56, 64, 87, 103, 194, 206, 207, 208, 209, 210, 212, 214, 216, 232
  as Minister of Defense, 254, 260, 261, 262, 276
  as State Planning Committee member, 237
  and United States, 351
  as vice-chairman, 336, 341
  wife. *See* Yeh Ch'un
Lin Po-ch'u. *See* Lin Tsu-han
Lin Tsu-han, 102, 147

Linwu (China), 77
Lin Yu-ying. *See* Chang Hao
Liping (Kweichow province), 78
List, Albert. *See* Li Teh
Li Ta-chao, 6
Li Teh (Otto Braun/Albert List), 54, 74, 76, 79, 80
Li Teh-sheng, 365, 367, 368, 370, 382, 390, 407, 408, 419, 421
Li Tso-p'eng, 346, 351, 352
Li Tsung-jen, 15, 21, 36, 38–39, 152, 216
Littlejohn, Robert, 201
Liu Chih-chien, 298, 312
Liu Chih-tan, 84, 85, 86, 87
Liu Feng, 319
Liu Hsien-ch'uan, 309, 315
Liu Hsing-yuan, 399
Liu Kuang-t'ao, 395, 399
Liu Lan-po, 425
Liu Lan-t'ao, 237, 425
Liu P'ei-shan, 319
Liu Po-ch'eng, 55, 62, 77, 79, 86, 103, 208, 214, 215, 216, 232, 346, 354, 365, 382, 396, 397
Liu Shao-ch'i, 72, 78, 79, 88, 99, 109, 112, 124, 133, 169, 235, 236, 242, 426
  as chairman of Chinese People's Republic, 250, 257, 258–259, 281
  and Chinese Communist Party, 244, 245, 246, 258, 262, 263, 269, 279, 280, 285, 286, 287, 294, 336, 345
  as Government Council vice-chairman, 232
  overthrow of, 295, 347
  rehabilitation of, 430, 432
  and Soviet Union, 249
  as Standing Committee chairman, 240
  and work teams, 283
Lo An (China), 65
Lochuan conference (1937), 102–104
Lo Jui-ch'ing, 264–265, 276, 279, 280, 282
Lo Mai, 88
Lominadze, Besso, 20, 21, 22, 25
Lo Ming, 66
London Evening News, 345
"Long Live Leninism," 255
Long March (1934), 49, 73, 76–78, 81–87, 90, 217
Lon Nol, 356
Lop Nor (Sinkiang province), 345
Losik, Alexander, 337
Lo Ssu-ting, 369, 370

Louis, Victor, 344–345
Loyang (China), 58, 211
Ludden, Raymond, 192
Lung-Hai railway, 179, 214
Lung Ling (Yunnan province), 153
Lu Ting-yi, 265, 279, 281, 425

MacArthur, Douglas, 175, 177, 231
McNamara, Robert, 272
Madagascar, 384
Ma Hung, 237
Malaya, 138
Malayan party, 51
Malaysia, 407
Malenkov, Georgi, 238, 239, 240, 244, 246
Manchukuo, 130
Manchuria, 32, 33, 141, 142, 179, 180, 182, 183, 337
  and Chinese Communists, 181, 188, 192–195, 197–204, 206, 208–209, 210, 212, 214, 229
  industrial base, 237, 238
  Japanese occupation of (1931), 54, 56, 113, 114
  and Nationalists, 183, 189, 190, 193–195, 197–204, 208–209, 210, 212
  railway system, 177
  and Soviet Union, 161, 162–163, 173, 174–175, 176, 177, 178, 180–181, 183–184, 186, 193, 194–195, 205, 218, 219, 238, 342
  See also Manchukuo; Northwest liberated area
Manchuria Democratic Joint Army, 192
Manchurian People's Government, 238
Mao Chih-yung, 395
Maoerhkai emergency conference (1935), 84–85
Maoists, 320, 324, 325, 384
Maokung (China), 82, 83, 84
Mao Tse-ching, 66
Mao Tse-tung
  and agriculture, 393
  brother. *See* Mao Tse-ching
  as chairman of Chinese People's Republic, 240, 241, 242, 250
  as chairman of Soviet Republic of China, 55, 64, 72, 87
  and Chinese Communist Party, 8, 21, 28, 29, 37, 38, 49, 52–53, 54, 55, 66, 72, 73, 76, 78, 79, 80, 81, 98–99, 106, 108, 109–110, 113, 116–117, 118–119, 120, 124, 132–137, 169–170, 205, 216–217,

Mao Tse-tung *cont.*
    234, 236, 237, 245–246, 249, 254,
    264, 265–267, 269–270, 278–281,
    282–285, 287–289, 338, 346,
    347–349, 355, 365, 370, 371, 376,
    377, 382
  and coalition government, 166–170,
    178–179, 190, 191, 220–221
  death (1976), 385
  as Eighth Route Army commander,
    109
  and Fukien rebellion, 70–72
  as Government Council chairman, 232
  and guerrilla warfare, 26, 29, 33, 34,
    36, 52–53, 63, 86, 103
  illness, 384
  and industrial development, 237, 392
  and Khrushchev, Nikita, 239, 240,
    244, 247, 256
  and Korean War, 229
  and Liu Shao-ch'i, 258–259, 283, 294,
    314, 345, 350
  and Long March, 76, 86
  and Malenkov, Georgi, 238–239
  and Marshall, George C., 191–192
  and mass organizations, 283, 286, 294
  and military, 253–255, 259–263,
    267–268
  and peasantry, 30, 48, 54, 67,
    268–269, 350
  as political commissar, 56, 64, 72
  program of the three red banners. *See*
    Communes; General Line; Great
    Leap Forward
  and proletariat, 375
  pseudonym. *See* Liang Hsiao
  rectification campaign (1957), 246
  and Red Army, 35–36, 37, 38, 40, 41,
    42, 43, 50, 54, 55, 56, 62, 63–64,
    70, 74, 75, 78–79, 83, 85–86, 103,
    136, 169, 207, 214, 216
  and revolution, 84
  Revolutionary Military Committee
    chairman, 76, 80, 85, 87, 88, 106,
    109, 120, 136
  as Shen-Kan-Ning Government
    commander, 109
  and Sino-Japanese War, 104, 107,
    109, 132, 134
  and soviets, 84
  and Soviet Union, 249–251, 255,
    276, 277, 343
  and Stalin's support, 105, 106
  "Thought of," 117, 169, 245, 261–262,
    280, 287, 325, 333, 372, 421

  three directives, 380
  three instructions, 383, 384, 389
  and united front policy, 90–93, 97,
    102, 103, 104, 105, 107, 108–109,
    111–113
  and United States, 360, 377–378, 385
  wife. *See* Chiang Ch'ing
  at Yenan conference (1944), 156, 158
  See also Cheng-feng rectification
    campaign; Great Proletarian
    Cultural Revolution; Lin Piao,
    incident; People's Liberation Army,
    Maoization of; Teng Hsiao-p'ing,
    and Mao Tse-tung
"Mao Tse-tung Thought Study Class,"
    325, 331
Mao Yuan-hsin, 388
Ma Pu-fang, 95
"March black wind," 306
Maring. *See* Sneevliet, Henry
Marshall, George C., 150, 154, 160, 172,
    184–187, 189, 191–193, 194, 195,
    196–205, 209, 210, 214, 218, 221,
    222
Marshall Islands, 138
Marx, Karl, 3, 4
Marxism-Leninism, 5, 117, 169, 245,
    332, 343, 372, 373, 422
May 16 corps, 326
Mekong River, 418
Mensheviks, 4
Midway, 129–130
Mif, Pavel, 47, 48
Mikoyan, Anastas, 243
Military Affairs Conference (1959),
    254
Military control committee, 305, 307
Million Heroes, 316, 317, 318
Ming Pao, 396
Min Mountains, 86
Min t'uan, 68
Molotov, Vyacheslav, 239, 246
Mongolia. *See* Inner Mongolia;
    Mongolian People's Republic; Outer
    Mongolia
Mongolian People's Republic, 344
Moscow conference of foreign ministers
    (1943), 142
Moscow group. *See* Internationalists
Moslem forces, 95
Mu Hsin, 321
Mukden (Manchuria), 56, 193, 194, 210
Muldoon, Robert, 383
Munich agreement (1938), 111, 113
Myitkyina (Burma), 153

Nagasaki (Japan), 177
Nanchang (Kiangsi province), 10, 13, 14, 21, 58, 114
  uprising (1927), 19–20, 22
Nanking (China), 10, 15, 32, 58, 110
Nan P'ing (China), 70
Nanyang Party, 51
National Congress (1938), 110
National Day, 336, 352
National Defense Council, 94, 95
Nationalist Army, 8, 9–11, 12, 20, 26, 33, 43, 50, 222
  and Japanese, 58, 96, 110, 118
  Left, 15, 17, 19–20
  in North China, 210–212
  on Taiwan, 216
  See also Manchuria, Nationalists in; National Revolutionary Forces; Red Army, and Nationalist Army
Nationalist-Communist United Front (1937), 102, 104–105, 111
Nationalist Party (Kuomintang) (China), 6, 25, 110
  bandit suppression campaigns, 50
  Bolshevik faction, 7. See also Chinese Communist Party, and Nationalist Party
  Central Executive Committee, 8, 10, 13, 14, 146, 208
  Central Supervisory Committee, 14
  and Chinese Eastern Railway, 32–34
  Communists expelled, 19
  encirclement campaigns, 53–54, 55, 58, 66, 67, 69–70, 82
  First National Congress (1924), 7, 8
  Second National Congress (1926), 8, 12
  Fifth National Congress (1936), 94
  Sixth National Congress (1954), 166, 170–171
  guerrilla warfare, 110
  Left, 10, 12, 13, 14, 15–16, 17–18, 19, 21, 104
  National Assembly, 165, 166, 167, 171, 180, 189–191, 200, 204
  Organization Department, 8
  police, 50–51
  Propaganda Department, 8
  Right, 10, 14, 17, 21, 104
  and urban areas, 29, 34–35, 221
  See also Political Consultative Conference; "Seventy-percent political, thirty-percent military plan"; Soviet Union, and Nationalist Government

National Military Council. See United National Military Council
"National revolutionaries," 5, 6
National Revolutionary Forces, 110, 115
  Eighth Route Army, 102, 103, 109, 115–116, 119, 123, 136, 167
  See also New Fourth Army
National Revolutionary Government. See Nationalist Party
National Soviet Congress (1931), 54–55, 56
"Nationwide revolution," 38, 39, 40, 41, 42, 46, 56–57, 58, 83, 91
"Negotiation on Equal Footing Is the Only Correct Way," 427
Nehru, Jawaharlal, 230
Neumann, Heinz, 20, 22, 25
New China Daily (Wuhan) (1938), 108, 109
"New democracy," 89, 95, 117
New Fourth Army, 108, 109, 116, 119, 120, 133, 136, 167
  Incident (1941), 121, 123–124
New "gang of four," 433
New Guinea, 138, 139. See also Port Moresby
"New life" movement, 67
New Order (Japanese), 114
"New Revolutionary High Tide and an Initial Victory in One or Several Provinces, A" (resolution; 1930), 40
"New Yenan." See Chiamuszu
New York Times, 369
New Zealand, 383
Niang, 68
Ni Chih-fu, 398, 407
Nieh Jung-chen, 56, 207, 398
Nienchuang, battle of (1948), 215
Nimitz, Chester, 175, 177
19th Route Army (Nationalist), 69, 70
Ninghsia province revolutionary committee, 330
Ningtu conference (1932), 62–63
Ninth Conference of Red Army Delegates (1929), 35, 36
Niu Huai-ling, 316
Nixon, Richard, 251, 356, 357, 359, 378
Nomonhon (Mongolian-Manchurian border), 114, 115
North Africa landings (1942), 128, 137, 138
North China liberated area, 231, 232, 233, 237
Northeast liberated area, 231, 232, 233, 237

"Northern Campaign," 9, 12
Northern Pacific route, 138
North Korea, 181, 230
    troops, 207, 220
    See also Soviet Union, and North
        Korea
North Vietnam, 272–273, 276, 356,
    357, 359–360, 362, 401, 402, 403,
    404–405, 417–418, 419–420, 438
Northwest liberated area, 231, 233
Noulens, Gertrude, 51
Noulens, Hilaire, 51
Novak, Robert, 409

Office of Far Eastern Affairs (U.S.),
    221
Office of Strategic Services (OSS)
    (U.S.), 157
100 regiments campaign, 122
"On New Democracy" (Mao), 117
"On Some Problems in Current Rural
    Work" (Mao), 265
"On Tactics against Japanese
    Imperialism" (Mao), 90
"On the Correct Handling of
    Contradictions Among the People"
    (Mao), 246
"On the New Historical Drama, the
    Dismissal of Hai Jui" (Yao), 280
"On the New Stage" (Mao), 111
"On the Ten Major Relationships"
    (Mao), 392, 415
"Open door" policy, 174, 176, 195
Operation Buccaneer, 143
Operation Milepost, 162–163
Organic Law and Common Program of
    the Chinese People's Political
    Consultative Conference (1949),
    232
Organic Law of the Great
    Administrative Areas' Governments
    (1949), 232
Organic Law of the People's Central
    Government (1949), 232
"Organizational Rules of Poor and
    Lower-Middle Peasant
    Associations" (Mao), 268
OSS. *See* Office of Strategic
    Services
"Our Study and the Current
    Situation" (Mao), 135
Outer Mongolia, 114, 131, 161, 332,
    344
Oyuwan soviet, 55

Pai Chung-hsi, 15, 21, 152
Pai Ju-ping, 367

Pakistan, 358–359
Pan shih tzu. See People's Liberation
    Army, "management group"
Pao, 68
Paoan (China), 93, 94, 96, 97
Pao Shan steel plant, 434
Paoting Military Academy, 11
"Paris Commune" concept, 303–304, 305
Paris Marxist study group, 6
Paris Peace Accords (1973), 359, 360
Patterson, Robert P., 221
PCC. *See* Political Consultative
    Conference
Peaceful coexistence, 239, 255
Pearl Harbor, 129, 131
Peiping. *See* Peking
Peking (China), 180, 216, 296, 297,
    298, 303, 304–305, 308
    Japanese provisional government in,
        110, 113
    revolutionary committee, 314
Peking Daily, 425
Peking-Hankow Railroad, 58, 59
Peking Military Region, 290(map), 349,
    429
Peking Municipal Committee, 284
Peking Review, 370, 400
Peking University, 283
P'eng Chen, 205, 237, 279, 280, 281,
    282, 289, 294, 425
P'eng Ch'ung, 398, 430
P'eng Teh-huai, 40, 42, 62, 70, 78, 79,
    85, 102, 236, 237, 242, 253,
    254–255, 259, 260, 261, 262
People's Daily (Peking), 249, 280, 283,
    293, 296, 304, 313, 318, 333, 337,
    368, 370, 375, 380, 381, 383, 417,
    421
People's Liberation Army (PLA),
    232, 233, 237, 254, 281, 297,
    304–305, 306–307, 310, 313,
    315–316, 318, 321, 324, 330–331,
    333, 334, 367, 429
    Cultural Revolutionary Group, 298,
        311, 312, 313, 319, 322, 329,
        479 n35
    formation training, 295
    General Political Department, 287
    "management group," 329
    Maoization of, 261–263, 267–268,
        269, 280, 298–302
People's Political Conference (PPC), 171
People's Republic of China (PRC). *See*
    Chinese People's Republic
People's Revolutionary Government, 69,
    70

Pescadores, 141
Philippines, 129, 138, 145
Phnom Penh (Kampuchea), 417–418
P'ingyuan province, 231
PLA. *See* People's Liberation Army
Po I-po, 237 246, 264, 425, 434
Po Ku. *See* Ch'in Pang-hsien
Poland, 115, 244. *See also* Soviet Union, and Poland
Political commissar system, 7, 9, 52, 55
Political Consultative Conference (PCC) (1946), 159, 179–180, 186, 189–191, 204, 218
Pol Pot, 362, 405, 418
Port Arthur (Manchuria), 239
Port Arthur-Dairen naval complex (Manchuria), 141, 173
Port Moresby (New Guinea), 129, 130
Potsdam Conference (1945), 174–175
PPC. *See* People's Political Conference
Pravda, 21, 96, 238–239, 364, 404, 424
PRC (People's Republic of China). *See* Chinese People's Republic
Problems of History, 242
"Program of Armed Resistance and National Reconstruction" (Chiang), 147
"Promote what is proletarian and liquidate what is bourgeois," 432
Provincial party committees, 352, 355
Pusan (Korea), 230
Pyongyang (North Korea), 404

Ratsiraka, Didier, 384
Rebel: cadre: military ratios, 330, 334, 372
Red Army (China), 25, 26, 28, 29, 34–35, 36, 37, 41, 42, 50, 51, 54, 76, 78–79, 90, 95, 206
  command of, 63–64, 85, 87, 102
  First, 40, 42, 43, 55, 56, 94
  First Field, 232
  First Front, 78, 81, 82, 83, 84, 85, 87
  Second, 40, 94
  Second Field, 214, 215, 232, 355
  Third, 40, 42
  Third Field, 214, 232, 355
  Fourth, 40, 77, 94, 206
  Fourth Field, 232, 355
  Fourth Front, 78, 81, 82, 83, 84, 85, 86
  General Political Department, 52, 55–56, 80, 87
  and Korean War, 230
  and Nationalist Army, 58, 59, 62–70,

74–75, 76, 77–78, 81–83, 84–85, 93, 96, 115, 189–190, 214–216
  North China Field Army, 232
  recruitment, 67
  regularization of, 63
  reorganization, 51–52, 55–56, 57, 63, 179
  strength, 169, 206, 217, 229
  unification of, 77
  Western Route Army, 94, 95, 98
  See also Long March; Manchuria Democratic Joint Army; National Revolutionary Forces, Eighth Route Army; New Fourth Army; People's Liberation Army
Red Flag, 38, 255, 273, 280, 303, 368, 369, 375, 380, 424, 432
Red Guard, 254, 292–294, 322, 326, 334, 348
Reformed Government of the Republic of China (1938) (Nanking) (Japanese), 110, 113
"Refutation of the New Leaders of the CPSU on United Action," 279–280
"Report to the Tenth National Congress" (Chou), 366
Republic of China. *See* Taiwan
Republic of Korea (ROK) army, 229, 230–231
"Resolution on Some Historical Questions" (Mao), 52, 53
"Resolution on Some Questions in the History of Our Party" (Mao), 170
"Resolution on the New Situation of the Anti-Japanese National Salvation Movement and the Democratic Republic," 94
"Resolutions on the Further Strengthening of the Collective Economy of the People's Communes and Expanding Agricultural Production," 265
"Review of the Errors in the Military Line of Comrades Po Ku, Chou En-lai, and List, A," 79–80
"Revised later ten points" (Liu Shao-ch'i), 269
Revolutionary committees, 304–305, 307, 314, 324–325, 326, 327–329, 330, 334, 337, 345–346, 348, 372, 399, 428
Revolutionary democratic dictatorship of the workers and peasants, 54
Revolutionary Military Commission, 64, 72, 76, 79, 80, 85, 87, 124
Revolutionary rebels, 294, 302, 304, 305,

Revolutionary Rebels, *cont.*
  306, 318, 323–324, 325–326, 329,
  330, 334
"Right opportunism," 64, 92
ROK army. *See* Republic of Korea army
Roosevelt, Franklin D., 130, 141–145,
  149–150, 151, 154, 159, 160–162,
  163
Roy, M. N., 5, 11, 15, 19, 20, 22
Russian Returned Students. *See*
  Twenty-Eight Bolsheviks
Russian revolution (1917), 3, 4
Russian Social Democratic Labor
  Party, 4
Rykov, Aleksey, 396

Saifudin, 399
Sakhalin. *See* South Sakhalin
San Francisco Conference (1945), 164,
  165
San Min Chu Yi. See Three People's
  Principles
Second All-China Congress of Soviets
  (1934), 70, 72, 73, 74
Second World, 373
Selected Works (Mao), 220, 392
Seoul (Korea), 177
"Seventy-percent political, thirty-percent
  military plan," 67–69
Shahsi (China), 114
Sha Hsien (China), 70
Shanghai (China), 10, 14, 15, 51, 180,
  295, 296
  Commune (1967), 303–304, 388
  Japanese occupation of (1932), 58
  Revolutionary Committee, 304, 307
Shangtuichi, battle of (1948), 215, 216
Shanhaikuan (China), 183, 194
Shan Hai pass, 65
Shansi-Chahar-Hopeh bases, 116
Shansi-Hopeh-Shantung-Honan border
  region, 116
Shansi province, 180
Shansi-Suiyuan border region, 116
Shantung base, 116
Shantung province, 180, 199, 211, 307
Shao Shih-ping, 86
Shcherbakov, J. S., 422
Sheng Wu Lien. See Hunan Provincial
  Proletarian Revolutionaries Great
  Alliance Committee
Shen-Kan-Ning Border Area
  Government, 102, 109, 135, 137,
  147, 167, 168, 179, 180
Shensi province, 86, 87, 330
Shen Tse-min, 48

Shih Ch'eng (China), 74–75
Short Course (Stalin), 242, 243
Shui Hu Chuan (Water Margin
  Chronicle), 377
Sian (China), 96
  conference (1944), 147
Siberia (Soviet Union), 362, 363, 369
Sihanouk, Norodom (prince of
  Cambodia), 361
Sihanoukville (Cambodia), 356
Singapore (Malaysia), 51, 407
"Single Spark Can Start a Prairie Fire,
  A" (Mao), 36
Sinkiang province, 173, 308, 337, 342,
  344
  revolutionary committee, 334
Sino-Indian border war (1962), 272
Sino-Japanese peace and friendship
  treaty (1978), 403
Sino-Japanese War (1931–1945), 90, 96,
  98, 101, 110, 113–114, 122–123,
  127–128, 132, 146, 151–152, 153,
  155
Sino-Soviet defense conference (1957),
  247
Sino-Soviet Treaty
  1945, 178–179, 193
  1950, 238–239
  1969 understanding, 400, 422–423
Sneevliet, Henry (Maring), 7
Snow, Edgar, 43, 357
Socialist Education Movement, 265, 266,
  267, 269–270, 283, 286
Socialist Republic of Vietnam. *See*
  North Vietnam
Solomon Islands, 129, 138
"Some Historical Questions in the
  Party" (Mao), 64
Soong, T. V., 164, 172, 173
Soong Ching-ling, 232
Sorge, Richard, 128
South China, 138
Southeast Asian Command, 145
Southeast Asian route, 138
South Hopeh base. *See* Shansi-Hopeh-
  Shantung-Honan border region
South Korea, 228, 230. *See also*
  Republic of Korea army
South Manchurian Railroad, 193
South Pacific route, 138
South Sakhalin, 161, 173
South Seas Party, 51
South Vietnam, 272, 356, 357, 359, 360
Southwest area, 232, 233
Southwest Government of Joint
  Defense, 152

Soviet Areas Conference (1930), 39
Soviet-Chinese nonaggression pact
   (1937), 101–102, 131
Soviet-Japanese neutrality pact (1941),
   101–102, 115, 127, 130–131
Soviet-Nazi pact (1939), 114–115, 121
Soviet People's Republic, 91
Soviet Republic of China (1931), 54, 55,
   58, 87, 90
Soviet Union
   and Afghanistan, 427, 428
   border incidents, 342, 344, 346, 347,
      357, 404, 425
   and China, 5, 6–8, 11, 14, 15, 16–19,
      24–34, 71, 88, 89, 115, 130–131,
      164, 172–174, 175, 177, 180–181,
      188, 195, 206–207, 218–221. See
      also Chinese People's Republic, and
      Soviet Union; Comintern, and
      Chinese Communist Party
   Communist Party (CPSU), 239, 240,
      242–244, 255, 256, 257. See also
      Comintern
   and Cuba, 273
   and Czechoslovakia, 88, 100, 332–333
   Far Eastern Army, 32, 127, 128, 332,
      337
   Fifteenth Party Congress (1927), 22
   foreign policy, 88–89
   and France, 88, 100
   and Germany, 71, 88, 100, 102, 111,
      114–115, 121–122, 127, 128, 131,
      138
   and India, 358–359
   and Japan, 3, 100–101, 102, 110–111,
      114, 122, 142, 161, 171–172, 176,
      358, 362, 364, 369. See also
      Soviet-Japanese neutrality pact
   and Lin Piao incident, 352–353
   and Middle East, 358
   and Nationalist Government, 96–97,
      101, 102, 111, 113, 122, 131, 184
   and North Korea, 229
   and North Vietnam, 272, 275, 342,
      357, 359, 360, 401, 402, 404–405,
      438
   and nuclear war, 239–240
   and Poland, 100
   Provisional Government (1917), 4
   Red Guard, 4
   soviets, 4–5. See also Chinese
      Communist Party, and soviets
   united front policy, 89
   and United States recognition (1933),
      88. See also United States, and
      Soviet Union
   and warm water ports, 142
   See also Manchuria, and Soviet
      Union; Spanish civil war; Yalta
      Conference
Soviet Workers' and Peasants' Republic.
   See Soviet People's Republic
Spanish civil war (1936), 88, 100
Ssu-ma Kuang, 370
Ssup'ingchieh (Manchuria), 193, 194,
   197, 206, 219, 220
Stalin, Joseph
   and Bukharin, Nikolai, 24, 25, 27
   and Chiang Kai-shek, 172–173, 195,
      219
   and Chinese Communist Party, 20,
      25, 27, 30, 37, 83, 242
   death of, 238
   and Hopkins, Harry, 172
   and Mao Tse-tung, 105, 238
   and Nationalists, 13, 17
   and personality cult, 242–244
   and Roosevelt, Franklin D., 141–142,
      159, 162
   and Soviet-Nazi pact, 115
   and Trotsky, Leon, 10, 11, 12, 16, 22,
      396
   and Truman, Harry, 174–175, 176
   and Yalta Conference, 163, 173–174
State Council, 189
State-War-Navy Coordinating
   Committee (SWNCC) (U.S.), 196,
   209, 222
Stilwell, Joseph, 130, 149, 150, 151, 152,
   153–155, 156
Strategic arms balance, 401
Struggle-criticism-transformation, 313,
   334
Stuart, Leighton, 203, 211, 214
Students. See Red Guard; Twenty-Eight
   Bolsheviks
Su Chen-hua, 374, 398, 412
Suiyuan province, 180
Sulzberger, C. L., 369
"Summary of Chairman Mao's Talks
   with Responsible Comrades of
   Various Places during His
   Inspection Tour, A" (Mao), 353,
   354
"Summation of the Experience of the
   Northwest Bureau's High-Ranking
   Conference," 137
Sun Chuan-fang, 10
Sungari River, 209
Sung Jen-ch'iung, 287, 288, 289, 412,
   430
Sung period, 370

Sung P'ing, 395
Sun-Joffe agreement (1923), 6, 7
Sun Yat-sen, 6, 7, 8, 104, 157, 159, 426
Sun Yat-sen University (Moscow), 37
Swatow (China), 22
"Sweep Out All Monsters and Ghosts,"
    283
SWNCC. See State-War-Navy
    Coordinating Committee
Szech'uan province, 82, 86, 308, 314,
    317
    revolutionary committee, 330

"Ta chai" principle, 350
Taierhchuang (Shantung province), 110
Taiwan, 190, 216, 228, 404, 409–410.
    See also Chinese People's Republic,
    and Taiwan
Taiwan Straits crisis (1958), 272
Tanaka, Kakuei, 362–363
T'an Cheng, 264
T'an Chen-lin, 66, 249, 305, 306, 325,
    365
T'an Ch'i-lung, 395
Tangku truce (1933), 65
Tangshan (China), 385, 388
T'ang Sheng-chih, 21
T'an P'ing-shan, 8
T'an P'ing-tzu, 312
T'ao Chu, 287, 288, 289, 296, 326
T'aoyuan area (China), 77
Tapieh Mountains, 211
Tatu River, 82
Teh (Mongolian prince), 110
Tehran conference (1943), 137, 138,
    140–141, 142, 144, 218
Teng, 68
Teng Hsiao-p'ing
    advancement of, 242, 245, 341, 355,
        361, 362, 370, 372, 376, 386, 395,
        396, 407–416
    and Chinese Communist Party, 66,
        72, 236–237, 244, 245, 246, 258,
        262, 267, 294, 346, 365, 368, 371,
        379, 381, 383, 386, 390, 391, 392,
        393–396, 397, 398, 399, 400, 401,
        405, 428
    as first vice-premier, 371, 377
    four upholds, 422
    and Mao Tse-tung, 251, 279, 345,
        349–350, 354, 360, 361, 362, 369,
        372, 375, 376, 377, 378, 380–383,
        384, 413, 414–415, 425–426,
        429–437
    military post, 64
    and modernization, 406, 407, 433

    and Soviet Union, 378, 404, 423,
        428–429
    as State Planning Committee member,
        237
    and Taiwan, 409
    three worlds theory, 373, 437
    and United States, 369, 377,
        406–407, 418, 419, 429
    and Vietnam, 421
Teng Tzu-hui, 237, 264
Teng Ying-ch'ao, 412
Thailand, 406
Third World, 373
"Three-all campaign," 132
Three People's Principles (Sun), 6, 7,
    104, 112, 157
Three Steels, 316, 317
Three-thirds system, 118
"Three way alliance," 303, 304, 305,
    307, 325, 345, 348, 372
Tibet, 334, 351
T'ieh Ying, 395
T'ien An Men Square riot (1976), 381,
    383, 396, 435
Tientsin (China), 180
Ting Sheng, 368
TMTT. See Mao Tse-tung, "Thought
    of"
Togliatti, Palmiro, 431
Tolun (Chahar province), 192
Tonkin Gulf incident (1964), 272
"Total capitulationism," 112–113, 122,
    123
Tou-p'i-kai. See Struggle-criticism-
    transformation
Trade and Finance Department, 268
Trans-Siberian Railway, 357
Trautman, O. P., 107, 122
Tripartite Pact (1940), 122
Trotsky, Leon, 10, 11–12, 16, 17, 22,
    24–25, 396
Trotskyites, 106
Troyanovsky, Oleg, 363
Truman, Harry S., 163, 164, 172, 174,
    175–176, 177, 184–187, 195, 208,
    228
Truman Doctrine (1947), 208, 222, 224
Ts'ai Ch'ang, 88
Ts'ai Ho-shen, 27, 31, 32
Ts'ai T'ing-k'ai, 69
Tsedenbal, Yumjagiin, 344
Tseng Shan, 105, 108
Tseng Ssu-yü, 319, 368
Tsinan (Shantung province), 212
Tsinghai provincial military district,
    309, 310

Tsinghua University, 333
Tsingtao (China), 180
Tsin-pu railway, 214, 215
Tsung Ts'ai. See Chiang Kai-shek, as
    director-general of Nationalist
    Party
Tsunyi (Kweichow province), 76, 78,
    81–82
Tsunyi conference (1935), 71–72, 73,
    78–81, 84
Tucheng (China), 81
Tu Cheng-nung, 88
Tu Li-ming, 194, 215, 216
T'ungchiang soviet, 62, 77
T'ungkao (China), 77
T'ungkiang area (Szech'uan province),
    82
Tung Pi-wu, 346, 354, 365, 371, 376
Turkey. See United States, and Turkey
Tu Yü-ming. See Tu Li-ming
Twenty-Eight Bolsheviks, 37, 39, 41, 46,
    47, 48, 107
Twenty-Three Articles, 270
Tyumen oil project (Siberia), 362

Ulanfu, 315, 365, 398
"United Council of China," 113, 114
United front departments, 120, 124
"United front from below," 71
United front policy. See Chinese
    Communist Party, and united front
    policy; Soviet Union, united front
    policy
United National Military Council, 156
United Nations, 160, 209, 230, 272, 273,
    358
United Nations Forces, 230
United States
    aircraft production (1943), 140
    and China, 127, 129, 130, 138, 141,
        144–145, 148, 149–159, 176, 178,
        181–183, 184–187, 188, 195–205,
        207–212, 214, 218, 219, 221–224.
        See also Chinese People's Republic,
        and United States
    and coalition governments, 144
    and Communism, 208
    and European front, 128, 137
    and Great Britain, 129
    and Greece, 208
    and Japan 128–130, 132, 138–140,
        145, 175–177
    Marines, 183, 199, 209, 222, 228
    Navy, 129, 130, 139, 140, 183
    Pacific Fleet, 129
    Pacific front, 137, 138–140, 145

    and Pakistan, 358
    Seventh Fleet, 229, 230
    and South Korea, 228–229
    and Soviet Union, 141–142, 144,
        160–162, 217–218, 223, 224,
        227–228, 401. See also Cold War;
        Détente; Korean War; Soviet
        Union, and United States
        recognition; Taiwan; Yalta
        Conference
    and Turkey, 208
    and Vietnam, 272–273, 275,
        276–277, 356, 359
Ussuri River, 342, 404

Very long range bomber (VLR), 140
Viet Cong, 272, 273
Vietnam War (1965), 271, 273, 275,
    276–277, 356, 359
Village level organizations. See Chia;
    Niang; Pao; Teng
Vincent, John Carter, 185, 200, 221
Vladivostok (Soviet Union), 142, 206,
    342
VLR. See Very long range bomber
Voitinsky, Grigorii, 6

Wallace, Henry A., 148–149, 150, 151
Wall Street Journal, 378
Wang An-shih, 370
Wang Chen, 412, 434
Wang Chia-hsiang, 55, 56, 62, 87–88
Wang Ching-wei, 8, 14, 15, 19, 22,
    113–114, 122, 123
Wang En-mao, 395
Wang Feng, 399
Wang Ho-shou, 425
Wang Hung-wen, 365, 366, 371, 377,
    379, 382, 384, 388, 397
Wang Jen-ch'ung, 412, 430, 434
Wang Li, 317, 318, 319, 320, 321, 326
Wang Ming. See Ch'en Shao-yü
Wang Pi-ch'eng, 432
Wang Shih-chieh, 147
Wang Tung-hsing, 365, 382, 387, 388,
    390, 397, 398, 407, 408, 412, 421,
    429
Wang Yun-ch'eng, 48
Wan Li, 395, 430
Warlordism campaign (1980), 432
Warlords, 6, 9, 36, 37, 82
Warlord War (1930), 41, 42
Warsaw Pact (1955), 332
Warsaw talks, 337, 356, 485 n66,
    487 n35
Washington Post, 409

"Water Margin" campaign (1975), 377
Wayaopao conference (1935), 87, 90–92, 93
Wedemeyer, Albert C., 155, 157, 158, 183, 209, 210
Weihaiwei (Shantung province), 199
Weihsien (Shantung province), 211
Wei Kuo-ch'ing, 365, 368, 382, 389, 394, 432
Wen Hui Pao (Shanghai), 280
West Central area, 237
Western Route Army. *See* Red Army, Western Route Army
West Germany, 227
Whampoa Military Academy, 7, 8, 9
"White Guard forces," 32
"White Paper" (U.S.) (1949), 228
"Whither China?" 328
"Why Khrushchev Fell," 273
"Will Russian Rockets Czechmate China?" (Louis), 345
Woodcock, Leonard, 409
"Worker-Peasant Mao Tse-tung Thought Propaganda Team," 333
"Worker-Peasant Red Army's Shensi-Kansu Guerrilla Contingent," 86, 87
Workers' General Headquarters, 317
Work groups, 283–284
World Congress of Communist Parties (1969), 331, 343, 344
World revolution, 3, 4, 5
Wu Chi (Shensi province), 86
Wu Fa-hsien, 320, 322, 330, 346, 350, 352
Wu Han, 279, 289, 334
Wuhan (China), 9, 10, 13, 14, 15, 19, 21, 58, 59, 316, 318
  Japanese control of, 113
  uprising, 20
Wuhan Military Region, 290(map), 308, 316–317
Wu K'o-hua, 399
Wu Kuei-hsien, 399
Wu Liang-ping, 73
Wu P'ei-fu, 6, 10
Wu River, 81, 82
Wu Teh, 365, 381, 382, 390, 394, 407, 421, 427

Yakutia natural gas and coal project (Siberia), 362, 369
Yalta Conference (1945), 159, 160–165, 173, 218
Yalu River (Korea), 230
Yang Ch'eng-wu, 312, 329, 330
Yang Shang-k'un, 87, 107, 279, 281, 425
Yang Teh-chih, 368, 419, 429, 430
Yangtze River area, 9, 58, 59, 62, 110, 114
  Japanese occupation of, 113
  as Nationalist territory, 179
Yang Yi-ch'en, 339
Yang Yung, 367
Yao Wen-yuan, 280, 282, 326, 333–334, 346, 365, 375, 382, 388, 397
Yao Yi-lin, 430, 433
Yeh Chien-ying, 87, 346, 352, 354, 365, 371, 379, 382, 383, 384, 385, 386, 387, 388, 389, 391, 393, 394–395, 396, 397, 400, 405, 412, 416–417, 425, 426, 427, 429, 430, 432
Yeh Ch'un, 322, 346, 350, 352
Yeh T'ing, 19, 108
Yellow River, 95, 110
Yenan (China), 98, 148, 211
  conference (1944), 156–158
  See also Shen-Kan-Ning Border Area Government
"Yen-Feng" insurgent coalition, 38–39, 41
Yen Hsi-shan, 36, 38, 41, 102, 103, 112
Yihuang (China), 65
Yingk'ou (China), 183
Yu Chiu-li, 398, 400, 430, 433
Yugoslavia, 255
Yü Li-chin, 329
Yun (Mongolian prince), 110
Yun Gan pass (Kwangsi province), 77
Yung Chi (Manchuria), 193. *See also* Kirin
Yunnan province, 82, 153, 308, 317
  revolutionary committee, 334
Yu Ta-wei, 197, 202, 203
Yütu (Kiangsi province), 76

Zinoviev, Grigori, 396